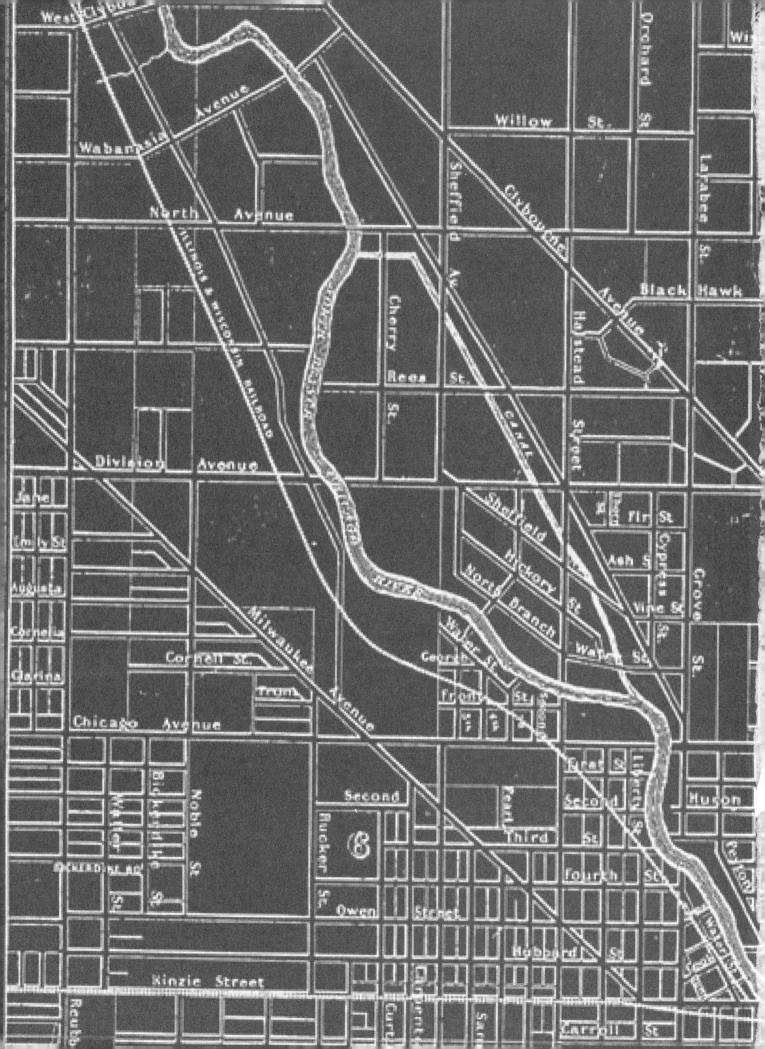

Confusion heard his voice, and wild uproar
Stood ruled, stood vast infinitude confined;
Till at his second bidding darkness fled,
Light shone, and order from disorder sprung.

Paradise Lost, Book 3
John Milton

ENI
WA

Edward M. Burke and Thomas J. O'Gorman

D O F
TCH

Edited by Thomas J. O'Gorman, Ellen Kuchuris and Erin Waitz
Produced by Chicago's Books Press
Designed by Sam Silvio, Silvio Design, Inc.
Printed in Canada by Friesens Corporation

ISBN 9788663-2-0 (Softbound)
ISBN 9788663-3-9 (Hardbound)

Front Cover
Mounted Chicago Police Ride a Snowy Street, (1907)
DN-0052152, *Chicago Daily News* Collection,
Chicago History Museum Photo Archive.

Back Cover
Traditional Six-Point Chicago Police Star, 1898,
Chicago Police Department Archive

Contents

POLICE

3561

CHICAGO

Dedicated to
The spouses, children and descendents of the
men and women of the Chicago Police Department
whose lives were taken in the service of the
nation's greatest city—Chicago.

Preface

As many of you may know, I have been a member of the Chicago City Council, serving as Alderman of the 14th Ward, for the past thirty-seven years. I have served with seven Chicago mayors—Daley, Bilandic, Byrne, Washington, Orr, Sawyer and Daley. During that time I have had a front row seat for Chicago's stunning urban miracle. I believe that no American big city has had such a remarkable and vibrant rebirth. Today, more than ever, it stands with an impressive urban character, square-shouldered, displaying what is best in the urban landscape of our nation.

But before I was ever was elected to public office, my career in public service began as a member of the Chicago Police Department. I suspect this will always be one of the proudest periods of my life. I was young, idealistic and filled with a sense of the future. In that way, I was like many of those we include among the five hundred thirty-four Chicago Police Officers whose narratives we tell in this book. They were all filled with a sense of the future and the promise of Chicago. For many in both the past and in the present, this was the doorway to the American way of life. For many others, it was an opportunity of sustaining and protecting a cherished way of life lived in the best city in America.

From its earliest days, Chicago has been shaped by its unique prairie geography. Our economy, our commerce and our rapid growth are all the product of our extraordinary location—this dramatic spot at the center of the nation, where the prairie meets the lake. It is no accident that we are the capitol of the American heartland. It was in our nature from the very beginning. Nelson Algren captured it best when he said that Chicago was "a city caught between twin seas—the rolling water and the western grass."

But it has always been the people of Chicago that most truly shaped its contours and invigorated its soul. Through their elastic imaginations and enormous capacity for hard work and heavy lifting, a city rose on the prairie not just once, but twice—the "Second City" outshining the first. Out of this engaging and creative urban self-understanding, our metropolis fashioned its own unique contributions to American life, offering everything from the meat on the table to the nation's most enduring political system of governance. Politics, here, has always been as much of an export as the Vienna hot dog or Cracker Jacks. The political character of Chicago continues to dominate our living, carved out of loyalties that never die and alliances that endure from one generation to the next. Like Major League Baseball, it commands our attention and never disappoints. It is the glue of local living.

Here in Chicago it has been said that courage is not just the absence of fear, but the understanding that there are more important things in life than fear. And here in Chicago, every person who dedicates their life to law enforcement commits themselves to the expression of such fearlessness. This resolute courage becomes the ground on which they trod; the companion that walks before them; the virtue of their living; and the prayer that surrounds their soul. Such fearlessness allows them to be effective, committed and engaging. It is often the very making of them as a police officer. This is true, whether it be after thirty years or three.

Each day, those who serve as sworn officers of the Chicago Police Department know, in the solitude of their heart, that there are more important things in life to be consumed with than fear. And because of that, they value the responsibility, the virtue and the valor with which they work each day, learned in families who treasure faith and freedom. Their lives are dedicated to safeguarding everyone's freedom and everyone's faith. The liberty and rights of all Chicagoans are protected by the heroic men and women of the Chicago Police Department, sometimes even at the cost of their own lives. Here in Chicago this has occurred five hundred thirty-four times.

None of us can ever really know what makes one heart more courageous than another. But I suspect it has something to do with what takes place in the deepest recesses of the soul, where the spirit which most defines us as human beings enwraps the character and sensibilities of man. This experience lifts us to noble heights by a sacrifice and wisdom that touches the very face of God. The heroic spark within the human heart fashions a vision that builds heroes out of ordinary men and women.

Each of these five hundred thirty-four carried with pride the emblem of their office—a bright, shinning star. Today, the brightness of their stars still shines, forever fueled by their heroic sense of generosity and courage. The hand of such virtue shaped not only their lives as Chicago Police Officers, but also their lives as human beings.

Over the course of history, each of them has been remembered by family and friends who recalled their passion and their kindness, their humor and their faith—a humanity that permits the goodness of others to thrive and grow. From them, devoted family members learned the lessons of life that nourish human hope, whether in the roll call room or around the family dinner table.

End of Watch is our way of acknowledging their sacrifice, and of recognizing that such heroic devotion to duty has shaped the very contours of Chicago's geography and spirit. Thomas J. O'Gorman and I recognize the heroism of these remarkable individuals as a great historical paradigm through which all Chicagoans can better understand our common, shared humanity. This can only be accomplished if we have the opportunity to understand the details and drama of such heroes' lives. It has been our task to fine-comb the seasons of Chicago life and to lift up the stories of these unique individuals against the background of their own times. I believe the real strength of Chicago life is found in the uncommon glory of our neighborhoods and people.

No other American city can boast of the urban character that Chicago can. The city's ability to survive, as it does, is due in no small part to what is Chicago's most valuable resource—our people. From Rogers Park to Woodlawn and from South Shore to Austin, the real secret of our urban vitality rests in the most celebrated collection of local communities anywhere. In our neighborhoods, the pace and proportions of urban life are made manageable. In our neighborhoods we find a place to call our own. We are grateful to those men and women, the five hundred thirty-four who gave their lives to guard and defend the people of Chicago. May all of them enjoy the reward of their goodness.

Things won are done; joy's soul lies in the doing.
Troilus and Cressida, I, ii

Honorable Edward M. Burke

Acknowledgements

Good name in man and woman, dear my lord,
Is the immediate jewel of their souls;
Who steals my purse, steals trash; 'Tis something, nothing;
'Twas mine, 'tis his and has been slave to thousands;
But he that filches from me my good name
Robs me of that which not enriches him,
And makes me poor indeed. [Othello, III, iii, 153]

It has always been our wish to reverence the reputations and sacrifice of the five-hundred thirty-four men and women whose stories we tell. This goal united all our actions and research. We had accomplices, muses, inspirations and valued friends in this common task. We are eternally grateful for their companionship and loyalty in this heartfelt effort.

This project owes a great deal of its life to **Ellen Kuchuris**, a most able assistant and Master of Political Science. A skilled researcher and woman of commodious industry, her careful management of our texts, and our tempers, was heavy lifting indeed.

Erin Waitz and **Megan Flaherty**, *Hawkeyes* from the University of Iowa, truly helped to bring the never-ending research to its conclusion. Their great hearts led them deep into the living and dying of our heroes, filled with respect and a nose for lost clues. In keeping track of the towers of documents and files they gave great shape to the work.

Sean Sweany of the University of Notre Dame, is an able journalist and classics scholar. He brought nuance and technical skills to the effort, educating everyone on the project by his facility with spreadsheets, data and an erudite love of history.

Megan Cleary from the University of Illinois and **Bridget Tully** from Georgetown University maneuvered their way around cyberspace and earth space, uncovering new avenues of documentation and pathways to important information.

The project behind *End of Watch* was a ten-year process. It began with summer interns copying the details of every policeman's death in historical Chicago newspapers of their times, and then creating the master-binders that served as our *tabula rosa* for all that followed. From this initial effort we fashioned our methodology and the vocabulary of our work. Our interns spent countless hours in the Harold Washington Library shifting through the details of old Chicago and helped to provide the framework for the narratives presented here in *End of Watch*. Today many of them have gone on to pursue noble professions. But they were present at the beginning, always supervised by Andrea Miller who helped early on as organizer and gatekeeper for this work. Her cool diplomacy and engaging knowledge of Chicago's reservoirs of historical information unearthed little known or obscure sources of materials. Without her, or her minions, this important structure would never have come about. **Amanda Augustine Vanek**, now a Chicago Police Officer herself, and other students all dipped their toes into the research pool and helped make it work.

Cook County Clerk **David Orr**, and Director of the Office of Vital Statistic **Timothy J. Dever**, gave great assistance providing documents without which our efforts might be less concrete. What friends they proved to be, providing us with more than 100 death certificates for Chicago's earliest police. These proved rich records not only of death, but of life. To them and their patient staff we are profoundly grateful.

Alderman **Isaac Carothers**, Chairman of the Chicago City Council Committee on Police and Fire, and the members of his committee, for all their leadership and efforts in conducting hearings to resolve the impasse of Constable James Quinn's exclusion from full recognition in modern times.

President Gary Johnson of the Chicago History Museum, the museum's valued Historian Russell Lewis and ever friendly Robert Medina, the museum's Rights and Reproduction Coordinator; each demonstrated how devoted to Chicago history they are. Without them, the beauty and scholarship of our efforts would never have been as keen. Their extraordinary generosity pays great homage to the men and women of the Chicago Police Department. Access to their photo archive reshaped the contours of *End of Watch*. Use of the *Chicago Daily News* Photo Collection, housed at the museum, provided us with stunning glass plate negatives that tell their own bold historical commentary throughout our pages. We are also grateful for their willingness to evaluate the historical documentation and corroborative evidence regarding Constable James Quinn and his full recognition by present day Chicago Police Authorities as a line of duty death.

The staff of the Municipal Reference Collection at the Harold Washington Library were an endless source of Chicago history, assistance and generators of statistics.

Chicago Police Superintendent Philip Cline, First Deputy Superintendent Dana Starks, Chief Counsel Sheri Mecklenburg and Inter-Governmental Affairs Director Robert Buckley all opened the history of the Chicago Police Department for us. The photography staff at Police Headquarters, the Photo Reproduction and Graphic Arts Department, provided a great service to those we honor through the hundreds of photographs they shared.

Mary Pat McCullough of the Fraternal Order of Police was a constant source of assistance locating badge numbers and pieces of lost information. Her savvy understanding of the how to get things done was a generous font of encouragement.

CPD. Sgt.(Ret.) Larry Augustine had a remarkable knack for helping retrieve obscure information or for connecting us to the right person at every turn.

The Hundred Club of Cook County and President Ralph G. Scheu often helped us from going in a wrong direction.

Professor Leigh Bienen of Northwestern University School of Law gave life to a remarkable project, *Homicide in Chicago 1870-1930*. She and her students made a lasting contribution to our understanding of the complexities of violent crime in our city. We cherished the richness of their research. Frequently it pointed us in the right direction or saved us from running down a wrong trail. Their data concerning the prosecutions of many homicide cases is one of a kind. We valued the website they developed, a treasure trove of accurate information. They shined a bright torch on many of the forgotten details concerning the violent deaths of many Chicago Police officers up to 1930.

President David Spadafore and the staff of the Newberry Library were essential in assisting in our search for census data and the location of old Chicago addresses before the 1909 renumbering of Chicago streets.

Former CPO Detective James Concannon, a rugged Chicago Police Veteran with a wide memory for lore and a knack for reviving Chicago characters of glory days, remains a giant without equal and a true friend. His daily reminiscences inspired us, and his stories of his noble friends on the job expanded our imaginations. He shared the grace of a lost time with us with exceeding generosity. In the process he quietly gave honor to the brave men he knew.

The families of many slain officers provided us with photos or mementos that deepened our understanding and the quality of our work. Father Thomas Mescall and the Mescall family; Mrs. Regina O'Brien and the O'Brien family; William R. Kushner, Chief of the Berwyn Police Department; and Martin Moylan and the Moylan family provided great resources for our work. We are also grateful to descendants of Constable James Quinn and Patrolman Casper Lauer, the families of Chicago's very earliest slain officers.

In Ireland, Desmond Fitzgerald, the 22nd Knight of Glin, helped connect us to Bernard Stack, historian of the village of Glin, County Limerick, the birthplace of "Terrible" Tommy O'Connor. He assisted us kindly reviewing records in Glin Parish Church, as well as making enquiries among families of present day O'Connors there.

The Irish Fellowship Club of Chicago's President, Kathy Taylor, provided us with an original copy of John Flinn's 1887 *History of the Chicago Police*. So we proceeded on our journey with a brittle, yellow historical roadmap that guided us through Flinn's urban synthesis. He was a fine writer and loved Chicago. As always, Kathy Taylor's generosity, and that of her dear mother, Dorothy, touched us all. We were not surprised to discover the Taylor family grew up on the city's Westside near Chicago Detective Martin Moylan, killed in 1952.

The *Chicago Tribune* provided many wonderful photographs of period crime scenes and related police photos. Editor Jim O'Shea and Debra Bade, Editor, News Research and Archives, were very helpful and speedy in the processing and delivery of photos to us.

Chicago Sun-Times publisher John Cruickshank was of great assistance, helping us get our hands on a very special photo.

We are indebted to individuals whose assistance was indispensable and whose identity will remain anonymous at their request.

We are grateful to book-artisan Sam Silvio for the luxurious quality of the design and workmanship of this volume *End of Watch*. He crafted the pages of our text into a sophisticated and artistic style worthy of the heroes we honor. We are so pleased with the quality of the book's cover that tells everyone immediately this is a work of noble purpose. Apparently, it is possible to judge a book as such.

We are grateful to publisher Neal Samors for all his efforts at keeping us on schedule and taking care of the thousands of details behind the publishing of this work.

Potter Palmer IV carries a pedigree of remarkable Chicago refinement. He is, as well, a high-priest of Chicago History and was most generous with his time and effort in seeing to it that Constable James Quinn, the first Chicago policeman to die on-duty, received a fair hearing. How proud his ancestors, the original Potter and Bertha, must be. All Chicagoans are grateful to the Palmers for the economic, cultural and social leadership they gave Chicago (and all those Impressionist paintings). Few may know that back in 1854, Potter Palmer I was a member of the jury that heard the case of Constable Quinn's killer, Bill Rees.

The Police Departments of many cities were good enough to provide us with current and up to date statistics on their own history. We salute their kindness in New York, Boston, Philadelphia, Washington D.C., Miami, Baltimore, Detroit, St. Louis, New Orleans, Los Angeles, San Francisco and London Metro.

At the suggestion of America's premier historian, story-teller and PBS narrator, the eminent David McCullough, we included in our project a comparison of the deaths of police officers in thirteen major urban centers (twelve plus Chicago). Mr. McCullough suspected correctly that we would discover some surprising information with which to make conclusions in an area of urban history not previously well-published. So *to* him we are much obliged for the bright challenge, and *for* him we hope we have accomplished a small goal for other historians to review and refine. Thank you Mr. McCullough for your love of American urban history that you know brims with the living of true heroes.

And to former DEA Agent (Ret.), and Chicagoan, Richard Barrett, whose proudest accolade remains that of being the son, grandson and great-grandson of courageous Chicago policemen, our very deepest and most humble thanks. An elegant student of history, Richard Barrett was an inexhaustible guide through the hallways of history for us in both the metropolis of Chicago and the Chicago Police Department. His adept facility with maneuvering through the Library of Congress and the Illinois State Archives is without equal. It paid off for us. He was a generous scholar and assisted in challenging the muddled history of Chicago's past. His fluency with the literature of history was a powerful resource for us in tracking down lost data, hidden truths, obscured facts and erroneous points of history. In addition, his willingness to assist in proofreading and editing was a great gift and act of friendship. His devotion to truthfulness and his ferocious loyalty to law enforcement heroes made him the champion of Constable James Quinn. Single-handed, he never gave up his conviction that James Quinn was shafted by history past and present. His impeccable scholarship confounded those critics who dismissed Quinn's sacrifice without the foundation of either scholarship or merit. Leaving no stone unturned, Richard Barrett wrote with the finger of judgment on the shabby bigotry of those who would deny Constable Quinn the vindication of history. His reward has been the empty silence, now, of those who possessed neither academic excellence nor credible scholarship.

Thomas Berry of the Catholic Cemeteries of the Archdiocese of Chicago was of singular assistance helping to locate the graves and cemeteries in which these fallen heroes rest.

Ryan Tubbs, Chief Information Officer of the Committee on Finance, was an enthusiastic computer wizard, making hard tasks easy. Dan Pascale for assistance with legal and commercial aspects with this project.

All of these remarkable helpers teach us what Shakespeare knew so well and spoke so well in *Richard III*—

An honest tale speeds best being plainly told.

Prologue

"End of Watch," in the language of law enforcement, means a tour of duty ends. For some, the truest and the most courageous, that moment, often, meant an eternal good-bye, a haunted separation beset by anguish, hurt and pain. In the hopeful healing of time and history, that moment is redeemed by a legacy of honor that brightens all darkness.

End of Watch is the story of those who no longer have a voice; men and women whose final moments of heroic living have been, at times, obscured by history and halted memory. Our work in this volume is both tribute and history; narrative and eulogy; poetic panegyric and solid Chicago fact. This is the saga of five hundred and thirty-four men and women, all sworn officers of the Chicago Police Department, each giving beyond the measure of human ability. At first glance, each of these officers might appear very different from one another when measured by the externals of time and culture, religion and race, ethnic origins and political loyalties. Yet over the long era of one hundred and fifty-three years of Chicago municipal history, they are fashioned from the same virtue and valor; the same conscious nobility expended in the safe-guarding of others. Whether their world was the rough-hewed wooden sidewalks and primitive police work of pre-Fire Chicago, or the shimmering metropolis of soaring skyscrapers and high tech crime detection, all these hearts are united by uncommon realities—a willingness to take great risks for others and devotion to the City of Chicago.

Our work, *End of Watch*, is an attempt to lift the veil of history to uncover the facts of each hero's life and death. We seek to know both the big picture and the small detail. Our reach is for the forgotten fact or the never-known story. All historians write, in one way or another, to save the reality of the past from the sentimentality of time or the easy romanticism of myth. We hope that we have accomplished this in honoring these heroes. We believe the heroes of the past are best honored by the truthfulness of thorough study and accurate research. To that end, we have struggled to achieve this at all costs—a goal sometimes made more difficult by the forces of history, like fire, flame, flood and spotty record keeping. We have been excited to discover the nineteenth century passion for detailed reporting of events both common and solemn. We were overjoyed to find the conflicts of early Chicago life and municipal growth reported with edgy, and often bold, exactitude. We were grateful that the events surrounding the deaths of Chicago Police personnel usually received significant attention and public honor—for each officer's death took place in a real time of tears and sorrows, family grief and heartbreak. We have sought to connect, whenever possible, the human story of each officer's family and cherished loved ones for whom this particular death was so personal and distressing. We have tried to tell, as well, the public side to the violence, criminal actions or tragic accidents that brought public outrage or regret. There is an old Irish saying that is sage advice when sorting through the baggage of the past.

May you never forget what is worth remembering, nor ever remember what is best forgotten.

For some this is a warning about the impact of people and events in our life; for others it remains a powerful wisdom, shielding wounds and emotions that never heal.

At the outset, we must explain how we arrived at the final number of our list of five-hundred thirty-four Chicago Police Officers. We began our work using the established list of four hundred forty-two officers represented in the Superintendent's Honored Star Case, located on the first floor of police headquarters at 35th Street and Michigan Avenue. On May 15, 2006, the Chicago Police Memorial Foundation issued a further supplemental list of all the officers whose names would appear on the new Police Memorial located along the lakefront near Soldier Field. This included an additional seventy-nine names beyond the roll of the star case officers. One additional name was discovered on the national police memorial website, known as the *Officer Down Memorial Page.* To this we added the names of twelve other officers we discovered during the course of our research. This brought the number in total to five-hundred thirty-four.

For the purpose of our research and written narrative, we amalgamated what we saw as the varied standards of evaluation for consideration by the Chicago Police Department, the Association of Chiefs of Police and other memorial associations. Good scholarship, as well as good judgment, became the bye-words of our efforts. We wanted to be as inclusive as possible and tell the very broadest possible human history. Our only intention was to place an officer's story before the reader. Perhaps there are times when our judgment conflicts with that of others. If so, we entreat your understanding. You will be the best judge of our efforts. Remembering, for us, is more important than judgment. And

more sacred! Valor is a hard virtue to measure. As Shakespeare
wrote in *Henry IV* Pt. 1 –

By heaven methinks it were an easy leap
To pluck bright honour from the pale-faced moon,
Or dive into the bottom of the deep,
Where fathom-line could never touch the ground,
And pluck up drowned honour by the locks.

In attempting to tell the story of these men and women, a secondary
tale emerges, an urban history told through the life and death of these
remarkable human beings. Whether a death took place in the era of gas
lamps and horse-drawn carriages, or under the shrill, piercing sound
of a siren and flashing Chicago-blue Mars light of the modern squad car,
the fatal sacrifice of these remarkable police officers tells a piece of the
truth about the City of Chicago and the people residing here.

We hope that in journeying through the narratives describing the
circumstances of each slain officer's death, our readers will come to a
fuller appreciation of the individual life of each. These heroes were each
someone's father, mother, husband, wife, brother, sister, neighbor, friend,
partner or colleague. Each death shattered the spirits of a large circle of
humanity, often with shocking speed—unexpected, unforeseen and with
enormous human pain. Long after the obsequies and rites of burial took
place, heartbroken spouses often had to endure the further pain of
criminal trials, judicial sentencing or the reliving of the most tragic event
in their life in the glare of the public press and larger media. For many
families, the death of their loved one was an intimate and personal loss,
a legacy enshrined in family history forever. For others, the passage of
time may have removed all active memory or details of an ancestor's
death in the line of duty. We hope that for families searching for the
accurate historical facts of a loved one's death *End of Watch* may revive
new understanding or appreciation.

To accomplish our goal of bringing five-hundred thirty-four
narratives to completion, we have relied on many sources for facts and
explanations, chiefly newspapers of the periods, often rich in the spirit
of the times and photographic detail. ProQuest, the indispensable
on-line search-engine, led us into the historical past in both the pages of
the *Chicago Tribune* and the *Daily Defender*. We have also relied on
municipal records such as death certificates. Frequently these documents

provided minutiae found nowhere else. Cemetery documents also proved to be an in-exhaustive source of family data and history that corroborated uncertain information. Church records also enabled us to elaborate on the personal history and neighborhood connections of many. Miraculously, the records of the Chicago Common Council, tracing the early legislative history of the city, thought to be lost for more than a century, were rediscovered in 1981 and became a golden flow of documentation for early municipal life and the Chicago Police Department.

Northwestern University School of Law's remarkable project *Homicide in Chicago 1870-1930*, directed by Professor Leigh Beinen, has made a lasting contribution to our understanding of the complexities of violent death in our city. In addition, students engaged in exhaustive research collecting data on the prosecutions of many cases, as well as their final determinations. This provided invaluable additional information to the details surrounding the death's of many officers. The website that developed out of this academic exercise (http://homicide.northwestern.edu) includes important details on the violent deaths of many Chicago Police Officers up to 1930.

From many contemporary newspaper accounts we were able to uncover critical details concerning the important role of African-Americans in Chicago law enforcement. It is striking that by 1890 there were thirty patrolmen and detectives of African-American heritage on the Chicago Police force. Just months before the Chicago Fire of 1871, James Shelton became the very first African-American to serve as a Chicago Policeman. Forty-three years later, Grace Wilson became Chicago's first African-American woman police officer in 1918. The first African-American police fatality took place on July 28, 1919 when Officer John Simpson was shot to death. This tragedy was related to the horrific race riots that erupted on the city's Southside during the summer months. Records also permitted us to chart the appointments of the first African-Americans to higher ranks within the Chicago Police Department. In all, more than fifty African-American police officers were killed in the line of duty. Chicago's first female officer killed on duty, Dorelle C. Brandon, on January 25, 1984, was also an African-American.

Sworn officers from among Chicago's Hispanic community entered the ranks of the Chicago Police Department later in the twentieth century. The first Hispanic to die in the line of duty was Officer Orestes E. Gonzales, shot to death on May 8, 1953. Officer Irma C. Ruiz became the first female Hispanic officer to die when she was shot September 22, 1988. With larger numbers of Hispanics now serving on the police force, the numbers of line of duty deaths has risen. That is graphically illustrated with four of the last seven Chicago Police to die on duty being of Hispanic descent. Officer Eric Solorio was, in fact, Chicago's last policeman to die on February 12, 2006, succumbing to injuries suffered in a fatal car crash one month previously.

Women first officially became sworn members of the Chicago Police Department on August 5, 1913. That was three years after the first woman in American history, Alice Stebbin Wells, received police power in Los Angeles in 1910; and twelve years before women were sworn-in to the New York Police Department in 1925. Ten Chicago women were given the oath that day. Seventy-one years later, Dorelle Brandon, Chicago's first female officer to die on duty, was killed in 1984. Five women in total have been killed in the line of duty in Chicago. All died between 1984 and 2003. Three were the victims of gunshot wounds; one died in a car accident and another drowned.

Many aspects of our search and enquiries were generously assisted by the Chicago Police Department. They were especially helpful in obtaining hundreds of photos of individual officers, crime scene photos, as well as those of historic station houses. They were a rich resource for research. Historians in both Ireland and France were helpful in tracking down hunches, suspicions and leads, forming a bridge into our Chicago tales. The Chicago History Museum was a thicket of historical enterprise providing without rival a doorway into every decade of Chicago living. Their archival material cemented our foundations for this historical travel. Their stunning collections of photography make the neighbor-hoods of Chicago come to life. And the treasury of their *Chicago Daily News* photo archive is a brilliant showcase of city life in its own right. What a luxurious history of Chicago these images display. The quality is without rival in any generation. These photos alone give voice and power to the personalities of the past in a way no written narrative can. Study them. See the detail of human life they expose in the light and shadow of everyday life. You can feel the grit. You can smell the humanity and ramshackle urban streetscape. Best of all, they enable every one of us to move through the textures that framed the context for many who lived before us, especially the heroes of the Chicago Police Department.

Hopefully, the reader will take time, too, with what is truly the most dramatic photo in our collection here—the Daguerre-type image of Officer Casper Lauer (see p.73), the second Chicago Policeman to die in the line duty in 1854. Photography was in its infancy, especially in early Chicago.

The very fact that someone managed to have the foresight to photograph the dead Officer Lauer in his coffin tells us something significant about the impact of Lauer's death and the sophistication of 1854 Chicago. The image is raw, unvarnished and startling—almost too real. We are exposed by its harsh and bitter truthfulness. It may be Chicago's most important photographic image. We are grateful, indeed, for the ability to use it with the permission and assistance of Officer Lauer's descendants who still reside in the Chicago area. They enrich all of us by their legacy of noble generosity. What might Officer Lauer think, knowing that one hundred fifty-two years after his brutal murder, Chicagoans are still viewing his image and discussing the valor of his sacrifice on the corner of Jackson and Plymouth?

End of Watch is an important historical dialogue; one that involves each of the officers whose stories we catalogue. Questions should be raised and debated about everyone included here. Notice the quality of the medical attention in the past. Think of all the officers who were taken to their family home to die when scant medical possibilities were available. Scrutinize the age of these police heroes, many were very young; fresh kids who might have escaped the shotgun blast, the knife point, the auto accident or bomb blast with more privilege and opportunity. Of the five-hundred thirty-four men and women who perished while "on the job," three-hundred eighty-two were the victims of gunshots; twenty-two died in motorcycle accidents; ten were fatally injured by a train, while eight were the victims of a bomb. More than fifty died in car crashes; twelve died from injuries sustained in a fight; while sixteen suffered fatal heart attacks. Two fell from a window to their deaths; three fell from their horse and were killed; and one even died as a result of severe radiation poisoning after the explosion of a gun scope he was testing (see p. 554). Thirty-nine were detectives; twenty-one had the rank of detective-sergeant; twenty-seven were sergeants; three lieutenants; one captain and one first deputy superintendent fell on duty over the decades, together with four hundred forty-two patrol officers. First Deputy Superintendent James J. Riordan remains the highest ranking police officer to be killed in Chicago history (see p. 555).

Remarkably, during Chicago's most unstable period of law enforcement, in the department's first forty years, from 1835 to 1875, only five Chicago policemen were killed. Such homicides were usually the exception when compared to the levels of local urban violence, even at this time when two-thirds of the male population carried concealed hand guns; and even during periods of extraordinary population explosions.

The Chicago Police Department is an urban institution with a long period of incubation counting several cycles of reform and reorganization. From the earliest days of elected constables to later eras of reconstitution under scrutinizing mayors, the Department of Police evolved in a slow and determined manner, inch-by-inch from 1835 onwards. Sometimes great achievements were made. At other times the frailty of human failure and hapless banality prevented a more speedy maturation and development. Surprisingly, in one of the most heinous moments of unbridled prejudice in Chicago bigotry, the Know-Nothing era when foreign-born American citizens were seen as unfit for civic employment, the institution of the Police Department made its most significant transition towards efficient administration. Though the Know-Nothings were short lived, the infection of their bigotry remained woven into the heart of law enforcement in the city. How ironic that Chicago's swelling population of immigrant citizens, most notably the Irish, made such great advancements in the police department in spite of the politics of prejudice.

In the one hundred seventy-one years since the start of the Chicago Police Department, one of the great indicators of police effectiveness has been the apprehension and arrest of law breakers (see pp. 552-553). No matter how sophisticated the tools of police work become, nothing beats putting a perpetrator behind bars. Measuring the numbers of those arrested has, at times been spotty, but the figures we were able to unearth provide an interesting look at some hard facts of Chicago crime and law enforcement. In 1853, there were 2,499 arrests made at a time when the population was near 59,000. In 1855, the number of arrests doubled to 5,008. In 1861, when the population climbed to well over 120,000, the number of arrests rose to 8,782. In 1864, in the hardest days of the Civil War, with a population of 169,000, arrests climbed to 14,014. Arrests soared to more than 25,000 in 1870, the year before the Great Fire when the population was almost 300,000. In 1879, as the population reached the 500,000 mark, arrests went over 30,000. In 1885, with a population of 650,000—more than 40,000 arrests were made. As Chicago's population dipped over 1,000,000 in 1890, arrests went past 60,000. It was not until 1913 that the number of arrests totaled more than 100,000. There were more than 2,300,000 residents by then. In 1924, during the hey-day of Prohibition, with the population almost at the 3,000,000 mark, Chicago counted 242,602 arrests. That was high indeed; but 1925 surpassed this figure, with 262,494 arrests. There begins a gradual decline in the number of arrests after this until 1937, a soaring year with Depression era statistics reaching almost 300,000 arrests. But that number was not crossed until after World War II, when there were 333,079 arrests in 1947. There were 7,319 Chicago Police on the streets at the time. Figures drop steadily during the 1950s. In 1959, there were just 69,122 arrests. The all time high was reached in 1982 when there were 412,965 arrests made by a force of 12,374 police. Since then arrests have stayed steady above the 250,000 mark. Winston Churchill once remarked that the true measure of citizenship is the willingness of ordinary people to perform with extraordinary courage. Each day the men and women of the Chicago Police Department deepen the truth of that wisdom in all that they do.

In attempting to catalogue the varying numbers of sworn officers in the police ranks from the beginning, we have had to rely on a wide variety of sources. The Chicago Police Department and publications in the Municipal Reference Library provided us with many of our numbers. The very earliest count was discovered in the records of the Common Council of the City of Chicago. Attempting to arrive at a verifiable number year-by-year often proved difficult. Two Chicago histories of the Police Department, John J. Flinn's *History of the Chicago Police* (1887), and Raphael Marrow's *In the Pursuit of Crime, 1833-1933* (1996), never had the opportunity to review many municipal documents concerning the city's police. Like most of their contemporaries, they presumed all such records perished in the Great Fire of 1871. However, now with the availability of such documents some eras have more accuracy in the number reported. We hope the reader will understand the dilemma that any historian faces in such circumstances. Wherever possible, we have attempted to verify such statistics. Competing sources at times proved conflicting. When possible we relied on the documents of the Common Council.

At the suggestion of historian David McCullough, we expanded our investigations to include the gathering of data on police officers slain in the line of duty in twelve other police jurisdictions for the purpose of comparison (see p. 556). We sought to understand where Chicago fit among the other great urban centers of law enforcement. Graphs and charts illustrating those discoveries are contained in an appendix at the end of our book. Included in the information collected was the "official" date of the establishment of each police department in these cities. Curiously enough, no matter how old a given city was, or how young in Chicago's case, most cities cite founding dates for their modern police force some-time in the early to mid nineteenth century. Chicago was incorporated as a town in 1833 and as a city in 1837. But 1835 has been generally accepted

This permitted police on the beat the ability to send a signal to their local station. The use of the telephone also transformed the effectiveness of police work. With the coming of automotive technology, police entered a whole new age as motorcycles and "flivvers" (flimsy primitive police cars) changed the manner in which crime and law breakers were engaged. But you will also discover in our narratives that, despite the advances made by the modernization of law enforcement, the criminal element in a metropolis like Chicago were equally quick to match the advances of those who pursued them.

History is an enterprise that entwines many layers of research and analysis. Its ultimate goal is a fresher, more expansive view of the truthfulness of who we are. If this be true, we hope we have accomplished our goal to bring the fullest possible perspectives of the sacrifice given by the men and women of the Chicago Police Department as recorded in this work. We also hope that we have assisted in bringing each individual police officer to a more recognizable understanding by the general public—for each of these individuals was a real human being. In their everyday lives, they brought laughter and delight, strength and stability to those they cherished and served. Many were ruled by expansive emotions, a nose for crime or a passionate distaste for law breakers. At home they sang, perhaps the tunes of the old country of their birth. They were people of prayer—vocal, robust and public; while some, most likely, were people of a quiet and personal devotion uttered in the silence of their own hearts when situations got rough or spun out of control. Many uttered their final human words in a prayer for mercy, or for the loved ones they left behind. Whether in the era of whiskers and handle-bar mustaches, or military crew-cuts, each of these officers was a full human being of incomparable measure. Each died too soon; often in their prime, in the fullness of their young lives. *End of Watch* celebrates their brash, bold, adventurous lives so filled with promise. For some, generations of family members never forgot and still recall their memory and sacrifice. For others, perhaps all living family is gone leaving no one to recall the full extent of their heroic sacrifice on behalf of the people of Chicago. Hopefully, *End of Watch* will channel a new awareness of these heroes— who they were and what they did. Say their names out loud. Learn where they perished. Visit their grave in a local Chicago cemetery. Light a candle in their memory. Let a word of prayer fall off your lips for them. Let your appreciation for their generous sacrifice bridge the gaps of time and the eras of the forgotten past. Do not permit the passion of their living and dying to go unnoticed. Each made an impact on their own time in the Chicago in which they lived. Armed with a more sensitive knowledge and understanding of each of their stories, let the barriers of time cease to divide. History has the power and the grace to unite by the grandeur of its own poetry and intelligence. If it reshapes your understanding of their sacrifice, then we have accomplished our goal.

We hope that *End of Watch* will bring honor to all these police heroes of the past. We also hope that it will bring honor to those who presently serve as sworn officers in the Chicago Police Department. It is our common prayer that no addenda will be necessary to augment the ranks of the dead remembered here in these pages. These five-hundred thirty-four Chicago Police souls stretch from Constable James Quinn in 1853 to Officer Eric Solorio in 2006. In the arch of that long span of time, the Union of our States was saved, the horror of human slavery was ended, Chicago rose-up from the ash heap more vibrant and resilient than ever, electricity was discovered, the 1893 World's Fair recalibrated the city's life, and the greatest inventions and discoveries of human intelligence reshaped our planet. When the atom was split beneath the football stands at the University of Chicago the clock of history was re-set and a new age began, eclipsing previous events of great Chicago technology, like the fete of reversing the flow of the Chicago River on the first day of the 20th century. No one should have been surprised, then, that the moon has been trod upon by human feet leaving ageless footprints in the dust. We have seen such glory in our own time, and in every time, in the vibrant stride of heroes, uncommon beings in common times. Their strength continues to shape those who loved them; those who still bear witness to their virtue; and those who remain safe by the eternal strength of their sacrifice.

We live in deeds, not years; in thoughts not breaths; in feelings, not in figures on a dial. We should count time by heart throbs...
Aristotle

Edward M. Burke and Thomas J. O'Gorman

The Chicago Police Department evolved much like the City of Chicago, changing with the forces of history and adapting to the pragmatic needs of the present. Its origins predate the incorporation of Chicago as a city. Between 1835 and 1871, the life span from pioneer days to the Great Fire, the Chicago Police Department matured into a well organized and highly professional expression of American law enforcement. Its early history during that period has often been forgotten and misunderstood. Only with the discovery of municipal records once

thought destroyed in the Great Fire
has it been possible to reconstruct
its beginnings and growth into
one of the nation's most effective
urban police forces. That early saga
provides the opportunity to
better understand the way in which
the Chicago Police Department grew
in modern times. Its early history
is a bright and resourceful tale.

Chicago is the capitol of the American
heartland—the robust center of the
nation's most vibrant economic muscle
and its most erudite architectural
grandeur. On the prairie, life unfolds

with a peculiar bonding to the soil. Here in the heart of the American continent, it stretches out for more than 230-square miles at Chicago. The start of Chicago's urban history opens when President Thomas Jefferson instructs his Secretary of War, Henry Dearborn, to construct a fortification at the strategic edge of the infant nation at the very juncture where the prairie meets the waters of the Great Lakes; at what today is the modern city of Chicago. Here, the land is miraculously shaped by the waters surrounding it.

Chicago first came to life in the primitive character of the stockade pilings of Old Fort Dearborn in 1803. Captain John Whistler, a Dublin-born engineer, was responsible for directing the timbered fort's construction. He was the first in a long line of prairie newcomers to alter the landscape that was to be Chicago. Built along the palisades joining river water and lake, the fort represented one of the nation's first endeavors to expand the contours of the Republic. The settlement here was rich in resources, especially the fur trade. Trappers and traders populated the meager, primitive environment tough skinned and ready for whatever came.

Township

Thirty years after the completion of the fort, on August 14, 1833, after the upheaval of intervening wars and treaties with Native peoples, Chicago incorporated as a town. It numbered a population of 350—more than three times its population just three years before. A Board of Trustees was elected; then, charged with the responsibilities of promoting the well-being of the town.

The boundaries of this settlement stretched between what is today DesPlaines Street on the West, State Street on the East, Kinzie Street on the North and Madison Street on the South—barely measuring one square mile. Just four years later, on March 4, 1837, the town officially incorporated as a city. On May 2 of that year, William Butler Ogden, a Democrat, was elected the city's first mayor. A fortuitous adventure thus began, setting in motion the most stunning saga in 19th Century American urban life. By 1840, Chicago bragged of almost 4,500 souls.

Fast-paced growth was a becoming a Chicago way of life. Such dramatic development would never cease. Chicago became the fastest growing city on earth in the last decades of the 19th century. Surviving great catastrophe, it became the most resilient landscape in the nation. This was a new kind of American city, a magnet drawing both new immigrants from weary Europe—men like Constable James Quinn from Ireland, Constable Casper Lauer from France and Policeman John Churchwood from England; as well as adventurous Yankees tired of the constrictions of New England Sabbaths—like financier Gurdon Saltonstall Hubbard, hotel magnate Potter Palmer, department store giant Marshall Field and railroad coach manufacturer George Pullman.

The Tools of Law Enforcement

Chicago's move to expanded municipal governance brought with it all the details and necessities of civilized living, even at the edge of the frontier. No sooner did the town incorporate than it fashioned a city jail, an indispensable tool for enforcing public safety. The log-cabin style structure was as much a symbol of development, as it was a practical tool of law enforcement. In addition, Chicago's first police force was soon organized with three constables being elected in August of 1835—Oresmus Morrison, Luther Nichols and John Shrigley. This was the germ from which all other policing would evolve in Chicago. This evolving nature of Chicago law enforcement permitted it the ability to meet the needs of the times from township days to chaotic twentieth century urban life. This is how the role of the constable was defined in Chicago in 1835:

It shall be the duty of the police constables to see that the peace of the town is kept, to quell all disturbances, and to take into immediate custody all disorderly and riotous persons, to report to the board of trustees all infractions of any of the ordinances of said town, to serve all processes where the trustees of said town are parties, to observe and carry into effect so far as practicable the directions of the board, or any individual trustee, to attend all suits wherein trustees are parties, to attend all fires within the limits of said town, and to protect the property that may be exposed from depredations and destruction. [Ordinance of November 4, 1835]

As the town of Chicago transformed into a city, it also set about furthering the framework for its official law enforcement organization, Chicago's police. The impact of this metropolitan institution cannot be under-estimated, especially in the early days of emerging urban self-understanding. It would become the centerpiece of any successful future municipal government.

A constabulary charged with the defense of "good order," quickly emerged. Following Chicago's incorporation as a city in 1837, an election was held to fill the newly created office of High Constable. John Shrigley of the township constables was elected. He was given three assistants by the Common Council, Joseph Brown, E, N. Churchill and James Matthews. Three further constables were appointed. They consisted of S.S. Bradley, Constable of the 4th Ward; Luther Nichols, Constable of the 1st Ward and Daniel Heartt, Constable of the 2nd Ward. These six fit the proportions of the law providing each of the city's newly drawn six wards; one constable per ward. Over the course of the intervening years, the Common Council, as the City Council was known then, was content to observe the economic realities of the time and permit a reduced force that dropped to three or four men at times. The full number was not made mandatory until 1848. This marked yet another transition in the organized police force in Chicago. On December 9, 1837 the pay for constables was set at one dollar and fifty cents per day.

John Kelly, a long-time Chicago police reporter, often wrote of conversations he had with old-time policemen whose memories were unbroken threads to the early days of city life. No one better demonstrated this than Alexander Beaubien. Born in Chicago in 1822 at Old Fort Dearborn, Beaubien was the first child baptized in Chicago by its first Catholic priest, Father John St. Cyr. Beaubien lived until 1907, dying at the age of 85. His career as a Chicago Policeman, the long-time lock-up keeper at the Harrison Street Station, was shaped by his remarkable longevity and frontier Chicago pedigree. He was the son of General Jean-Baptiste Beaubien, and a nephew of Mark Beaubien whose tavern was among the first commercial enterprises in Chicago history. Officer Alexander Beaubien recalled Chicago's earliest police with precision:

I remember Jack Shrigley very well, for I was fifteen years old when he took office as high constable. On account of his exalted position I used to think he was the leading citizen of Chicago. He was a man of great prowess and very clever with his dukes. Once I saw him lift a barrel of whiskey off the ground to a platform four feet high. The city's first calaboose was at Madison Street and Michigan Avenue (at that time on the lake shore proper), and I often saw Shrigley dragging prisoners there after he put them to sleep with his fists. [John Kelly, *Chicago Police Digest*, March 1942]

Shrigley was succeeded in 1839 by his assistant, Samuel J. Lowe who would administer the police until he was elected Sheriff of Cook County in 1842. Before he left the post, the Common Council amended the City Charter creating the office of City Marshal and made it an elected position. Orson Smith, Lowe's successor, was the first to hold that position. Smith remained Marshal until 1845 and is credited by many with influencing progress and the expansion of the police force. Philip Dean then spent two years as Marshal before being succeeded by Ambrose Burnham in 1847.

Political Chicago

Recognizing the unique bond between Chicago's mayors and the force of organized police is an essential construct of Chicago life. With mayors only holding a one year term of office, the life cycle of the police were often tied to a mayor's political success or defeat. The effectiveness of each appears to be forever linked. Success and efficiency in both were often opposite sides of the same urban coin. That relationship through the decades has been frequently controversial and combative. But it was also affirming and reflective of reasoned approaches to ever-changing types of urban crime.

Alexander Beaubien, Albert Lemmersaid,
James Sinclair, W. H. Gale, George C. Foote
and Samuel Flanders standing for portrait
under a tree at an Old Settlers Picnic (1905).
DN-0001190, *Chicago Daily News* Collection,
Chicago History Museum Photo Archive.

Chicago's early mayors were plain-speaking, earnest men, whether they were Democrats or Whigs. In fact, Mayor Francis C. Sherman, Chicago's fifth mayor, validated this observation in his inaugural address, March 4, 1841, when he told his listeners of his limitations—"No portion of my life has been devoted to those studies and pursuits which qualify one for addressing the public." There was little pretense in Chicago's beginnings. But each of Chicago's early municipal leaders shared a common purpose, as Sherman put it, to deepen the principles that "naturally tend to peace and good order." A sturdy jail is a great way to start.

New Patterns of Law and Order—The Watch

Further effective legislative action was taken in 1845 to strengthen the work of Chicago's law enforcement officers. Assisting the constables in their efforts was the Night Watch. Their responsibility was to patrol the city streets during the evening hours—6:00 P.M. to 6:00 A.M. Night time lawlessness was on the increase in the city and the additional force of manpower provided much needed protection. The City Marshal found it impossible to keep convincing the constables of the need to work around the clock. This change to a regular night time police marks an important transition in refining and growing the police force as the city expanded.

This new force of peace officers had the potential to increase surveillance and intelligence during the long, and often, dangerous nighttime hours. This patrol was constituted specifically to arrest anyone found "at unusual hours, or under suspicious circumstances." Provisions were made for the Night Watch to incarcerate the suspect of any crime in the County Jail. Particular attention was called to "All drunk and disorderly persons." Adding to the muscle of the Watch was the provision that "resisting" arrest carried a high fine, as much as twenty-five dollars; a very heavy sum then.

The introduction of the Night Watch marked a further tightening of the grip of the rule of law in Chicago. As thousands of newcomers made their way to the prairie boomtown, it was necessary for Chicago's political leadership to further bolster the resources of the police. Law enforcement was becoming more systematic. Lines of authority and responsibility were continually undergoing refinement. In just a very short period, Chicago was proving its ability to reinforce the safety and success of the public's right to order and well-being.

Chicago legislators initiated a more expanded law enforcement vocabulary with the introduction of new police personnel. "Police Constables" were individuals elected by the citizens of an individual ward. "Special Police Constables" were "elected" by the Alderman of the Common Council. In reality they were more likely nominated and approved by a hand vote in the Common Council.

Legislation specified that in each of the wards of the city, the elected constable was to have his own office. The object of their attention was also further expanding, charged as they were "the protection of life and property, and the preservation of the peace and order of the city." There was much to protect with the growing commercial success of Chicago's merchant class. There was nothing like economic achievement and the acquisition of possessions of value to expand the task of police work in Chicago.

Chicago's election of its municipal government was an annual event occurring in March. So each new mayor had the opportunity of reshaping the important issue of police protection. In an ordinance "to regulate the Police of Chicago" the Common Council reiterated the necessity of having the dual force of Constable and Night Watch.

That the Mayor and Aldermen, Marshal and Police Constables, whether elected by the people or appointed by the Council, and the Watchmen of said City, shall constitute the Police thereof; And upon them respectively the peace, good order and quiet thereof, and of prosecuting or otherwise punishing violations of the laws of said city. [Ordinance, July 6, 1849]

The ordinance was detailed in placing responsibility for urban order on those who are elected. The Mayor, in fact, was charged to "superintend and direct the Police generally." Aldermen of the city, too, were required to be "conservators" of the peace in their respective wards. They were to take an active role in maintaining order. The High Constable, or City Marshal as he became known, was "constituted the Chief of Police." All other officers were "subject" to his authority. The Chief of Police was further required to keep and maintain a central office in which he could conduct business with some officers of his constabulary present in the office to attend to police business. Perhaps the most significant element of the legislation was the recurring theme of deepened attentiveness on the part of the city's constables. A more determined spirit of "duty" was woven into the expectations placed on all who served, along with "their hours and times of duty." Enforcement of the city's laws was becoming systematically professionalized in Chicago. The city was becoming more conscious of its need for civility. The rough ways of the past were becoming less tolerated. Provisions were spelled out providing for "watchmen" to be appointed as needed when the situation determined it. They were authorized to "disperse all improper crowds; arrest all persons who shall make improper noises, otherwise disturbing the quiet and order of the city." By 1849 the city was booming and wealth was a resource in which many Chicagoans came to delight. The Chicago Board of Trade was flourishing, cargoes crisscrossed the city's waterways and the railroad was coming to life. Chicago had made great strides in its first decade as a city.

The I&M Canal—A Waterway to the Future

By 1850, the population had grown to almost 30,000 citizens, 6,000 of whom were Irish-born. Most of them had arrived in Chicago as a result of the construction of the Illinois and Michigan Canal, the ninety-mile water-way connecting the Illinois River with Lake Michigan. Hand dug with the familiar tools of Irish enterprise, the pick and the shovel, the I&M Canal, as it was known, changed Chicago life forever. The city became joined through its waterways directly to the greatest water highway of them all, the Mississippi River. With such easy access, agri-commerce and manufactured goods could conveniently pass in abundance through the south branch of the Chicago River, the Illinois River and then the Mighty Mississippi. The canal emboldened Chicago's mercantile opportunities and transformed it into the most financially successful urban metropolis in the nation. The commerce of the nation's interior found its passage to the Gulf of Mexico through the waterways of Chicago.

After the completion of the I&M Canal in 1848, Chicago was on its way to breath-taking success, owed in many ways to the muscle and backbone of the Irish. In large numbers the canal-digging Irish made Chicago their home. Many settled along the route of the canal and populated the neighborhood of Bridgeport, the terminus of the project. Chicago and the prairie would never be the same. Neither would the character of Chicago law enforcement. By 1850, the number of constables had increased to nine, elected from each of the city wards. James L. Howe, a pioneer Chicago baker, was elected the City Marshal. And though it was commonly held that not much would come from the service of this baker-turned-police officer, even his biggest critics ate their words when a very definite decrease in crime occurred during his time in office.

The growth of Chicago's Catholic immigrant population, and the sense of confidence that it placed in Chicago's future, was reinforced substantially when the Roman Catholic Diocese of Chicago was established in 1843. The Irish-born William Quarter, just 37 years old, became its first bishop. Just ten years later in 1852, Irish nuns, the Sisters of Mercy, established Mercy Hospital, Chicago's first chartered hospital, at Rush Street near the Chicago River. The medical facility arrived just in time, in the midst of the series of cholera epidemics that raged between 1849 and 1855. More than six hundred Chicagoans died from the disease in 1849; with an additional four hundred dying in 1850; two hundred in 1851; six hundred in 1853 and more than 1400 in 1854. Urban expansion and unprecedented population explosion were not without their human toll. Sanitation conditions and caution with the city's water supply became a controversial municipal issue at the time, with improvements developing that reduced Chicago's dependence on unhealthy sources of water. This would remain a serious concern for decades.

The Crime Rises—The Police Expand

As the city expanded, so too did the necessity of responding to the growth of crime. Chicago Mayor James Woodworth, the tenth to occupy the office, was crystal clear in his second inaugural address, March 16, 1849, in declaring a new and improved way of fighting crime. The mayor called for the development of a new, more sturdy city jail, "a Bridewell," he called it, referring back to the landmark English prison. He wanted Chicago to have "a House of Correction." It was his intention, he said, to follow the City Charter and construct a more formidable city jail. Woodworth's focus was not just criminals, but the Chicago Police. He saw this as the most advantageous way "to give force and effect to our police organization." Even though he would have to wait for city finances to stabilize to build his jail, he proposed the immediate acquisition of land and materials with which to begin the project. He went on to suggest that the very people who would occupy this correctional facility should be the ones to build it. "What better," Woodworth proposed, "than to use that class of individuals dominated by rogues, vagabonds, stragglers, idle and disorderly persons infesting the community, and who are now permitted to go at large for the want of a proper place to confine them." The mayor laid out a wide view of Chicago law breakers, as well as the dominating civic imperative to create a safer city by developing the means to control those who threaten the public good.

Probably nothing did more to enhance the ability to deter crime on the nighttime streets that the gas lamps that were installed in 1850. Their glare added scrutiny to every foot of city pavement and provided the Night Watch with renewed opportunity for catching sight of any wrong-doer. This was nothing short of a revolution in technology and furthered the passion for things modern in Chicago life.

The Rights of a Common Citizenship

The Common Council was once again proposing new regulations for the police. In 1851, it reinforced its past support of local law enforcement and further clarified the type of individual seen as best serving the ideals of the local rule of law. One significant new component of these regulations was added by the new second Illinois State Constitution— the necessity of being a U.S. citizen in order to hold elected office. This provision came on the heals of the growing waves of immigrants that by 1850 were changing life in Chicago.

The population of Chicago peaked at roughly 30,000 individuals that year. Six thousand residents were Irish-born, and another six thousand were born in the German states, meaning that 40% of the population was made up of these two foreign-born ethnic groups alone. This was also the year that the first groups of Poles began to arrive in Chicago. It is not hard to understand the concerns that local leaders felt as such large numbers of foreign-born residents began to take such a foot hold. The Common Council was quick to respond to the realities of life, passing an ordinance that read—

No person shall be appointed a Watchman or Police Constable who is not a citizen of the United States. [Ordinance May 17, 1851]

In point-of-fact, this was no less than what the new 1848 Constitution of the State of Illinois made mandatory. It required that all persons seeking elective office, "any" public office, be a citizen of the United States. So the 1851 Common Council legislation was in no small part a response to the new Constitution. Police constables were no exception.

In addition to this litmus test, several other changes reinforced the authority of those in Chicago law enforcement. Watchmen were given the unbridled authority to enter any premises based on any reasonable suspicion that a law of the city was being violated. This applied to any house, store, shop, grocery, or other building in Chicago. If a Watchman was suspicious, there were no restrictions on his power to investigate anywhere.

The City Marshal was also given the responsibility of establishing a set of general rules for the regulation of the police. Written copies of these regulations were to be available to all members of the force. The rules were to be binding on all.

Penalties were also adopted to prevent anyone from impeding a police officer in the discharge of his duties. And in addition, anyone sentenced to imprisonment for this offense was to be subjected to hard labor while in custody in the Bridewell.

All this legislation appears to be tightening, once more, the impact of professional law enforcement. Police regulations show themselves to be an evolving urban phenomenon in Chicago. The legislation anticipates the growth spurts of Chicago as a city. The *Rules* were pragmatic and supportive of the peace officer. The evolving nature of Chicago's urban character is a powerful determinant in the shaping and reshaping of Chicago police authority.

Policing in the Sun—The Day Police

1853 was a busy year for Chicago's police. On March 14, the Common Council named and swore-in the Night Watch for 1853. The Common Council also for the first time introduced the idea of establishing a Day Police. They saw the Day Police as being able to provide significant support in the rail depots, bridges and harbors of Chicago, all areas of heavy traffic. These were important areas of commercial significance. Chicago's grain market had already become the largest in the world. The Common Council decided to give the issue of the Day Police to the Council's Committee on Police for further study.

On March 28, 1853, the Committee on Police went ahead with the decision to establish the Day Police. It produced a document, referred to as a "Report on the Committee on Police," naming nine men authorized by the Committee to become the Day Police. Later on April 7, 1853, Casper Lauer, of the Night Watch, was sworn-in as a member of the Day Police bringing the total to ten.

The establishment of the Day Police demonstrates the changing face of Chicago crime, as well as the increasing need for an expanded police presence in Chicago's bustling urban metropolis. Perhaps no other single development in the history of the city's Police Department had such a long-lasting and modern effect upon it as the Day Police. The constabulary continued to be an elected office during this period. But the Common Council recognized the need for expanding the presence of the police in the city both day and night.

At this juncture, the Common Council understood that the old May 1851 Ordinance that "regulated, established and created" the Police department needed to be updated. Any shortcomings in it or in the "Report" creating the Day Police were now rectified by a new ordinance. The ordinance of May 12, 1853 did just that. Section 1 stated:

That there be and hereby is established a Police Department, to consist of the Marshal, Police Constables, Policemen and Watchmen of the city, who shall be known as Police Officers. The Mayor, Aldermen, and the Watchmen of the city shall be ex-officio members of the Police Department.

What this legislation accomplished added a new component—"policemen"—to the workings of the city's law enforcement apparatus. The word, "policeman" had actually never been used before in the city's municipal legislation. The Day Police reshaped everything, even Chicago's everyday vocabulary. The very word "policeman," describing the newest members of the force, had no previous use here. "Policeman" was a new concept. The Council also saw to it that its legislation included a process by which policemen could be added to the ranks. As it states in Section 6 of the Ordinance:

The Common Council shall, from time to time, upon the recommendation of the Mayor and Committee on Police, appoint suitable persons to be policemen."

Given the sweeping change that this Ordinance brought about, on August 8, 1853 it was necessary for the Common Council to legitimize all the pre-existing members of the Day Police. The August vote made the Day Police legal, including the ten men who had been nominated to serve on the Day Police. Jasper Cutler, Michael Grants, John Beach, Luther Nichols, S.H. McDearman, Casper Lauer, S.P. Putnam John Daly, George Rommeiss and James Daly were all listed as having been elected by the Common Council, not the voters, to their new posts. Luther Nichols carried enormous political influence in city government and the Police Department. He had been around since Chicago was a town. His influence in the careers of S.P. Putnam, John Beach, James Daly and Casper Lauer cannot be understated. And while the newspapers reported the election of Day Police on August 9, 1853, no other corroborative evidence exists to substantiate that the election in the Council ever took place. With ten names on the list, although only nine were called for by the Ordinance, it seems likely that the inside influence of Luther Nichols may have been the guiding hand in the successful appointment of these individuals.

The Dos and Don'ts

The *Police Rules*, a 32-page pocket volume of policy governing the authority and responsibilities of the Police Department, debuted in August of 1853. It was a precise volume, a codified tome easily accessible to each and every member of the force. They were obliged to know and understand all that was expected. This slim book set a new tone, a more developed sense of professional conduct. To insure this, every police officer was furnished with a copy of the *Police Rules*, "which," Rule 18 instructed, "he must frequently peruse, so that he may become perfectly acquainted with his duties." In many ways this was a substantive effort to re-envision Chicago's urban police. Nothing said that better than Rule One—indicating that a policeman was always on duty.

All of the Police officers shall devote their whole time and attention to the business of the Police Department, and not follow any other calling; and although certain hours are allotted to each man's duty, on ordinary occasions, yet all the of officers must be prepared to act at a moment's notice, whenever their services may be required.

Police work in Chicago was to be a singular endeavor, a full time profession. Every member was expected to forego any outside employment. The *Rules* made this cogently clear. It also established the changing face of Chicago as a metropolis. This was no longer the rough-house, boom-town of the prairie with little regard for the bounds of civilized living. This was a Chicago of growing civility. Law enforcement was not just corralling local drunks. It was about process and procedure, not merely who was the toughest man with his fists. The saga of fast-growing Chicago is deepened in the "rules of conduct" for Chicago's police. It marks a further chapter in the development of professional police services, a very specified reality of mid 19th century life that police jurisdictions were dealing with from

Paris to Philadelphia, and from London to New York. Law enforcement was moving from a reactive enterprise to a proactive one. As Section 92 of the *Rules* stated:

> *The first duty of a Police Officer is to prevent the commission of a crime; and for this purpose, he has the power to arrest any person, who from his acts, conduct, situation and character, he has just cause to suspect is about to commit a felony.*

Police Homicide—The First to Fall

This was the everyday environment of the Chicago Police—Constable, Night Watch and Day Police from which the city's first two police casualties emerged, Constable James Quinn, December 5, 1853; and Day Police Officer Casper Lauer, September 18, 1854. Each lawman reflects the changing times in the life of Chicago. Each homicide provides a sobering moment for recognizing the deepening disregard for public order and the growing threat of urban crime. The city had long since lost its small town persona. And the forces behind these tragic deaths, Quinn's as a result of two severe beatings by a notorious saloon owner, and Lauer's the result of a fatal stabbing at the hands of a violent and deranged drunk, offer a sad insight into the ever-changing character of Chicago. Given the small numbers of police personnel at the time, to have two police homicides within a nine month period was a public outrage. Each killing was a deliberate and uncontrolled act of physical violence, and each a very publicly witnessed event. Each man died, as the city's Common Council ruled, "in the discharge of their duty." Not only had Chicago's police become more organized and regulated, but the professionalism of the police would appear to have been internalized by each of these remarkable men. Their deaths offer great evidence for what was changing and unfolding on the city's streets. Perhaps their most lasting impact was emotional, as can clearly be seen in the far-reaching next step in the re-regulating of the Chicago Police.

The effort began when Darius Knight became City Marshal in 1854, making sure that his protégé, Luther Nichols, received the appointment of the city's first Assistant Marshal. It was an important appointment not only for local law enforcement, but for Nichols, a former soldier of the Illinois Blackhawk Indian Wars. His star in the police transitions yet to come would not only rise, but shine as well. Darius Knight remained as Marshal, an important part of the Dr. Levi Boone's "Know-Nothing" ticket in the city's upcoming mayoral election.

Staying Modern—An Evolving Institution

The evolving character of the institution of the Chicago Police Department was always both fluid and pragmatic. City leadership during this early period demonstrates an intelligent comfort with the on-going process of reshaping and re-regulating the sworn officers of the peace over time. Given the newness of the city's urban self-awareness, this approach was far from guarded, but instead offered the understanding that the organization of the police was not a finished product, but more a work in progress. It was a pragmatic structure for the moment in times of ever increasing population, ever expanding commercial enterprise and more violent urban crime.

During the years 1850-1860 Chicago nearly quadrupled in size and population. Nothing compounded the necessity for a dynamic police force more than the growth of sheer human numbers. Even more ominous, as the decade unfolded, the American nation was slipping further and further into the chaos of civil conflict over the issue of slavery and states' rights. Chicago was morphing into a large industrial metropolis. Nothing aided in that process more than the establishment of Chicago as the rail hub of the nation. The centrality of Chicago's geographical location and the smooth maneuvering of Chicago's favorite son in Washington D.C., the diminutive Senator Stephan A. Douglas, "the Little Giant," greatly shaped the destiny of the city. Douglas was the city's most ardent champion in

Chicago's 14th Mayor, Dr. Levi Day Boone,
1855-56, a descendant of pioneer
Daniel Boone, Stalwart of The Know-Nothings,
Chicago Public Library Archive.

creating a rail network to traverse the nation with Chicago as its central point. The dramatic expansion in the technology of the steam engine and railroads transformed Chicago more than any single element in its history. With every component of Chicago life ballooning in size and importance, the city found itself at yet another juncture in the refining process of its professional law enforcement body.

Ethnic Cleansing—The Know-Nothings' Madness

The further re-organizing of the Chicago Police that came on April 20, 1855 must be understood in light of the forces of local history at the time, as well as the bold personalities of Chicago's government leaders. The continuing waves of immigrants arriving in Chicago, and the rest of the nation, had fomented an ugly and bitter bigotry. Suspicions of foreigners and general distrust of the non-American population in large cities sparked a congealing of narrow, reactionary trends in social and political thought. In addition, revolution in many European capitols in 1848 heightened anxieties. Bomb-throwing anarchists and left-wing socialists brought many foreign cities to a standstill and sent chills everywhere. American "Nativitists" wanted no opportunity for such European-bred mayhem to touch the streets of American cities.

The Know-Nothing movement was an "America First" type phenomenon—exclusive, rigid, middle class, secretive and Protestant. The objects of its disdain, more often than not, were Irish Catholics. While the movement began in New York around 1843, where it was known as the American Republican Party, it thrived with particular ferocity in Illinois where it was rumored that Abraham Lincoln was once a member. When members of the movement were asked about their party and what it was about, the frequent response of members was, "I know nothing;" hence the origins of their name.

No one made Know-Nothing blood boil more than the pope at the time, Pius IX. The Pontiff was demonized by Nativisits, and was the vigilant object of their suspicions. All Catholics, particularly the clergy and the Irish, were perceived by Know-Nothings as having an allegiance to his papacy that bordered on the demonic. Wherever large numbers of Irish Catholics thrived, the Know-Nothings flourished with Boston and Chicago becoming prime targets of their secret hatred. Know-Nothings worked behind the scenes to thwart the success of Irish Catholics, excluding them from advancement, justice and, very often, their civil rights. No one in Chicago was more expressive of the Know-Nothing ethos than Dr. Levi Boone, the physician elected Mayor of the City of Chicago in the spring of 1855 on the Know-Nothing ticket. His chief target was not only the Irish, but any individual not born in the United States. In his inaugural address, March 13, 1855 he was frank about his suspicions and the goals he intended to accomplish as mayor:

I cannot be blind to the existence in our midst of a powerful politico-religious organization, all its members owning, and its chief officers bound under an oath of allegiance, as well as the spiritual supremacy of a foreign despot, boldly avowing the purpose of universal dominion over this land, as asserting the monstrous doctrine, that this is an end to be gained, if not by other means, by coercion and at the cost of blood itself. Against such doctrines and such schemes, gentlemen, I wish to be known as taking my stand, and to their defeat I must cheerfully consecrate my talents, my property, and if need be my life.

His rage against Roman Catholicism was coming to a head. Boone, an actual grand-nephew of the American pioneer Daniel Boone, was declaring all-out war on "papists." He would soon institutionalize his bigotry by excluding any U.S. citizen of foreign birth from employment by the City of Chicago. It did not take him long to require this in the reorganization of the Chicago Police. Ironically, this came at a time when half the population of Chicago was foreign-born.

Often Boone was assisted in his political bigotry by Chicago newspapers, especially the *Tribune* which always seemed to delight in finding irregularities and suspicious behavior in the immigrant Catholic population or in the leadership of their religion. The paper helped to encourage the fears and intolerance of Chicago's native-born, middle class population. When three new Roman Catholic bishops were consecrated in New York in November 1854, for instance, the *Tribune* went to great lengths to publish an English version of the Latin oath each bishop was required to swear on the Gospels. Just one week later, November 11, 1854, the *Tribune* ran another version of the oath, this time with the addition of italicized inserts that they claimed were a truer version of the oath. It asked readers to compare the two versions. The paper believed, it said, that the words of the oath under scrutiny will show people the true intentions of "popish imposition" that is the agenda of the papacy to gain control of politics in America. The paper went on to say— "They can have a good idea of the motive of the priesthood in practicing such imposition." The *Tribune's* analysis exaggerated every nuance possible in the oath, so that any reasonable reader could only but see the papal "imposition on the American people." This, and a constant barrage of anti-Catholic accusations, helped to create a climate most inhospitable to foreign-born Catholics. Any perceived conflict between Catholics and Protestants was quickly reported and robustly analyzed by the *Tribune*, far beyond the proportions of the incident. Even private disagreements within mixed families of Catholics and Protestants became an opportunity to point out the egregious hidden motives of the Catholics involved. Any event anywhere in the country that could reinforce misgivings about Catholics was liberally reported on a continuous basis, helping to create a climate of bigotry and fear.

The *Tribune* was soon going all the way, encouraging the establishment of a police force comprised exclusively of native-born citizens. This is what it printed in an editorial, June 24, 1854:

The late excitement in Brooklyn, when certain (Catholic) Irish members of the police refused to do duty in opposition to their own countrymen, or openly connive at their outrageous conduct; as well as many other instances consistently occurring, shows the necessity of having the police force substantially composed of native born citizens. It is evident there is a rancorous state of feeling pervading certain classes of our population, in this and other cities, based on religious or national sympathies and which is momentarily liable, under the influence of some comparatively trivial exciting cause, to result in open rupture.

This extremism provided Levi Boone with a political environment in which the panic of bigotry could disenfranchise foreign-born American citizens from public service. The madness of the Nativist fallacy was stewing to its full strength; or as the *Tribune* put it:

Careful and anxious investigation and reflection, since the election, have impressed me with the conviction that, in the present state of public sentiment, and under existing circumstances any police force, in the city to be safe to itself, or security to others, must be constituted of men known as born in this country. [June 24, 1854]

Orchestrating the fears of the general population of Chicago regarding the competency of its naturalized citizenry to serve as police officers with ability or honor; the newspaper helped a groundswell to build, strengthening the growing prejudice. Confidence in the abilities of naturalized citizens was quickly eroding due to the constant assault of the *Tribune*. The newspaper captured the bigoted spirit of the age with peculiar vengeance. Not only was the city's leadership attempting to exclude immigrants from city employment; but they were encouraging the actual barring of American citizens who were already serving as police. In Chicago that excluded more than half the population. In an open appeal "To the Citizens of Chicago," the *Tribune* centered its focus in an unabashed style. The following opinion piece by W. Daniels left no doubt what they wanted:

The time is near at hand when the present police officers are to leave their situations and new officers are to take their place. I hope that the citizens will look into the matter and choose men for that office that are fit for the business. As near as I can learn, there are some thirty or forty of the police who are green Irish men that have got the shells off their back. They begin to run after honest men as they pass up and down the street minding their own business. I think it is strange that men cannot walk the street without being molested by some Irish watchman. [March 18, 1854]

Ironically, Constable James Quinn—born in Ireland, and Day Policeman Casper Lauer – born in France, both Roman Catholics, died before the examination of their foreign births could dismiss them from the police. Mayor Boone would have had little tolerance for these two U.S. citizens who died in the line-of-duty prior to his election.

Nothing the *Tribune* wrote was as much a prequel to bigotry as a bitter editorial it published against the Night Watch in 1854. They railed at them for not being more forthright in suppressing crime. The indictment was for failing to stop a robbery at Sherman & Co. located at Lake and Clark Streets. Because the burglars were able to break through stringent security devices, the newspaper pointed out that the Night Watch should have uncovered the robbery while it was happening, although it does not inform the reader as to what the police patrol may have encountered elsewhere on their beats. Instead, it focused on the real cause of the police failure—the Irish.

The burglars went about their work with coolness and carefulness, and every one must see that had the watch been vigilant they must have discovered their operations. It is too well known to need proof that our night police is almost entirely composed of Irishmen. They have proved themselves, not only in this, but in numberless other instances, utterly incapable of discharging the duty required of them. There would not be half the crime committed in the streets of our city were our night police composed of men who would, in the first place, learn their duty, and then do it, regardless of fear, favor or affection. We have Irish policemen in our city who live in constant violation of this duty, as laid down in the published police rules of the city, and this violation and disregard of duty is winked at by those whose policy leads them to court the favor of those whom they should expose. [June 26, 1854]

Assessing responsibility for the causes of social turmoil or criminal behavior to a minority is an old canard. On the one hand the city's municipal government was attempting to expand the ranks of the police to keep pace with urban growth by placing too many demands on the small-sized police force. But on the other, they were actually using the fact of increased crime to brand those same small ranks of police with responsibility for the crimes themselves. The Irish, particularly, were caught in the middle, stuck between Nativist social prejudice and urban cultural upheaval.

There is a remarkable story which provides a clear example of the deep seated bigotry which was so ripe during this period of Chicago life, and demonstrated so dramatically by Mayor Levi Boone. So pervasive was its effect that even the heroics of those who place their own lives on the line for others could expect little acknowledgement. This is the story of two Chicago policemen—one Irish-born, Night Watch Officer Patrick Delaney; the other, German-born Night Watch Officer Carl Affeld. Their saga was reported in the *Chicago Tribune*, September 5, 1853. Both men came to the rescue of a man named Dunn who was set upon by armed robbers at Washington Street near Wacker Drive. Following their attempt to rescue Dunn, each officer was shot by the suspects. Delaney took a bullet in the groin and Affeld was hit in the arm. Each survived and required time for recuperation. Delaney was absent nearly seven weeks. Delaney returned to work in October 1853. Neither Officer, however, is listed on the rolls of Chicago Police in 1855 during Boone's term as mayor. But remarkably both appear back in the ranks of the Chicago Police in 1856 after Boone was defeated by Thomas Dyer. It is not a surprise that Dyer is heavily criticized for recalling to the police those officers who were naturalized American citizens, like Delaney and Affeld. This places Mayor Boone's open aggression against non-natives and his strategic attempts to rid the city of their influence in context

Foaming Mad—Lager Beer Riots

Nothing demonstrates the strident character of Mayor Levi Boone's urban policy more than his most enduring legacy, the Lager Beer Riots. When Boone and the Know Nothings came to office, the new mayor chose Inauguration Day 1855 to announce his offensive on immigrants. The first place he would begin was in tightening controls on the sale of alcohol, certain to hit immigrants hard. Knowing he could not muster the political capital to completely outlaw the sale of liquor, Boone did the next best thing. He asked his colleagues in the Common Council to join him in a crack-down. "I wish to bespeak your active co-operation," he said, "in closing all places where liquor is sold upon the Sabbath day." He took aim, then and there, at the very heart of Chicago's foreign-born population whose cultural traditions had little time, or even more meager respect, for teetotaling. No one was more outraged than the huge community of Chicago Germans.

Mayor Boone then set into motion a series of legislative actions that earned him the enmity of a wide variety of local foreign-born Chicagoans. No one was threatened more than the city's German saloon keepers by the Sunday prohibition against serving alcohol on the Sabbath. German immigrants were decidedly hard working and Sunday was the only day on which they could enjoy the German beer gardens in their communities with their families. Boone went further by raising the cost of a license to sell alcohol from $50 to $300. This enflamed the city's German community. Their defiance of the Mayor's orders led to high numbers of arrests. Meanwhile in the non-ethic enclaves of native-born Americans the same laws were not being enforced.

When some of the defiant Germans who had been arrested were scheduled to appear in court, hundreds of angry German protesters made their way to the courthouse on the Southside of the river at Randolph and Clark Streets. Fearing a great melee, Boone ordered the swing bridge over the river at Clark Street moved so as to block the approach of marchers to City Hall. He also had police strategically placed upon the structure of the bridge. They opened fire on the marchers. The result was one marcher killed and one policeman severely injured. This marked Chicago's first serious act of civil unrest. More than anything, it was a testament to Boone's Know-Nothing extremism. This was the very first attempt since the Revolution of 1776 to call the very quality of American citizenship was being called into question. Such misguided excess would have been inconceivable to the Founding Fathers. Full citizenship was what the Republic was all about, with no distinction between native and foreign-born citizens.

Reshaping Chicago—Police Reorganized Again

Because Chicago's mayor only served one year terms, annual elections necessitated the annual appointment and reappointment of police personnel. Mayor Boone's reorganization had been really a two part process. First he reappointed those he found acceptable for the reconstituted police. This included the Day Police and the Night Watch that came into being before his election. Second, he announced the complete overhaul of the entire command. Within days of the changes in a now "all-American" Chicago Police Department, the *Tribune* was singing the praises of the reconstituted force.

> *The Police force of the city has been reorganized, and the new members appeared on duty for the first time yesterday. They are a fine looking body of men and will no doubt do a good service.* [March 23, 1855]

The all-Protestant, all-American-born force was mid-wifed by the American Law and Order Ticket—the Know-Nothings. In the re-organized force, as of the mid days of March, Day Police and Night Watch were still separate. Darius Knight (a Know-Nothing) was Chief of Police, Luther Nichols (a Know-Nothing) was named Captain of the Day Police and S.P. Putnam (a Know-Nothing) was appointed Captain of the Night Watch. Each man was a tried and true American. Among the ten men and one Lieutenant under Captain Nichols command, and among the twenty-six men and one Lieutenant under Captain Putnam's command no Irish or ethnic names appear on the roster. Boone lost no time in disposing of "foreigners."

But shortly into his term, he announced even bigger plans. Mayor Boone had another goal for his administration, the complete re-structuring of the Chicago Police. News of this "new" police first appeared in the *Tribune*, just days in advance of the Common Council's vote. Pleased with the expulsion of the Papist immigrants from the force, the newspaper voiced its opinion on what it felt was the most significant priority—an expansion in the number of active policemen and a merging of the Day Police with the Night Watch:

> *We understand that the draft of an ordinance for the increase and regulation of the Police Force of the city is in the hands of the Committee on Police, and will be brought before the Council at an early date.*
>
> *Our Police Force though composed of the very best kind of men, is entirely too small for the necessities of a city so populous as our, and there can hardly be a doubt as to the propriety of its increase. We do not know whether the ordinance makes any provision for uniting the police, but we hope that also will be attended to. Let us, in this matter, learn wisdom from the experience of other cities.* [April 28, 1855]

On April 30, 1855 the Common Council, at the behest of the Mayor, passed legislation to re-regulate the Chicago Police in a wide and sweeping manner. Far beyond any past organizational plans of re-regulation, the changes adopted marked an entire new strategy in Chicago's urban police structure. But it was not the landslide vote that many might have predicted. Only eight out of fifteen aldermen voted in favor of the sweeping changes offered by Boone. Seven hard-liners refused to budge on the alterations. But, for all the insensitive repression laid down by Boone and his the Know-Nothings, the plan was bright, modern and logistically well developed—something that the city needed.

Among the many new components presented in his plan were the division of the city into three distinct police districts and the expansion of police ranks of command. Structurally, there was one Captain to oversee the operations of the Department, three or more Lieutenants, three or more Second Lieutenants; three or more Sergeants, plus the biggest change of all—the merging of the Night Watch and the Day Police into one entity, the Chicago Police. Ultimately, this meant the establishment of 24-hour police protection. Vigilance widened to last around the clock with no more time lags in the protection of the populace.

The pre-existing Market Houses of the city were put to use as the first police stations. The 1st District Station (South Division) was located in the basement of the Courthouse/City Hall, at Clark and Randolph Streets, the site of the present City Hall. There, thirty-three policemen were under the command of 1st Lieutenant Luther Nichols, a man with a long history in law enforcement in Chicago. The expanded number of officers and the merging of the Day and Night Police now meant that the newly constituted police had three watches, such that at any given time two-thirds of the department was off-duty. This was a big improvement over the "twelve hours on—twelve hours off" policy of the past.

The 2nd District (North Division) was located at Randolph Street between Union and DesPlaines Avenues. There, another veteran Chicago man of law enforcement, S.P. Putnam, was named 1st Lieutenant with twenty-one men under his command. There, ten men shared the three eight-hour watches.

The 3rd District (West Division) was located at Michigan Avenue and Wacker Drive, where yet another police veteran, 1st Lieutenant Michael Grants, commanded twelve men who functioned in three four-man watches.

The entire structure of the Chicago Police was re-centered in the heart of growing Chicago neighborhoods, under the command of a Lieutenant. He would be the local boss, at the "Station," relying on the endeavors of a 2nd Lieutenant to bring orderly life to the routines of police work. One of the many details for which the 2nd Lieutenant was responsible was the attention paid to the grooming and personal appearance of every man under his command. Police work in this model was decentralized and localized to the neighborhoods. The key word by which the 2nd Lieutenant was to engage the rank and file of the command was efficiency. The expectations of the past were gone. The expanded force had all new guidelines. Overseeing the cleanliness and order of the everyday details of the Station House was the Sergeant.

Built into the new police structure was the ability to expand the ranks as needed, especially in the moments of "tumult, riot, or the threat of insurrection." Also proscribed was the policy by which officers could be removed. Added to the prescriptions of duty for every member of the force was the oath to the Constitution of the State of Illinois, an indication of the source of the city's home rule powers. In this highly organized and command-centered structure, Chicago's police continued to retain the authority to enter any building or structure in the city. The new changes in local law enforcement came down to control, control and control; and the expansion of a unified force to one hundred three men who worked around the clock in three distinct shifts, very much the way police work is performed today.

The *Chicago Times* was critical of the re-organization. The newspaper particularly disliked the expanded size of the police department, and the division of the work force into three shifts. But the *Tribune* took issue with it:

The objection, if seriously made, shows the ignorance of the writer of what constitutes the very life and efficacy of a police force, namely the existence of a body of men at such a spot and in such a condition that they can be brought into active and efficient service at a moment's warning. It is not the mere and actual presence of policemen that deters evil-doers from the commission of crimes, but rather a knowledge of the fact they will probably be discovered, and so strong a force instantly summoned that escape or resistance will be impossible. [May 4, 1855]

The most lasting and unifying element of the re-regulating of the police force was the appointment of Cyrus P. Bradley as Captain of the City Police. The *Tribune* called the appointment, "an excellent one," understandable since Bradley was among the celebrated Know-Nothings in the city. He was confirmed by the Common Council by an almost unanimous vote; actually receiving more votes than the Police Ordinance, itself, received. Having served as Sheriff of Cook County and Chief of the Volunteer Fire Department, Bradley came to the position with powerful credentials.

Captain Bradley and all his men came to the Common Council on Saturday May 27, 1855 at 4:00 P.M. to take the oath of office administered by Mayor Boone. Before swearing them in, the mayor offered a few words on the occasion, He sounded the call to a new era in Chicago Police work. Boone set the tone, not just for the day, but for the future of this newly professionalized department. It marked a fresh perspective for Chicago's new Police Department and the power they were to exercise. These were Boone's elite American troops. He lost no time in defining them by their unique status as native sons.

Gentlemen, I am glad to see such promptness on the part of the police. Promptness is one of the chief requisites in a policeman. Our object has been, in the selection of a police force, to select gentlemen – gentlemen with whom we could associate, and in whom your fellow citizens could have confidence and respect. You have been selected from a very large number of applicants as the finest individuals we could find. I have every reason to believe that we shall be satisfied with the men we have chosen.

Boone then went on to list the elements of both character and behavior essential to every part of the new Chicago Police Department. These elements also just happened to be significant components of the Know-Nothing manifesto, ebullient with Calvinist morality. The moment allowed Boone to remind everyone that the "conduct" of the rabble Irish Papists would no longer tolerated by the new Calvinist regime. He continued:

It is expected that no policeman imbibe in intoxicating liquor while on duty. In former times, policemen have been known to go to common drinking places, and to drink in bars.
Under the new rules, it will be expected that the policemen will entirely abstain from the use of liquor, except as medicine. If, therefore, there are any who think this rule too stringent, they need not take the oath of office.

The mayor had more behavior modification in mind and he was blunt in saying it. This was a new day and not the same old police force. Continuing, he said:

Let me allude to another thing. It has been said that some of you are in the habit of using profane language. I trust this will be entirely avoided in the future. It is a habit, to say the least, not very gentlemanly.

Boone had one more warning for them before the oath, reinforcing the kind of conduct he expected.

One more thing. Avoid when on duty, everything like playfulness or boyishness. Preserve on all occasions, a dignified demeanor, and such a one that will cause you to be respected. [May 28, 1855]

After speaking, Mayor Boone administered the oath and a brand new era in the history of the Chicago Police Department came to life. Sadly, it also set loose the waves of institutional bigotry.

Reestablishing Equilibrium—A Return to Normalcy
Chicago's Know-Nothing revolution was short lived. Foreign-born citizens and Democrats sought their revenge at the polls in the election of March 4, 1856. Considered one of the most galvanizing campaigns in Chicago's history, a new political muscle swept Boone and his anti-Catholic, anti-immigrant party out of office. The issue of the rights of naturalized American citizens cemented a special unity among the forces which defeated the Know-Nothings. They elected the city's 15th mayor, Thomas Dyer to lead them out of the morass.

Chicago Police Chief Cyrus Parker Bradley, appointed June 1855, photomechanical print, Chicago History Museum Photo Archive.

CYRUS PARKER BRADLEY

APPOINTED - JUNE - 1855.

Mayor Dyer made it clear from the beginning he would have no part in the fragmenting extremism of Boone's past administration.

I intend to appoint no man to office who is not, in my opinion, fitted for the place. While I shall have due regard for political friends, I intend, so far as I can, to demonstrate that good, and faithful and competent officers can be obtained, even while political associates are preferred. While I shall make no difference against naturalized citizens on account of their birth, I shall equally respect the native citizens. Birth of place shall not influence me for or against applicants for office. It is needless for me, perhaps, to say that I entertain no sentiment or feeling in sympathy with those who would make birthplace or creed a test for office, or for the exercise of political right. [March 11, 1956]

In a city that had grown to a population of 84,113, this was good news for the tens of thousands of Chicagoans who were naturalized U.S. citizens; and it was good news for those Chicago policemen who had been expelled from the force because of their foreign births. Dyer could not have been clearer in what he said on inauguration day. Such a reversal of fortune did not sit well with the *Chicago Tribune* which boldly accused the Irish of stealing the election. It was quick to point fingers at the very citizens whose exclusion from office it had so intensely applauded. The Irish and other naturalized foreigners may have been prevented from municipal employment, but they had not been deprived of their constitutional right to vote. Voter turn-out sent Boone out of office and the Tribune into shock.

Great surprise will be felt by readers acquainted with city politics, when they know what an enormous vote was cast at the election yesterday. When, however, they learn that a greater part of the increase over the vote of last year is due to illegality, backed up by perjury, they will cease to wonder at the figures presented. When they learn that the Irish in the forenoon took and held the Seventh Ward, that the challengers who were sent there were either driven away, or were, by fear of violence, deferred from doing their duty, that the voters rejected in other Wards were poured in there by scores and hundreds; that the same men voted under assumed names in many cases twice, and in some three times; that men never seen in the Wards before, voted by the dozens. [*Chicago Tribune*, March 5, 1856]

Though it offered no end of accusations, the newspaper provided no real evidence to support the claims of the Irish Catholic high-jacking of the election. The *Tribune* was careful to blame all foreigners, not just the Irish. The outcome of the 1856 election for them was a "Catholic" assault.

In close union with these was the entire Catholic population under instruction and surveillance. It went as a unit. Not a man who believes in the supremacy of the Papal Power, that did not go straight out and directly [vote] for the triumph of slavery. Not a man who gives up his conscience to the control of the priesthood that did not use the ballot to beat down freedom. [*Chicago Tribune*, March 5, 1856]

Mayor Dyer's defeat of Levi Boone was the product of the alliance of many forces in Chicago, not least of which was the various citizens of foreign birth. They had a powerful issue to bring them together. It was a pragmatic and tactile reality that was near at hand. Imagine how many votes the Irish and German policemen who were fired from the Chicago Police Department by Boone were able to rally across the city? The tide was turning and everyone knew it. No one was filled with more foreboding than the *Chicago Tribune*. It was quick to warn the new mayor against any drastic action regarding the police:

We fear that, in this important branch of the city government, a change for the worse is to happen under the rule of Mr. Dyer. His promises to the rapscallion who electioneered for him, who secured him the fraudulent votes to which he owes his election, who stood at the polls to over awe the opposition and bully the timid, must be kept, and we shall probably have as the first fruits of the "great victory," just such a police as the mob which rallied in our streets after the battle would elect. What eradicators of law and order they will be, let their shouts, blasphemies and orgies on the day of the "big drunk," bear witness. Before the end of the year, reveries will be the legal tender in Chicago. [Chicago Tribune, March 12, 1856]

But a new police force could not be stopped. By April 30, 1856, Mayor Dyer and the Police Committee had appointed seven new policemen to replace seven others who had been removed for bad conduct. "At this rate, the *Tribune* reported, we shall have an entirely new police force about every three months." The newspaper was also quick to criticize a "Dyer" detective who had, himself, been pick-pocketed while on duty. "This must be a cute detective," it offered, continuing a non-stop tirade against ever growing changes in the Police Department.

Within two weeks of Dyer's swearing-in, rumors were circulating that the appointment of "new" policemen was at hand. By April 3, 1956 twenty-two men were appointed: Jacob Sauter, Michael Finnucane, Charles Dennehey, Francis Hammelsheim, James Maloney, George Ernst, Henry Hoffmeiter, John Doyle, Daniel W. Killop, Peter Scott, Charles Affeld, M.O. Lang, John Enwright, Patrick Quigley, John Gorman, John Hennebery, Jacob Large, John Large, John Ludwig, Patrick Coneidiac, John Shcaffer and James Mellen. Their overriding surnames of Irish and German origins left no question that a tidal wave of change had been set in motion. It was rumored that another forty men had been appointed and their names would be soon announced. In the meantime swarms of applicants made their way to the City Hall in the attempt to secure a position with the reconstituted Police Department. The *Tribune* reminded its readers that those who had been discharged from the force, Know-Nothing appointees, represented the cream-of-the crop.

The men selected were placed upon duty last night, and a corresponding number of old policemen discharged, among them a number of the very best officers we ever had in Chicago. [Chicago Tribune, April 4, 1856]

The biggest bang was yet to be heard. That occurred when Mayor Dyer set out to remove 1st Lieutenant Luther Nichols from his post at Division 1. Nichols held fast and refused to budge, saying that his appointment did not come from the mayor, but rather from the Common Council itself. The vitriol and bad feelings that had been building permeated the air within the Chicago Police Department. At Division 2, the post of 1st Lieutenant was offered to a Mr. Abbot. He promptly refused the promotion given the heightened emotions of the time. Something similar occurred at the 3rd Division where the mayor sought to appoint Jacob Sauter as 1st Lieutenant. Sauter, a long time friend of Nichols, was also a fellow Know-Nothing and resigned from the force rather than take up the appointment. Chicago's law enforcement community was highly stress-ridden. Accusations concerning the fitness of some new appointees continuously surfaced. The *Tribune* was almost gleeful when it could report that Mayor Dyer found it necessary to discharge the Irish-Catholic 2nd Lieutenant Finnucane from duty. The newspaper referred to him as the "private Lord of the 3rd Division."

Typical of the newspaper's passion for sowing the seeds of "dis-information," were their reports from unnamed correspondents. Nothing portrayed that more than this question from such a correspondent:

Can you inform the public whether or not one of the new policemen was at one time the doorkeeper of the notorious "Brown House," and whether or not he was ever bound over in this city on a charge of passing counterfeit money! [Chicago Tribune, April 10, 1856]

The *Tribune* relished the opportunity to put such unsubstantiated accusations before the bewildered public. The response to this "correspondent" was nothing less than a blatant act of treachery that sought to spread the seeds of suspicion. The publisher wrote:

We know nothing about the matter, and therefore cannot enlighten our correspondent in that regard. We will, however, look up the facts and publish them. [Chicago Tribune, April 4, 1856]

It is difficult to believe that the newspaper could succeed in such intentional deception of the public's right to know. So intertwined was it with the policy of exclusion, that the *Tribune* lost its objectivity. The newspaper was angry and stopped at nothing to continue the alarming denigration of half Chicago's population. When the latest transformation of the Police Department was nearly in place, it became even more unrelenting in its willingness to affix blame for the upheaval.

Nearly, if not quite, all the old policemen are now turned out, and new ones put in their steads. Some of these are good men, but we regret to say that a very large majority are totally unfit to occupy the posts they do.

Lest our citizens should forget to whom they are indebted for the appointment of these men, we remind them that Mayor Dyer and Aldermen Sexton, LaRue and Diversey, are the gentlemen to whom their gratitude is due. [Chicago Tribune, April 10, 1856]

No one had been more supportive of Mayor Levi Boone and his Know-Nothing campaign to reconstitute and expand the Chicago Police without foreign-born citizens than the *Tribune*. It applauded his wide sweeping changes and decentralizing of command. The *Tribune* never criticized him when he discharged all the long-serving foreign-born naturalized U.S. citizens, like Officers Delaney and Affeld, when his new police ordinance became law. However, as soon as the tables were turned, and Boone and his Know-Nothings were sent packing, the *Tribune* decided it was time to roll back the clock and amend the police ordinance to create a further barrier for foreign-born U.S. citizens. The newspaper then moved from its previous criticism to advocating a legislative change to remove the Police Department from any influence of the mayor.

We have seen enough of the action of the Mayor and his Police Committee to be satisfied that if the appointment of the police is left to them, there is no reason to expect that but a few, if any, fit men will be selected, and it becomes the duty of the Common Council who have the remedy in their own hands to apply it and so amend the Police Ordinance as to require that all policemen shall be elected by the Common Council. [Chicago Tribune, April 14, 1856]

Among Mayor Dyer's more controversial early actions was to remove the Police Department's First Captain, Cyrus P. Bradley, from his post and then abolish the post entirely. This, then, triggered an immediate reaction from the "Bradley boys," those special appointees who served as detectives on his staff. Bradley was credited with giving the city its very first detectives when he created this elite squad. Their sudden resignations "en masse" permitted the *Tribune* the chance to warn the public of the terrible consequences to come. Its skill at bringing panic to the public was without equal, as its headline of April 18 attested: *Let Every Man Guard His Own Life and Property*—the banner read. The paper went on to make sure that Chicago's citizens were aware of how bad conditions had become:

On yesterday all the detective officers in the city resigned their places, and Chicago is now left without a police who know anything about catching thieves. [*Chicago Tribune*, April 18, 1856]

The detectives' letter of resignation sent to City Marshal James M. Donnelly was signed by the departing officers and made clear their intent. Their action was taken, they claimed, because they "have been forced by the late actions of the Common Council in attempting to disgrace Captain Bradley by expelling him from an office that they well know he did not want, and would not accept." The eight detectives who signed the letter were— Charles Noyes, William M. Douglass, William S. Tenbroeck, Friend Noyes, Cyrus Keeler, B.C. Yates, J.H. Williams and Jacob Rehm.

To make sure that Mayor Dyer's new appointments to the police would have an uphill battle in their ability to achieve public confidence, the *Tribune* again took aim at them with wild, unsubstantiated and reckless claims.

A gentleman who has enquired into the matter informs us that twenty-three of the new police are keepers of rumshops, several of which places are among the very lowest and most filthy in the city. This knowledge of the facts alone ought to be sufficient to stamp the Dyer administration as one utterly reckless of the good name of the city and should serve as a new incentive to the Common Council, which has the power, to repeal the present Police Ordinance and substitute one requiring all policemen to be elected by ballot by the Council. [*Chicago Tribune*, April 22, 1856]

On the following day the newspaper presented a litany of further unsubstantiated claims against the new police. It cited examples, usually brought by "a responsible source," of malfeasance, incompetence, weak character and stupidity; all reinforcing for the public its stereotypical assessment of the Irish and other non-native citizens. Any possible pretext that could serve its ability to editorialize against the short-comings of "Catholics" was used liberally to reintroduce the prejudice that voters so summarily tossed out of office with Levi Boone.

When, finally, Dyer recommended a candidate to fill the post of Captain of Police, J.W. Connett, he quickly became the newspaper's prime target. Though Connett received the recommendation of the Police Committee, he was not popular with the Common Council. He was sworn-in on April 22, 1856 and served as captain the entire length of Dyer's term, though City Marshall Donnelley would continue to run the Police Department. The *Tribune* used the opportunity to indicate that several individuals had been "promised" the post of captain as a reward for political support, further denigrating Dyer's attempts to restore public confidence in the new police which numbered some one hundred twenty-four officers at the time.

Ironically, after leaving his post as Captain, Bradley joined B.C Yates, J.H. Williams and Charles Noyes and formed a partnership under the name C.P. Bradley & Co., in a private detective agency.

For the remainder of Dyer's term in office, the rancor continued at every juncture. It was a reactive time. The press, the disdained Know-Nothings, and all the animosity stirred up among the city's immigrant population made it difficult to govern the expanding urban metropolis of Chicago. It would take a man of steely heart and broad shoulders to reverse the chaotic forces of confusion and meanness that had become a part of everyday life in Chicago. There was, however, one man who cherished the opportunity to bring the city around, a veteran of the U.S. Congress and tough newspaper publisher, John Wentworth. At six foot seven inches, "Long John," as he was known, had just the right frame to tackle the gripping dilemmas of Chicago, particularly its Police Department.

Long John Wentworth—Chicago's First Micro-Mayor

When Wentworth was sworn-in as Chicago's 16th Mayor on March 10, 1857, the first of his two non-consecutive terms, no issue was more pressing than that of the Chicago Police Department. His election marked a new and engaging era for Chicago law enforcement. He was the first to acknowledge the difficulties the city encountered because of the severe actions of the Know-Nothings under Boone. Under Dyer, overcompensating for these injustices was predictable. But Wentworth was no dreamer, as his first words as mayor indicate:

Our citizens have ceased to look to the public police for protection, for the detection of culprits or the recovery of stolen property. It cannot be relied upon for the preservation of order, as was evinced on the day of our recent election. I am not prepared to state any specific plan now which will give efficiency to our police and regain the public confidence. But, I will, in a few days, nominate to you some person for Chief of Police, and then I hope he will be rigidly scrutinized as to his qualifications and rejected if not thought to reach the necessary standard. [March 10, 1857]

In these early days of the Wentworth administration, the new mayor made it clear he was looking for first-class citizens of the City of Chicago to serve as members of the police. He indicated that he wanted to know how long an applicant had lived in the city when considering his qualifications. In fact, he made it a requirement that any applicant to the police had to have two recommendations from citizens of outstanding business merit. He took a different tack than his predecessors. His solution was to employ those who had a real stake in Chicago's success. He wanted to know "how long they have resided in the city, where they reside, and whether they are men of family." Only bona fide residents would be considered. He wanted men whose homes were respectable, and who lived in a variety of locations across the city. For Wentworth, those who served as police had to demonstrate a sense of social and ethical commitment to Chicago. It was no less than he required of himself.

With the Wentworth administration in control, only twenty men of the original 1855 Mayor Boone police force remained as members of the department. Under Wentworth the ranks of sworn officers had soared to one hundred seventeen, but with the dynamism of the city's growth the number appeared insufficient to handle the volume of urban crime. Wentworth soon devised a plan to fill the gap. Rather than increase the numbers of police, he would decrease the numbers of law breakers. His prime target was the Sands, the near-north side hot bed of vice and gambling in the 9th Ward, between the river and Grand Avenue, from the Lakefront to State Street. This was the very neighborhood where, almost five years earlier, Constable James Quinn was beaten to death in the Rees saloon. With predictable fanfare, the mayor ordered the wholesale destruction of the Sands. On April 20, 1857, Wentworth led the assault himself, charging ahead of more than thirty police armed with gigantic steel hooks and chains. No structure, no bordello, no gambling den, no saloon escaped total destruction. One by one, the mayor and the police pulled down the wooden shacks lining the streets and then set them ablaze. Wentworth was on the march and no thief, prostitute, gambler, or saloon keeper was safe. The mayor's raid even netted him the notorious Smith brothers, the kings of Chicago vice.

Wentworth led his cohorts and their prey to the city jail in the basement of the courthouse, where he roared in a voice that carried clear to the crowds on the sidewalk that he "intended to teach them a lesson that they would remember." He saw to it that everyone caught in the raid was booked and put behind bars and declared that if anybody licensed by the city to carry on a trade or commercial enterprise showed up with bail, their licenses would be instantly voided. [Antiques Digest, 1857]

Chicago's 16th Mayor, "Long-John"
Wentworth, 1857-58, 1860-61, used a heavy
hand running Chicago's Police. Chicago
Public Library Archive.

Many of the most notorious bosses of vice and thievery managed to escape further west into the Irish area around Goose Island to set up shop again. But the Sands was no more, thanks to Mayor Wentworth. His "hands-on" approach to police work was just beginning. At the same time it was the start of his reputation as a serious urban crime fighter. Wentworth was often denounced for his heavy-handed assault on local lawbreakers. As Ralph W. Marrow and Harriet I. Carter put it—

He broke up dens of thieves and demi-reps, compelled notorious characters to make their appearance in police court each morning; drove harlots from the streets; protected respectables; shielded women from the approaches of scoundrels; and banished many human scourges who were want to loaf about the streets. [In Pursuit of Crime, 1996]

Wentworth ignored his detractors and was confident in his leadership of the Police Department. Like no mayor before him, he was the man in charge of his police. Ironically, despite his bold and open pursuit of lawbreakers, Wentworth kept all of the city's police in civilian dress. He had no interest in uniforms. The effect was that Chicago's police were less visible, seldom deterring crime by their physical presence on the streets. The only external emblem of their authority was the police badge they were required to wear. Before the year was up, Wentworth also put the police in a special cap with a lettered badge spelling out the word P.O.L.I.C.E. Over the years a myth later sprang up recalling these as "leather badges." But no such badges were ever used. The lettered badges were suppose to distinguish police from the city's most vicious criminals, a gang of renegade hackmen, as wagon drivers were known. This gang of notorious felons was hard-core. No crime or villainy was beneath them, everything from rape to murder. Working alongside genuine hackmen, police pursued crime while wearing the required hats with the lettered badges of their profession. Keeping the Chicago Police in their "hats" was an attempt to subvert the criminal element among the hackmen and drivers. But it was an uphill battle. *The Daily Democrat* was highly critical of the mayor over this. They found it unacceptable that the police looked just like the runners, porters and expressmen on the city streets. They wrote—

The badge of the police is composed of silver-plated letters spelling out the word POLICE in an arc of a circle upon a patent leather base, giving below the registered number of the officer. We questioned at the outset in our own minds the taste of those who devised this badge. We think it might have been given a much neater form, and in this respect believe no advance has been made upon the old "stars," save the two obvious ones, that the number of the officer is made conspicuous and that it is worn upon the cap. It would have been much better to have retained the star, modifying it in these respects, and in view of the other really most weighty objection we shall urge, we trust the Police Committee may be induced to make some change in the badge. [Daily Democrat, May 14, 1857]

As Wentworth's term was coming to an end, his public criticism was expanding, just like the city's crime, and the worsening economic conditions of the times with a serious depression approaching. He was getting the lion's share of the blame for everything that went wrong in Chicago. In the spring of 1858, troubled Chicago voters elected Republican John Charles Haines as the city's 17th Mayor. With little personal interest in aggressively pursuing the city's vice merchants, the new mayor declined to aggressively pursue lawbreakers as Wentworth had. Haines however does have a most remarkable claim to fame regarding the Chicago Police.

Mayor Haines was a well-known speculator in the investment rage of the day—copper. Because of his interest in this burgeoning American metal enterprise, Chicagoans began to use the sobriquet "Copperstock Men," when referring to the police. The name is said to have been later shortened to "coppers," and even more colloquially to "cops." Under his administration, police courts were expanded to keep up with the steady increase in crime.

Haines was re-elected mayor in 1859. During his second term, he created a new "official" uniform and placed police in crisp blue frock coat and blue caps trimmed with gold. Shiny brass badges completed the very antithesis of the simple Wentworth style. This handsome haberdashery, however, did not make up for the fact that the city's population of some 95,000 people were being served by a police force of roughly one hundred thirty-six men. Only some thirty officers were on the street at any given time, creating what many believed to be a law enforcement crisis. Long John Wentworth was not content to remain quiet.

In the election of March 1860, "Long John" Wentworth was returned as the city's mayor and with him returned his revolutionary approach to police management. He wasted no time in letting everyone know what the future was to hold. He spoke plainly at his second inauguration.

Economy in the administration of public affairs is always desirable, because it is the surest guarantee against corruption. But at the present time it is an imperious necessity.
[Wentworth, March 22, 1860]

No sooner had he returned to office than he quickly abolished the trappings of his predecessor and took police personnel out of uniform. They were back in civilian dress. Wentworth also convened a special police board of complaint consisting of the City Marshal and the three lieutenants of the city's police districts. The new board met in the basement of the City Hall, mandated by the mayor to answer every, and all, complaints of citizens concerning the police. In addition, Wentworth brought in new, stringent budgetary measures that brutally reduced the size of the corps of police to about half its 1859 strength. The source of his authority he saw as simple—Section 2 of Chapter XL of the Municipal Laws, that specified—

"The Mayor shall be the head of the Police Department, and shall superintend and direct the police generally. [Wentworth, March 22, 1860]

Armed with what he believed was an established right to conduct the business of the police, Wentworth went on a blood-letting campaign, firing many long-time officers. He also made significant changes in the *Rules,* the official catalogue of procedures and responsibilities all members of the police carried with them. He set his stamp on everything with a heavy hand from daily routines to the chain of command. Nothing was beyond his tinkering.

It has been suggested that orders could be issued directly to the Lieutenants of the Division, and thereby saving the salary of the Captain of Police, which is fifteen hundred dollars per annum. I am willing to try the experiment of getting along without a Captain and hope I may succeed. I therefore shall not nominate any person to that office at present. [Wentworth, March 22, 1860]

By 1860 the population of Chicago had reached more than 112,000. This was an explosive urban metropolis. The city was setting records. Its newest railway station, the Illinois Central, was majestic and acknowledged as the largest railway station in the world. Chicago had already become the "crossroads" of the nation due to the network of rails that carried passengers and freight across America, always through Chicago. All these elements of Chicago's urban life would come together in what just might be Wentworth's most audacious political accomplishment, the 1860 Republican National Presidential Convention. In this endeavor, the Chicago Police Department was an essential component.

Just one month after his re-election, Wentworth welcomed his fellow Republicans to Chicago for what would be their most critical attempt to stabilize the Union. Each day the Union drifted further towards revolt. Southern states were at the brink of seceding from the Republic. In what was only the second national convention for the Republican Party, they arrived some 40,000 strong with 500 delegates enthused for the convention. Delegates found Chicago hospitable and determined to join in the battle to help save the nation. Wentworth had an even more difficult political agenda – to make his friend, downstate lawyer Abraham Lincoln, the party's nominee. Wentworth and Lincoln had served together in the United States Congress, though Lincoln only had been elected once as an Illinois Congressman. Blueprints for Lincoln's convention selection had been worked out in the offices of Joseph Medill, the publisher-owner of the *Tribune*. Wentworth had ensured that the convention hall, known as the Wigwam, was hurriedly constructed in less than five weeks along the south branch of the Chicago River. In this barn-like building Lincoln would command victory and defeat the powerful forces of New York Senator William Henry Seward, on the third ballot. Essential to that success was Wentworth's role as the convention's host.

Ironically, the reform-minded mayor left out no political trick or shenanigan to help Lincoln become the party's nominee. In the process, he commandeered the Chicago Police Department in its first-ever engagement at a national political convention. Slavery, tariffs and the trans-continental railroad were the hot political issues of the day that surfaced in the convention's daily engagements. Sadly the Union was imperiled and no one could prevent the tragedy that would soon beset the nation. But in insuring Abraham Lincoln's nomination for president of the United States on May 18, 1860, Long John Wentworth achieved what must be the outstanding accomplishment of his political career. What peril might have befallen the nation had Lincoln not been president at the darkest hour in American history? At the mayor's command, the Chicago Police Department was on hand to ensure order and safety in the streets when Wentworth released his throngs to capture the nomination for Lincoln. When Seward supporters arrived to take their seats in the Wigwam, many found that their credentials were not valid. Instead, Chicago Police were admitting Lincoln's supporters who suddenly found themselves with forged tickets admitting them to the convention hall. The absence of Seward stalwarts within the hall took much of the wind out of the push to nominate their candidate. Meanwhile, Wentworth saw to it that the Lincoln crowds were able to shout and holler for their man with a new found strength. Wentworth's police guards ensured only those chosen by the mayor could make their way to the hall. Lincoln, though not present, gladly accepted the nomination from downstate Springfield.

Many Chicagoans thought Mayor Wentworth petulant and eccentric. Just when the city was expanding as never before, he reduced the effectiveness of the police by his sweeping reductions in their numbers. He continued interference in the everyday life of the Police Department. As a result of his cuts large swaths of the city were left without the protection of the Police Department in the critical months before the Civil War. In response, sprouting up all around the city were private police, "watchmen" as they were known, willing to take on the protection of vulnerable business enterprises. As Wentworth's second term came to its end, the Chicago Police Department had been reduced to a captain, six lieutenants and some fifty patrol officers. Outrage was the common sentiment of the day. Indignation against the mayor was at an all time high.

Faced with an overriding fear for the safety and well-being of Chicagoans, the Illinois State Legislature had adopted a plan to stop Wentworth's interference once and for all. They crafted legislation that provided for the establishment of a Police Board mandated by law with the responsibility of administering the affairs of the Chicago Police Department without the interference of the mayor.

There shall be organized in the city of Chicago an executive department of the city of Chicago to be known as the board of police which shall consist of three commissioners...to be elected by the people. [Illinois General Assembly, February 22, 1861]

Wentworth knew the significance of this new law and was outraged at the challenge to his authority. Rather than see the actions of the State Legislature as something that would revolutionize police administration in Chicago, Wentworth took this action as a personal insult and offense. He was not through with interfering with the Chicago Police Department yet.

Nothing earned Wentworth the condemnation of history more than his final act as mayor, one that remains the strangest in Chicago Police history. On the evening of March 21, 1861, the mayor called together the entire Chicago Police Department in his City Hall office. The first meeting of the newly mandated Police Board was set to convene at the same time in another area of the Courthouse. Frederick Tuttle, William Wayman and Alexander C. Coventry were the men appointed by Governor Richard Yates to serve on this board. Wentworth kept his men with him until the early hours of the morning, well past 2:00 A.M. Once the board had adjourned and left the building, the mayor announced that rather than permit them the opportunity of dismissing his appointed officers, he was discharging the entire police force then, and there. It was an arrogant and antagonistic act of defiance, devoid of all grace or civility. Wentworth was angry and he permitted his anger to shape his decisions. What that meant was that from his dismissal of the force until 10:00 A.M. that morning, the City of Chicago was without police protection.

In the light of day, after just hours, some police officers who had been dismissed by Wentworth were invited back to work and quickly sworn-in. Order was restored. But Wentworth was seen by many Chicagoans as being disloyal to the city, having placed it in danger, however briefly, to satisfy his own personal needs. Ultimately he lost the public opinion battle because of his recklessness. The Police Board had its work cut out. It had an entire police force to put together. Jacob Rehm, a policeman of long-standing reputation was given the post of Deputy Superintendent. R.J. Paulson was appointed as captain. Three sergeants were likewise designated—William Turtle, W.W. Kennedy and John Nelson.

The establishment of the police board had a further potential for good order and stability built within it – the permanency of police personnel. With mayors changing almost annually in Chicago, each mayor traditionally brought a change in the command and administration of the police. This constant upheaval wore away any possibility of strength or effective administration. Now separated from the highly political influence of the office of mayor, the Chicago Police Department had, for the very first time, the chance to grow calmly and professionally. When Julian S. Rumsey assumed the office of mayor on May 6, 1861, replacing Wentworth, he had no grand design for the city's police force. What would occur there was now beyond the scope of his office. He acknowledged this in his inaugural address.

I am not at present prepared to make any specific recommendations. I have no policy to promulgate, more than is indicated in what I have already said. [Rumsey, May 6, 1861]

This was a whole new day in Chicago. For the very first time, the city had a mayor who would no longer be involved in the internal administration of the police. It was good for everyone. But as the new mayor was sworn-in, every Chicagoan was only too aware of the looming catastrophe that was engulfing the nation. Less than one month earlier, April 12, 1861, Confederate forces fired on the Union garrison of Fort Sumter in Charleston Harbor. The American Civil War had begun. Rumsey spoke for all Chicagoans when he attempted to express how the war was redefining what it meant to be an American. It was changing how everyone lived. New priorities eclipsed the issues of the past.

Now in the general anxiety to preserve our common country for ourselves and our children, and as an asylum for the oppressed of all nations, patrizan [sic] feeling and nationalities are seemingly forgotten. With me it is certainly so, and until that great issue is settled, the man who is for our country in this time of her sorest need, is my political friend; he who is not for her, is my enemy.
[Rumsey, May 6, 1861]

Shortly after Rumsey took office, the news spread that Cyrus Bradley had accepted the position of General Superintendent. Despite the history he would bring to the position, chiefly his ties to the Know-Nothings of Levi Boone, Bradley was also perceived as an effective law enforcement administrator. Free of the intrusions of the office of mayor, he would be allowed far more independence than he had known before. And he could safely look ahead at more than a year at a time. No matter who was elected to the office of mayor in the coming election, Bradley did not have to seek the approval of his mayoral successor. The Chicago Police Department had never experienced such independence before. But there was no escaping the trauma that was dividing the nation. Mayor Rumsey was quick to bring his concerns about "Southern Sympathizers" to the attention of the Common Council. Given the fluid nature of Chicago's geography as the nation's transportation hub, he was suspicious of "secessionists and spies" swarming around Chicago in hopes of gathering information for the Confederacy. He went so far as to propose legislation to the Common Council, requiring that any citizen of the United States "not ready to take an oath of allegiance to the United States be requested to leave the city immediately."

Chicago was a hotbed of southern sympathizers. As the war progressed, and the numbers of Confederate prisoners grew at the city's infamous military prison, Camp Douglas, the realities of the war became apparent.

In 1861, with Long John Wentworth out of office, Chicago Police were returned to uniforms—dark blue frock coats with buttons emblazoned with the words "Chicago Police." Dark gray trousers with a blue stripe down the leg added to the distinctive outfit, together with blue cap with a bell crown, specially designed for the protection of the head. Each cap carried the officer's number.

That same year General Superintendent Bradley also returned to an element of professional law enforcement that had long been one of his favorites—a detective division. During his previous service under Mayor Boone, he had a corps of detectives in his office. They later resigned in protest when Bradley was dismissed. He first began with a detail of detectives that he established as the first official Detective Division. Bradley's new appointments were to constitute the very first regular bureau of detectives. Organized under the command of S.C. Storer, this group consisted of Horace Elliott, Ike Williams, William Douglas, Henry Kaufman, Joseph Dixon and Asa Williams. He later added William Tenbroeck, Samuel Ellis, James Morgan and John Wall. This was a welcomed addition to the stabilization of the department. Chicagoans were quick to regard the Detective Division with high esteem.

Francis Cornwell Sherman, who had been Chicago's fifth mayor back in 1841, was returned to the office of mayor twenty-years later in the election of 1862. He was a Democrat. Bradley remained in office despite the outcome of the election. Chicago's population neared 140,000. The city was facing new challenges due to the war and from continuing urban growth. Bradley solidified the Police Department's sense of discipline. He was a tough taskmaster. He needed to be. Among the responsibilities of the police was the rounding up of deserters from the military. Chicago was a growing crossroads of military activity. Troops passed through Chicago on their way to the frontlines and when they were eventually able to be furloughed, they again passed through Chicago. Most people moving through the city were armed. It was common for civilians to carry weapons about their person. Two-thirds of the male population of Chicago was believed to carry a gun.

Mayor Sherman was elected to a one-year-term in 1861. But he went on to became the first Chicago mayor to be elected to a two-year-term when the Illinois General Assembly extended the term of office. He served what was actually his third term from 1863 to 1865, the most critical years of the war era. By 1863 Chicago had not only grown in population, it had expanded geographically, extending from seventeen square miles to twenty-four. Such expansion placed an ever-growing burden on the Chicago Police. It was almost physically impossible to protect such a large area in very dangerous times. Bradley resigned his position as General Superintendent of Police on February 20, 1863, shortly before the April municipal elections. Having also accepted a military appointment as Provost Marshal, Bradley found he could not discharge responsibilities. Jacob Rehm, tried and true, was given the position of General Superintendent.

With its headquarters, called the Central Station, set up in the City Hall on the southwest corner of Washington and LaSalle Streets, the divisions of the Police Departments jurisdictions were further defined and reorganized. The system of precincts was introduced into the administration of the department, just as the number of wards in the city also expanded to sixteen. The Police Department's 1st precinct was located in the Armory at the corner of Franklin and Adams Streets. John Nelson was appointed the captain and M.C. Hickey designated as the 1st sergeant. Thomas Clayton was made 2nd sergeant with thirty-six patrolmen attached to the station. Further, a sub-station from the 1st precinct was established at 26th and State Streets on the south end of the city.

The 2nd precinct was located in the west end of the city at Randolph and DesPlaines Streets in the West Market Hall. William Turtle was appointed captain with William Kennedy acting as 1st sergeant. George Miller served as 2nd sergeant with twenty patrolmen assigned to the station.

The 3rd precinct was located in the north end of the North Market Hall east of Clark Street at Illinois Street. Frederick Gund was made captain with John N. Norton acting as 1st sergeant and Charles H. Jennings as 2nd sergeant. Eighteen patrolmen were assigned to the station.

This, however, was only the beginning of what would prove to be a complex moment in city history. Superintendent Rehm resigned his office on March 14, 1863, but the police board refused to accept it. This was further complicated when one of the board member's term of office expired and his colleagues elected him the president of the board. The mayor wound up being an ex-officio member of the board and Cyrus Bradley was appointed acting secretary adding further complexities. By July 3, 1863 the board was ready to accept Superintendent Rehm's resignation. Promptly, each member of the board nominated his own particular candidate resulting in a stalemate. More than eight months would go by before any candidate was appointed. And in a strange turn of events, during these months, acting secretary Bradley assumed the responsibilities of superintendent. All this coincided with the mayoral election of 1863 in which Mayor Sherman was re-elected, to serve a two year term. The controversy over the appointment of a new superintendent would not be resolved without the intervention of the courts and a long series of political plots and schemes, not least of which was the appointment of Long John Wentworth to the board of police.

During this potent period the Chicago Police Department suffered its first death of a patrolman in the line of duty in ten years. Officer John C. Churchwood died March 25, 1864, four days after he set out to arrest a drunken Union soldier, Duncan McGillis, who was reported causing a disturbance at the Soldier's Home, 541 West Randolph Street. The English-born Churchwood suffered extraordinary trauma while making the arrest. The incident, long forgotten in the history of the Chicago Police Department, focuses attention on the ever-growing numbers of military personnel who were present in Chicago during the Civil War. Resources were strained within the department while the city attempted to cope with the growing numbers of military personnel who brought their own brand of disorder to Chicago.

While William Turtle, the nephew of board member William Wayman, was appointed Superintendent of Police by dissenting members of the board in April 1864, he would spend the next twenty-one months embroiled in constant turmoil. During this same time, the city faced one of the most dangerous and terrifying summers when the Democratic National Presidential Convention convened in Chicago, August 29 to 31.

When the convention met in Chicago, it opened against the background of great unrest. The Civil War was unpopular and unsuccessful for the North. Lincoln detractors were legion. Rumors abounded that during the convention the city's water supply was going to be poisoned. Strife in the streets became so intense that federal troops were called out to protect the population. A mass of rogues and ruffians, thieves and gamblers came by horseback, wagon and train to swarm the streets of Chicago. Chicago police were out in force in the biggest test of their ability to keep order. There were also stories making their way around Chicago that there was to be a rescue of the 8,350 Confederate prisoners from Camp Douglas on the Southside. They were guarded by just 736 Union soldiers. Many of the prisoners were young native-born Irishmen from the South. Their detention did not sit well with Chicago's robust Irish community. Many feared an Irish assault on the camp. No one was more concerned than the commandant of the camp, General J.B. Sweet, who in a moment of desperation telegraphed the federal government for assistance. One thousand soldiers of the 109th Pennsylvania Regiment entered the city to reinforce security. Fears that Chicago would burn to the ground by the actions of anti-war protesters were taken seriously by regular Chicagoans. Anti-Lincoln Democrats, known as the "Copperheads," had high-jacked the presidential nominating convention and later gave their name to the gathering. A serious strain was placed on the municipal apparatus of the city like never before. No one felt it more than the Chicago Police. President Lincoln was demonized and his nemesis, General George B. McClellan, received the nomination for president from the Democrats. Though Chicago may never have known a moment more tinged with urban terror, none of the cataclysmic horrors came to pass. The military, bolstered by the street work of the Chicago police, were able to stay the hand of catastrophe in one of the darkest moments of the war. Ironically, one of the great cultural attractions during the convention was the appearance of the famed actor John Wilkes Booth at the McVicker's Theater.

As spring arrived in 1865, the last vestiges of the South's abilities to continue the war evaporated. The city of Richmond fell. With unusual dignity and nobility, President Abraham Lincoln accepted the surrender of the Confederacy on April 9, 1865. General Robert E. Lee surrendered to General Ulysses S. Grant and America was utterly changed; so was Chicago. Within six days, President Lincoln, with so many significant ties to Chicago, was dead from an assassin's bullet. The nation was plunged into grief. Following the president's funeral in Washington, D.C., on April 21, 1865, his remains were placed aboard a special train to transport him back to his native Springfield, Illinois. The seventeen hundred mile journey carried him through many of the nation's most important cities—New York, Baltimore, Philadelphia, Buffalo, Cleveland, Indianapolis, Michigan City and Chicago. Lincoln's Chicago funeral procession, May 1, 1865, rivaled that of New York City's. Chicagoans lined the streets from the railroad terminal. *The Chicago Tribune* reported that the cortege passed out of Park Row into Michigan Avenue led by—

Police Officers in single rank, in uniform, wearing mourning rosettes on the left breast and a crape bandage on the arm. [*Chicago Tribune*, May 2, 1865]

They were followed by a large band of musicians from the Great Western Light Guard playing the *Lincoln Requiem*. Then followed the Chief Marshal, Colonel R.M. Hough and the

Assistant Marshals, among who was Chicago Superintendent of Police William Turtle.

Turtle had recognized the importance of preserving good order throughout the city; so in addition to the police in the procession, he detailed one-hundred-twenty police to guard the approaches to the principal streets. The *Tribune* reported that the Chicago Police "performed very efficient service during the day." It later went on to say that "some of the specials, doubtless impressed with the dignity of their position, seemed hardly to know their duty." Throughout the moving tribute to the president, Chicago's police force of one hundred-seventy-nine men were out in full force sustaining order, keeping their eyes peeled for any sign of trouble and searching the funeral crowd for pick-pockets, misfits, troublemakers and thieves.

Thirty-seven thousand people marched down Michigan Avenue, turning up Lake Street, then onto Clark Street in tribute to the martyred president as his body was carried to Court House Square and the laying-in-state in the City Hall. Ten-thousand school children served as an honor guard wearing black sashes. Mayor Long John Wentworth, one of Lincoln's most robust supporters, the man who helped secure the nomination for him, served as a pallbearer. More than one-hundred-twenty-thousand people watched the solemn rites for the slain president. Seven-thousand people an hour were passing the bier. On Tuesday, May 2, 1865 the body of the president was returned to his funeral train for the one-hundred eighty-four mile trip to Springfield, Illinois for burial. Mayor John B. Rice was sworn-in May 3, 1865. the day following Lincoln's funeral. He captured the spirit of the city in his inaugural remarks—

Gentlemen, the commencement of our official life is shrouded in gloom. The world is appalled, our nation is in mourning; let us all here, as upon an altar, cast aside now and forever all passionate exaggerations, all asperities, all exacerbations, and keep our minds on those cardinal points, devotion to our country, to humanity and justice, with a constant effort for the right, so that when our days are ended, this city's voice may justly proclaim of each of us— he did his duty. [Rice, May 3, 1865]

In the years immediately following the Civil War the ranks of the Chicago Police swelled. There were 179 sworn officers in 1865; an additional one was added in 1866 for 180. As the number of post war arrests climbed to more than 23,000 in 1866, the numbers of police increased steadily—to 268 in 1867; 291 in 1868; to 368 by 1869; 374 in 1870 and to 450 policemen in 1871 on the eve of the Great Fire. Despite the increasing numbers of added police, between the end of the Civil War and the Fire of 1871, there were no policemen killed during that six year period.

Policemen were poorly paid and had little opportunity to provide for themselves or their families in case of catastrophic injury or illness. In a pragmatic move, Chicago's rank and file patrolmen banded together to form the Policemen's Benevolent Association in 1868. With a growing population and an expanding array of new urban neighborhoods, new police stations were proposed for the south and north sides of the city. On Cottage Grove Avenue between 25th and 26th Streets, in the heart of the Irish neighborhoods, and on Chicago and Milwaukee Avenues, in the Polish community, new stations brought an important new police presence. Arrests in the city reached more than 26,000 in 1870.

The population of Chicago had grown to 298,977 in 1871, reflecting the remarkable peacetime prosperity that the city knew. Continued urban expansion marked it as the nation's most muscular and dynamic economic prospect. After his visit to Chicago in 1871, the social reformer Henry Ward Beecher said that the city "fairly smokes and roars with business." More ships arrived at the port of Chicago in 1871 than the combined number for the ports of New York, Philadelphia, Baltimore, Charleston, San Francisco and Mobile. And yet, for all its modernity and financial success, the city was, for all practicality, shaped out of wood. It had 57 miles of wood-paved streets; more than 560 miles of wooden sidewalks; and

Chicago Police direct swelling
crowds at President Abraham Lincoln's
Chicago Funeral, May 1, 1865.
Chicago History Museum Archive.

thousands upon thousands of freshly built wooden houses. All of this boded ominously as the summer of 1871 progressed, proving to be hot and dry. The autumn was equally dry. Chicagoans saw more than twenty-five fires break out around the city, then, further creating a hazardous climate, until October 8, 1871. When the first smoke of that fire was glimpsed by the lookout atop the City Hall, he could also see the last of the city's fire equipment returning from an earlier fire that took four city blocks south of the city. That blaze pushed Chicago resources to the limit. When the fire of October 8 broke out, along DeKoven Street, there was no reason to believe that this would be any worse than the dozens of other recent blazes. But as the conflagration got underway, it had something no other fire possessed—the growing prairie winds that would turn it into an inferno. The fire was soon out of control. Before it would end by the surprise of a gentle rain falling on October 10th, it would take three-fifths of the central city with it. With no problem jumping the Chicago River, it burned all the way to Fullerton Avenue. Remarkably, although the toll in destruction was high, the number of victims was small by comparison, less than 300 dead. A temporary morgue was set up on Milwaukee Avenue in a livery stable to accommodate the families of the victims. The Chicago Police were on duty to keep order and assist those attempting to identify the dead. The *Chicago Tribune* reported—

At the door were stationed Officers George Mitchell, Parker, Smith and Special Policemen, and a long line of persons anxious to obtain a glimpse of the remains. That the bodies were burned beyond recognition they were told peremptorily, but a morbid curiosity and a feeling of certainty that they, at least, could recognize what no one else could, kept a crowd at the door. At 8 o'clock a string was formed reaching possibly half a block. The police allowed the men to go in by tens, and then, after a look, let them go again. At this rate it was found that 100 persons came in every 20 minutes or so, or 300 per hour.

The Officers maintain the strictest order, and none but the quietest and most decorous behavior is allowed. [*Chicago Tribune*, October 12, 1871]

While Chicago's police assisted in a variety of tasks in the immediate aftermath of the Great Fire, official law enforcement had been taken over by the United States Army under the command of Lieutenant General Philip H. Sheridan. In the official proclamation of Marshal Law it was agreed that—

The police will act in conjunction with the Lieutenant General in the preservation of the peace and quiet of the city, and the Superintendent of the Police will consult with him to that end. [*Chicago Tribune*, October 12, 1871]

Thieves were particularly aggressive in attempting to find and loot safes within the burned out shells of businesses and banks. Orders given to the militia and the police were as strict as possible to discourage such crime. Six companies of soldiers reinforced the orders to prevent wholesale looting. Special police were inducted from among citizens to also help maintain order. However, it was soon discovered that many of the criminal element had infiltrated this unit and the Board of Police disbanded this group immediately.

The city's recovery began quickly, the moment it was learned that cities around the nation had already begun to send supplies and necessities so that the people of Chicago could survive. A large warehouse belonging to the firm of Toby & Booth on Eighteenth Street was set up to accept provisions arriving in the city. During the first day and night, sixty full train car loads of supplies were rushed to Chicago. Hard as it might be to imagine, all things familiar were swept away. One hundred cars arrived on the second day. Life was beginning again among the ruins.

Mayor John Wentworth addresses Montgomery and Emmett Guards at the second City Hall and Courthouse (1855). Chicago History Museum Photo Archive.

Caricature of "outward bound" Irish immigrant (1854). Daguerreotype by A. Hesler, Chicago History Museum Photo Archive.

Constable James Quinn,

became the first Chicago police officer to die in the line of duty on December 5, 1853. His death, much like his life, was reflective of the conflicts and passions of life in Chicago at the mid-point of the 19th century. Like many other Chicagoans, Quinn was an immigrant who settled in the city. Born in 1814 in the rural Irish countryside near Garrythomas, County Kilkenny. Quinn married Margaret O'Shea on April 29, 1847 in the Roman Catholic parish of Wind Gap, County Kilkenny. Leaving Ireland for Canada as the trauma of the Great Famine hit Ireland, the Quinn's first child, Mary, was born in Toronto, Ontario. After the arrival of the Quinns in Chicago, two subsequent children were born, son Patrick in August of 1850 and daughter Katherine in 1853. The family resided in Holy Name Parish. Their home was located at the northwest corner of Grand Avenue and St. Clair Street, next to the lakefront neighborhood known as "the Sands."

In 1853 Quinn was elected to the office of constable by his neighbors and local residents of the 9th Ward. It was not, however, a good time to be either foreign-born or Roman Catholic in Chicago. Prejudices, particularly official municipal prejudices, were powerful and unforgiving. It was the era of the "Know-Nothings," a hate-based political party that pledged to exclude all those who were Catholic and not American-born from elected positions of public honor and trust. Quinn's defeat of the Know-Nothing candidate in the area of the Sands made him a marked man, someone who had purposely challenged the status quo. With the city's police Captain, Luther Nichols, the Cook County Sherrif Cyrus P. Bradley, and many other officials all sworn members of the secret Know-Nothings Party, Quinn was a visible thorn-in-the-side of his biased opponents. The fact that he carried the election in his 9th Ward with a majority of Irish Catholic voters further alienated Quinn from the local political powerhouses. All of this is critical to understanding the circumstances of Quinn's death and the ironic response he was to receive in death from Chicago's official leaders.

On Friday evening, December 2, 1853, Quinn was ordered to carry out the arrest of a suspected thief, Paul Parmilee. Armed with an official warrant, Quinn went off in search of this suspect. Quinn located him on the notorious waterfront Sands, and proceeded to make his arrest. Following this, the prisoner requested he be allowed to enter a nearby saloon to gather a few possessions before heading off to the police station. Quinn obliged the prisoner and entered the den with him and was immediately attacked by the notorious owner of the saloon, Bill Rees, with the result that Parmilee escaped and Quinn sustained serious injuries.

The following evening, Saturday, December 3, 1853, despite his injuries, Quinn was back on duty and received yet another warrant instructing him to arrest Parmilee. Quinn returned to the Sands in search of him and in doing so encountered Rees in a saloon where he once more challenged Quinn. Refusing to fight Rees, he was further brutalized by him, compounding the seriousness of his prior injuries.

Despite those injuries, Quinn went to headquarters and made his report to the Night Watch captain who subsequently kept all twenty-six nightwatchmen on duty. He authorized them to work "extra services" to descend on the Sands *en masse* to search for and arrest Rees and Parmilee. Quinn returned home just before noon and was confined to his bed. Early that evening Dr. Henrotin treated Quinn and found him to be in great pain. On the following morning, Monday, December 5, 1853, Constable Quinn succumbed to his injuries. It was determined that his ribs were broken, puncturing vital internal organs. He left behind his wife of six years, Margaret, as well as three children under five years of age. His funeral took place at Holy Name Church and burial was in the old Catholic Cemetery on Dearborn Street between North Avenue and Schiller Street, in what is today are the grounds of the home belonging to the Cardinal Archbishop of Chicago. The whereabouts of Quinn's remains have been lost.

1853

On December 12, 1853, the Common Council, as the Chicago City Council was then known, at a regular meeting passed an Order closing "houses of ill fame" in the city, in response to the murder of Quinn in Rees' "saloon." The Council indicated that this was necessary because "A member of the Police of the City has been lately killed in the discharge of his duty." This marked the very first time that the city's municipal government so recognized a "line of duty death" within the Chicago Police. The full brunt of the police force descended upon the Sands and carried out large-scale arrests. On January 9, 1854, a Grand Jury indicted Rees for the murder of Quinn, with his trial commencing on February 1, 1854. Rees was subsequently found guilty of manslaughter and sentenced to five years in the Illinois State Prison at Alton. He was delivered there on February 15, 1854.

On February 24, 1854, Margaret Quinn, feeling the economic hardship resulting from her husband's death, filed a petition with the Common Council for assistance because her husband "died while faithfully and honestly discharging his duty as an officer of the City of Chicago." On March 6, 1854, the Council's Committee on Judiciary issued a report "concurring" with the widow's petition and recommended a payment of fifty dollars. This was the first time death-duty benefits were awarded to the widow of a Chicago police officer.

Quinn's descendants went on to become valuable contributors to Chicago life. His only son, Patrick, known as Paddy, played Major League Baseball in its early days, with the 1874 Chicago Champions, the Franklin Baseball Club. He later played on Cap Anson's Chicago White Stockings, the precursor to the Chicago Cubs. Several of Constable Quinn's grandsons served on the Chicago Fire Department; one, William J. O'Brien, died in the line of duty on July 15, 1917 in a gas explosion. Grandsons Joseph and James O'Brien also were career firefighters. Another grandson, John J. O'Brien was a Chicago Police Department Captain who served from 1901 until his retirement in 1935. He was well known and beloved by all with whom he worked.

Patrolman Casper Lauer,

became Chicago's second policeman to die in the line of duty nine months after the death of Constable James Quinn. In some ways the two men share very similar stories, but closer scrutiny shows they could not have been more unalike. Like Quinn, Lauer was an immigrant, born March 8, 1820 in Bielsbrueck, in the wine growing region of Moselle, in the province of Lorraine, France. His family, culturally German, though citizens of France, came to the United States in 1839. The following year, 1840, at 20 years of age, Casper came to Chicago with some of his brothers, while his mother and other family remained in Buffalo, New York. Nine years after his arrival in Chicago, Lauer became a Chicago Policeman. He served on the force for five years before his death. But he had already made a name for himself by his service with the Volunteer Chicago Fire Department.

Through his membership in this elite brigade, Lauer quickly assimilated into Chicago life and came to know important contacts in its municipal leadership. The Chicago City Directory of 1851 gives his address as Fort Dearborn, the old stockade fortress built along the palisades of the Chicago River. Though no longer used as a military outpost, what remained of the fort at the time was used as a residence for those with municipal responsibilities and connections to political power. Lauer's address would indicate his friendship with Luther Nichols, the Captain of Police, was paying off. That friendship stretched back to 1840 when Nichols was Chief Engineer of the Fire Department and Lauer worked on engine No. 2, the Metamora. By 1854, Lauer had moved his family to Clark and Polk Streets in the heart of the city. His wife, Eva Oehmen Lauer, had given him two children both born in Chicago; Nicholas, on January 19, 1851, and Joseph, in 1854.

1854

The Village of Garrythomas, County Kilkenny,
near the birthplace of Constable James Quinn.

Lauer served the police department in two positions, first as a member of the Night Watch from 1851 to 1853, and then as a Day Policeman from 1853 until his death. Lauer's brother, John, also served as a member of the Night Watch. Like Constable James Quinn, Casper Lauer's early death in the line of duty is a recent discovery, only unearthed through the efforts of his descendants and historical researchers in the past several years. Lauer's patrol jurisdiction was south of the river in an area that today is the very heart of the business district.

On September 18, 1854 Lauer was summoned to a domestic disturbance involving an intoxicated man, Patrick Cunningham, fighting with his elderly parents. Upon his arrival at the scene, Lauer arrested Cunningham and began to escort him to the nearby police station. At the intersection of Jackson Street and Plymouth Court, in the area today that borders the federal plaza, the perpetrator produced a knife. Cunningham was able to overpower Lauer and stab him in the ribs with the knife. Despite the severity of his wounds, Lauer was able to inflict two powerful blows to his suspect's head with his official police-issue baton. Cunningham was knocked to the ground, bleeding heavily.

After Lauer secured the knife, he ordered people in the crowd that had gathered to prevent the suspect from escaping. Quickly flagging down a passing wagon, Lauer had himself transported to the nearest drug store—the closest available source of medical attention in 1854. He did not survive for long.

Officer Lauer's Requiem Mass was celebrated in St. Peter Church in the heart of the city and burial took place in St. Boniface Cemetery, the German Catholic burial ground on North Clark Street. A large number of Chicagoans, including Mayor Isaac Miliken, were in attendance. The City Marshall, Darius Knights, today's equivalent of the Superintendent, issued a proclamation expressing the deep sorrow and sense a loss felt by the Department. As a sign of their respect, members of the Chicago Police Department all wore a badge of mourning. Lauer was given a hero's salute. Officer Lauer was photographed in his coffin in an early Daguerreotype. His portrait presents an eerie image of a sad moment in Chicago's early history.

Patrick Cunningham was tried and found guilty of voluntary manslaughter on January 21, 1855 and sentenced to eight years in prison. The short term was the maximum allowed under the voluntary manslaughter statute of the time but he would not serve the full sentence. Cunningham was taken to the State Penitentiary at Alton on February 18, 1855 where he stayed for almost three years before being transferred to the Illinois State Penitentiary at Joliet on June 9, 1858. Cunningham's sister, Mary, began petitioning Illinois Governor John Wood to pardon her brother. Others, including the prosecutors of the case, the trial judge, the warden of the State Penitentiary at Alton and lawyer Abraham Lincoln, also sent petitions seeking Cunningham's release. Patrick Cunningham was pardoned by Governor Wood on August 8, 1860 after serving almost six years of his eight year sentence.

Patrolman John C. Churchwood,

1st Precinct, 39 years old, died in the line of duty on Friday, March 25, 1864 in the midst of the American Civil War. His death was virtually forgotten in Chicago history until recent research revealed his story. Churchwood was born in Surrey, England and immigrated to Chicago with his wife, Helen, and son, John, Jr. In Chicago the Churchwoods lived on Carroll Street between Morgan and Carpenter Streets in the 6th Ward.

On March 21, 1864, Officer Churchwood was summoned to the Soldiers' Home at 541 W. Randolph Street, a free residential facility operated by the Methodist Church in Chicago where the many Union soldiers passing through the city could find respite from the fatigue of the war. Churchwood went there to arrest a soldier from the 51st Illinois Infantry Regiment on a charge of disorderly conduct. The soldier in question, Private Duncan McGillis, 39, was a diminutive man with a drinking problem. Following his arrest, McGillis was being escorted to the police station when he asked Churchwood if he could retrieve some possession from his room to take with him. Churchwood obliged the suspect and accompanied him upstairs in the Soldiers' Home to his quarters. McGillis and Churchwood then both took a serious tumble as a result of McGillis' inebriation. As a result of the fall, Churchwood seriously injured his hand, breaking the bones in his thumb. The injury quickly became inflamed, causing a serious infection in his entire arm. Within two days it had worsened to such an extent that doctors wanted to amputate the arm above the elbow. Churchwood refused their suggestion of an operation with the result that soon his entire body had toxified to such an extent that death appeared imminent. Just four days following his injury, Officer Churchwood died. The County Coroner, Justice Conrad Diehl, held an inquest into the death of Officer Churchwood and the jury returned a verdict of death from Erysipelas, the infection that killed him. Since McGillis was intoxicated at the time of Officer Churchwood's death, the jury did not find him responsible.

Officer Churchwood received a hero's funeral two days later, Sunday, March 27, 1864. At 10:00 A.M., the entire Chicago Police Department, with their stars draped in "somber crape," gathered at the 1st Precinct Central Station and marched as a unified body to the Carroll Street home of the deceased. There, a religious service was conducted befitting his status as an important member of the Washington Lodge A.P.A.—the American Protestant Association. Together with many other friends, the police procession then traveled down Randolph Street to Clark Street and then north to the old cemetery at what is today Lincoln Park. At that point the marchers left the funeral cortege, which continued up Clark Street to Graceland Cemetery on Irving Park Road. Officer Churchwood, the *Chicago Tribune* reported "was a most efficient and respected official." The newspaper later went on to condemn Private McGillis and strongly express the sense of outrage that many Chicagoans felt following Churchwood's death. Churchwood, they wrote, "has fallen victim to the unprovoked brutality of a man who has sworn to protect the same law he was trying to uphold, but one who, with too many comrades, seems to think that a soldier's mission is simply the operation of brute force on the battlefield, and that a soldier's honor is not tarnished by contact with a brothel or drunkard's cell. They forget their high mission, and instead of being keepers of the peace, become a terror to well-disposed citizens." It had been ten years since the people of Chicago experienced the death of a Chicago Policeman in the line of duty. Even in wartime, it was a harsh and bitter experience for everyone. Sadly, no record exists today identifying the location of the grave of Officer Churchwood in Graceland Cemetery.

1864

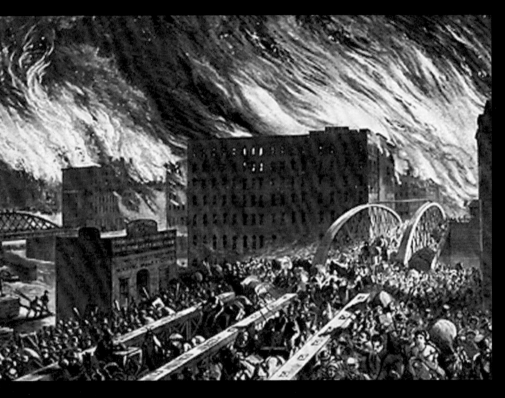

Chicagoans escape the Great Fire
of 1871 over the Randolph Street Bridge,
by John R. Chapin, *Harper's Weekly*.
Chicago History Museum Archives.

Burning of Chicago Chamber of Commerce,
LaSalle and Washington Streets, *Harper's Weekly*.
Chicago History Museum Archives.

The Crosby Opera House burns shortly after
its renovation, *Harper's Weekly*.
Chicago History Museum Archives.

a79 End of Watch

Patrolman Patrick O'Meara,

STAR #94, 1st Precinct, Deering Street Station, 38 years old, was killed in the line of duty August 4, 1872, in O'Brien's Saloon at 35th Place and Halsted Street. He was murdered by a thug named Christopher Rafferty, whom the *Chicago InterOcean* once referred to as a "roughian." O'Meara, who worked one of the city's toughest beats, was born in Ireland in 1834, came to the United States as an infant and settled in Bridgeport by 1856. In 1860, he married Julia Thompson, a fellow Irish immigrant. His cold blooded murder outraged Chicagoans. It was an atrocity further deepened by the fact that the killer had escaped. Local neighborhood folk took to the streets frantic with excitement following his murder, forming small posses that headed out to the prairie grass to hunt for the killer. Local police officials soon persuaded people to permit Chicago detectives to track Officer O'Meara's murderer down themselves.

Chicagoans read with anguish the careful details recounted in the city's newspapers. They learned that Christopher Rafferty, a 24-year-old bricklayer, had been engaged in a Westside street riot with three friends during the previous week. Rafferty, his brother and another man were arrested for their part in the violence while a fourth man of their company escaped. After being examined by the police the three men were released on bail. Rafferty claimed a witness to his innocence, a man named Donovan. But Donovan refused to appear on Rafferty's part or provide an alibi attesting to his innocence. Upon his release, Rafferty went looking for this witness intent on revenge. When he found him he beat Donovan severely with a brick. The victim then swore out a warrant against Rafferty. It was in the apprehension of Rafferty for this crime that O'Meara was killed.

At 12:30 A.M. O'Meara accompanied another Chicago Policeman, James Scanlan, to Daniel O'Brien's Saloon on Halsted Street at 35th Place in an area known as "Hamburg." The neighborhood was well known for the brutality of its cutthroats and hordes of filthy women. Both Irish cops new Rafferty on sight and quickly spotted him in his hang-out. Rafferty was buying drinks for the house when officers approached him seated at a table. When Rafferty first saw O'Meara, he offered him a cigar. Scanlan took out the disorderly warrant and told Rafferty it was for him. Rafferty appeared to cooperate as he stood and walked to the door with police. Suddenly, he made a dash for the door, spewing curses at the police and pulling a revolver from his pocket. He pointed the barrel at O'Meara's chest and pulled the trigger. O'Meara's last words were, "Stay, Chris, don't shoot." He would never utter another word. His body hit the floor. Pointing his revolver at Scanlan, he fired once more, just missing the policeman's head. Scanlan then jumped on him and a desperate scuffle ensued. When Rafferty tried to pull the trigger again, Scanlan stopped the hammer with his hand. No help came from the crowd inside the saloon who quickly exited to the street. Rafferty was able to subdue Scanlan and escape the saloon into the night of the prairie.

Rafferty did not elude police for long. Later on the morning of August 4, police received a tip from a female tavern owner in the town of Willow Springs. The woman claimed she had recently sold whiskey to a man who resembled Rafferty. Five officers boarded the evening train to Willow Springs and were able to confirm Rafferty's presence in the area when they arrived. The officers then hired a farmer with a wagon to help them search the area and split into three groups in order to cover more ground. Rafferty was eventually located by Patrolman Dennis Mahoney and the farmer, walking by himself. He appeared to be heading towards Joliet. Mahoney quickly jumped into the back of the wagon and told the farmer to offer the criminal a ride. Rafferty accepted the offer and had barely seated himself in the wagon when Mahoney grabbed and handcuffed him. Rafferty was taken back to the

The men of the Deering Street Police Station,
(Loomis Street, 1872). ICH-i25473,
Chicago History Museum Photo Archive.

Patrick O'Meara Family
(Photo Courtesy of Family).

Inset: Patrolman Patrick O'Meara (1872).
ICH-i257413, Chicago History Museum
Photo Archive.

city and locked up in the Harrison Street Station. He was tried and convicted of Patrick O'Meara's murder one month after his capture. But in a strange turn of events the case was overturned. A new trial was ordered in Lake County, Illinois. In Waukegan, Rafferty was, again, found guilty of O'Meara's murder. He was subsequently hanged in 1874. Ironically, he was quietly buried in Calvary Cemetery, the same Cemetery in which his victim had been laid to rest. Officer O'Meara left behind his wife and five children. For more than a century, he was considered the first officer to die in the line of duty.

Shortly before he was hanged, O'Meara's killer is said to have penned the following ballad.

Ballad of Chris Rafferty

Come all you tender Christians, I hope you will draw near,
And likewise pay attention to a few lines I have here.
For the murder of O'Meara I am condemned to die,
On the 28th of February, all on the gallows high.

My name it is Chris Rafferty, that name I never denied.
I left my aged parents in sorrow for to cry.
Oh little did they think in my youth and bloom
That I would come to Chicago to meet with my sad doom.

My parents reared me tenderly as plainly you may see
Constantly good advice they always gave to me.
They told me: quit night-walking, and shun bad company
Or State's Prison or the gallows my doom would surely be.

Scanlan and O'Meara, they came in a saloon.
They said to me, "Chris Rafferty, we want you right soon."
It was then I pulled that fatal pop and shot him through the heart
Which leaves a loving wife and husband for to part.

On the day of my trial it would pierce your heart to see
My companions and associates they were all standing by.
I bid them take a warning by my sad fate,
And to leave out their night-walking before it was too late.

On the day of my execution it would pierce your heart to see
My sister come from Bridgeport, to take farewell of me.
She fell into my arms, and bitterly did cry,
Saying, "My darling, dearest brother, this afternoon you die."

O now my trial is ended from this world I must depart,
For the murder of O'Meara I am sorry to the heart.
Come all you young and older men, take warning by my sad fate,
And leave off your night-walking before it is too late.

Patrolman Christian Jacobs,

STAR # unavailable, Webster Avenue Station, 35 years old, observed two suspicious men in front of a local pool hall while on his beat on the night of August 18, 1873. Jacobs decided to investigate what they were doing. As he moved toward the men, they took off in the opposite direction. Jacobs ran after them but soon discovered a third man who pulled a gun and shot him at the intersection of Larabee, Lincoln and Webster Avenues. Within hours, Jacobs was dead. The policeman was a German immigrant and lived at 1968 N. Burling Street, one block east of Halsted Street. Charles McLain, alias Brockey, was later taken into custody as the man who had shot Jacobs. McLain was a notorious burglar and villain. Officer Jacobs was the son of John and Rosina Jacobs. Burial took place Graceland Cemetery, at Clark Street and Irving Park Road.

1873

Patrolman S. Wellington McArthur,

STAR # unavailable, 30 years old, was stabbed in the early hours of June 15, 1877 in a lumber-yard near the Lake Street Bridge. McArthur and his partner, Officer Henry Smith, heard someone yell that they had been stabbed, so they ran to the scene. The two officers found two sailors who appeared to be under the influence of alcohol and in some sort of fight. One of them, Frank Sheppard, had already stabbed the other, named Anderson. As McArthur attempted to separate the two men, Anderson stabbed him in the abdomen and then fled the scene. Immediately, Officer McArthur was taken to the West Madison Street Station where he was treated and remained for the next few days. Shortly after the stabbing, Sheppard was apprehended and held without bail. Sheppard claimed that the stabbing was the whiskey's fault, making no attempt to deny what had happened. He even went on to say that he thought that the officers were the men that had earlier attempted to rob him. A jury found Sheppard guilty of manslaughter. He was sentenced to 25 years at the Illinois State Penitentiary at Joliet.

Policeman McArthur had only been serving on the Chicago Police for one month. Originally from Whitehall, New York, McArthur had also served on the police force there. Two weeks later, on June 29, the patrolman died at his home. The young officer, who lived at 128 N. Peoria Street, left behind a pregnant wife and young child.

Patrolman Gilbert E. Reynolds,

STAR # unavailable, West Madison Street Station, 37 years old, was accidentally shot on December 5, 1877 while cleaning equipment with fellow Officer Thomas Brannock before their shift started. Brannock's service revolver accidentally dropped from his overcoat, hit the floor, and fatally wounded Officer Reynolds in the abdomen. A doctor arrived at the station, but little could be done. Four hours later, Officer Reynolds succumbed to his wounds. The patrolman had been an officer for six years, serving some of his time with the 12th Street Station. He was survived by his wife and daughter.

1877

View of DesPlaines Street (c. 1890).
DN-0004626, *Chicago Daily News* Collection,
Chicago History Museum Photo Archive.

Patrolman Albert Race,

STAR #7, 1st Precinct, Central Avenue Station, 30 years old, lost his life in the line of duty on October 4, 1878. He was shot at point blank range while investigating a burglary at 10:00 P.M. at 1328 S. State Street. Officer Race, while on patrol, recognized some suspicious behavior in front of the Lesser Friedburg Pawn Shop, watching a variety of goods being unloaded from a horse drawn wagon. When he stepped up and asked one of the men what he had, he was told "none of your business." The man raised a revolver and fired at him. As Officer Race fell dead to the ground, the perpetrator fled the scene in the direction of Lake Michigan. The assailant spooked the policeman's horse so badly that it ran away wildly, south on State Street. Officer Race was carried to a nearby Freidigki's Drug Store, where he was pronounced dead.

When police inspected the murder scene and recovered the horse and wagon, they uncovered a large quantity of silk and velvet fabric, stolen just a short time before from the E.S. Jaffray and Co. Dry Good Store.

Investigators on the scene saw the pool of blood on the side walk where Officer Race had fallen. The pawn shop was locked and had its curtains drawn. One eyewitness, William Harmon, a young man working at a near by grocery store, acknowledged that two men, one tall and one short, had been sitting in the wagon. He also acknowledged that the smaller of the two men was the shooter and believed he would recognize the assailants on sight.

Chicago Police Detectives Dan Considine and James Flynn questioned Lesser Friedburg and his wife. Friedburg was a well known fence for stolen goods. It was not long before merchandise inside the pawn shop matched merchandise found in the murder wagon. The Friedburgs were locked up at the Harrison Street Station.

Further investigation by Chicago Detectives of the Jaffray Silk robbery led police to discover it was the work of Johnny Lamb, alias James Williamson, Philo Durfee, George Freeman, Jim Griffin, Charles Dennis, and Jimmy Driscoll. Friedburg had guaranteed to pay this gang 85 cents a yard for the fabric. In addition, he loaned one of the men a revolver. While delivering the merchandise, Officer Race walked up upon the men. Nine days after Race's murder, Johnny Lamb was arrested on charges of murder and burglary. George Freeman was arrested in St. Paul, Minnesota while on the run and was transported back to Chicago. Both Freeman and Lamb were identified as the perpetrators. Freeman betrayed Lamb by turning in states evidence. Lamb was convicted and sentenced to hang. However, Lamb was granted a new trial and was ultimately acquitted for Race's murder.

The *Chicago Daily News* reported that Officer Race was a "fine-looking" man who stood 6 feet 2 inches tall, weighing about 175 pounds. Race was of German descent and came to the United States when he was 22 years old. He never married and had lived in Chicago for eight years. "His superiors," the paper noted, "unite in praising him for his sobriety and strict attention to duty. He was a man of more than average intelligence and thoughtfulness." Officer Race's body was taken to Elton's "dead room," it was reported, where it was placed "upon ice" for viewing. It was said that the grief among his brother officers was "profound." Officer Race was taken to Pittston, Pennsylvania for burial.

Patrolman James Keon,

STAR # unavailable, 35 years old, was patrolling a Northside alley when he fell into an excavation hole on November 20, 1878. The officer suffered fatal injuries from the fall and on December 1, 1878 he died in his home. Patrolman Keon was laid to rest in Calvary Cemetery, Evanston.

Children of Polish immigrants play in front of St. Stanislaus Kosha Church located near the Rawson Street Station, an area that was home to thousands of Poles (c. 1880). DN-0005624, *Chicago Daily News* Collection, Chicago History Museum Photo Archive.

Patrolman Timothy Mahoney,

STAR #230, 2nd Precinct, Deering Street Station, about 40 years old, was one of the many dedicated officers who were native-born to Ireland. On June 11, 1881, he was shot around 11:00 P.M. while attempting to arrest two burglars at the corner of 37th Place and Halsted Street. He died a short time later in the early hours of June 12. Patrolman Mahoney was walking his beat at 37th Place and Halsted Street when Richard Jones and his wife of 3815 S. Emerald Avenue entered their home and discovered two burglars fast at work. The burglars took off and Jones followed. He soon met Patrolman Mahoney and described the men he was following. Mahoney recalled having just seen the men and took off after the offenders. When Mahoney caught up to them, a scuffle ensued and three shots were quickly fired. The policeman fell to the ground and exclaimed, "My God, I've been shot!" As he lay on the ground dying, his murderer and his accomplice fled into the darkness in separate directions. Many Chicagoans, remembering the deaths of Albert Race and Patrick O'Meara, were outraged at Mahoney's murder. The *Chicago Tribune* called the deed, "Foul Murder." The paper alerted all Chicagoans to the acts committed by the "Marauders," who they said disappeared in darkness and blinding rain. Eventually a man named William Elliott was arrested for Mahoney's murder, but he was later released. Officer Mahoney was buried in Calvary Cemetery, Evanston.

Detective Patrick M. O'Brien,

STAR #188, 2nd Precinct, 12th Street Station, 32 years old, died August 3, 1881 at 3:20 P.M. from wounds received in the line of duty. O'Brien was shot on August 1 while pursuing an assailant named Thomas Cahill, who allegedly shot a person on the street. Cahill was pursued to his home at 50 W. Rebecca Street, where he barricaded himself inside. The offender then pushed his revolver through a crack in his door and pulled the trigger, resulting in O'Brien's fatal wound. O'Brien was carried to the nearby 12th Street Station where doctors on the scene diagnosed his wound as fatal. O'Brien was a ten-year-veteran of the Chicago Police Department. Born in Rutland, Vermont, he was brought by his family to Chicago as a child. He rose through the ranks from a patrolman following a beat along 12th Street to detective duty in his civilian clothes. The *Chicago Tribune* reminded readers that like O'Brien's great friend, Patrolman Timothy Mahoney, killed just seven weeks earlier, he was also a "thief-catcher." His nose for crime investigation led his superiors to promote him to detective rank. His partner in that post was Officer Thomas Dooley.

O'Brien and Mahoney were recalled as being very similar men as well as being the warmest of personal friends. They shared a love of police work, as well as an Irish heritage. Both were members of the same division, number 7, of the Ancient Order of Hibernians. O'Brien was also a member of the Police Benevolent Association, The Police and Fire State Association and of the Fidelity Court of the Ancient Order of Foresters. Tragically, O'Brien left a wife and five small children aged nine months to nine years. They lived at the corner of Maxwell Street and Thirteenth Street. In addition, Patrolman O'Brien left behind his widowed mother who resided in his home with his family. The *Chicago Tribune* acknowledged Mrs. O'Brien was, "burdened with sorrow with her son's demise." Officer O'Brien was interred in Calvary Cemetery, Evanston. Thomas Cahill, the shooter, was taken into custody, tried and convicted and spent the rest of his life in the Illinois State Penitentiary at Joliet.

1881

The Rawson Street Station, one of Chicago's earliest Northside Police Stations.
Chicago Police Department Photo Archive.

Cahill Brothers Saloon (c.1880s).
DN-0000882, *Chicago Daily News* Collection,
Chicago History Museum Photo Archive.

Austin Avenue Police Station on Chicago's
Westside (c.1890). DN-0003820,
Chicago Daily News Collection,
Chicago History Museum Photo Archive.

Old Station at 113 W. Chicago Avenue
made of Illinois Limestone.
Chicago Police Department Photo Archive.

Patrolman Daniel Crowley,

STAR #296, 3rd Precinct, Cottage Grove Station, 34 years old, died on August 4, 1881, the day after Detective Patrick O'Brien. Crowley's death came from the severe infection of a gunshot wound to the thigh received July 25, 1881. He died at home in his own bed at 838 S. Miller Street. The policeman had been born in Ireland and left behind a wife, but no children, to grieve him. Crowley had been assigned the task of following up on some petty larceny cases during which he dressed in civilian attire. Early in the evening on the night of July 25, 1881, Crowley arrested Neil Hennessy and Johanna Lyons for the theft of some articles of clothing from Mrs. Mary McCormick. He subsequently arrested the notorious Minnie Daley for the theft of some property from the home of Mr. P. O'Meara at 528 W. Harrison Street. Minnie was also wanted on several other charges in conjunction with Johanna Lyons. Minnie was accompanied to the station by her mother, Mrs. Daley, hoping to bail her out if the chance presented itself. Suddenly, when the Daleys and Officer Crowley were walking north on DesPlaines Street, at Quincy Street near Old St. Patrick's Church, a man heavily under the influence of alcohol stepped up to Minnie, slapped her intimately on the shoulder and let fly a steady stream of foul mouth vulgarities. Mrs. Daley, taking umbrage to the assault and insult, slapped the man. As a result, the man became fouler in his speech. Officer Crowley engaged the man, cautioning him on his behavior and telling him to move away. Crowley showed the man his badge and star, repeating his warning to step aside. Without uttering a single word, the man removed a revolver from inside his coat, aimed it point blank at Crowley's chest and pulled the trigger. With a lightening response, Crowley brought his police cane down on the assailant's hand. The blow, at the exact moment the shot was fired, struck the revolver, causing the bullet to enter Crowley's thigh.

Despite his leg wound Crowley pursued his assailant, chasing him down to Jackson Street and then west another two hundred feet. Throughout the chase, Crowley returned fire from his own weapon, which misfired due to a rust pivot in its mechanism. Crowley's assailant was soon out of sight. The policeman then returned to the Daleys to escort them to the station, but collapsed from exhaustion at the next corner.

Several physicians attended Crowley and were even successful in extracting the bullet from the deep, fleshy part of his thigh. But they were not optimistic in their prognostication, since this particular kind of wound in most cases resulted in severe internal infection. As they predicted, the infection spread to Crowley's stomach and intestines, finally taking his life ten days after the shooting. He was originally interred in Calvary Cemetery, Evanston, but was later moved. An assailant named Edward Kelly was apprehended and convicted of the shooting of Officer Crowley. He was subsequently sentenced to five years in the penitentiary.

Patrolman John Huebner,

STAR #490, 4th Precinct, Rawson Street Station, was killed in the pursuit of armed burglars as dawn broke on February 4, 1882. He was a German born officer. In 1882, the Rawson Street District was a four square mile expanse of prairie. Houses sparsely dotted the flatland terrain north and west of the city. Officer Huebner was one of six policemen assigned to this large urban track. In the pursuit of his patrol duties, Huebner was proceeding west on Potomac Street (1300 North) and Greenview Street (1500 West) after hearing shots coming from that direction. There the policeman came upon two burglars in the commission of a crime at the corner of Potomac and Greenview Streets. Immediately, a scuffle ensued.

Seizing the smaller of the two offenders, Huebner threw him to the ground. Just then the other one said, "Let him go, you ___, or I'll kill you!" In an instant, four fatal bullets were pumped into Huebner's body in rapid succession. As the men ran off, and with death imminent, Patrolman Huebner raised himself and fired his revolver three times before finally dying. Officer Huebner was buried in Graceland Cemetery.

James Tracy was later caught and charged with the murder of Patrolman Huebner. He was found guilty of the charge and hanged in September of 1882.

There was an odd controversy concerning Tracy following his death. When James Tracy was sentenced to hang, he donated his body to science. He gave a group of doctors permission to revive him after he was declared legally dead. With the cooperation of the Cook County States Attorney and the warden of Cook County Jail, doctors transported Tracy's corpse to a laboratory in the jail, where they attempted to resuscitate the convict.

In a *Frankenstein*-like procedure, the doctors attempted the resuscitation by attaching primitive electrodes to Tracy's body and administering electricity. These electric shocks made his heart and even his leg muscles contract.

Revival, though, proved to be out of the question, because Tracy's neck had snapped in the hangman's fall. There was only a moment of spine-chilling anticipation when an electric shock made the cadaver's eyes open.

Patrolman Clarence E. Wright,

STAR #255, 3rd Precinct, DesPlaines Street Station, 25 years old, was killed instantly on the evening of Wednesday, November 29, 1882 while attempting to serve a warrant on William Allen, alias Joe Dehlmer. Wright was well liked by his colleagues; a "bright, quick, a good officer, and a gentlemen, and was highly thought of by his superior officers and fellow brother policeman," the *Chicago Tribune* reported. Only minutes before his murder took place, Officer Wright was sitting at the lock-up-keeper's desk in the cell room at the DesPlaines Street Station. While speaking to a friend on duty there, Officer Jennings, Wright was summoned by his superior, Lieutenant Ward, and asked to serve William Allen with an arrest warrant for disorderly conduct. He was told that the suspect could be found at his nearby home at 500 W. Washington Street. William Allen was characterized by the *Chicago Tribune* as a "desperado." When Officer Wright reached Allen's apartment, the door was slightly opened by a woman. Before Wright could utter a single word, Allen raised his revolver over the woman's shoulder and fired. Wright fell over backwards and was instantly killed.

The *Chicago Tribune* characterized the shooting as "a plain, cold-blooded, out-and-out murder, with no extenuating circumstances and no sensational features." It was the type of violent act that enraged Chicagoans' civility, reminding them how dangerous law enforcement in the city remained.

Officer Wright was unmarried and lived with his mother, brother and sister at 3835 S. Indiana Avenue. An indication of how well Wright was loved and respected by his fellow officers occurred when the dead man's mother was brought into the room to view her son's remains. It is said that she was so broken hearted and the scene was so pitiful that veterans of the Chicago Police Department chocked back tears as they witnessed it. Wright was buried in Graceland Cemetery.

On December 4, 1882, the *Chicago Daily News* reported the grim details of Bill Allen, Wright's murderer. The newspaper focused on his race, African-American, as a significant component of the reportage. The fury that swept the city in the aftermath of Officer Wright's death was palpable. Chicago Police left no stone unturned in hunting Allen down.

The details of Allen's capture become even more significant because it would eventually result in another death of a Chicago policeman. A series of events began at 1:00 P.M. on Sunday afternoon, December 3, 1882 when Officer Patrick Mulvihill stopped by the saloon of his brother, Jerry Mulvihill, at 210 N. Halsted Street. There, Officer Mulvihill discovered that the city's most sought after murderer, Bill Allen, was hiding at the home of Bill Lambert at 414 N. Halsted Street. Both Mulvihill brothers raced to the location. Officer Mulvihill went in the alley-way, while his brother secured the front of the premises to cut off Allen's escape. Allen spotted Jerry Mulvihill as he passed his window and began firing through a rear window at Officer Mulvihill. Mulvihill returned fire. At that point Allen fired once more at Officer Mulvihill striking him in the thumb with a bullet that deflected to his forehead. When Mulvihill fell, Allen made his escape. Despite his wounds both Officer Mulvihill and his brother continued to return fire at Allen.

Jerry Mulvihill took off after Allen down Green Street as far as the Northwestern Railway tracks. Police across the city were alerted and joined a great crowd of Chicagoans who joined in the search for the "desperado." Allen was discovered by Sergeant John Wheeler of the Union Street Patrol when the murderer jumped out of a large packing crate in the chicken coop at the rear of a building at the corner of Green and Kinzie Streets. Wheeler and a young boy, named Fred Lane, blocked the door to prevent Allen from fleeing. Wheeler shoved his revolver through the door and began firing at Allen. The killer screamed "I'm hit, that's enough." Wheeler continued firing three more times before the door was opened. Allen was pulled out, weak and bleeding. He fell to his knees, shouting, "that's enough I give up." Allen was dragged into the center of the yard where several policemen had gathered. They were joined by an excited crowd of onlookers who began firing indiscriminately at Allen.

The crowd managed to grab the body of Allen away from the police, placing a rope around his neck. The *Chicago Daily News* headlined it as the "FRANTIC ATTEMPTS OF A MOB TO LYNCH THE DEAD DESPARADO." But police soon quelled the mob and regained custody of Allen's body. They transported it to the DesPlaines Street Station in a patrol wagon. At the station, crowds grew so riotous demanding to see Allen's body, that it was placed on exhibition in the women's department of the station. This permitted the body to be seen by on lookers through a rear window. Six bullet wounds in Allen's torso and legs could clearly be seen by the crowds. "THE BRUTAL MURDER OF POLICEMAN WRIGHT TERRIBLY AVENGENED," said the banner above Allen's photo in the press.

The *Chicago Daily News* also reported, without much detail, that two Chicago Police Officers, John Fletcher and T.J. Foley, had been discharged from the force as a result of their involvement in Allen's death. Both policemen were friends of Officer Wright and were with him when he was gunned down by Allen.

Patrolman Patrick Mulvihill,

STAR # unavailable, DesPlaines Street Station, 24 years old, was born in Ireland, and died on July 22, 1884 in direct connection to the events he initiated in the apprehension of a notorious "cop killer," Bill Allen. Mulvihill expired at 8:00 P.M. at 440 N. Halsted Street at Hubbard Street, not far from the site of Allen's capture and death. Chicagoans followed the details of Mulvihill's long struggle to regain his health following his shooting in *The Daily Press*.

In attempting to apprehend the "cop killer" Bill Allen, a bullet ricocheted off Mulvihill's thumb and was embedded in his forehead. After the removal of the bullet, doctors and attendants pronounced a full recovery. Over the ensuing weeks Mulvihill appeared on the road to health. At one point, with the help of doctors, he was able to return to the DesPlaines Street Station, galloping up the stairs and joking with friends over his enormous appetite. In January of 1883, however, his health began to decline. Doctors believed an abscess in the brain was behind his deterioration. After much consultation, highly complicated brain surgery was initiated, remarkable for its technical nuance during this era of medicine. He went on to make a remarkable recovery from the complex surgical procedure. Doctors were encouraged by the quick return of his good health. But eventually the severity of the wound and the increased infection claimed Officer Mulvihill's life. Eighteen months after the original shooting by Bill Allen, Mulvihill died. The details of his illness were sympathetically watched by all of Chicago. His death ended a tragic episode in urban mayhem. His Solemn High Requiem High Mass took place at St. Stephen Church, at Ohio and Sangamon Streets, a largely Irish community near the North Branch of the Chicago River. The funeral procession later traveled to the Northwestern Depot where young Mulvihill was transported for burial to Toronto, Iowa, not far from the town of Clinton along the Mississippi River.

Patrolman Cornelius "Con" Barrett,

STAR #63, 1st Precinct, 34 years old, met his death at the hands of a "madman" in Chicago's Polk Street Railway Station on Sunday, May 31, 1885. He was one month from his third anniversary as a Chicago policeman. Reports that an inbound Wabash Avenue train had been highjacked by a "lunatic" were substantiated as the locomotive pulled into the depot located between Plymouth Court and Federal Street. Louis Reaume, the suspect, unleashed "a reign of terror" in the Polk Street Station, firing his revolver at a squad of policemen who had arrived to apprehend him. One of his bullets hit Officer Con Barrett. It would take him less than fifteen minutes to die. Before Reaume was overpowered, he received three bullets in the back.

Barrett collapsed in the station before his killer reached the Fourth Avenue door. A reporter from the *Chicago Tribune* was the only person near Barrett when he fell. The reporter rushed to his side to comfort him and held his head for the short time it took him to die. The reporter had been on the platform when he saw the officer fall and found that his heart was still beating even though he lay unconscious. As he died, the first of the panicked passengers stampeded away from the gun fight in which the murderer was killed. A doctor arrived to attend to Barrett's wound but found he was too late. The policeman's body was placed on a stretcher and carried to the nearby Harrison Street Police Station where it was placed in the squad room. The deceased's fellow officers gathered around the corpse to pay their respects, drawing back the sheet over his body from time to time to view it. The body was later taken to a larger room, nearby, to better accommodate the huge crowds that came to pay their respects. Policemen guarded the doors of the room where the body laid. The *Chicago Tribune* called Officer Barrett "a victim of demoniac insanity." The mourners came with heads uncovered for hours until Barrett's body was taken to Birren and Carroll's undertaking at 171 W. Chicago Avenue. Patrolman Barrett was unmarried and lived with his sister. He was interred at Calvary Cemetery.

1884

Patrolman Michael W. O'Brien,

STAR #389, 3rd Precinct, DesPlaines Street Station, 25 years old, died on Wednesday November 11, 1885. His death was made even more insidious by the macabre identity of his shooter, "a crazy, one-eyed, cobbler." O'Brien was shot and killed at 8:30 P.M. by Max Ritterberg, an "insane shoemaker," while patrolling his beat at Halsted and Adams Streets. The *Chicago Tribune* also characterized the shooter as a "Socialist crank." O'Brien heard a gunshot coming from a tiny shoe shop on S. Halsted Street. Quickly running to the scene of the shooting, O'Brien ran into the shop and discovered Ritterberg standing in the middle of his shop with his hands behind him. An employee, Joseph Boubek, was also there. Ritterberg protested O'Brien's questions and denied that a shooting had occurred in his shop. Just as O'Brien reached out to take hold of the shoemaker, Ritterberg pulled a gun from behind his back, thrust the weapon into O'Brien's chest and fired it at him. The *Chicago Tribune* reported in detail the actions of the dying O'Brien. The *Chicago Tribune* reported that despite his wound, he still managed to run across the street to a police patrol box and attempted to retrieve its key from his pocket to summon help, but he collapsed before he could do so. The officer then exclaimed to a crowd that had gathered, "My god, I'm shot!" and fell into the arms of bystanders. One of the onlookers, C.K. Taggert, a railroad employee, took O'Brien's keys from his pocket and called for a patrol wagon. A nearby salon keeper named Minucciani also called for a wagon from a private box. As O'Brien was dying he was carried into James H. Kirkley's Drug Store, where an examination of his wound was made by a doctor named Stuart. He discovered that the bullet had entered the body near the right breast and exited in the center of O'Brien's back. Sadly, Stuart acknowledged the wound was mortal. Officer O'Brien was conscious enough to ask for a priest to attend him. Someone ran over to Old St. Patrick's Church, just one block away at Adams and DesPlaines Streets, and returned with a priest who gave Extreme Unction to the dying officer.

When the patrol wagon arrived at the scene, Officer O'Brien requested to be taken to the home of his father, 542 W. 13th Street. One hour later, O'Brien died. The young O'Brien lived at 803 W. Congress Street and was soon to have been married.

Meanwhile, Max Ritterberg, O'Brien's killer, fled the scene of the crime and hurried to his own home, where in the presence of his family he put his pistol to his head and fired, committing suicide around the time O'Brien lay dying. Officer O'Brien was laid to rest in Calvary Cemetery.

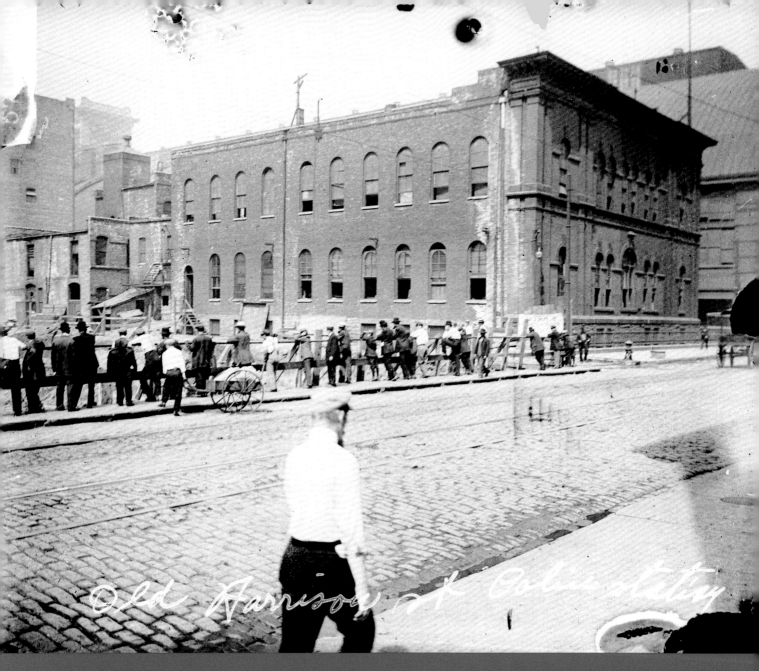

Harrison Street Police Station located at Harrison and LaSalle Streets (c.1890). DN-0057228, *Chicago Daily News* Collection, Chicago History Museum Photo Archive.

Near the scene of Patrolman Michael W. O'Brien's death at Adams Street near Halsted Street, in the distance is Old St. Patrick Church. DN-0063523, *Chicago Daily News* Collection, Chicago History Museum Photo Archive.

1886

The Haymarket Square Riot Police Deaths

Patrolman Mathias J. Degan,

STAR #648, 3rd Precinct, 34 years old, was the first Chicago Policeman to die in the line of duty during the riot at The Haymarket Square, a wide expanse and market place just west of Halsted Street on Randolph Street. The square was the site of a labor rally, protesting the events that occurred on the previous day, May 3, at the McCormick Harvester Plant where a labor riot had taken place over the issue of the eight-hour-day. The movement for shorter work hours had become filled with radicals and anarchists who precipitated much of the labor violence. The Haymarket Square Riot was the tragic finale of this labor unrest.

Officer Degan joined some two hundred other Chicago Police Officers at the Haymarket Square who were attempting to control the large crowd that had assembled when a dynamite bomb was thrown and exploded. Struck by shrapnel, Officer Degan died almost instantly. He had been a Chicago Policeman for only a year-and-a-half. With other policemen killed, wounded or maimed, Degan was carried to the nearby DesPlaines Street Police Station, where he died. Degan was a widower and was survived by a son. His funeral took place on May 7, 1886 from his home at 1500 South Canal Street. The remains of this Chicago hero were interred at St. Boniface Cemetery on North Clark Street, the Roman Catholic German Cemetery.

Patrolman John J. Barrett,

STAR #557, 3rd Precinct, 34 years old, was transported to the County Hospital immediately after the explosion in the Haymarket. He was wrecked by the blast at the corner of Randolph and DesPlaines Streets on that wet Tuesday evening. He died from the effects of the bomb on May 4, 1886 at 11:30 A.M., two days after being fatally wounded in the riot. Barrett had been a Chicago Policemen for just 18 months. Few of his attending physicians or Chicago Police brass could believe that he lasted as long as he did. He had a hole in his liver and he was breathing through a tube that had been inserted. Wounds throughout his body, particularly on his head and along his shoulders, made his death inevitable. Barrett's grieving wife, mother and sister gathered around his bed. They were with him as he took his last breath. Barrett was the first of two Chicago Policemen to die at the County Hospital that day, with Patrolman George Miller lasting several hours longer. Later in the afternoon, Barrett's remains were transported up to the Birren & Carroll Funeral Home at 171 W. Chicago Avenue. Family members had requested that he be taken to his home at 848 W. Erie Street, but the Cook County Coroner refused permission. Barrett was considered one of the finest men on the force and his death deeply affected the mood of troubled Chicagoans. Police superiors spoke of him in the highest of praise and recalled for the press Barrett's commitment to duty and his virtuous heroics. He was the second Chicago Policeman to die in the events of the Haymarket battle. Barrett was buried in Calvary Cemetery in Evanston.

In the aftermath of the Haymarket Riot, a widespread police sweep of the city took place with the detainment of many labor organizers and radicals. Eight men were arrested and charged with conspiracy. Though the bomb thrower was never identified, and little direct evidence could be proved, Judge Joseph E. Geary imposed the death sentence on seven of the eight on trial. The verdict was upheld by both the Illinois and U.S. Supreme Courts. Four of these men were hanged on November 11, 1887–August Spies. Albert Parsons, Adolph Fischer and George Engel. Another, Louis Lingg committed suicide in prison, exploding a stick of smuggled dynamite in his mouth. Two others had their sentence reduced to life. Ultimately, Illinois Governor John P. Altgeld, pardoned the remaining three in prison.

DesPlaines Street Station where triage
was set up for the wounded in the aftermath
of the Haymarket Riot (May 4, 1886).
Chicago History Museum Archive.

Haymarket labor rally poster.
ICH-i06215, Chicago History Museum
Photo Archive.

Fatal explosion of bombs at Haymarket
Square (May 4, 1886).
Chicago History Museum Archive.

Attention Workingmen!

GREAT

MASS-MEETING

TO-NIGHT, at 7.30 o'clock,

AT THE

HAYMARKET, Randolph St., Bet. Desplaines and Halsted.

Good Speakers will be present to denounce the latest atrocious act of the police, the shooting of our fellow-workmen yesterday afternoon.

THE EXECUTIVE COMMITTEE.

Achtung, Arbeiter!

Große

Massen-Versammlung

Heute Abend, ½8 Uhr, auf dem

Heumarkt, Randolph-Straße, zwischen Desplaines- u. Halsted-Str.

☞ Gute Redner werden den neuesten Schurkenstreich der Polizei, indem sie gestern Nachmittag unsere Brüder erschoß, geißeln.

Das Executiv-Comite.

Patrolman George F. Miller,

Star #551, DesPlaines Street Station, 29 years old, died as a result of gunshot wounds received during the Haymarket Square Riots on May 4, 1886. The officer's death was thought of as quite gruesome because he suffered such a long, horrific death that lasted over a period of two days. Miller, only a year-and-a-half on the force, was so horrifically wounded in the initial explosion that he was only kept alive with opiates that deadened his excruciating pain. Miller's lingering death permitted his brother and sister to travel to Chicago from Rochester, New York, Miller's hometown, to be with him at the end. The *Chicago Tribune* reported to shocked and distraught readers that Miller "spoke calmly of the end in his conscious moments." With loved ones around him, he "saw death as a release" from the brutal effects of the bomb. He finally died at 10:45 P.M. on May 6, 1886, 48-hours after he had been shot. He was the third Chicago Policeman to die in the line of duty following the tragic events on Randolph Street in the Haymarket Square. The young officer was assigned to the city's DesPlaines Street Station. After the riot, it served as an emergency medical center for the injured because of its proximity to the Haymarket battlefield. Miller was survived by his parents and his siblings who had remained at his bedside throughout the horrifying ordeal of his death. His family carried his remains back to Oswego, New York where he was buried in St. Paul Cemetery.

Patrolman Timothy Flavin,

STAR #691, 4th Precinct, Rawson Street Station, 27 years old, had only been on the force for 16 months when he became the fourth Chicago policeman to die from wounds suffered at the Haymarket Square Riot. Flavin, a native of County Kerry, Ireland, came to the United States around 1880. He was the father of three small children, the oldest just five years old. Officer Flavin was seriously wounded in the immediate firefight of bullets that erupted in the Haymarket Square following the explosion of a bomb. He had been shot multiple times and was taken to County Hospital where doctors eventually amputated his leg on Friday, May 7, the third day after the riot.

Doctors had high hopes of a full recovery until his condition began to deteriorate. Around 3:00 P.M. on Saturday, May 8, Flavin began a rapid decline that took his life later that day. Father A. J. Burns and three Religious Sisters of Mercy were at his bedside throughout his final hours. They cared for him as death approached in a solidarity of faith and Irish fraternity. His long ordeal demonstrated to everyone the dramatic courage and fortitude that was a deep part of Officer Flavin's character. Flavin's bright sense of Irish humor endeared him to many and made him a popular man on the force. The nobility of his personal courage left a powerful legacy to all who knew him. Flavin was buried in Calvary Cemetery in Evanston.

Patrolman Michael Sheehan,

STAR #545, DesPlaines Street Station, 29 years old, became the fifth victim to die from the Haymarket Riot when he succumbed to his wounds in his home at 711 W. Barber Street at 5:05 P.M. on May 9, 1886. He had been shot twice during the riot, once in the leg and then through the back. The bullet did terrible damage inside him, piercing his abdomen and liver. He was unmarried and had been a member of the Chicago Police Department for just over a year. Although his parents lived in England, Sheehan had been born in Ireland in 1857. After moving to the United States in 1879, he lived in Chicago for seven years. Sheehan was laid to rest in Calvary Cemetery.

Haymarket Square rear Randolph and
Halsted Streets (c.1890). DN-0056709,
Chicago Daily News Collection,
Chicago History Museum Photo Archive.

Police Officers of the
Gresham Street Station (1890's),
ICH-i39638, Chicago History
Museum Photo Archive.

Patrolman Nels Hansen,

STAR #822, 3rd Precinct, 37 years old, was a Swedish native and a resident of the city's Scandinavian enclave of Swede town, on the city's Near North Side. Hansen died in the Cook County Hospital on May 14, 1886, more than a month after the riots. It had been thought that his recovery was progressing well and it was the subject of continued interest in the newspapers. But after many weeks, his health began to decline. His cause of death was septicemia, an infection caused by the bullet wounds he received. Hansen had been on the force only 18 months when he died. The policeman was married and the father of two children. He was sadly buried along the edge of a road in the potter's field at Rosehill Cemetery, not far from today's Scandinavian neighborhood of Andersonville. Hansen only received a gravestone in 2003, one hundred seventeen years after his heroic death. He was the sixth policeman to die in the Haymarket riots.

Patrolman Thomas Redden,

STAR #621, 3rd Precinct, 49 years old, died 12 days after he was severely wounded in the events of the Haymarket clash. In the early hours of May 16, 1886 he expired at Cook County Hospital, where he had put up a valiant struggle for life. His left leg had been fractured as a result of the bomb explosion, while his right arm and left cheek each sustained bullet wounds. Officer Redden had been a member of the Chicago Police Department for 12 years. He was survived by a wife and two children and became the seventh officer to die as a result of the trauma of the Haymarket. Redden was laid to rest at Calvary Cemetery.

1887

Patrolman Michael O'Brien,

STAR #216, 3rd Precinct, Deering Police Station, 43 years old, was working with his partner, Officer William Dillon, when he was shot and killed on April 3, 1887 while attempting to disperse a crowd creating a disturbance behind a tavern at 2741 S. Archer Avenue, near Quinn Street. The tragic shooting took place around 11:30 P.M. at a well-known Irish watering hole known as Burke's Saloon. O'Brien was an eight-year-veteran of the Chicago Police Department when he was shot through the right lung by an ex-convict named Timothy O'Grady. The shooter was well known to the officers. He stuck out in the crowd of drunk and disorderly roughnecks whose noisy carrying-on had been creating unusual havoc for the beat cops. As the policemen approached the crowd, mayhem ensued with people running in every direction—some around the corner into an alley and some through the saloon itself to make it out the front door. O'Brien went after them in quick pursuit. He caught up to O'Grady along the sidewalk and immediately recognized him as a man known to have concealed weapons on his person. A scuffle ensued when he attempted to apprehend O'Grady, but the offender managed to break away. O'Grady raced around the corner onto Quinn Street and made his way down a flight of stairs that led to a side street. He soon found himself trapped between O'Brien, who was chasing him, and Dillon who had stationed himself at the rear of Burke's Saloon. O'Grady quickly fired four or five rounds at O'Brien. Neither officer could get off a shot without the risk of hitting each other in the direct line of fire. O'Grady made the most of this stand off, disappearing down the main sidewalk over to O'Malley's Packing House, also on Quinn Street, just half a block away. Each officer was hot on his trail and succeeded in getting off one shot each at the fleeing O'Grady.

Seemingly, the culprit had vanished, though the two officers remained at the corner on Quinn Street for some ten minutes before O'Grady was finally seen attempting to sneak through the alley. O'Brien shouted to him, "Hold on there!" O'Grady responded with one shot from his revolver. O'Brien and Dillon both returned fire as they raced after him. O'Grady turned once more and fired at O'Brien who suddenly shouted, "Bill, I am gone! Send for the priest." Dillon then discharged all his rounds at the escaping O'Grady and returned to his partner, who by now was choking on his own blood. The bullet had pierced his right lung and exited through his back. Dillon carried O'Brien to the front of Burke's Saloon and immediately went to the patrol box to summon the patrol wagon. O'Brien was unconscious when he arrived at his home at 2726 S. Hickory Street. By the time Doctors Kennedy and Egan arrived, he had lost a great deal of blood. After examining the wound, they concluded that it was fatal. Officer O'Brien lingered through the night before death finally came. He left a wife and two children. He had earlier been attached to the 22nd Street Police District. Officer O'Brien was buried in Calvary Cemetery.

The *Chicago Tribune* reported that news of the fatal shooting of Officer O'Brien was quickly sent to detectives' headquarters. Two of the city's most well regarded detectives, Bonfield and Treharn, were roused from their sleep to pursue O'Grady. It was known that he lived with his father, a fine respectable man who ran a blacksmith business. Their home was located at 2723 S. Archer Avenue, not far from the murder scene. O'Grady was subsequently captured and charged with O'Brien's murder. He was later found guilty of the crime and sentenced to prison.

But then the case took a strange turn. Dyer Scanlan was a well-known neighborhood tough who, like O'Grady, was a man engaged in many nefarious affairs. He was arrested and convicted of the 1888 shooting of Chicago Police Officer Martin Nolan, who took six slugs from him. Scanlan was sentenced to ten years for that crime. While he was in prison, he began to believe that he was dying of tuberculosis. Faced with his own mortality, Scanlan confessed to the murder of Officer O'Brien at Burke's Saloon in 1887, the crime for which O'Grady was then serving a prison sentence. When the facts came out, Illinois Governor John P. Altgeld gave O'Grady a full pardon in the death of Officer O'Brien. Scanlan never died of tuberculosis and was released from prison in 1895. He returned to the rough, tough life of Chicago's "Tenderloin."

Detective William S. Hallaran,

STAR #214, 1st Precinct, Central Avenue Station, 36 years old, was a popular, well-respected detective when he perished at the hands of a tough, professional criminal and young killer, Mike Lynch, on July 16, 1887. Hallaran was known all over Chicago as *Billy*, but his real moniker as most Chicagoans knew it was that of "thief-catcher," and "thief-hater." He had, as the *Chicago Tribune* wrote, "sent many of them over the road," to prison.

Five years earlier, Hallaran and his partner, Officer Leonard, had been instrumental in sending Lynch and his partner, "Uncle" Hogan, to the penitentiary, on charges of burglary. This became the source of his fatal enmity with the ex-convict. It was Hallaran's testimony that secured their convictions. Ironically, Hogan had received a 20-year-sentence for his crime, while Lynch received a sentence of 10 years. But Lynch had his sentence shortened to just four years through the intercession of Hallaran. The policeman was well-aware that Lynch was suffering from consumption, a disease that made it likely he would not live out his term. Lynch was hardly out of prison before he was up to his old tricks, providing the Chicago Police with ample cause to keep their eyes on him. Hallaran and his partner, Officer Ryan, were given the task of surveillance on Lynch. So suspicious were they of his involvement in fresh burglaries that they were able to obtain a warrant for vagrancy on him. After their evening roll-call at the station, the two officers made their way to Lynch's home near the corner of 2800 S. Fifth Avenue. Lynch's own mother and sister would later testify to police that someone came to the house and told Lynch that Officer Hallaran was coming after him. Lynch is said to have acknowledged the oath he swore to kill Hallaran if he ever came upon him again. They also reported that he retrieved a revolver from his room before leaving the house that night.

Homes in Swede Town (1880-1885).
ICH-i01417, Chicago History Museum
Photo Archive.

Officer Hallaran arrived just in time to see Lynch fleeing the house. The policeman then boarded a streetcar and followed after him until reaching the corner of 25th Street and Wentworth Avenue. He came upon Lynch, and was in the process of putting his hands on him, when a small child suddenly dashed between them. In that split second, Lynch recognized Hallaran and pulled out his gun. In an instant, says the *Tribune*, "the young desperado fired." Hallaran, mortally wounded, fell backwards, rolling down some ten feet below where they stood. "The murderous young thief," the newspaper said, "meanwhile made his escape." He was only out of prison 10 months when he gunned the officer down.

Chicago newspapers called the killing "a premeditated deed." The shooting that claimed Hallaran's life took place around 7:00 P.M. The detective was shot through the front of his neck and the bullet struck his spinal column, instantly paralyzing him. First on the scene was Officer John McDonald of the Harrison Street Station, who had been riding past the murder spot on a streetcar. Hearing the gun fire, he jumped from the trolley to reach the dying man's side.

Unconscious, Hallaran was first taken back to the 22nd Street Station where doctors were summoned. His wounds were examined by two physicians, Doctors Andrews and Steele. Their conclusion was that the wounds would prove fatal. Almost miraculously, Hallaran came out of his unconscious state, though it was determined he was completely paralyzed from the shoulders down. Surgery to remove the bullet was out of the question, so precarious had been its passage into his body, between the windpipe and jugular vein. For a brief moment, the dying man had recovered sufficiently to be able to answer some questions.

As Hallaran's murder was announced to police around the city, cordons of officers fanned out across the metropolis with one mindset: the apprehension of Lynch. Two patrol vehicles, the Cottage Grove Avenue Wagon and the 22nd Street Wagon, began a "dead run," visiting every conceivable haunt of the perpetrator Lynch. Detectives roamed the streets. Within an hour of the crime, Lynch had been fingered. He was hiding out at the house of a friend, named Kerns, who lived at 2631 S. Shields Avenue. Based on this reliable information, both patrol wagons made their way to the residence from different directions, quickly surrounding the premises. Lynch's partner in crime, a desperate character named Ryan, was recognized by police as he rushed out of the house. He had been sought the previous week, so he was taken into custody. After that, police made their move on Lynch as Officers Webber, Corcoran, O'Brien and Sergeant Ptack of the Canalport Avenue Station made their way into the hideout. They found no sign of Lynch until they reached the attic where he appeared ready to make a fatal standoff with a revolver in hand. The gun turned out to be a .38-calibre bull-dog, with one chamber empty. However, once faced with the reality of the armed men before him, his only response was surrender. As the *Chicago Tribune* reported, "he probably read in their grim looks an unspoken desire for an excuse to revenge the cowardly assassination of their brother officer." The tall, slim, black mustached Lynch was then apprehended, handcuffed and arrested. He was taken to the station and brought to the bedside of his dying victim.

Looking face to face with his murderer, Hallaran was asked if this was the man who shot him. He responded in the affirmative. Lynch is said to have had a sullen expression on his face during his encounter with Hallaran. "What did you do it for?" shouted the booming Irish voice of Lieutenant John D. Shea, the burly former chief of detectives, a man more feared than any other in Chicago by criminals and thieves. He placed an unholy fear, it was said, a fear so strong it was physical, in the soul of any offender. This death bed scene was no exception. Lynch began to mumble a line of excuses about what had happened to the imposing Shea. There was no letting up on the part of the Lieutenant. "Well, why haven't you gone to work to support your mother and sister then, instead of running around with thieves and letting them support you?," he asked. Lynch gave no response.

Cook County Courthouse and Jail located at
Hubbard and Illinois Streets (c.1900).
Chicago History Museum Photo Archive.

Talk of Hallaran's condition so enraged members of the Chicago Police that quiet whispers of a lynching began to circulate. But police brass made sure that talk was what it remained. Those bound by oaths ensured that no harm would come to Lynch. Captain Buckley had him removed to a far away sub-station where he remained in high security.

Hallaran was taken to Michael Reese Hospital where he lingered before dying at 12:25 A.M. on July 17, 1887. Gathered around his death bed were his wife and two small children. Also at his side were his aged mother and father, their hearts broken at the tragedy before them. Chicago Police Lieutenants Duffy and Shea stood with their fallen comrade, as did Officers Ryan and Foley. His death came quietly and peacefully. He had been on the force five years.

Detective Hallaran was a native of New Haven, Connecticut and bore the lessons of hard work and duty learned at the hands of an industrious father. Before joining the Chicago Police, Hallaran worked for Chicago meatpacker Nelson Morris. He often accompanied important shipments of cattle to Europe. He was at home doing security on the sea and in various ports of call. His high intelligence and abilities were quickly noted once he joined the force and a fast promotion to detective was forthcoming. He was a man at ease with important duty and his own merit helped carve a career for himself of considerable recognition. Hallaran was also a man of strong opinion that he expressed with ease and power—a dynamic sense of honesty that at times was almost a fault. He made his home with his family at 3705 S. Armour Street. Hallaran was buried in Calvary Cemetery.

Lynch was subsequently convicted of Detective Hallaran's death and sentenced to 35 years at the Illinois State Penitentiary at Joliet. Lynch was later judged to be insane and placed in a mental asylum until June 7, 1898, when records indicate that he either escaped or was released.

Patrolman Philip L. Robinson,

STAR #777, 3rd Precinct, 29 years old, had only been on the Chicago Police Department for two months when he was shot on the night of August 31, 1887. He lingered for five days until September 5, 1887, before finally dying. His brief, but heroic, tenure was marked by noble character and a sense of honor that even long service cannot bring. He paid the ultimate price for his vigilance. When he was informed by two citizens that they had been fired at by a man on the street wielding a gun, he was off in hot pursuit. Robinson is said to have seen the offender fleeing the scene. As the officer reached the offender, he called out for him to halt at the Sangamon Street viaduct near 16th and Halsted Streets. At this point, the offender, a Chinese man named Chow Lam, is said to have turned and fired three times at the policeman. Robinson returned fire and continued to pursue. The gunman then fired the fatal shot, hitting the officer. Robinson was taken to Cook County Hospital, where he remained conscious but weak up until his death. Around his bedside were two fellow officers and his wife. He faced his impending death stoically; expiring around 11:00 P.M. on September 5.

Meanwhile, Chow Lam was captured and taken into custody. He is said to have sat trembling in his cell at the West Chicago Avenue Station, convinced that he would be taken out of his cell and hanged before he could receive his due in court. As a Chinaman, The *Chicago Tribune* reported, he was also gripped by the fear that he would have his head shaved in prison, removing his sacred "queue," the long braided plait of hair that was essential for men in Chinese culture. Without it he believed he would be barred from any entrance into paradise. In the end he had little to worry about. He was acquitted of the murder of Officer Robinson. Mrs. Robinson and her two children were said to have received no benefit from the Policemen's Benevolent Association because her husband had only been on the job for two months. They did, however, receive a $30 a month pension under a state law that had only recently been passed. Officer Robinson was buried in Rosehill Cemetery.

Chicago Police Funeral Honor Guard (c.1900).
DN-0001794, *Chicago Daily News* Collection,
Chicago History Museum Photo Archive.

A Chicago Policeman rides through downtown
Chicago (c.1900). DN-0051059, *Chicago Daily News*
Collection, Chicago History Museum Photo Archive.

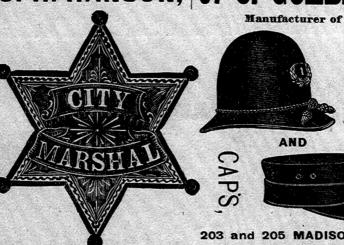

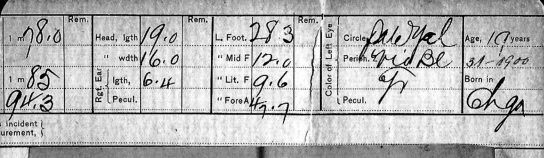

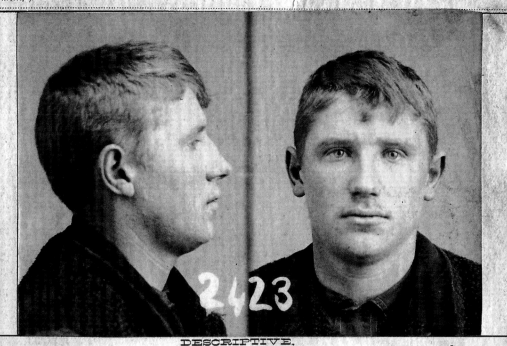

DESCRIPTIVE.

Chicago Police Department "mug shot" of Charles Erickson sentenced to 6 months in the Cook County Jail, November 1888. (Private Collection)

Patrolman John Keegan,

STAR #768, 3rd Precinct, West Madison Street Station, 38 years old, was found at 6:00 A.M. on November 4, 1887, shot to death on the floor of the prairie in the vicinity of Van Buren and Sacramento Streets. Few clues were discovered that could shed any real light on the final moments of Officer Keegan's life. He was laying on his breast, grasping his weapon, a .44-caliber Colt revolver. Officer Keegan had suffered a severe head wound with the cranial interior terribly shattered and torn, the *Chicago Tribune* reported. Powder burns were discovered on the flesh of the forehead, indicating that the muzzle of the gun was very close when it was fired. One bullet was missing from the chamber. Initial reports stated that the brain was taken out near the base of the skull by the force of the impact of the gun shot. Doctors speculated that the shooting bore all the signs of a suicide during their initial examination.

Officer Keegan had last reported to his station at 11:45 P.M. on Thursday night, November 3, having "pulled" the patrol-box located at the corner of Albany and Van Buren Streets. He was obliged to make such a report every hour. It was thus believed that his death occurred sometime between then and 1:00 A.M.

Friends and colleagues of Officer Keegan were hard pressed to come up with anything that could have pushed him to an act of such desperation. The policeman lived with his wife and two children at 2534 W. Washington Boulevard and to all observation had a happy domestic life. He never indicated or spoke to anyone about suicide. He was a member of the Catholic Order of Foresters, a benevolent insurance organization, and had just recently made all necessary payment to bring his account up-to-date. This was a sign which some took as an indication he was about to do himself in. At the scene of the shooting, no sign of struggle was evident. In the end, the official report indicated that Officer Keegan was shot to death by an unknown assailant. He was laid to rest in Calvary Cemetery.

Patrolman Timothy Sullivan,

STAR #811, 14th Precinct, 8th Station, 51 years old, was the last victim of the Haymarket Square Riot of May 4, 1886. He had suffered a gunshot wound, but was able to survive for more than two years before he succumbed to his injuries. Sullivan died on June 13, 1888. Bright's Disease, a severe deterioration of the kidneys, was given as the cause of death, exacerbated by the long decline his body endured from the gunshot wound. Officer Sullivan was a native of Ireland and lived at 1503 W. Grand Avenue. He was buried from Annunciation Church on W. Wabansia Street. His Funeral Mass was celebrated by the pastor, Father W. S. Hennessy. Officer Sullivan was laid to rest in Calvary Cemetery on June 17, 1888.

His death came seven months after four of the ring-leaders of the Haymarket event were executed for their part in the riot. Albert Parsons, August Spies, George Engel and Adolph Fisher were all hanged on November 11, 1887. One other convicted conspirator, Louis Lingg, committed suicide in his cell on the eve of his execution. Using a stick of dynamite smuggled into his cell, he effectively blew his head off. Three others, Samuel Felden, Oscar Neebe and Michael Schwab, were convicted, but later pardoned for their crimes by Illinois Governor John P. Altgeld in June of 1893.

Chicago City Hall and Courthouse (1885).
ICH-i00440, Chicago History Museum
Photo Archive.

Chicago Police march in a funeral procession (1903).
DN-0000308, *Chicago Daily News* Collection,
Chicago History Museum Photo Archive.

St. Bridget Church on Archer Avenue located in the Bridgeport neighborhood was the spiritual home of many Chicago Irish Police Officers killed in the line of duty (c.1900). DN-0056556, *Chicago Daily News* Collection, Chicago History Museum Photo Archive.

Patrolman Adam W. Fryer,

STAR #752, 12th Street Station, was killed in the line of duty at 2:30 A.M. on August 9, 1889 by two well-known neighborhood criminals, John McGrath and William Martell, who had vowed to shoot any police officer who attempted to arrest them. The bandits' latest unlawful escapade had begun a few evenings before when the two men spent the evening at a saloon near 15th Street and Union Avenue. By the end of the night, officers had been called to the establishment to break-up a fight between Martell, McGrath, their associates and another group of patrons. Two patrolmen were dispatched and attempted to restore order, but they met stiff resistance from Martell, McGrath and those with them. The lawbreakers began by simply cursing at the officers, but the situation soon deteriorated and they began wildly shooting. Astonishingly, the officers managed to escape uninjured and immediately went back to their station to swear out a warrant against the group's ringleaders.

The offenders were spotted again in the early morning hours of August 9, 1889 at Polk and DesPlaines Streets by Patrolmen Moore and Hallihan. The two officers were out on their usual patrol and had actually walked past McGrath and Martell before their identities registered. Moore and Hallihan immediately turned around. McGrath quickly spotted the officers and realized that he and his partner had been recognized. The bandit attempted to get his weapon, but Moore was quicker and had his revolver pointed at the two criminals before they could retrieve theirs. Neither man said anything to the officers. They chose to turn and flee instead, with the patrolmen in hot pursuit. As the chase took the men north on DesPlaines Street, Moore fired his weapon. Unfortunately, that tactic only served to increase the speed of the bandits who swerved down an alley and had disappeared when the officers reached the other side.

Moore and Hallihan decided to continue their search and were proceeding down Jefferson Street to Harrison Street when they heard two ominous cracks of gunfire. They quickly hurried towards the direction of the sound and discovered Patrolman Fryer collapsed on the sidewalk at the southeast corner of Harrison and Clinton Streets. Fryer had heard the shot fired by Patrolman Moore and had gone to the emergency box to call for back-up. He was unsure from what direction the shots had come, but as he stood and waited for reinforcements he heard the sound of pounding footsteps coming towards him. McGrath and Martell came into view and Fryer ordered them to stop, but once again they chose to speak with their guns. Both men drew their weapons and fired on Patrolman Fryer at close range. One bullet entered the officer's neck and severed his carotid artery and jugular vein before lodging in his brain, while the second entered his abdomen.

Two watchmen, who had been a block from the scene of the shooting, quickly came to Patrolman Fryer's aid. However, there was nothing that could be done for the officer. Fryer died without speaking, less than five minutes after the men reached him. But he did manage to convey his wish that they retrieve the patrol box key in his pocket and call for help. They were about to perform this final request when the DesPlaines Street patrol wagon pulled up just as Fryer took his last breath.

Meanwhile, McGrath and Martell had continued their flight and boarded a Halsted streetcar at Randolph Street. McGrath went home, informed his brother, James, of his plight, and the McGrath boys set off for the rail yard where they soon lost the police officers among the stationary railcars. McGrath and Martell were both eventually arrested, and the two local toughs were quickly brought to trial. A guilty verdict was returned along with a life sentence in the Illinois State Penitentiary at Joliet for both men. However, a new trial was granted shortly thereafter and both men were acquitted. No time was ever served for the cold-blooded killing of Patrolman Fryer. The officer was layed to rest in Graceland Cemetery.

Patrolman James McDowell,

STAR #763, 7th Precinct, 44 years old, was making a routine report at 11:00 A.M. on October 3, 1889 at the corner of 43rd and State Streets. While at the corner, the officer was approached by a customer who had just exited J. J. Phelan's Saloon, Andrew Gilligan. Gilligan informed McDowell that he had asked Phelan who the promoters of a new gas company were and that Phelan had directed his inquiries to McDowell. The officer and Gilligan then proceeded to a back room of the saloon where they held a conversation. A few moments later McDowell emerged with Gilligan following closely behind. Neither man looked particularly satisfied. According to the *Chicago Tribune*, once McDowell had reached the bar, he turned to Gilligan and told him, "You had no right to call me a liar." This was a statement Gilligan did not respond to verbally. Instead he reacted by pulling out a revolver and firing at Patrolman McDowell, who stood no more than three feet from him. McDowell lunged at the criminal and the two began wrestling. Phelan joined the fray and managed to wrestle the gun from Gilligan, but not before he was able to shoot at least one more time. The two men were having trouble bringing Gilligan under control and only managed to do so with the help of another patrolman who arrived on the scene. The Fiftieth Street patrol wagon soon arrived and McDowell and Gilligan were both transported to the station.

Patrolman McDowell died on the afternoon of October 3, 1889 in Mercy Hospital. He left behind a wife and four children. The officer had joined the Chicago Police Department in 1875 and served for 14 years before his death. Patrolman McDowell was buried in Mount Carmel Cemetery. Gilligan refused to answer any questions at the station but a search of his clothes revealed a bank book that showed a credit of $50 at the Oakland Bank where he apparently had a reputation as a neighborhood tough. He claimed McDowell had hit him after they got into an argument and he had only fired in self-defense. However, witnesses disputed this account. Gilligan was eventually sentenced to two years in the Penitentiary.

Patrolman Thomas Carroll,

STAR # unavailable, died on September 19, 1891, after inhaling nitric fumes. Chicago Fire Department Captain Patrick L. Mullins was the only other victim to die of the fumes. The nitric fumes were a result of a chemical explosion that took place.

Patrolman George Schlinger Jr.,

STAR #1671, 24th Precinct, was fatally shot and killed on October 10, 1891 at 161 N. Peoria Street by career criminal Mike Moriarty. The offender was seized, tried and convicted of the officer's death and sentenced to life in the Illinois State Penitentiary at Joliet. Schlinger, who died almost instantly at the scene of the shooting, was given a proper funeral for a fallen hero by the Fraternal Policemen's Benefit Association and the American Lodge, #271, Knights of Pythias, an association in which Schlinger was a member. The funeral was held at 10:30 A.M. on October 13, 1891 at Sigmund and Company, located at 192 W. Chicago Avenue. It was a simple service but the high regard the community had for the officer was evident in the overwhelming number of floral arrangements that filled the room. Six of Schlinger's fellow officers served as pallbearers while a full company in dress uniforms marched behind the hearse as it made the journey to Cavalry Cemetery where Patrolman Schlinger was buried.

1891

Bridewell Prison at 26th Street and California Avenue, prison for criminals who have committed less serious offenses (c.1890). DN-0000314, *Chicago Daily News* Collection, Chicago History Museum Photo Archive.

Funeral train taking mourners to the cemetery (c.1890). DN-0050021, *Chicago Daily News* Collection, Chicago History Museum Photo Archive.

Entrance to the Illinois State Penitentiary at Joliet, home to many of the Chicago Police Department's many cop killers (c.1890). DN-0055584, *Chicago Daily News* Collection, Chicago History Museum Photo Archive.

Chicago Police Department patrol wagon (1890's). DN-0003714, *Chicago Daily News* Collection, Chicago History Museum Photo Archive.

Patrolman William H. Schnell,

STAR #2188, 35th Precinct, 27 years old, was killed in his home on January 2, 1892 when the service revolver he was cleaning unexpectedly fired. Schnell was a resident of the Humboldt Park neighborhood and a member of Court Benevolent, No. 30, I.O.F. and the Policeman's Benevolent Society. His funeral service was held at his residence at 357 N. Francisco Street. He was then taken by carriage to his interment at Graceland Cemetery. The young officer had been on the force for eight months and was survived by his mother, Caroline Schnell.

Patrolman Jasper H. Cole,

STAR #1703, 27th Precinct, 28 years old, was on duty February 10, 1892 when a tragic accident took his life in the DesPlaines Street Station, which he considered a home away from home. Patrolman Cole had just arrested a robbery suspect and brought him back to the station to be questioned by his captain. Another patrolman, William Welbasky, was in the captain's office at the time and Cole stayed to speak with him as the questioning began. After only a few inquiries, Cole realized that their presence was presenting a distraction that was preventing their superior from getting the information he needed. Patrolman Cole suggested they both leave in order to expedite the questioning. They both exited the room. In the main room of the station, the men headed towards the east window and began to discuss the particulars of the case.

After a few moments, their conversation turned to the case of another criminal, Frank Henderson, who had attempted to shoot his mother and sister. Welbasky informed Cole that he had in his possession the gun Henderson used. Cole asked to see it and reached to retrieve it from the other officer's pocket at the same time as Welabsky's fingers closed around it in order to produce it. Their hands tangled in Welbasky's pocket and the gun accidentally discharged a bullet that entered Patrolman Cole's brain through his right eye. Another policeman, Officer Mahoney, came running out of his office as Cole fell to the ground unconscious and immediately called for a doctor. The doctor arrived shortly thereafter, but quickly discovered that there was nothing he could do and pronounced the wound fatal. Cole never regained consciousness and died shortly before 6:00 P.M. in the station's main room. His body was taken to Klaner's Milwaukee Avenue Morgue.

Cole had joined the force only four years earlier in 1888. He had originally been assigned to the East Chicago Avenue District but was transferred after a temporary suspension of duty following the switchmen's strike in 1891. He was reassigned to the West Side and his superiors spoke of him in glowing terms, remembering a dedicated, tenacious officer who took his job very seriously. Patrolman Welbasky was never detained or held accountable for the tragic accident. Policeman Cole was laid to rest in Calvary Cemetery.

1892

Patrolman John Powell Jr.,
STAR #1168, 21st Precinct, 32 years old and
Patrolman Henry L. McDowell,
STAR #1609, 27th Precinct, 30 years old, were both part of a raid on an illegal horse track taking place in Garfield Park on September 6, 1892. It was the second day that the police had attempted to shut down the operation, conducted in defiance of a city edict. Following the same strategy used one day earlier, the police invaded the park and loaded the patrol wagon with track employees, bookmakers and customers, none of whom seemed very surprised by their circumstances. The probability of a raid was well-known to all who were at Garfield Park that day, but few could have foreseen the tragic results brought about by one man.

The wagons were getting ready to pull away from the park with their odd assortment of criminals when a police whistle, shrill and loud, was heard coming from the other side of the park. The sharp crack of a gunshot followed only seconds later and an officer lay mortally wounded. Patrolman Powell had been part of a large group of spectators, police officers and various characters milling around the park, when he decided to move away from the group and do one more patrol of the area. He had barely gotten to the sidewalk when he saw James M. Brown, a well-known Texas bandit, emerge from a small lane at the end of the park. Powell moved towards him and was about to command him to halt when Brown noticed him, raised his weapon and fired without saying a word.

The first bullet struck Powell in the arm, while Brown, seeing that the officer was not incapacitated, fired again. The second bullet hit Powell in the hand before passing through to his stomach. He fell to the ground fatally injured. As Brown turned to flee, he saw Patrolman McDowell turning onto Lexington Avenue from the park's Jan Huss Avenue, effectively blocking his escape route. McDowell saw the fallen officer a little further down the road and the weapon in Brown's hand. He immediately attempted to diffuse the situation. According to the *Chicago Tribune*, McDowell called out, "Don't shoot any more! Put up your gun! I will not shoot!" Brown, apparently attempting to further the desperate reputation that had followed him from Texas, replied "But I will," and fired at McDowell. The officer realized that Brown was not going to surrender peacefully and fired almost simultaneously, beginning a short-lived gun battle. Brown's gun had not fired on his first try and he fell to his knees as McDowell's bullet found its target. Relentlessly, Brown continued to shoot and the officer had no choice but to return fire. After only a few moments, the smoke cleared and both men lay on the park ground fatally wounded.

The details surrounding McDowell's encounter with Brown are drawn from an antemortem statement that he was able to give to the Justice of the Peace, Jarvis Blume, before he died in Cook County Hospital on September 7, 1892, only half a day after Patrolman Powell died at the scene. McDowell was able to give a description of Brown and depicted a man past middle age, with a gray beard wearing a gray suit and a black slouch hat. The officer, who had joined the force only a year before as a sub-patrolman, made it clear that he did not threaten Brown in anyway. He claimed that Brown had fired at him completely unprovoked after he had called for a truce, making him responsible for the deaths of the two officers. Patrolman Powell was buried in Oakwoods Cemetery and Patrolman McDowell was buried in Rosehill Cemetery.

Patrolman Thomas McNamara,

STAR #unavailable, 40 years old, was killed in a West Harrison Street Saloon on October 16, 1893 by Frank P. Sherman. The two men had quarreled in the establishment and Sherman shot the officer in the head. McNamara's injury proved fatal and he died only a few hours after the altercation. He was buried at Calvary Cemetery, Evanston. Sherman was indicted for his murder on October 30, 1893.

Detective Edward J. Carney,

STAR #83, Central Station, was walking with his partner, Detective John Conway, on December 2, 1893 when they observed two suspicious men at the corner of 39th Street and Langley Avenue and stopped to inquire about their business. A recent series of crimes in the area had left Carney and Conway under orders to question any pedestrians who were found in the residential area in the late hours of the night. The men took offense at the questioning and became confrontational, leading the officers to place them under arrest. The two suspicious characters resisted and revealed the large Colt revolvers they were hiding. They used these weapons to beat Conway over the head while the other offender shot Carney in the right leg just below the knee.

The bandits, A. F. Holmes and James G. Potter, left the scene but did not get far before they were found and locked up at the 35th Street Station. Upon questioning, they identified themselves as private investigators employed by Thiel's Detective Agency. The alleged private detectives were held by the Criminal Court. Though bond had been posted for the two men they were not originally allowed to leave. Detective Carney was taken to his brother's house at 2931 S. Union Avenue. Doctors were called to decide whether to remove the bullet, but determined that extracting it would do more harm than good. Unfortunately, the injury became inflamed with blood poisoning and became so painful that on December 8, 1893, Carney was taken to Chicago Hospital at 15th Street and Champlain Avenue. Doctors at the hospital realized that the deterioration of Carney's condition left them no choice but to operate, which they did in a long painful surgery. The detective was put under anesthesia and the surgeons were able to extract the bullet. However, Carney never recovered from the shock to his body from the shooting and the operation, despite valiant attempts to revive him. He died that same evening at 6:30 P.M. His brother John, a police officer from the Fiftieth Street Station, attempted to commit suicide several days later because of his sorrow, but his attempt failed and he was hospitalized.

These events were reported to Central Station, which immediately sent a bulletin out to all stations notifying them of Carney's death and issuing arrest warrants for Potter and Holmes for the murder. The men had earlier been released from custody, but now scores of officers flooded the streets, intent on arresting the murderers of their fellow officer. Carney was surrounded by grieving colleagues who refused to accept his death. Some headed directly to Thiel's Detective Agency where they were told that both men had left the city. Police later found and arrested the two offenders and prevented their release on bail. Officer Carney was laid to rest at Calvary Cemetery, Evanston.

1893

Patrolman John Dempsey,

STAR #unavailable, 7th Precinct, 38 years old, was struck by a Grand Trunk Railroad train while guarding a railroad crossing on July 13, 1894. Dempsey was protecting the crossing at the intersection of 26th Street and Stewart Avenue when he was caught unaware by the train. He was taken to Mercy Hospital where he died the next day on July 14, 1894. He was survived by his wife and laid to rest at Calvary Cemetery, Evanston.

Patrolman William Feeley,

STAR # unavailable, Stockyard District, 27 years old, was killed in the line of duty on July 31, 1894 when he fell from a Chicago and Grand Truck Railroad engine into the path of an oncoming train. The accident took place near the corner of 49th Street and Damen Avenue. Officer Feely was immediately killed from the impact of the oncoming train. Feely and fellow officers were assigned to patrol the tracks between Ashland Avenue and the Panhandle Crossing during the fierce upheaval of the Stockyard Riots that accompanied the labor problems that summer. He was the second Chicago Police Officer to die in a railroad accident during the Pullman Strike and the Great Northern Railroad Strike that year. The labor unrest and violence began on May 11, 1894. By July the federal government had intervened by issuing injunctions to halt all boycott activities. Soldiers worked with local Chicago Police to keep trains and rail lines running. Officer Feely was survived by his wife and lived at 35th and Peoria Streets. He was buried in Mount Olivet Cemetery on 111th Street.

Patrolman Andrew Hauswirth,

STAR # unavailable, Sheffield Avenue Police Station, was shot to death on the corner of Ashland Avenue and Altgeld Street while he and his partner, Patrolman Patrick Moore, tried to arrest two men. On the morning of September 28, 1894, the two policemen heard two shots fired from the direction of Ashland Avenue and Dunning Street. They ran towards the sound and saw two men coming from a yard. They ordered the men to halt, but instead the men ran north on Ashland Avenue. The officers called out a second time before they took off in pursuit.

Unexpectedly, one of the men turned and opened fire on the officers. He fired twice, and one of the bullets struck Hauswirth in the groin. Hauswirth returned fire, hitting the shooter in the back. The injured offender fell to the ground while the second escaped down the street.

After firing several rounds, Hauswirth eventually fell to the sidewalk. Policeman Moore immediately called for backup, and Officer Hauswirth was rushed to St. Joseph Hospital where he died. The wounded shooter was transported to Alexian Brothers' Hospital and died shortly there after. The second offender escaped, never to be found.

Patrolman George Krum,

STAR #1452, 22nd Precinct, 37 years old, was killed while responding to a disturbance at a house of ill-repute, known to be a safe haven for thieves and suspicious characters, at 700 W. 20th Street on November 1, 1894. Krum apparently heard an argument taking place inside the residence around 1:30 A.M. and attempted to intervene. One of the participants, a bandit named Cornelius "Con" Burns, stepped forward and shot the officer three times. Krum, though mortally wounded, still returned fire, emptying all the chambers in his revolver. He managed to strike Burns three times before falling to the ground at the bottom of the stairs, which lead to the second floor of the house. Other officers, Patrolmen Hartagan and Baldwin, had been in the area and rushed to the address at the sound of gunshots. There, they found Krum's lifeless body. They immediately searched the second floor and found Mrs. Margaret Ward, her thirteen-year-old daughter, Elsa, James Quinn and Con Burns hiding in a small room.

1894

Burns, suffering from bullet wounds to the heart, right groin and thigh, was transported to Cook County Hospital, while the rest were held at the Canalport Avenue Station. Burns was a known convict who had done several stints in the Bridewell Jail. He came from a family of criminals that included a brother who had shot a police officer several years earlier and was jailed for five years for the crime. The police who accompanied Burns to the hospital were aware of the fatal severity of his injuries, but still attempted to get a statement from him. Burns also knew that he would not recover and refused to speak. Doctors confirmed what everyone already knew and pronounced his case hopeless, stating that any of the wounds he had sustained could prove fatal on its own. He died shortly after arriving at the hospital without ever giving his own account of what had taken place. Policeman Krum left behind his wife and was buried in Forest Home Cemetery.

Patrolman Edward A. Duddles,

STAR #2507, 39th Precinct, Larabee Street Station, 44 years old, was patrolling on the evening of January 3, 1895 when he heard a woman screaming. He headed towards the sound at 448 W. Division Street and found a robbery in progress. Before Duddles could draw his weapon, the burglars opened fire and the officer fell to the ground fatally wounded within seconds of his arrival. An account of the evening's events was given by Mrs. Lundvall, an inhabitant of the address on Division Street, the woman whose screams Officer Duddles had heard. Mrs. Lundvall had returned to her apartment that evening between 8:00 P.M. and 8:30 P.M. and found the door locked. Assuming that her husband was inside, she knocked and rang the bell but received no response. As she waited, she heard movement within and decided to pry open the door. Once she had gained entrance, she noticed two men moving down the hallway at the back of the apartment and discerned that they were robbers. She dispatched her son, Freddie, to the police station to summon help. Before she and her daughter, Lillie, could exit, the men emerged from the back of the residence with their guns leveled at the innocent residents. They told Mrs. Lundvall that they would shoot her if she screamed, so she stayed silent as the two men made their way towards the door.

The burglars were eager to exit quickly and practically ran over young Lillie in their haste, causing the little girl to stumble down the stairs that led to the main door. Lillie screamed as she fell and Mrs. Lundvall cried out in alarm at the rough treatment of her child, causing the robbers to turn and fire at her. The bullet missed the frightened woman and lodged into the ceiling just as Patrolman Duddles burst in. The offenders were startled by the officer's entrance. Their fingers were already poised on their triggers and they opened fire, striking Duddles several times. The officer was dead in a matter of moments. Lillie was only feet from the officer when he was hit and her cloak and dress were stained by the officer's blood, sending the young girl into hysterics.

Unfortunately, due to her agitated state and the speed at which everything happened, Mrs. Lundvall was unable to give a comprehensive description of her assailants. She was able to tell investigating officers that there was a third man present, who had apparently served as a lookout. She had seen him before attempting to enter her apartment and it was believed that he warned his comrades inside that she was returning before he fled the scene. John Carey and William Roach were eventually arrested and confessed to their parts in the tragic events surrounding Patrolman Duddles' death. James MaGee was found guilty of complicity in Patrolman Duddles death after a jury trial. Each man was sentenced to life at the Illinois State Penitentiary at Joliet. Patrolman Duddles, who had begun his career at the East Chicago Avenue Station, lived at 2147 N. Southport Avenue and left behind his wife and six children. He was born in England and had been a member of the Chicago Police Department for 12 years. Officer Duddles was laid to rest in Rosehill Cemetery.

Measuring a prisoner at the
Illinois State Penitentiary at Joliet
(late 1890s). G1987.192,
Chicago History Museum Photo Archive.

Patrolman John Monahan,

STAR #3179, 19th Precinct, was working his regular beat at the 23rd and Halsted Street car barns on January 27, 1895 when he was killed in a tragic accident. Monahan, a native of Ireland, was standing at the entrance to one of the car barns at 12:20 A.M. when car #1835 was being switched onto the tracks that led into that particular barn. The officer did not notice the change and was unable to escape when the car suddenly swung around the curve and into the building, pinning Patrolman Monahan between the wall and the streetcar in a space that measured only six inches. Besides the obvious injuries sustained by such a crushing force, the officer's head had been thrust through the car window at impact and his jugular was severed by the broken glass. Workers at the car barn immediately stopped the car and attempted to free Monahan, though he lived for only a few moments after being rescued.

Monahan, a seven-year-veteran of the force, was a widower with three children. He had been experiencing some professional difficulties before his death and on the evening of January 26, 1895 he had been arraigned before the police board on a charge of intoxication. The board recommended that he be dismissed from the force, but no final steps were taken. He was on duty early the next morning when he was killed. Monahan was laid to rest in Cavalry Cemetery.

Patrolman John B. L. Blumberg,

STAR #922, 14th Precinct, 38 years old, was patrolling the historic Pullman district on November 7, 1895 when he was killed in the line of duty. Blumberg was guarding the Pullman crossing of the Illinois Central Railroad Company, located at 111th Street and Cottage Grove Avenue, when two trains approached the area at the same time. Blumberg, who was born in Sweden in 1857, was busy directing passengers disembarking from the southbound train to safety and apparently did not notice the approach of Engine 215 as it traveled northbound at 3:00 P.M. He did not recognize his own perilous position as he concentrated on the train which was already in the depot. He realized the danger only when it was too late to avoid being struck by the incoming train. He died a short time after the accident, leaving behind a wife and three small children, after five years of dedicated service on the force. He was buried in Oak Woods Cemetery at 67th Street and Cottage Grove Avenue.

 # Patrolman Patrick Fenton,

STAR #1169, 19th Precinct, 36 years old, was fatally shot on February 27, 1898 by an offender, Michael Clark, who was later found insane and committed to an asylum for life. Clark was a sheep butcher at the stockyards who lodged at 522 W. 42nd Street, a rooming house run by Mrs. Ellen M. Cleary. She described Clark as an ideal tenant up until about two months before the shooting when he began acting "flighty" according to her account. He had been fired from his job and left the residence about two weeks before the incident only to return on February 26. That day, Mrs. Cleary informed him that she needed his room and that she would like him to pack his belongings and leave the following day. He seemed to have no objection when Mrs. Cleary gave him this news, but when she went to remind him the next day he appeared to be having one of his spells. She left his room without pressing the point because she was frightened.

Mrs. Cleary left Clark alone until his brother, Frank Clark, came to visit in the afternoon at which point she informed him of his brother's strange behavior and her need for the room. Clark would not see his brother and, after pressing for entrance, Frank left to retrieve their oldest brother, Tom, who had more influence with Michael. When the men returned they again attempted to enter Clark's room. He finally opened the door only to threaten to shoot his brothers if they did not leave. They retreated and moved to the front of the house where they discussed the situation with Mrs. Cleary. She told them she was afraid to have Clark in the house. They promised to remedy the situation quickly by bringing back a police escort to bring their brother to the asylum.

Sullivan's Sample Room, 5058 S. Wentworth Avenue (1895). G1981.0293.093, Chicago History Museum Photo Archive.

In the evening, Frank and Tom returned with Patrolman Fenton, a native of Ireland born in 1866, and his partner, Patrolman Daniel Carey. They once again tried to persuade Clark to let them in. When their requests seemed to fall on deaf ears, Fenton warned Clark that he would have to break the door down. Clark indicated he had no problem with that. Fenton threw himself against the closed door twice, falling into the room as the hinges gave way on his second attempt. At the same moment the officer entered the room, a shot was heard. Fenton cried out that he had been hit. Carey rushed into the room to help his partner and another shot was heard. Fenton staggered from the room into the hallway and fell dead at the feet of those congregated there, shot through the heart. A moment later Carey stumbled into the hallway also bleeding from a gunshot wound, while Clark jumped through the unopened window of his bedroom.

Clark landed safely 15 feet below and sustained only minor cuts to his wrists and ankles. He fled, wearing only his pajamas, the three blocks to St. Cecilia Church where Father Kelly looked after him until the police came and took him into custody. Once they reached the station, investigators tried to question Clark but he refused to cooperate and exhibited all the mannerisms of a madman. He answered all questions asked of him with bloodcurdling screams that could be heard well outside the walls of the station. He provided officers with no useful information about the motivation for his actions. Clark was officially found insane and committed to the Chester State Hospital for Insane Criminals, located downstate along the Mississippi River, on June 30, 1898. Michael Clark hanged himself at Chester on February 14, 1900. Patrolman Fenton was buried at Mount Olivet Cemetery.

Patrolman Bernard A. Kuebler,

STAR #238, 3rd Precinct, 29 years old, was on patrol with his partner, John O'Brien, on October 10, 1898 when he was informed of a robbery that had taken place in the area a short time before. He and O'Brien continued walking their beat, considering the evidence that had been found at the scene, when they came upon two men who fit the provided description of the burglars. The officers approached the men in an alley behind 200 W. 23rd Place near the 2300 block of S. Wentworth Avenue, now the heart of Chinatown, intending to discern if they were indeed the bandits from earlier in the evening. According to one eyewitness, Kuebler and O'Brien had actually passed the two men before Kuebler turned about five feet later, as if following a sudden impulse, and one of the bandits immediately fired at the officer.

The bullet entered Kuebler's upper lip and moved upward before lodging in his brain, killing him almost instantly. O'Brien turned just in time to see his partner fall to the pavement of the unlit street, darkened only moments before the confrontation when the bandits, Owen Bowland and Edward Kelly, had broken the streetlight. He immediately followed the fleeing men, one of whom turned and fired at him. Using the flash from the weapon as his target, O'Brien discharged his own weapon several times and hit Bowland in the leg and lungs.

Bowland was taken to Mercy Hospital where he was given only small odds for survival and Kuebler's fellow officers started to try and reconstruct the night's events. Originally it was believed that Bowland had shot Patrolman Kuebler for several reasons. Bowland was a small man by all accounts and the angle at which the bullet entered the officer's lip was cited to indicate that the shooter must have been a shorter individual. In addition, it was believed that only one of the men had a gun. Since O'Brien shot in the direction of the flash that came from the bandit's gun and he wounded only Bowland, it was believed an assumption of his guilt was safe. However, when the police reached Bowland where he had fallen, no weapon was found in his possession. The area from where the criminal had been hit to where he had staggered and fell was thoroughly searched and no gun was discovered. An examination of his person also produced no weapon, although a strange collection of belongings comprised of a rosary, crucifix, some rings and a coupon good for one five cent cigar was found. The police puzzled over the gun's absence, but finally theorized that Bowland must have had enough time to hand the weapon over to Kelly who had managed to escape.

Kelly was a well-known character in police circles and there was no shortage of officers willing to join the search for him. As the hunt began, Sergeant Tom Cronin attempted to question Bowland, who was completely uncooperative. He even went so far as to seem pleased about Kuebler's death, telling the officers who were guarding him that, "He has always hounded me and I am glad he's done for," according to the *Chicago Daily News*. Kuebler's reputation as an enforcer who relentlessly pursued the guilty had made him many enemies, some extremely vindictive, who probably echoed Bowland's pronouncement.

The final court records tell a different story than the original police speculation though. In the end it was Edward Kelly who was held responsible for Patrolman Kuebler's death. Kelly was eventually arrested and brought back to Chicago from Hammond, Indiana and sentenced to life in the Illinois State Penitentiary at Joliet on July 12, 1899. Owen Bowland, a young man not even 18-years-old, recovered from his wounds despite the dire initial predictions and was acquitted of all charges. Patrolman Keubler was laid to rest at Graceland Cemetery.

 ## Patrolman Bartholomew Cavanaugh,

STAR # unavailable, 4th Precinct, Cottage Grove Avenue Station, 42 years old, fell to his death on December 15, 1898 while investigating a burglary. The officer was at the Hodge Building, located at 22nd Street and Indiana Avenue, following up on a report of a possible break-in when he attempted to climb a staircase in an area behind the building. According to the reconstruction of events put together by investigators, Cavanaugh must have lost his footing and fallen to the alley below. He broke his neck and lay helpless until fellow officers discovered him a few moments later. A wagon was called for but the officer died before he reached Mercy Hospital. Officer Cavanaugh lived at 3548 S. Fifth Avenue and was survived by his wife, Anne, and three children, Loretta, Bernard and Alice. He was buried at Mount Olivet Cemetery.

Patrolman Edward J. Wallner,

STAR #1533, 23rd Precinct, Hubbard Street Station, 29 years old, was learning to work with a new partner, John W. McCauley, on January 5, 1899 when they ran into six wanted hold-up men. The officers had just come to the intersection of 21st and Wolcott Streets when they noticed the suspicious gang of men. When the bandits became aware of the officers, they immediately fled south on Wolcott Street and disappeared down an alley. The officers followed the robbers into the alley at 1900 W. 21st Street, between 21st Place and 22nd Street, and found themselves face to face with six criminals with their weapons drawn standing less than ten feet away. Patrolman Wallner ordered them to surrender, but they opened fire instead. A fusillade of bullets then rang out with the bandits taking advantage of the refuge provided by the darkened alley. One of the first bullets fired struck Wallner, who immediately fell mortally wounded. McCauley continued to fire until a shot to the groin incapacitated him.

Moments later a squad of back-up officers appeared on the scene to find their fallen comrades alone in the deserted alley. They had been alerted by Officer Robert Cline, who had been near the scene when the shooting began and immediately called for aid. Both injured officers were taken to Cook County Hospital, but Wallner could not be saved. He was a well-respected officer whose brother was also on the force, working as a desk-sergeant at the DesPlaines Street Station. This was the second tragedy the Hubbard Street Station had encountered in less than a week. Only a few days before his own death, Wallner had served as a pallbearer at the funeral of John Ware, who had been his partner for many years. As the officers of the Hubbard Street Station walked under the black crepe hung to honor Patrolman Ware and learned of Patrolman Wallner's death, it was easy to conclude that the symbol of mourning now hung there for both men who had shared so much in life. Officer Wallner was buried at St. Boniface Cemetery. Four men, Charles Peterson, Frank Ford, Michael McFadden and Ed Lally were eventually charged with Wallner's death and each man received a life sentence at the Illinois State Penitentiary at Joliet on June 2, 1899.

Patrolman Edward Leach,

STAR #2766, 11th Precinct, 58th Street Station, 36 years old, was shot by a fellow officer on February 10, 1899 after the men exchanged heated words about Irish politics. Patrolman Leach and Patrolman Patrick Furlong both ended their shift in the early morning hours of February 10 and hurried together to the saloon of William Wagner at 6001 S. State Street in an attempt to avoid the cold winter morning. Once inside, the two officers, who had both joined the force through civil service appointments made by Mayor George B. Swift, met up with a group of fellow officers who were discussing world events.

The conversation soon turned to Irish politics, a subject on which the men held opposite beliefs. Furlong sympathized with the plight of the Irish and vehemently disapproved of the actions the British had taken against them. Leach saw things differently and claimed that the British had been justified in the policy held. What had began as a friendly discussion soon boiled down to an intense argument strictly between Leach and Furlong. According to witnesses, the quarrel took a tragic turn when Leach lost his temper completely and struck Furlong while calling him vile names. Furlong responded to the insult by taking out his service revolver and firing at his friend. Two bullets struck Leach, one in the abdomen while the other entered his right breast and passed straight through his body.

Chaos broke out in the small saloon, but one patron was cognizant enough to exit the establishment and summon officers from the Woodlawn Street Station, the closest to the saloon. Once police arrived and surveyed the situation, they called their colleagues at the 50th Street Station, where Furlong and Leach were based. They waited for them to arrive and handle the next steps. The circumstances at the saloon were considered so serious that

Desk-Sergeant Dan Brown left the station unattended and was taken to the scene in the patrol wagon. When he arrived he found Leach unconscious and bleeding. He directed that the officer be sent to the Chicago Hospital at 49th Street and Cottage Grove Avenue. Leach died at the hospital later in the day without providing any explanation for the events that had taken place in the saloon. He was buried at Oak Woods Cemetery. Furlong was taken into custody and transported to the 50th Street Station where he was stripped of all official police insignias and treated as a normal prisoner. Furlong was sentenced to the Illinois State Penitentiary at Joliet for 14 years on May 17, 1899, but was released only a year and a half later on December 22, 1900 on the orders of Governor John R. Tanner.

Patrolman John F. McDermott,

STAR #1885, 29th Precinct, Warren Avenue Station, was discovered fatally injured on the morning of April 11, 1900. Mary McDermott discovered her brother behind his house at 3451 W. Fifteenth Street with a gunshot wound to his head and quickly called for help. The patrolman was transported to the Cook County Hospital where he regained conscious but could not explain his injury. McDermott's revolver had been laying only a few feet from him when his sister found him. Investigating officers speculated that he may have fallen down the back stairway at his home and accidentally discharged his weapon. Patrolman McDermott died later the same day without ever explaining the circumstances surrounding his shooting.

Desk-Sergeant Timothy S. O'Connell,

STAR #266, 12th Precinct, 31 years old, was killed in the line of duty on April 29, 1900 at the 18th Street Viaduct while returning home from duty. O'Connell, a native of Ireland, was believed to have been waylaid by three men who attempted to rob him. The officer withdrew his revolver, causing two of his assailants to flee while the third turned and pulled his own weapon, shooting the officer before he could fire. Captain John Wheeler of the Chicago Police indicated that the police believed a man named George Hencheck, a man at one time employed in a bicycle shop, and well-known to the local precinct, as the leader of the thieves. At the time of his arrest, a revolver was found in his possession though he denied any knowledge of the incident.

Two others, Peter McClain and Frank Goodhoe, were believed to have knowledge of the shooting and were detained. They were released when they provided solid alibis that placed them at a party celebrating the completion of a new boat set to accompany Admiral George Dewey along the new Drainage Canal, which had opened the previous January. Hencheck was later acquitted of all charges. Officer O'Connell, who lived at 609 W. 18th Street, was survived by his wife and buried in Calvary Cemetery, Evanston.

1900

Patrolman William F. Messenger,

STAR #711, 2nd Precinct, 38 years old, was reviewing court sheets with Desk-Sergeant James J. Scully at the desk of the Harrison Street Station, 130 W. Harrison Street, on the afternoon of April 24, 1901 when Richard D. Houghtelling entered the station. Messenger, a Chicago native, had earlier exchanged words with Houghtelling that morning in response to two women who complained of his behavior to Messenger and his partner, Patrolman J. F. Reicks. The two officers had then asked Houghtelling to move along and stop following the women, before going on their way. At approximately 12:20 P.M., Houghtelling entered the Harrison Street Station with the apparent intent of demanding Messenger retract his accusations from earlier in the day. Messenger refused and proceeded to walk from behind the wicket, the protective screen that shielded police from the waiting area of the station, and ordered Houghtelling to leave the premises. He was barely through the wicket when Houghtelling fired a gun, hitting Messenger in the chest and left side.

Scully immediately fired at Houghtelling from behind the wicket and then proceeded through the door, shooting as he went. Messenger was also firing as Houghtelling moved towards the LaSalle Street entrance of the station. When he realized his gun was empty, Houghtelling, who was wounded during the exchange, attempted to escape down a corridor, but was detained by the lockup-keeper and bailiff. He was laid out on the office floor and then moved to the steps before finally being taken to the Cook County Jail Hospital. Houghtelling died from his gunshot wounds the following day. Messenger was taken to St. Luke Hospital where he too died from his injuries the following day. Officer Messenger was laid to rest in the mausoleum of Graceland Cemetery.

Patrolman John T. Reddy,

STAR # unavailable, Englewood Station, 37 years old, had just returned to the station from a trip to the County Jail in the police "blue" wagon when he fell to the ground dead at the feet of his fellow policemen on December 11, 1901. He was a well-known character on the Southside, remembered best for his happy disposition and his girth. Weighing in at over 300 pounds, Reddy was by far the heaviest policeman in Inspector Hunt's district, according to the *Chicago Tribune*. Patrolman Reddy lived at 6053 S. Halsted Street and left a widow, as well as his parents, Edward and Margaret Reddy. His remains were taken to Van Duser's Undertaking Rooms at 6138 S. Wentworth Avenue. He was buried on December 14, 1901 at Calvary Cemetery, Evanston.

1901

Chicago Police Officer in distinctive bell-shaped cap with spike (1899). DN-0002013, *Chicago Daily News* Collection, Chicago History Museum Photo Archive.

Patrolman Patrick Duffy,

STAR #1190, 19th Precinct, 35 years old, observed a wanted offender outside the Tenth Presbyterian Church at Emerald Avenue and 46th Street on May 1, 1902. Duffy approached the man and began questioning him. During a five minute exchange the offender exhibited suspicious behavior, evading the officer's questions and shifting his eyes from side to side. As they spoke another man approached outside of Duffy's view. At the end of his conversation with the first offender, Duffy reached out to detain the man by taking his arm. This action caused the second man to shout in alarm. Duffy, now aware of the second man's presence, turned toward him at which point the second man removed a revolver from his pocket and placed it next to Patrolman Duffy's head. He pulled the trigger and shot the officer through his right eye. Duffy fell silently to the sidewalk, dying almost instantly. Officer Duffy was buried in Mount Olivet Cemetery.

The incident was witnessed by four citizens, one of them a ten-year-old child, who provided accounts of the men's actions. Hugh Reilly was the first to be arrested in connection with the shooting and on September 20, 1902 he was sentenced to fourteen years in the Illinois State Penitentiary at Joliet. Over eight years later, Vincent Brisco was arrested for his part in Patrolman Duffy's shooting and was also sentenced to fourteen years in the Illinois State Penitentiary at Joliet on December 9, 1910.

Patrolman Charles Pennell, STAR #1852,

28th Precinct, West Lake Street Station, 38 years old and

Patrolman Timothy T. Devine,

STAR #1814, 28th Precinct, West Lake Street Station, 42 years old, were both killed in the line of duty on August 12, 1902 while attempting to apprehend two burglary suspects. The officers were found lying at the entrance to an alley at Jackson Boulevard and Ashland Avenue, each having received a fatal gunshot wound. Devine was dead when they were discovered, while Pennell succumbed to his wounds about an hour later at the Cook County Hospital.

Before his death, Patrolman Pennell was able to give only a brief, halting description of their assailants, describing two men, one six feet tall with a silk hat, the other approximately five foot eight. He tried to convey more, but was unable due to the gravity of his injuries. He died at Cook County Hospital a short time later. Officer Pennell was buried in Mount Carmel Cemetery and Officer Devine in Calvary Cemetery.

Reconstruction of the events from witnesses who heard the shots led the police to believe that the officers were ambushed by a hail of bullets fired by the two assailants. A trail of blood found in the alley led investigators to believe that the officers were able to wound one of the assailants when they returned fire. Devine was found with his gun in his hand and Pennell's weapon was discovered about twenty feet from the officers near a fence in the alley. Both weapons had been fired at least twice.

The perpetrators remained at large and the mystery unsolved until November 30, 1905 when Charles Kruger, sentenced to death in Pennsylvania for killing a constable there, confessed to the Chicago murders. Louis Stowkowski had been already arrested in August of 1902 in connection with the crime based on information given by a jailhouse informant linking him to Pennell and Devine's deaths, but final records indicate the majority of blame lay with Kruger.

1902

Patrolman Fred Heilman,

STAR # unavailable, 5th Precinct, 35th Street Station, 49 years old, was attacked by a mob of men and women at 32nd and Halsted Streets on August 24, 1900 after leaving the 35th Street Station. The officer was attempting to force the group from the rear of a saloon when he was beaten with his own club. Seven people, Michael and Thomas King, Marquette Schott, James and Mary Bowling, Fred Wittick and Maggie Wittick were arrested in connection to the beating. Policeman Heilman did not succumb to his wounds until three years later on January 18, 1903. The fallen officer was survived by his wife, Lizzie, and siblings, Michael, Hazel Hayden, Annie Shoemaker, and Mary MacKenhoupt. He resided at 6336 S. Champlain Avenue and was buried at St. Boniface Cemetery on January 31, 1903 after his Funeral Mass at Holy Cross Church. Heilman had at one time been the wagon driver for the Chief of the Chicago Fire Department, Denis Swenie, before becoming a police officer.

Patrolman Michael J. O'Rourke,

STAR #426, 5th Precinct, 42 years old, was shot on October 22, 1903 after confronting a suspect wanted on an assault charge. He died from his wounds two days later on October 24, 1903. The accused had been involved in a domestic dispute earlier in the day and the officer, a native of Ireland, was providing security for the offender's former sweetheart when the altercation occurred.

Miss Nellie Murray had recently ended a relationship with the assailant, Fred Sierre, and had been unable to retrieve her personal effects from Sierre's apartment. She requested a police escort and Officer O'Rourke was dispatched to make sure she was able to recover her belongings. Sierre spied the pair as they approached and, fearing arrest, he escaped through a window. A few moments later, O'Rourke spied Sierre in an alley near the apartment. Leaving Miss Murray in a nearby doorway, the officer approached Sierre who removed a revolver from his pocket and fatally shot the officer in the abdomen.

Sierre was arrested on October 24, 1903 and brought to the patrolman's hospital bed where O'Rourke was able to identify him as the shooter despite his failing condition. O'Rourke died four days later, on October 26, and was buried at Mount Carmel Cemetery.

When Sierre was returned to his holding cell, after O'Rourke's identification, he made two suicide attempts. Both times he invited death by climbing to the top of his cell and attempting to smash his head against the concrete floor. The first attempt was not successful, but on the second try he was able make contact, at which point he fractured his skull. He was discovered lying unconscious in a pool of blood and rushed to Provident Hospital. There he was assessed by physicians and sent back to his cell in the care of the officers on duty. Three and a half months later, on February 5, 1904, Sierre was acquitted of responsibility for the murder.

Detective John Quinn,

STAR #2797, 41st Precinct, 37 years old, was killed in the line of duty on Sunday November 22, 1903 while attempting to arrest hold-up man Gustav Marx, wanted on charges of robbery and attempted murder. Marx, 21-year-old with a lengthy rap sheet, was approached by Detective Quinn and his partner, Detective William B. Blaul, at the Greenberg Saloon, 1957 W. Addison Avenue near Damen Avenue, around 10:30 P.M. Marx was well-known to Detective Quinn, who had arrested him several times in the past for various crimes. Quinn was spotted by the offender as he attempted to make his way to the back of the saloon where he was confronted by Detective Blaul.

According to witnesses, Quinn did not appear to be expecting any resistance from the offender and simply stated that he wanted him to come with them. In response, Marx drew

Chicago Police Funeral Honor Guard and
public at Holy Name Cathedral (c.1903).
DN-0000240, *Chicago Daily News* Collection,
Chicago History Museum Photo Archive.

The site in Miller's Station, Indiana where Patrolman Joseph Driscoll was killed and the "Car Barn Bandits" were captured. DN-0001561, *Chicago Daily News* Collection, Chicago History Museum Photo Archive.

Detective James J. Keefe,

STAR #1620, 21st Precinct, 43 years old, had his life cut tragically short on January 5, 1905 when he and four other officers went to arrest two known felons wanted on charges of armed robbery. Information reported to the police placed Harry Feinberg and Frank Gaghen at Gaghen's brother Edward's house at 190 W. 25th Street. Officers were dispatched to ascertain the truth of the report and arrest the men if they were found to be there. Four of the officers surrounded the house, while the fifth approached the front door and began to question Edward Gaghen.

As Edward denied entrance to the officers at the front, Keefe made his way to the back door and knocked loudly. Gaghen left the front door and admitted Keefe in through the back door to the kitchen. The officer made his way through the apartment to a closed bedroom door off the kitchen. The occupants of the room suddenly opened fire through the closed door and fatally wounded Keefe with the first bullet. According to the *Chicago Daily News,* Keefe cried out for his fellow officers as he fell, calling "Help me boys, I'm shot! For God's sake, come to me," before he fell to the ground.

Keefe's fellow officers returned fire and wounded both of the suspects before arresting them. After being rushed to Mercy Hospital within thirty minutes of the shooting, Patrolman Keefe died due to serious wounds in his stomach and chest. Frank Gaghen was eventually tried for his murder and sentenced to life in prison in the Illinois State Penitentiary at Joliet on April 6, 1905. Keefe was a highly respected member of the Chicago Police Department, a man who was acknowledged to be one of its most brave and courageous members. He had spent more than ten years working out of the Detective Bureau and among his citations was the Carter Harrison Award in 1899. He was interred at Calvary Cemetery.

Sergeant Richard F. Cummings,

STAR #101, 42nd Precinct, 48 years old, was killed in the line of duty on May 1, 1905 while guarding Montgomery Ward & Company wagons in an area beset with labor problems. Cummings was stationed on Washington Street, near Dearborn and Clark Streets, and given control of a group of officers charged with keeping the peace in the tension-filled area. Tempers flared between strike-breakers and sympathizers as the officers attempted to perform their duties. During the confusion, a horse-drawn wagon from Marshall Field & Company attempted to circumvent Cummings and enter a heavily congested area. The side of the wagon crashed into the officer and threw him to the ground. The impact caused life threatening injuries to the officer, leading to the arrest of the driver, James Odessa, who was later acquitted on all charges.

The Employers' Association designated resolutions of sympathy for the fallen officer and presented his family with $1,000. Cummings' death was the second in two days that could be linked to strike violence. It was the first police fatality. Officer Cummings was buried in Calvary Cemetery.

Patrolman Patrick E. Blackwell,

Star #1235, 15th Precinct, 38 years old, was directing traffic in the busy intersection of State and Van Buren Streets on May 10, 1905 when he fell back into an open freight elevator shaft in the street and sustained life threatening injuries. Blackwell was assigned to the rear of Siegel, Cooper and Company Department Store and charged with easing the traffic congestion there. In the course of his duties, he signaled for a wagon to move and stepped back to allow its passage. As he did so, he was bumped by the wagon and accidentally knocked down the elevator shaft. He died ten days later on May 20, 1905 and was buried in Mount Olivet Cemetery.

Patrolman Patrick Riordan,

STAR # unavailable, 19th Precinct, was on patrol as a watchman at the railroad crossing at 41st Street and Stewart Avenue when he was struck by a train on June 17, 1905. Officer Riordon had been directing a group of workman at the crossing when he jumped onto the northbound tracks to avoid a southbound train and failed to notice that trains were approaching from both directions. He was hit by the northbound train and suffered fatal injuries. He was a widower; and buried at Mount Olivet Cemetery on 111th Street.

Sergeant John P. Shine,

STAR #44, 17th Precinct, 42 years old, was responding to a report of a gunman terrorizing the Englewood neighborhood on October 10, 1905, when he was shot and killed. One death and several injuries were already attributed to the man, who was said to be the wandering the streets brandishing a gun at frightened citizens. Shine discovered that the man had barricaded himself in his nearby apartment at 6100 S. State Street. He decided to approach and attempt to apprehend the assailant. Locating the apartment, the officer knocked and demanded entry. The offender, Robert Newcomb, did not verbally respond; instead he shot through the closed door and fatally wounded the officer, who died two hours later at Englewood Union Hospital. Shine was buried in Calvary Cemetery.

After the shooting, Newcomb remained barricaded in his apartment while it was surrounded by more than one hundred policemen intent on apprehending him. The officers fired a hail of bullets into the apartment, keeping Newcomb under siege until he surrendered and was arrested. Though described by the *Chicago Daily News* as "crazed" and "maddened," Newcomb was tried and convicted of various crimes. He was hanged on February 16, 1906.

Patrolman Jacob Sebastian,

STAR # unavailable, Cragin Station, 56 years old, was fatally shot on November 8, 1905 while delivering election reports to the Cook County Board of Election headquarters with Patrolman Robert Adlum. The Board's headquarters were located in City Hall, which was extremely busy that day as election judges and clerks returned their own reports and civilians gathered outside on Washington Street to discuss election results. Upon entering the building, Officer Adlum tripped and his revolver flew from his pocket as he attempted to break his fall. The weapon discharged and the bullet entered Officer Sebastian's abdomen, causing a fatal wound. Officer Sebastian was rushed to the Chicago Emergency Hospital. Before he allowed doctors to operate, the officer insisted that his wife be notified of his condition. Sebastian, a 23-year-veteran of the force, lived at 1343 N. Cicero Avenue. Doctors eventually removed the bullet and Sebastian was initially given a favorable prognosis but his injury ultimately proved fatal.

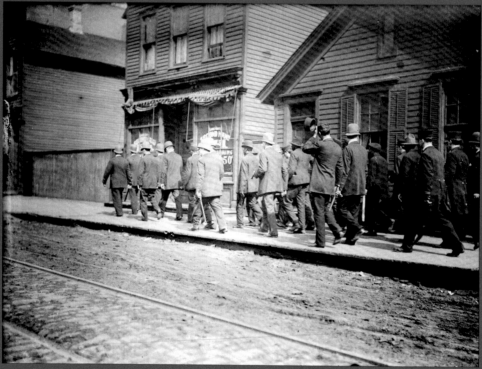

Detective Austin B. Woolsey,

STAR # unavailable, DesPlaines Street Station, 43 years old, succumbed to an injury suffered in the line of duty on February 13, 1906. The detective had been injured four years earlier on November of 1902 while attempting to arrest a blind man, Thomas Brody, in the DesPlaines Street Station. He suffered a concussion to his brain caused by a blow from Brody's cane and never recovered. Detective Woolsey was survived by his wife, Bessie, and son, Joseph. He lived at 310 S. Sacramento Avenue and was laid to rest in Rosehill Cemetery in Council Bluffs, Iowa.

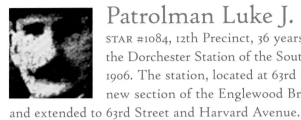

Patrolman Luke J. Fitzpatrick,

STAR #1084, 12th Precinct, 36 years old, was approached by a train conductor at the Dorchester Station of the Southside Elevated Railroad on November 19, 1906. The station, located at 63rd Street and Woodlawn Avenue, was part of a new section of the Englewood Branch that had opened only 16 days earlier and extended to 63rd Street and Harvard Avenue.

The conductor informed Fitzpatrick that four wanted safe blowers had just reached the station on the Hammond train. The officer moved towards the suspects, eventually identified as Charles Hanson and Guy Van Tassel, who opened fire at his advance. Fitzpatrick was mortally wounded but able to return fire. The offenders made their escape and the officer was removed to St. Bernard Hospital, where he died the same day. He was laid to rest in the cemetery of St. James at the Sag Bridge, where large numbers of early Irish were buried while working on the great project of the Illinois and Michigan Canal in the 1840s.

Hanson was eventually apprehended following a shootout with another officer. During the search after his arrest, it was discovered that he had various safe blowing tools in his possession. He refused to give information on his three companions and was sentenced to life in the Illinois State Penitentiary at Joliet on April 30, 1907. Van Tassel was eventually apprehended in San Francisco and returned to Chicago in June of 1907. He was tried and convicted for his part in Patrolman Fitzpatrick's murder and given his own life sentence on December 10, 1907. It is said that he was spared the gallows by the appearance of his aged mother in court. Charles Hansen remained in prison until 1947 when he was released after serving 39 years. He was set free on the grounds that his original trial was in violation of an Illinois State Statute that guaranteed trial within four months. During his long prison term, Hanson had studied law.

1906

A man being carried to a patrol wagon by two policemen during the 1902 Teamster strike. DN-0000515, Chicago Daily News Collection, Chicago History Museum Photo Archive.

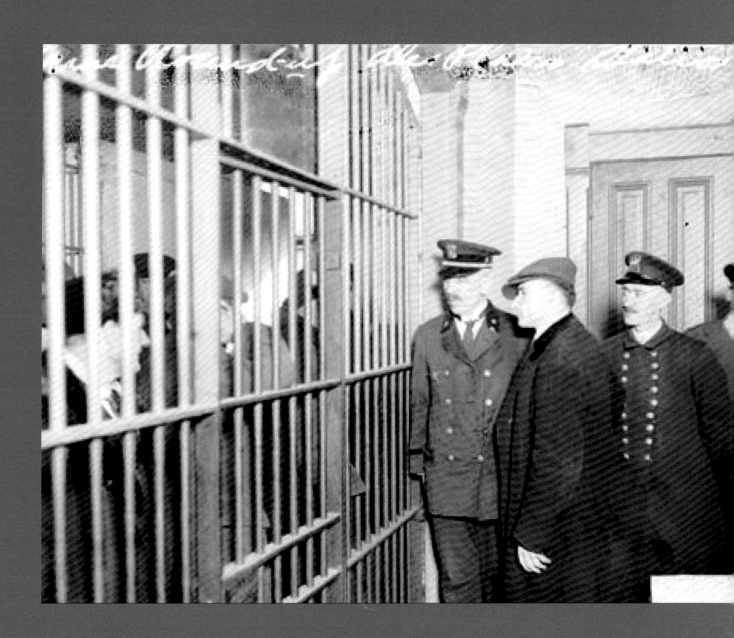

Patrolman Edward W. Smith,

STAR #3002, 31st Precinct, Austin Station, 31 years old, was shot and killed by an unknown gunman on August 4, 1907 on his way home in a homicide that may have been related to his police work. Smith, a mounted officer in the downtown service district, was killed on the corner of Washington Boulevard and Washtenaw Avenue. After the shooting, the officer managed to stagger the final block to his home where his wife discovered him, wounded and bleeding, attempting to open the front door.

Two theories were recounted by the *Chicago Daily Tribune* as possible explanations behind the officer's death. The first, attributed the attack to someone Smith had been with earlier in the day; the second placed the blame on highway men. The latter was the one held by Smith's superior, Lieutenant C.C. Healey. The officer had been out and about all day in his civilian clothes and was making his way home around 12:30 A.M. when the assault took place. According to the paper, he managed to only tell his wife, "That fellow shot me," before slipping into an unconscious state from which he never recovered.

His wife was questioned extensively by investigating officers but could tell them very little and had no knowledge of any enemies who would want to kill her husband. As the neighborhood was searched for the assailant, Mrs. Smith told officers that her husband had left their home at around with 3:00 P.M. with a man with whom she was not acquainted. That was the last time she saw him. She hoped that this man might be able to offer some insight into her husband's death.

Some neighbors claimed Theodore Girard, a civil engineer who might have been with the Panama Canal at one point, was the man in question. Police searched for him the night of the murder, but it is not known if he was ever found. Patrolman Smith's murder remains unsolved. His body was laid to rest in Rosehill Cemetery.

Patrolman Robert McAneney,

Star #1412, 12th Precinct, 47 years old, was shot and killed on his way home from work on November 16, 1907. He was shot in his chest, near the corner of Wentworth Avenue and 63rd Street within 100 feet of his home. The official police theory contended that McAneney was killed by an ex-convict he had helped send to prison. One suspect was Charles Smith, a convict who had been released from the Illinois State Penitentiary at Joliet two years earlier. Patrolman McAneney had helped put him away. The other, Freeman Caniff, had been sent away 20 years before due to McAneney's police work. He had been released only months earlier. Patrolman McAneney's wife had died only seven months before her husband was shot and had expressed anxiety at Caniff's release. But McAneney claimed not to feel any trepidation. The officer was a widower with seven children, the oldest of whom was set to undergo surgery relating to injuries sustained in a streetcar accident at the time her father was killed.

Patrolman Helge Hullgren was in a restaurant near the Englewood Station when the shooting took place and was the first to reach the fallen officer. McAneney's still buttoned overcoat and holstered weapon made it appear that the officer had been caught unaware by the shooter. The bullet had already taken McAneney's life when Hullgren reached him. The officer did not see a suspect at the scene, although two other witnesses came forward to provide descriptions.

The cashier of an all night restaurant on Wentworth Avenue, Miss Jeanette Holly, was able to describe a man of about 35 years of age, 5 feet 8 inches tall, who wore a short, tan coat and a hat that obscured his face. John Keeney, a ticket seller at the 59th Street "El" Station was able to provide details about the same man. He claimed that the individual ran into the station in such a state of agitation that he scattered his fare all over the floor before rushing through the turnstile and catching the northbound train. All signs of the suspect were lost after that sighting.

The Chicago Police Department
"Beauty Squad"—Distinguished by their
impeccable appearance and bearing (1908).
DN-0005989, *Chicago Daily News*
Collection, Chicago History Museum
Photo Archive.

A bustling shopping arcade on
Milwaukee Avenue, west of Ashland Avenue,
located in the heart of a predominately
Polish neighborhood. DN-0055533,
Chicago Daily News Collection, Chicago
History Museum Photo Archive.

Another theory about the attack, published by the *Chicago Daily Tribune*, gave jealousy as motive for the assault. That account claimed that a married railroad man was driven to the act by the anger he felt over McAneney's interest in a woman. The newspaper asserted that an arrest of the railroad man was possible that morning but acknowledged that the police would not confirm the prominence of this theory. Officer McAneney's body was sent to Niles, Michigan for burial in Calvary Cemetery there.

Two year later, in 1909, a convict serving a sentence for robbery in the Illinois State Penitentiary at Joliet, James O'Neill, confessed to the unsolved mystery of McAneney's murder. Seized by a haunted conscience O'Neill, who had once spent two years studying for the priesthood at Holy Cross Seminary, said, "I have been unable to sleep since the night I killed him. I awake in a cold sweat and see him staggering toward me clutching at his wound, the blood running between his fingers. I was going crazy and I am glad I told it."

Patrolman William R. Mooney,

STAR #2590, 27th Precinct, 52 years old, was shot on January 2, 1908 by a burglary suspect at the intersection of Sangamon and Van Buren Streets at 7:30 P.M. Mooney and two other officers had gone to take a robbery victim's statement when they noticed a suspicious character. The two other officers detained the suspect, moving him to nearby patrol box, while Patrolman Mooney continued to take the victim's statement. As they spoke in the doorway of the victim's home, three men approached the house that Mooney believed may have been involved in the earlier incident. He commanded the men to come closer so the victim could attempt to identify them. They were reluctant. When the officer grabbed the nearest man by the arm the other two escaped.

Patrolman Mooney fired into the air to gain the attention of his associates at the patrol box. They observed the fleeing suspects and shot at the men but were unable to wound them. One policeman took off in pursuit of the suspects at the same moment another shot rang out. Both officers looked over in time to see Mooney fall to the ground, apparently felled by the revolver in the hand of the suspect he had detained. The first officer continued his pursuit of the two other suspects, while the second took off in pursuit of Patrolman Mooney's killer, dragging his original prisoner with him on the chase.

A fierce gun battle between one of the officers and the two suspects ensued, but he was unable to apprehend them. Mooney's shooter also managed to make his escape. In the meantime, Patrolman Mooney, who was born to Irish parents in Canada, was taken to Grace Hospital where he was able to provide a description of his assailant before succumbing to his injury on January 2, ending 16 years of service with the Chicago Police Department. Innocent bystanders who had been wounded during the ensuing gunfire were also brought to Grace Hospital and laid in beds next to the fallen officer. William Brown and Thomas McCann were eventually arrested in connection with the shooting and each received a sentence of 14 years in the Illinois State Penitentiary at Joliet. Officer Mooney, who worked out of the DesPlaines Street Station, was survived by his wife and buried in Forest Home Cemetery.

An "X" marks the site of Patrolman Robert McAneney's murder on November 16, 1907. DN-0005386, *Chicago Daily News* Collection, Chicago History Museum Photo Archive.

The home of Patrolman McAneney located on the 6300 block of S. Wentworth Avenue (1907). DN-0005339, *Chicago Daily News* Collection, Chicago History Museum Photo Archive.

Patrolman McAneney's sons, John and Robert (1907). DN-0005341, *Chicago Daily News* Collection, Chicago History Museum Photo Archive.

William Brown, the accused murderer of Patrolman Mooney (1908). DN-0005622, *Chicago Daily News* Collection, Chicago History Museum Photo Archive.

William Brown
arrested for murder of
Policeman ... Mooney

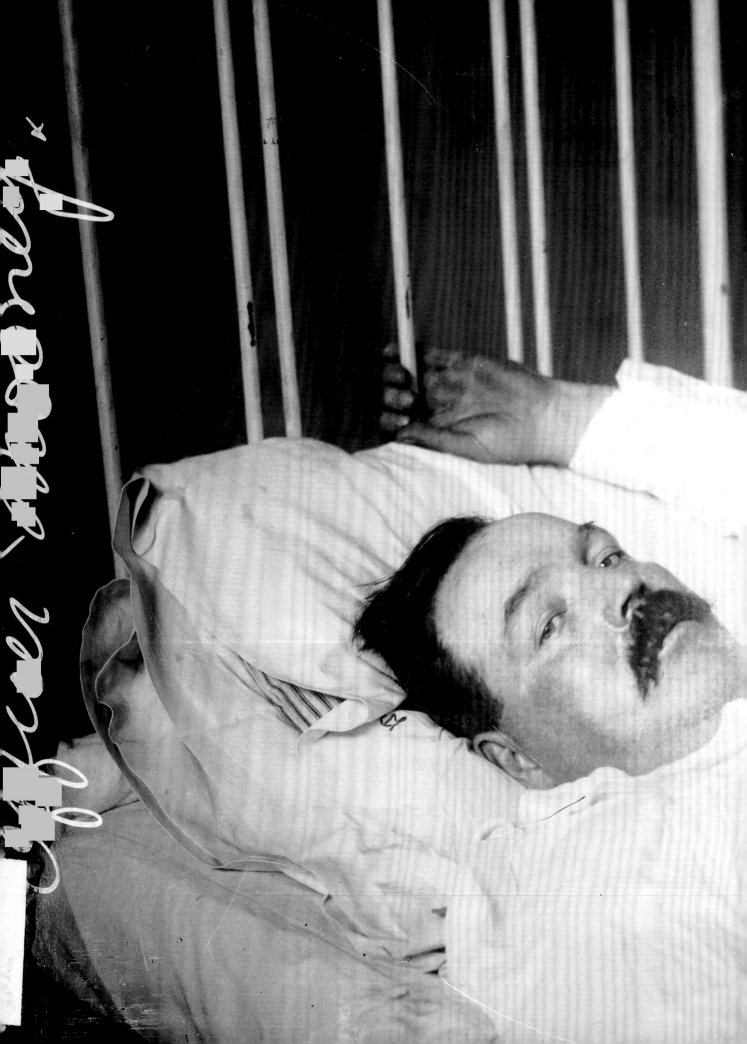

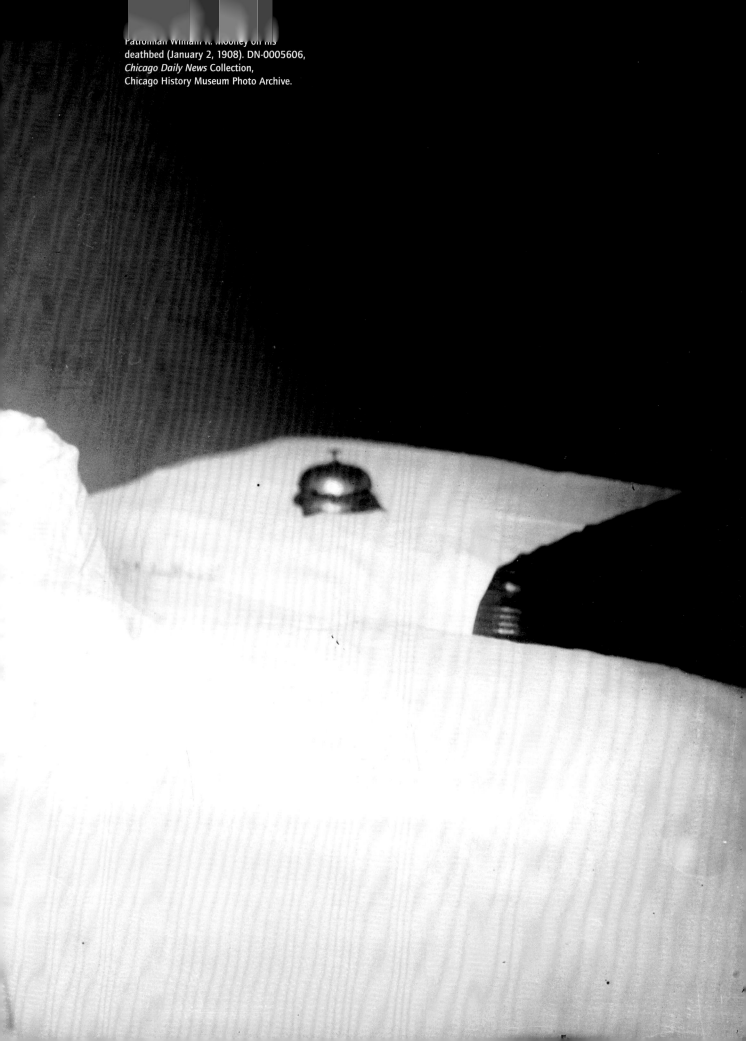

Patrolman Michael D. Callahan,

Star #2842, 29th Precinct, 29 years old, was shot in the line of duty on January 2, 1908 while attempting to apprehend two cronies of Patrolman Mooney's killer. During the citywide manhunt for Mooney's killer on the morning of his death, Callahan stopped four known criminals, Bert McCagg, David Anderson, John Dennin and Joseph Lemke, at the corner of Hoyne Avenue and Washington Boulevard and questioned them. Callahan was traveling with his partner, who remained a half-block behind him as was their custom on patrol, when he saw two pairs of suspicious looking men.

The officer believed the men were up to no good and he approached them. His hunch later proved correct when it was discovered that the men had spent all day in a rented room planning night-time holdups. When Callahan spotted them, they were patrolling for victims and did not appreciate the officer's questions. Instead of responding to his queries, the four men opened fire, fatally shooting Patrolman Callahan in the abdomen.

The policeman was able to return fire and fatally wound McCagg, but the others managed to escape. Callahan was rushed to Roosevelt Hospital where he later died. The three assailants who had managed to flee the scene were eventually apprehended although charges against Lemke were eventually dropped. Anderson, a twenty-year-old cocaine addict who boasted of his crime-record in other cities, was sentenced to hang for his role in the crime but was never executed. Dennin received 14 years in the Illinois State Penitentiary at Joliet. Officer Callahan was interred in Calvary Cemetery.

Chicago Police Officers at the entrance to
Cook County Jail, 54 W. Hubbard Street (1904).
DN-0001860, *Chicago Daily News* Collection,
Chicago History Museum Photo Archive.

Detective-Sergeant William J. Russell,

STAR #85, 34 years old, Detective Bureau, was killed on June 12, 1909 at 10:30 P.M. while attempting to apprehend a known criminal in Barney Bertshce's Saloon at 739 W. Randolph Street. Russell and his partner, Detective-Sergeant Thomas Stapleton, observed George Bissett, an ex-convict known as "the Gimlet Burglar," in Bertshce's Saloon and entered the establishment to question him. Bissett did not want to answer the officers' questions and began to back away as they approached.

Bissett had made his way to the saloon that night in search of Bertsche and another man by the name of La Blanche. The shooter believed the men had double-crossed him in a business deal concerning a valueless concession stand at a neighborhood amusement park. Neither of the men were there that evening, but he was unable to exit the saloon before the officers spotted him. Russell confiscated a weapon from Bissett and tense words were exchanged after which Bisseet opened fire with a second gun. Patrolman Russell was hit in the head at pointblank range with the first bullet; he was killed instantly. Bissett continued to fire, striking Russell again and wounding Stapleton who was able to return fire and injure Bissett.

Bissett was able to make his way out of the saloon, but collapsed into the arms of a uniformed policeman outside, Sergeant Kilgore, who promptly arrested him. He hovered between life and death before recovering enough to be tried and sentenced to life in prison on December 31, 1909. However, at retrial on March 21, 1911 he was defended by the celebrated attorney Clarence Darrow and acquitted of all charges. Detective-Sergeant Russell was buried in Mount Carmel Cemetery.

Patrolman Henry Schnable,

STAR #1062, 5th Precinct, 31 years old, lost his life on July 1, 1909 while endeavoring to capture a burglary suspect in a vacant lot at 3436 S. Wabash Avenue under the Southside elevated train tracks close to 34th Street, only one block north of where Chicago Police Department Headquarters stands at 35th Street and Michigan Avenue today. Schnable had encountered the suspect leaving a building in an alley near 33rd Street around 1:50 A.M. He ordered him to halt. The man disregarded the officer's order and began to shoot at him as he attempted to escape. Patrolman Schnable returned fire and it appeared he had hit the offender, Tegee McNeil.

McNeil's injury was later discovered to be part of a ruse to draw the unsuspecting patrolman closer, according to the testimony of another officer who arrived on the scene. This allowed the offender to wound Schnable at close range, guaranteeing the fatality of the shot. A set of burglary tools, including a chisel, dark lantern, screwdriver and large red handkerchief, were later discovered during a search of the alley where a burglary had occurred. McNeil managed to flee but was later caught. An indictment was sought but was rejected by the grand jury. Officer Schnable was laid to rest in Oak Woods Cemetery.

Patrolman John P. Kearney,

STAR # unavailable, died after falling off his horse on July 1, 1909. Officer Kearney had been assigned as protection for a wagon driver who had been threatened by striking union workers. Kearney's horse suddenly bolted when an automobile passed by, throwing the officer to the ground. Patrolman Kearney sustained fatal injuries in the fall and died the next day on July 2, 1909. He was buried at Mount Olivet Cemetery on 111th Street.

Detective John A. Wren,

STAR #3987, 5th Precinct, 38 years old, was shot in the line of duty in the early morning hours of March 4, 1910. Wren approached three suspicious men with his partner, Patrolman Patrick Quinn, around 4:30 A.M. at the corner of Chicago Avenue and Hudson Street. As he attempted to search them, the men drew weapons and proceeded to open fire, wounding both Wren and Quinn. The officers returned fire but were not capable of stopping the men.

Wren was hit twice in the abdomen. Though doctors at Passavant Hospital operated to save his life, there was no chance for recovery. He died on March 5, 1910. Quinn was also wounded by the offenders. He was quoted in the *Chicago Tribune* describing the assailants as "three men, all with overcoats, caps, and black moustaches." However, the dark setting and general confusion at the scene left him unable to offer more exact descriptions, although he did believe he would be able to identify the men if they were brought before him. At one point, three men were held at Shakespeare Avenue Station; Mike Mekevitt, Joe Glumaky and Fred Vogt, all previous offenders. The men had been arrested after a robbery, but denied any knowledge of the shooting. Another offender, Barrato Cornico, was later arrested as a possible suspect. Quinn identified the man, but several of Cornico's friends corroborated his alibi and nothing came of the arrest. Officer Wren, a 12-year-veteran of the Chicago Police Department, was survived by his wife, Margaret, and buried in Calvary Cemetery.

One theory advanced at the time of Wren's death attributed his murder to the "Black Hand" gang, a term given by police for various Mafia affiliated groups responsible for crimes in the Italian neighborhoods of Chicago. The association was never proven, but Wren's death did lead to a resolution to form an Italian Detective Squad, charged with infiltrating and understanding the ways of the Italian community in order to facilitate tighter crime control in the area.

The plan for such a squad had previously run into trouble because the educational requirements of the civil service exam did not allow police management to use the men needed to get the job done. The proposed resolution to this dilemma was the establishment of a special fund that would be utilized to sufficiently educate the men that would comprise the squad. Patrolman Wren's death was believed to be the incident needed to actually make that fund and the Italian Detective Squad a reality.

1910

89th Street Police Station,
15th Precinct (1910).
ICH-i39635, Chicago History Museum.

Detective John Wren's homicide scene,
murdered by the Black Hand.
DN-0056850, *Chicago Daily News*
Collection, Chicago History Museum.

Police arrest cocaine fiends (c.1910).
DN-0006057, *Chicago Daily News*
Collection, Chicago History Museum.

Dome of the old Federal Building (1910).
ICH-i39641, Chicago History Museum.

Patrolman Patrick Melia,

STAR #2243, 20th Precinct, 31 years old, lost his life at 1:00 A.M. on the morning of April 27, 1910 in a Chicago rail yard. Melia was on patrol at the Santa Fe Line, at 48th Street and Lawndale Avenue, when he discovered thieves in the process of robbing a train car. He approached the offenders, one of whom pulled a double-barreled, sawed-off shotgun from underneath his coat and fired at the officer. Patrolman Melia, a two-year-veteran of the force, died within a matter of seconds and his killers escaped. Officer Melia's body was transported to Cincinatti for burial in St. Joseph Cemetery.

Steve Zacek eventually confessed to Melia's murder and implicated three associates as co-conspirators. On May 19, 1920, Zacek hanged himself in his 19th Precinct cell before he could be sentenced for his crime. Two of the men he named, Joseph Priabela and Steve Orth, were detained for their roles in Patrolman Melia's death on May 25, 1910. Priabela received a sentence of 25 years to be served at the Illinois State Penitentiary at Joliet, while Orth was given a life sentence at the same facility. Joseph Flash, the third man named by Zacek, died in Iowa before he could be questioned about his role in the crime.

Patrolman Edward G. Shea,

STAR #3399, 31st Precinct, 55 years old, was killed in the line of duty on August 16, 1910 while guarding the dangerous Austin Boulevard "EL" crossing on the Oak Park Line. He had taken up the post barely two weeks before the accident because the officer who usually worked that patrol was badly injured in a collision with the same train. The train was identified as "dead," meaning it was run each morning with no passengers, and considered by many in the neighborhood to be quite unsafe.

Shea was diligently keeping the tracks clear in a heavily congested area when the train appeared on the eastbound track. Shea stepped to the westbound track to continue directing traffic when the train, running at full speed, jumped to the westbound track with no warning. The quick turn of events left the officer confused and unable to escape the path of the speeding train in time. Despite the confusion, the 18-year-veteran of the force fulfilled his duties in keeping others safe until the very end. His were the only injuries sustained in the accident. When the train struck the patrolman, his weapon discharged and he sustained a bullet wound in the hip in addition to his other injuries. The train dragged the officer more than seventy-five feet. He was dead by the time rescuers reached him. Officer Shea, who made his home at 3011 S. Wallace Street, was survived by his wife and two children, George and Myrtle. His Requiem Mass was celebrated St. Matthew Church. He was laid to rest at Mount Carmel Cemetery.

The tragedy was compounded by the fact that Shea and local residents had often complained about the hazardous crossing, and the dead train in particular. The train ran on the Chicago and Oak Park elevated rail lines but crossed at street level on Austin Avenue, creating a dangerous intersection. Many blamed the rail switching system, and the ability to switch trains at high-speed, for the accident. A resident petition calling for the elevation of the tracks began circulating soon after Shea's death.

Chicago Police Officer Patrick Melia.
Chicago Police Department Photo Archive.

D'Amico Grocery Store located in the "Death Triangle." DN-0056709, *Chicago Daily News* Collection, Chicago History Museum.

"Death Triangle," the center of the Black Hand in Little Sicily located at Cleveland and Oak Streets. DN-0056708, *Chicago Daily News* Collection, Chicago History Museum.

Rear view of the tenements in the Westside Maxwell Street District (c. 1910). ICH-i35464, Chicago History Museum.

Detective Jesse C. Gilman,

Star #3953, 38th Precinct, 56 years old, and his partner Detective William Burns, set out to investigate a complaint filed by a man against his employee on December 23, 1910. The victim asserted that his employee had taken a shot at him the night before near his business on N. Franklin Street. The officers decided to stake out the entrance to the place of employment in the early evening and wait until the man arrived in order to question him. As they waited, they noticed someone lurking in the shadows near where they stood and set out to question him. The suspect, George Carcio, kept his hands in his pockets as he initially spoke with the officer. After an exchange of no more than a few words, the suspect suddenly fired a shot through his coat pocket, fatally wounding Detective Gilman in his left femoral artery.

Gilman immediately fell to the ground bleeding profusely while his partner took off after the suspect. A running gun battle that extended over half a mile ensued, ending with Burns firing a fatal headshot at Carcio near Ontario and Wabash Streets. Ten minutes after the pursuit began Gilman was discovered by fellow officers and rushed to Passavant Hospital, the same facility Carcio was taken to after being wounded. Carcio died shortly after his arrival at the hospital. Gilman succumbed to his injuries the next day at 4:00 P.M. on December 24, leaving behind his wife Florence. He was buried in Mount Olivet Cemetery.

Detective Burns was lauded for his efforts by Assistant Chief Schuettler, whose words appeared in the *Chicago Daily Tribune*,

"I am proud of you, Officer Burns, for your performance this evening...Your example should be one for emulation by other members of the department. This killing was justifiable in every sense, and you did your duty in pursuing and getting this man rather than attending to your wounded brother officer."

Schuettler words seemed designed to address any who might question Burns' choice to pursue the offender rather than attending to his partner. The shootings and subsequent chase took place at the end of the workday in an area crowded with shoppers and workers on their way home. Many on the street only narrowly escaped Gilman and Burns' fate as the bullets flew around them during the chase. A horse fastened to a nearby delivery wagon was not as lucky, dying as a result of a fatal shot received during the on-going gun battle.

Patrolman Thomas E. Tighe,

STAR #2700, 24th Precinct, 34 years old, was patrolling his regular beat on February 10, 1911 when he received a report of a woman who had made a complaint against three men who had insulted her near 13th Place and S. Leavitt Street. When Tighe arrived at the corner, the woman was gone, but there were three men standing there whom Tighe ordered to disperse. One of the men, Michael Bradshaw, took exception to the officer's command and spoke to him offensively.

Tighe placed the abusive offender under arrest and was attempting to lead him to a patrol box in order to contact the station when Bradshaw's two friends intervened, claiming that there were no grounds for arrest. Tighe took a moment to address the men, a moment the suspect took advantage of. Bradshaw was able to break away from the officer's hold and knock him to the ground before fleeing with his friends. Tighe quickly was up on his feet and gave chase. Upon seeing the policeman in pursuit, one of the assailants turned and fired his weapon several times, striking Tighe in the abdomen. Tighe returned fire. A trail of blood ran east down Hastings Street in the direction the men had fled, indicating that the officer may have wounded one of the men.

Tighe, a four-year-veteran of the Chicago Police Department, was taken to Cook County Hospital. There he provided details of the incident before slipping into unconsciousness, unable to identify which man had been the shooter. Patrolman Tighe's injuries finally took his life one month later on March 11, 1910. Four men, Henry Etchingham, Michael Bradshaw, and two others identified only by their last names, Carr and Wayne, were eventually held in connection to the crime. Bradshaw and Etchingham were identified as the possible shooters. Bradshaw, Carr and Wayne were eventually acquitted on all charges. Etchingham was deemed to be the triggerman and received a thirty year sentence that was to be served at the Illinois State Penitentiary at Joliet. Officer Tighe was buried in Mount Carmel Cemetery.

Patrolman Patrick Fogarty,

STAR #1352, 10th Precinct, 40 years old, was off-duty when he was attacked on July 2, 1911 and fatally wounded at 743 W. Pierce Street by his own service revolver while struggling with an offender. Fogarty died only 45 minutes after the 2:15 A.M. shooting at Grace Hospital. He never made an official statement about the incident. However, Sergeant Barren claimed to have spoken with the officer. According to the *Chicago Daily Tribune*, the sergeant claimed that, "Fogarty told me three men had met him in Connelly's Saloon and followed him. He gave me descriptions of his assailants, but became delirious before I could gather the details." The usefulness of this statement to the investigation was not assessed.

A great deal of the details surrounding this incident remained shrouded in mystery since the incident took place outdoors in the early morning hours after a night of drinking. Many of the witnesses who gave statements were inebriated. It appeared that Fogarty had spent the night in the company of his nephew, Michael Hannon, taking in a picture show and visiting several saloons with a small group. He was badly intoxicated when he left his nephew's boarding house and was just outside the front door when he was attacked. Hannon heard the shot and was the first to reach Fogarty's side, only twenty-five feet from the residence. It was a short struggle struggle with the offender.

Hannon's inebriated state left many holes in the account he gave to investigating officers. It led police to offer their own theory about the events that led to Fogarty's death. There was conjecture that the shooting was an act of revenge by a man Fogarty had arrested, although one newspaper believed the distance between the location of the shooting and where Fogarty had his beat made that proposition flawed. Nonetheless, there was a statement given by Bernard Friedman, of 731 W. Pierce Street, a witness to the shooting, which alleged that:

"I heard one of Fogarty's assailants say 'You are the fellow who tried to arrest us.' Two men rushed upon the policeman. The first man struck him on the jaw, knocking him against the railing guarding the stairway. Then the other fellow struck Fogarty and knocked him to the walk. Fogerty (sic) tried to reach for his pistol, but the first thug was too quick for the officer and shot him. Then they ran. It was over in a minute. I believe I will able to identify the men."

John Gay was arrested on suspicion of being involved in Fogarty's murder on July 14, 1911 and confessed to the crime the same day. Another suspect, Paddy Ryan, was also wanted by the coroner for questioning about his role in the shooting but he was never found. Gay was sentenced to the Illinois State Penitentiary at Joliet on the charge of manslaughter on January 13, 1912. Officer Fogarty was laid to rest in Mount Olivet Cemetery. He was a five-year-veteran of the force and was survived by his wife, Hanna.

Patrolman Thomas Schweig,

STAR #3427, 32nd Precinct, 34 years old, was on duty at 1639 W. Ohio Street shortly after 2:00 A.M. on July 15, 1911 when he was fatally shot by three unknown assailants who escaped without detection. The officer was scheduled to start his furlough later that day and was fatally shot not far from his own home at 561 N. Ashland Avenue. One theory placed the blame for the shooting on highwaymen, heartless criminals who had fired bullets through the officer's head and heart without leaving behind a single clue.

A citizen stumbled upon the fallen officer and immediately notified the local precinct. The officer's weapon was found clutched in his hand, but it was still fully loaded, indicating he had been unable to return fire. Inspector Healy was tapped to head the investigation into Schweig's murder and confirmed both the shortage of clues and the officer's excellent reputation. Officer Schweig's interment took place in Mount Olivet Cemetery.

Patrolman Charles T. Jones,

Star #3594, 33rd Precinct, Rawson Street Station, 53 years old, was patrolling in plain clothes on November 10, 1912 with his partner, Patrolman Charles Gierman, when they came upon a group of about twenty men loitering on the corner of Bloomingdale and Honore Streets. When the youths spotted the officers they scattered in all directions and fled. One group of about five made their way down the alley to 1733 N. Honore Street and locked themselves in a shed located there.

The officers took hold of a nearby fence rail and used it to break down the barricaded door. Once the officers had entered, the five assailants attacked them, seizing their revolvers. The offenders immediately began using the officers' own weapons to start shooting at them in a one-sided gun battle. The defenseless officers had no recourse. Patrolman Jones fell to the ground bleeding profusely from five different bullet wounds. He died of internal hemorrhaging en route to St. Elizabeth Hospital. Gierman was not hit by the barrage of bullets, but was so badly beaten that he could not pursue the offenders, all of whom escaped before he was able to get to his feet.

Growing crime in the area comprising Bloomingdale, Honore, Blackhawk and Noble Streets, plus the addition of yet another police death, led to the spread of a dragnet through the area. Twenty-five detectives were dispatched with a directive that ordered them to round up any suspects who might possibly be involved in Jones' slaying. Within hours, the lockup was full. Many suspects were held for examination.

Although Patrolman Gierman asserted that he might be able to identify at least one of the assailants, no one was ever convicted. However, two men, were later arrested, Arthur Reich for murder and Edward "Bottles" Rahn as an accessory. Both were acquitted at trial. Reputed to be members of one of the numerous gangs recently infesting the city, especially Chicago's Westside, they stirred up a great deal of notoriety for themselves.

Four members of a similar gang had recently been hanged for their role in the murder of Fred Guezlow, a local truck gardener. Prior to Officer Jones' death a group of young men also brutally attacked and slashed Patrolmen Julius Bender and Edward Sullivan. Gangs were becoming infamous for a rash of assaults that had been sweeping the area when the attacks on police began. Police once busy protecting ordinary citizens now found it necessary to protect themselves. Officer Jones was buried in Forest Home Cemetery.

1912

Patrolman Peter M. Hart,

STAR #1224, 10th Precinct, 32 years old, was sent to a residence at 1617 S. Wabash Avenue on January 20, 1913 that police believed belonged to known gang member Robert Webb. Webb was the chauffeur for the Perry Auto Gang, the city's first automobile bandit gang, and had been in police custody three times in the previous eleven days. Hart was dispatched to wait in Webb's apartment and arrest him when he returned home. The officer did manage to surprise Webb when he came through the door, but a struggle ensued and moments later Hart was shot and killed by a bullet from his own gun. Hart was later buried in Mount Olivet Cemetery.

Webb fled from the fallen policeman and managed to make his escape, taking the building stairs to the roof, then slipping back inside through a skylight and accessing the back porch stairs which led him to the street. The only clue he left behind was a set of footprints in the snow that allowed the police to speculatively retrace his steps.

Information on Webb's possible whereabouts was provided by James A. Perry, a member of the same auto bandit gang. He was known to be a close associate of the killers. Webb, Perry, and Frank McErane had orchestrated a three month city-wide crime spree that culminated in Officer Hart's shooting inside Webb's apartment. The three men developed a pattern of stealing a different car every three or four days. They made themselves into a regular neighborhood nuisance well known at the local precinct. In one particular act of bravado, the three actually shot at police during a getaway from a jewelry store robbery, just to ensure there was no doubt to whom credit for the crime belonged. An example of their brutality was demonstrated several days later when they shot and stabbed another policeman, Fred Sticken, who had pulled them over to inform them they had a broken taillight. Officer Sticken survived and his attack led to renewed efforts by the police to bring the bandits into custody.

These determined efforts soon led to Perry's arrest and a twenty-page confession that included the home addresses of his conspirators. After Hart's ill-fated journey to Webb's residence, police brass promised Webb's immediate capture. It would be three weeks before Webb was apprehended on February 13, 1913 and later convicted of Officer Hart's murder. He was sentenced to life in the Illinois State Penitentiary at Joliet on July 31, 1913, but his story was not yet over. Webb escaped from the prison farm on July 16, 1925 and quickly returned to his familiar, criminal ways. He was arrested again at 43rd Street and Cottage Grove Avenue on September 4, 1925, where a large amount of cash, probably acquired in hold-ups, was found in his possession. He was returned to the Illinois State Penitentiary at Joliet.

Patrolman Andrew Gartley,

STAR #4133, 44th Precinct, 38 years old, was fatally assaulted on May 30, 1914 when he attempted to end a barroom brawl. Gartley, who lived at 820 W. Lill Avenue, was on patrol when he entered a tavern at 2581 N. Lincoln where he planned to cash his paycheck. As he waited, a fight broke out behind him between five patrons. The officer attempted to intervene, an effort not appreciated by any of the combatants, who all turned on him. Patrolman Gartley was severely beaten. Once rescued, he was taken to Alexian Brothers Hospital but never woke. Gartley died on June 1, 1914. His injuries included a broken jaw and severe internal bleeding caused by many blows and kicks that rendered him unconscious. Three men, Daniel McNamara, David Kerr, and James Shearin, were detained in connection with Gartley's death, but they were all released on October 28, 1914 and the crime was never solved. Officer Gartley was laid to rest at Montrose Cemetery.

Detective-Sergeant Stanley J. Birns,

STAR #322, 35 years old, Detective Division, was killed on July 16, 1914 in a tragic case of miscommunication and false identification. Detective Birns was assigned to a team of officers performed raids in the Vice District under the command of First Deputy Superintendent of Police M.C. Funkhouser. Unbeknownst to these officers, Chief Morals Inspector Dannenberg had assembled his own squad to carry out similar raids that evening as well. Dannenberg's men were originally supposed to carry out raids on the Northside but ended up on 22nd Street sometime around 9:00 P.M.

Dannenberg's men initially raided a notorious hot spot known as "The Turf" where they discovered four prostitutes openly soliciting business. The officers summoned the Clark Street Wagon to pick-up the four women and one man they arrested. They then headed east to meet Dannenberg on Michigan Avenue. As they walked, the officers were followed by a group of "macques," neighborhood regulars who followed members of the vice squad and attempted to deny them the element of surprise on their raids by being loud and drawing attention to them.

Four of the Inspector's men, Police Officers Fred Amart and Joseph Merrill, Railway Fireman James Carroll and Investigator Johnson, had just reached the stairway to Swann's Poolroom on 22nd Street when they first crossed paths with Funkhouser's men at approximately 9:35 P.M. Chaos reigned a moment later as gunfire erupted and pedestrians scrambled to escape the bullets exchanged by the two groups. The sound of revolvers and automatics split the air. The sound of gunfire brought policemen pouring in from all directions, from the vice squads as well as the men from the 22nd Street Station and Bill Schubert's gambling crew.

After the wounded and dead were identified and transported to the hospital or the morgue, Detective Johnson was taken into custody at the 22nd Street Station and accused of firing the shot that killed Birns. Detective Amart accompanied Johnson. Both men were questioned at various times by Funkhouser, Chief Gleason and Captain Ryan, all ranking members of police leadership. All of the officers involved were exonerated at the conclusion of questioning.

Birns was a three-year-veteran of the Detective Squad who had been promoted only two years after joining the force. Originally a laborer, Detective Birns was an excellent investigator by all accounts and had recently solved a case that involved recovering a railcar full of stolen horses in Kansas. He had been planning how to spend the reward money received from that case when he was killed. Birns was buried at St. Adalbert Cemetery.

1914

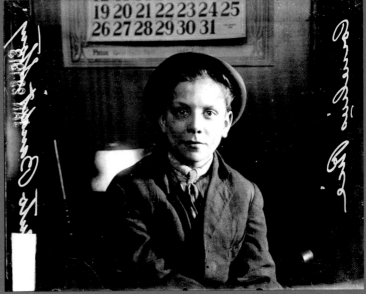

Robert Webb, murderer and auto thief,
killed Patrolman Peter Hart (1913).
DN-006291, *Chicago Daily News* Collection,
Chicago History Museum.

James A. Perry, leader of the infamous
Perry Auto Gang (1913).
DN-0060122, *Chicago Daily News* Collection,
Chicago History Museum.

Cornelius Rice, an adolescent member
of the Perry Auto Gang (1913).
DN-0060168, *Chicago Daily News* Collection,
Chicago History Museum.

Mrs Agnes Walsh.

First Chicago female Police Officers
Clara B. Olsen, Mabel Rockwell, Lulu Burt,
Anna Sheridan, Theresa Johnson, Anna Loucks,
Agnes Walsh (1914). DN-0062443,
Chicago Daily News Collection, Chicago
History Museum.

Patrolman John Rowe,

STAR #3045, 28th Precinct, 53 years old, was the second man murdered by a group of armed robbers on August 16, 1914. Three young men, Michael Geary, Arthur McNally, and William Dohney, 22, 17 and 16 respectively, had spent the night of August 16 robbing elevated train stations. Three branches of the Garfield Park "El" had already been robbed when the bandits made their way to the Damen Avenue Station where the ticket agent, John W. Stevens, a Civil War veteran, had received a report of the earlier robberies stating that one agent had already been shot in the leg. He resisted the men when confronted. They fatally shot him. Officer Rowe ran into the suspects as they exited the Damen Avenue Station after shooting Stevens. Rowe realized that these were the bandits who had been causing such havoc. He attempted to detain Geary, who then shot him.

The offenders then fled down an alley where they encountered Patrolman Nels Larsen, who had been drawn to the area by the sound of the shot that had killed Rowe. Larsen chased the killers, firing his gun as he ran, wounding Geary, who went down. McNally tripped over Geary and fell, forcing him to surrender to the policeman. Dohney continued down the alley where he was spotted by Detective Sergeant Thomas Comerford, who had been patrolling the area and heard the shots fired by Officer Larsen. Comerford chased Doheny, but when it was obvious the man had escaped, he returned to the area where the shots had originated to investigate further. There he discovered the body of Patrolman Rowe. Rowe was transported to the Cook County Hospital, but died before receiving medical attention. He was buried at Forest Home Cemetery.

Less than $50 was stolen on that August evening that cost the lives of two men who dedicated their lives in service to their country. The events guaranteed three young men prison sentences that would deny them years of freedom. Doheny was caught three days later and on October 31, 1914, he and McNally were sentenced to Pontiac Reformatory, due to their young age, to serve a sentence that ran concurrent with the one they received for the Stevens murder. Geary was held as the leader of the crew and he received a life sentence at the Illinois State Penitentiary at Joliet on October 30, 1914. It also was to be served concurrent with his sentence in the Stevens case. Escaping from Joliet in 1920, he could not resist a return to his life of crime. He was soon arrested again and returned to prison for his part in a bank heist.

Patrolman George H. Trumbull,

STAR #899, 4th Precinct, 37 years old, was shot and killed while attempting to arrest an offender who had assaulted two men on State Street near 26th Street on August 17, 1914. The killer, Simon Hogan, had been visiting at a private home earlier in the day when he began an argument with the lady of the house. Other residents were trying to throw Hogan out when he pulled a revolver and started beating two of them with it. During the fight, a woman ran into the street to call for help and drew the attention of Policemen George Trumbull, Lewis Hall and Lewis Schroeder, all walking nearby. The three men followed her to the home and arrived just as Hogan exited the front door.

Officer Trumbull spotted the gun and made a lunge for Hogan. The assailant immediately opened fire with five shots aimed at the officer. One of the bullets found its mark, causing Trumbull to fall to the ground as a bullet lodged right below his heart. Hall and Schroeder drew their weapons and set off in pursuit of Hogan, firing as they ran. Hogan managed to evade them, although his luck seemed to change moments later.

As Hogan was fleeing Hall and Schroeder's bullets, he ran into two other patrolmen who detained him, questioning what he was running from. Hogan, telling the officers the truth, said that there had been a shooting on 26th Street and he was running to escape harm. The patrolmen released Hogan and went off in the direction he had pointed out to search for the gunman. Moments later they ran into Hall and Schroeder who asked which way a man matching Hogan's description had gone. Realizing their mistake, the patrolmen joined Hall and Schroeder in their search for Hogan but they were unable to locate him.

The patrolmen's mistake may not have been the only police error that night. Many witness accounts claimed that Hall and Schroeder did not immediately come to Trumbull's aid after the first shot was fired. These reports stated that Trumbull's associates ducked into a doorway as the bullets whizzed past and only emerged when Hogan had finished shooting. Only once the offender had fled to the end of the street did they come out and begin their pursuit, according to these witnesses. Hogan may have been able to evade the police that day, but his luck did not last. He was eventually convicted of Patrolman Trumbull's murder and sentenced to life in the Illinois State Penitentiary at Joliet on November 27, 1914. Trumbull was buried at Oak Woods Cemetery.

Detective-Sergeant John J. Prendergast,

STAR #375, 35th Precinct, 38 years old, was heroic to the very end, saving a life on August 30, 1914 even while he sustained injuries that ended his own. Pendergast and an offender that he was escorting to the station were standing at the intersection of Pulaski and Milwaukee Avenues waiting for a streetcar when a speeding vehicle came bearing down on them. The automobile contained five men who appeared to be drunk, unaware of the pedestrians in front of them. Detective Pendergast shouted a warning to the other citizens on the corner and made sure his offender was pulled to safety but could not get himself out of the way in time. The officer died almost instantly after impact with the car which was estimated to be traveling at 50 MPH.

The driver of the car never slowed and witnesses were unable to discern a license plate. However, two arrests were eventually made in the case. On September 12, 1914 George Teleff and Frederick Bartells were held on charges of manslaughter concerning the death of Pendergast. The October Grand Jury returned a "No Bill" for Bartells and sent Teleff on to trial. He was acquitted on all charges on January 23, 1915. Prendergast was buried at St. James at the Sag Cemetery.

Detective-Sergeant Frank Dealy,

STAR #539, 32nd Precinct, 48 years old, fell in the line of duty as he patrolled his regular beat on October 5, 1914. Dealy observed two suspicious men on the corner of Halsted Street and Grand Avenue and decided to approach to inquire about their business. It was a decision that proved fatal when the two men drew revolvers and began to shoot as the officer drew near. The assailants fled, chased by patrons from nearby restaurants and saloons who had been drawn outside by the sound of the gunshots. The shooters eventually escaped their pursuers by weaving between railroad freight cars and creating a trail that could not be followed. Meanwhile, Dealy was transported to St. Elizabeth Hospital by concerned citizens. He died there four hours later in the company of his wife and children. He was laid to rest in Mount Carmel Cemetery.

Dealy did not usually travel his patrol alone, but he set out by himself that night while his partner sat at the front desk of the station for the regular desk sergeant who was ill. His partner, Christopher Hughes, had just been relieved and was on his way to meet Dealy when the call reporting the shooting came into the station. The search for the killers started almost

Simon Hogan convicted killer of
Patrolman George Trumbell (1914).
DN-0063348, *Chicago Daily News* Collection,
Chicago History Museum.

immediately and eight suspects were arrested, including the man Dealy had initially identified as the shooter, Chris Maratio. Dealy was at first able to give an account of the shooting but questioned his memory right before he lapsed into unconsciousness. He never woke again and could offer no further elaboration. Two men, Joseph Colucci and John "Schultz" Sulinsky, were eventually brought before the November Grand Jury on charges related to Dealy's death but a "No Bill" was returned for both men.

Patrolman William J. Rosenstreter,

STAR #3980, 38th Precinct, Chicago Avenue Station, 28 years old, was investigating a disturbance at a saloon on the northwest corner of Illinois and State Streets when he was fatally shot by Charles Williams on Friday, November 6, 1914. Williams was with a group who had spent the day drinking at Brothers' Saloon. As he and his friends left, Williams turned and shattered the front window of the establishment, an act witnessed by Rosenstreter and another officer, Edward Baynes.

After seeing this act of vandalism, Rosenstreter approached Williams and attempted to place him under arrest. Instead of cooperating, the vandal removed a revolver from his pocket, placed it against the Patrolman Rosenstreter's neck and fired once. Baynes immediately wrestled the revolver from Williams and called an ambulance for his fallen partner, but it was too late. Patrolman Rosenstreter died four hours later at Passavant Hospital. He had been a member of the police force for less than a year. He was buried in Eden Cemetery on Irving Park Road in suburban Schiller Park.

Williams was arrested and confessed to the shooting on November 7, 1914, but would provide no motive. In addition, two accomplices, Edward Carey and Mrs. Bessie Fallon, were held. On September 15, 1915, Williams was acquitted.

Patrolman Austin L. Fitch,

STAR # unavailable, Englewood Station, was a 27 years old, motorcycle policeman whose motorcycle overturned after striking a pedestrian, Henry Horner, of 2045 S. Michigan Avenue, on November 16, 1914. Officer Fitch was thrown from the motorcycle and sustained severe internal injuries due to the violence of the accident. He died at Mercy Hospital on November 24, 1914 at noon from the fatal skull fracture he received the previous week. Horner broke his collar bone and lacerated his scalp, but survived the accident. The grandson and name sake of a very successful early Chicago Jewish grocery merchant, Horner would go on to a distinguished career in politics, serving as the Governor of Illinois from 1933 until his death in 1940. Officer Fitch, the son of Austin J. and Frances Fitch, lived at 6035 S. Honore Street. He was buried in Mount Greenwood Cemetery.

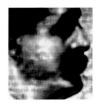

Patrolman John B. Sausman,

STAR #953, 4th Precinct, 54 years old, was patrolling with his partner, Dan Langan, on January 5, 1915 when they stumbled upon a robbery in progress at the corner of 29th Street and Indiana Avenue. The officers observed two men, William F. "Bob" Mason and James O'Neil, holding up a pedestrian. They rushed to the victim's aid. The two men worked as a team and during the commission of this particular crime Mason was going through the victim's pockets while O'Neil held the gun that kept the terrified citizen still.

Sausman and Langan cautiously approached the offenders and placed them under arrest, unaware that Mason was also carrying a weapon concealed in his coat pocket. He fired a single bullet from the revolver and struck Sausman in the temple. The officer fell to the ground fatally wounded. Mason and O'Neil immediately fled, and Langan went in pursuit of O'Neil, apparently unaware that Mason had been the one to fire the fatal shot. Lagan shot at O'Neil as he ran and dodged return fire from the assailant. Neither man would admit defeat and both even stopped to reload at one point during the chase. The gun battle finally ended when Langan managed to wound O'Neill in the lung and abdomen. Mason escaped and an order for his apprehension was issued the next day. It was not known if he was ever caught. Officer Sausman was laid to rest in Forest Home Cemetery, on DesPlaines Avenue in suburban Forest Park.

Patrolman Thomas Colquit,

STAR #108, Lincoln Park Police, was on patrol in Lincoln Park on February 10, 1915 near the Ulysses S. Grant monument when he was struck and killed by a car carrying Illinois Congressman George E. Gorman. The Congressman was on his way to a political meeting when his vehicle hit Patrolman Colquit. All accounts claim the car was not speeding or being driven erratically. The vehicle immediately stopped and came to the officer's aid by transporting him to Columbus Memorial Hospital. Colquit, a 17-year-veteran of the police force with seven children, died several hours later. He was interred in Calvary Cemetery, Evanston.

Patrolman James F. Mitchell,

STAR #2949, 11th Precinct, 15th Street Station, 26 years old, spotted a group of men, Alfred Holland, James Hamilton, John Welch, James Kneeley and Daniel Holland, loitering at 49th and Federal Streets on November 15, 1915. He decided to question them and upon doing so felt compelled to search them for weapons. As he began his check of each man, Alfred Holland turned and fled. The policeman commanded him to stop just as Holland drew a weapon and fired, striking the officer. Mitchell, who had joined the force only one month prior after years as a salesman, was transported unconscious to Washington Park Hospital where he died several hours later. He was later laid to rest in historic Mount Olivet Cemetery on 111th Street.

Mitchell's partner, Patrolman John C. Burke, who would soon meet the same unfortunate fate, immediately gave chase as the remaining men scattered. Burke apparently made the choice to pursue Hamilton as he fled from the Holland home at 4940 S. Federal Street because a bullet from his gun was found in Hamilton's leg when he was arrested. All five men, including Daniel Holland, Alfred Holland's son, were eventually detained and held for questioning. On July 8, 1916, Holland was convicted of manslaughter and sentenced to the Illinois State Penitentiary at Joliet.

Patrolman Ludwig Rudolph Skala,

STAR #11, West Park Police, lost his life in a motorcycle accident on November 21, 1915. Skala had just reached the intersection of Jackson Boulevard and Ashland Avenue when his motorcycle engine failed, causing the machine to stop dead. The loss of movement hurled Skala over the motorcycle's handlebars to the ground. Upon impact he fractured his skull. Though he was immediately taken to Cook County Hospital, he died shortly after arrival. He was buried in St. Adalbert, the famed Northside Polish Cemetery on Milwaukee Avenue.

Patrolman John C. Burke,

STAR #1287, 11th Precinct, 15th Street Station, 29 years old, met the same fate as his partner, Patrolman James F. Mitchell, when he was killed on December 16, 1915. Burke was on patrol when he spotted a man wanted for questioning in multiple delivery truck hold ups. The offender saw Burke crossing 57th Street and fired three shots at him. The fatal bullet hit Burke in the chest right above his police star and he died instantly. Earlier that morning, according to the *Chicago Daily Tribune*, Burke had told his wife, "Don't wait for dinner for me, Rose. I'm going to get that red pepper robber and I'll be late," a testament to the officer's ambition and dedication.

The assailant, who had been frightening neighborhoods on the north and south sides for months, finished firing and disappeared into the alley. He was never seen by law enforcement again. Officers had been told to be on the lookout for the bandit when a 19-year-old delivery boy, Herbert Gergston, told an associate, George Dykema, that he had been robbed of $1.40 moments before. Dykema relayed the report to Burke and described the robber. Looking for a five foot ten inch tall, well-dressed man with a round face and a dark fedora, Burke took off in the direction the witness said the robber had gone. He noticed a man matching that description as he started up the alley near Prairie Avenue. His decision to investigate further led to his tragic death.

It was originally believed that Fred Logue, the alleged "Red Pepper" bandit, was the one who killed Patrolman Burke. But when Logue was found and arrested, he admitted to every accusation expect the murder of Patrolman Burke. Finally, a man by the name of William J. Lyle was arrested in Nashville, Tennessee. A warrant for his arrest noted Lyle had used the same tactics used by the "Red Pepper" bandit. Three delivery boys, victims of the highwayman, were able to identify Lyle as Burke's killer. Burke had been married for only two months when he was killed. He was laid to rest in Mount Olivet Cemetery.

General U.S. Grant memorial in Lincoln Park,
site of Patrolman Thomas Colquit's death.
(1905, ©CHM). Chicago History Museum.

Crowds in the Loop on State Street awaiting
news of the Eastland Disaster (1915).
DN-0064584, *Chicago Daily News* Collection,
Chicago History Museum.

Chicago Police Officers restrain growing
crowd awaiting news of the Eastland Disaster.
DN-006498, *Chicago Daily News* Collection,
Chicago History Museum.

Patrolman Bror A. Johnson,

STAR #242, Traffic Division, was directing traffic on January 21, 1916 when a distraught citizen told him of a robbery in progress. Johnson left his post and headed to Thomas Cook & Son Steamship Agency at 15 E. Jackson Boulevard. He had just reached the business when one of the robbers emerged. Upon seeing the policeman waiting for him, the assailant fired twice, fatally wounding Johnson. He was immediately transported to St. Luke Hospital but died en route. He was later interred in Calvary Cemetery, Evanston.

Thomas Cook & Son was located in a heavily congested area full of shoppers and end of the day workers who scrambled for cover at the sound of gunfire. Bullets flew inside as well, striking cashier E. L. Walsh in the chest. After shooting the policeman and clearing their getaway route, the bandits exited the business and made their way to a black automobile. Police quickly converged on the scene at the sound of the shots and some arrived in time to pursue the robbers, who abandoned the black car at the corner of Wabash Avenue and Jackson Boulevard. They proceeded on foot, escaped into the city and were never apprehended. Patrolman Johnson spent his last few moments surrounded by concerned citizens who waited with him as the ambulance arrived. The robbers made off with $900 of Cook & Son's money.

Patrolman Stuart N. Dean,

STAR #72, 29th Precinct, Warren Avenue Station, 60 years old, had his life taken on July 18, 1916 by a crazed gunman who had already killed three people. Dean was part of the first wave of officers who attempted to enter a barricaded home at 320 N. Claremont Avenue where Henry McIntyre, and his wife, had holed up after his murderous rampage. Police approached the residence under intense fire as the McIntyres kept up a constant barrage of bullets from the front window. Deciding that rear entry would be more advantageous, the original squad of officers kicked down the back door and entered.

The kitchen was empty, as was the hallway where they battered down another door. Tragically, McIntyre lay waiting on the other side and shot Patrolman Dean through the heart as soon as the door was down. As police tended to their wounded friend, the McIntyres pushed the broken door back into place and fortified it with various pieces of furniture. A bureau and several chairs provided a prime vantage point from which the offenders continued their assault on police while providing coverage that kept officers inside from having a clear shot. According to the *Chicago Daily News*, Captain Wesley H. Westbrook ordered police to stand down saying, "One is enough. Take it easy," a testament to his respect for the lives of his men at a time when death by gunfire was all too common.

Police did not retreat completely. Instead they joined the multitude of other policemen who now ringed the residence waiting for McIntyre to show his face. After what seemed like an endless period of time with no McIntyre sighting, Captain Westbrook decided that McIntyre would need to be forced out. He set off three rounds of dynamite near the entrance of the house as a diversionary tactic. As confusion reigned, a team of police raced inside. The scene they came upon was gruesome. Mrs. McIntyre's body lay just outside the barricaded door, riddled with bullets which had blown away part of her skull. Henry McIntyre was still on his feet but extremely dazed and confused by the police presence. Still, he attempted to raise his weapon and take aim at police. They did not allow him a single shot before firing on him, fatally wounding him. He died a short time later at Park Avenue Hospital. Patrolman Stuart N. Dean was later interred in Arlington Cemetery in Elmhurst. He was a longtime veteran of the force.

Detective-Sergeant John J. Bialk,

STAR #474, 40th Precinct, North Halsted Street Station, was shot on September 21, 1916 while trying to arrest a boarder who had shot his landlady, Mrs. Nellie M. Acker. Charles M. Depew was living in the residence at 1925 N. Park Avenue when police were dispatched to investigate reports of his threatening behavior. Earlier in the day, Mrs. Acker had given a statement at the North Halsted Street Station claiming that DePew had chased her out of her home the day before. The statement also contended that DePew had threatened to kill her and other boarders, putting Mrs. Acker in mortal fear for her life. She had been driven from her home with nothing but the clothes she was wearing. She requested a police escort to enter her home with her and throw DePew out. She was told to return home and wait for an officer who would meet her there shortly.

Sergeant Bialk was dispatched to the Acker home a short time later where he confronted the boarder. DePew responded by shooting Mrs. Acker, causing a fatal wound. When Bialk attempted to disarm him, Depew shot the officer in the stomach, mortally wounding him as well. Thirty minutes after Bialk had left his station, a call was received there reporting the shootings and describing a crazed DePew, running around the home waving his gun at other residents. Additional officers were dispatched to the scene where DePew surrendered without a fight.

The officers did not question DePew immediately but instead took him directly to Alexian Brothers Hospital where Bialk had been transported. They feared that the seriousness of Sergeant Bialk's condition would deny them an identification of the shooter if they delayed. Officer Bialk lost his life on September 24, 1916 and was interred in St. Adalbert Cemetery on the city's Northwest side. DePew was held by the coroner for the murder of Bialk eight days later on September 29, 1916, but was later acquitted of all charges on January 9, 1917.

Patrolman John F. Maher,

STAR #215, South Park Police, became another casualty attributed to the modern technology of motorized vehicles on October 7, 1916. Maher, a 15-year-veteran of the police jurisdiction responsible for the maze of thorough fares in the city's Southside parks and assigned to enforce traffic rules and regulations, was on motorcycle patrol on October 6 when he attempted to pull over a speeding vehicle. The vehicle ignored the officer and continued at a reckless speed. Maher set off in swift pursuit and reached a speed of between 40 and 50 MPH when he collided with an auto at the intersection of 37th Street and Michigan Avenue.

Patrolman Maher was thrown to the ground and suffered fatal internal injuries. The driver of the automobile, Mrs. Modie J. Spiegelman, wife of the treasurer of Spiegel Home Furnishing Company, was uninjured but her car suffered damage. Maher's motorcycle was almost completely wrecked. The crash occurred at 5:30 P.M. during a period of heavy congestion leaving many pedestrians and motorist as witnesses to the accident. Despite these many bystanders, the driver of the speeding car was never brought to justice. After the crash Maher was taken to Mercy Hospital where he died early the next morning. He was laid to rest in Mount Olivet Cemetery on 111th Street.

Patrolman John F. Kenny,

STAR # unavailable, Motorcycle Division, was on routine patrol on November 11, 1916 when his motorcycle was struck by a Borden Dairy delivery truck. Kenny, who resided at 4054 W. Fifth Avenue, suffered severe injuries that led to the amputation of his right leg shortly after the accident. He died twelve days later, on November 23, 1916, at Washington Park Hospital. Officer Kenny left a wife, Hannah Ford Kenny, along with four sons and a daughter. He was buried at Mount Carmel Cemetery.

Captain Wesley Westbrook and Chief Charles Healy at the scene of Patrolman Stuart Dean's murder (1916). DN-0066867, *Chicago Daily News* Collection, Chicago History Museum.

Chicago Police at the McIntyre House where Patrolman Stuart Dead was murdered (1916). DN-0066868, Chicago Daily News Collection, Chicago History Museum.

Patrolman Bruno H. Frederick,

STAR #4813, 1st District, West Chicago Avenue Station, lost his life during a period of high crime in Chicago when policemen were told by their superior officers to shoot first and think later, according to the *Chicago Daily News*. Frederick was shot in a dance hall full of unsavory characters on November 30, 1916. He was attempting to shut down a nightlife spot at Morgan Street and Grand Avenue. While trying to arrest Alex Maggio, Frederick was set upon by an angry mob. The officer was beaten and then shot five times. He died the next day as a result of his injuries. Frederick was buried in German Waldheim/Forest Home Cemetery in suburban Forest Park. On December 14, 1916, Joseph Bousk and Daniel Matteo were held for their roles in the officer's death. Bousk was sentenced to 14 years in prison at the Illinois State Penitentiary at Joliet. All others arrested in relation to the incident were acquitted.

Frederick's death, coupled with the shooting of Patrolman Miles F. Brown of the 50th Street Station, led to the intensified use of teams of officers known as "flying squadrons," who spent the Thanksgiving weekend of 1916 rounding up over 250 suspects believed to be involved in various crimes. Burglars, pick-pockets and thieves were all locked in police cells for the weekend after officers confiscated the weapons that were found on the majority of them. The "flying squadrons" were a fairly new development that Acting Chief Schutter believed could do a great deal of good in combating the city's crime problem. He told the *Chicago Daily News* that the Chicago Police could clean up crime, "If the courts will give them a lift in disposing of the cases taken before them." It is unknown whether his veiled reference to growing suspicions of judicial corruption and repeated incompetence within the justice system during this era was ever heeded or acted upon.

Patrolman Edward J. Mulvihill,

STAR #2432, 21st Precinct, Maxwell Street Station, 39 years old, was killed on December 18, 1916 by Louis "Deliciacano" Doveno. The suspect escaped the scene of the officer's death, at 1041 W. Vernon Park Place, and was never arrested or charged. Mulvihill left behind a wife and two young sons, Jeremiah and Edward, Jr., who honored their father's wish that they serve as Christmas morning acolytes at St. Finbarr Roman Catholic Church only four days after his funeral mass was offered there.

Mulvihill had apparently made the mistake of intervening in a dispute between Doveno and Florence Ward, a woman Doveno wished to marry but who did not share his interest in the idea. Miss Ward and her mother had made an arrest appeal regarding Doveno because he had threatened to kill or maim the girl with acid if she refused his proposal of marriage. Mulvihill located Doveno and attempted to execute the arrest warrant, but Doveno fled when he saw the officer approach. Mulvihill pursued him until Doveno turned and fired at him, striking the officer and causing him to fall. Once Doveno saw that Mulvihill was gravely wounded, he returned to where the officer lay and delivered the fatal shot.

Three suspects were arrested near the site of the shooting by Detective-Sergeants Yancey and Fleming, who had been nearby when the shooting occurred. Four other suspects eventually joined them. All seven swore they knew nothing about the shooting or Doveno's whereabouts. It was believed he may have been hiding in the Italian District with friends or relatives, but no one was saying if they knew. Eventually all seven suspects were released and the officer's murder was stricken from court records on November 13, 1919 without any charges or convictions in the case. Following his Requiem Mass at St. Finbarr, Officer Mulvihill was buried in Mount Carmel Cemetery in suburban Hillside.

Patrolman John L. Donner,

STAR #125, Lincoln Park Police, 46 years old, was trying to apprehend a speeding motorist in Lincoln Park on May 7, 1917 when he collided with a vehicle at Sunnyside Avenue and Sheridan Road. The officer, who was going about 60 MPH, had no time to break or swerve. He was killed instantly upon impact. Donner, who lived at 2661 N. Marshfield Avenue, had been patrolling on Sheridan Road when he saw a car speeding in the southbound lanes. He pursued the vehicle, but soon found his path blocked by a bus also traveling south. He moved into the northbound lanes in an attempt to overtake the bus and crashed head on into a car driven by George E. Orr, a general manager for the National Security Company. Orr's car, which was traveling at normal speed, had been hidden from Donner's view by the bus. The officer was thrown from the seat of his motorcycle and flew through the air before crashing into Orr's vehicle and fracturing his skull. Officer Donner, an eight-year-veteran of the force, left behind a wife and son. He was buried in St. Lucas Cemetery on North Pulaski Road. His funeral was attended by officers from the South and West Park forces, as well as men from his own department.

Patrolman Charles "C.P." Larson,

STAR #4830, 33rd Precinct, 29 years old, had been a police officer for 18 months when he came upon two offenders attempting to break into the Star Theater at 1447 N. Milwaukee Avenue in the early hours of May 11, 1917. Larson noticed the two men in the basement stairwell at the theater, made his way down the stairs, told them to move away from the door and attempted to question the men. One of the two offenders, possibly a participant in the "film operators" war, took a shot at the officer. The assailant's aim was off in the dimly lit stairwell and he managed to only wound the officer in the arm, providing enough time for he and his companion to dash past Larson and up the stairs to the street.

Larson recovered enough to follow the men and draw his service revolver. He fired on the two fleeing suspects, wounding one, but they returned fire and struck the officer again three times, including a fatal shot that penetrated his lung. By now, the chase had led the men to Wood Street and North Avenue, where the fatal bullet felled Larson. He was discovered by other patrolmen who had responded to the call of shots fired. Larson was taken to St. Elizabeth Hospital, where he died two days later on May 13, 1917. Before his death, a suspect, Edward Schieve, was brought to the hospital and Larson identified him as one of the shooters.

Schieve proclaimed his innocence, admitting that he had been at the Star Theater that night but denying that he was the shooter. He had offered to provide the police with the name of the shooter but no records exist of arrests being made in the case. It is unclear whether anyone was ever brought to justice for Patrolman Larson's sacrifice. He was laid to rest in Mount Olive Cemetery on West Dakin Street.

1917

Chicago Police Department wagon, (1915-1917).
ICH-i24075, Chicago History Museum.

Patrolman Peter R. Bulfin,

STAR #1746, 17th Precinct, 42 years old, was the father of seven children ranging in age from 21 months to 16 years when he lost his life in the line of duty on July 13, 1917. Bulfin regularly accompanied Edward Wyatt, a clerk at Chicago City Bank & Trust Company, as a bodyguard when Wyatt transferred large amounts of money from his bank to the Live Stock Exchange National Bank in the Stockyards. That particular July day, Wyatt was carrying over $10,000 when four men approached the vehicle Bulfin and Wyatt had just entered at 6233 S. Halsted Street with the intention of robbing them. The men leveled their guns and told Bulfin and Wyatt to put their hands in the air. Wyatt complied, but Bulfin attempted to reach for his service revolver and was shot through the heart by one of the robbers before he could raise his weapon. Another of the bandits then seized the box of cash that Wyatt had dropped when he had ducked for cover. Simultaneously, a cashier from within the bank who had heard the gunfire started shooting at the bandits from inside the establishment. Startled by the gunfire, the robber only grabbed one bag from the box, making their take only $20 for each man, including the driver of the getaway car. The men sped away past terrified pedestrians, shooting as they went to discourage any pursuit. Thomas Malloy was later held for driving the vehicle used in the raid and Frank Brown was held for questioning. Both men claimed to be business agents. They denied involvement in the attempted robbery and any prior knowledge of the raid. Another suspect, Jack King, was later arrested, but no further action was taken. Officer Bulfin was laid to rest in Mount Olivet Cemetery on 111th Street.

Patrolman John Gibbs,

STAR # unavailable, Motorcycle Division, was killed on July 28, 1917 when his motorcycle collided with an automobile driven by Frank Lennen of 706 N. Troy Street. The incident occurred at the intersection of Chicago and Kedzie Avenues. Upon impact, Gibbs was thrown about 40 feet from the collision site. His skull was fractured when his head crashed into the curbstone. Gibbs was unmarried and had been a resident at 920 N. St. Louis Avenue.

Detective-Sergeant Martin J. Corcoran,

STAR# 469, 42nd Precinct, Town Hall Station, was on patrol on August 13, 1917 when he noticed two men, Albert Johnson and William Pisano, carrying a basket of what appeared to be stolen jewelry and other pinched goods. He pursued and finally stopped them in front of the H.H. Garage at Waveland Avenue and Broadway Street. His intention was to ascertain the origin of the objects in the basket. But he was never given the opportunity because Johnson pulled a revolver and shot the officer three times before any words were exchanged.

Robert F. Hoffman, owner of the H.H. Garage, witnessed the officer pursue and stop the two men. He also observed the shooting. As Corcoran fell, Hoffman ran out to the sidewalk and took off after the fleeing offenders. Pisano and Johnson ran in opposite directions and Hoffman chose to pursue the escaping shooter. As he ran, he picked up the revolver that Johnson had discarded while running down the alley. Hoffman managed to wound Johnson with his own gun after firing only two shots. He dragged the offender back to the garage where Corcoran had been laid out in the company's office. Both men were then taken to Alexian Brothers Hospital.

Johnson and Pisano were believed to have been the offenders responsible for the robbery of Donald R. Innes, 3757 N. Pine Grove Avenue, earlier in the evening. Corcoran had heard a report of the burglary and suspected Johnson and Pisano might be the culprits when he spotted the basket full of goods. When he observed them that night he ordered them to halt but they fled instead. In his pursuit, Corcoran fired after them. He believed this might frighten them enough to make them halt in front of the garage to answer his question. Sadly, that was not the case.

Johnson and Pisano were both eventually arrested and charged for their parts in the crime. Johnson was originally arrested after he was treated for his gunshot wound. Let out on bond, he then proceeded to jump bail, but was arrested again and eventually sentenced to be hanged on June 14, 1918. He appealed his conviction all the way to the highest court in the nation. The United States Supreme Court affirmed his conviction and he was finally put to death on February 28, 1919. Pisano fled to Houston, Texas but was discovered and extradited from Camp Logan. He was sentenced to the Pontiac Reformatory on a burglary charge. Officer Corcoran was laid to rest at St. Joseph Cemetery on Thatcher Road.

Patrolman Joseph P. Tiernan,

STAR #3014, 29th Precinct, Warren Avenue Station, 42 years old, was shot in the early morning hours of August 23, 1917 when he came upon two burglars attempting to break into the West End Dry Goods Store at 1775 W. Madison Street. He was attempting to place both men under arrest when one of them produced a weapon and fatally wounded him. The officer died the next morning at a local hospital. He was survived by his wife, Margaret (née Tierney) Tiernen. His son Joseph had preceded him in death. The funeral procession began at his residence, 5585 W. Monroe Street, and proceeded to St. Catherine of Siena Church on Washington Boulevard in Oak Park. Officer Tierney was later buried in Mount Carmel Cemetery in suburban Hillside. The shooter, Harry Lindrum, was eventually caught and held on August 27, 1917. He implicated his co-conspirator Harry Sutherland. On November 3, 1917, Harry Sutherland was given 25 years in the Illinois State Penitentiary at Joliet. Lindrum was sentenced to hang on December 14, 1917, but was later given a reprieve by the governor. His amnesty did not last long and he was finally executed on February 15, 1918.

Patrolman Joseph A. O'Connor,

STAR #3704, 1st Precinct, Central Station, 34 years old, was in the company of Miss Alma Scanlon, a woman who was not his wife, on October 30, 1917 when he placed W.M. "Olson" Osborne under arrest at the northwest corner of Market and Madison Streets in front of the Galt Hotel. Osborne had directed an insulting remark at Miss Scanlon and O'Connor took exception and placed the offender under arrest. Soon after he was taken into custody, Osborne produced a gun and fired at the officer. Patrolman O'Connor returned fire and mortally wounded Osborne. Witnesses to the altercation included several apprentice seamen from the Great Lakes Station, one of whom, A.J. Gritten, sustained a non-life threatening bullet wound to the neck. Mrs. Scanlon went to the police station directly after the incident to provide her statement to investigating officers. Osborne was originally taken to the Iroquois Memorial Hospital, but died four days later on November 4, 1917 at the Bridewell Hospital, only hours before O'Connor succumbed to his wounds at St. Luke Hospital. Family and friends rallied around the dying officer during his hospitalization, attempting to convince him that he would recover. O'Connor would not entertain the idea according to the *Chicago Daily Tribune* and told his loved ones, "That's all right boys; don't kid me—I'll be in Mount Carmel in a few days," a prediction that proved tragically true. His Funeral Mass was celebrated at Our Lady of Angels Church and he was later buried in Mount Carmel in suburban Hillside, just as he had foreseen. His wife Mary, who resided with her husband at 3701 W. Ohio Street, was at his bedside during his final days and publicly forgave her husband for being in the company of another woman at the time of the shooting.

Detective-Sergeant Joseph H. Urban,

STAR #518, 35th Precinct, 39 years old, died in the in the line of duty on December 6, 1917 due to a tragic misunderstanding. On December 1, 1917, Detective Urban entered a local store, the National Tea Company, at 2830 W. Armitage Avenue, after hours in order to investigate a series of neighborhood robberies. Another patrolman, Charles Weinecke, was on rounds in the area at the time and observed Urban in the store. Thinking that Urban was one of the burglars who had been troubling the neighborhood, he went to investigate. In the confusion created by the lack of knowledge on the part of both officers, Weinecke fired once, fatally wounding Detective Urban. He was taken to St. Elizabeth Hospital, where he died on December 6. Patrolman Weinecke was exonerated of all responsibility for the officer's death. Urban was laid to rest in St. Adalbert Cemetery on North Milwaukee Avenue.

Patrolman Michael J. McGough,

STAR #2982, 18th Precinct, Gresham Station, 39 years old, was fatally shot the same day as Detective Urban, December 6, 1917. McGough was on patrol when he spotted a man stealing coal at a railroad yard and tried to place him under arrest. The thief resisted, answering McGough's attempt to place him in custody with a fatal gunshot. The offender, Charles Markino, a night watchman employed by the Chicago and Western Indiana Railroad located on Wallace Street between 80th and 81st Streets, pleaded poverty as the motive behind his crime. He claimed that his family was freezing and their hardship had pushed him to the desperate act of stealing from his employer. His effort to gain sympathy, or at least understanding of his actions, failed and he was sentenced to the Illinois State Penitentiary at Joliet for an undetermined amount of time on December 20, 1919. McGough, a native of Castlebar in County Mayo, Ireland, was able to give his own account of events before he died on December 7, 1919. His funeral was held on December 10, 1919 at St. Leo Church and he was interred at Mount Olivet Cemetery. He was survived by his wife, Elizabeth Foley McGough, and his children, Mary and John.

Chief of Police Herman Schuettler
with bomb experts examining
an explosive device at headquarters (1917).
DN-006942, *Chicago Daily News*
Collection, Chicago History Museum.

Crowd at State and Washington Streets
(1919). DN-0077873, *Chicago Daily News*
Collection, Chicago History Museum.

Detective-Sergeant George Clausen,

STAR #3400, 22nd Precinct, 42 years old, was a ten-year-police veteran who had recently been promoted from Expert Horse Trainer to City Detective when he died in the line of duty on April 13, 1918. Clausen and his partner, Detective Luther Beauchamp, were making their nightly rounds when they stopped at a patrol box and phoned into the station.

The operator who took their call informed them of a robbery at the saloon of Louis Porter at Damen Avenue and Harrison Street, phoned in only moments before. The officers assured the operator that they would be on the lookout for the hold-up men and returned to their patrol. The officers were unaware of how tragic that promise would prove to be.

Only a half a block separated the policemen from their quarry. Mere yards from the patrol box at 2625 W. Madison Street, where Clausen and Beauchamp were standing, was the saloon of James L. Flannigan, the establishment the robbers chose as their next target. Three bandits entered the saloon and ordered the dozen patrons to line up against the wall. Two of the offenders busied themselves emptying the pockets of the patrons while the third kept his gun pointed at Flannigan. Overall, the robbers collected more than $150 between the cash register and patrons' wallets. Once they had finished, they began to slowly back towards the door to ensure that no one in the establishment entertained the idea of recouping their money and valuables. Although an intelligent move in theory, a front door exit left them vulnerable to attack. Once Clausen and Beauchamp arrived, they were able to glance through the saloon's screen door. There they saw the patrons lined up against the wall without the offenders initially noticing them. They quickly entered the saloon and were met by the robbers' raised guns and were ordered to put their hands in the air. The officers ignored this command, reached for their weapons and a gun battle began.

As the saloon's customers dove behind the bar and took cover under tables, Clausen and Beauchamp returned the bandits' fire. Both officers were hit and fell to the ground, but Beauchamp was able to continue firing his weapon while several bullets that had wounded Clausen quickly proved fatal. Only one man was ever held responsible for firing at the officers in Flannigan's Saloon and he lived only a few hours longer than Detective Clausen. Dan Maloney, identified later as Clausen's shooter, had the bad luck to be the last of the group to attempt to leave the saloon. Completely disregarding the bodies of the fallen officers, his comrades stepped over Clausen and Beauchamp and exited. As Maloney followed, Beauchamp was able to summon the last of his strength and fire a final shot that proved fatal for the robber. He fell next to the officers. Other men who were held in connection to the saloon brawl were Arthur McNally, James Pemborton, James Griffith and Harry Smith. All but Smith had prior police records. The police also sent out warrants for J.P. Sweeney and Charles M. Clark. A Charles M. Clark had been taken into custody the night of the shooting, but it was later determined that he was not the Charles M. Clark sought and he was released.

In June of 1918, John Brandt was taken into custody and charged with taking part in Detective Clausen's murder. He was arrested after a chance encounter with Detective Beauchamp who had returned to his regular beat after recovering from the injuries sustained the night of his partner's death. Beauchamp recognized Brandt as one of the men he and Clausen had fought with in April and arrested him and his companion, Miss Rose Moore. Brandt denied the officer's identification and claimed that he had been working as a teamster the night of Detective Clausen's murder.

Detective Clausen lived at 125 S. Whipple Street. Funeral services, attended by high-ranking officials such as Captains Thomas F. Cronin and Michael J. Gallery and Lieutenants Patrick McWeeney and William Ambrose, were held at Sacramento Avenue Methodist Episcopal Church. Clausen was laid to rest in Oak Ridge Cemetery where six members of the Policemen's Benevolent Association served as pallbearers. Funeral services at the cemetery were performed by Garfield Lodge of the Masonic Order, No. 686. Detective Beauchamp's doctors refused to let the injured officer pay his last respects despite his pleas, deeming his health too precarious to allow him to leave the hospital.

Patrolman James F. Looney,

STAR #821, 7th Precinct, 39 years old, was leaving the saloon of George Hedel at 1150 W. 22nd Street on April 18, 1918 when he noticed two suspicious men enter. After identifying the shady characters as hold-up men, he attempted to draw his weapon but was shot at close range by one of the offenders before he was able to do so. His assailants escaped and were never found or held accountable for his death. Looney's injury did not immediately prove fatal, but he developed gangrene from the wound and died two weeks later on May 1, 1918. He was buried in Calvary Cemetery in Evanston, Illinois.

Patrolman Peter H. Ostiller,

STAR #3376, 17th Precinct, was on foot patrol at the busy intersection of Roosevelt Road and Halsted Street when he was struck by a motorist on June 12, 1918. The driver, Henry Stephan of the Commonwealth Edison Company, had swerved to avoid crashing into a street car but could not avoid hitting the officer. Ostiller, who lived at 3210 W. Arthington Street, was rushed to the hospital and died from his injuries later the same day. Stephan was also severely injured in the crash. Patrolman Ostiller was interred at Waldheim Cemetery, Progressive Order of the West.

Patrolman Matthew J. Foley,

STAR #170, South Park Police, was patrolling in Jackson Park on September 12, 1918 when he noticed a speeding vehicle. He took off in pursuit but lost control of his motorcycle and crashed to the ground. He was taken to Illinois Central Hospital, where he died several hours later. Patrolman Foley resided at 5545 S. Union Avenue and his Funeral Mass was celebrated at Visitation Church. He was laid to rest in Mount Olivet Cemetery on 111th Street.

Patrolman John F. Schuetz,

STAR #4381, 31st Precinct, 56 years old, was returning home for dinner on January 27, 1919 when he surprised two burglars outside of the duplex apartment building that he owned at 1331 W. Hollywood Avenue. His wife, who was standing by the kitchen window as she prepared the evening meal, heard him confront his assailants on the sidesteps that led down to the basement. She heard a short conversation and two shots, followed by the sound of the officer's body falling down the passageway. Mrs. Schuetz and her daughter then heard the sounds of fleeing footsteps down the alley as they rushed down the stairs from their second floor apartment. They discovered Schuetz lying unconscious, shot just above the left eye and bleeding profusely. They were quickly joined by concerned neighbors who called an ambulance that took Schuetz to Lake View Hospital.

Schuetz, a 23-year-veteran of the force and a model officer by all accounts, lived for an hour after the shooting, but was unable to speak a single word before his death. His assailants disappeared down the alley adjacent to his home and were never seen again. No real conclusions about the motives for Patrolman Schuetz's murder were even reached. However, the *Chicago Daily News* offered two theories that the police were considering. The first examined the idea that Schuetz had been accosted by enemies. However, that theory could not be credited because not a single friend, family member or acquaintance could remember Schuetz ever having an enemy. The second premise theorized that Schuetz had discovered two robbers who were attempting to burglarize the apartment on the first floor and tried to apprehend them, leading one of the men to fatally shoot him. The murder of "Honest John," as he was known by friends and colleagues, remains as senseless and puzzling a crime as any the department had ever seen. Officer Schuertz was buried in St. Boniface Cemetery on N. Clark Street. His death was one of thirty-five murders that remained unsolved in 1919.

Detective-Sergeant James L. Hosna,

STAR #324, Detective Division, 36 years old, went to the saloon of Patrick "Paddy the Bear" Ryan at 1403 S. Halsted Street on the night of February 15, 1919 with the intention of arresting burglar George Vogel for his part in a wagon robbery. Hosna headed to the saloon, a well-known hangout of Westside criminals, and waited for Vogel, confident that he would eventually come in. Hosna's assumption proved correct when Vogel pulled up later in the evening in an automobile driven by his childhood friend from the Southwest side, Frank Krueger. According to the disjointed account of events that Hosna was able to give from his hospital bed, he said hello to Vogel when he entered and asked if he had taken part in the wagon job that was being investigated. Hosna stated that Vogel did not bother to reply, but instead pulled his gun from his coat and fired point-blank at the officer four times. Hosna never had the chance to retrieve his own weapon and fell to the saloon floor mortally wounded. Vogel then stepped up to the fallen officer and fired two more bullets into his back. Believing that he had inflicted all the damage he possibly could, Vogel jumped into Krueger's automobile and they fled the scene. The car was later found wrapped around a lamppost at the corner of 14th Place and Morgan Street.

Krueger denied all knowledge of the incident the next day when the police came to his home to question him. He even went so far as to deny having been in Vogel's company the night of February 15, although several eyewitness accounts contradicted him. Krueger was not the only one to claim ignorance of the confrontation. Both Patrick Ryan and the saloon's porter, Charles Pitts, spent long hours in the interrogation rooms at the Maxwell Street

Chicago Police control crowd
at Eastland disaster, July 24, 1915.
DN-0064969, *Chicago Daily News*
Collection, Chicago History Museum.

Eastland disaster, Chicago Police
Officers unload blankets.
DN-0064969, *Chicago Daily News*
Collection, Chicago History Museum.

Chicago armory on Washington Boulevard, temporary morgue for Eastland victims. Today this building houses HARPO Production for Oprah Winfrey. DN-0064993, *Chicago Daily News* Collection, Chicago History Museum.

Chicago Police at Eastland Chicago River scene. DN-0065006, *Chicago Daily News* Collection, Chicago History Museum.

Station being questioned by Hosna's angry colleagues. But both insisted that they had not seen the shooting. Even without their corroboration, a massive manhunt was under way in the city. Every man in the detective bureau, aided by hundreds of plain clothes policemen, combed the city under the direction of Chief of Detectives James L. Mooney. The *Chicago Tribune* reported that the directive to "Get Vogel dead or alive" was sent to every police station in the city. Vogel thwarted any satisfaction officers might have taken in his capture when he voluntarily turned himself in to the State's Attorney's Office on February 19, 1919, although the sheer determined vengeance that drove the task forces to search for him might have played a role in that decision. His incarceration was short-lived and ire must have risen again when he was acquitted of all charges on June 13, 1919 after arguing that he shot Hosna in self-defense. Vogel contended that he had shot Hosna after an argument over "graft," which left him feeling threatened. The offender claimed that Patrolman Hosna had demanded $300 from a known auto thief and had become angry when Vogel had taken it from him because of his inebriated state. The Chicago Police Department vehemently denied Vogel's claims.

After the shooting, Detective Hosna was taken to Cook County Hospital where his family began a 12-hour vigil that would last until the early morning of February 16, 1919 when he died. According to the *Chicago Tribune*, his last words, which were whispered to his father, wife and two brothers, were "I know I died game anyway...But get Vogel. He didn't give me a chance." With Vogel's acquittal, Hosna's dying wish would remain unfulfilled. Hosna requested that his children be brought to see him about a half an hour before he died, however, they did not reach the hospital in time to say good-bye. The officer was later buried at Bohemian National Cemetery.

Patrolman Robert M. Love,

STAR #80, West Park Police, 45 years old, was investigating complaints of boys throwing rocks in Shedd Park at 23rd Street and Millard Avenue when he was struck and killed instantly by a Chicago, Burlington & Quincy Railroad train on April 9, 1919. Earlier in the evening, residents had complained of young hooligans throwing rocks at their homes and in the park. Love, a 12-year-veteran of the force, had been dispatched to see if he could locate the boys. One of the theories proposed to explain his death claimed that he had indeed found the young men. This supposition claimed that his determined pursuit of the offenders had not allowed him to hear the train until it was too late to reach safety. Love's body was discovered a short while later when local resident Harry Tibbets noticed the officer's cap as he was passing by the park. He had just retrieved the cap and begun to search for its owner to return it when he found Patrolman Love. Officer Love was laid to rest in Rosehill Cemetery.

Patrolman Henry A. Mandleco,

STAR #1403, 12th Precinct, Kensington Station, 29 years old, had just made his last "pull" at one of the patrol boxes on his beat on April 23, 1919, and was officially off-duty for mere moments when he spotted two men driving a car that contained stolen cargo. Most thieves do not travel around boldly showcasing the spoils of their endeavors; but in this case, the two crates of live chickens spotted by the policeman would have been difficult to conceal. Mandleco noticed the pilfered goods and left the sidewalk. Elmer B. Munns, a nearby druggist and resident who had been walking with him, followed Mandleco. The officer stepped into the intersection at 102nd and Halsted Streets and ordered the bandits to halt. When the car showed no signs of decreasing its speed, he raised his weapon and prepared to fire. Before he ever got the chance, a well aimed shot from one of the car's passengers tore through his heart and killed him instantly. The truck swerved around the body of the fallen officer and turned onto Halsted Street, racing off into the night.

Munns, who had left his place on the sidewalk as soon as Mandleco fell, picked up the officer's gun and emptied it in the direction of the fleeing offenders, possibly wounding one of them. A little over a week after Patrolman Mandleco's death, an arrest was made in the case when Joseph Boshart was apprehended on May 2, 1919. In addition, an arrest recommendation was made concerning Peter Schaefer, who may have been the car's other passenger. He was never found and the arrest action was stricken from the record on May 4, 1920. On October 17, 1919, Boshart was sentenced to life in prison. His sentence might have come as some small comfort to Mandleco's father, Henry C. Mandleco, a 30-year-police veteran who also worked out of the Kensington Station. He was probably more than aware of how seldom justice was well served. He remained proud. Henry A. had just finished his two year probation period required for every new recruit and was recently established as a full officer before he was killed. He was part of the proud tradition of protection and service his father had begun in their family. Officer Mandleco was buried in Mount Greenwood Cemetery on 111th Street.

Patrolman Cornelius Wilson,

Star #2902, 3rd Precinct, Cottage Grove Station, 29 years old, was another officer whose commitment to safeguard the city ended when he was off-duty at 2:00 A.M. on the morning of May 1, 1919. Wilson had just ended his shift and was on his way home dressed in civilian clothes when he spotted three men who were suspected of committing several armed robberies at the corner of 37th and State Streets. He approached the offenders and began asking questions, which they apparently did not appreciate because two of the men produced guns and began shooting at the officer. Wilson was able to return fire during the duel that followed and fatally wounded one of the robbers. However, he too sustained life-ending injuries that did not allow him to pursue the other men as they fled his gunfire.

As Patrolman Wilson lay dying in the street, a motorist came upon the scene. Seeing the officer's critical condition, the concerned citizen put him in his vehicle and transported him to the closest hospital. Wilson's injuries, however, were too severe and he died en route. As one Good Samaritan attempted to aid Wilson, another notified the Cottage Grove Station of the events that had taken place. An ambulance was immediately dispatched to recover the fallen officer. By the time it arrived, Wilson was already on the way to the hospital, so the ambulance driver and his partner decided to search the area for clues as to what had taken place. They discovered the dead burglar's body about a half block down the street.

A further search revealed a mask, gun and a type of stocking cap that indicated the man may have been a former soldier. A week after Patrolman Wilson's murder, two members of the Hooded Bandit Gang, a group of criminals who had spent the past six months robbing banks, pedestrians, coal yards and pay rolls, confessed to the officer's murder. On May 14, 1919, Herman Dykes and Dan Harlan were formally charged with Patrolman Wilson's death. Harlan had confessed to his part in the crime while at the Cook County Hospital where he was being treated for a gunshot wound sustained after Wilson's murder. On August 25, 1919, both men were sentenced to life in the Illinois State Penitentiary at Joliet. Officer Wilson was buried in Campbellsville, Kentucky.

Patrolman Richard J. Burke,

STAR #1236, 15th Precinct, Deering Station, 35 years old, entered a tavern at 33rd and Halsted Streets that was still operating after legal closing time in the early morning hours of June 16, 1919. The officer lost his life when he announced that he would be forcing it to close. The details of what happened in the tavern are vague, though it appeared that some of the patrons of the establishment did not possess the best character. They were startled by the appearance of the officer and his declaration. They also feared that after he closed the place, he might wish to take a closer look at those inside since more than a few of the patrons were suspected of illegal activities. They confronted Patrolman Burke and in the chaos that ensued, the officer was fatally shot with his own gun.

Unidentified patrons then dumped Burke's body onto the sidewalk outside the saloon. Afterwards several men jumped into a taxicab and sped away, according to an account given by Miss Harriet Galewski, a witness and resident at 749 W. 33rd Street. Galewski had gone to her window when she heard the gunshots and had been able to observe the events. An on-duty patrolman who was stationed nearby also heard the shots and watched as the taxicab raced down the street. He fired his revolver at the vehicle and when it halted, he arrested the six passengers and the driver, assuming that the shooter might be among them. On July 18, 1919, John O'Brien was held on charges for firing the fatal shots, while William "James" Kelly was arrested as his accomplice. Kelly's case was stricken from the record but O'Brien paid for his crime when he was hanged on February 20, 1920. Officer Burke was laid to rest in Mount Olivet Cemetery.

Patrolman John W. Simpson,

STAR #4774, 4th Precinct, Wabash Avenue Station, 28 years old, was the first African-American policeman to die on duty in Chicago and one of the two police officers who died during the violent race riots that swept the city during the summer of 1919. Few details are known about Simpson's death because of the disorder and turmoil that characterized those dark days. Simpson was found bleeding profusely from a gunshot wound to the abdomen outside the 31st Street Police Station at 31st Street and Wabash Aveune on July 28, 1919. He was rushed to Mercy Hospital but his injuries were too grave. He died on the operating table. His killer was never identified. Officer Simpson was buried in Lincoln Cemetery.

The events that led to Simpson's death mark a sad chapter in the history of Chicago that highlight the divide between those of different races. An unseen racial line running from sand to surf divided the beaches of 25th and 29th Streets. The 29th Street beach was used by white Chicagoans while African-American beachgoers used the one on 25th Street. On a hot summer Sunday in 1919, Eugene Williams, an African-American teenager, accidentally drifted south of that unseen boundary while taking a break from the heat in Lake Michigan. According to various accounts, whites on the 29th Street beach began throwing rocks at the swimming teenager, in anger at the young man's transgression of the racial line. Reports differ as to what caused the young man to finally slip under the water. One report states that the drowning was caused by a rock thrown at William's head, while a second claims it was due to fatigue produced by fear of entering the shallow waters where an angry white crowd had gathered. Either way, the fact remains that he drowned that day not far from shore. His senseless death rocked the city and led to the worst racial violence seen then. When the riots and bloodshed were over, thirty-eight Chicagoans were dead. The Southside's neighborhoods were devastated. An Irish gang known as the Ragen Colts, which dominated several Chicago neighborhoods—including Bridgeport, Hamburg and Canaryville, in the early 20th century, bore much of the responsibility for the violence of riots. Later they became part of the mob under Al Capone. In the end over one thousand citizens were left homeless and impoverished by the riots. Chicago's reputation suffered damage that would not quickly fade.

Patrolman Daniel J. Carton,

Star #3216, 23rd Precinct, 32 years old, was wounded during the race riots on July 30, 1919 while attempting to maintain order in a saloon at 43rd Street and Union Avenue in the Canaryville neighborhood. Tensions were running high in the city at the time and disagreements easily turned to bloodshed at the drop of a hat. These tensions led Carton to intervene in a common barroom scuffle in the hope that he could prevent it from igniting further violence. John Ward was bent on violence though, and shot the officer when he intervened. Injured, but still determined to perform his duty, Carton managed to fire a critical shot that found its mark and fatally injured Ward, who died the following day. Patrolman Carton survived for six weeks, but finally succumbed to the wound and died on September 15, 1919. He was buried in St. Mary Cemetery in DeKalb, Illinois.

Chicago Police Officer John W. Simpson,
first African-American policeman to die in the
Line of Duty in Chicago.
Chicago Police Department Photo Archive.

Race Riot crowds in the street (1919).
G1964.1048.C, Chicago History Museum
Photo Archive.

Crowd at 35th and State Street
during the Chicago Race Riots (1919).
DN-0071297, *Chicago Daily News*
Collection, Chicago History Museum.

Patrolman during Chicago Race Riots
stand with Federal troops.(1919).
DN-0071298, *Chicago Daily News* Collection,
Chicago History Museum.

Patrolman Morgan Donahue,

STAR # unavailable, Fillmore Street Station, 40 years old, was murdered at the Hoffman and Egan Saloon at 59th and Halsted Streets on August 25, 1919. Donahue was at the saloon that night with 15 of his brother officers. Though events surrounding this night have forever remained fishy, one thing is clear, two men were shot, Officer Donahue and Anthony Kelly. Kelly lived at 4208 S. Union Avenue and was a foreman at Wilson & Company's meatpacking plant in the stockyards. Two other people were injured during the brawl.

Hoffman and Egan bought the saloon 16 days before, more than one month after the dry law went into affect. The events surrounding the Englewood saloon prove that the dry laws of prohibition were not being respected and that law enforcement officials were aiding in the corruption. There were two different theories that emerged as to how the clash began. The first theory was that Donahue attempted to take a bottle of beer from the saloon; the second theory suggests that the patrons at the bar believed the policemen to be "dry" investigators. After the initial clash, Officer Donahue began to fight with Kelly, who was making every effort to take control of his beer bottle. Donahue's partner, Officer John P. Donegan, shot Kelly because he believed that Kelly was trying to kill his partner and that Donahue needed to be defended. Kelly was hit in his right leg and chest. Donahue, too, was shot. Three men took the officer to the Englewood Union Hospital where they left him outside the front door before promptly fleeing the scene. Before Donahue even entered the hospital for treatment he died.

Immediate action was taken by Chief of Police Garity as he suspended four officers for their possible involvement in the incident. The officers included Detective-Sergeant Edward Powers of the East Chicago Avenue Station, Detective-Sergeant Frank Welling of the Detective Bureau, Detective-Sergeant William Egan of the Maxwell Street Station and Patrolman John P. Donegan of the Fillmore Street Station. Powers and Donegan admitted that they had been at the saloon and Donegan acknowledged his involvement. Egan claimed that he had not been in the saloon at all that night, while Welling, on the other hand, admitted to being at the saloon but claimed that when the fight broke out he fled the scene, only to return once it was all over. No further action was ever taken against the suspended officers and after a short period of time they were able to return to their jobs.

Detective-Sergeant William "Packy" Doyle, a motorcycle policeman, was the first person to give a coherent account of the murder, though authorities continued to have a foggy picture of what went on. It seems that Doyle and Powers both tried to break up the brawl, but after little success they each ran to a call box to request back up. The Englewood and Stockyard Police Stations each received word about the events at the Hoffman and Egan Saloon. Officers quickly began to leave for the scene. One officer, Joseph Donahue, age 25, went along after hearing that his brother had been shot. While en route, it was learned that Morgan Donahue had died. With the news of his brother's death, Joseph felt that he no longer had anything to live for and attempted suicide. Fellow officers took the gun from his hand and calmed the officer down.

Edward Hoffman, one of the proprietors of the saloon, was arrested and held without bail for killing Officer Donahue on September 29, 1919. The Coroner's Jury held Hoffman to the Grand Jury on a charge of murder. Hoffman admitted to firing a gun, but said that he shot the ground in hopes of ending the dispute, denying that he shot the officer. Hoffman was pinpointed as the killer because he had a .45 caliber gun, the same type which killed Donahue. Later, a mysterious gunshot appeared on the floor, made by a .45 caliber gun, matching Hoffman's prior claim. In the early spring of 1920, the Grand Jury voted "No Bill" for Hoffman. Nobody was ever noted as having been charged for the deaths of Patrolman Donahue or Anthony Kelly. Officer Donahue was buried at Mount Olivet Cemetery on 111th Street.

Interestingly, both Donahue brothers, as well as Officer Donegan, all had been probationary policemen. Morgan and Donegan had been on sick leave when Morgan died. Donahue resided at 5130 S. Lowe Avenue and was survived by his mother, brothers and sisters. Donahue and his brothers still lived at home with their widowed mother. Donahue and Kelly had both previously been soldiers in the U.S. Army during World War I.

Detective-Sergeant George C. Burns,
STAR #207, 20th Precinct, Filmore Street Station, 39 years old, and **Detective-Sergeant Bernard J. Lenehan,** STAR #536, 20th Precinct, Filmore Street Station, 48 years old, lost their lives in the line of duty after being shot during a hold-up at Thomas Mulhern's Saloon at 3301 W. Madison Street on October 3, 1919. The two detectives had been at Mulhern's for only a few moments, chatting with bartender Eugene Morrissey, when bandits entered through a side door around 1:00 A.M. with handkerchiefs over their faces and weapons drawn. One of the bandits struck a patron, Vernon Lambert, on the knee with his weapon and he cried out, causing the policeman to turn towards the noise. The assailants recognized Burns and Lenehan as police officers and opened fire as the detectives reached for their service revolvers. Burns was shot four times in the stomach and side before he could retrieve his weapon. Lenehan was able to use his gun against the intruders, but was fatally shot at close-range in the forehead when he attempted to restrain one of the robbers. When the gunfire faded, both officers lay fatally wounded while the killers escaped by car. A witness reported seeing an automobile that matched the getaway car's description stalled at Spaulding Avenue and Jackson Boulevard. Unfortunately, it was gone when officers arrived to investigate.

In the meantime, Burns was rushed to St. Anthony Hospital where he died within a half hour of his arrival; Lenehan was taken to Garfield Park Hospital. Lenehan managed to cling to life for two days before dying on October 5, 1919. The loss of these men was a great blow to the Chicago Police Department and the city itself; but nowhere was the pain of their deaths felt more acutely than in the detectives' homes where 14 children became fatherless that day. Burns was father to six children; and Lenehan, who lived at 4055 W. Grenshaw Street, had eight. Vernon Lambert was locked up at the Detective Bureau over his connection to the killings of Burns and Lenehan. It was never clear whether Lambert was a witness or one of the bandits. Detective-Sergeant Burns and Detective-Sergeant Lenehan were both laid to rest at Mount Carmel Cemetery, Hillside.

Officers investigating the tavern shootout combed the city for the owner of a hat with the trademark "Gus the Square Hatter," left at the scene along with a white handkerchief and a .38 caliber Smith and Wesson blue steeled revolver. Police made public the serial number of the weapon, 22560, believing that someone who had once owned it might come forward and provide a clue to its current owner. They also provided descriptions of the holdup men. Both were believed to be around 35 years old, while the first was about 5 foot 10 inches tall with dark hair and a smooth face. The second man was described as slightly shorter with light brown hair and a clear complexion. A reward of up to $1,500, gathered from donations by Burns and Lenehan's fellow detectives, was offered for any information leading to the arrest of the bandits. One of the criminals involved was eventually tentatively identified as John Kristoveck, a left handed shooter who was killed by police after he shot and killed Police Patrol Sergeant Edward Marpool a year later.

The passage of the Volstead Act in 1919 prohibited the brewing and distilling of alcoholic beverages and their sale, unleashing a wave of fierce crime in the U.S. (1920). DN-0072930, *Chicago Daily News* Collection, Chicago History Museum.

Chicago crime boss Alphonse Capone (1929).
DN-0087660, *Chicago Daily News* Collection,
Chicago History Museum.

Prohibition ushered in a new genre
of crime when liquor was outlawed in 1920.
Chicago Tribune Photo Archive.

Patrolman Michael Duffy,

STAR #141, 11th Precinct, 41 years old, was fatally shot when he responded to a call on November 28, 1919, reporting a drunken patron waving a pistol inside of the Merry Widow Saloon at 6135 S. Halsted Street. The offender, George Rogers, also known as Roy Schilling, as well as three other aliases, had been quarreling with a female companion when he became extremely irate and produced a gun. Rogers knew that the patrolman had been summoned to arrest him. He wasted no time using his weapon, shooting Duffy shortly after he entered the saloon. Duffy, a 14-year-veteran of the force, died November 30, 1919 at St. Bernard Hospital. He was survived by his wife, Mary, and four children, Michael, Vincent, Ambrose and Marion. Patrolman Duffy lived at 5812 S. Aberdeen Street. His Requiem Mass was offered at Visitation church on W. Garfield Boulevard and he interred at Mount Olivet Cemetery.

Rogers was held for Duffy's murder on December 12, 1919 after confessing to the crime. The offender had formerly been employed as a switchman in Stickney, Illinois but was better known for his forays in the illegal endeavors of safe-blowing and robbery. Investigators believed that Rogers, "a mysterious, more or less seedy individual," according to acquaintances interviewed by the *Chicago Daily Tribune*, had stolen the murder weapon at 63rd Street and Kedzie Avenue, where he frequently spent the night. He often gravitated towards that spot because chauffeur Robert Fritz was employed there and the men were associates. Fritz was believed to have been Rogers' driver the night of the murder and was held by the police for questioning. Fritz's place of employment was not Rogers' primary residence though. According to reports, his true home was a shack near 63rd Street and the Grand Trunk Rail Line tracks. He disappeared from that area ten days before the shooting after waving around a great deal of money and talking of grand plans. On June 11, 1920, Rogers' sentence of life in the Illinois State Penitentiary at Joliet for the murder of Patrolman Duffy ended any plans he might have made.

Patrolman Harry J. Busse,

STAR #289, South Park Police, 30 years old, was patrolling his regular beat in a city park on Thursday, January 26, 1920 when he ran into Charles Shader, a member of a robbery gang, who was on his way to pull off another heist. While questioning Shader, the two became involved in a physical altercation and the criminal drew a pistol and fired at the officer, fatally wounding him. Busse died the following day. He was a World War I veteran and served with the South Parks Police for four years. His Requiem Mass was held at St. Martin Church. He was afterwards interred at St. Mary Cemetery. Busse was survived by his mother, sister and brother.

Shader, only 19 years of age, already had a long criminal history when he took Officer Busse's life. Several months before his encounter with the policeman, he had shot and killed his own father. He claimed self-defense in regard to the crime of patricide, stating that he had only taken such drastic measures because his father was beating his mother. He could not easily defend the other crimes to which he had confessed, a long list of robberies and hold-ups undertaken with the help of Frank Lee and Emmett McCaskle, 16 and 9 years old respectively. Shader attempted to place the blame for these crimes squarely on the mother whom he had committed murder in order to protect. He claimed that he and the two other boys had not wanted to commit the illegal acts but had been compelled to by Mrs. Shader. His attempt to shirk responsibility for his many offenses was unsuccessful and he was sentenced to life at the Illinois State Penitentiary at Joliet for Officer Busse's murder. He never served the sentence though because of his participation in a jailbreak, which led to the murder of Deputy Warden Peter Klein at the state penitentiary. Klein was beaten and stabbed to death with a knife and scissors on May 5, 1926. Six of the seven suspects, including Shader, earned a death sentence. On October 10, 1928, Shader received the dubious honor of being the last man hanged in Illinois.

The passage of the Volstead Act in 1919 prohibited the brewing and distilling of alcoholic beverages and their sale, unleashing a wave of fierce crime in the U.S. (1920). DN-0072930, *Chicago Daily News* Collection, Chicago History Museum.

Patrolman Dennis Wilson,

STAR #3511, 3rd Precinct, Cottage Grove Station, 27 years old, was patrolling in plain clothes on April 9, 1920 when he heard a gunshot. Wilson rushed in the direction of the sound and discovered three men quarreling, one of whom was brandishing a revolver. Learning that the three men had been quarreling and knowing that one shot had already been fired, Wilson attempted to disarm the gunman, William Hargraves. Hargraves was a barber who worked in the shop at 2946 S. State Street, where the confrontation took place. Officer Wilson ordered Hargraves to drop the gun, but he refused to comply. Instead of handing Wilson the weapon, Hargraves opened fire on the officer, who was able to return fire with his own weapon. When the gun duel was over, Wilson lay dead. He had been killed instantly by a shot through the heart. Hargraves lay beside him suffering from a fatal wound that would take his life the next day. The other two men involved in the quarrel had fled when the gunfire began and were never found. Officer Wilson was laid to rest in Lincoln Cemetery.

Patrolman William A. Roberts,

STAR #3566, 5th Precinct, Hyde Park Station, 30 years old, confronted a suspicious man on May 14, 1920 and lost his life in the line of duty. Roberts spotted Horace Dalton in front of 5052 S. Drexel Boulevard carrying a bag and acting shifty. He stopped Dalton at 1:51 A.M. and attempted to question him, unaware that he had just robbed an Illinois Central Railroad mail car that ran between Kankakee and Chicago. Afraid that his crime would be discovered, Dalton refused to answer questions and instead produced a revolver. Dalton and Roberts then proceeded to engage in a gun battle that ended only after the bandit ran out of bullets and fled the scene. The officer, who continued to fire despite being knocked to the pavement, was taken to Washington Park Hospital by a passing motorist who had heard the exchange of gunfire. He was treated for gunshot wounds in both his head and side. Officer Roberts died at the hospital at 10:30 A.M. the same morning. He was laid to rest at Mount Olivet Cemetery.

Before his wounds rendered him unable to speak, Wilson was able to give an account of his confrontation with Dalton and informed investigators that he and the offender had exchanged ten shots. Witnesses who observed Dalton get away down 51st Street to Cottage Grove Avenue and hail a cab filled in the rest of the story of his escape for investigators. Dalton was then traced to a residence at 816 E. 51st Street. Officers surrounded the lodging house and ambushed Dalton, killing him. He died at 3:15 A.M. on May 14, 1920, seven hours before Roberts succumbed to his injuries.

Patrolman William R. King,

STAR #417, 3rd Precinct, Cottage Grove Station, 43 years old, responded to a report of a man causing a disturbance on a streetcar on May 25, 1920. He removed the offender, Freeland Bettis, from the streetcar and placed him under arrest. He then led Bettis to a patrol box on the southeast corner of 37th and State Streets in order to place a call for a police wagon that would take the offender to the station. He turned his back to Bettis as they stood at the patrol box. The offender took advantage of the momentary lapse in attention by removing a gun from his coat and fatally shooting the officer from behind. King died several hours later. He was buried at Walnut Ridge Cemetery in Jeffersonville, Indiana.

After the shooting, Bettis ran to his home at 3538 S. State Street where police cornered him a short time later. He had discarded his weapon along the way and claimed to have no knowledge of the incident, but the testimony of several witnesses left little doubt of his guilt. He was arrested the same day as the shooting and sentenced to life at the Illinois State Penitentiary at Joliet on March 10, 1921 by Judge Kersten.

Detective-Sergeant Frank J. McGurk,

STAR #557, Detective Bureau, 44 years old, was serving as a replacement for Acting Lieutenant William Freeman on August 3, 1920 when he was killed in the line of duty. Freeman regularly guarded the Illinois Vinegar Manufacturing Company, 4800 S. Oakley Avenue, during the dispersal of the payroll. He was unable to fulfill the duty that evening so McGurk and his partner, Detective Patrick Mulvihill, volunteered to replace him. McGurk, who had been injured during the race riots the previous year, was a well respected officer who, along with Mulvihill, had led the police efficiency list 15 times. He was known for his dedication to the job. Detective-Sergeant McGurk was standing near the payroll window when three men disguised as workmen emerged from a stairway that led to the basement. According to the *Chicago Daily Tribune*, when he saw their weapons appear, McGurk shouted, "These fellows aren't working here," and immediately confronted the gunmen.

The leader of the bandits, all of whom wore handkerchiefs over their faces, ordered McGurk to put his hands up but the detective reached for his service revolver instead and the three men opened fire. McGurk was knocked down by the force of the bullets but still managed to return fire until his injuries caused his trigger finger to go numb. Detective-Sergeant McGurk's actions kept the bandits from obtaining the payroll. He died later that same day from the wounds he sustained. The offenders fled empty-handed and police were left to speculate as to whether their near success was aided by an employee of the Vinegar Company who attempted to pull off an inside job. Officer McGurk was interred in Mount Carmel Cemetery.

It was eventually determined that the fatal shot that ended McGurk's life had been fired by Stanley Galus. Galus had illegally enlisted in the Canadian Army under an assumed name to avoid detection but was discovered and sent back to the United States. When investigators finally tracked him down, they had to extradite Galus from Fort Omaha, Nebraska to Chicago to stand trial. He was indicted and sentenced to life at the Illinois State Penitentiary at Joliet on January 8, 1921 while all charges against his co-conspirators were dropped.

Washington Park Bank Robbery

Detective Frank McGurk searching the home of bank robbers in 1916. He was later killed in 1920. DN-065748, *Chicago Daily News* Collection, Chicago History Museum.

Detective Frank McGurk examines evidence in the home of bank robbers in 1916. He was later killed in 1920 (1916). DN-065748, *Chicago Daily News* Collection, Chicago History Museum.

Detective-Sergeant William E. Hennessy, STAR #2461, 3rd Precinct, Cottage Grove Station, 29 years old and Detective-Sergeant James A. Mulcahy, STAR #536, 3rd Precinct,

Cottage Grove Station, 29 years old, were partners who both tragically lost their lives in the line of duty on August 23, 1920. They were investigating patrons at the Beaux Arts Club, a notorious den of skullduggery located in the old Pekin Theatre Building at 2700 S. State Street, when a fatal altercation took place. Hennessy and Mulcahy, veterans of the Marines and Navy respectively, had been at the club only a short time when a patron began a quarrel with the officers. The offender, Hirsche Miller, attacked Mulcahy. Hennessy immediately came to his partner's aid, prompting Miller to retrieve a gun from his jacket, which he used to fatally shoot both officers.

Investigators from the police department and the State's Attorney's office immediately leapt into action, vowing to find the officers' killer. Their search led them along Chicago's infamous Whiskey Trail, the path that the city's million dollar illicit liquor trafficking enterprise followed. The Trail wound its way around the seedier side of the city through cabarets, crooked politics and gambling houses before finally leading the law to Miller. Miller, an ex-boxer and bailiff of the Municipal Court, was a known runner for a whiskey ring along the Trail. His exploits made him an unrepentant criminal who freely admitted to killing Hennessy and Mulcahy but denied any blame for their deaths since he claimed he did not know that they were police officers. The coroner held him on August 31, 1920 along with accomplice Samuel J. Morton. Both were indicted for their roles in the crime by the August Grand Jury. Despite Miller's confession, both men were acquitted of any blame for the detectives' deaths on January 7, 1922. Detectives Hennessy and Mulcahy were both laid to rest at Mount Olivet Cemetery.

Sergeant Edward W. Marpool,

Star #618, 25th Precinct, 55 years old, was working the late shift on the night of October 26, 1920 when a citizen complaint came into the station. The report described two armed men who were wandering the streets and were believed to be dangerous. Marpool, who had just finished handing out assignments to his patrolmen, decided to go and investigate. The sergeant searched the area where the offenders were last seen and noticed two suspicious men accompanied by female companions in an alley on Custer Street, just east of Western Avenue, around 1:15 A.M. He cautiously approached the offenders, intending to arrest them if he found weapons in their possession. According to the *Chicago Tribune*, one of the women cried, "Don't shoot Harry," as Marpool drew near, but her words went unheeded. One of the bandits drew a revolver and fired at the sergeant who stood only a few feet from him. The whole group then fled, leaving him lying mortally wounded in the street. Marpool was discovered shortly after the shooting but died on the way to the Alexian Brothers Hospital. He was buried at Mount Carmel Cemetery.

Marpool's fellow officers immediately sprang into action and over 300 of them soon swarmed a blocked-off section of the city where his killer was believed to be. The heavy police presence paid off, although time and patience were necessary to catch what proved to be a very slippery criminal. Marpool's shooter, John Kristoveck, engaged police in four gun battles over the course of three hours as they methodically hunted him down. At 4:30 A.M., only a few short hours after he took Sergeant Marpool's life, he was gunned down at the corner of Milwaukee and California Avenues. On September 21, 1921 it was discovered that his accomplice, James Morrison, was serving a sentence in a federal prison in Atlanta, Georgia related to a U.S. Post Office hold-up. Morrison's troubles with the law followed him until his death, which came in 1938 when he was a resident at the U.S. Hospital for Defective Delinquents.

Patrolman Joseph L. Pijanowski,

STAR #1427, 19th Precinct, Maxwell Street Station, 29 years old, was fulfilling his assignment as bodyguard to former Alderman William Held on November 14, 1920 when he was injured in the line of duty. Held had been receiving death threats for some time when he requested protection from the police department. Pijanowski, who had drawn the late shift, was outside Held's home with the former Chicago City Council member at 2544 S. Kedvale Avenue around 1:45 A.M. when a suspicious man approached them.

A few words were exchanged and then shots rang out, jarring and harsh in the quiet of the early morning hours. In the darkness, Pijanowski and Held lay wounded on the sidewalk as the attacker fled. Held's wounds were not life threatening, but the same could not be said of those suffered by Pijanowski. Both were taken to St. Anthony Hospital. Held, working as a clerk in the police court was questioned about his alleged involvement in illegal liquor deals.

He denied any complicity. Officer Pijanowski died four days later on November 18, 1920 and was buried in St. Adalbert Cemetery. Shortly after Patrolman Pijanowski's death, Raymond Knight was arrested and charged with the shooting. He confessed and claimed that robbery was his only motive and had no knowledge of the prestige of his chosen target. He provided police with the names of the men who had accompanied him that evening. Albert E. Willer and Henry J. Schmidt were held on November 30, 1920. The case against Schmidt was eventually dropped, but Knight and Willer were not able to escape punishment and both men received life sentences in the Illinois State Penitentiary at Joliet on January 14, 1921.

Patrolman Charles R. Conlon,

STAR #104, Traffic Division, 69 years old, had just ended his shift and began his regular walk home on December 16, 1920 when he stepped into a situation that illustrates the reality that policemen are never off duty. Conlon had just stopped at a newsstand to buy his regular, nightly paper when its owner of 15 years, and Conlon's good friend, William H. Pope, informed him of the armed robbery in progress in the store behind him. Only moments before, two armed men had entered the Home Drug Company, also known as the Ashland Block Pharmacy, at the corner of Randolph and Clark Streets for the purpose of robbing it.

Over forty customers were in the store when the men entered and all were caught by surprise. One of the men stood at the Randolph Street entrance and kept watch while the other brandished his weapon at the cashier and demanded the contents of the cash register. However, the woman behind the counter, Miss Mandy Linthal, was a gutsy cashier. She flatly refused to give the bandit the keys to the register, leading him to viciously attack her and threaten her life.

As the robber was attempting to obtain the key from Miss Linthal, Mr. Pope was informing Patrolman Conlon of the events transpiring inside. Conlon immediately drew his service revolver and entered the store via the Randolph Street entrance. The bandit who was supposed to be keeping watch had fled at the officer's advance and the criminal at the cash register was clearly startled when Conlon announced his presence and ordered him to drop his weapon. The man turned his attention from Miss Linthal without recovering any money and escaped through the Clark Street exit with Conlon close on his heels. Once outside in the busy Loop area and surrounded by over 100 pedestrians and theater patrons, Conlon shouted for the man to halt, firing at him when he failed to do so. Hearing the shot, the bandit turned and fired in return, emptying his revolver at the the policeman. One of his bullets found its mark and Conlon fell with a fatal wound to his abdomen in front of a candy store at 187 N. Clark Street. He was quickly taken to Iroquois Hospital, but died shortly after his arrival. Officer Conlon's burial took place in Mount Carmel Cemetery.

His killer, Thomas Heavy, would not live much longer. He and his companions had robbed a Westside drug store earlier in the evening, fleeing with large amounts of morphine, cocaine and heroin. There was speculation that these drugs had been ingested, becoming the fuel driving this tragic crime spree. Heavy had not traveled very far from where Officer Conlon lay mortally wounded when he ran into Patrolman John Dodd. The patrolman recognizing Heavy as the shooter, ordered the offender to stop. Heavy did not listen. Dodd fired again, killing him almost instantly. Conlon was a 28-year-veteran of the force only two weeks away from retirement when he lost his life in the line of duty.

Patrolman Timothy O'Connor,

STAR #2079, 11th District, Englewood Station, 50 years old, was fatally injured in the line of duty on December 18, 1920 as he guarded a garage that housed delivery trucks for Marshall Field and Company. The officer was stationed in a delivery barn at 7005 S. Wentworth Avenue, assigned to add extra protection during the Christmas rush, when six armed men entered the facility. They immediately opened fire when they spotted O'Connor, wounding the officer three times and stealing $5,000 in the chaos that ensued. The bandits fled in a waiting getaway car and were never brought to justice. After the shooting, Patrolman O'Connor was taken to St. Bernard Hospital, where he died two days later on December 20, 1920. He was buried in Mount Carmel Cemetery. Two men, Ed Kaufman and Dominic Monaco, were arrested on December 29, 1920 and charged with being apart of the robbery team. They were released without trial on January 27, 1921.

Patrolman John J. Mullen,

STAR #4275, 29th Precinct, North Halsted Street Station, 25 years old, was shot in the line of duty in the Hawaii Café at the Lincoln Gardens on the corner of Wells Street and Lincoln Avenue at 12:57 A.M. on January 1, 1921 when he responded to a report of an armed, intoxicated man in the café. Mullen entered the establishment and was in the process of placing John W. McEvilry under arrest when McEvilry's associate, Eddie Morris, came up behind the officer and shot him point-blank in the back, fatally wounding him. Officer Mullen was laid to rest in Mount Carmel Cemetery.

Morris and McEvilry had entered Hawaii Café at the Lincoln Gardens earlier in the evening along with two young women and sat at a table near Mrs. May Rhoden. Around 12:45 A.M., the women left the café just as a patron seated at Mrs. Rhoden's table told a joke. The woman laughed loudly enough to gain McEvilry's attention, and he mistakenly believed that she was laughing at him. According to the *Chicago Daily News*, McEvilry shouted, "I'll show you whether to make fun of me because the girls ditched me," before waving a revolver at Mrs. Rhoden. The terrified lady ran screaming to the proprietor of the café, John Ballash, who sent for the police. Officer Mullen was only a half a block away from Lincoln Gardens when he received the report and he hurried straight over. As he walked in, Morris was leaving, but Mullen stopped him and requested that he stay while McEvilry was questioned. Morris did follow the officer back in, but instead of calmly waiting while Mullen spoke to McEvilry, the bandit took out his revolver and shot him.

Other officers who had heard the report of the armed man made their way towards the café and were close by when the shot was fired. Their proximity made McEvilry's escape impossible, though he tried to flee, and he was arrested on the spot. Morris did manage to escape but was found a month later hiding in a haystack in Beverly Hills, California on January 8, 1921. He returned to Chicago to stand trial. He was sentenced to life in prison the same day McEvilry's trial ended in an acquittal on February 16, 1921.

Patrolman Martin J. Collins,

STAR #263, South Park Police, was on patrol in the South Park System on January 4, 1921 when he observed an intoxicated motorist at Garfield Boulevard and Ashland Avenue. He moved toward the vehicle and ordered the driver to pull over. The driver, David Stephenson Groh, of the Groh Detective Agency, ignored Collins' order and pushed the officer away from his vehicle. After shoving the policeman, he attempted to drive off, but Collins could not clear the automobile before Groh hit the accelerator. Witnesses at the scene reported that Groh ran into Patrolman Collins with his vehicle and crushed him against another car after he pushed the officer away from the driver's side window. Patrolman Collins was taken to German Deaconess Hospital at 54th and Morgan Streets where he died later the same day. Collins lived at 519 W. 45th Place. He was interred in Mount Olivet Cemetery on 111th Street.

Groh and his wife, who was a passenger at the time, were taken into custody and were tried for the murder of Collins. Assistant State's Attorney Samuel Bristoe asked for the death penalty.

Detective-Sergeant Patrick J. O'Neill,

STAR #2963, Detective Bureau, 45 years old, was on the trail of a murderer when he died in the line of duty on March 23, 1921. O'Neill was the head of a squad of five detectives who were acting on a tip that claimed to provide the whereabouts of wanted murderer, Thomas, "Terrible Tommy" O'Connor. The detectives surrounded the residence of William Foley, O'Connor's brother-in-law, and prepared to inquire if he was in residence.

They were there to collect O'Connor on bond forfeiture in connection with the murder of O'Connor's friend, Jimmy Cherin. Cherin's body had been found over a year earlier on a country road southwest of the city, and O'Connor was believed to be responsible. Detective-Sergeant O'Neill was stationed at the back of the home at 6415 S. Washtenaw Avenue when his colleague knocked on the front door. He saw O'Connor emerge through the back door onto the porch seconds later.

To say that O'Connor was unhappy to see O'Neill would be an understatement. According to the *Chicago Daily Tribune*, O'Connor looked to where O'Neill stood below him and exclaimed, "You dirty----, I am going to get you anyway. You've hounded me long enough," before opening fire on the detective. O'Neill was shot five times and fell to the ground unconscious as his colleagues looked on in horror. The events of the next few moments were disputed with witnesses claiming O'Neill's body lay unattended for a number of minutes. However, the officers on the scene claimed that their immediate attention to O'Neill is what allowed O'Connor to escape. Detective-Sergeant O'Neill was buried in Mount Carmel Cemetery. O'Connor remained on the run for three months before he was arrested in St. Paul, Minnesota on July 30, 1921. On October 14, 1921, O'Connor was sentenced to hang on December 15, 1921. However, he would never see the hangman's noose thanks to a successful jailbreak on December 11, 1921, which freed him until his death on the lam sometime in 1951.

"Terrible" Tommy O'Connor in a crowd (1921). ICH-i29640, Chicago History Museum.

Detective-Sergeant Patrick O'Neill's widow and their three children, Patrick, Jr.; Mary and Joseph (1921). DN-0073063, *Chicago Daily News* Collection, Chicago History Museum.

Sergeant Thomas J. Egan,

STAR #595, 5th Precinct, New City Station, 28 years old, was keeping watch over the home of Police Superintendent Charles Fitzsimmons at 5533 S. Hyde Park Boulevard on August 20, 1921, when an armed offender approached him and announced his intention to rob the officer. Walter "Martin" Grzybowski had been lurking in the shadows near where Egan stood for some time when the sergeant turned to confront him. Realizing that he had been spotted, Grzybowski emerged, pointed his weapon at the officer's face and announced a robbery.

Egan, a battle scarred veteran of more than a dozen shootouts, immediately drew his revolver and fired. Two of his bullets found their mark in the bandit's abdomen but did not disable him completely. As he fell, Grzybowski was able to fire his own weapon three times, including a deadly shot that lodged in Egan's heart. According to the *Chicago Tribune*, Chief Fitzmorris was preparing for bed when he heard Egan shout "Chief I'm shot! O, Chief hurry," and raced outside in his nightclothes with service revolver in hand. Fitzmorris found Egan and Grzybowski lying unconscious in the street. Sergeant Egan regained consciousness long enough to tell the chief that robbery had been the assailant's motive. Though Egan was lucid for only a moment, it was long enough to convince Fitzmorris that his home had not been the target of the night's violence. The chief then turned and reassured his neighbors, who had emerged from their homes at the sound of gunshots, many armed themselves, that they could return to their beds in peace.

Egan and Grzybowski were both taken to Illinois Central Hospital where Egan died five days later on August 26, 1921. Grzybowski recovered but committed suicide before he could be tried for his crime. Egan, a second generation police officer who served on the force with his father and three brothers, had only recently been promoted to sergeant and was highly respected as a tough, but honest officer. He was buried at Mount Olivet Cemetery.

Patrolman Paul Schutz,

STAR #4349, 11th Precinct, Englewood Station, 29 years old, was a member of a flivver squad sent to investigate a shooting at The Galloper's Club, 6265 S. Western Avenue, on October 16, 1921. The gentleman's club had enjoyed an excellent reputation up until that evening with a clientele made up almost entirely of all neighborhood business men. Before the night was over, it would see great carnage, including the death of two men and the wounding of three others. When Schutz and fellow police reached the Galloper's Club, they quickly realized that several arrests would need to be made and quickly began rounding up the suspects. They had been at their task only for a moment when they were ambushed by a gang of suspicious characters who appeared to have been lying in wait for them.

Gunfire erupted and the officers attempted to exit the confining rooms of the club and reach safety. Patrolman Schutz had reached the alley outside of the establishment, at 63rd Street and Western Avenue, when he was fatally wounded. He survived long enough to identify his shooter, Charles Cleaver, who was arrested later that night. Cleaver was indicted on December 27, 1921 but was later acquitted of all charges as was another man indicted as an accomplice in the cases. The details of the tragic events that led to Patrolman Schutz losing his life in the line of duty are not clear, but the haunting words the *Chicago Daily News* attributed to Chief Charles Fitzsimmons, claiming the attack as "a deliberate attempt to murder a policeman," highlight an intriguing mystery that has never been solved. Schutz was buried in Mount Greenwood Cemetery.

Patrolman James Harrington,

STAR # unavailable, 11th Precinct, Marquette Station, 52 years old, was thrown from the third floor of Robert Emmet Memorial Hall at 2179 W. Ogden Avenue on December 4, 1921 when he attempted to close down a dance that was operating there illegally. The event being held at the hall was still in full swing in the early morning hours, well after the established city curfew of 10:00 P.M. Harrington attempted to enforce the city ordinance that set closing times for such places. For his troubles he sustained injuries that claimed his life later the same day. Joseph Lucey of 4244 W. Ogden Avenue, found Harrington on the ground with two other men that had been at the hall. He was arrested and taken to the detective bureau for questioning. John Sullivan was also arrested, but nothing came of Lucey or Sullivan's arrests. Later, on December 6, 1921, Philip Ottova, Attilloi Puscinelli, Sittimo Ginnetti and Eugene Cesaratti were all arrested and indicted for their part in the mob action at the dance hall, but they were acquitted of all charges on February 1, 1922. No one was ever convicted of Patrolman Harrington's death. He was buried at Mount Carmel Cemetery.

Detective-Sergeant Charles Paldina,

STAR #493, Detective Division, 33 years old, was a dedicated, resourceful officer who rarely rested when there were criminals on the streets. The very morning of the day he was slain in the line of duty, January 20, 1922, he vowed that he would get the man he and his colleagues had been hunting over the past month. Paldina knew Charles Neuman's days of freedom were numbered but could not have foreseen the tragic end the day held for both his nemesis and himself.

Following a promising lead, Paldina proceeded to a saloon at 901 S. DesPlaines Street where he had been informed Neuman could be found. As the detective approached, he was spotted by the bandit, who came out to meet him in front of the saloon with his gun blazing. Shooting through his coat, Neuman was able to wound Detective-Sergeant Paldina in the stomach three times before the officer was able to use his own weapon and return fire. Despite his wounds, Paldina held his own in the gun battle that followed, emptying his revolver into Neuman as he chased the fleeing bandit, who continued to fire all the while. Neuman's escape came to an end only two blocks from the saloon where he collapsed from the damage done by Paldina's five bullets. They had found their target. Both men were taken to Cook County Hospital, but both died before they could receive treatment. Paldina was laid to rest at Mount Carmel Cemetery.

Eddie Neuman's criminal past followed him even to the grave. In an ironic twist of fate his body was identified at the Cook County Morgue by Abe Hubschman, the owner of Star Loan Bank, a pawnshop that Neuman and four accomplices robbed of over $25,000 in jewelry several years earlier, a crime for which they were never tried. Hubschman must have relished the small sense of justice he gained when he was able to confirm the death of one of the men who had robbed him.

Patrolman Ernest H. Cassidy,

STAR #2692, 7th District, 26 years old, was performing one of his regular duties as a police escort for a bank officer when he was cut down in the line duty on April 3, 1922. Cassidy and Phillip Sommer, treasurer of the Royal Building and Loan Association, began their nightly walk of the single block to the bank at 9117 S. Commercial Avenue where Sommer planned to deposit $4,200 in cash and $3,800 in checks. He was carrying it in a black satchel. Their short distance was "brilliantly" lit and full of pedestrians at 8:30 P.M. The men fell into their customary routine with Cassidy following three steps behind Sommer.

Irving Park Police Station (c. early 1920's).
DN-0074399, *Chicago Daily News* Collection,
Chicago History Museum.

The treasurer made his way down the street in high spirits, smiling at acquaintances and exchanging pleasant greetings. One short conversation he had would prove to be chilling in retrospect. Sommer answered an associate's query about his regular evening walk. According to the *Chicago Daily Tribune*, the man inquired as to whether Cassidy was transferring funds and Sommer replied, "Yes. You know last week I had a dream I was held up. So on that Monday I had them give me two policemen. Nothing happened. So I reduced the guard to one again," tragically unaware of the events that would transpire in just moments.

In a strange twist of events, there were no pedestrians within 100 feet of the men's final destination as they approached. This relative emptiness turned out to be a small bit of luck that probably saved lives when five bandits pulled up to the curb in a black touring car with its curtains ominously drawn. One leapt from the car and stood behind Cassidy while he ordered the officer to put his hands up. Training and instinct had Cassidy reaching for his weapon, but it had not even cleared the holster when the bandit pulled the trigger on his own revolver releasing a bullet that went straight through the policeman's heart. He fell to the sidewalk, dead before the doctor arrived a mere ten minutes later. He was laid to rest at Mount Carmel Cemetery.

Sommer did not fare any better than his bodyguard. After shooting Patrolman Cassidy, the bandit turned his attention to Sommer, whom he fatally shot before running away with the $8,000 the treasurer had been about to deposit. Neither Sommer nor Cassidy ever regained consciousness and, therefore, could not provide any details of the events that transpired. Witnesses crowded the street attesting to the fact that the men had been attacked without provocation or warning. On May 4, 1922, Charles Conroy was held without bail for the murder of both men, but released when the charges were withdraw.

Patrolman Thomas J. Clark,

STAR #3509, 16th District, Maxwell Street Station, 27 years old, was patrolling the plant that housed the Henneberry Printing Company and its surrounding neighborhood at 22nd and Jefferson Streets on May 9, 1922, an area that had been rocked by labor disputes, when he came upon three men in an old model Ford. Two men got out of the vehicle and began throwing bricks through the windows of the factory. Clark took immediate action. He ran the offenders off the property and then continued on his patrol, attentively surveying the surroundings in order to prevent the band of labor activists, who had been committing violent acts all over the city, from causing any more harm. Henneberry was under heavy guard because, as was well known at the time, many of the glaziers and other union workers were unhappy with the factory's decision to become an "open shop." Resentments were simmering near the boiling point and tragically bubbled over on the evening of May 9, 1922.

A short time after he had originally run the men off the property, Patrolman Clark came upon the same car parked only a little further down the street. He approached the car determined to question the men, but he was not given the chance. The car's occupants waited until the officer was close enough that their shots would prove fatal. They then gunned him down before he was close enough to speak with them. They waited to see the wounded officer fall to the ground dead before speeding off down Jackson Boulevard to continue their reign of terror. Officer Clark was interred at Mount Carmel Cemetery.

Sergeant Terrence Lyons,

STAR #11, West Park Police, became another victim of Chicago's labor troubles, just hours after Patrolman Clark. Even after the late hours of May 9 had given way to the early morning hours of May 10, 1922, the mayhem was not over. Lyons was usually assigned to patrol in and around city parks and had just left the station in Union Park with his detail when he encountered the deadly bandits. Lyons and his men were driving north on Ashland Avenue when they were stopped by the light at Jackson Boulevard. When the light turned green, they noticed a car speeding rapidly towards them from the east that had no apparent intention of obeying the traffic signal. Lyons signaled for the reckless vehicle to stop, but the driver accelerated instead and the car's passengers swore at the officers as they flew by.

Sergeant Lyons decided to pull the vehicle over and sped after it, traveling west along Jackson Boulevard. When the policemen pulled alongside the vehicle, they realized that the occupants inside matched the description of three suspects given by a night watchman at the Sharp and Partridge Plant where a bombing had taken place earlier in the evening. Before they could apprehend the suspects a burst of automatic gunfire erupted from the old model Ford and Lyons fell unconscious at the wheel. A policeman riding in the backseat quickly jumped behind the wheel and steered the car to the Cook County Hospital, but it was too late for Sergeant Lyons. He died during the short ride to the hospital from the multiple gunshot wounds he had sustained. Lyons was laid to rest at Mount Carmel Cemetery.

According to the *Chicago Tribune*, Police Chief Charles Fitzmorris went on record immediately after the shooting stating his belief that the violence that had been terrorizing the city, and which had taken the lives of the two policemen, could be traced back to labor agitators who were unhappy with the Landis Agreement. The Landis Agreement, named after its federal arbitrator Judge Kenesaw Mountain Landis, was a settlement designed to end the ongoing wage dispute between Chicago Building Contractors and the unions to which their workers belonged. Landis handed down his judgment in January of 1922 with the directive that it not be enforced until June 1 of the same year. The wage rates set by the judge were 18% to 25% higher than those prescribed by an earlier 1918 agreement in effect at the time. Unfortunately, they were not high enough to satisfy many labor leaders.

Labor officials and union members began to show their displeasure in early March with a campaign of harassment and persecution targeted at contractors who had already begun to use the Landis scale. By the beginning of May, a gang of ten "dynamiters" had a terrified city holding its breath and attempting to guess where they might strike next. According to various reports, the team of bombers had been contracted to carry out some twenty bombings with their wages being paid directly from union dues. On May 9, 1922, two bombs were thrown shortly before Patrolman Clark spotted the old model Ford near the Henneberry Plant. The night's distinction as the most violent and deadly, thus far, spurred Chief Fitzmorris to action.

The old model Ford that had figured so prominently in the deaths of Officers Clark and Lyons was found abandoned the morning after the crime spree. A search of the vehicle provided only one clue to the identities of the labor bandits but it was a valuable one. The bloody fingerprint of John Miller, a local bartender and well-known union muscle man, was found on the dashboard of the auto. Based on this evidence, Fitzmorris called for the arrest of Miller, his wife, and all officers and representatives of the Building Trades Union, a number that reached over two hundred. Over a dozen indictments were handed down implicating various players in the violence but, in the end, only two men were held responsible. John Miller was found guilty of the death of Patrolman Clark and sentenced to 25 years in prison, one of the cars passengers, Charles "Slim" Duschowski, was sentenced to life in prison for the murder of Sergeant Lyons. Duschowski's life of crime did not end there though. The unrepentant murderer was part of the prison break that led to the death of Joilet Prison Deputy Warden Peter Klein. Duschowski enjoyed his freedom for only a short time. He was apprehended soon after his escape and hanged for his part in the Klein murder on July 2, 1927.

Patrolman Robert Gibbons,

STAR #138, Lincoln Park Police, was killed instantaneously at the corner of Lake Shore Drive and Fullerton Avenue on June 26, 1922. The officer was traveling at a high rate of speed when he lost control of his motorcycle and crashed into a yellow taxicab. The taxi was unable to stop in time and the wheels of the vehicle rolled over the officer's fallen body. Witnesses at the scene reported that the accident happened so fast that they were unable to provide an accurate account of the events. He was buried in Calvary Cemetery in Evanston.

Patrolman Patrick H. Doherty,

STAR #1978, 2nd District, Cottage Grove Station, 30 years old, was off-duty and out of uniform on August 10, 1922 when he noticed two men on the street who matched the descriptions of wanted armed robbers. Doherty was an officer who was well-known for patrolling his beat, the "bad lands" as he had termed it, even when he was not technically on-duty. He was a familiar face in the neighborhood and it surprised no one who knew him that he decided to approach the offenders and attempted to place them under arrest. Witness accounts of the events that led to his fatal shooting were varied and vague due to fear of neighborhood vice bosses, but some details were substantiated.

According to the most trustworthy accounts, Doherty was passing along 28th and State Streets when he noticed the two men and called out. In response, the men shot at Doherty from the opposite side of the street. The patrolman engaged in a gun battle with the offenders, firing twice as they continued to fire at him. It could not be determined whether the weapons were indeed fired from such a distance or if the stories were told that way in order to protect witnesses from having to identify Doherty's assailants. Whatever the distance though, three bullets did enter Patrolman Doherty's body, causing a mortal wound that brought about his death soon after. The claim that shots came from the shadows and that identities were obscured provided a plausible cover for witnesses who wanted to do their civic duty but still had to live in the neighborhood in which the violence had taken place.

Doherty's death heightened racial tensions in the city when over 100 officers were sent into the largely African-American area surrounding 31st and State Streets to search for the officer's killers, who were reported to have been African-American. Further violence did not result, however, and the policemen, mostly reserve officers, were able to keep the crowds under control and restore order within an hour. The mystery surrounding Doherty's death left room for a great deal of conjecture. The theory that seemed to receive the most support claimed that the policeman's death was a planned hit. In the neighborhood where Doherty patrolled it was an open secret that the local criminal kingpins talked of plotting his death to end his interference in the vice activities upon which they depended. However, none of the allegations citing crime boss involvement in Doherty's death were ever verified. On August 12, 1922, David Thompson and Louie Roberts were held by the coroner but both were acquitted on November 28, 1922. No one was ever found responsible for the murder of this dedicated and heroic officer. Doherty was buried in Mount Olivet Cemetery at 111th Street.

Chicago Motorcycle Policemen (c. 1920).
DN-0074647, *Chicago Daily News* Collection,
Chicago History Museum.

Patrolman Ralph S. Souders,

STAR #360, 12th District, 29 years old, survived the horrors of World War I and went on to serve his fellow citizens faithfully upon his return until he lost his life in the line of duty on December 19, 1922. Souders still held the rank of probationary policeman, having joined the force only three months before, when he was assigned to guard a franchise of the Great Atlantic and Pacific Tea Company at 5361 S. Morgan Street. A wave of robberies had swept the local A & P stores in the weeks preceding the officer's death and extra security had been added. Souders was in the back room of the store when the bandits entered through the rear door and caught him by surprise. The two who were in their mid-teens trained their guns on the officer. Souders did not stay motionless as they had commanded, but tried to disarm one of the young criminals, lunging for his weapon. At his sudden movement, both fired their weapons with one bullet piercing Souders heart, killing him almost instantly. The suspects then fled the store without any merchandise or money. Officer Souders was interred in Mt. Carmel Cemetery.

The identity of the bandits was discovered by the police almost immediately. Chief Fitzmorris immediately had all available officers combing the city looking for Souders' assailants. Manpower for this search was readily supplied by the numerous new recruits that had been added to the force in the two months since Patrolman Doherty's death. After that tragic shooting in August, Chief Fitzmorris had made it clear that the reserve officers he had been forced to call upon left the city at a disadvantage to the criminal element and demanded more officers be added. An angry and grieving citizenry, weary of the violence and lawlessness that was creeping through the city, strongly supported Fitzmorris' request and soon 1,000 new recruits were added, including Patrolman Souders.

Souders' colleagues wasted no time bringing Bernard Grand and Walter Krauser into custody. The boys confessed to their crime on December 21, 1922. Grant was sentenced to hang on June 15, 1923 with Kauser to follow four months later on October 19, 1923. Both men appealed their sentences to the Supreme Court. The Court affirmed Grant's death sentence while reversing Krauser's on February 21, 1925. The knowledge that Grant would indeed hang at some point did not seem to satisfy Krauser and on June 22, 1925 he expedited his co-conspirator's sentence when he murdered Grant in the county jail. This act coupled with his part in Souders' death earned him a life sentence at the Illinois State Penitentiary at Joliet on November 28, 1925. Souders was interred in Mount Carmel Cemetery.

Patrolman William J. O'Malley,

STAR #2, 20th District, Warren Avenue Station, 25 years old, was making his end of shift call from the patrol box when he received a report of a shooting that had taken place nearby. In a decision that would cost him his life on the night of December 30, 1922, O'Malley, accompanied by Patrolmen S. R. Kennedy and W.M. Murphy of the Warren Avenue Station, decided to investigate the incident and began making their way to Paulina Street and Jackson Boulevard. The policemen only reached Hermitage and Van Buren Streets when they spotted three men loitering on the corner. After approaching and questioning these characters, O'Malley attempted to place one of the men, John Reiss, under arrest for the earlier shooting. Reiss produced the weapon he had used only an hour before and fired at the officers, hoping to cause enough confusion to allow his escape. Tragically, one of the killer's bullets struck Patrolman O'Malley's police star before lodging in his chest, and mortally wounding him. He was rushed to the Cook County Hospital where he died shortly after his arrival. He was laid to rest in Calvary Cemetery in Evanston.

As his fellow officer fell to the sidewalk, Patrolman Kennedy whipped out his service revolver and shot Reiss, who died later that same evening. The killer paid the price that many considered appropriate for his crimes. There was no hope of understanding his motivation for the original shooting that night. It was lost with him. The sequence of events recounted to police by those at the scene did little to explain what led to the violent evening. According to those involved, Miss Minnie Finkelstein, her brother Isadore, Miss Bessie Klass and Leo Kaufman, all were innocently making their way home after a high school dance when they encountered Reiss. The hoodlum had walked past them, mumbling a muffled, "Pardon me," and then suddenly shot at the group without warning. One bullet struck Miss Finkelstein, who collapsed. As Miss Klass attempted to aid her, the two young men they were with fled from Reiss. It was not known how these boys escaped Reiss, but the police did not see them when they came upon Reiss a short time later. The girls were questioned extensively by police, but could shed no further light on Reiss' rationale for opening fire.

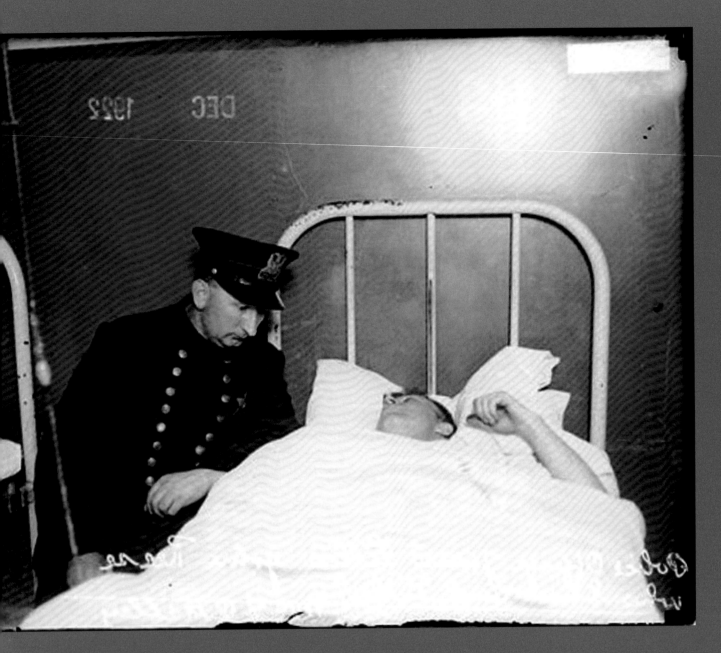

Patrolman Lillie with offender James Reese,
killer of Patrolman William O'Malley (1922).
DN-0075357, *Chicago Daily News* Collection,
Chicago History Museum.

Patrolman Blanton W. Sutton,

STAR #5275, District 2A, Stanton Avenue Station, 30 years old, encountered a well-known suspicious character in a pool hall at 60 W. 37th Street on June 4, 1923. Sutton was on his way out of the establishment when the offender, Eugene Jackson, entered. Something about Mr. Jackson's attitude did not sit right with Sutton and he decided to confront him. The decision cost him his life.

According to one of the pool hall owners, identified in the *Chicago Daily Tribune* as Mrs. Forbes, Sutton had entered the poolhall searching for a particular person whose identity she did not know. The policeman walked up and down the length of her poolroom several times before making his way towards the exit convinced that the person he was looking for was not there. Near the front door he stopped to talk to Mrs. Forbes. While she and Patrolman Sutton were conversing, Eugene Jackson, a laborer, entered and scowled at the officer. According to the proprietor, Sutton took offense at Jackson's actions and remarked, "That man wants to be arrested. Maybe we'd better take him over to a whaling," before following Jackson to the back of the room.

Sutton caught up with Jackson near a pool table in the rear of the establishment and began to question him. After only a few inquiries the officer began a search to determine whether the offender was carrying any weapons. Instead of allowing the search, Jackson backed away and drew a gun. Patrolman Sutton wasted no time in responding and quickly drew his own weapon. Two shots were heard in quick succession and then Sutton fell to the floor, mortally wounded. In addition, an innocent patron playing pool, James Wisger, received a fatal wound from a stray bullet that lodged in his back as he played. Sutton was removed unconscious from the poolhall and died on route to Provident Hospital. Jackson was arrested not long after Sutton's death and committed suicide while in police custody. Officer Sutton was buried in Lincoln Cemetery.

Patrolman Vincent Spiro,

STAR # unavailable, Motorcycle Division, 24 years old, was seriously injured while attempting to stop a speeding automobile, on July 10, 1923. Officer Spiro died from his injuries ten days after the accident on July 19, 1923. John Coleman, the man who is believed to have been driving the automobile, was arrested by police from the Englewood Station. He was charged with assault with a deadly weapon. Spiro had lived at 8014 S. Peoria Street.

Patrolman Lawrence C. Hartnett, Jr.,

STAR #3044, 21st District, Maxwell Street Station, 28 years old, was killed in the line of duty on October 27, 1923 while making a raid on an illegal liquor operation run out of the grocery store by the Montana family. Hartnett, along with Sergeant Stephen Barry and Patrolman F. Fuerst, set out the evening of the 27th to investigate a report of an illegal bootlegging operation being run at 914 W. Polk Street. The drab, non-descript building that the three officers approached showed little indication of the illegal activities it housed, but they knew that appearances could not always be taken at face value when dealing with bootleggers.

They raided the shop and discovered the tip had been correct. As the officers entered, the family did their best to pour the evidence down the drain. Despite these efforts, the officers found a jug of wine, several cans of alcohol and over sixty bottles of moonshine. The matriarch of the family, Madelina Montana, attempted to stop the officers by throwing scalding water at them, but the policeman pressed on. In desperation, Joseph Montana, Jr., grabbed a revolver and ran to where the officers stood outside discussing the best way to proceed. He opened fire on the officers, gravely injuring Hartnett and Barry before leaping

1923

over their prostrate bodies, disappearing down an alley that ran alongside the house.

Despite his injuries, Sergeant Barry was able to flag down a passing auto. The driver quickly transported the wounded officer to the Cook County Hospital where it was discovered that his injuries were treatable. His good luck did not extend to Patrolman Hartnett, a six-year-veteran of the force with a five-week-old baby at home. He died shortly after the shooting.

At once, an all-points-bulletin calling for the immediate apprehension of 17-year-old Montana Jr. and his father was broadcasted across the city. Police immediately flooded the Italian quarter where the moonshine operation was located, apprehending the offenders the next day. In fact the whole Montana family, Joseph Sr. and Joseph Jr., Madelina, Rosena and John, were all arrested and charged with various illegal activities, including a murder charge for Joseph Jr. On April 24, 1924 in a bench trial the entire family was acquitted of all charges. Officer Hartnett was laid to rest at Mt. Carmel Cemetery.

Patrolman John McGonigal,

STAR # unavailable, Warren Street Station, 64 years old, was killed shortly before 7:30 P.M. on November 14, 1923 by an explosion of six barrels of grain alcohol that had been confiscated and stored after a raid two months prior. It is believed that a spark from the officer's pipe ignited the grain alcohol.

Mayor Dever immediately spoke out in regard to the explosion. The mayor issued an executive order directing alcohol, moonshine and other alcoholic liquids, seized in raids removed from police stations every evening. The confiscated goods were to be stored at the municipal pier or other locations where the loss of life would be prevented should the alcohol explode.

Officer McGonigal was the only person injured in the explosion. He was about to clean "Dr." Spencer Brown's prison cell, when the explosion took place. The cell block, capable of holding up to 150 prisoners, was only holding one prisoner at the time. Vincent De Genova of 2147 S. Tilden Street was only slightly injured due to the thick wall surrounding the cell.

The patrolman was survived by his wife, Emma Holmes McGonigal, of 26 S. Damen Avenue. The couple's only son had died two years prior to the explosion. McGonigal had been a lockup keeper for the Warren Street Station for 35 years.

Patrolman Daniel J.Carey,

STAR #116, South Park Police, 29 years old, was struck by a car at Michigan Avenue and 32nd Street in the South Parks on December 13, 1923. Carey was on his motorcycle and had stopped traffic at the intersection in order to shoot a horse that had gone lame and was holding up traffic. The operator of the vehicle apparently was not paying attention and barreled through the intersection at high speed, striking the officer. Carey, one of six children, survived for two days before succumbing to his injuries on December 15, 1923. He was buried in Mount Olivet Cemetery, 111th Street.

The Montana Family at their trial for the murder of Patrolman Lawrence Hartnett (1923). DN-0076881, *Chicago Daily News* Collection, Chicago History Museum.

Patrolman Vincent Skiba,

STAR #1707, 7th District, 52 years old, and his partner, Joseph C. Lamb, were on patrol on January 7, 1924 when they recognized three bandits at the corner of Merrill Avenue and 79th Street who were wanted for armed robbery. The bandits were not willing to go quietly and opened fire on the officers. They wounded Skiba and Lamb before disappearing into the surrounding prairie with Lamb firing at their retreating forms. Lamb was only superficially wounded and stood by helplessly as a passing priest, Father Henry Weber, assistant pastor of St. Philip Neri Roman Catholic Church, administered Last Rites to Skiba. He was then rushed to South Shore Hospital, but died before he could receive care. Skiba was laid to rest at Holy Cross Cemetery.

News of the shooting swept quickly through the department. Friends of Skiba and Lamb, together with squads of officers under the direction of Chief of Detectives Michael Hughes, scoured the streets only moments after hearing of the incident. One group of police pulled alongside a streetcar on which one of the bandits was believed to be riding and pulled Eddie Duncan into custody. He quickly turned in his co-conspirators, naming Henry Wilson and Samuel Dalton as the men who had been his companions when Skiba and Lamb were shot. Wilson and Dalton were soon apprehended and all three men confessed and were indicted. Duncan was sentenced to the Illinois State Penitentiary at Joliet for life on February 25, 1924, two days after Dalton and Wilson were sentenced to hang. They were executed on April 18, 1924 at Cook County Jail.

Patrolman William F. Bunda,

STAR #3848, 16th Precinct, Maxwell Street Station, 30 years old, was patrolling on March 31, 1924 when he noticed three men chasing a lone citizen. Bunda intervened, stopping the men at the southeast corner of Miller and Polk Streets. He then commenced a search for weapons. It was then that one of the bandits drew a revolver and fired, fatally wounding him. Though critically injured, Bunda was able to draw his own weapon and shoot one of his assailants, effectively incapacitating the man. He then managed to detain the other two suspects until help arrived. Rushed to Cook County Hospital he desperately battled his injuries for seven days before dying on April 7, 1924. Bunda was buried at St. Adalbert Cemetery.

The three men Officer Bunda apprehended, John Pettitto, John Simonetti and James Vitaliano, were all officially held by the coroner on April 15, 1924. Vitaliano had initially been held at the Bridewell Hospital while he recovered from the wounds sustained when Patrolman Bunda fired at the offenders. The May Grand Jury returned No Bills on Simonetti and Vitaliano. Pettitto was indicted for Bunda's murder, but received an acquittal on November 26, 1924.

Patrolman James A. Williams,

STAR # 942, 2nd District, Cottage Grove Avenue Station, 45 years old, was killed on July 16, 1924 when he interrupted four men attempting to rob the home of Miss Flora Davis at 2819 S. Wabash Avenue. When Williams appeared at the scene, the robbers immediately opened fire. One of the burglars, Nathan Pauletto, shot four bullets into Williams' back and two more into his side. As the strong-willed policeman fell to the ground, he fired at the fleeing robbers but only managed to hit one, Pauletto. The offender received a debilitating wound to the abdomen. His accomplices deserted him at the crime scene.

Officer Williams was rushed to Michael Reese Hospital, where he later died. His shooter, Pauletto, was treated at Bridewell Hospital. Sergeants Patrick Lee and Frank McNamara enraged by Williams' brutal murder and successfully tracked down the remaining assailants. They soon arrested Walter Harris, of Bunker Street, as a suspect. During the interrogation, Harris eventually admitted to the robbery but denied being a part of the shooting. He did, however, give the names of Pauletto, Charles Holis and Clarence Mitchell as his accomplices. All four men were arrested and sentenced to life at the Illinois State Penitentiary at Joliet. Officer Williams was laid to rest in Kansas City, Kansas.

Patrolman Frank C. McGlynn,

STAR #2229, 14th District, 27 years old, was escorting D.T. Healy, an employee of Stearns Lime and Cement Company on July 18, 1924 when he died in the line of duty. McGlynn was killed while helping Healy transport the company's $6,000 payroll to the factory. As they entered the company plant, located at 2700 S. Leo Street, in the Bridgeport neighborhood, they were met with a hail of bullets fired by hold-up men who had overpowered the office staff and waited for the payroll messenger to arrive. The offenders never spoke a single word of warning before opening fire. As a result, Officer McGlynn was unable to remove his own weapon from his holster before he was incapacitated by three bullets to the chest. As one of the bullets entered McGlynn's heart, Healy bolted from the building, yelling at the top of his lungs as he ran. The officer fell to the sidewalk just outside the doorway he and Healy had just barely entered. The revolver he attempted to draw fell next to him, never fired.

The three bandits who had awaited the payroll at the cement company then emerged from the building, white handkerchiefs hiding their features. They jumped into a waiting automobile where a fourth accomplice waited. Healy watched the car pull away from curb as he held on tightly to the bag containing the payroll for which McGlynn was gunned down. Word of Patrolman McGlynn's death was quickly flashed over police wires. Squads of officers carrying shotguns spread across the city in search of his killers. The first arrested was George Meade. He wasted no time in implicating Raymond Carroll as one of his accomplices. Carroll was brought back to Chicago from Saugatuck, Michigan where he had been hiding. Both men were held by the coroner on July 31, 1924. Another accomplice, George Dempsey, was then implicated as the owner of the getaway car and brought back to Chicago from New York City. On May 8, 1925, Meade and Carroll were sentenced to life in the Illinois State Penitentiary at Joliet by Judge Lynch. Charges against Miller were dropped on March 25, 1927. Patrolman McGlynn, known among fellow officers as "Handsome Mac," was a six-year-veteran of the Chicago Police Department. He was survived by his wife and son. Officer McGlynn was laid to rest at Mount Carmel Cemetery.

Street panorama of 63rd Street and
Cottage Grove Avenue (c.1920's).
DN-0074047, *Chicago Daily News*
Collection, Chicago History Museum.

Suspects in the DesPlaines Street Police Station (c.1920). DN-0071640, *Chicago Daily News* Collection, Chicago History Museum.

Sergeant Harry J. Crowley,

STAR #160, 38 years old, was an honored and well respected Chicago Policeman who received the *Chicago Tribune* Award for heroism in September of 1921. However, his days of heroism quickly ended on the night of November 8, 1924 when he was shot to death by two men.

On that night, Crowley accompanied Miss Margaret Price to a "soft drink parlor" owned by John Quail at 539 W. Polk Street. The two friends were sitting at a table towards the back, enjoying a beer, when suddenly two armed bandits entered the establishment wearing matching blue handkerchiefs over their faces. The thugs demanded that patrons throw up their hands as they attempted to rob them. Instinctively, Officer Crowley drew his pistol and confronted the men.

Simultaneously, both the officer and one of the robbers fired their weapons. A bullet pierced Crowley directly in the heart. His assailant took a bullet in the right side of his chest. Both dropped to the ground bleeding, but Crowley managed to continue firing in hopes of wounding the second offender. He was unsuccessful in his attempts. The second man fired three more shots at the fallen officer as he fled out the door. Crowley died before any help could arrive. The man who shot Crowley was identified as Calisto Hernandez. He later died from the wound Crowley inflicted. The escaped offender, Joe Estrado, was eventually arrested in Rockford, Illinois on December 17, 1924. He was brought back to Chicago on December 18. He was found guilty of the murder of officer Crowley and was sentenced to life in prison in the Illinois State Penitentiary at Joliet on February 9, 1925. Crowley was buried in Mount Carmel Cemetery.

Patrolman Peter Mellody,

STAR #1334, District 2A, Stanton Avenue Station, 54 years old, was killed during the early hours of Thanksgiving Day morning, November 27, 1924, while responding to a burglary. He was shot twice due to a misunderstanding between himself and a private watchman.

While Mellody was on his way home to celebrate the holiday when he was side tracked by the burglar alarm at the Vernon Drug Company's store located at the southeast corner of 35th Street and Vernon Avenue. He decided to investigate the situation. John Breen, the private watchman of the store, was standing in the doorway when Melody arrived. Mellody mistook Breen to be the burglar and attacked him with his club.

Breen responded by firing two shots, one in the officer's hip and the other below his heart. Mellody was rushed to Lakeside Hospital, where he died. Breen was treated at the same hospital and later arrested. Breen was eventually exonerated after proving he had acted entirely in self-defense, saying, "He hit me on my head," Breen said, "I had to shoot. It was self-defense." Officer Mellody was buried at Calvary Cemetery, Evanston.

Patrolman Edward J. Cleary,

STAR #4220, 16th District, Maxwell Street Station, 31 years old, was killed on November 29, 1924 in the vicinity of 1113 W. Maxwell Street, after attempting to arrest an unknown suspect. The investigation of the officer's murder lasted until 1928. Sadly, no one was ever found guilty of the crime.

Isabella Stepnec of W. Liberty Street reported a man loitering outside the entrance of her home. Officer Cleary was sent to investigate the situation and indeed found a suspicious man lurking around. When Cleary tried to make the arrest, the man shot the officer and made his escape. The coroner made a recommendation that Minnie Lovejoy, another resident of W. Liberty Street, be arrested for being an accessory based on the belief that she knew the identity of the shooter. She was arrested on December 1924. Several years had passed before Joe, alias Mike, Johnson was arrested on March 25, 1927. He was later held without bail by Judge Allegretti on April 12, 1927. The investigation continued, with police making another arrest on April 15, 1928. The accused, James Gibson, was eventually acquitted on January 15, 1928. Officer Cleary, who had resided at 4357 S. Princeton Avenue, left behind his mother and father. The patrolman's Requiem Mass was said at St. Cecilia Church. He was buried in Mount Olivet Cemetery.

Patrolman William A. Perrin,

STAR #846, 10th Precinct, Gresham Station, 27 years old, was killed November 30, 1924 in a case of mistaken identity. The officer was patrolling his usual route when he approached a resident of the area who mistook Perrin for a holdup man and opened fire on him. The policeman was mortally wounded and died almost instantly. Perrin was later buried in Mount Olivet Cemetery.

The night Officer Perrin was killed Hugh A. Stewart and his wife drove up to the front of their home, located at 8515 S. Paulina Street. The wife exited the car and entered their home while Stewart remained in the car intending to park the sedan in a garage behind the house. Before Stewart could pull away from the curb, a squad car packed with three policemen pulled up next to him. Stewart mistook the officers for thugs aiming to rob him. As a result, Stewart drew his automatic weapon and fired upon the innocent patrolmen. He fired eight bullets, four of which struck Perrin in the heart and head. The rest seriously injured the remaining two officers. After an investigation under Detective William Schoemaker, it was determined that the incident occurred because of the many holdups that had taken place in the area and the fearfulness of local residents. On December 1, 1924, Stewart was exonerated by the coroner.

Patrolman William Holmes,

STAR #4042, District 2A, Stanton Avenue Station, 44 years old, was the last victim of a night of crime during the early hours of December 24, 1924. It was only 12:20 A.M. on Christmas Eve when the officer was walking his beat with his partner, Patrolman Jesse McKinney. The two policemen responded to a robbery at 37th Street, reported by a female resident. They discovered two men attempting to burglarize a home and quickly tried arrest them. The robbers resisted, firing their guns, killing Holmes and wounding McKinney. One of the bandits, George Williams, was killed during a shootout with other officers while the other escaped. Holmes was interred in Bloomington, Illinois.

Motorcycle Park Police Squad (c.1920's).
ICH-i23645, Chicago History Museum.

Mounted Chicago Police Officer and
early patrol car (c.1920). ICH-i39632,
Chicago History Museum.

Police Officer Kleback's
squad (c.1920's). ICH-i39637,
Chicago History Museum.

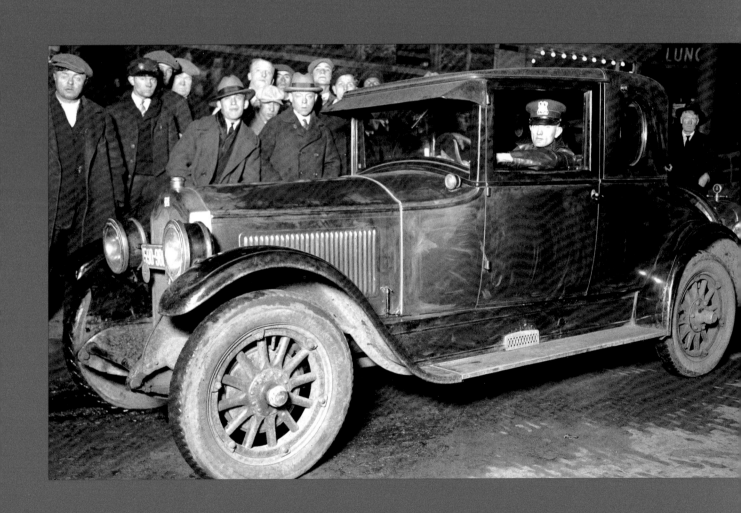

Cadillac turned a corner too quickly and crashed into a light pole. The police officers immediately jumped from their vehicle and ran toward the stopped Cadillac.

They were met with a hail of gunfire, killing Patrolmen Olson and Walsh instantly. A bullet to the chest brought Sergeant Conway down as well, leaving Sweeney as the only cop to continue the fight. Help eventually came in the form of Patrolmen Albert Rickey and George Oakey, passengers on a nearby streetcar who witnessed the shootings. They hailed a taxi and instructed the driver to take the fallen officers to St. Bernard Hospital and then rejoined Sweeney in pursuit of the gangsters. During the chase, Genna turned and attempted to shoot Sweeney but his gun malfunctioned. He did not get another chance to wound an officer. Genna was running towards 59th and Artesian Streets with the police close behind when Sweeney fired a shot that found its mark. Genna stumbled and went down. Though gravely wounded, he was still conscious and managed to crawl into a building through a basement window. Sweeney continued in pursuit of the other men as Officer Rickey followed Genna into the basement. There he found Genna lying on the basement floor bleeding profusely from a hemorrhaged femoral artery in his thigh. Rickert called an ambulance, but the blood loss was too great. Genna died on the way to the hospital.

As soon as news of the bloody battle reached precincts across the city, police from all parts of Chicago converged on the spot. One of the squad cars racing towards the scene was close enough to hear the exchange of gun shots. They drove up just in time to see Sweeney pursuing two men who jumped onto a westbound streetcar. The officer in command of the vehicle, Sergeant Stapleton, ordered the driver to pull up alongside the streetcar as he leapt onto it. Stapleton apprehended the two men who turned out to be Scalise and Anselmi. Amatuna was nowhere to be found. He had fled the scene after the Cadillac crashed before the gunfire began.

Scalise and Anselmi were eventually acquitted of Patrolman Walsh's killing, but were tried twice for the murder of Patrolman Olson. Their first trial ended in a guilty verdict that earned both men a 14-year-sentence for manslaughter. However, they were granted a second trial around a defense of justifiable homicide. The gangsters' attorney claimed his clients had simply been defending themselves against "unwarranted police aggression." He asserted that it was no crime to kill a cop if one is detained against his will or a weapon is drawn against him, situations in which he maintained the men should not be answerable to the law. This argument may seem preposterous today, but the reputation of the police department at that point in time was hardly blameless, becoming further sullied as the trial progressed. The culmination of the trial came when the defense attorneys produced a small book taken from Mike Genna's body that detailed approximately four hundred policemen who were on Genna's payroll. Payments of $8,000 a month, an exorbitant amount for that time, were spread all across the city, leaving confidence in the justification of the officers' actions very shaken. The little black book actually disappeared during the trial but the damage had been done, especially after Chief Collins admitted the truth of its contents. Two years after that violent day in June, Scalise and Anselmi were free men; though not for long. Scalise and Anselmi were soon found dead on the side of the road in Indiana. They had been beaten to death by Capone in early May 1929 after they betrayed him.

Patrolman Patrick J. McGovern,

STAR #4336, 31st Precinct, Townhall Station, 35 years old, was shot and killed during the afternoon of June 22, 1925 at 2:45 P.M. He fell at the corner of Ainslie Street and Sheridan Road. The officer's life was brutally taken while protecting George Haney, treasurer of the Pantheon Theater. It was Officer McGovern's weekly routine to escort Haney from the theater to the North Shore Trust and Savings Bank at 5000 N. Sheridan Road.

On the afternoon of the 22nd, McGovern carried $4,080 wrapped in a newspaper under his arm. The money represented two days' receipts from the theater. As McGovern and Haney walked down the crowded street, three men were waiting for them in a parked car on the north side of Ainslie Street at Sheridan Road. The men pulled on their caps when McGovern and Haney came into sight. One of the thieves, described as short and having a mustache, stepped out of the vehicle and approached the two men. The thief blocked McGovern's path, drew his .38 caliber pistol and pointed it at him. He demanded the money by saying, "Stick 'em up or I'll blow your brains out!" McGovern instinctively reached for his weapon. Before he could remove it from his holster, the assailant raised his pistol and shot McGovern three times in the chest. McGovern fell dead on the street with his hand still on his pistol. Several arrests were made concerning McGovern's death but no one was ever found guilty of the crime.

McGovern was a dedicated officer of nine years as well as an honored World War I veteran. He was the fifth Chicago policeman in 16 days to be killed in the line of duty by a gunman. McGovern lived with his sister, Mary, at 2060 N. California Avenue and was the main source of income for his family. His parents still resided in County Cavan, Ireland, where the slain officer had been born. Sadly, Officer McGovern was not the first member of his family to lose his life in the line of duty. His brother, James McGovern, a Chicago firefighter, died during a fire on Canal Street on March 15, 1922. McGovern also had a brother who was a detective for the Chicago Police Department. He was laid to rest in Mount Olivet Cemetery.

Patrolman William J. Allison,

STAR #304, South Park Police Station, 40 years old, was on routine patrol on his motorcycle on June 15, 1925 at Western and Archer Avenues when he was killed in the line of duty. The officer was riding in the middle of traffic when two automobiles collided. Allison was pinned between the two autos and was crushed by their collision. He was rushed to St. Anthony Hospital, but died eight days later on June 23, 1925 from the many injuries he sustained in the collision. He was buried at Oak Ridge Cemetery.

Sergeant Harry J. Gray,

STAR #886, 9th District, Englewood Station, 43 years old, was fatally shot on October 28, 1925 during the arrest of the notorious fugitive, Martin J. Durkin. The murder of Sergeant Gray was not at the hands of Durkin himself, but rather his girlfriend, Elizabeth Andrews, alias Betty Werner. Officer Gray died at 5;15 AM on October 29, 1925.

Durkin was wanted for auto theft and the murder of FBI Special Agent Edwin Shanahan on October 11, 1925. It resulted in a $500 reward for his arrest. Werner had left her husband to be Durkin's common law wife. The Chicago Police Department became involved in the search for Durkin after he had seriously wounded three other Chicago Police Officers. Durkin's mother, father and two sisters were arrested for helping him escape to California after shootings in 1924. On October 27, 1925, the day before Sergeant Gray's fatal shooting, Chicago police teamed up with the FBI in hopes of apprehending the fugitive. Gray was put in charge of the squad.

Reputed Chicago gangster Sam Genna
confers with a group of associates (1925).
DN-0079183, *Chicago Daily News* Collection,
Chicago History Museum.

Gangsters John Scalise and Albert Anselmi
consult with their attorneys (1925).
DN-0082639, *Chicago Daily News* Collection,
Chicago History Museum.

Flivver Squad members from
First South Park District (1925).
DN-0079674, *Chicago Daily News* Collection,
Chicago History Museum.

The FBI knew Durkin had a girlfriend and that the couple often visited her uncle, Lloyd Austin of 240 W. Englewood Avenue. When confronted by several FBI agents and a squad of Chicago policemen, Austin immediately gave permission for them to hide in his apartment until Durkin arrived. Police were not only hiding in the flat, but were also stationed throughout the neighborhood. As soon as Durkin arrived with Werner, Sergeant Gray placed him under arrest. It did not go smoothly, as a great commotion and a struggle between the two ensued. During the fight, Sergeant Michael Naughton accidentally shot and killed Lloyd Austin.

In retaliation for the accidental killing of her uncle, Betty reached for a revolver and fatally shot Sergeant Gray. Durkin was shot at by both officers, but wore a bullet proof vest that prevented any life threatening injuries.

Gray was taken to Mercy Hospital where his wife was already a patient. She was able to sit at her husband's bedside until his death on November 2, 1925. Sergeant Gray's last words were reported as, "O, if Naughton had only known how to use a shotgun, or if he had let me take it." Gray was laid to rest in Forest Home Cemetery.

In the aftermath of the shooting, Werner helped Durkin escape for a second time. He fled to California where he wounded another policeman, before returning east. He was finally arrested on January 20, 1926. Durkin was discovered on board a railroad train near St. Louis, Missouri and was arrested by U.S Department of Justice agents. He was taken back to Chicago the following day and locked up in the Cook County Jail. Durkin was tried, convicted and sentenced to 35 years for the murders and 15 years for auto theft. He was released from prison in July of 1954 and died in 1981.

Werner's uncle was survived by his pregnant wife, Marion and their 18-month-old baby. Funds were set up at many of the Chicago Police Stations so that Mrs. Austin could receive aid. Since her husband's death was an accident, police felt an obligation to support the Austin family.

Patrolman Frederick M. Schmitz,

STAR #1253, District 1A, South Clark Street Station, 42 years old, was killed November 9, 1925 when a bomb exploded in his basement window while he was working on his furnace. The bomb was believed to be intended for another member of the Chicago Police Department, Captain Ira McDowell, Schmitz's next door neighbor. Captain McDowell, known for being a strict enforcer of the law, had driven the gamblers and bootleggers from the district.

Officer Schmitz was a traffic policeman and lived at 5233 W. Van Buren Street. During the afternoon of November 9, while Schmitz was in his basement, his three children were playing on the first floor. Six or seven sticks of dynamite planted in the front basement window detonated not long after Schmitz entered. The children were startled by the loud explosion and nervously called down to their father. When there was no response, the oldest called for the fire department. The investigation of the incident uncovered neither a motive nor a suspect. Officer Schmitz was buried in St. Boniface Cemetery.

BETTY WERNER

Martin Durkin, the offender responsible
for the death of Sergeant Harry Gray (1925).
DN-0080068, *Chicago Daily News* Collection,
Chicago History Museum.

Patrolman George W. Thompson,

STAR #2009, 2nd Precinct, Cottage Grove Station, 32 years old, was fatally shot at 11:00 P.M. on November 14, 1925 after stopping two suspicious men for questioning. Officer Thompson and his partner, Patrolman Napoleon Sutton, were walking their usual beat when they spotted two men in the area between Dearborn and Federal Streets. The officers stopped the men because they thought they looked like criminals. They immediately asked the suspicious men where they were going and flashed their stars. At that moment, the men became nervous and defensive. The two then drew their revolvers and began shooting. Officer Thompson fell in a matter of seconds, but he managed to continue firing. After Officer Thompson fell, one of the assailants also slumped to the ground due to a fatal wound. Upon seeing his partner in crime, Floyd Battles, bleeding and falling to the street, the second gunman, Claude Huddelston, surrendered and was arrested by Sutton. Battles was believed to be the man who killed Officer Thompson. Although Huddleston was arrested that day, he was later acquitted on March 16, 1926. Thompson was buried in Mount Glenwood Memorial Garden Cemetery.

Patrolman James H. Carroll, (left)
STAR #517, 6th District, 37 years old and
Patrolman James A. Henry,

STAR #3275, 6th District, 31 years old, were partners and among the many officers of their district ordered to stand watch in the neighborhood surrounding Lloyd Austin's Englewood Avenue apartment in the hunt for Martin Durkin in October of 1925. Several members of the Chicago Police Department and the FBI had been involved in the stake out for the fugitive wanted for car theft and severely wounding three Chicago police officers, as well as the murder of a FBI Special Agent.

Officers Carroll and Henry were assigned to stand watch outside a saloon owned by John McKeone, located at 5253 S. Halsted Street. Though they should have been standing outside the establishment, for several nights they had been watching from inside the saloon. On November 28, 1925, the two officers were sitting near a stove in the barroom. Responding to a knock at the door, George Howard, the bartender, let in three men who claimed to be policemen. These bandits displayed their weapons and demanded that everyone put their hands up because they were going to rob them. Officers Carroll and Henry came to the rescue and confronted the offenders. Shooting erupted almost instantly and both officers sustained fatal gunshot wounds. Officer Carroll was shot in the head and died at the scene, while Officer Henry received a bullet in the abdomen and died four days later, December 1, 1925. It was reported that Officer Carroll discharged six bullets, all of which were later found in the wall. The offenders escaped without a scratch and were never arrested. Carroll was laid to rest at Mount Hope Cemetery and Henry was buried in Mount Olivet Cemetery.

Patrolman Edward F. Finnegan,

STAR #3444, 15th District, Brighton Park Station, 27 years old, was patrolling in his automobile on March 27, 1926 when he arrested two men, Richard Evans and Otto Hacker, for speeding. Finnegan drove back to the station with Hacker sitting next to him and Evans right behind him. Unbeknownst to Finnegan, Evans was carrying a concealed weapon. He drew the gun and shot him in the back of the head. As the car sped down Washtenaw and Pershing Roads, the men threw the policeman from the vehicle. Tragically, Finnegan's body dragged along the pavement because his blue uniform got caught on the running board. When the body finally dropped, it landed almost right in front the Brighton Park Station. Evans and Hacker did not slow the vehicle in the slightest, but instead continued to make their escape.

While this tragic event was taking place, Finnegan's partner, Officer Edward Ruback, was following behind in his car. As the two men sped past the police station, Ruback jumped out of his vehicle and began to fire a round of bullets. Lieutenant Bert Cleghorn and Joe Leonard, a police operator, heard Officer Ruback's shots and ran outside. They planned to shoot at the speeding car as well but a crowd of children from a nearby playground stood in the way. Officer Finnegan was declared dead before he ever reached a hospital. He was interred in Holy Sepulchre Cemetery.

Evans and Hacker escaped that day, but were later picked up in Midland, Texas and turned over to the Sheriff on September 20, 1926. Evans was sentenced to hang on October 22, 1926, but the hanging was postponed until October 29, 1926. Hacker was acquitted on January 18, 1927.

Patrolman Edward F. Mashek,

STAR #3975, 24th District, 24 years old, died of chronic nephritis, a disease of the kidneys, on April 8, 1926. The condition was triggered by a gunshot wound he received on July 2, 1923 at 8:13 A.M. The policeman was sent to guard the Royal Blue Store, 5725 W. Division Street, because the manager, Clarence F. Mounts, complained of recurring hold-ups. Mashek was stationed there for only a week and had already stopped robberies. On July 2, Mashek was fatally injured protecting the manager of the store when three armed men tried to rob it.

That morning, Mounts opened his store and stood in the front portion alone, going about his normal routine while Officer Mashek was in the back. A green car pulled up in front of the store; one man remained behind the wheel and two armed men went into the store. The robbers ordered Mounts to walk toward the back of the store with his hands up. Upon seeing the holdup, Mashek immediately responded by drawing his weapon and confronting the robbers. Before Mashek had a chance to fire, he was shot in the abdomen. The officer landed face first on the floor and his gun flew out of his hand. Seeing the critically wounded officer sprawled across the floor, the two robbers raced out of the store, jumped into the green getaway car and sped off. Mounts immediately picked up the officer's gun and chased after the thieves. He hailed a car in the street and chased after their getaway car for a mile and a half, firing several shots.

Two girls, Peggy and Mary Nottingham, also known as Peggy McCann and Mary Kelly, were picked up for questioning with regard to Mashek's shooting. After 48 hours of questioning the two finally signed a 62-page confession, which incriminated Adolph Austwick and William Curry. Austwick, age 20, who was believed to have been the shooter, was held with the bond set at $65,000. Curry, age 19, was held as an accessory, with bond set at $25,000. It was believed that Curry was also involved with other robberies in the city. Officer Mashek had been married one month prior to the shooting. His bride remained by his bedside until his death. Mashek was interred in Bohemian National Cemetery on Pulaski Road.

Patrolman Eugene Hulton,

STAR # unavailable, 10th District, Wabash Avenue Station, was in a patrol automobile on April 24, 1926, on his way to the scene of a hold up when it was struck by a street trolley at 48th Street and Indiana Avenue. Officer Hulton was seriously injured internally. Both his legs were also fractured. Hulton had been in the car with Officers Frank Ballou, William Phillips, and Charles Frabel. All four officers were taken to Washington Park Hospital. The only critically injured officer was Hulton. On April 25, Officer Hulton succumbed to his wounds. He left behind his wife and son.

Patrolman Frank J. Blazek,

STAR #4901, 10th District, Wabash Avenue Station, 29 years old, was found dead after midnight on April 29, 1926. His body was discovered in his police vehicle in front of 4913 S. State Street. According to police evidence, Blazek had attempted to arrest "Lovely" Joe Crown, a notorious criminal responsible for some thirty-seven crimes.

Blazek had started his shift with his partner, Officer John Gorman, who ended work early after getting permission from his captain. Officer Blazek continued on the route alone and noticed a suspicious man walking in the night. When he realized that the strange man was Crown, the wanted suspect, he stopped and placed him under arrest. While attempting to transport Crown to the station, Crown put up a struggle. He grabbed Blazek's gun and shot him. A bystander alerted police and reported that after shooting Officer Blazek, Crown had beaten him over the head, fracturing his skull. Police searched the area and Blazek's vehicle for evidence and found a narcotic vial and a hypodermic needle in the rear seat, which was suspected to be Crown's.

On May 11, 1926, Crown was arrested. Three days later he was held by the Coroner after confessing to the murder and robberies. On October 1, 1926 justice was served and he was sent to the Illinois State Penitentiary at Joliet for life. Officer Blazek was laid to rest in Resurrection Cemetery in Justice, Illinois.

Patrolman Michael A. Madigan,

STAR #5347, 14th District, Deering Street Station, 33 years old, was fatally shot on June 5, 1926 while searching a "soft drink parlor" for liquor. Madigan was assigned to vice and liquor duty with his partner, Patrolman Michael Connaughton. The officers were searching a "soft drink parlor" owned by James Beninato, located at 2724 S. Union Avenue. The policemen were very suspicious of Beninato because he was a known bootlegger. While Madigan and his partner were conducting their search, Beninato shot Madigan twice in the head and once in the back, shattering his spinal cord. Madigan had been in the process of opening a cupboard when Beninato reached for his revolver and fired at the cop.

Patrolman Connaughton attempted to defend his partner and shot Beninato, but not fatally. Madigan and Beninato were taken to People's Hospital at Adams and Paulina Streets. Officer Madigan died from his wounds on June 18, 1926. Beninato, a father of ten children, was arrested and was later acquitted.

Madigan lived at 3130 W. Arthington Street and had been on the force four years. He had a reputation of being a fearless lawman, and had won the *Chicago Tribune's* $100 monthly bravery prize. Madigan had only been married to his 19-year old bride, Mary, several months when the incident occurred. His wife stayed by his bedside until the end. She was the sister of Officer Frank McGlynn, who was killed in the line of duty on July 18, 1924. The two had met at McGynn's funeral in July of 1924. Officer Madigan was buried in Mount Carmel Cemetery in Hillside.

Detective Patrick J. Daley,

STAR #1178, 23rd District, West North Avenue Station, 31 years old, was shot to death on June 27, 1926 at 2:20 A.M. near 900 N. Springfield Avenue at Iowa Street. He was killed by an unidentified man while walking home from the West North Avenue Station. Daley was working as a detective in civilian clothing; the reason some believed he was attacked. Daley lived with his cousin, Sergeant Dennis Lyons, at 910 N. Springfield Avenue. Lyons was startled by the gunfire and ran outside, discovering Daley motionless on the sidewalk. Lyons looked at the body and discovered that Daley was shot in the chest and heart. The frantic sergeant called for help at once. A Detective Bureau Squad rushed to Daley's aid and escorted him to a hospital, but he died on the way.

Daley's body fell in front of the home of Dennis Sherlock. According to Sherlock, he heard someone fumbling around his front door some time around 2:30 A.M. Before opening the door, he called to the person outside but received no answer. Police theorized that Daley must have spotted the burglar and ordered him to stop. Sherlock believed he heard another voice command an order just before shots rang out, disrupting the silence of the night. The police killer disappeared into the darkness never to be found. Patrick Daley was interred at Mount Carmel Cemetery.

The Silver Shield of 1899 that replaced the traditional star for just one month. The star was quickly brought back. Chicago Police Photo Archive.

Chicago Police
Officer John J. Byrnes.
Chicago Police Department
Photo Archive

Sergeant Floyd A. Beardsley,

STAR #881, 9th District, Kensington Station, 47 years old, had been on the force for twenty years when he was fatally shot at 2:15 P.M. on October 31, 1926 while attempting to arrest two auto thieves.

Detectives from the Kensington Station had been searching the area intensely for the notorious car thief Timothy Hennessy, who was a known member of an organized gang of auto thieves. Beardsley and his partner, Sergeant Andrew Harrah, found Hennessy's partners in crime, Stanly Gracyas and Henry Perry, at a garage at 312 E. 116th Street. The two young men were attempting to transport a previously stolen car that was being temporarily stored by Hennessy in his recently rented garage space. Beardsley and his partner successfully arrested Gracyas but Perry escaped. Beardsley instructed Harrah to investigate the scene and the prisoner's rooming house. Once Beardsley and Gracyas were alone, the prisoner drew his gun and fired at Beardsley. After fatally wounding him, the offender jumped into a car and escaped. Sergeant James J. O'Brien appeared on the scene and fired at the escaping car. Gracyas returned fire and shot O'Brien in the right hand. Detectives eventually found the two thieves after an extended search. Gracyas was arrested for the murder of Beardsley, and Hennessey was charged as an accessory. Perry was arrested one block from the garage and also charged as an accessory.

Beardsley, who was in charge of the detectives at the Kensington Station, was interred at Cedar Park Cemetery. Funeral services for the detective were held at Carson's Morgue, which was located at 119th Street and Stewart Avenue. The sergeant was survived by his wife, father and brother.

Patrolman Julian A. Bonfield,

STAR #2310, 3rd District, Wabash Station, 38 years old, was fatally shot responding to a robbery. On December 15, 1926, two armed men held up 25 women and four men at the University Extension Conservatory, a mail order music store located at Langley Avenue and 41st Street. After hearing the reports of the robbery, Officer Bonfield rushed to the scene and met the thieves outside. One of the men had stolen a fur coat from a woman and draped it over his arm. When Bonfield commanded them to halt, the offender with the fur shot through the coat and struck Bonfield in the neck. Seeing that the officer was seriously injured, the men ran off. Patrolman Bonfield died on his way to Chicago Hospital.

On December 16, 1926, Elin Lyons was arrested and positively identified as the killer. It did not take long for Lyons to confess to the robbery and shooting. Lyons also identified Willie Brown as his partner, but Brown was never found. Lyons was hanged in the Cook County Jail on June 24, 1927. Patrolman Bonfield was the son of a retired police captain and the nephew of another who commanded police during the Haymarket Riots. Bonfield lived at 7138 S. South Chicago Avenue with his wife May. In addition to his wife, he was survived by his parents and four siblings. He was buried in Oak Woods Cemetery.

Patrolman Edwin Halloran,

STAR #214, Sheffield Avenue Station, 37 years old, was cranking a police flivver, a small police vehicle, on December 27, 1926 in front of the station when the vehicle's crank handle kicked back and bruised his left arm. It was not until January that the injury seemed serious when blood poisoning began to develop. The officer was taken to St. Mary Hospital. There, his arm was amputated. Little could be done to save Halloran's life and on January 14, 1927 he died from "septicemia of a pangremous condition of the forearm," which had been induced from the flivver handle incident. The policeman was survived by his wife, Irene, and his parents John and Mary (nèe Fergus), in Ireland. Halloran was interred at Calvary Cemetery, in Evanston on January 17, 1927.

Chicago Police Department "Flivvers,"
an early squadcar (1924).
DN-0088168, *Chicago Daily News* Collection,
Chicago History Museum.

Patrolman David J. Cairns,

STAR # unavailable, Traffic Division, 45 years old, was directing traffic at 79th Street and Stony Island Avenue when he died on February 4, 1927. The officer was struck by an automobile driven by Charles Smith. Smith was apprehended two blocks later by another motorist who pursued and caught him. Officer Cairns was buried at Evergreen Cemetery, on 87th Street.

Patrolman Joseph A. Bender,

STAR #2958, 11th District, 30 years old, was returning home late in the evening of February 10, 1927 after attending a double wake at 5611 S. Wood Street for a mother and daughter, Mary Kelly Mooney and Mary Mooney Koppelmann, when he was accosted by two offenders. Bender was in civilian clothes but carrying his police weapon when he left the wake to return home. Some attending the visitation had noticed a suspicious car outside the wake but had not done anything to investigate. The car pulled away from its spot when Patrolman Bender exited and followed him towards his nearby home at 1642 W. 57th Street. He had almost reached his door when the car pulled up beside him and two men drew his attention.

No one attending the wake or present on the street was close enough to see exactly what happened, but it was believed that Bender's natural inclination to defend the law led to his death. When the two men reached Bender, they told him to put up his hands and announced their intention to rob him. Instead of acquiescing, Bender reached for his own weapon as one of the men opened fire. The off-duty policeman was struck just above the heart by a well-aimed bullet and fell to the sidewalk as his killers fled. Several other policemen who had been attending the same wake heard the shots and attempted to pursue the car, but they were on foot and could not get close enough to shoot the offenders without endangering innocent passersby.

Bender was quickly transported to the German Deaconess Hospital, on Morgan Street, but died several hours after his arrival on February 11, 1927. According to the *Chicago Daily Tribune*, he was able to shed some light on what happened and told those riding with him, "They tried to stick me up and I wouldn't have it." It was noted that the crime bore similarities to one recently committed at 5639 S. Hamilton Avenue, where Elmore Bell had been shot in front of his home. Captain John Egan stated that he believed the two crimes had been committed by the same men. William Gall and Victor Walinski were later arrested for the crimes on February 18, 1927. They confessed and received life sentences at the Illinois State Penitentiary at Joliet on September 19, 1927. Patrolman Bender left behind a wife and an eight-year-old son. He was interred at St. Mary Cemetery.

1927

The new Cook County Jail at 26th Street
and California Avenue (1929).
DN-0087862, *Chicago Daily News* Collection,
Chicago History Museum.

Patrolman Joseph Bender's son and widow
(1927). DN-0082685, *Chicago Daily News*
Collection, Chicago History Museum.

Joseph Bender, Jr. identifies his father's
murderers, William Gall and Victor Walinski
(1927). DN-0082686, Chicago Daily News
Collection, Chicago History Museum.

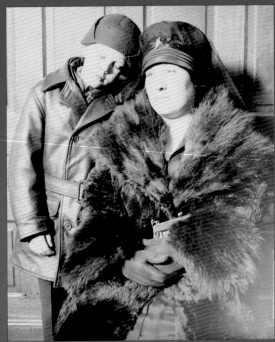

Patrolman Leo Grant,

STAR #3751, 11th District, 30 years old, and a World War I veteran was shot and killed at 3:43 A.M. on Ewing Avenue between 98th and 99th Streets on March 12, 1927 by three convicts who had escaped from the Illinois State Penitentiary at Joliet. Grant and his partner, Officer William H. Frost, had been on the lookout for the men, Robert Torrez, Gregario Rizzo and Bernard Roa, all of whom had been convicted of murder and sentenced to death. The policemen spotted the assailants and approached them, causing the convicts to begin shooting. A gun battle ensued during which Patrolman Frost and Rizzo were both wounded and Patrolman Grant was fatally injured. Rizzo and Torrez were arrested at the scene and returned to the Will County Sheriff; but Roa, the triggerman, managed to escape and was never apprehended. Grant was taken to the South Chicago Hospital and died there a short time later. Grant left behind a three-year-old son, Leo Jr., and a grieving wife, Helen, who was at his South Chicago Hospital bed when he passed away. Grant's funeral was held at Drexel Park Presbyterian Church and he was interred at Mount Hope Cemetery.

Investigating officers quickly discovered that the men had inside help in their prison break. They had managed to escape from the Illinois State Penitentiary at Joliet during a previous incident with four other men. During that attempt, one of the men had brutally knifed and killed Deputy Warden Peter Klein when he had tried to impede their flight. The three who would be involved in Grant's death had been recaptured and were brought back to face the death sentence they had originally been given. Instead, they plotted an escape once again. This time they were able to gain help from the inside, paying Edward F. Gibbons, a guard at the Illinois State Penitentiary at Joliet, and an ex-colleague, $1,500 to aid them in breaking out. After this second prison break, the three men ran into Officer Grant, fatally shooting him. Gibbons' part in the plot was soon discovered and a warrant was sworn out for him by Will County Sheriff Albert Markgraf. He was arrested when he reported for duty early the next morning. In addition, the State's Attorney ordered the arrest of any person who had recently visited the men at the Illinois State Penitentiary at Joliet. Despite these efforts, Bernard Roa was never found.

Patrolman James Cooley,

STAR #792, 2nd District, Cottage Grove Avenue Station, 52 years old, was coming to the aid of two robbery victims on January 23, 1927 when he was fatally injured in the line of duty. Two citizens approached Patrolman Cooley around 10:30 P.M. and reported that they had been held up, asking if the officer would help them locate their assailant. Cooley agreed and soon came across Thomas Pemberton in front of 2916 S. Prairie Avenue. The victims identified Pemberton as their attacker and Cooley approached to make the arrest. The officer drew his weapon, pressed it against the offender's back and announced he was under arrest. Before he could say anything more, Pemberton whirled around with his own gun drawn and mortally wounded the officer in the head at close range. He then quickly fled the scene, but was apprehended several hours later and booked on robbery and assault to murder charges the next day.

The gravity of Cooley's injury was not immediately evident and may have been aggravated by the amount of time it took him to reach a hospital. The two robbery victims, Dr. Paul M. Anderson and James L. Kotrich, who had originally requested Cooley's help, quickly loaded the injured officer into their vehicle and sped towards the hospital. Unfortunately, Dr. Anderson drove recklessly, ignoring stoplights until he collided with another vehicle at Monroe Street and Michigan Avenue. Kotrich was injured in the crash. Anderson was taken into custody and held at the Cottage Grove Avenue Station where officers questioned him on

Helen Grant with her husband, Patrolman Leo Grant, on his death bed in the Cook County Hospital (1927). DN-008302, *Chicago Daily News* Collection, Chicago History Museum.

his driving. He claimed he had been trying to reach Iroquois Memorial Hospital because it was the only facility that came to mind. Whatever his intent, his actions caused an hour to elapse before Officer Cooley was transported to St. Luke Hospital. The father of six survived there for three months before succumbing to his injuries on April 4, 1927. The charges against Pemberton were then amended to include murder but he was acquitted of all charges on October 21, 1927. Cooley was laid to rest at Holy Sepulchre Cemetery.

Patrolman James Kakacek,

STAR # unavailable, 14th District, Deering Street Station, 30 years old, was shot by a fellow officer on April 15, 1927 at 7:45 P.M. in a poolroom located at 500 W. 25th Place. Officer Kakacek and his partner, Officer William Allen, were at 30th and Wallace Streets when they were given word via wire tap to head to the poolroom. Two Mexican immigrants wanted for robbery were thought to be there. Patrolmen Charles Wetter and Patrick Mullen of the Flivver Squad also were sent to the poolroom from the Deering Street Station, unaware other police were sent to the location. Kakacek and Allen, in their civilian clothing, arrived first. The proprietor of the poolroom, Joseph Lapinelli, pointed out the two suspects. Before the two officers could get far in their search, Officers Wetter and Mullen came in and shooting began. Wetter shot Kakacek mistakenly, as he believed he was a robber. Immediately Allen yelled out, "Don't shoot any more. You've killed one of our men." It was too late, Kakacek had already been critically wounded. Wetter was taken into custody and questioned by Captain John Horan, but later he was released. Wetter was exonerated by the Coroner's Jury on April 17, 1927. The two Mexican immigrants, Anthony Bautasia and Elis Redon, both of 231 W. 25th Street, were arrested and then released.

Sergeant Kazimer Wistert,

STAR #247, 32nd District, 50 years old, was approached on the street by an individual, on July 10, 1926, who identified a man committing an armed robbery. Wistert rushed to the scene and interrupted the crime, causing the offender to flee. The officer followed the man into the hallway of a building at 2204 W. Wilson Avenue and discovered that he had climbed to the landing above. From there the bandit took aim and fatally shot Wistert in the chest before fleeing. The offender was never discovered or apprehended. The patrolman was quickly rushed to Ravenswood Hospital. He lingered between life and death for almost a year before dying on June 7, 1927. Wistert was a 20-year-veteran of the force and left behind a wife and four children. He was buried at St. Joseph Cemetery.

Shackled camera-shy prisoners in lock-up (1927). DN-0082968, *Chicago Daily News* Collection, Chicago History Museum.

Patrolman Thomas J. Healy,

STAR #5416, Traffic Division, 25 years old, was off-duty and in plain clothes on August 2, 1927 when an offender, Porter Simpson, approached and offered to take him to an illegal gambling house. Healy, eager to raid the illegal establishment, agreed to follow the bandit. He followed Simpson to a secluded area at the rear of 71 E. 42nd Street. Simpson then produced a gun and announced his intention to rob the policeman. Healy, expecting a move such as this, already had his gun drawn. The two men exchanged shots, fatally wounding each other. Simpson died shortly after the fatal exchange of bullets. Healy was rushed to Chicago Hospital where he survived for four days before dying on August 6, 1927. He was laid to rest in Holy Sepulchre Cemetery.

Sergeant Patrick F. Delaney,

STAR #417, 16th District, 50 years old, was on patrol on October 4, 1927 when he heard shots fired. He proceeded in the direction of the sounds and came upon three suspicious men in front of 1337 W. Hastings Street. Delaney began to question the men and while his attention was centered on one, another pulled a gun and fatally shot him. The men fled, with the policeman emptying his gun at their retreating backs. Sergeant Delaney staggered to a nearby police call box where he relayed his injuries to the dispatcher at the Maxwell Street Station. He collapsed before completing his report and a patrol wagon was immediately dispatched. When officers reached their fallen comrade, they found him unconscious at the foot of the patrol box and instantly rushed him to Cook County Hospital. He died there at 4:30 A.M. Delaney, a 21-year-veteran of the Chicago Police Department, was buried in Mount Carmel Cemetery.

Four people were eventually held responsible for the policeman's death. Arthur Lucas, Shelby Brown and Willie Richardson were charged with murder on October 11, 1927, with Miss Sidney Norment held as an accessory. Brown, only a teenager, crumbled under pressure, telling police interrogators Lucas was hiding in a barn at the rear of his home, where he was later found. On March 12, 1928 Lucas, 24, of 1308 W. 14th Street, entered a plea of guilty and received 14 years in the Illinois State Penitentiary at Joliet. The cases of the three other offenders were dismissed.

Detective Walter Schwass, suspect Roy Doll and Captain Dan Lynch at the Maxwell Street Station (1927). DN-0083639, *Chicago Daily News* Collection, Chicago History Museum.

Gangster Joe Aiello, who tried to kill Al Capone twice, and gang members in police custody (1928). DN-0084475C, *Chicago Daily News* Collection, Chicago History Museum.

Sergeant Thomas Lynch,

STAR # unavailable, Fillmore Station, was accidentally shot by a fellow officer while chasing a gangster on November 23, 1927. Sergeant Lynch was the second fatality since new gang wars had broken out in Chicago. Lynch's squad, which consisted of F.T. Barnes, George Maher, Harry Lange, and Charles Wetter, was driving down Washington Boulevard when they took notice of a nearby automobile. The drivers of the unknown automobile immediately sped away from the approaching police vehicle. The officers chased the fugitives through the neighborhood while firing several shots. The police chase ended at Lake Street and Hamilton Avenue where Sergeant Lynch was shot in the left side of the head. He was rushed to Robert Burns Hospital, where he died later that day. The killers were suspected to be members of the "42 Gang" from the Halsted and Taylor Streets neighborhood of "Little Italy," possibly connected to the Capone-Aiello gang war. Several Chicago speakeasys were raided by the Chicago Police after Lynch's death, but no one individual was ever charged with his murder. Sergeant Lynch was laid to rest at Mount Carmel Cemetery.

Patrolman Vincent Gillespie,

STAR # unavailable, attached to the Vice and Gambling Detail of Chief of Police Michael Hughes' office, 28 years old, he was shot on the night of November 29, 1927. After being fatally shot, the officer managed to drive himself to St. Luke Hospital on S. Michigan Avenue where he died the next morning, November 30.

The details of Gillespie's death remained a mystery for some time. Before he died, he regained consciousness long enough to share with Lieutenant Michael Grady his story of that night. Gillespie claimed that he was shot by two African-Americans while at 31st Street and Cottage Grove Avenue. However, the story proved to be false after Gillespie's wife stepped forward with the true facts. Just before Gillespie died, he sent for his wife and shared with her the real story. She in turn related it to Frank J. Loesch, the man in charge of the grand jury.

According to Mrs. Gillespie, her husband confessed he was shot by a detective-sergeant whom he refused to name. The two policemen had been in a "resort" at 36th Street and Indiana Avenue when a quarrel erupted between them. At the end of the argument, Gillespie tore off the police star from his coat and spat at the detective-sergeant, "Here, you can take this right to your 'higher up' for all I care," he said, as he stormed away. According to an eyewitness, the detective-sergeant shot Gillespie in the back as he walked away.

Unfortunately, Gillespie's killer was never identified nor prosecuted. Due to matters concerning election problems and fraudulent voting, the State's Attorney's office could not take on the investigation of the Gillespie's case. It was then handed back to the police department, which was unsuccessful in solving the mystery. Patrolman Gillespie, who resided at 742 S. Albany Avenue, was survived by his wife.

the curb and sped away. Witnesses spotted them down the street switching cars, then taking off in the getaway vehicle. As the bandits made their escape, Chiska was being rushed to Keystone Hospital at 1623 N. Kostner, where he received several blood transfusions from his fellow officers. He survived for a short time thanks to the heroic efforts of the members of Squad Six of the Fire Department, who kept him alive using a pullmotor. Tragically, their efforts were in vain. Sergeant Chiska died later that afternoon. He was laid to rest in Bohemian National Cemetery.

On April 28, 1928, Stanley Walker and Joseph Papciak were booked for the murder of Sergeant Chiska. The arrest of Steven Cygan was recommended the next day. Cygan was eventually apprehended and it was determined that he had been the actual shooter of Sergeant Chiska. He received a death sentence after his conviction and was electrocuted on October 13, 1939. Papciak received a 20-year-sentence in the Illinois State Penitentiary at Joliet, following his conviction, but there is no record of Walker receiving any jail time.

Patrolman Jesse Sneed,

STAR #5078, 4th District, Cottage Grove Avenue Station, 32 years old, stopped to question two suspicious young men on April 7, 1928. His vigilance led to his death in the line of duty. Sneed was patrolling at 12:45 A.M. and had just reached the northwest corner of 31st Street and Vernon Avenue on the Southside when he came upon the two suspects. He detained them and began making inquiries about their business. One of them then drew a gun from his pocket and shot the officer. The two assailants then left the scene where the fallen officer lay mortally wounded.

Sneed was discovered shortly after the shooting and rushed to Michael Reese Hospital, where he lingered between life and death for four days before succumbing to his wounds on April 11, 1928. Sneed was buried in Lincoln Cemetery.

Two men, Clarence Lewis and Ralph Banks, were arrested for the murder and tried in the closing months of 1928. On September 28, 1928, Banks was acquitted on all charges, while Lewis received a life sentence at the Illinois State Penitentiary at Joliet on November 26, 1928.

Patrolman Emil Shogren,

STAR #985, 17th District, Stanton Avenue Station, 32 years old, was riding as part of Sergeant John Shortwall's detail on April 18, 1928 when the squad pulled up to a stoplight and noticed two shifty looking men. Shortwell and Shorgren exited the car at 39th Street and Michigan Avenue, intending to question the men. They had not yet reached the suspects when the men opened fire. The two policemen immediately returned fire, but it was too late for Shogren. He suffered a fatal bullet through the heart in the initial barrage. Officer Shogren was buried in Oakhill Cemetery.

The two perpetrators then turned and ran with Shortwall in hot pursuit, shooting as he chased after them. The other police who had remained in the car exited at the sound of gunfire and joined the sergeant as he attempted to apprehend the killers. One of Shortwall's shots found its intended target. The first bandit fell to the sidewalk with a bullet in his jaw as his companion continued his escape. Police continued their chase and cornered the second bandit at the rear of 3958 S. Michigan Avenue. He turned and attempted to battle police but was quickly killed by Patrolman Frank Pietrowiak.

Shorgren was rushed to the hospital, but the father of three small girls was pronounced dead on arrival only 45 minutes after reporting for duty. Investigators then returned to the scene and identified the dead bandit. A railroad pass card found in the deceased man's pocket informed them that he was Robert Nash, a career criminal who was responsible for the murder of Charles Cook only eleven days earlier on April 7. The wounded assailant, Joseph Copps, also had a lengthy criminal record. However, he never did any time for his role in Patrolman Shorgren's death, despite being charged as an accessory.

Patrolman Arthur F. Esau,

STAR #4967, 38th District, Town Hall Station, 32 years old, possessed police instincts honed by twelve years on the job. He sensed something was wrong as soon as he entered a local drugstore at 3404 N. Clark Street at 10:05 P.M. on April 27, 1928. Esau became suspicious when he did not see a clerk behind the counter. Going behind the counter he discovered a holdup in progress. The two perpetrators spotted Esau and immediately fired at him. Though not in uniform, they quickly identified him as a policeman.

The offenders had entered the store only moments before Esau, forcing the clerk, Louis Terman, into the backroom along with customer Jack Weber. Terman, who was the brother of the drugstore's owner Jack Terman, tried to resist but was overpowered. According to Terman and Weber, who were witnesses, the assailants drew as close as they could to Esau and fired without a word.

After watching Esau fall, they fled to a waiting car and sped off into the night. A pedestrian outside the drugstore heard the shots and called police, who raced to the scene. When a squad led by Sergeant Robert McComb reached the store, they discovered Patrolman Esau dead at the scene. The clerk and the customer were still bound and gagged. A survey of the scene led police to believe the robbers were the same men who had robbed Harry Reveille's men's clothing store at 3152 N. Lincoln Avenue earlier in the evening. A clerk and customer at that location had also been bound and gagged. It was believed there may have been a connection to two additional robberies. The first took place at the store of Harry Walburn, 2739 N. Clark Street, while the second occurred on the Southside. A hat taken from Walburn's store and a coat from the Southside hold-up were both left behind during the clothing store robbery, leading officers to believe they were all connected.

On May 10, 1928, Charles Walz, age 18; Anthony Greco, age 19; and their female companions, Dolly Kazor and Gertrude Pialkowski, were all booked for Esau's murder. The women were included in the charges as accessories after confessing to their parts in the crime. Their cases were eventually stricken off the record. On October 19, 1928 Walz and Greco received death sentences that were to be carried out on December 14 of the same year. They managed to delay their fate for several months with appeals, but were eventually electrocuted on February 20, 1929. Walz and Greco were the first to die in the electric chair at Cook County Jail. Patrolman Esau was laid to rest in Eden Cemetery in Schiller Park, Illinois. He was survived by his wife, daughter, Janice, and his parents, Charles and Adeline.

The electric chair at Cook County Jail.
DN-0083971, *Chicago Daily News* Collection,
Chicago History Museum.

Patrolman Arthur Esau's widow and daughter,
Janice (1928). DN-0085210, *Chicago Daily
News* Collection, Chicago History Museum.

Gertrude Pialkowski and Dolly Keslor were
accused of Patrolman Esau's, murder but
were later acquitted (1928). DN-0085756,
Chicago Daily News Collection, Chicago
History Museum.

Chicago Police Officer Arthur Esau.
Chicago Police Department Photo Archive.

Patrolman William A. O'Connor,

STAR #3470, 15th District, Englewood Station, 37 years old, had just foiled a robbery at Harold Grady's "soft drink" parlor at 7135 S. Halsted Street. He was attempting to place the offenders under arrest during the last hours of June 3, 1928 when he was killed in the line of duty. The thieves he encountered were concluding a series of robberies begun earlier in the evening on the Southside. O'Connor had just finished his shift and was on his way home when a patron from the soft drink parlor who managed to escape told him of the events unfolding in the shop. He reported that the bandits had lined all of the customers up and gone down the line robbing each of them. They had been in the process of robbing Grady of $70 when the man managed to sneak out to seek help. O'Connor followed the customer back to the establishment and was about to enter with his pistol drawn when the bandits made their exit.

One of them attacked the patrolman, striking him on the head with the butt of his weapon. A struggle then ensued between the two men. The bandit was ultimately able to shoot a bullet, striking O'Connor in the head. The offender broke free and ran off with his companion. Astoundingly, O'Connor followed close behind. The officer shot at the bandits' retreating backs. They turned and returned fire, delivering a fatal wound. The patrolman fell to the sidewalk in front of 7143 S. Halsted Street. He was quickly taken to Engelwood Hospital, where he died at 5:00 A.M. the morning of June 4. Compounding the tragedy of the situation, O'Connor was supposed to have gone on vacation on June 1, but had been asked to delay so that he could be on duty for the elections on June 4. O'Connor was buried in Calvary Cemetery in Evanston.

Alfred Malette, John Dempsey and Edward Demker were all apprehended and confessed to their involvement in the crime on June 14, 1928. They were then turned over to the Sheriff until August 7, 1928, when Dempsey and Demker were each sentenced to the Illinois State Penitentiary at Joliet for 50 years. Malette was condemned to join them for 20 years. Dempsey did not remain with his comrades long. On October 26, 1928, he was taken from the penitentiary to testify on behalf of two men on trial for robbery and escaped from the courtroom. He was discovered in Las Vegas, Nevada and brought back to the Illinois State Penitentiary at Joliet on October 10, 1931.

Patrolman Thomas McNamara,

STAR # unavailable, 6th District, 37 years old, was fatally injured in the line of duty on July 4, 1928 after being struck by a vehicle at 50th Street and Drexel Boulevard around midnight. According to witnesses, the driver of the car that struck McNamara exited his vehicle, stared down at the unconscious officer and then got back in his car and sped off. One of the bystanders at the scene thought quickly and managed to copy down the license number of the automobile before it raced out of sight. After the accident, Patrolman McNamara, who lived at 4453 S. Berkley Avenue, was rushed to Washington Park Hospital where he succumbed to his injuries the next day on July 5.

Investigators quickly discovered that the car observed at the scene belong to David Greenfield of 4170 S. Drexel Boulevard. Greenfield appeared at an inquest being held into the officer death with his attorney and peacefully surrendered. The inquest was then continued until July 11 and the offender was held at the Hyde Park Police Station until the findings of the police investigation into the incident could be presented. No true bill was returned for Greenfield and he was released. Officer McNamara was buried at Holy Sepulchre Cemetery.

Detective Jeremiah E. O'Connell,

STAR #1977, 7th District, 38 years old, was walking his beat around midnight on July 29, 1928 with Patrolman Harold O'Doyle when a citizen informed them that a known armed robber was nearby. O'Connell and O'Doyle followed the informer to an alley near 33rd and LaSalle Streets. They found him in the process of holding up Minister George Van Pertiolay of Mount Vernon Baptist Church at 101 W. 35th Street.

The officers immediately stopped the robbery and attempted to place the bandit, Aaron Woodworth, and his accomplice, Joe Harris, under arrest. A struggle ensued with Woodworth pulling a revolver. A gun battle began that ended with O'Connell fatally wounded and O'Doyle injured. In addition, the original victim of the crime, Van Pertiolay, was caught in the crossfire and lay dead on the sidewalk when the smoke cleared. Police rushed to the scene and wounded Woodworth, who was then taken into custody with Joe Harris. O'Connell was rushed to Lakeside Hospital, where he died on July 30, 1928. He was interred in Holy Sepulchre Cemetery.

Woodworth recovered from his wounds and was officially held for Patrolman O'Connor's death on September 25, 1928. Joe Harris was released on all charges on September 26, 1928, with Woodworth answering for the crimes alone. It was determined that he would pay the ultimate price. His execution date was set for June 14, 1929. Woodworth chose to appeal his sentence to the highest court in the land, hoping for mercy or clemency. On January 7, 1930, the Supreme Court affirmed his conviction and his death sentence. He was finally executed by electrocution on April 11, 1930.

Patrolman Luke Howe,

STAR # unavailable, 55 years old, was the victim of a tragic car accident on August 25, 1928 caused by Michael J. Kinney, 22 years old, of 2017 E. 72nd Street. Officer Howe, along with three additional officers, was escorting a burglary suspect, Thomas Fay of South May Street, to the station.

As the police car reached the intersection of Dorchester Avenue and 50th Street, it was suddenly struck by Kinney's vehicle, traveling at nearly 60 MPH. The devastating collision killed Officer Howe and injured Kinney, Fay and three fellow police officers, Frank Murphy, Maurice Hearne and James Doolan. Officer Howe was buried at Holy Sepulchre Cemetery.

Patrolman Leonard T. Jagla,

STAR #1151, 38th District, Town Hall Station, 31 years old, was patrolling with Lieutenant Albert Mikes and Patrolman Frank Dwyers around 8:30 A.M. on the morning of September 4, 1928 when they noticed three suspicious men enter a cigar store at 905 S. Kedzie Avenue. The officers decided to follow up on their hunch that the men were up to no good and tried to enter the store. They found the front door locked and realized there was a robbery in progress. Patrolman Jagla rushed to the back of the building to cover the rear entrance as his colleagues pounded on the front door.

The bandits had already robbed one customer and were planning to make the proprietor their next victim when they were startled by the banging at the door. The offenders abandoned their plans and made their way to the back entrance, where they met Patrolman Jagla. According to the *Chicago Daily Tribune*, Jagla could be heard telling the men to "Stick'em up," followed by a hail of bullets. The fatally wounded officer fell to the ground as the three men made their escape.

One of the them, Morris Luce, chose to flee in the wrong direction and jumped over a fence right into the waiting arms of Patrolman Dwyer. Coming face-to-face with the officer's revolver took all of the fight out of Luce, who quickly told Dwyer, "I surrender. Your buddy's been shot," and offered no further resistance. The officers on scene called for help and Jagla was rushed to St. Anthony Hospital. He was dead upon arrival. Doctors believed that of Jagla's four bullet wounds, the one which entered just above his heart caused the fatal injury. Jagla was buried in St. Adalbert Cemetery in Niles.

After learning of Jagla's death, officers immediately turned their attention to Luce. He was aggressively questioned as to the identity of his accomplices. Warrants for the arrest of James

Ray Bullard, who killed Patrolman James O'Brien, with his wife and daughter during trial (1929). DN-0087410, *Chicago Daily News* Collection, Chicago History Museum.

Nolan and Loe Hendricks were issued. Nolan was discovered in Houston, Texas on November 18, 1928 and turned over to the Sheriff there before being sent back to Chicago. On December 15, 1928, Nolan and Luce each received sentences of 14 years to be served at the Illinois State Penitentiary at Joliet. There is no record of Hendricks ever being caught or punished.

Patrolman James J. O'Brien,

STAR #1544, 15th District, Englewood Station, 36 years old, was on patrol with his partner, Patrolman Raymond Nelligan, at 1:45 A.M. at the southwest corner of 62nd and Halsted Streets on September 16, 1928 when he spotted a wanted car thief. O'Brien approached the offender, Ray C. Bullard, and attempted to arrest him. Instead, he found himself in the middle of a gun battle that cost him his life. Nelligan was also wounded in the barrage of gunfire as both policemen managed to return fire and hit Bullard. The offender then fled the scene as the officers lay critically wounded. O'Brien and Nelligan were rushed to St. Bernard Hospital. O'Brien died later that day from a wound to his abdomen, while Nelligan endured a long recovery from a chest wound. O'Brien was interred in Holy Sepulchre Cemetery. Two years prior O'Brien had been wounded by an automobile thief who shot and killed his partner, Sergeant Floyd Beardsley. At the time the two had been attached to the Kensington Station.

Bullard escaped the scene but did not enjoy freedom long. Three hours after the shooting, police received a phone call reporting that a man fitting Bullard's description was seeking treatment for a bullet wound from a doctor in Oak Lawn. He turned him in. Captain of Detectives John Egan immediately sent a patrol car to retrieve the offender, who quickly confessed to his crime once he was in police custody. Bullard was officially held by the coroner on September 17, 1928 and later sentenced to 30 years in the Illinois State Penitentiary at Joliet on February 2, 1929.

Patrolman Michael J. Lynch,

STAR # 5343, 4th District, Stanton Avenue Station, 40 years old, was on duty on December 8, 1928 protecting the A & P Grocery Store at 458 E. 37th Street when armed bandits entered and announced a robbery. His reaction displayed the bravery and reckless disregard for his own life that he often exercised in the course of his duties. His desire to protect the store employees and customers led him to confront the robbers directly, instead of remaining concealed as he had been ordered to do. Lynch was one of several officers from the Stanton Avenue Station who had been detailed to several local stores due to a recent spate of robberies by a gang that had been terrorizing the neighborhood for weeks. Police were under specific instructions on how to respond if they came into contact with the offenders, but Lynch could not follow those orders in good faith.

Lynch emerged from the shadows where he had been keeping watch and confronted the gang that consisted of Henry Dixon, Clarence Cook and Ira Borner. Dixon immediately shot at the patrolman, firing several times from close range. The robbers quickly left the scene. Lynch died only a short time after their exit. On December 11, 1928, the offenders were found and confessed to their crimes. Cook and Borner were captured and arraigned as accessories in Patrolman Lynch's death. Dixon faced multiple murder charges when it was discovered that the officer's death was not the only one that he had committed. He was also charged with the double murders of druggists Peter Lynch on November 14, 1928 and drugstore patron William Piun on November 10, 1928. The cases against Cook and Borner were eventually dropped, but the victims received a measure of justice when Dixon was sentenced to life in prison the Illinois State Penitentiary at Joliet on August 9, 1929.

Lynch, who resided at 7756 S. Ada Street, left behind his widow, Veronica McFadden Lynch; and four children, Joseph, Thomas, Marie and Rita. His Requiem High Mass was offered at St. Sabina Church. Burial took place at Mt. Olivet Cemetery.

Young Patrolman James Mescall
at the scene of Chicago's notorious
"Big Jim" Colosimo's death.
Courtesy of the Mescall family.

Detective James R. Mescall,

STAR #2245, Detective Bureau, Wabash Avenue Station, 39 years old, died on December 3, 1928 following a long convalescence stemming from a tragic automobile accident involving the patrol car in which he was riding. Mescall was a heroic figure among the Chicago Police, one who often found himself photographed or written of in Chicago newspapers. In the chaotic frenzy of the 1920s, the robust, Irish-born Mescall frequently cut a dashing figure in the world of Chicago law enforcement. Born in 1887 in the rustic, rural, Shannon-side village of Cooraclare, County Clare, Ireland, Mescall arrived in the United States as a 15-year-old boy in 1903 and came to Chicago. Early on he found both romance and opportunity. He married an Irish-American girl from the Bridgeport neighborhood, Loretto McKain, and joined the Chicago Police Department where he quickly displayed a refined eye for police work. In 1915, his work became historic when he was one of the first responders called out to the great disaster of the sinking of the steamer Eastland in the Chicago River at LaSalle Street. With the death toll rising well above 800, it became the worst maritime disaster in American waters. Five years later, he was once again at the threshold of history when he was called to the scene of the slaying of the notorious "Big Jim" Colosimo in 1920. Chicago newspapers ran a photo of young Mescall standing over the dead mobster's corpse in his South Wabash Avenue restaurant. Mescall's steady ability to engage Chicago hoodlums led to his invitation to join an elite squad of Chicago Police led by Detective Chief Michael Hughes, who pursued gangland public enemies armed with the ubiquitous "Tommy gun." The *Chicago Tribune* cited him for "unusual bravery" on February 14, 1922 when it described his fight with three robbers that occurred the previous day. He even managed to capture one of them. The Mescall family, who made their home at 78th and Sangamon Streets, in St. Leo Parish, displayed the familiar Irish passion for public service with distinguished careers in both the Chicago Police and Fire Departments. Mescall's only son, James E. Mescall, was himself a Chicago Police Lieutenant, while his daughter, Mary, later wed Chicago Police Detective Martin F. Walsh. Cousins Tim and Pete King were respectively a Chicago Fire Fighter and Chicago Policeman.

Mescall was riding in a detective Cadillac patrol car in early 1925 when, at the intersection of 39th Street and Lake Park Avenue, he and his detective partner were broadsided by a Rolls Royce limousine driven by an intoxicated chauffeur. The driver lost an ear in the crash while Mescall sustained injuries that would prevent him from returning to active duty. Ultimately, he never recovered. More than three years later, he succumbed to the affects of the accident. With his family at his side, he died on December 3, 1928 after suffering a cerebral hemorrhage. His Requiem High Mass was celebrated at St. Leo Church, 7747 S. Emerald Avenue. He was buried in Calvary Cemetery. In 1968, forty years later, Loretto McKain Mescall, his widow, died and was buried beside him.

On May 25, 2006, seventy-eight years after his death, Detective James R. Mescall was honored, belatedly, by the Chicago Police Department when his STAR-#2245-was placed in the Star Case at Police Headquarters.

Patrolman John Sacht,

STAR # unavailable, Maxwell Street Station, was on patrol with his partner, Officer John Barry, on January 1, 1929. The two had been examining an abandoned automobile at Polk and Morgan Streets when a speeding limousine barreled down the street. The vehicle struck Officer Sacht and dragged him nearly a block before his body rolled under the wheels and was crushed. In the early hours of 1929 there were also two other deaths suspected to have been caused by the person driving the limousine.

Shortly after the accident, police came across a limousine which belonged to Wilbert B. Ashby, a prominent Chicago architect. The limousine was damaged, with a crushed left fender and a smashed headlight. Ashby's chauffeur, James Norton, filed a report at the DesPlaines Street Station indicating the limousine was stolen. Ashby and his wife were held for questioning, but were later released saying they knew nothing about the accident.

Patrolman Henry Lange,

STAR # unavailable, 37 years old, died on January 3, 1929 at St. Luke Hospital. Lange fractured his skull on December 21, 1928 as a result of falling from his horse in front of 333 S. Franklin Street. Patrolman Lange lived at 3353 W. Evergreen Avenue.

Patrolman John Keough,

STAR # unavailable, Racine Avenue Station, 52 years old, was directing traffic at the Ogden Avenue Bridge when he meet his death on January 29, 1929. Keough was attempting to stop Frank Monticello, 27 years old, of 908 W. Taylor Street. Monticello was a truck driver who ran the traffic signals. Keough raced into the street to stop him and slipped, only to fall under the wheels of another truck. The policeman was taken to Alexian Brothers Hospital, where he died. Monticello was held by the police but no further action was ever noted. The fallen officer had been on the force for 20 years and resided at 207 N. Lockwood Avenue. Patrolman Keough left behind a wife and five children.

Sergeant Arthur Vollmar,

STAR #886, 38th District, Town Hall Station, 37 years old, was patrolling on his motorcycle on School Street around 7:40 P.M. on February 22, 1929, with his partner, Patrolman Carl Panlowski, riding in the sidecar.

A citizen informed them he had just been held up. The victim, Dr. Walter A. Birgerson, said the robber stole $8 from him in front of his home and then took off. Birgerson followed the robber until he saw the police. Describing a heavyset man with a beard, Birgerson pointed the officers in the direction the bandit had gone.

The suspect had last been seen heading west about a block from where Birgerson had hailed the patrolmen. It was not long before they caught up with him on their motorcycle. The suspect saw police approach and attempted to flee by jumping on a moving streetcar going south on Clark Street. His getaway failed, so he drew a revolver and took aim at his police pursuers. Vollmar and Panlowski returned fire as they continued their chase. The shooter suddenly stopped, turned and took deadly aim. Vollmar was hit and immediately toppled from the motorcycle, which careened across the street and scraped a parked car before striking a female pedestrian.

Panlowski then leapt out of the sidecar and continued the pursuit on foot as the offender disappeared down a nearby alley. Near the edge of the alley, the officer emptied his weapon at the retreating figure. The offender stumbled once before escaping entirely, leading Panlowski to believe he may have wounded him. He wanted to continue his pursuit but

Four police officers surround Antonio Sakis (1929). DN-0089896, *Chicago Daily News* Collection, Chicago History Museum.

Two motorcycle officers, William Byer and Lieutenant Lowell Smith. DN-0079763. *Chicago Daily News* Collection, Chicago History Museum.

had to abandon it when he suffered a minor heart attack. In the meantime, Vollmar was taken to the John B. Murphy Hospital where it was determined he had died due to a gunshot wound to the head. Sergeant Vollmar was laid to rest in Irving Park Cemetery.

On April 29, 1931, Ralph Yarck was brought in for questioning from Alton, Illinois on suspicion of involvement in Sergeant Vollmar's death, but the case was dropped the next day. No one was ever convicted of the crime.

Patrolman Edward DeMay,

STAR # unavailable, 4th District, Motorcycle Police, 37 years old, was injured on March 5, 1929 while patrolling the streets of Chicago on his motorcycle. DeMay was in pursuit of a speeding automobile, traveling at 35 MPH when his motorcycle slipped on the cobblestone. The slick pavement caused him to slide the length of the street car track crushing the metal of his motorcycle. The officer sustained fatal injuries to his left leg which would prohibit him from ever riding a motorcycle again. On March 7 the officer succumbed to his wounds. DeMay was survived by his wife and four-year-old daughter.

Detective Raymond E. Martin,

STAR #2313, 31st District, Bomb Squad, 33 years old, lost his life in the line of duty on May 15, 1929 when he acted as a decoy in a police sting set up to capture the kidnappers of a prominent real estate agent. Martin agreed to act as a stand-in for Moses Blumenthal, the brother of kidnap victim Philip Blumenthal, and make the ransom payment of $15,000. Detective Martin was said to have borne an uncanny resemblance to Moses, an x-ray technician. He even wore a sling to authenticate an injury Blumenthal had recently sustained. But the disguise was not enough to fool the kidnappers.

Philip Blumenthal, a former bootlegger who moved on to find success in the field of real estate, had been kidnapped with ransom set at $30,000. A $15,000 down payment to guarantee Philip's release had been paid by Henry Finkelstein, a surviving member of the Bugs Moran gang. Philip was freed after two days of confinement on the promised word that the rest of the money would be delivered. The crime was then reported to police, who formulated a plan to capture the kidnappers. It was built around the use of Detective Martin as a red herring, with police and the Blumenthals waiting for the kidnappers to call and dictate the next drop off point where the next $15,000 was supposed to be exchanged.

Detective Martin donned his disguise as Lieutenant George Baker, the head of the bomb squad where Martin had recently been assigned, and three other officers took concealed positions. From their hidden locations they could observe and aid the detective if assistance became necessary, or so they believed. Unfortunately for Martin, events unfolded too quickly for police to prevent tragedy. All police personnel were in place when the offenders pulled up to collect their money at 4:50 P.M. It took them only moments to see that it was not Blumenthal they were dealing with, so they immediately opened fire. Martin returned fire as the kidnappers ran to the getaway car, continuing to shoot even as he fell to the ground. The other officers emerged from hiding as soon as the first shot was fired and joined Martin in firing at the offenders. Luck seemed to be with the criminals though, and they escaped unharmed with the $15,000 Martin had been carrying.

Martin was taken to Francis Willard Hospital, but his wounds were too severe for the facility to treat. He died a short time later. Later, Martin O'Leary, David Miller, Ernest Rossi and Fred Fisher would be identified as the suspects involved in both the kidnapping and the shooting, though they were never brought to conventional justice. On August 22, 1929, Fisher and Miller were murdered during a fight in a gaming establishment in Ludlow, Kentucky. The fate of the other two kidnappers remains unknown. Detective Martin was interred in Irving Park Cemetery.

Detective Joseph J. Sullivan,

STAR #5431, Detective Bureau, 28 year old, had followed in his father Sergeant Jeremiah Sullivan's footsteps when he had joined the Chicago Police Department in 1922, seven years before his death in the line of duty on May 22, 1929. Sullivan was found shot to death in his auto in front of 3133 W. Polk Street. Police were initially baffled by his murder. Various theories were proposed to account for his death. The most credible was that his murder was the work of enemies he had made while assisting Lieutenant William Cusack's Detective Bureau Squad. Although this theory was seen as the most probable, it could not be verified with exact details. As police superiors were attempting to put the pieces of the case together, a call was received by Deputy Commissioner John P. Stege.

The anonymous caller claimed that Detective Sullivan's death had actually taken place inside the infamous saloon of Joseph "Red" Bolton at 1610 W. Polk Street and that his body was placed in his car after his death and driven to the location where he was later discovered. Bolton's speakeasy was not identifiable from the outside, so Stege sent Captain John Egan to locate the saloon and investigate. Egan arrived at the address the informant had given and discovered a lamp shop used as a façade to hide the saloon. He made his way inside and found himself in an empty room with no signs of a recent struggle.

Bolton's Saloon was not unknown to local law enforcement officials. Only two weeks before Sullivan's death, a lieutenant from a Westside station had been severely beaten in the saloon. Some speculated Sullivan may have gone to avenge his fellow officer, who was also a good friend. The saloon's manager, Elmo Clarke, and bartender, William "Dinky" Quan, were believed responsible for the first attack on the lieutenant. Police quickly began looking for them to question their part in the detective's death. "Red" Bolton and Bernard McComb, another patron of the saloon, were also wanted for questioning. Bolton turned himself in later that night but did little to help the authorities to reconstruct the events of the early morning. He claimed to have left the saloon around 12:30 A.M., before Sullivan entered. He admitted there were still patrons there but refused to name them. Bolton was eventually booked as an accessory to the crime but he was discharged on June 14, 1929.

Investigating officers fared only slightly better when they questioned Clarke after he turned himself in for questioning. He told the police that Sullivan had been there only a short time before the shooting, but claimed he knew nothing else and could not identify who pulled the trigger. The unidentified informant who had made the original call to Deputy Commissioner Stege had pointed to Clarke as the shooter, but there was no evidence to back-up the claim. Police officers had to release Clarke. Quan was finally caught about six months later, but he was released in November of 1929 when the grand jury did not indict. On December 27, 1929, Quan encountered another kind of justice when he and two companions were killed by Sergeant P.B. O'Connell and Squad 21-A at 14 N. Sacramento Avenue.

Two subsequent theories related to Detective Sullivan's death concerned the recent death of Detective Raymond Martin and an attack on a post-office employee. Some sources, including Sullivan's fiancée, Miss Alice Bates, claimed that the detective had gone to Bolton's Saloon to question a suspect he believed was involved in the Blumenthal kidnapping. Still others claimed that the search for Willie Doody, a notorious baby-faced criminal wanted for the shooting of Post Office Inspector Evan L. Jackson several weeks earlier, had led Sullivan to the notorious Westside saloon. Historical records offer no definitive explanation for Detective Sullivan's presence at Bolton's, but the threads of these theories point to the officer's death in the performance of his duty. Sullivan's funeral was held at St. Francis Assisi Catholic Church and he was laid to rest in Mount Carmel Cemetery. He resided with his father at 1037 S. Mayfield Avenue.

Detective Joe Sullivan's car at 3133 W. Polk
Street where his body was discovered (1929).
DN-0088271, *Chicago Daily News* Collection,
Chicago History Museum.

Alice Bates, fiancée of murdered
Detective Joseph Sullivan (1929).
DN-0088298, *Chicago Daily News* Collection,
Chicago History Museum.

Young Willie Doody escorted to lock-up by
Baliff Joe Chemma (1929). DN-0089824,
Chicago Daily News Collection, Chicago
History Museum.

Patrolman Herbert N. Hagberg,

Star #1028, 41st District, 32 years old and

Patrolman John L. Conley,

Star #4636, 30th District, 41 years old, had just reported to the W. North Avenue Station on May 31, 1929 when a report of a domestic disturbance was received. Hagberg and Conley, along with Patrolman Joseph J. Murphy, were sent to the residence at 2431 W. Thomas Street with strict instructions to either quell the disturbance or take the man into custody if he could not be calmed. The details of the report stated that Ferdinand Preuse was believed to have shot his wife inside their home on Thomas Street in a crazed, drunken fit. Preuse was a World War I veteran whose expert marksman skills were noted on his service record, a fact unknown to the officers who went to investigate.

The three patrolmen made their way to the one-and-a-half story dwelling which was located in an overcrowded immigrant neighborhood known as the Ukrainian Village. There, two homes often sat on lots meant to accommodate only one. Hagberg and Conley exited the car and left Murphy to keep watch as they went to survey the situation. The officers moved into the passageway that ran between the front and rear residences and crept close to the back of the house. About 20 feet into the walkway, Conley came to a corner of the house and cautiously turned left. There he found a window located at eye-level and after making sure he heard no sounds from inside the residence, he peered through the glass, shading his eyes in an attempt to see into the darkened room.

Suddenly, the sharp sound of shotgun fire split the afternoon air. Patrolman Conley threw his arms back as his body was propelled backward from the force of the blast. As he fell to the ground, a gaping wound in his chest could clearly be seen. Patrolman Hagberg had been close behind Conley. He too became Preuse's victim when another shotgun blast was heard only seconds later. Hagberg frantically brought his hands towards his head, only to discover that the blast had blown away a portion of his face. He whirled blindly from the window, screaming in pain before falling quiet only 15 feet from where he had been shot.

Patrolman Murphy left his vehicle at the first sound of gunfire and rounded the corner of the house as concerned neighbors also reached the scene. Preuse opened fire on anyone who came into range and he killed one alarmed resident, John Chorazak, who had come to investigate. In addition, the crazed gunman also gravely wounded Patrolman Murphy and two other innocent bystanders. Preuse then escaped before police reinforcements could reach the scene, but he would not remain at large for long.

Preuse's crazed state of mind did not seem to be in question. His end erased what little doubt there may have been about his mental health. According to authorities, Preuse fled from his home to a nearby railroad yard housing the tracks of C. & N.W. Railroad. The next morning, his decapitated torso was discovered on the tracks in front of 4245 W. Kinzie Street, some three miles from where the tragedy began. It was believed that he had jumped into the path of an oncoming train, taking his own life and any hope of understanding the actions that took the lives of two courageous policemen. Patrolman Hagberg was laid to rest in Memorial Park Cemetery and Patrolman Conley was buried in All Saints Cemetery.

Patrolman Earl K. Leonard,

STAR #4558, 25th District, 32 years old, was a motorcycle officer patrolling Laramie Avenue near Madison Street on the Westside around 10:10 P.M. on June 9, 1929 when he watched motorist John Bartoli drive his vehicle through a red light. Leonard immediately pursued Bartoli, finally pulling him over on Quincy Street near Lotus Avenue. Bartoli's car was packed with nine passengers, four women and five men, who watched as Leonard questioned and then placed Bartoli under arrest. After securing the suspect, Leonard began to walk him toward the patrol box on Madison Street to call for a wagon to come pick up the offender.

One of the passengers in Bartoli's car, Patrick Joyce, refused to allow his friend to be arrested. He reached under the car seat, produced a pistol to the horror of the other passengers and informed them, "One bullet will finish that copper," according to the *Chicago Daily Tribune*. His companions attempted to dissuade him from exiting the car. When words failed, the men tried to detain him physically, but he was not to be stopped. Joyce left the car and promptly caught up with his friend and Leonard just feet from the patrol box. He then fired one deadly shot at Patrolman Leonard. The bullet hit the officer in the right temple, causing him to crumple to the ground as Bartoli and Joyce made their escape.

News of Leonard's shooting quickly reached almost every officer in the city due to a radio call broadcast by *The Tribune*-owned WGN. Several detective squads rushed to the scene. The wounded officer was taken to the Frances Willard Hospital, a nearby alcoholic treatment hospital, but nothing could be done for him. The seven-year-veteran of the Chicago Police Department died a short time later. He was buried in Woodlawn Cemetery in Forest Park, Illinois.

Officers at the scene of shooting found an abandoned vehicle near where Leonard had been found. They were able to trace the vehicle to an owner who claimed that he had lent it to Patrick Joyce. A statement given to police by Karen Patten shed further light on the situation. She explained that all those involved had been at her Westside home. They left to take one of the female passengers to her home on Quincy Street near Lotus Avenue, where Leonard eventually stopped the vehicle and made the arrest.

This disjointed information eventually led officers to investigate Joyce's past. They discovered that he had a lengthy criminal record that included multiple robbery charges, although he had spent only six months altogether in Bridewell Prison. Joyce's mother and brother were brought to the station for questioning early on the morning of June 10, but the suspect was not caught until four days later on June 14, 1929. On August 9, Joyce was sentenced to the Illinois State Penitentiary at Joliet for life. An arrest warrant had also been issued for Bartoli, but he was not apprehended for over two years. On October 28, 1931, Bartoli was arrested in Moberly, Missouri and the Chicago Police Department was notified of his capture. Unfortunately, the State's Attorney did not have enough evidence to guarantee a conviction of Bartoli. On November 3, 1931, Moberly Chief of Police Sam Sparkman received a telegram instructing him to release the offender.

Patrolman John J. Sweeney,

STAR #411, 29th District, Racine Avenue Station, 37 years old, had been on the force for ten years when he was gunned down in the early morning hours of July 7, 1929. Three wagon patrolmen, Peter Arnold, Thomas Buckley and Joseph Moffat, had been sent to 836 N. Noble Street around 2:50 A.M. the same morning to arrest a man whose wife had sworn out a complaint against him. While they were at the house on Noble Street, they heard shots fired and rushed out to investigate. Moments later, they were hurtling down an alley between Noble and Rose Streets, just off Chicago Avenue, before stopping abruptly as they discovered Sweeney's unconscious form. The patrolman was bleeding from a bullet wound through the heart. The empty alley was immediately searched but yielded no suspects or clues.

Patrolman Sweeney was quickly rushed to the nearest hospital, but he died before arriving. His death remained a complete mystery for over two weeks. Police combed the area surrounding the scene hoping to discover a viable lead. They brought in many neighborhood residents for questioning but nothing solid was uncovered. Then on July 25, 1929, John Wysocki, a career thief, confessed to killing Patrolman Sweeney. Apparently, Wysocki had been in the process of robbing a Checker taxi driver just as Sweeney decided to investigate what appeared to be suspicious activity. The officer foiled the robbery and attempted to put Wysocki under arrest, leading the offender to draw a gun and shoot Sweeney in the chest. On August 3, 1929, Wysocki was sentenced to 78 years at the Illinois State Penitentiary at Joliet. The patrolman was originally attached to the Chicago Avenue Station. Sweeney was interred in Mount Carmel Cemetery.

Patrolman William Gallagher,

STAR #1162, 26th District, 35 years old and

Patrolman Jesse D. Hults, STAR #3629,

32nd District, East Chicago Avenue Station, 45 years old, were attempting to rescue a kidnapping victim on September 25, 1929 when they were gunned down in the line of duty. The man the officers were attempting to rescue, Charles Kirkman, was the leader of an alleged Southside cult, the Moorish Science Temple. The group had apparently been experiencing internal conflicts and this was not the first public sign of problems. The international treasurer of the organization, Claude Greene, was shot and killed before a meeting on March 14, 1929, only six months before Gallagher and Hults. After Kirkman was taken from his home at 442 W. Elm Street, two of his fellow cult leaders attempted to free him themselves before turning to the police for help.

Consequently, Patrolmen Gallagher and Hults found themselves approaching an apartment building at 4139 S. Martin Luther King Boulevard at 11:45 A.M. on September 25, ready to demand Kirkman's release. They entered the building and proceeded down a dimly lit hallway until they reached the apartment where it was believed the cult leader was being held. They demanded entrance and the order to open the door had barely been given when a hail of gunfire erupted from inside the apartment. Gallagher and Hults both fell mortally wounded from the storm of bullets as the other officers with them returned fire. A fierce struggle between police and assailants then began, with police resorting to sawed-off shotguns, revolvers and tear gas bombs to force the kidnappers out of the residence. The mêlée then moved to the streets where officers eventually traded more than one hundred shots with the cult members, who continued to fire at the police as they fled the scene. The crowd that had gathered to watch as the battle raged witnessed a sequence of events that would leave three people dead and two gravely injured.

Patrolman Gallagher and Charles Kirkman both died at the scene. Patrolman Hults was rushed to Mercy Hospital where doctors discovered that he had received seven bullet wounds and concluded that nothing could be done to save the officer's life. As doctors surveyed Hults' condition, over one thousand extra policemen were called on to patrol the Southside to prevent escalation and further violence. This precautionary measure proved unnecessary as the residents of the area quickly settled down, wishing no repeat of the bloody scene they had witnessed that morning.

Sixty people were taken into custody directly after officers took control of the situation. Suspects were aggressively questioned to discover the root of the cult's quarrel and the names of those who were responsible for the deadly shootout. Investigators quickly learned that the association was nothing more than a racket run to make money for those posing as the temple's leaders. Deputy Commissioner Stege publicly proclaimed that all of the costumes, titles, and regalia associated with the Moorish Science Temple were nothing but deceptive props used to twist the religion of Islam into a ploy to scam innocent believers. The leaders whom officers were able to interview admitted to charging several thousand cult members 50 cents weekly in dues that largely went into their own pockets.

Deacon Stephens, the cult member who was identified as Officer Hult's shooter, was killed by a member of Officer Frank J. Reynold's squad shortly after shooting the patrolman. The sixty suspects being held were soon joined at the station by 20 of their cult associates who were ordered held by Deputy Commissioner Stege after he was informed of Hult's death. The patrolman, a 21-year-veteran of the force, succumbed to his wounds on the evening of September 26, 1929, only a short time after promising his superior, Lieutenant Andrew Barry, "Don't worry Andy. I'll beat this and be back on the job soon," according to an account in the *Chicago Daily Tribune*. The same day, Ira Johnson was identified as Patrolman Gallagher's killer and held by the coroner along with five associates charged as accessories. On April 18, 1930, Johnson was sentenced to life at the Illinois State Penitentiary at Joliet, while his five companions each received lighter sentences for the secondary part they played in the death of both officers. Patrolman Gallagher was buried in All Saints Cemetery and Patrolman Hults was interred in Elmwood Park Cemetery.

Patrolman Fred Mudloff,

STAR #186, Lincoln Park Police, was patrolling his beat by motorcycle on October 4, 1929 when his machine hit a rough spot. The officer lost control of the bike and was thrown head first into the pavement. Mudloff was rushed to the nearest hospital, where it was discovered that he had fractured his skull. He was in the hospital for two days before succumbing to his injuries on October 6, 1929. Patrolman Mudloff was survived by his wife, Regina, and a two-year-old daughter who watched as he was buried amid an elaborate police ceremony on October 9. Mudloff's funeral cortege was comprised of officers from the South Park, West Park and Chicago Police Department. The well-respected officer, a member of the Lincoln Park Police Benevolent Association, was laid to rest at St. Adalbert Cemetery.

Police autos (1929).
DN-0087660, *Chicago Daily News* Collection,
Chicago History Museum.

Chicago Police Department squad cars (1929).
DN-008170, *Chicago Daily News* Collection,
Chicago History Museum.

Halsted Street Bridge over the north branch
of the Chicago River, the scene of Officer
Thomas Murtha's death (1929).
DN-0061137, *Chicago Daily News* Collection,
Chicago History Museum.

Depression Era unemployed men in front of the *Chicago Daily News* building (1928). DN-085378, *Chicago Daily News* Collection, Chicago History Museum.

Detective Jerry E. Murphy,

STAR #4447, 25th District, Fillmore Street Station, 37 years old, met death on January 15, 1930 in a blaze of gun fire during a robbery at a Chicago apartment building on the city's Westside. Events unfolded quickly when police were summoned to 4049 W. Jackson Boulevard. Lieutenant Edward Conroy, a well-known police veteran, led police in the early morning siege. Around 4:30 A.M. a resident of the apartment building, Harry Sucherman, had set off an alarm when three burglars entered his home, took $80 from his trouser pocket and forced him to open a wall safe. When he pressed a button, it rang in the apartment of his brother, Nathan, just across the hall on the first floor. He immediately rang the police. Officers from the Fillmore Street Station were quickly dispatched, uniformed and plain clothes cops alike, under the command of Lieutenant Conroy. He had the building surrounded before the burglars could exit the scene. Conroy was at the front of the Jackson Boulevard building with Sergeant Lynch, while Detective Murphy and a colleague named Loeffer were at the rear. Conroy confronted the burglars as they prepared to make their getaway. "Come out and surrender," Conroy shouted to the trio of thieves – Al Holzman, Meyer Wolf and Sam Waterman. The bandits stood on the landing, realizing that an easy exit was now impossible. They responded with a volley of gunfire that cracked the stillness of the early morning. It was then that Detective Murphy entered the building through a rear window and made his way to the lobby where the burglars were holding police at bay. Before he had time to fire his gun, he fell dead from a gunshot wound.

Tear gas bombs were tossed into the lobby, forcing the thieves, now turned murderers, to seek higher ground. One bandit attempted to enter the apartment of Dr. A.A. Hirsch by passing himself off as a policeman. Mrs. Hirsh shouted down to police in the street, "They're banging on my door. Shall I let them in?" At that point, Lieutenant Conroy shouted back to her to call the station for reinforcements and to admit no one to her flat. Within minutes, two squads from the Detective Bureau arrived. They rushed the building and discovered the bodies of Detective Murphy and two of the robbers. A third invader shouted down from the third floor that he was willing to give himself up. He immediately put down his weapon and surrendered to police.

The suspect identified himself as Sam Wasserman, alias Sam Waterman. He gave his address as 1256 S. Troy Avenue and his age as 32. His dead accomplices were identified as Al Holtzman, of Hoopeston, Illinois, a town 100 miles southeast of Chicago, and Sam Wolf, a well-known local crook. Despite Wasserman's insistence that he only met his accomplices the previous Monday, Chief of Detectives John Stege discovered that he was, in fact, an ex-con from Michigan who had been arrested with Wolf the previous year.

The Cook County States Attorney indicted Wasserman for the murder of Detective Murphy, though the suspect insisted that he was not the actual killer. Assistant States Attorney Abraham Lincoln Marovitz made it clear that even if Wasserman was not the trigger man, he was guilty of the detective's death because he and his accomplices were engaged in the commission of a crime when the death took place.

The Cook County Morgue grew crowded later that day with victims identifying the dead burglars as the perpetrators of crimes against them. Mrs. Sally Goodman of 1901 S. Springfield Avenue identified the body of Holzman as one of three men who had robbed her the day before of $200. After forcing their way into her home, the trio subjected her to torture until she told them where her money and jewelry were hidden.

While the bodies of Holzman and Wolf lay on slabs in the morgue and Wasserman sat in his cell, Lieutenant Conroy was being patched up at Garfield Park Hospital. He had sustained a gunshot wound in the shoulder during the siege. At the same time, the body

View of 63rd Street and Cottage Grove Avenue
(1930). ICH-i39630, Chicago History Museum.

J. WASSERMAN

of Detective Jerry Murphy was stretched out in his coffin in the Murphy family home at 4172 W. 24th Place. His Funeral Mass was held at Epiphany Catholic Church. He was later laid to rest at Mount Carmel Cemetery.

Patrolman Louis C. Szewczyk,

STAR #2521, 8th District, South Chicago Station, 35 years old, was on patrol with his partner, Patrolman Daniel Collins, around 11:45 P.M. on January 27, 1930 when they spotted three suspicious men at the southeast side of 90th Street and Buffalo Avenue. The officers approached the men and announced that they were policemen. One of the men, Max Garcia, waited until Szewcyzk and Collins were about eight feet away and then drew a pistol and fired. The first shot hit Szewcyzk in the chest near the heart, as his partner drew his own weapon and fired in return. Garcia then turned and fled north on Buffalo Avenue with Collins in close pursuit. Garcia's two companions escaped in the opposite direction. Collins and Garcia exchanged shots as they ran, covering three blocks and emptying both weapons before the officer overtook the offender and disarmed him.

Szewczyk was rushed to Illinois Steel Company Hospital but his wound proved too severe. He was pronounced dead on arrival. Patrolman Szewczyk worked as a plain clothes policeman and was survived by his wife and two children, who were both under the age of five at the time. He was buried in Holy Cross Cemetery in Calumet City.

Police quickly captured and questioned Max Garcia. The offender identified Joseph Garcia and Alphonso Reyes as his companions on the street corner and both were soon arrested. All three men were held by the Coroner on January 28, 1930 on the charge of murder. On May 16, 1930, Max Garcia was sentenced to 25 years in the Illinois State Penitentiary at Joliet. The cases against Joseph Garcia and Alphonso Reyes were tossed out.

Patrolman Harry S. Olsen,

STAR #219, Lincoln Park Policeman, 30 years old, was on routine patrol when he lost his life in the line of duty on February 8, 1930. Olsen was driving a motorcycle with a mounted sidecar, racing south along Lake Shore Drive near Webster Avenue in pursuit of a speeding motorist, when his machine struck a rut that forced him to veer and skid. He was hurled headlong into the path of an automobile driven by B. Strauss of 5220 S. Kimbark Avenue. Knocked unconscious, Olsen was taken to nearby Columbus Hospital, where he died a short time later. A veteran of World War I, he served with the 58th Brigade's 122nd Field Artillery Regiment under the command of Brigadier General James A. Shipton. This was also the regiment in which the *Chicago Tribune's* Colonel Robert McCormick served in France. Olsen left behind his widow, Ethel Johnson Olsen of 5507 N. Artesian Avenue, as well as his parents, Andrew and Augusta Olsen. In addition, he was mourned by three siblings, Earl Olsen, Mrs. C.W. Shaves and Mrs. H. C. Luepke. His burial took place in Mount Olive Cemetery. He was a member of the Lincoln Park Police Social and Benevolent Association.

Detective John J. Ryan,

STAR #5618, 36th District, Hudson Avenue Station, 30 years old, fell in the line of duty at 11:30 A.M. on February 24, 1930 during a savage gun battle with a veteran Chicago criminal, ex-convict Joseph Fallon. Fallon had a criminal record stretching back eighteen years. He was well known to local police. Detective Ryan paid a visit to the Chicago rooming-house operated by Fallon's sister, Mrs. May McGovern, at 1598 N. Clybourn Avenue, accompanied by two uniformed patrolmen, in the hope of discovering the whereabouts of the fugitive. He was wanted on a warrant for robbery and bond forfeiture. Ryan's tip on Fallon's location was supplied by former 43rd Ward Chicago Alderman Titus Haffa. Fallon had skipped out on $25,000 bond that had been put up by a friend of Haffa's. After an extended search of the premises by the three policemen, Fallon was not to be found. The two uniformed police then left the house while Ryan decided to remain at the scene to see what unfolded. Only minutes after his colleagues left, Ryan heard the sound of a closet door opening. As Fallon attempted a quick get-away, he exited his hiding place with his guns blazing. Ryan pulled out his own revolver and managed to get off three shots before he was hit and mortally wounded. Fallon was hit in the leg sustaining a wound that would eventually prove fatal. May McGovern managed to escape with her brother in a Checker Taxi Cab, taking him to a flat at 2419 W. Harrison Street on the city's Westside. Detective Ryan was subsequently taken to St. Joseph Hospital where he died a short time later. Captain Thomas Condon of the Hudson Street Station jumped into action, calling a large force of detectives into the District to hunt down Fallon. He issued the order to "shoot first" to any officer discovering the suspect. Fallon was soon discovered at his Westside hideout by Captain Condon and a squad of detectives. He was transported to the Bridewell Hospital at the Cook County Jail. He had taken three bullets from Ryan's revolver and died at 9:35 P.M. Police said that Fallon was a close "buddy" of the late criminal, Russell Clark, who was himself shot and killed by police five years earlier in a robbery.

Detective Ryan lived at 2466 W. Chicago Avenue and was mourned by his wife, Angeline, as well as his two children, five-year-old John Jr. and three-year-old William. He had been on the police force for three years. During that time he had acquired a reputation for "fearlessness." Twice during his last eight months he had been given "credible mentions" by his superiors. He was laid to rest in Mount Olivet Cemetery on 111th Street on the city's Southside.

May McGovern and the taxi driver, Tony Patti, were booked by police as accessories, with McGovern being held by Judge William F. Helander to the Grand Jury with bond set at $5,000. The following day, another suspect, Charles Rafters, was also booked and later held on $5,000 bond by Judge John Sbarboro. Patti and Rafters were each later discharged, while McGovern was acquitted the following May by Judge Philip J. Finnegan.

Patrolman George R. Neil,

STAR #5166, 18th District, 38 years old, was in plain clothes when he became embroiled in a dispute in a Back of the Yards diner located at 5435 S. Halsted Street on Monday, May 19, 1930. Neil was brutally attacked by four men thought to belong to an Irish club devoted to the violent hatred of African Americans. Neil saw the four men order an African-American customer off his seat and begin to beat him. Neil announced he was a Chicago Police Officer. The patrolman then told the victim he did not have to move. The four men then began to attack Neil with unvanquished fury. One man threw a stool at Neil while the others pummeled him. Another man grabbed Neil's revolver and fired twice, seriously wounding him in the stomach before fleeing the scene. On Thursday, May 22, 1930, Neil succumbed to his wounds at the German Deaconess Hospital at 54th and Morgan Streets. Later that day, John Kelly of 5630 S. Morgan Street and Daniel Lynch of 5634 S. Peoria Street were booked on the charge of murder. The coroner also ordered the arrest of two of their known associates, William O'Malley and William Connors. Officer Neil, himself a resident of the nearby Bridgeport neighborhood, was buried at Mount Greenwood Cemetery at 2900 W. 111th Street. His killers were never convicted of his death.

Patrolman John J. Guiltanane,

STAR #1325, 13th District, Morgan Park Station, 36 years old, died in a flurry of bullets while attempting to subdue two suspects in the midst of an armed robbery at the Morgan Park Auto Sales Company at 2345 W. 113th Street on the city's far Southside at 12:55 A.M., July 18, 1930. Patrolman Anthony P. Wistort was also wounded in the gun battle when the two bandits were caught by surprise. Both officers were attached to a special squad at the Morgan Park Station. They had been on an early morning patrol doing follow up surveillance after a local gas station had been robbed near 115th and Halsted Streets. The perpetrators of that robbery had been seen escaping in a small sedan with only one headlight working.

The officers decided to visit a local auto parts store on the chance that the criminals may have been on the lookout for a headlight. After reaching the store they parked outside and went in. The night porter, Elisha Alford, was standing with his face to the wall and his hands in the air. He was being searched by a man with a drawn gun. Guiltanane and Wistort ordered the gunman to surrender. He did so with no resistance. The bandit's partner was waiting outside in the small sedan and was captured with no resistance. A third policeman, Officer Fred Jurgens, making his rounds in the neighborhood saw his fellow policemen and hurried over. They asked him to pull the nearby police box for a police wagon. At the moment that the suspects, Harry Yetter and William Neveraski (aka Nevere), were being placed under arrest and escorted to the rear of the Police Ford, they pulled out their concealed weapons and began to fire madly at the officers. Guiltanane was hit in the lungs and Wistort in the abdomen. Wistort was taken to Little Company of Mary Hospital in nearby Evergreen Park. But death came quickly for Officer Guiltanane. Officer Jurgens later stated that he returned to the garage as soon as he heard the gunfire, but that the suspects had vanished. Sergeant J.J. Kelly, also of the Morgan Park Station, discovered a license plate concealed in a side pocket of the small sedan. It was issued to Andrew Vanosky of 1638 W. 63rd Street, whom police immediately began to pursue. Yetter was caught and arrested later that same day. On July 2, 1931, almost a year after Officer Guiltanance's death, Yetter was convicted and sentenced to the Illinois State Penitentiary at Joliet for life. In May of 1936, Neveraski was arrested for his part in the shootout and murder. On July 19, 1936 he was sentenced to 199 years in the Illinois State Penitentiary at Joliet by Judge Burke. Six years earlier, mourned by his mother, Officer John J. Guiltanance was buried in Mount Olivet Cemetery.

Patrolman Thomas Locashio,

STAR #184, Lincoln Park Motorcycle Policeman, 30 years old, was killed while on duty Monday, September 8, 1930. Locashio was fatally injured when he collided with an automobile on the city's Outer Drive extension (now Lake Shore Drive) at Barry Avenue. The auto was driven by a 17-year-old, Charles Goldstein, of 5136 W. Irving Park Road. Locashio was immediately taken to nearby Columbus Hospital, where physicians determined that his neck had been broken, his skull fractured and serious internal injuries were sustained. He died on Tuesday, September 9, 1930. Goldstein told police that he was turning west off of the Drive at Barry Street when Locashio, traveling south on his motorcycle, struck his vehicle. Locashio lived at 4546 N. Clark Street and was the father of two children. He was laid to rest in St. Boniface Cemetery at 4901 N. Clark Street, but moved the following month to Rosehill Cemetery at 5900 N. Ravenswood Avenue.

Patrolman William I. McCann,

STAR #34, 13th District, Morgan Park Station, 34 years old, was accidentally killed in the line of duty at 2:00 A.M. on September 16, 1930 while responding to a call from a concerned resident of a building at 1434 W. 111th Street. What compounded the tragic circumstances of his death was the fact that he was shot by the very resident who called for police assistance. McCann and his partner, Patrolman Adolph Avery, were riding in their squad car, equipped with the very latest radio apparatus, when they received a call stating that Leon Davis, of 1434 W. 111th Street, had phoned the station to report burglars were in the building's basement. The patrolmen arrived at the scene less than two minutes after hearing the report. However, as they approached Davis' door, he mistook them for the burglars. Fearing for the safety of his wife, Laura, and their three-year-old son, Leon Jr., Davis opened fire through a side window of his flat. The gunshot struck Officer McCann in the forehead just above his right eye and he fell mortally wounded. McCann was immediately taken to Roseland Community Hospital by a fire truck that happened to be passing after answering a nearby alarm but was pronounced dead upon arrival. Officer Avery stated that he was about to return fire when he heard the cries of Mrs. Davis and her son from within their apartment. Davis admitted that he had fired the shots, stating "When I heard the footsteps outside...I never thought that the police could get there so quickly." Officer McCann was buried in Holy Sepulchre Cemetery on 111th Street. He had lived at 7301 S. Green Street and left two sons, William, age 13, and John, age 12. Davis was later held on a charge of manslaughter, but was released when it was determined that his fatal actions were unintentional.

Patrolman Gilbert Wilson,

STAR # unavailable, Mounted Police, 27 years old, met his unfortunate fate at the lower level intersection of LaSalle Street and Wacker Drive on October 2, 1930. Wilson had just started his shift when his horse was alarmed by the noise released from a garbage wagon. The horse reared up and threw the patrolman under a truck carrying three trailers, which crushed him. Officer Wilson had been on the force for 22 months and was unmarried. He resided at 4921 N. Northwest Highway

Detective William P. Rumbler,

STAR #2358, 35th District, East Chicago Avenue Station, 33 years old, was an off-duty plain clothes detective on October 12, 1930 when he was killed. Rumbler had stopped to visit a friend, James Purcelli, who owned a "Soft Drink Parlor" at 3174 N. Milwaukee Avenue. At around 9:25 P.M., he was sitting in a chair talking to his friend when the first of three bandits entered the establishment, asking for someone by the name of "James Darwin," Purcelli later informed the police. As Purcelli told them he did not know anyone by that name, two other men entered and ordered Rumbler, Purcelli and two workers in the rear of the shop to "put up their hands." After complying with this request, one of the bandits began to search Officer Rumbler, leaving the policeman no alternative but to reach for his gun and begin firing at them. They returned fire in what newspapers called a "fusillade." Rumbler was hit by a fury of bullets and fell to the ground riddled by eleven gunshot wounds. He was taken to Belmont Hospital where he was pronounced dead just minutes later. When police arrived at the scene under the command of Lieutenant James Doherty, two caps believed to belong to the killers were discovered. One of them had a bullet hole in it, as well as blood stains. Police immediately ordered a watch placed on all hospitals and doctor's offices in the belief that one of the four bullets that Rumbler had been able to fire found its mark. Purcelli was taken to the Shakespeare Avenue Police

Station for questioning. He informed police that he and Rumbler had been friends for many years and he had just dropped in for a visit on the night of the killing.

Police disclosed Rumbler's partner, Detective John Kratzmeyer, had recently received death threats related to their actions taken against beer runners. But police dismissed the idea that these threats were related to the officer's death. Rumbler had been on the force for 10 years and had been married twice but had no children. He was laid to rest in Irving Park Cemetery at 7777 W. Irving Park Road.

After the shooting, Rumbler's assailants escaped in an automobile. The following day, police responded to a "radio flash" that a wounded man had been taken to 2032 W. Erie Street. When police arrived, they discovered Walter Evenow who quickly confessed to the crime and went on to implicate two others, John Senow and Frank Mallen, as his accomplices. On January 20, 1931, Senow was caught in Cleveland, Ohio while attempting to pass a bad check. After his arrest, he was transported back to Chicago. He was named in an indictment along with Evenow and Mallen, although Mallen remained at large. On May 21, 1931, Senow and Evenow were sentenced by Judge Williams to 60 years in the Illinois State Penitentiary at Joliet after being found guilty of the death of Detective Rumbler. In 1955, after serving 24 years and 25 days of his sentence, Evenow was paroled. Mallen was never found.

Patrolman Peter J. Connolly,

STAR # unavailable, 17th District, 35 years old, was burned to death on October 19, 1930. Connolly was eating at a restaurant located at 1545 W. 47th Street when a waitress asked the officer to look at the hot water boiler which was malfunctioning. While the policeman was reading the instructions on the boiler it exploded and severely burned him. His injuries resulted in his death.

Patrolman Joseph M. Fitzpatrick,

STAR #210, Traffic Division, 43 years old, died in a gun battle with five bandits. Officer Fitzpatrick was a highly regarded member of the force who had spent many years working at Madison and Canal Streets directing traffic before being assigned to the busy intersection of Monroe and Dearborn Streets. At this important downtown post his sunny Irish disposition made him hundreds of friends, particularly among the notables in the financial and business community who always addressed him as "Fitz." On Saturday, October 25, 1930, around 5:45 P.M., Fitzpatrick went to visit his sister who resided at the Hayes Hotel, 6345 S. University Avenue, not far from his own home at 907 W. Garfield Boulevard. As the off-duty policeman was exiting his automobile, he was set upon by five armed bandits who order him to "Stick 'em up." Rather than follow their command, "Fitz" pulled out his own gun and began firing at the bandits. He was able to get off three shots before he was hit just under the heart with a fatal bullet. The assailants escaped in an automobile and were never found again. Taken to Saint Bernard's Hospital, Fitzpatrick died on arrival. He was mourned by his wife and daughter, Marie Leona, age 8. His Requiem Mass was celebrated at Visitation Church and he was laid to rest at Mount Olivet Cemetery.

Police investigating the slaying were later able to recover a brown coat with a pistol in the pocket. The gun was believed to have been used in the killing of Officer Fitzpatrick and was turned over to ballistic experts. Unfortunately, nothing further developed and nobody was found responsible for the officer's murder.

Detective Hubert J. Dillon,

STAR #4957, 22nd District, Maxwell Street Station, 35 years old, was killed in the line of duty on November 23, 1930. Dillon, squad leader at the station, perished when he was shot through the heart by a 33-year-old assailant, McKinley Carter of 639 W. Maxwell Street. Detective Dillon had been on the force for 10 years and lived at 5071 W. Jackson Boulevard. Dillon was fatally shot by Carter as he stepped out of his police automobile while responding to a call with his squad about reports of a fight between two African American men at 630 W. O'Brien Street. Immediately, two of Dillon's companions, Patrolmen Patrick Gaynor and Robert Irwin, opened fire on the assailant and fatally wounded him. The shooter's companion, Mayo McCulley, of the O'Brien Street address, jumped forward to attack the police with a knife. He was seized and taken into police custody. Officers Gaynor and Irwin commandeered a passing automobile to transport Detective Dillon to Mother Cabrini Hospital on South Racine Street. He was pronounced dead on arrival. Dillon was buried at Mount Olivet Cemetery.

Later, McCulley told police that he and Carter had been drinking and started to quarrel with each other. Neighbors, he acknowledged, called police to report the brawl. He went on to stress that he did not know that Carter was in possession of a gun.

Patrolman James S. Corcoran,

STAR #5044, 26th District, DesPlaines Avenue Station, 33 years old, was killed in a fatal gun battle on November 25, 1930. His death occurred at 11:36 P.M in front of a drug store at 2843 S. Indiana Avenue. Dressed in plain clothes, he had been shot twice by an unidentified man. His gun, police discovered, was missing from the scene. Early reports indicated he had been involved in a fight with his assailant and a third man, also unidentified. Corcoran was taken to Michael Reese Hospital and pronounced dead. He was later laid to rest in Mount Carmel Cemetery.

Police were able to ascertain that prior to his death Corcoran had been seen inside a near-by "speakeasy" that operated disguised as a tailor shop at 312 E. 29th Street. In the absence of the proprietor, Mabel McKinney and Arline Ray were in charge of the establishment. Police took McKinney into custody and brought her to Michael Reese Hospital, where she identified Corcoran as one of three men who had been in the illegal establishment earlier in the evening. She said that they had been served beer and complained it was too sweet. After half an hour, she said, the three men left together. Soon after this, William Bredenbeck, a nearby druggist, telephoned police to report the shooting outside his store. He stated that when he rushed out of the drug store following the gun shots, he noticed two men wrestling on the ground and he could see a police star in plain view. Following the shooting he saw one of the men flee. Arline Ray went on to say that later one of the men Corcoran left with returned, appearing quite agitated. He left quickly without speaking to anyone.

This was all the information police had to go on. The case was veiled in mystery for almost two months until a strange set of circumstances occurred. On January 31, 1931, Mrs. Donna Bevier lodged a complaint with police in the 3rd District against another woman, Peggy Smith. Smith was furious with Bevier's actions and retaliated against her by telling police that Bevier knew the killer of Officer James S. Corcoran. When police questioned Mrs. Bevier, she admitted that she knew a notorious panderer named Thomas DeSett. Police went after him and found him in suburban Maywood at the home of his brother. DeSett acknowledged that he had a fight with a man at the Indiana Avenue address months earlier on November 25th. He signed a statement to that effect. Mrs. Bevier went on to admit that she had been given a gun by DeSett and that she threw it into the Chicago River for him from the Halsted Street Bridge. She intimated that her lover, DeSett, was a common robber. Investigating officers then offered the opinion that DeSett attempted to rob Corcoran on that evening and the policeman resisted, perishing in the ensuing struggle and gun battle. Though DeSett was charged with intentional manslaughter, on July 8, 1931, he was found not guilty of the crime. Officer Corcoran Mount Carmel Cemetery.

Patrolman Raymond Kavanagh,

STAR # unavailable, Motorcycle Division, was pursuing a speeding vehicle on December 28, 1928 when his motorcycle collided with a curb. The resulting crash fractured Kavanagh's skull, but he was able to recover from the injury and return to work. Two years after the crash, Kavanagh underwent surgery for seizures caused by his head injury. Tragically, his condition was fatal and he died in the operating room on December 18, 1930.

Patrolman John Vondruska,

STAR #6048, 25th District, Fillmore Station, 32 years old, was killed on New Year's Day, January 1, 1931. His death occurred at 7 A.M. in the Yellow Cab Company's garage at 4950 W. Flournoy, amid a blaze of bullets fired by five armed bandits who set out to rob the cab company's payroll of $8000. Ironically, Vondruska had been placed at the garage to prevent this very kind of robbery. Upon first hearing the bandits order him to "Stick 'em up," Vondruska began firing at the gang of robbers, who arrived in two automobiles. William Smith, a Yellow Cab Chauffeur, was wounded in the leg during the shoot-out while attempting to come to the officer's aid. Police determined that at least one of the bandits used either a machine gun or an automatic pistol when he opened fire on Vondruska, inflicting his mortal wound. A sawed-off shot gun was also employed in the battle. Five witnesses to the shooting were able to identify two of the shooters, Mike DeSteffano and George Conrad, from police photographs. On July 29, 1930, another member of the gang, Mike Mecurio, was found guilty and sentenced to 20 years in the Illinois State Penitentiary at Joliet by Judge Joseph David. Officer Vondruska was laid to rest in St. Adalbert Cemetery.

Patrolman Hugh Kennedy,

STAR # unavailable, West North Avenue Station, 37 years old, was found dead on January 13, 1931 in an empty lot located at 52nd Street and Ogden Avenue, near Cicero. Kennedy had been shot once in the head, and it was later determined that he suffered from a broken back and internal injuries as well.

The motive and circumstances of the brutal murder of Officer Kennedy remain a mystery. After police investigations concluded various theories were proposed to explain how the officer was killed. At first, it was believed that Kennedy had been taken for a ride by gangsters. However, according to Captain McGurn, Kennedy had no known enemies. A second theory was expressed by the coroner, which was inspired by the officer's broken back and internal injuries. The coroner believed that Kennedy had been struck by an automobile, picked up by the driver, and then thrown out of the vehicle once the driver discovered that Kennedy was dead.

The coroner's theory was logical; however it did not explain the shot to his head. Police investigations continued. Eventually police were led to Vito Lotresci, 45, and his son, Sam, 24 years old. The Lotresci home had reportedly been robbed by four youths. The four young men confessed that they had indeed robbed the Lotresci home, and stolen a revolver that had belonged to Officer Kennedy. This linked Lotresci to the murder. The elder Lotresci claimed that the weapon had been found six years earlier by his son Sam. Sam confirmed his father's statement; however the two stories were not accurate. But without further proof the case against them was dropped. Officer Kennedy was buried at Calvary Cemetery, Evanston.

Patrolman Patrick J. Murray,

STAR # unavailable, Irving Park District Police, 62 years old, was crossing the street at the intersection of Crawford Avenue and Byron Street when he was struck by an automobile on March 15, 1931. Murray, of 3800 W. Eddy Street, was with a companion, Officer Peter Novak, age 60, of N. Avers Avenue, when they were both struck and dragged 15 feet by an automobile. Witnesses at the scene believed two men and two women had been inside the vehicle at the time of the accident. It appeared the vehicle made no effort to stop. Once Novak was free of the vehicle, he was rushed to Belmont Hospital. Novak was was able to receive treatment. Murray was instantly killed. Later that day, police found an automobile, stolen from the former Sheriff Charles E. Graydon, that was believed to have been the the hit and run vehicle from the incident. The automobile was found at Oakley Boulevard and Emmerson Avenue and appeared to have been in an accident of some sort. The vehicle had blood stains on it, as well as fender dents, believed to have come from the two bodies it struck. It is not known if anyone was ever charged for the death of Officer Murray or for the disappearance of former Sheriff Graydon's automobile. Officer Murray was buried at Holy Sepulchre Cemetery on 111th Street.

Sergeant Patrick J. Costello,

STAR # unavailable, 43 years old, died after fracturing his skull while on duty as traffic supervisor on April 3, 1931. The officer had just left the intersection of Halsted Street and Roosevelt Street. He was attempting to jump on a westbound Roosevelt Road trolley when he lost his grip and fell to the pavement. He was taken to Alexian Brothers Hospital, where he died. Costello had been a chauffeur for Morgan Collins during his administration as Commissioner of Police. Sergeant Costello was laid Holy Sepulchre Cemetery on 111th Street.

Patrolman Patrick J. Gallagher,

STAR #4966, 38th District, Town Hall Station, 41 years old, was fatally shot on April 14, 1931 by a successful Chicago grain trader in a strange turn of events. Gallagher and Patrolman Carl Johnson had been sent to the Windsor-Wilson Hotel at 915 W. Wilson Avenue in responce to a complaint from John Pendrick, the hotel's night clerk, concerning a drunken party in Room 328. While attempting to quiet the noisy gathering, Gallagher, a 15-year-veteran of the police force, was shot in the abdomen by 59-year-old Frederick Guy Sprague, the owner of the Grain Traders Company, a commodities brokerage house at 39 W. Adams Street. When the police first arrived, Sprague told them he was celebrating his birthday but that he would send his guests, two men and two women, home. Upon leaving, the policemen heard the noise start back up again. Returning to Sprague's apartment, they knocked on the door. According to Officer Johnson, Sprague opened the door and fired two shots, one hitting Gallagher and the other going wild. Officer Johnson quickly disarmed Sprague. The wounded officer was immediately taken to Lakeview Hospital where he died at 2:30 A.M. Officer Gallagher, the father of four children, had once been the recipient of the *Chicago Tribune* award for police heroes. He and his family resided at 1042 W. Waveland Avenue, just down the street from Wrigley Field. He was laid to rest at Calvary Cemetery.

Police said that Sprague, the shooter, was intoxicated when he was taken into custody. He quickly retained the services of Attorney Barrett O'Hara. The following day he was held by the Coroner, but on November 20, 1931 he was found not guilty of the crime.

Patrolman Harry W. Fielder,

STAR #unavailable, Marquette Station, died on April 14, 1931 after being fatally struck the previous evening by an ambulance taking burn victims to the hospital. At approximately 6:30 P.M., a fire was accidentally started by workers attempting to locate a leak in a sewer tunnel located at 22nd and Laflin Streets, 35 feet below ground. More than 60 laborers and firemen eventually became trapped in the tunnel, overcome by the smoke and fumes that rendered squad after squad of firefighters unconscious. Ambulances sped through the night, taking the injured to various hospitals and then returning to make the trip again.

Fielder was on routine patrol two blocks from the scene at 22nd Street and Damen Avenue when he was hit and fatally injured by an ambulance rushing a firefighter to the hospital. The officer left behind his wife, Josephine; children, Margaret and Marion; and parents, Charles and Minnie. The funeral was held at Resurrection Church and the officer was interred at Mount Carmel Cemetery.

Patrolman Anthony L. Ruthy, (left)
STAR #4158, Traffic Division, 43 years old and
Patrolman Patrick Durkin, STAR #1549, Traffic Division,
38 years old, were both fatally shot in a Michigan Avenue shoot-out with a would-be bank robber named Frank Jordan, aka Carl Carlson. The gun battle took place on Thursday, April 30, 1931 and immediately claimed the life of Officer Ruthy. Durkin was critically wounded, but did not die until two days later, Saturday, May 2, 1931.

Frank Jordan, 33 years old, lived at 2140 W. Jackson Boulevard and, according to the *Chicago Tribune*, was a doughnut peddler in Rock Island, Illinois until some eight months earlier when he decided on a more lucrative career as a bank robber. He was being sought in connection with a bank robbery in Neponset, Illinois by two Burns Detective Agency operatives, Alex Benson and John Woods. The men had located Jordan around 5:30 P.M. in the Federal Life Building. After following him to the corner of Randolph Street and Michigan Avenue, Detective Benson, by pre-arrangement, signaled to Patrolman Durkin for assistance in making the arrest. Durkin grabbed Jordan's arms from behind, but the suspect was able to free himself from the hold and reached his .25 caliber revolver, which he used to shoot Officer Durkin. Patrolman Ruthy, busy directing traffic at the Randolph Street and Michigan Avenue intersection, saw the commotion and went to Durkin's aid. The streets were filled with crowds of workers heading home, providing Jordan with the opportunity of blending in with the crowd of pedestrians and motorists. Ruthy, the detectives and a number of civilians pursued Jordan down Randolph Street to Garland Court and on to Washington Street. Finally on Wabash Avenue, Ernest Schaublin, of 2804 W. Logan Boulevard, was able to leap on Jordan, knocking him to the ground. Before the assailant could be fully subdued, he managed to fire-off the remaining bullets in his gun. No civilians were hit. but Officer Ruthy was fatally wounded. He died within minutes of his arrival at Saint Luke's Hospital.

Officer Ruthy lived at 1621 E. 55th Street and had become well known to Chicagoans when he was a witness in the famous trial of the Vincent Brothers who were tried for the murder of Alfred Lingle, a *Chicago Tribune* reporter and friend of Al Capone. That assassination had taken place on June 9, 1930, less than a year before Ruthy's own death. Lingle had been killed near the Illinois Central Railway pedestrian tunnel that leads to Michigan and Randolph. Ironically, that spot was not more than 100 feet from where Officer Ruthy was himself gunned down. After Ruthy's death, Acting Police Commissioner Alcock was emphatic that there was no relation to Ruthy's murder and his testimony in the sensational Vincent trial. At the time, Officer Ruthy had trouble remembering all the details of the murder he was suppose to have witnessed because of a head injury he had sustained during that incident. At the time of his death he was directing traffic, police said, to provide him with a light workload during his recovery. Funeral services for Officer Ruthy were held on May 4, 1931 from the mortuary at 1735 W. 35th Street. Six of his fellow policemen from the Traffic Division served as pallbearers under the direction of Captain Joseph J. O'Connell. Seven lieutenants and sergeants served as honorary pallbearers. He was laid to rest in Holy Sepulchre Cemetery.

Meanwhile, Chicagoans waited for word on the condition of Officer Durkin. He had been a member of the department for 17 years and received blood transfusions from his brother officers in an attempt to save his life. Doctors were encouraging early on but after lingering for two days, the officer died on May 2, 1931. He was survived by his widow, Beatrice, and his three children, Mary, 14; Edward, 12; and Eleanor, 9. The family resided at 6738 S. Prairie Avenue. Durkin was laid to rest in Holy Sepulchre Cemetery.

Initially, Frank Jordan was held for the murder of Officer Ruthy and was indicted by the Grand Jury and taken before Chief Justice McGoorty for arraignment. A second indictment was added following the death of Officer Durkin. Hours earlier, the gunman had confessed to Chicago Mayor Anton Cermak, who led the initial interrogation. He told the mayor of the bank hold up that netted him some $4000 back on April 22. Police found that it was one incident in a long record of criminal acts. It was also discovered that he had served time in the Illinois State Penitentiary at Joliet. Police also arrested Mrs. Gladys Jordan, wife of the accused, in their Jackson Boulevard flat. She admitted that she had been at the scene of the crime, armed in an automobile. On May 29, 1931, Jordan was found guilty of the double homicide of Officers Ruthy and Durkin and was sentenced to die by Judge Joseph Sabath. He was executed in the electric chair in Cook County Jail on October 16, 1931.

Patrolman Michael J. McGinnis,

STAR # Unavailable, Motorcycle Division, 37 years old, crashed into the rear of a truck on May 25, 1931. McGinnis, a motorcycle policeman, had been pursuing a speeding vehicle north on State Street when he crashed at 35th Street. The officer was taken to Chicago Memorial Hospital where he died in the early hours of May 26. Frank Sigman of 1028 S. Newberry Avenue, who had been driving the truck, was arrested but no further charges were brought against him. McGinnis left behind a wife and two children. He was buried at Holy Sepulchre Cemetery.

Patrolman Edward F. Smith,

STAR #4567, 25th District, Fillmore Station, 33 years old, was on duty doing surveillance at 1:30 P.M. on Memorial Day, May 30, 1931, at the John Marshall High School at Kedzie Avenue and Adams Street when he was tragically killed by a 15-year-old boy. Mrs. Mae Crabtree of 3303 W. Warren Boulevard, a janitor at the school, and her 9-year-old son, Charles, waved down Officer Smith after seeing three individuals break into the Westside high school. She said that the burglars were still on the premises. Officer Smith, Mrs. Crabtree and her son made their way inside the school and began a search of the classrooms. Smith heard the sound of splashing coming from the school's swimming pool. While he made his way in the direction of the pool, Mrs. Crabtree was about to summon assistance from the Fillmore Station when she said she heard the policeman order someone out of the pool, telling them to get dressed. She then heard several shots ring out and caught sight of two boys rushing out of the school through a nearby window. Several squads quickly arrived from the station and entered the pool area, where they found Officer Smith lying dead. He had received several bullet wounds in the heart and back of his head. A trail of blood leading out of the pool area showed Smith had been able to fire and wound one of the suspects. The trail ultimately led to the second floor and came from a wound that the shooter had received in his finger. It took just six hours for police to piece together the events that had taken place and make an arrest.

Policeman Edward Flynn of the Fillmore Station began to question several boys who had appeared at the scene. One of them, Leonard Zylch, age 12, of 3321 W. Adams Street, was the son of Chicago Policeman Walter Zylch. He told investigators that he had spoken to two boys who had witnessed the killers escape. The Zylch boy was taken by Officer Flynn and three other police investigators to a home at 3359 W. Adams where they found 12-year-old William Datz and 13-year-old Harold Landis. They told police about the boys they had seen, giving them their names and addresses. Police then quickly went to 736 S. Claremont Avenue where they forced their way in to the house. There, brothers Varner and Earl Corry soon admitted their role in the shooting. They took Flynn out to a back porch where they showed him the place they had thrown the revolver used to shoot Officer Smith. The 15-year-old Varner and 13-year-old Earl also gave officers the name of 15-year-old Schuyler Pearson, who had been with them.

Varner Corry told police the details of the shooting at the Fillmore Station. "We were swimming in the pool when the policeman came in," he said. "He told us to dress. I started to put on my clothes, and was half-way dressed when I took hold of my revolver. I pointed it at the policeman and told him to put up his hands. Then he reached for his revolver, and I thought he was going to shoot, so I fired four or five times. I don't know how many. He got his gun and shot at me and hit me in the second finger of my right hand. I went to the second floor, and got down a drain pipe. I don't know how my brother or Schuyler got away."

Captain Patrick J. Collins, together with the Chief of Detectives John Norton and Deputy Detective Chief Lawrence Rafferty, questioned the three boys until midnight, along with Assistant State's Attorney E.A. Ferrari. They discovered the boys had broken into the school some two months earlier and stolen the revolver used to kill Officer Smith from the school gymnasium office. Varner told them that his father had ordered him to return the gun, but he carried it around with him instead.

A Grand Jury held all three boys over on a charge of murder, while the State's Attorney ruled that they would be tried in Criminal Court, not Juvenile Court, given the seriousness of the offense. Charges against Earl Corry and Schuyler Pearson were eventually dropped. Varner Corry was indicted On July 28, 1931 he was found guilty of the death of Officer Smith and sentenced by Judge Joseph Sabath to the Illinois State Penitentiary at Joliet for 18 years.

Officer Smith was married and left four children. He was laid to rest in Mount Carmel Cemetery.

Sergeant John Cronin,

STAR # unavailable, 25th District, Fillmore Station, 65 years old, was a long-time Chicago policeman with 40 years on the job when he was struck by an automobile while inspecting a car parked near his station on June 3, 1931. The car was driven by Leo Goldstein, an auto salesman. Cronin, who resided at 4926 W. Adams Street, was rushed to Garfield Park Hospital after the accident and succumbed to his injuries a short time later. Sergeant Cronin was the beloved husband of the late Mary Cronin and was survived by his three children, Catherine, John and Thomas. His Requiem Mass and Funeral were held at Resurrection Church on W. Jackson Boulevard and he was interred at Calvary Cemetery.

Patrolman Edward M. O'Donnell,

STAR #3363, 26th District, DesPlaines Street Station, 35 years old, was escorting Lillian Rice, the assistant cashier of the Paul Schultz Baking Company, 25 N. Green Street, to the Mid City Trust and Savings Bank at Madison and Halsted Streets with cash and checks for deposit on the afternoon of June 9, 1931. O'Donnell had been detailed to protect Miss Rice for the block-long walk to the bank. As they made their way there, two bandits stepped up to them at Green and Madison Streets. One grabbed the brief case containing the money, while the other shot Officer O'Donnell who attempted to thwart the robbery. He fell to the ground mortally wounded and died at 2:40 P.M. Officer O'Donnell, who lived at 4907 W. Fulton Street, was pronounced dead at Cook County Hospital, leaving a wife and two children. He was laid to rest in Mount Carmel Cemetery.

At the scene, gun shots alerted Frank Roger, a sporting goods salesman, who was parked in a nearby car. He immediately ran to the side of the fallen officer. As the assailants fled toward Washington Boulevard, Roger took Officer O'Donnell's gun and pursued them at a fast pace. It was not long before he caught up to them as they hid under a parked car at the rear of 32 N. Halsted Street. Roger shouted, "Come out from under there and come out with your hands up." He was in full command of the situation. Roger was soon joined by West Park Patrolman Patrick J. Dorgan and Patrolman Ernest Schafer of the 26th District, who both aided in the capture of the bandits. They were soon identified by police as 25-year-old Mike Trotta of 924 N. Ashland Avenue and 29-year-old Nick Floridia of 1933 W. Taylor Street. The men were unarmed when they were captured, but police searching the area soon discovered their weapons on the roof of a nearby barn. Police, however, never recovered the money that was stolen, leading to speculation that a third bandit had been involved in the robbery and was able to escape with the briefcase. Trotta and Floridia admitted that the weapons were theirs and soon confessed to the robbery and shooting. On August 6, 1931, Trotta and Floridia were found guilty of their crime. Both were sentenced to 145 years in the Illinois State Penitentiary at Joliet by Judge Charles A. Williams. In 1959 Floridia's sentence was commuted by Governor Stratton from 145 to 90 years. In 1961 he was eligible for parole. The governor also shortened Floridia's sentence because of good behavior.

Patrolman Thomas J. Johnson,

STAR #387, South Park Police, 29 years old, was fatally injured in a motorcycle accident on Sunday, June 21, 1931. Officer Johnson's motorcycle was struck from behind on the Outer Drive at 23rd Street by an automobile driven by William Devine of 8126 S. Luella Avenue. Officer Johnson was taken to nearby Michael Reese Hospital where he died the following day, Monday, June 22, 1931. Devine was arrested and arraigned before Municipal Judge Francis Borrelli on charges of reckless driving. Funeral services for Johnson took place at his parents' home, 6500 S. May Street, before proceeding to St. Brendan Church on South Racine Avenue. Officer Johnson was survived by his wife, Jean, and his parents. The patrolman was interred in Mount Olivet Cemetery.

Patrolman James J. Casey,

STAR #2807, Traffic Division, 39 years old, was fatally shot during an altercation with an escaped convict at 10:00 P.M. on June 30, 1931. Casey had responded to a complaint from Miss Frances Bosky of 4339 S. Greenwood Avenue, and her friend, Bert Boff. Bosky, a waitress, told Officer Casey that she had been harassed by Coy Thompson, of 4222 S. Berkley Avenue, when she left her place of employment near 43rd Street and Oakenwald Avenue. She noted that Thompson had insulted her and her escort, Mr. Boff, when she rebuffed Thompson's rude advances. When Boff stood up to "the masher," she claimed that Thompson pulled a gun on them. Officer Casey arrested Thompson and disarmed him. The suspect then suddenly pulled another revolver on the policeman and shot him eight times. Thompson then fled the scene. It was later found that he had escaped from jail in Mayfield, Kentucky. About 20 minutes later, a neighbor informed Police Officers James Curtin and T.F. Curtin that Thompson was hiding in a building at 4301 S. Oakenwald Avenue. He was soon apprehended and placed under arrest. Officer Casey, who lived at 4463 S. Lake Park Avenue, died the following day, July 1, 1931. He was laid to rest in Mount Olivet Cemetery.

Following the discovery of the gun Coy Thompson use to kill Officer Casey, the suspect was held by the coroner. On July 6, 1931, he entered a plea of Not Guilty. He was later found guilty of murder and sentenced to 100 years in the Illinois State Penitentiary at Joliet by Judge Philip J. Finnegan. Twenty-nine years later, in 1960, he was paroled.

Patrolman Joseph V. Isaacs,

STAR #5914, 12th District, the Kensington Station, 28 years old, was on his annual furlough when he intervened in an argument at a Chicago roadhouse, the Spanish Point Tavern, in the Roseland community at 11851 S. Michigan Avenue around 4:00 A.M. on Saturday, October 9, 1931. Isaacs was dressed in civilian clothes, sitting at the counter with two friends, Thomas Liskas, a cab driver with whom he had come, and John O'Leary, a night watchman who joined them at the saloon. While they were sitting at the counter, an argument arose between some women at the back of the tavern. A man, later identified as Thomas Scupino of 1610 S. 51st Street in suburban Cicero, came up to them and warned them to keep quiet. Officer Isaacs told Liskas that the man was armed. Later reports indicated that it sounded as if a woman was being beaten in the back. Officer Isaacs drew his own revolver and attempted to intervene. As he did, one of the women, Victoria Feltrin, grabbed Isaacs' wrist. In the struggle the policeman was disarmed. It is believed that he was then shot with his own gun. Scupino and another woman exited the tavern through a back door and fled in a taxi, leaving his hat and coat at the roadhouse where police found them. Scupino went to the Lexington Hotel at 2135 S. Michigan Avenue, the once infamous Chicago headquarters of Al Capone. At 6:00 A.M. he reported his car stolen to Cicero police.

Officer Isaacs, of 6542 S. Lafayette Avenue, died at 2:30 A.M. on the following day, Sunday, October 10, 1931. He was mourned by his wife, Alice Monan Isaacs, his sons, Joseph and Robert; his parents Nellie and W.J. Isaacs, and his brothers, Charles and Francis. His Requiem Mass was celebrated at 9:00 A.M. at St. Bernard Church in the Englewood neighborhood, on Tuesday, October 12, 1931. He was laid to rest in Holy Sepulchre Cemetery.

It was not until October 28, 1931 that Scupino was finally arrested. At the time, he would provide police with a signed statement. In a closed inquest, Scupino was exonerated by the coroner of any responsibility in the shooting because neither Liskas, nor O'Leary, could identify him as the man they had seen fleeing the roadhouse. Captain Michael Grady, however, obtained a murder warrant for Scupino and had him arrested again after the inquest. Two days later, October 30, 1931, Victoria Feltrin was held by the coroner as an accessory before the fact. On November 4, 1931, Scupino was held to the Grand Jury without bail by Judge Leon Edelman. Both suspects were released in December 1931.

Detective James Caplis (top center) with
fellow detectives, before his murder (1931).
DN-0086326, *Chicago Daily News* Collection,
Chicago History Museum.

Patrolman Michael W. Oakley,

STAR #5445, 40th District, Summerdale Station, 36 years old, was returning to his home at 1908 W. Courtland Street at 1:30 A.M. on December 12, 1931. He was walking down N. Damen Avenue in civilian dress, near Bloomingdale Street, when he was set upon by a young man who stepped out of an area between a building and the railroad track elevation. The assailant was holding a handkerchief to his face with one hand and a revolver in the other. He attempted to rob Officer Oakley, who had his hand on his own revolver in his overcoat pocket. The policeman fired his gun while it was still in his pocket. He then attempted to pull his gun from his pocket just as the assailant fired at him and inflicted a mortal wound. As Oakley fell to the ground, he managed to get off four more shots at his unknown shooter as he fled the scene. Officer Oakley was taken to nearby St. Mary of Nazareth Hospital, where he died at 8:30 A.M. on the following day, December 13, 1931. Before he died, Oakley said that he thought he had wounded the gunman. On January 5, 1932, a Coroner's Jury returned a verdict of "Murder by Unknown Person in the act of a hold up."

Officer Oakley had been on the force for 10 years. He was survived by his mother, father and sister, and laid to rest in St. Adalbert Cemetery.

Detective James J. Caplis,

STAR #1511, Detective Bureau, 31 years old, was fatally shot dining in a Northside Chinese restaurant shortly before Christmas of 1931. Caplis, who was off duty, was at the Beach View Gardens, located on the second floor of a building at 804 W. Wilson Avenue in the Lakeview neighborhood. He was dining with his girlfriend, Miss Marie Pelzer of 4733 N. Kedvale Avenue. More than 50 other diners were also enjoying late night Chinese food around 1:00 A.M. Beach View Gardens was a popular establishment that boasted a live orchestra. In fact, Verne Buck, the orchestra leader, had just lowered his baton and more than a dozen diners who had been dancing were returning to their tables when an armed gang made their way up to the second floor restaurant after taking the doorman, Leon Johnson, captive. The five men arrived by automobile and left it near the main entrance on the Clarendon Street side of the building. Forcing Johnson to walk in front of them, the bandits entered the restaurant with shotguns and revolvers drawn, splitting up and securing various parts of the establishment. Then, after forcing musicians to lay down their instruments, they made their way to a cashiers' cage where they confronted restaurant manager, M.S. Bow, and assistant manager, J.D. King. The bandits called out to all customers, "All right, no trouble. We mean business."

What customers did not know at the time was that the hold-up gang had already planted two men and a woman, with weapons ready, in the restaurant before they stormed in. As patrons were being forced to move against one of the restaurant walls, Officer Caplis began to move away from the crowd. Drawing his own revolver, he raced to another side of the room and made himself a target once he ensured that other patrons were out of the line of fire. He then fired at the nearest bandit, who quickly fired back. As the gun battle began, the bandits began to flee the premises still shooting at Caplis. The gunmen then moved towards the stairwell with Caplis firing after them. When one of them fired a shotgun blast, he hit Peggy Griggs, a 20-year-old woman who was in the dining room. Another shotgun blast intended for Caplis also missed. As the bandits reached the top of the stairs and fled, they aimed one final shot at Caplis. It hit the officer in the back before he had a chance to shoot them on the stairs. More than a dozen men carried the gravely wounded Caplis to nearby Lakeview Hospital. He died a short time later from his injuries.

In June of 1928, Caplis had been the recipient of the *Chicago Tribune* Monthly Hero Award. Once again, in the early hours of December 21, 1931, he demonstrated great courage in confronting the gunmen who put the lives of so many people at risk. He was laid to rest in Calvary Cemetery.

Through information received from a police "stool pigeon," it was soon learned that two women, one aged 16 and another aged 17, had been a part of the robbery of the Beach View Gardens. Dorothy Evans and Marcella Royce were quickly rounded up. Soon their confessions led to the capture of others involved in the crime. On December 27, 1931, two 17-year-old men were in custody and admitted their role in the slaying of Officer Caplis. In the end, Frank Freeman, Jack Burlison, Nicholas Bruno, Tony Pape and Ralph DeFillipis were all arrested. DeFillipis, police discovered, furnished the arsenal of weapons. Also captured were Rocco De Fillipis, alias, De Ferro; Frank Piazza; alias Prazza, and Herman Glick, alias Herman Cohen. All were indicted for murder.

Frank Freeman, alias Red Freeman, was found guilty and received 99 years at the Illinois State Penitentiary at Joliet. Harlborn Burlison, alias Jack Burlison, also received 99 years. Tony Pape, alias Tony Boy, received 14 years in the Illinois State Penitentiary at Joliet. Nicholas Bruno was sentenced to 20 years in Joliet, and Frank Piazza received 14 years there as well. Dorothy Evans and Marcella Royce had charges against them withdrawn. Herman Glick was later murdered on April 5, 1932. Rocco Ferra, alias Rocco the Barber, was never found.

On March 25, 1965, Freeman was paroled from Menard State Prison after serving 33 years. During his prison term he spent 25 years in the psychiatric division and his remaining time working as a nurse in the division infirmary. Freeman had been sentenced to 99 years, but was released early under the revised Illinois Criminal Code, under which inmates serving sentences of 20 years or more became eligible for a parole hearing after serving 11 years of a sentence.

Patrolman Arthur W. Wittbrodt,

STAR #271, South Park Police, 35 years old, was killed on January 16, 1932 when he was thrown from the running board of a car that he had ordered to drive him to the scene of an accident he was to investigate. He was riding on the outside of the borrowed vehicle when its driver hit the brakes suddenly to avoid hitting another car at the intersection of 53rd Street and Michigan Avenue. Wittenbrodt was hurled to the pavement and died from the injuries he sustained on impact. The patrolman left behind a wife, Pearl Pisrowski Wittbrodt, and two children, Rita and Arthur J. He was the son of Francis and the late Herman Wittbrodt, and brother to Robert Wittenbrodt, Mrs. August Volcusrdmen and Mrs. Paul Pistach. Patrolman Wittenbrodt's funeral proceeded from his residence at 5304 S. Wolcott Avenue and he was interred at St. Mary's Cemetery.

Patrolman Martin Knudson,

STAR #1457, 28th District, Austin Station, 45 years old, was guarding a newspaper circulation garage when he was killed in the line of duty on February 5, 1932. Junior newspaper carriers for the *Chicago Evening American* paid their bills at the paper's circulation headquarters, located at the rear of 856 N. Trumbull Avenue, every Friday. Patrolman Knudson was on duty there at 6:20 P.M. as the young men came to settle their accounts. Warren Strouts, the garage manager, was talking to one of the paper boys, Stephen Brodin, 13, when a maroon car with four passengers pulled up to the garage's Iowa Street entrance. Three of the passengers dashed out of the vehicle and into the garage with guns drawn and ordered everyone inside to put their hands up. Knudson was seated on a bench out of the bandits' line of sight when they gave their order.

He rose from his seat and faced the robbers as he drew his own weapon, leading two of the bandits to immediately open fire. The patrolman was hit but he continued to advance on the robbers, emptying his revolver at their backs as they ran off to the getaway car, where a fourth bandit waited behind the wheel. As Officer Knudson dropped his empty gun and fell to the ground witnesses saw one of the bandits stagger. This led police to believe Knudson may have wounded one. Patrolman Knudson, a 15-year-veteran of the police force, was taken to Franklin Boulevard Hospital where he repeatedly told staff and fellow officers, "I shot one of them, I shot one of them," according to the *Chicago Tribune*. Officer Knudson died at 8:20 P.M. the same evening, leaving behind his wife, Sophie, a teacher in the Schubert School, and two children, Marian, 10, and Martin Jr., 5. Knudson was buried in Mount Olive Cemetery.

Knudson's belief that he had wounded one of the criminals was proven correct only ten minutes after his death when investigating officers found a vehicle matching the getaway car's description abandoned at the rear of 3717 W. Lexington Street. Inside the car, police discovered the body of James J. Stewart, 18, who lived about ten blocks from where his body was found. Stewart's body was identified by his father, who told investigators that his son had recently been employed as a helper at the Red Star Line trucking enterprise. Ballistic tests on the bullets found in Stewart's body confirmed that they had been fired from Patrolman Knudson's own gun. A similar test done on the bullets that killed Knudson confirmed that they had been fired by the weapon found on Stewart's body. On February 6, 1932, the Coroner recommended the arrest of Stewart's accomplices. Only one, Frank Severina, was ever found. He was discovered in New York City and brought back to Chicago, where he was sentenced to life in the Illinois State Penitentiary at Joliet on April 19, 1933.

Patrolman George T. Barker,

STAR #175, 35th District, Chicago Avenue Station, 32 years old, was celebrating the 13th wedding anniversary of friends when his attempt to stop a robbery left him dead in the line of duty on March 13, 1932. Barker was not officially on duty at the time of the shooting. In fact, he was still on medical leave related to a shooting in July of 1931, when he resisted a robbery in front of his home. However, he did not let his previous injury or inactive status prevent him from doing his job when he saw civilians in danger. Robbers entered the restaurant of Irving Grossman, located at 1438 W. Madison St., around 1:40 A.M. and announced a hold-up. Barker was at this "Soda Parlor" celebrating the anniversary of James and Helen Bingley with a group of friends that included actresses Sue Ross and Wilma Thompson. They were gathered at the bar located at the back of the establishment with Mr. Grossman as the two armed bandits entered.

When Barker confronted the bandits a gun battle ensued. The patrolman was able to prevent the thieves from completing the robbery but he was wounded in the stomach and chest. Barker was rushed to the Cook County Hospital, where he originally identified himself as Joe Anson before giving his real name. The officer died there later the same day, survived by his wife and two children, who buried him in Calvary Cemetery in Evanston.

The three shots that Barker fired also seemed to have found their mark, according to a physician who practiced near the restaurant. He reported that two men came in shortly after the shooting seeking medical attention for gunshots wounds, but had left when he informed them that he would have to report their injuries to the police. The men were soon identified as Nick Konemogloos, alias Nick or John Petros; and Charles L. Hughes. Konemogloos was eventually identified as Officer Barker's killer and was brought back from New York City by State's Attorney officers on January 20, 1933 to stand trial for murder. On May 8, 1933, Konemogloos was sentenced to life at the Illinois State Penitentiary at Joliet, where he died in the 1960s.

Patrolman Raymond C. Kelly,

STAR #5396, 5th District, Wabash Avenue Station, 31 years old, lost his life in the line of duty on April 3, 1932 when he attempted to arrest a man who had shot and killed his wife and wounded another man. The wounded man, the killer's boarder Marganto Fernandez, was shot in the left arm. Somehow he managed to escape to the second floor of the apartment building where he was lodging and call for police assistance. Patrolman Kelly, and his partner Patrolman Robert Fawcett, responded to a radio report of the events at about 3:25 P.M. They were informed that they would be confronting the offender, Edward Wash, who after drinking all day flew into a homicidal rage. Police reached the apartment building at 5742 S. State Street and learned Wash's approximate location in the building from a crowd that gathered out front to observe the commotion. Kelly and Fawcett went to the fourth floor and each knocked at a different door in the hallway, trying to find the madman's whereabouts. Wash opened the door that Kelly knocked on and instantly began firing his weapon, fatally injuring the officer. Kelly still managed to discharge his own weapon and forced the offender to retreat. Wash continued to fire through the closed door of his apartment as Fawcett intervened, continuing the gun battle as he carried Kelly out of the line of fire.

Once outside, the patrolman rushed past the reinforcements pushing their way through the crowd out front that had swelled to several thousand. He placed his wounded partner in their vehicle and raced towards the hospital in the company of two other officers, Detectives McKeown and McGuire. Patrolman Kelly died en route to Washington Hospital as reinforcements gathered outside the Wash residence and considered the safest way to subdue the murderer. Wash was not deterred from his murderous rampage by the more than 50 officers outside his home. He continued shooting as police on the scene launched tear gas into his apartment. Detective Martin McGuire returned to the scene after Patrolman's Kelly's death was confirmed and fatally shot Wash. Patrolman Kelly was interred at Mount Olivet Cemetery.

Patrolman Robert H. Granger,

STAR #5788, 5th District, Wabash Avenue Station, was touring his district by car with his partner, Patrolman Alonzo Spaulding, on April 9, 1932 when a citizen approached the African-American officers and told them of a robbery in progress. The informant, Judson Slappey, reported a man attempting to recoup his losses after a craps game by robbing each of the players at gunpoint. Slappey managed to escape and led the officers to the apartment of Clarence Harris at 5730 S. Prairie Avenue. They entered with their weapons drawn at 10:40 P.M. There they found William Mills, who was also African-American, wielding a weapon and trying rob the men with whom he had just played a dice game. Granger ordered Mills to drop his weapon just as Mills turned his gun on the officers and fired. Granger fell dead almost instantly, but Spaulding, who was also hit, managed to empty his revolver at Mills' retreating back and hit the killer in the shoulder before he escaped. Officer Granger was laid to rest in Holy Sepulchre Cemetery.

Mills did not avoid detection for long. He was found at 5652 S. Indiana Avenue with three bullet wounds soon after the shooting. He was arrested by Lieutenant Al Booth and officially held by the Coroner for Granger's murder on April 11, 1932. He was later found guilty and sentenced to life at the Illinois State Penitentiary in Joliet on September 15, 1932. One additional man was wounded the night of Officer Granger's murder in a strange corollary to the case. Herbert Cross, a civilian, was visiting William Mills' sweetheart at 5740 S. Prairie Avenue on the evening of April 9, 1932 when he heard the gunshots that took Patrolman Granger's life. Unsure of the events transpiring down the street, he waited a few moments and leapt out the window of the residence, trying to escape before trouble found him. Believing the man sneaking out of the building might be the cop killer, Sergeant Thomas Casey ordered him to halt and then fired his weapon, superficially wounding Cross. He questioned him about his actions before letting him go.

Patrolman William G. Gagler,

STAR #1634, 4th District, Stanton Avenue Station, 38 years old, was on patrol with Patrolman Frank Bergan and Sergeant Grover J. Gormley on June 18, 1932 when they spotted the wife of a man wanted for larceny. They were passing the suspect's residence at 3117 S. State Street when they observed Mrs. Spear sitting on a truck in front of her home. Gormley ordered Bergen to stop the squad car so that they could determine if Mr. Spear was in the area. They approached her and asked if her husband was home. Gormley had attempted in the past on two occasions to serve Spear with a warrant against him for consuming gas not coming through the gas meter, but had missed him both times. Mrs. Spear told the officers that her husband was inside the building. They then entered the apartment building, located Spear and informed him that they had a warrant for his arrest. Spear did not resist, but requested that he be allowed to retrieve his hat and coat from his apartment upstairs before being taken into custody. The officers gave him permission and Gagler was sent to accompany him. They were ascending the stairway when Spear suddenly sprinted ahead. He ran to a chair, retrieved a revolver from underneath it and turned, firing at Patrolman Gagler six times. According to the *Chicago Daily Tribune,* he shouted "nobody's going to take me," as he shot at the officer. Gagler had his own weapon drawn as they climbed the stairs and was able to return fire four times before falling. By the time Bergen and Gormley reached Gagler, Spear had fled.

The wounded officer was rushed to Mercy Hospital where it was discovered he had been hit four times, twice in the arm and once each in the leg and stomach. Five fellow officers who had come to the hospital to check on their colleague's condition offered to donate blood for the transfusion doctors deemed necessary to save Gagler's life. Their efforts were in vain though, and Patrolman Gagler died at 7:55 A.M. on the morning of June 19, 1932. He was survived by his wife and four children. They buried him in Mount Carmel Cemetery.

Spear was located not long after the officer's death at the Cook County Hospital, where he had gone to seek treatment for bullet wounds sustained. He was quickly locked up at the Bridewell Hospital where he died at 9:00 P.M. on June 26, 1932.

Acting-Sergeant Frank J. Cunningham,

STAR #60, 22nd District, 33 years old, was on patrol July 4, 1932 when he and his squad noticed two cars parked haphazardly outside of Jerry Heinig's "Soda Parlor," at 2025 S. Laflin Street, where they had decided to eat shortly after 1:00 A.M. Accompanied by fellow officers, Detectives Dan Masterson, John Hickey and George Davis, Cunningham entered the establishment first, unaware that a hold-up was in progress. As he opened the door, the sergeant witnessed four bandits, all but one with handkerchiefs over their faces, herding the restaurant's customers into a backroom. One of the bandits informed the police a hold-up was in progress and ordered them to join the other patrons lined against the wall. Cunningham and Hickey immediately ordered the bandits to drop their weapons, producing their own guns as they did so. The bandits answered with a volley of shots. Cunningham fell to the ground. Hickey immediately returned fire while young Heinig, the proprietor's son, picked up Cunningham's gun from where it fell and joined the gun battle. The young man received a non-fatal gunshot wound as three of the bandits made their way toward the back exit.

The last bandit tried to duck past Detective Hickey, still busy firing at the other robbers. He found Detective Masterson waiting for him outside. Masterson followed the still-armed bandit towards a parked car, allowed him to enter and then forced the man to surrender without another shot being fired. The captured bandit, Harry King, alias Jerry Keane, was taken to the station, as were the revolver and four empty shells found beside him in the vehicle. In the interim, Sergeant Cunningham and the Heinig boy were rushed to St. Anthony Hospital. There King was brought before Cunningham for identification as his shooter. The sergeant positively identified King as the man who had shot him. However, he was not officially held by the coroner for the shooting until July 19, 1932, the day that Cunningham died from the bullet wound below his heart. No record of King's conviction for the robbery and shooting is recorded, nor is the fate of his three accomplices. Patrolman Cunningham was interred in Saint Joseph Cemetery.

Patrolman Richard J. Keogh,

STAR # unavailable, Motorcycle Division, 38 years old, was fatally injured when his motorcycle collided with an automobile at high speed at Rosedale and Milwaukee Avenues on September 27, 1932. Officer Keogh had been attempting to stop a traffic violator when John Kostak crashed into his motorcycle. Police took Kostak into custody shortly after the accident. Officer Keogh had served on the force for 14 years, spending most of his time in the motorcycle division. Married and the father of two children, he died shortly after arriving at the hospital.

Patrolman Patrick Madden,

STAR #3540, 29th District, North Racine Avenue Station, 54 years old, was on patrol with fellow policemen of the auto detail on November 20, 1932 when they received a radio report from headquarters. A complaint of shots being fired on Walton Street near Holt Street had been lodged by a concerned resident at 12:10 A.M. All available men were ordered to the scene to investigate. Madden and his fellow officers were the first to arrive at 1451 W. Walton Street. There they discovered a loud, unruly gathering, which they raided. One man was observed discarding a loaded revolver in a bedroom. Police placed several men and women under arrest. Madden was waiting outside to load suspects into the wagon when he was approached by a man who claimed the original reported shooter was hiding under a nearby porch. The patrolman placed the wagon in charge of another officer and went in search of the offender, whom he discovered as the informant had described.

Patrolman Madden pulled the man out and placed him under arrest just as two other officers, Vernon Johnson and Stanley Pabish, pulled up and asked if he needed help. Madden told them that he had the situation under control and was simply going to escort the offender back to the waiting wagon. The officer then asked them to go to the call box and relay the events that had transpired at the scene. Madden and the other officers believed that his prisoner, Frank Bialek, was a regular Saturday night drunk who, once subdued, would not be any more trouble. As a result, no one searched the prisoner for a weapon.

As Officer Madden and Bialek were walking, another police car pulled to the curb, containing Patrolmen Otto Buck and Roman Orzechowski, and asked the state of the situation. The officers heading to the call box had informed them that Madden had the situation under control, but Orzechowski exited the car just to be certain. He approached just in time to see Madden and Bialek start to struggle in front of 1437 W. Walton Street. Bialek managed to escape Patrolman Madden's grip, but the burly officer was able to briefly regain his hold. In a matter of seconds, Bialek had broken free again and drew a weapon. Orzechowski ran to assist his fellow officer, watching in horror as Bialek fired a bullet that lodged in Officer Madden's skull. Patrolman Orzechowski pulled his own gun but was not able to act before the offender turned and fired in his direction. He was hit in the abdomen by a shot fired less than ten feet away and fell to the sidewalk. Other police at the location rushed toward the sound of the gunshots with their revolvers drawn and sent more than a dozen bullets chasing after Bialek as he disappeared down an alley.

As some police looked for the shooter, the scene was carefully searched by others for any clues to his identity. A coat was discovered that led officers to determine Bialek's identity. Armed with this identification, squads combed the street looking for the 24-year-old red-headed bandit who had left one officer dead at the scene and another so gravely wounded that he was given only a slight chance to live when he was taken to St. Mary of Nazareth Hospital. Patrolman Madden was laid to rest at All Saints Cemetery in DesPlaines. Officer Orzechowski survived his wound. Bialek managed to evade capture for one month before he was given up by his former girlfriend, Carrie Rachmacy, who agreed to help the police lay a trap for the murderer. On December 20, 1932 he was taken into custody and officially held for murder by the coroner on December 23.

In 1933 he was sentenced to 99 years in prison, at the age of 24. In late December of 1956 Bialek was released from Stateville Prison, after serving some 23 years.

Patrolman William D. Lundy,

STAR #2179, 17th District, New City Station, 57 years old, stopped for a moment's rest from his patrol at the grocery store of Mrs. Vera Walush at 4312 S. Ashland Avenue around 3:00 P.M. on December 9, 1932 when two men entered to rob the store. Lundy was seated at the back of the store when the men came in with guns drawn, announcing a hold-up. However, Lundy did not draw his own weapon in an attempt to avoid bloodshed.

Joseph Majcek, wrongly convicted of Chicago Police Officer William Lundy's murder, spent years behind bars until his case was taken up by the *Chicago Sun*. Courtesy of the *Chicago Sun-Times* Photo Archive.

The offenders did not initially see the officer. Lundy chose to use this to his advantage and attempted to wrestle away the bandits' guns and place them under arrest. One of the offenders struggled free and opened fire on the officer. Lundy sustained six bullet wounds, including one to his heart. Incapacitated by his injuries and the fact that he had never drawn his gun, Lundy was unable to return fire. The bandits fled the scene unharmed in a car with an Ohio license plate. The policeman died shortly after the shooting, leaving behind a wife and three children. He had been a member of the Chicago Police Department for over 25 years and was eligible for retirement with a pension, but chose to remain on duty. Lundy was buried in Holy Sepulchre Cemetery.

His killers did not remain at large for long thanks to an informant who spun a tale of envy and anger for investigating officers. They were told that the burglary had been planned by a female nemesis of the proprietor Mrs. Walush. She engineered the robbery for revenge against her enemy. This led to the arrest of Joseph Majczek. He was booked for murder concurrent with a recommendation for the arrest of Ted Marcinkewicz, the second offender who eventually surrendered to officials. Both men were convicted for their part in Officer Lundy's death. In 1946 a *Chicago Sun* reporter began an exhaustive investigation and led a crusade to exonerate Majcek and Marcinkewicz. Majczek's mother scrubbed floors to raise money to prove her son's innocence. The newspaper championed the cause that led to Majczek's release. So powerful was this story, actor Jimmy Stewart starred in the film version of Majczek's frameup, "Northside 777." It was the first feature film shot in Chicago. Marcinkewicz requested that he be allowed to finish out the remaining years of sentence.

Patrolman Maurice Marcusson,

STAR #1865, 11th District, Bureau of Identification, 34 years old, was on duty on the 9th floor of the McNeil building at 323 W. Jackson Boulevard at 4:50 P.M. on January 20, 1933 when he was fatally shot. Marcusson was guarding the office of the Market Loan Company when he was told of three suspicious characters loitering in the corridor. The men had aroused the suspicion of the building's elevator engineer, who sent a porter to the office in order to alert the officer. Marcusson left the office, approached the men and tried to question them. Once he announced himself, all three bandits pulled out weapons and opened fire. Marcusson had been prepared and had his own weapon in hand. Although he was fatally injured, he managed to wound one of the offenders, Tony Rocco, who was captured as he tried to flee the building. The other two criminals managed to successfully escape. Rocco was questioned by Captain Willard Malone on January 23 and admitted to firing at Marcusson but refused to name his companions. Eventually, angered at taking the fall for his friends, Rocco named George Chevas, the driver, and two men he knew only as Basile and Paul as his partners in crime. In addition, he recanted his claim to be the shooter.

Marcusson, who was married with two children, was rushed to St. Luke Hospital after the shooting. He lingered for three days before succumbing to his injuries on January 23, 1933. He was interred in the Temple Judea Waldheim Cemetery. Rocco faired better than Marcusson, making a rapid recovery in the Bridewell Hospital that allowed him to be indicted with Basile on January 31. On September 22, 1933, Rocco was sentenced to 199 years in the Illinois State Penitentiary at Joliet for murdering Officer Marcusson. Basile received a life sentence in Joliet on October 14, 1932 for his role in crime, the same day that Chevas was found not guilty. There is no record of Paul ever being found or tried for the policeman's murder.

Patrolman Roscoe C. Johnston,

STAR #3227, 5th District, Wabash Avenue Station, 42 years old, was in the office of the Gordon Baking Company, located at 5324 S. Federal Street, at 9:35 A.M. when three armed robbers entered. The bandits did not see Officer Johnston when they came in and immediately commenced rounding up the bakery's employees. Two of the offenders had entered with their weapons drawn and took the purchasing agent and phone operator upstairs to the cashier's cage. A third man with a sawed-off shotgun soon joined them. They were in the middle of stealing the bakery's receipts when Officer Johnston stepped onto the scene. Johnston had been waiting in the bakery's upstairs storeroom from the time the offenders entered in order to make sure that he was not surprised by additional members of the gang. When he was sure all the men were inside and occupied, he emerged from the door behind the cashier, M.H. Axelrod, at the moment the thieves ordered Axelrod to give them a bag containing $200. Johnston saw that announcing his presence would only give the bandits time to react so he simply opened fire, hoping to wound or incapacitate them. Johnston's decision to shoot without speaking led the offenders to drop the money bag and flee empty-handed, but not before the thief with the sawed-off shotgun fired at Johnston's head and killed him. The three men fled to their car where a fourth bandit was waiting behind the wheel. They sped off never to be seen again, although the blood stained vehicle was discovered in front of 4217 S. Halsted Street an hour later. The car offered no clues, as it turned out to be a stolen car that was outfitted with license plates lifted from another vehicle. Johnston, an African-American, was a 14-year-veteran of the force who had been detailed to the bakery because it had been robbed of $5,000 the summer before. Johnson was survived by his 17-year-old daughter, Lorraine, a senior at Englewood High School. Lorraine, now an orphan, received $443 dollars from the *Chicago Tribune's* Police Hero Fund. She buried her father at Holy Sepulchre Cemetery.

Patrolman Arthur D. Mutter,

STAR #1000, 14th District, Gresham Station, 44 years old, stopped at the Beverly Club, a restaurant and "Soda Parlor" at 8041 S. Ashland, after he finished his shift on April 18, 1933. He lost his life while attempting to disarm an offender in the restaurant. Mutter had been at the Beverly Club almost an hour and a half, standing at the cigar counter, when he observed two men eject their companion after an argument. The man who had been expelled, a taxi driver who wore a Checkers Cab cap, returned only a moment later armed with a sub-machine gun. He headed back towards the table where his acquaintances sat, passing Mutter as he went. The patrolman, who was still in uniform, halted the offender's march towards his pals and attempted to disarm him. They struggled and Mutter succeeded in forcing the man to point the muzzle of the weapon towards the floor. Mutter then gained control of the weapon, but the gunman's companions quickly joined the fight and overpowered the officer. All three men struggled briefly, the officer scuffling fiercely with the tallest man in the group. Finally, one of the cab driver's friends drew a pistol and shot Mutter twice.

Events that followed are not clear. It was claimed that the men fled the restaurant by car. That account could not be confirmed though, and their identities were never discovered. Matthew Hogan, owner of the Beverly Club, his brother Thomas, together with Elmer Lantz, the bartender, and Edward Haywood, a patron, were all held by the police for questioning. They provided no concrete clues to further the investigation. While they were being questioned, Patrolman Mutter struggled to survive at Auburn Hospital, where he had been taken after the shooting. His wounds proved too grave and he died the same night, leaving behind his widow, Mrs Gussie Mutter, and five children. He was buried at Holy Sepulchre Cemetery.

Patrolman Stanley J. Lutke,

STAR #6510, 40th District, Summerdale Station, was on foot patrol in the early morning hours of April 30, 1933 when he noticed suspicious activity taking place in the Argyle Smoke Shop located at 5018 N. Broadway Street. Lutke crossed the street and peered into the shop's windows in an attempt to determine if his assistance was needed. He discovered that his instincts had been correct; the owner of the store, Edward Searmore, was being held-up at that very moment. Lutke came upon the scene just as the robber was finishing the crime. The patrolman decided to wait just outside the front door of the business in order to surprise the suspect and achieve an easier arrest. However, the bandit spotted the policeman and bolted out the entrance, leaving Lutke no choice but to shoot at his fleeing form. The patrolman fired five shots and the thief stumbled, but continued his escape down Broadway. Lutke followed in determined pursuit, reloading his weapon as he went. Tragically, the patrolman failed to notice a second bandit exit the shop behind him.

A driving rain fell that night, partially obscuring the officer's view into the shop and he had not seen the additional offender. As Lutke followed the first man, the second criminal took advantage of the policeman's forward gaze to sneak up behind him. He crept within five feet of Lutke before the patrolman became aware of his presence. The officer whirled to confront his offender just as the man fired a single shot, striking Lutke in the forehead. The married father of four was rushed to Edgewater Hospital but his wound was fatal. He died there at 3:05 A.M. His assailants were never found. Lutke was laid to rest in Saint Adalbert Cemetery.

Patrolman Oscar E. Brosseau,

STAR #174, 25th District, Fillmore Station, 55 years old, was assigned to keep the peace outside of a bakery during a labor dispute on June 1, 1933 when he was brutally beaten by demonstrators. He was stationed in front of the Royale Bakery at 1240 S. Kedzie Avenue, and charged with keeping the picketers, from the local 237 of the Jewish Baker's Union, in order. The bakery employed non-union workers and the union members were protesting this practice. At 9:50 P.M. the mob turned violent and attacked Patrolman Brosseau. The officer was severely beaten with a baseball bat and sustained fatal wounds. He was rushed to St. Anthony's Hospital and lingered for three weeks before succumbing to his injuries on June 20, 1933. His official cause of death according to the coroner's report was "from pulmonary embolism result of a fracture of the patella bone, due to external violence." On July 7, 1933, the coroner's jury recommended the arrest of his assailants on the charge of manslaughter. Sam Goodman, Al Goldberg, Morris Kauffman and Nathan Stein were all arrested on June 22, 1933 as accessories to murder. All were discharged by Judge Hayes on July 25, 1933. Patrolman Brosseau was survived by his widow, Mrs. Nellie Brosseau, his mother Mrs. Virginia Brosseau, one sister and two brothers, one of whom, George Brosseau, was a policeman out of the Warren Avenue Station. Brosseau was interred at Mount Carmel Cemetery.

The grief stricken Lutke family
three months after Officer Lutke's death.
Chicago Tribune Photo Archive.

Patrolman Harry J. Redlich,

STAR #5406, 27th District, Warren Avenue Station, 38 years old, was directing traffic at Madison Street and Kedzie Avenue around noon on July 8, 1933. Redlich was told by Mrs. Charlotte Taylor, the secretary for the advertising agency of Thomas W. Compton, that her employer was currently being robbed by bandits who had stolen $90 just one month before on June 7. Mrs. Taylor had been in the corridor outside of Room 307 in the Madison-Kedzie Building, located at 9 S. Kedzie, when she saw the offenders get off the elevator. She watched them go into her office and, after realizing she recognized them from the earlier incident, she sprang into action. After informing the building elevator operator, Steve Jadro, of the events taking place, she raced to the street and found Officer Redlich.

Redlich followed Mrs. Taylor back to the office and discovered the bandits in the process of holding up Mr. Compton and Jack Kiefus, a salesman. The perpetrators, John Bongiorno, alias Joe Lippo; and Ross King, alias Kenneth Smith; were both ex-convicts on parole. Bongiorno served six years for his part in a Chicago hotel hold-up, while King had served six years of a 7 to 15 year sentence at Marquette Prison in Michigan for a robbery conviction. Prison had apparently failed to turn the men from crime. As Redlich stood outside of Room 307, he could see Bongiorno's shadow on the glass of the office door. The officer drew his gun and ordered the bandit to step out of the office. Bongiorno came out unarmed and tried to persuade Redlich that he was an insurance agent. The officer, unconvinced, told the bandit to move over by the elevator. While Bongiorno argued his identity his partner, whom Redlich had not seen, took the spoils of the robbery, $60 in cash and $20 in stamps. The second offender leapt out the office window to a ledge about 10 feet below and crept back into the building through a second story window. He returned to the stairs to where his partner and Redlich stood. Redlich's back was to King and the bandit took advantage of the fact the officer was concentrating on searching Bongiorno for weapons. Without any warning, he fired five shots at Patrolman Redlich, three of which entered the patrolman's back. The 12-year-veteran fell to the hallway floor and died there a short time later. He left a widow and 8-year-old daughter, Jacqueline, to mourn him. Redlich was buried in Acacia Park Cemetery.

Bongiorno and King both escaped from the building unharmed, but they did not remain at large for more than a few hours. King was driving a stolen truck when he was chased through the streets by the Detective Bureau squad that took him into custody. Borngiorno was arrested in the basement of 3031 W. Warren Boulevard. On July 8, 1933, a special Coroner's Jury turned the two bandits over to the Grand Jury on a charge of murder. The day after the arrests, an angry public demanded the death penalty be sought during the suspect's trials. On September 16, 1933, Bongiorno was sentenced to the Illinois State Penitentiary at Joliet for 199 years, where he stayed until being paroled in the 1960s. King was the one who would pay the price the public demanded, receiving a sentence of death on September 18, 1933. He was electrocuted on October 16, 1933.

Patrolman Elmer R. Ostling,

STAR #1189, 27th District, Warren Avenue Station, 34 years old, and **Patrolman John Skopek,** STAR #6614, 27th District, Warren Avenue Station, 34 years old, were on patrol, riding west on Washington Boulevard, on July 22, 1933 when they spotted a car that matched the description of an automobile stolen three weeks earlier. The vehicle had since been used in the commission of several crimes. The passengers in the car spotted the officers and sped off, causing Ostling and Skopek to begin pursuit. The officers ultimately ran the fugitive car to the curb in front of 2838 W. Washington Boulevard at 9:30 P.M., exiting their own vehicle in order to question its occupants. The officers were within a few feet of the car when two of the men inside exited and opened fire. The barrage of bullets riddled both officers, but they each managed to shoot once before falling to the pavement. Skopek's shooter was so close when he fired that his gun's flame actually burned the policeman's face. After being hit six times by bullets from .45 caliber and .380 millimeter weapons, Skopek fired his single bullet and fell dead to the pavement. Ostling was hit five times by bullets from a .45 caliber gun and then fired his one shot. Seconds later, he slid off the curb and under the wheels of the stolen vehicle. The bandits got back in the car, aiding one of their own who had been wounded by the officers' return fire. The car then sped away from the curb, running over Patrolman Ostling's prone body, racing west down Washington Boulevard before turning north on Francisco Avenue.

Traffic became snarled at the scene of the crime as hundreds of concerned citizens crowded around the fallen policemen. Four civilians took it upon themselves to put Ostling in his patrol car and drive him to the Franklin Boulevard Hospital, while a bystander took Skopek's lifeless body to Washington Boulevard Hospital in his own auto, hoping he could be saved. Skopek, was survived by his wife, and son, Robert, age 7, and was buried in Resurrection Cemetery. Ostling, father to a 10-year-old daughter, Corinne, hung on for only a brief time. As his death neared, he lay in his hospital bed repeating, "They didn't give us a chance, they didn't give us a chance", according to the *Chicago Daily Tribune*. He died just as his wife, who was accompanied by Patrolman Otto Jicha, neared his hospital room. Patrolman Ostling was laid to rest in Mount Olive Cemetery.

The stolen vehicle the officers had pursued was eventually discovered in front of 1829 W. Huron Street. The blood spattered back seat lent credibility to the theory that the officers had been able to wound one of the offenders.

Sam Turriano and James Progue, both ex-convicts with lengthy criminal records, eventually confessed to the crimes after a botched prison escape undertaken by Progue and Edward Moorehead, another passenger in the stolen vehicle. All of the offenders had been sentenced to the Illinois State Penitentiary at Joliet in 1934 for their part in unrelated crimes, but Turriano served a shorter sentence than his two friends. He was transferred to Pontiac Reformatory in July of 1934 and paroled in December of 1936. He was not incarcerated when Progue and Moorehead attempted to breakout on October 8, 1937.

Moorehead was shot by guards during his escape attempt and died two days later on October 10. The first information that pointed to these men as the shooters of Ostling and Skopek surfaced in February of 1937. Progue entered a guilty plea for his part in the murders of the two policemen on November 11, 1937. Turriano followed suit on December 12, 1937. Both men received sentences of 199 years to be served in the Illinois State Penitentiary at Joliet.

Patrolman John G. Sevick,

STAR #6576, 41st District, Rogers Park Station, was in the courtroom of Judge Charles E. Malthrop on the 5th floor of the Criminal Court Building, 54 W. Hubbard Street, at 11:15 A.M. on July 24, 1933 when he confronted an armed prisoner who had escaped from the deputy sheriff. Court business was going on as usual that summer day when two bandits, John Scheck and Carl Grundhoefer, attended a hearing in which they received a continuance regarding the charges of murder and bank robbery in Niles Center for which they were currently in custody. They had been removed from the jail and moved to the courthouse in order to attend their hearing. They had spent the day in the court's bull-pen. While there they were able to receive visitors and Scheck, a young man 20-years-old, was visited by his 22-year-old sister Mary, who had carried a gun to him. After the hearing, she passed it to her brother through the prison bars.

News accounts paint Scheck as a true psychopath with deep hatred for all involved in law enforcement. He also had a reckless courage that made him a likely flight risk. In addition, reports indicate that security at the courthouse was very lax.

According to witness statements, the escape attempt began after Scheck and Grundhoefer's hearing. Deputy Sheriff John Kavanaugh had just unlocked the bull-pen door to begin the process of transferring the prisoners from the courthouse back to the jail when Scheck produced his gun and overpowered him. Commanding the deputy at gunpoint, they forced Kavanaugh to lie down on the ground and then dashed past him in a wild attempt to secure their freedom. They had just reached Judge Malthrop's courtroom when Kavanaugh notified his fellow officers of the events that had taken place. After spotting the men striding nonchalantly past Judge Malthrop's bench, Sevick intercepted them as they reached the outer door of the courtroom. The officer ordered them to halt, but was met by gunfire from Scheck's smuggled gun. Sevick managed to return fire, but was mortally wounded by two bullets near the heart. He died only a few minutes after the escape attempt began. Sevick was laid to rest at Forest Home Cemetery.

Scheck also lodged two bullets in the walls of Judge Malthrop's packed courtroom before dashing out. His capture came only after a desperate chase through the building after which he was taken to the Bridewell Hospital with a bullet in his back, which left him in critical condition. After shooting Sevick, Scheck raced through the hallways exchanging shots with the officers that followed. Using Grundhoefer as a human shield, he wound his way through the courthouse before finally being caught after a failed attempt to assassinate Assistant State's Attorney Charles Dougherty.

Grundhoefer was also taken back into custody and held as a party to Patrolman Sevick's death along with John Scheck, Mary Scheck, Joe Scheck, Rose Scheck, Janet Haddon and John Soder. The most incriminating evidence tying all those in custody to the crime was the smuggled gun, which the police discovered had been modified. The barrel of the weapon had been cut off with a hacksaw and the missing piece was found in the basement of the Scheck home when it was searched. The August Grand Jury did not bring a murder charge against Grundhoefer or accessory charges against anyone else but Rose Scheck. Despite reports that Mary Scheck had been the gun smuggler; Rose went on trial and was found not guilty of being an accessory on September 15, 1933. On August 31, 1933 John Scheck was sentenced to death, but instead received a reprieve on October 13.

Patrolman Patrick J. Ryan,

STAR #4940, 32nd District, Shakespeare Avenue Station, 46 years old, had only half an hour before his shift ended when he stepped into the Kimball Tavern at 3328 W. Armitage Avenue around 11:45 P.M. on August 8, 1933. He ordered a sandwich and had just sat down to enjoy it when he was approached by an intoxicated patron, Peter "Piccolo" Pace. The 23-years-old, and his companion, had been drinking their own homemade wine at the tavern when the uniformed officer entered. After observing Ryan order and take his seat, Pace approached the patrolman and offered him a glass of their wine. Ryan politely declined and Pace became enraged by his refusal. He threw the glass of wine in the officer's face and a struggle began as Ryan attempted to place him under arrest. As they grappled, Pace withdrew Ryan's gun from its holster and fired, hitting the patrolman in the stomach twice.

Ryan fell immediately, overwhelmed by wounds so grave that he died within moments of the shooting. Pace then turned the gun towards the startled witnesses seated in the tavern. He brandished the weapon, threatening to shoot the tavern owner, Edward Bergman, if he attempted to block his escape. He then fled the tavern with his companion. Patrolman Ryan's gun was later found in a nearby alley where it was believed Pace dropped it as he left the scene.

Pace was arrested without a struggle a short time later by Sergeant William Gormley. He was still drunk when the sergeant apprehended him, and confessed to the shooting during the cab ride to the station. However, his account of the events that transpired in the tavern was different than the story told in statements by other witnesses. Pace claimed that after he threw the wine at the officer, Ryan had produced his pistol and shot twice, leading him to attempt to take the gun. Bystanders admitted that the struggle between the two men made it difficult to see how the gun went off when the officer was shot. However, no records mention more than two shots being fired and both of those bullets are accounted for by the injuries Officer Ryan sustained. Pace's self-defense story was not believed by the court that tried him. He was sentenced to 199 years in the Illinois State Penitentiary at Joliet on October 13, 1933. Officer Ryan was a 15-year-veteran of the Chicago Police Department when he lost his life. He was survived by his wife, Hannah; and four children, Joseph, 16; Marie, 13; Adelaide, 11; and Jackie, 7. Ryan was buried in Mount Olivet Cemetery.

Patrolman Joseph P. Hastings,

STAR #6384, 35th District, was on patrol at Navy Pier on August 14, 1933 when he heard a shot fired from one of the nearby businesses. He went to investigate and discovered a robbery in progress which he attempted to thwart. Hastings misjudged the number of gunmen at the scene and subsequently lost his life in the line of duty. The robbers' chosen target was the office of the Bureau of Streets, which the Illinois Emergency Relief Commission had been using as a pay station to compensate men working on the pier, located on Hastings' regular beat. The office was crowded with over 50 employees of the Commission's "make work" division, men who had been left unemployed and destitute by the Great Depression and now relied on organizations like the Commission to offer work that would provide a paycheck. George Turner was the paymaster employed by the Commission who passed out checks. Thomas B. Rawls was a Currency Exchange official who cashed payroll checks.

Six city clerks were on the second floor office going about their work, in addition to the waiting workers, when the bandits burst in with their weapons drawn. Turner had not yet handed out the first check, so the cash box that the offenders snatched from Rawls still held its original $600 plus some coins. One of the Bureau clerks, Jerome Hartnett, grabbed a phone in a desperate attempt to call for help as the criminals advanced on Rawls. He was seen by one of the offenders who fired a shot in his direction, missing his head by only an inch. The bandits, identified as Morris Cohen and Hymie Sinnenberg, then ordered everyone in the office to lie on the floor. As they waited for everyone to comply, Officer Hastings arrived on the scene, drawn by the sound of the bullet that had been fired at Hartnett. Another Bureau clerk, Charles Eddy, described the rest of the events that led to the officer's tragic death. According to Eddy, Hastings entered the office and only seemed to notice the offender that was rifling through the cash box. He aimed his weapon at the man he could see, but was spotted himself and fired upon by the other gunman. Hastings fell wounded but managed to fire twice before his strength gave out. The robbers grabbed the fallen officer's gun and fled to the front of the office, firing one more time. They then fled the scene with the cash box. After they exited, they dropped one of the weapons. It was picked up by bystander George Stumpf, who emptied it at the backs of the retreating gang. As he did so, several of the men in the office loaded Hastings into a vehicle and headed for Henrotin Hospital. Their efforts, however, were in vain. A fatal bullet had nicked Hastings' star, passed through his heart and exited his back. The fallen officer was waked at the home of his brother-in-law, John J. O'Hara, at 624 W. 43rd Street, before being moved to St. Gabriel Church for a Requiem Mass. Hastings was interred in Mount Olivet Cemetery.

The search for Patrolman Hastings' killers began immediately and it was not long before Cohen was found in a car at the Ambassador Garage at 1350 N. Clark Street, bleeding from a gunshot wound. Cohen initially denied his part in the crime. He eventually confessed that he had planned the holdup himself and enlisted the help of an accomplice whose name he did not know. When presented with pictures of various suspects both he and other witnesses identified the other man with him at the office that day as Hymie Sinnenberg. He, however, was never apprehended. His arrest was recommended by the coroner, but he and the money were never discovered. On August 23, 1933, Cohen was sentenced to death for his part in the slaying of Officer Hastings, who had married four months prior to his death. Cohen was electrocuted on October 13, 1933 at Cook County Jail.

Patrolman William E. Hoard,

STAR #223, South Park Police, 40 years old, was on patrol with his partner, Denis Osborne, on September 10, 1933 when they noticed a speeding motorist and took off in pursuit. As they approached the Outer Drive at the 23rd Street entrance to the 1933 World's Fair, the "Century of Progress," celebrating the 100th anniversary of Chicago's founding, a car suddenly emerged from a parking lot and shot across the road in front of them. Osborne noticed the car in time and was able to stop his motorcycle after skidding more than 40 feet, but his partner was not as fortunate. According to Osborne, it appeared that Patrolman Hoard never saw the vehicle and did not slow from his pursuit speed of 70 MPH before smashing into the vehicle and sustaining life-ending injuries. He was rushed to Chicago Memorial Hospital, but died before he arrived. The vehicle he hit was driven by Sterling Peacock, a resident of Evanston, and Vice-President at N.W. Ayer and Sons, Inc. Peacock was accompanied in the vehicle by his wife and two other couples, none of whom were injured. Patrolman Hoard was buried in Evergreen Park Cemetery on W. 87th Street.

Patrolman Miles Cunningham,

STAR #1150, 26th District, DesPlaines Street Station, 38 years old, approached the scene of an automobile accident at the corner of Adams and Halsted Streets around 12:25 A.M. on September 22, 1933, unaware that the occupants of one of the vehicles had just robbed two Federal Reserve Bank messengers. Cunningham was on patrol with his partner, Maurice Fitzgerald, when they observed two vehicles, one of them a Hudson sedan, crash at the intersection. The impact sent the sedan swerving into a light post, effectively disabling the vehicle. Cunningham approached the inoperative auto to offer assistance and was met with a hail of gunfire. One of the bandits had seen the officers conversing at the southeast corner of the intersection and warned his companions of their advance. Cunningham was hit six times by the volley of bullets and died only a short time after being rushed to the Cook County Hospital. Neither Cunningham nor Fitzgerald were able to return fire. The bandits quickly seized a passing vehicle and fled from the scene.

Ten minutes before the shooting, two bank employees, Victor Plontkoski and Otto Wizran, were making their way down Jackson Boulevard, halfway between Clark and LaSalle Streets, with a small vehicle they used to push the mail from the old post office to the bank at the northwest corner of Jackson and LaSalle. They were in the company of two guards, Proctor Lisle of Wheaton and John McGilien of Dobson Avenue, when they were suddenly accosted by the occupants of two automobiles that pulled up to the curb next to them. One of the vehicles, a small sedan, contained four men. Three of them, all in masks, exited the vehicle while the driver, a red-headed man with a light complexion, stayed behind the wheel, as did the solitary occupant of the second vehicle. The masked robbers confronted the messengers and their guards with their machine guns drawn and left them no choice but to hand over the two full sacks of first class mail and money they were transporting. The guards had no chance to draw their own weapons and could only watch helplessly as the bandits peeled away from the curb.

The criminals' vehicle crashed only moments later and their confrontation with Patrolman Cunningham was over in a matter of seconds. Though they were successful in fleeing twice that night, three of the bandits involved would pay for their crimes. They had taken the life of a husband and father of two who had stood in his station only 20 minutes before his death joking about how he would spend a long overdue paycheck he had just received. The men Cunningham met that night had long criminal histories associated with some of the city's most infamous crimes. Although they would not be brought to trial for his death, they would all eventually end their days incarcerated or dead because of their lives of crime.

The Hudson sedan used in the robbery on the night of September 22 was discovered to have been owned by George R. "Machine Gun" Kelly. He was apprehended on September 26, 1933 in Memphis, Tennessee and later sentenced to life in prison for the kidnapping of Charles Urschel of Oklahoma. An associate of his, Gus Winkler, was also sought on suspicion that he was involved in Patrolman Cunningham's shooting because the vehicle involved had been equipped with a special smoke screen device in a garage owned by a former associate of his. Winkler, one of the killers known to have been involved in the St. Valentine's Day massacre, was discovered when police followed his chauffeur to a residence on Lake Shore Drive where he was living under the assumed name of M.M. Michael. Evidence of Winkler's involvement was augmented by the fact that ballistic tests proved that one of the guns that had shot Cunningham had been used in the Kansas City Union Station massacre, a crime in which Winkler had been involved. Verne Miller was the final suspect named as part of the robbery and murder that evening. He was another well known criminal in the city, famous for shooting his way out of a police trap set in a Chicago hotel in November 1933. A World War I hero, Miller turned to a life of violent crime after his return from France. He had been on the lam for less than a month when his body was discovered in a ditch outside of Detroit. He had been beaten to death. Officer Cunningham was laid to rest in All Saints Cemetery.

DIVISION OF INVESTIGATION
U. S. DEPARTMENT OF JUSTICE
WASHINGTON, D. C.

Fingerprint Classification

23 27 W 0

7 W OI 14

WANTED

GEORGE R. KELLY, aliases GEORGE KELLY, R. G. SHANNON.

KIDNAPING

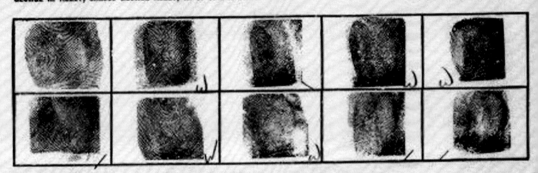

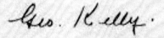

Geo. Kelly.

DESCRIPTION

Age, 35 years
Height, 5 feet, 9½ inches
Weight, 177 pounds
Build, medium muscular
Eyes, blue or gray
Hair, dark brown
Complexion, medium ruddy
Expert machine gunner

Remarks: Sometimes wears
octagon shaped rimless
glasses.

CRIMINAL RECORD

As George Kelly, No. 1968, received State Prison, Santa Fe, New Mexico, March 14, 1927; crime, violation National Prohibition Act.

As George Kelly, No. 5296, arrested Police Department, Tulsa, Oklahoma, July 24, 1927; charge, state vagrancy.

As George Kelly, No. 2332, arrested Sheriff's Office, Tulsa, Oklahoma, January 12, 1928; charge, National Prohibition Act.

As George Kelly, No. 29362, received United States Penitentiary, Leavenworth, Kansas, February 11, 1928, from Tulsa, Oklahoma; crime, Possession of liquor (Indian Cy); sentence 3 years.

George R. Kelly is wanted for the kidnaping of Charles F. Urschel at Oklahoma City, Oklahoma, on July 22, 1933.

Law enforcement agencies kindly transmit any additional information or criminal record to nearest office, Division of Investigation, U. S. Department of Justice.

If apprehended, please notify the Director, Division of Investigation, U. S. Department of Justice, Washington, D. C., or the Special Agent in Charge of the office of the Division of Investigation listed on the back hereof, which is nearest your city.

(over) Issued by: J. EDGAR HOOVER, Director.

Detective-Sergeant William T. Shanley,

STAR #760, Detective Bureau, 43 years old, was involved in a sting operation to capture a member of the infamous Dillinger Gang, led by public enemy #1, John Dillinger, on December 14, 1933 when he lost his life in the line of duty. Shanley was with Patrolmen Frank Hopkins and Martin Mullin at a garage at 5320 N. Broadway Street when he was fatally shot. Shanley had been on patrol with the two officers when a radio call, a fairly new technology at the time, was received from Chief of Detectives William Schoemaker. The Chief informed the men that they were to be on the lookout for a green roadster somewhere on the same block where the garage was located. The officers discovered the car at a garage run by Frank Kuhn and Arthur Ulness. The garage owners stated that the vehicle had been dropped off so that a damaged fender could be repaired and that the man and the woman who brought it in would be back to retrieve the car shortly. Shanley relayed these findings to Schoemaker and offered to await the offenders' return. The Chief agreed to let the officers remain at the garage, but warned the detective-sergeant to be extremely cautious because at least one of the individuals they would encounter was considered desperate and extremely dangerous. Shanley wrote down Dillinger's name on a piece of paper, which was later found in his pocket. He then reported the new assignment to his fellow officers.

Around 3:45 P.M., Shanley asked Hopkins to notify Mullin that their squad car had to be returned to the Detective Bureau before the next shift came on at 4:00 P.M. Mullin was keeping watch from the vehicle, which was parked at Catalpa and Broadway Streets. Hopkins immediately left to relay the message. Shortly after, a man, assumed to be John Hamilton, and a woman, Mrs. Elaine De Kant Dent, entered the shop. The events that unfolded were reported by a mechanic, Sam Tower, employed by the garage. According to him, the couple entered the garage and walked up to the car. Shanley approached Hamilton and asked if the car belonged to him. Hamilton answered in the negative and stated that it belonged to his wife, indicating Mrs. Dent, who then produced a license receipt. This apparently did not satisfy Shanley and he began to search Hamilton for a gun while instructing the suspect to keep his hands in plain sight. As he leaned down to pat Hamilton's hip pockets the offender pulled his weapon from a shoulder holster and shot the detective-sergeant twice.

Shanley reeled from the force of the bullets and yelled he was wounded, telling onlookers to send for help. He then fell to the floor with the license receipt still clutched in his hand. As he fell, Hamilton grabbed Mrs. Dent by the arm and dragged her out of the garage. Further events were recounted by Patrolman Hopkins, only 200 feet away when the couple emerged from the garage. He moved towards them as Hamilton fled through a vacant lot. Mrs. Dent ran towards Hopkins and the officer quickly seized her, struggling and cursing as he dragged her back to the garage. The moment he stepped inside he spotted Shanley lying on the floor in a pool of blood. He ran to his side but could do nothing to aid him. Sergeant Shanley died 15 minutes later at Edgewater Hospital. He was later interred at All Saints Cemetery.

Shanley, who had once received the *Chicago Tribune* Hero Award, was one of 12 officers who lost his life in pursuit of the notorious Dillinger Gang in 1933 and 1934. John Dillinger and his equally ruthless counterpart, Baby Face Nelson, were both eventually shot and killed in separate incidents. The rest of the gang was ultimately killed, executed or sentenced to lengthy prison terms. Hamilton had been considered especially dangerous when Shanley confronted him because of his leadership role in a gang of murderous thugs who had broken out of the Indiana Penitentiary in Michigan City on September 26, 1933. He was wounded in the Battle of Little Bohemia Lodge on April 30, 1934 and died a short time later.

Patrolman Thomas Murphy,

STAR #2533, 17th District, Stanton Avenue Station, 40 years old, was fatally shot on December 31, 1933 at 11:57 A.M. while on duty protecting the Eastman Coal Company at 3443 S. LaSalle Street. After a previous robbery at the coal yard three weeks earlier netted bandits $200, police stepped up security to thwart further assaults from the robbery gang. Officer Murphy had been assigned to protect the premises from further crime.

Not long before the holdup and shooting the same band of robbers was responsible for a daring daylight robbery of the Sunday collection from Little Flower Church at 8001 S. Wood Street. As church ushers were carrying the money from the church to the rectory, they were set upon by the gang. They rode off with more than $1,600. The gang then made their way to the coal company.

Murphy was standing in the office near the doorway when he heard the office manager, Fern Else of 7127 S. Wabash Avenue say, "Here they come again–the same bandits." Two of the three bandits were peering through a side window into the office, brandishing their weapons and ordering those inside to "Stick 'em up." A third man who tried to enter through the office door discovered that it was locked and preceded to fire his weapon through the door. It was at this point that Officer Murphy began to fire his own weapon. The two men at the window ran away, but the third man moved around to a window on the opposite side of the small office and shot Officer Murphy in the back. A fourth man, at the wheel of a Ford V-8 auto, drove away northbound on LaSalle Street before heading west on 33rd Street. All the members of the gang escaped.

Officer Murphy was taken to Mercy Hospital where he lingered for one month before succumbing to wounds. He died at 2:00 A.M. on February 1, 1934. He became the sixteenth Chicago Policeman to die as a result of a gun battle since the start of 1933. The policeman was married and lived at 5527 S. Wolcott Street. He was interred in Holy Sepulchre Cemetery.

Murphy's son John, then 5 years old, later became a member of the Chicago Police Department and served for more than 25 years. His grandson, Michael, is presently a sergeant on the force.

Patrolman John R. Officer,

STAR #700, 5th District, Wabash Avenue Station, 43 years old, was among the city's most well-known African American members of the Chicago Police Department when he was gunned down in a fierce battle with three bandits in a shoe store owned by William Friedman. The crime took place at Bill's Bootery, 302 E. 43rd Street, around 8:52 P.M. on the evening of April 13, 1934. The perpetrators were in the process of herding Friedman, his clerk, Albert Pearson of 4344 S. Calumet Avenue, and six store patrons into the basement when Patrolman Officer entered the store. The thieves were just about to flee with $200 when Officer noticed that no one seemed to be in the usually busy shoe store. He moved toward the rear of the premises with his gun drawn. It was then that he was fired on by the three bandits. Officer was able to get off five shots before he was shot in the heart. He slumped to the floor and died. Immediately, the gang made their escape by high-jacking an automobile belonging to Jack White of 350 E. 59th Street. His car had been parked near the curb. White and Miss Hazel Anderson were about to enter the shoe store when they were forced to chauffeur the criminals to Lake and Paulina Streets on the city's Westside. The stickup-men gave White $3 for the lift. They also left him with the warning that if he talked to anyone about what happened, he would be killed. Police learned two more bandits were to have taken part in the robbery, but they became alarmed when a police car pulled up near the shoe shop.

One week later, on April 20, 1934, police apprehended the gang of five—Alonzo Haywood, alias Alonzo McNeill of 1928 W. Maypole Avenue; George Walker of 335 E. Garfield Boulevard; Henry Moore, also of 335 E. Garfield Boulevard; Noble Easley of 5237 S. Prairie Avenue and Henry Clements, also of 335 E. Garfield Boulevard. Haywood was arrested at his home, with the other four apprehended at the Garfield Boulevard address. Haywood, Walker and Moore were the three men who robbed the shoe store. It was determined that Walker and Moore were the actual individuals who shot and killed Patrolman Officer. All of these men confessed to their involvement in the robbery and homicide. They were identified by witnesses.

Patrolman Officer lived at 523 E. 67th Street and was buried at Sand Hill Cemetery in Princeton, Indiana.

Mounted Chicago Police Officer talks
with children (1945).
ICH-i26750, Chicago History Museum.

Patrolman Victor H. Sugg,

STAR #3701, of the 36th District, Hudson Avenue Station, 35 years old, was discovered lying in the street in front of 2365 N. Lincoln Avenue at 3:15 A.M. on April 15, 1934. He was taken to Alexian Brothers Hospital at 1200 W. Belden Avenue. There it was determined that he had suffered a severe skull fracture. Officer Sugg lingered for nine days in the hospital before succumbing to his injuries on April 24, 1934. An investigation was immediately launched to discover the cause of his injuries. Witnesses recalled that the police officer had been speaking with three intoxicated, but unknown, young men, who struck the policeman, knocking him to the ground. Sugg sustained his fatal injury when he hit the pavement, smashing his head against a brick wall. The Coroner's Inquest brought back a verdict of murder.

Officer Sugg lived at 6059 W. Matson Avenue and was buried in St. Boniface Cemetery. Later, his remains were transferred to All Saints Cemetery in suburban DesPlaines.

Patrolman Patrick J. Redmond,

STAR #1583, 12th District, Kensington Station, 29 years old, was shot and killed during an armed robbery on May 9, 1934. The slain officer had been assigned to guard a payroll exchange that took place at a local tavern at 644 E. 113th Street in the Southside community of Roseland. Employees of the nearby Pullman Company were in the process of cashing their checks at the tavern owned by Frank Ghodotti. He had withdrawn more than $2000 for the purpose. There were some fifteen Pullman employees in the backroom of the tavern in the late afternoon. With them were Albina Ghodotti, the owner's wife, and Antonio Fraccaro, the owner of the building in which the tavern was located. Fraccaro had his son Emil with him. Officer Redmond was with the group in the backroom as four bandits entered the tavern. "This is a stickup, everybody," one of the gang shouted. Just then, Redmond emerged from the backroom and the gang opened fire on him with the sawed-off shotguns they were carrying. Redmond was immediately hit on the left side of his abdomen. The blast shattered his left arm as well. As he fell to the floor, he shot his gun twice, but the bullets went astray and hit the tavern windows. The criminals quickly fled the scene, abandoning their plans to rob the payroll. As they left, Emil Fraccaro grabbed a shotgun that was hanging on the wall of the tavern and fired at the fleeing killers. Despite his quick thinking, they escaped in a car, speeding west on 113th Street.

With remarkable courage, Redmond was able to give police a description of the men before being transported to Roseland Hospital where doctors tried in vain to save the young patrolman's life using blood transfusions—a procedure still in its infancy. Calls went out to every police station in town for blood donations. In spite of a great outpouring of volunteers, Officer Redmond died before he could receive the blood he needed, lasting less than three hours.

Patrolman Redmond was married, with a wife and two children. He resided at 8016 S. Langley Avenue. In addition, his brother, Lambert, a policeman, was also assigned to the Kensington Station. The slain officer was laid to rest in Holy Sepulchre Cemetery on 111th Street. He had been a member of the Chicago Police Department for two years.

Patrolman Stanley L. Bobosky,

STAR #1446, Motorcycle Division, 40 years old, and his partner, Patrolman Richard Zimmerman, were in uniform and working a special assignment in the city's resurgent campaign to reduce the number of auto thefts. These crimes were an urban issue reaching dramatic proportions. Bobosky and Zimmerman were driving as they spotted three youths riding in a V-8 Ford sedan shortly after midnight on July 6, 1934. The officers then stopped for a red light at Western Avenue and Lake Street on the city's Westside beneath the "EL" track.

As the three youths drove up, Bobosky exited the police squad and walked over to their car to question them. "Who owns this car?" Bobosky asked, placing one of his feet on the running board of the auto. Just then, the driver of the car pulled out a revolver and shot Bobosky in the abdomen. The men then fled the scene. It was 12:30 A.M. when Zimmerman took Bobosky to Washington Boulevard Hospital. Doctors determined that the bullet had entered through his left side, passed through his abdomen and exited through his right side, causing a mortal wound. At 3:30 P.M., Officer Stanley Bobosky died from his injuries. He was mourned by his wife, Madeline, and two children, Robert, 10, and Dorothy, 4. Bobosky was buried in St. Joseph Cemetery.

Patrolman William F. Penney,

STAR #5356, 1st District, Detective Bureau, 38 years old, was conducting an investigation at the Modern Tavern, 722 S. Halsted Street, on July 24, 1934 when he become involved in an argument with several men. The men attacked and severely beat the patrolman before fleeing the scene. Penney left the tavern too, but returned moments later when he realized the keys to his automobile had been lost during the struggle. The bartender gave Penney his keys that had been left behind. Penney later returned to the tavern for a third time to arrest the men who had assaulted him earlier in the day. The patrolman brought three friends back with him and approached the tavern door with two of them at around 9:50 P.M. The third friend remained in Penney's vehicle. They found the front door locked and had turned to make their way back to the car when the front door opened and a shotgun emerged. Two blasts were fired and Patrolman Penney was killed instantly along with one of his companions, while the other sustained minor injuries.

Patrolman Penney, who was in civilian clothes at the time of his death, was identified at the scene by the policeman's star found in his pocket. He had been out of uniform that day because he was a prosecution witness in a conspiracy case. Police later determined that the shotgun had been fired by Steve Vrionis, a bartender at the Modern Tavern who lived in an upstairs apartment. The murder weapon was found in a room adjacent to Vrionis' apartment. There is no confirmation that he was ever apprehended. Officer Penney had been assigned to the Detective Bureau for ten years. He was survived by his wife and three children. Officer Penney was interred in Holy Sepulchre Cemetery.

Patrolman Anton Zapolsky,

STAR # 5369, 1st District, Central Station, died on July 30, 1934 from wounds he received in a downtown shootout three days earlier. Zapolsky was on duty in the Loop with his partner, Patrolman Leonard McPhail, when they encountered an escaping automobile thief pursued by a police squad. Observing Charles Lewis, alias Miller, of 2434 W. Moffet Street, running in the vicinity of Wacker Drive and Clark Street, Zapolsky and McPhail joined in the pursuit. While attempting to apprehend the suspect, he opened fire at the policemen and hit Zapolsky in the abdomen. The wounded officer was taken to Henrotin Hospital.

Lewis, who had originally had been caught trying to steal a parked car, was shot and killed at 206 W. Randolph Street by Patrolman John Fogarty of the Detective Bureau. Lewis' body was later identified in the County Morgue by 58-year-old Casimir Maciong, of 311 N. Drake Avenue, who told police that Lewis was responsible for the murder of his son, Zygmund, some six weeks earlier. He told police that his son named Lewis as his killer as he was dying in Cook County Hospital. He claimed that Lewis had been paid to kill his son by a bootlegger.

Officer Zapolsky died from the wound he sustained three days after the shootout. He was mourned by his wife, Minnie; his children, Dorothy and Thomas; and his brother, William. He was waked in his residence at 4421 S. Marshfield Avenue. His Solemn Requiem High Mass was celebrated at Holy Cross Church. Burial took place in St. Casimir Cemetery on 111th Street.

Lieutenant James F. Day,

STAR #261, 14th District, Gresham Station, 71 years old, had been a member of the Chicago Police Department since 1891 when he was found dead on Wednesday, September 19, 1934. The Lieutenant's body was discovered in a vacant lot at 8545 S. Green Street, just 100 yards from the Gresham Police Station on the city's Southside. An initial police investigation revealed that he had been struck from behind during a robbery, suffering a serious head injury. An autopsy revealed that in addition to the fatal injuries to his head, Day had suffered a heart attack during the assault. Mrs. Minnie Day, his wife, indicated to Gresham Police Captain William J. O'Brien that her husband had cashed his paycheck and was carrying a large amount of cash on him when he left their home at 5409 S. Michigan Avenue that evening. The Lieutenant's revolver and empty wallet were found at the scene. Lieutenant Day was buried from St. Ann Church on Garfield Boulevard and laid to rest at St. James at the Sag Cemetery.

The *Chicago Tribune* reported that a 26-year-old former inmate of an insane asylum, William Duba, who was arrested for loitering at 63rd Street and St. Louis Avenue, confessed to police that he had beaten Lieutenant Day in the head with a large tree limb. The Oak Lawn resident provided police with intimate details of the assault and robbery. Police were dubious of his "confession," based on his record of mental instability. He was able to lead police to the very spot where they had found Lieutenant's Day's body. Police were conducting their own search for a suspect with a bruised eye who was earlier seen by Officer William Burke running from the spot where Day's body was found. The suspect, Willie Randolph, was caught, arrested and on November 30, 1934 was found guilty of the murder of Lieutenant Day before Judge Charles F. McKinley and sentenced to life in the Illinois State Penitentiary at Joliet.

Mounted Chicago Police Officer writes
a parking ticket (1934).
ICH-i19703, Chicago History Museum.

Patrolman Louis F. Furst,

STAR #6347, 5th District, Wabash Avenue Station, 44 years old, was directing traffic at 59th and State Streets on Saturday, September 22, 1934, in the late morning, when a witness to an armed robbery, Miss Irene Lewan, an employee of H.J. Coleman Company, came running to him for assistance. Lewan had been eating her lunch in a back room of her office at the time of the hold-up. She managed to sneak out a back entrance to summon help. Furst ran to the Coleman Company, just a few doors to the north at 5857 S. State Street. As he did, he encountered the armed suspect who had just robbed the business of $200. The gunman brandished the nickel-plated revolver that he used to hold-up the manager, Byron Bailey, and the clerk, Miss Mary Kowal. When the gunman, later identified as 21-year-old Jay Franklin, alias, Taylor, of 5330 S. Prairie Avenue, saw Furst coming he fled to a nearby real estate office. As soon as Officer Furst came into view, Franklin wedged his foot against the glass door and fired simultaneously with Furst.

Sadly, Furst's shot missed the gunman. Franklin then fired five bullets at Furst. The first shot hit Furst in the head, fatally injuring him. The killer then fled. Officer Furst died at 11:45 A.M. Two policemen on patrol in the area heard the gun shots and quickly arrived at the scene along with an off-duty officer from the Wabash Avenue Station. They caught sight of the gunman as he fled. The officers were aided in their pursuit by a squad car from the Detective Bureau. Franklin eventually stopped and hid in a second floor apartment at 5821 S. Grove Avenue; telling the occupant of the apartment that he was hiding from his wife. He then made his way to the apartment's pantry hoping to outwit police. Meanwhile, two policemen ran up the front stairs, while two ran up the back stairs to the rear porch. When police ordered Franklin to surrender, he answered with a burst of gunfire. The four policemen then returned fire on Franklin. Patrolman Carl Nelson, of the 5th District, killed the offender.

Officer Furst lived at 1435 E. 60th Street and was survived by his wife, two sons and daughter. He was buried at Oakland Cemetery in Carbondale, Illinois.

Patrolman Thomas E. Torpy,

STAR #525, 5th District Station, Wabash Avenue Station, 38 years old, became the second officer from his station to die in the line of duty on the same day, Saturday, September 22, 1934. At 2:45 P.M. Torpy and his partner, Patrolman Robert Galbraith, went to an apartment located at 4733 S. St. Lawrence Avenue to arrest 27-year-old Clifton Myrick. The suspect was wanted in connection with his involvement with a gang that carried out some 40 robberies and two murders. Five members of the gang, including Myrick's bother, John, were already in police custody. Torpy and Galbraith set up a detail at the apartment to apprehend the other Myrick brother. When the suspect walked out of his apartment, he saw police had him covered with their guns and quickly slammed the door of the flat. Torpy grabbed the door knob, opening the door, at which point Myrick opened fired, hitting Torpy twice. The patrolman continued to pursue Myrick down a stairway where the assailant shot him two more times, the last bullet piercing his head. Torpy tumbled down the stairs while Galbraith pursued Myrick, firing at him as he went. When police finally subdued the suspect, he had been shot five times. As Myrick was being transported in a police wagon to the Bridewell Hospital, he attempted to seize a gun belonging to Patrolman John Hogan. In the struggle that followed Patrolman Clinton Towne, of the 5th District, shot Myrick two times, killing him.

Officer Torpy was survived by his wife, son and step-daughter. He was laid to rest in Holy Sepulchre Cemetery. He was a 12-year-veteran of the Chicago Police Department.

Patrolman Alfred M. Stokke,

STAR #2571, 38th District, Town Hall Station, 38 years old, was assigned to guard the Meisel Tire Company at 4465 N. Broadway Street on January 24, 1935 when he was killed in the line of duty. Information had been sent to the police indicating that a robbery would take place there. Stokke was sent, in uniform, to prevent the crime from happening. He was keeping watch from the backroom when a car occupied by three gunman pulled up to the front of the store shortly before 5:00 P.M. They entered and held up Carl Adams, the store's owner, and Frank Smith, a customer; stealing $50 from the cash register before Stokke surprised them as they attempted to hustle Smith into the backroom. Simultaneous shooting began and Stokke was hit in the head and groin. The robbers then quickly fled the scene by car. The patrolman was transported to Lakeview Hospital where he received a blood transfusion. All the medical efforts were in vain and he died at 11:05 P.M. His children, Ernestine and Frank, stood at his bedside.

Before he died, the 17-year-veteran told Captain Patrick O'Connell that he believed he had wounded two of the men before they escaped. On September 3, 1935, Alex Goralski, Eugene Wroblewski and Anthony Adams were arrested and confessed to Patrolman Stokke's murder. The men were tried on October 8, 1936, found guilty and received sentences of 75 years each.

Patrolman Edwin E. Peppard,

STAR #5967, Marquette Station, 30 years old, died two hours after jumping from the fourth floor of a burning building, at 1207-09 S. Damen Avenue, on April 15, 1935. Officer Peppard arrived to the scene of the fire with Officers Joseph Carroll and Frank Jenousek. Soon after, the officers were joined by Officers Arthur Richter and Frank Braddock. The patrolmen ran into the building to save those who were still inside. Peppard who was trapped was left behind as everyone else ran for the stairs to exit the building. Officer Richter saw Peppard's clothes catch on fire. Before firemen could raise their ladders up to save Peppard, he leaped out the window. Peppard, a six-year-veteran, fell to his death, leaving a wife and child behind.

Patrolman Thomas Kelma,

STAR #427, 22nd District, Maxwell Street Station, 38 years old, was off-duty enjoying a card game with friends in the rear room of Ray Curran's Tavern, 2023 S. Ashland Avenue, on May 31, 1935 when two gunman entered around 9:30 P.M. One ordered Kelma and his friends to raise their hands while the other moved towards the card table. Kelma had his back to the door and was unaware of the criminals until they announced themselves and demanded that one of his tablemates, Joseph Jira, hand over his winnings. Once he realized the situation, the patrolman reacted quickly, overturning the card table, drawing his weapon and firing at the bandits. The thieves had not been expecting resistance and when they encountered it they lost their resolve. They fled to a waiting Ford sedan, where an additional accomplice awaited them, without taking any money. Kelma followed close behind and was met by a barrage of bullets fired by the car's passengers. He stood fast against the lethal volley, returning fire until one of the bandits' bullets found its mark and struck him near the heart. The offenders left the fallen officer bleeding to death on the sidewalk outside the saloon.

A police squad headed by Sergeant Richard Adamek arrived shortly after the shooting. Kelma was rushed to St. Anthony Hospital, where he was pronounced dead. The ten-year-veteran was survived by his wife and two children, who saw justice done when Edward Derlack, Thomas Arelando and Jerry Reporto were arrested for their parts in the crime. Derlack was sentenced to 199 years, while Arelando received a 14-year-prison term. Reporto was condemned to spend the rest of his natural life at the Illinois State Penitentiary at Joliet. Frank Banko was also wanted in connection with the officer's death but his case was closed when he died shortly after the shooting. Officer Kelma was laid to rest at Bohemian National Cemetery.

Patrolman William H. Stringfellow,

STAR #2272, Traffic Division, 52 years old, had been assigned to patrol and traffic duty in the vicinity of Union Station, specifically the corner of Jackson Boulevard and Clinton Street, for more than ten years when he was killed in the line of duty at 11:17 A.M. on October 3, 1935. Over the years Stringfellow made it his practice to escort cashiers from the station's various businesses to the nearby Mercantile Trust and Savings Bank at 541 W. Jackson Boulevard. On October 3, he was escorting John Beahan, a cashier for the Fred Harvey restaurant, from the establishment's basement offices to the street when they encountered the bandits who would end his life. The two men were ten feet from the main floor ramp leading out to Clinton Street, just north of Jackson Boulevard, when Beahan noticed a man on the ramp who appeared to be innocently tying his shoe. Beahan was only a few paces behind Stringfellow when the stranger, a "shoot first" bandit, suddenly straightened and fired several shots at the officer. Stringfellow immediately fell to the ground fatally wounded, unable to draw or even reach his own weapon. Beehan, startled by the gun fire, fell to the ground and hit his head, dropping the money bag he carried in the process. The shooter grabbed the bag, containing between $3,700 and $5,300, and ran to Clinton Street, where he was joined by three companions. The four men then jumped into a nearby sedan and sped away. Not a single word was ever spoken by the killer according to Beahan.

The deserted ramp where the crime occurred quickly filled with customers from inside the station. Among them was Dr. Walter Aye of Pennsylvania, who pronounced Patrolman Stringfellow dead at the scene from two gunshot wounds. Stringfellow was a lifelong state resident, born in Sycamore, Illinois on June 27 1883. He joined the Chicago Police Department on November 13, 1914. Stringfellow was survived by his wife, Elizabeth, and son, Raymond, 23 years old elevator operator at Union Station, though was off-duty the day his father was killed. The Stringfellow family resided at 6817 N. Ottawa Street. Investigators believed that Stringfellow's killer may have been part of a gang that was involved in an attempted robbery at University State Bank, 1354 E. 55th Street, the Monday before. That crime had been characterized by a great deal of shooting and police believed the patrolman's calculated, unprovoked killing was a pattern set by the same group. Fred Belter, an employee of the Fred Harvey restaurant, was held and questioned as a suspect in the crime. Officer Stringfellow was laid to rest at Acacia Park Cemetery.

Patrolman Joseph Klocek,

STAR #400, Chicago Park District Police, was patrolling his beat on October 8, 1935 when he lost his life in a tragic motorcycle accident. Klocek was traveling on 84th Street between Yates and Philips Avenues when his motorcycle hit a loose stone, causing it to skid out of control. The patrolman was thrown to the pavement and sustained fatal injuries. Children en route to Coles Elementary School witnessed the tragic accident. Klocek was laid to rest at Forest Home Cemetery.

Patrolman Joseph Isola,

STAR #653, Chicago Park District Police, 46 years old, was walking his beat on Washington Boulevard when he was fatally shot in the line of duty after coming to a citizen's aid on November 1, 1935. Charles McGavin, a former member of Congress, and Joseph Posch, the owner of a restaurant at 1350 W. Lake Street, were walking down Ada Street, just north of Washington Boulevard, when they were attacked by two robbers. The robbers concentrated on Posch, leaving McGavin free to run for help. He found Patrolman Isola patrolling a short distance away and brought him back to the scene, where the crime was still in progress. While McGavin was gone the robbers beat Posch severely and stole $28. When the offenders saw Officer Isola approaching with McGavin they opened fire and a fatal shot lodged just below the patrolman's heart.

Isola was rushed to Garfield Park Hospital where he died on November 2, 1935. Posch was in critical condition with a fractured skull when he was taken to the Cook County Hospital. It was determined that he would likely lose sight in his right eye. McGavin disappeared shortly after the shooting but was later found at his residence, a hotel at 900 W. Madison Street, and taken into custody shortly before Isola's death. McGavin represented the 8th Illinois District in Congress from 1905 to 1909. His political career, short but impressive, began when he was appointed Assistant City Attorney in 1903. Police who located McGavin took him to the Detective's Bureau to view pictures of suspects, but he was unable to identify any of the bandits from the pictures he was shown. The police planned on keeping him in custody until he testified at the inquest into the patrolman's death. Officer Isola was buried at Mount Olive Cemetery.

Patrolman Arthur Swanson,

STAR #547, Chicago Park District Police, 39 years old, had been a police officer for ten years when his motorcycle hit a slick spot at 3600 S. Michigan Avenue on May 14, 1936 and spun out of control. Another officer riding with Patrolman Swanson was seriously injured but survived the accident. Swanson's injuries proved to be fatal and he died a week after the accident on May 21, 1936. The patrolman resided at 20 W. 109th Street with his wife, Hedrig, and children Russell and Rita Mae. In addition, he was survived by his father, Charles G., and siblings Alice, Elmer and Carl. Officer Swanson was waked at 6659 S. Halsted Street and was laid to rest at Oakhill Cemetery.

Patrolman Jerome M. McCauley,

STAR #6700, Accident Prevention Division, 36 years old, was on patrol in car #177 with his partner, Edward Brieske, on May 29, 1936, when they spotted a group of suspects in a stolen car at the intersection of Elston and Damen Avenues. A radio message that relayed information concerning criminals who had held up stores at 4200 W. Fullerton Avenue and 4063 N. Milwaukee Avenue had just reached them. The communication reported that the men had stolen $200 at the second establishment and gave the last three digits of their license plate number as 953. When the officers reached the intersection of Paulina and Dean Streets at around 8:45 P.M., they recognized the occupants of a car being driven southeast on Elston Avenue as the suspects described in the radio broadcast and set off in pursuit.

With sirens shrieking and Brieske in the driver's seat, they sped along the congested street after the stolen vehicle, narrowly missing other vehicles and a street car as they turned onto Wood Street. At the intersection of Wood Street and Webster Avenue, the police were slowed by street construction that allowed them to get within 50 feet of the suspects. Brieske jumped out of the vehicle and fired at the robbers who returned fire as they made their way past the construction barrier. As Brieske returned to his car, he noticed that one of the bandits' bullets had struck the car but put it from his mind as he resumed pursuit. McCauley joined in the gun battle as the cars approached the Bloomingdale Street viaduct. His fire was also met with a response of bullets. One of the robbers' bullets came through the windshield, fatally wounding Patrolman McCauley with a bullet above his right eye with an exit wound behind his right ear. It caused him to drop his pistol onto the street as the chase continued.

Brieske remained unaware that his partner had been shot as he weaved his way through traffic. He then heard a low groan, looked to his right and discovered McCauley lying on the floor of the vehicle. Upon discerning his partner's injury, Brieske immediately stopped his pursuit and headed to North Avenue Hospital where McCauley, a three-year-veteran of the force, died one hour after he arrived. The robbers continued their escape, heading east on Julian Street before abandoning their vehicle in front of 1550 N. Orchard Street. Descriptions of the suspects were provided by Mrs. Sidney Lewis, who had been robbed by the gang during the second hold-up at the Midwest Poultry Store. She told investigators that all the men involved in the crime were fairly young. It was then learned that the car in which they had been riding had been reported stolen on May 9, 1936 by its owner Herbert Max, of at 2420 N. Lawndale Avenue.

McCauley, a World War I veteran, was survived by his wife. On June 18, 1936, Frank Korczykowski was arrested after being identified as one of the men involved in the crime spree that night, followed by Paul Jenkot and Andrew Bogacki six days later. On September 28, 1936 Jankot was sentenced to 199 years in the Illinois State Penitentiary at Joliet. Bogacki and Korczykowski were found to have played more fatal roles in the shooting and both were sentenced to death on August 17, 1936. They were electrocuted on Halloween of the same year in the Cook County Jail. Officer McCauley was laid to rest at Mount Carmel Cemetery.

Patrolman John Freichel,

STAR #3710, 23rd District, Marquette Street Station, 42 years old, had just enjoyed a glass of beer while off-duty at a local tavern, located at 759 S. Kedzie Avenue, when he was fatally shot on August 23, 1936. The saloon's bartender, Jerry Flanagan, told investigators that Freichel had arrived a little before 4:00 P.M. and had stayed only a short time. As he left the tavern, Sam LaSasso, a local hoodlum whom Freichel had arrested several times before, was entering. LaSasso recognized the patrolman as he opened the screen door. According to witnesses, the criminal mumbled a few words about getting even before firing three shots at the officer. He then turned and exited through the door he he had just entered. He continued east down Polk Street before turning down the alley running behind the tavern as Freichel, staggering because of two fatal bullet wounds, drew his weapon and attempted to exit through the back in order to cut off LaSasso's escape. He collapsed next to the tavern's rear door.

As Freichel lay helpless in the back of the tavern, LaSasso raced north through the alley to Lexington Street and then west to Kedzie Avenue before stopping, pointing his weapon at his head and firing one shot. He then fired two shots into his body, all in an apparent attempt to commit suicide. Once discovered, he was taken to the Cook County Hospital, arriving only a short time after Freichel was admitted to Bethany Hospital. Patrolman Freichel died later the same day while LaSasso held on for two weeks before dying on August 27, 1936. Freichel, a fifteen-year-veteran of the force, was married with one daughter at the time of his death. The policeman was laid to rest in St. Mary Cemetery.

After both men died investigators interviewed LaSasso's friends and family to try and ascertain the motives behind his actions. The killer's 17-year-old sister Emily was interviewed at their family home and told police that her brother had been unsuccessful in finding a job and had told her he was disgusted with his life. LaSasso was only 30 years old at the time of his death but had a criminal record dating back to 1926, including several arrests made by Patrolman Freichel. Other LaSasso relatives told investigators that LaSasso had vowed to kill himself. They believed his decision to kill Freichel happened in the heat of the moment. The criminal held a long standing grudge against law enforcement officials, Freichel in particular, a feeling of resentment exacerbated by his persecution complex. It was believed that Freichel's tragic death was simply a matter of him having been in the wrong place at the wrong time.

Sergeant Frederick Fischer,

STAR #36, Chicago Park District Police, 39 years old, was writing an accident report at North Lake Shore Drive and Fullerton Parkway in Lincoln Park on October 21, 1936 when he was struck by a passing vehicle. Fischer was filling out a report on Arthur Cohen, whose car was hit by George Levinson, when a third vehicle came along and pushed Levinson's car into the officer. Cohen's wife, who was injured during the first accident, was the only other person hurt. Fischer sustained fatal injuries that led to his death the next day, October 22, at Columbus Hospital. Fischer was survived by his wife, Ciara; mother, Mathilda; and siblings, William, Max, Martha Amerski, Arthur and Charles. His funeral services were held at the 3301 W. Fullerton Avenue and he was interred at Waldheim Cemetery. Fischer was a member of the Chicago Park Policemen's Benevolent Association.

Patrolman Michael Toth,

STAR #7334, 17th District, New City Station, 32 years old, and his partner Thomas Bourke were assigned to squad car #182 on November 8, 1936 when they received a radio report of a complaint made by a tavern owner. Walter Godula, proprietor of a tavern at 4830 S. Wood Street, called "Police 13-13," precursor to the modern 911, and reported a disturbance. The officers decided to investigate, parking their vehicle mere feet north of the tavern before heading inside at about 12:15 A.M. They headed towards the west end of the bar where they saw two men matching the radio description of the suspects involved in the disturbance. Toth told one of the men to get his hand out his pocket as Bourke approached the other, club in hand. Disliking Bourke's aggressive approach, the suspect drew a revolver and placed it next to the officer's head, removing Bourke's own gun from its holster at the same time. Toth was also facing trouble as the suspect he had approached fought and forced him into a darkened back room. Suddenly gunshots were heard from the room in which Toth had disappeared. Bourke broke free from his assailant and dashed out of the establishment to 4800 S. Wood Street, where he called the station for back-up. He then ran back inside and discovered his partner sitting on a chair near the front door, bleeding profusely. The gunman and his accomplice had fled, leaving behind the weapon used to fatally shoot the officer. Patrolman Toth was quickly picked up and transported to German Deaconess Hospital by the 17th District wagon. It was determined that he had been shot twice, once in the stomach and once in the hand. He died at the hospital at 7:00 P.M. that same night. Toth was laid to rest at Resurrection Cemetery.

Police investigators pieced together the events surrounding Patrolman Toth's death. According to Godula's statement, the two bandits entered his establishment at around 11:30 P.M. and consumed several drinks. They then proceeded to try and sell Godula two pistols for $20, speaking in Slovak as they made the offer. He countered that he would pay $15 but they declined and continued drinking. Nervous that two men he knew to be armed were slowly getting more and more inebriated in his establishment, the proprietor snuck away and contacted the police. Here Godula's account deviates from police. According to the *Chicago Daily Tribune*, Godula told whoever answered his call that there were "two bad men in his place with guns," a contention the police denied. Police claimed Godula's report was not that specific, claiming he simply described a disturbance. That was how it was broadcast on the radio. He had not mentioned that the men were armed. Bourke was later quoted saying, "If we had known they were armed we would gone in with guns drawn," a move that might have save Patrolman Toth's life.

Toth, who left a wife and two children, emerged as a hero when witness accounts described the officer stepping in front of his assailant's gun when the offender pointed it at Bourke after wounding Toth. Frank "Doc" Whyte and Stanley Murawski were arrested on December 15, 1936 and charged with Patrolman Toth's murder. They were both found guilty and sentenced to death by electrocution, which took place on April 16, 1937.

Patrolman Arthur J. Sullivan,

STAR #3911, 23rd District, Marquette Station, 37 years old, was investigating a complaint on January 14, 1937 when he was shot and killed. Sullivan was off-duty and on his way home when a citizen, who knew him to be a policeman, approached and claimed he had just spotted the man who recently robbed him. Casimer Kulis, a drugstore clerk who worked in a pharmacy at 3001 W. Cermak Road, had been seated in a restaurant when he noticed Joseph Schuster, a paroled convict, pass by the window. Kulis then spotted Sullivan and ran out to the street, telling the patrolman Schuster was the man who had robbed him of $27 the day before.

Sullivan and Kulis then followed Schuster into the Kedzie Avenue Station of the Douglas Park "EL" near 20th Street at around 11:45 P.M. The men followed Schuster up to the platform where Sullivan confronted him with Kulis' allegation. The suspect protested saying Kulis was mistaken.

Sullivan did not believe his protests of innocence. He began to search Schuster before escorting him down the station stairs, intending to take him in. Unfortunately, Sullivan's routine pat-down failed to reveal a loaded revolver Schuster was carrying in a shoulder holster. The officer had noticed the hard protrusion but taken Schuster's word when the bandit claimed it was only his ribs. When the men reached the landing, Schuster drew his weapon. He placed it next to the officer's temple and fired a single shot that entered Sullivan's head and killed him instantly. Schuster then aimed the weapon at Kulis but it misfired. He fled back up the station stairs and jumped down onto the tracks, running along the rails and climbing down a pillar to escape.

Sullivan was survived by his wife and four children, who ranged in age from two to fifteen years old. Schuster only remained at large for two days before the police apprehended him, although he was not officially arrested until January 20. He was found guilty and sentenced to death on March 3, 1937 and electrocuted in the Cook County Jail on April 6, 1937. Officer Sullivan was laid to rest at Mount Carmel Cemetery.

Sergeant Sidney Thomas Sullivan,

STAR # unavailable, DesPlaines Street Station, 49 years old, was struck and killed by a vehicle on Roosevelt Road on January 31, 1937. Sergeant Sullivan was on his way to interview an informant about a recent rash of taxicab robberies in the DesPlaines Street District when his vehicle skidded on an ice patch and slid into a ditch. As the sergeant began to walk for help he was struck by another car sliding on the ice.

Sergeant Sullivan had been on the force for 23 years and was survived by his wife, son, daughter, and brother. Sullivan's son, grandson, brother and two nephews all went on to distinguished careers with the Chicago Police Department.

Patrolman Bernard B. Klinke,

STAR #229, Chicago Park District Police, 40 years old, was struck and killed by an automobile on February 22, 1937 while directing traffic on his regular beat. Klinke was at the intersection of 3400 N. Sheridan Road with a red lantern, a method many officers used where there were no signal lights. Witness reports of the incident stated that the officer had blown his whistle to stop northbound traffic and swung the lantern in that direction. He then moved towards the curb to offer assistance in crossing the street to Mrs. Lee Schiff and her daughter, Gladys. At the same moment, George H. Gamber was driving northbound.

Gamber, a 57-year-old retired mail carrier, hit Klinke right before the officer reached the sidewalk. The distraught driver claimed that he had not seen the lantern or heard the officer's whistle as he neared the intersection. Gamber was booked on a charge of manslaughter and held in custody in order to assure his appearance at the inquest the next day. Klinke, a 13-year-veteran of the force, was remembered by his colleagues as a courageous officer who was cited for bravery in 1925 for his part in catching one of the Drake Hotel robbers. He was also the first officer to receive the *Chicago Tribune's* $25 weekly award, which was presented for outstanding acts of courtesy by city policemen. He was recognized with the inaugural award in 1933 for the overwhelming enthusiasm he displayed aiding visitors at the World's Fair, the Century of Progress Exposition.

1937

Patrolman Martin Wolski,

STAR #359, Chicago Park District, 36 years old, was in uniform patrolling McKinley Park on March 26, 1938 when he noticed some suspicious activity. Wolski was making rounds of the park in an automobile driven by his brother-in-law, Louis Czapski, and spotted a strange sight as they reached the area, commonly known as Lover's Lane at 3500 S. Damen Avenue. An old model sedan was parked a short distance ahead of them. Both of the vehicles front doors were open and two young men stood on the pavement next to it. Czapski brought the car to a short bend in the road about 100 feet from the parked car in order to conceal its presence from the young men. Wolski informed his brother-in-law that he did not like the look of the situation and got out to investigate. He ordered Czapski to stay in the car while he explored the situation. Wolski approached the car with only a flashlight in hand, despite his suspicions.

Police are not sure exactly what happened after Wolski left his vehicle except that it was only a short time before shots were fired. Czapski heard about six shots and immediately leapt from the car. He rushed to Patrolman Wolski's aid. When he reached the other vehicle, he found the officer laying in the road dying. His hat was on the ground nearby and his gun, which had been fired twice, was at his side. The suspects Wolski had approached quickly disappeared north through the park. It was believed they may have been two youths in their late teens who had been holding up "spooners" in the park. In April of the same year, four members of a gang, Bruno Murzydlo, Victor Labuckas, Bruno Panavas and Felix Loraitis were sentenced to one year in prison each for park robberies. Wolski, a 13-year veteran, was rushed to the Evangelical Hospital. He died from gunshot wounds to the head, shoulder and hand without ever regaining consciousness. No one was ever caught for the shooting. Wolski was laid to rest at Resurrection Cemetery.

Patrolman Patrick E. O'Malley,

Star #1346, 39th District, Damen Avenue Station, 31 years old, was off-duty in civilian clothes waiting for a friend when he was called to duty and fatally shot on August 21, 1938. O'Malley was killing time at Neely's Cocktail Lounge, 2405 N. Clark Street, which was closed that Sunday morning. The front door was locked and O'Malley was relaxed as he talked with the bar's proprietor William Neely, Neely's wife and their friend. Their pleasant Sunday morning was shattered when four gunman entered through the back door and announced a stick-up. O'Malley quickly stepped away from Mrs. Neely and drew his weapon. He shot rapidly at the bandits who fired in return. Seconds later, one of the robbers, Ossie Townsend, fell to the floor dead. His companions quickly fled the scene, running out to their vehicle where a fifth bandit waited in the driver's seat.

Patrolman Walter Frank was passing near the lounge when he heard the shots and ran to the scene. He found the front locked and quickly made his way to the back at the instruction of those inside. He observed the three bandits scrambling into the waiting vehicle and drew his own weapon as one of them fired at him. He fired three shots before the offenders sped away. He then rushed inside to discover Patrolman O'Malley bleeding from bullet wounds in his chest, stomach and shoulder. Help soon arrived and O'Malley was rushed to North Chicago Hospital.

Shortly after Patrolman O'Malley was taken to the hospital, a man with a gunshot wound was dropped off at a nearby doctor's office. It was ascertained that he was one of the suspects involved in O'Malley's shooting and taken into custody. It was not known whether Patrolman O'Malley or Patrolman Frank had injured the man, George Hamar, but it was clear once questioning was underway that he had no problem giving up the men who had abandoned him at the doctor's office. Hamar quickly confessed his part in the crime and named as

1938

his accomplices Howard Poe, Henry "W. Nash" Napue, and Lucius "Red Light" Webb. Poe was later electrocuted on August 1, 1938 for his part in the crime. Hamar was sentenced to 199 years in prison. Webb was also sentenced to 199 years for his part in the hold-up and homicide, but was released after Governor Stratton reduced his sentence to 57 years.

Patrolman O'Malley died from his wounds on August 30. His parents, Mr. and Mrs. John O'Malley were at his hospital bedside, as were his siblings, including his brother, Policeman William O'Malley. News of O'Malley's death quickly spread through stations across the city where other officers listened to the tale of his efforts against the four bandits. All were hoping for his recovery. According to the *Chicago Daily Tribune*, O'Malley was best described by Captain Thomas Duffy who declared that "O'Malley was the type of brave young police policeman that the City needs." Officer O'Malley was buried at Mount Carmel Cemetery.

Patrolman John A. Olson,

STAR #5397, 28th District, 45 years old, was escorting Harold Osmundsen, a cashier at the Metropolitan Life Insurance Company branch office at 3208 W. North Avenue, to the Pioneer Trust and Savings Bank at 4000 W. North Avenue on October 20, 1938 when he was attacked and killed. At around 9:50 A.M. the men set out on their usual route with Osmundsen carrying a black satchel containing $2000 to be deposited at the bank. A half block east of the bank, at Harding and North Avenues, a young man who had been lounging in a doorway suddenly stepped forward and aimed a gun at Olson and the cashier. He demanded the money Osmundsen was carrying and grabbed the black satchel before running south down Harding Avenue.

Olson immediately set off in pursuit of the robber but had only taken a few steps when a second suspect, idly looking at a store window, smashed a lead filled rubber hose into the back of the officer's head. Stunned, Patrolman Olson stumbled only momentarily before resuming his search for the first bandit. He was in the process of drawing his service revolver when the second offender stepped up and shot him once in the back. The shooter then disappeared east on North Avenue while his companion vanished down a nearby passageway. The hose the killer used to incapacitate Patrolman Olson was found near the scene soon after the shooting, as was a zipper jacket worn by one of the bandits. In addition to these items, investigators also discovered the the murder weapon, an Iverson Johnson Revolver, near the tragic intersection.

Neighborhood storekeepers and shoppers were able to provide fairly accurate descriptions of the two suspects, though none provided a solid identification. Patrolman Olson had been rushed to Danish-American Hospital after the shooting but died shortly after arriving there. The 16-year-veteran of the force was survived by his wife, Dorothy; and 3 children, Richard, Alice and LaVerne. The fallen officer was laid to rest at Irving Park Cemetery.

Detective-Sergeant Edward J. Lynn,

STAR #132, 25th District, Fillmore Station, 37 years old, was answering a report of a tavern patron with a concealed weapon when he was gunned down on November 30, 1938. Lynn had been called to the Blue Goose Café at 10 S. Pulaski Road around 8:30 A.M. when the proprietor, Thomas Williams, discovered a customer was armed. The man in question, James Wood, had fallen asleep and tumbled off his tavern stool. When Williams went to help him up he believed he felt a weapon in his pocket. Shortly after, Williams saw Lynn and his partner, Detective-Sergeant Allen Mulvey, walk by on their way to breakfast. He motioned them inside and informed them of his suspicions. Williams told the detectives that Woods had also been in his establishment the evening before and created a disturbance. When he returned that morning, he proceeded to fall asleep at the bar. The detectives, on duty in civilian clothes, decided to investigate the situation and approached Woods' stool.

Detective Lynn stepped up to another patron who was seated near Woods, informed him he was a police officer and then began patting him down for weapons. Upon hearing this Woods, who had appeared to have fallen back asleep, drew his weapon and began firing at the officers. Witnesses reported hearing Woods yell, "You're not going to get me," as he fired. The first shot fired hit Lynn in the head, but he still managed to draw his own revolver and shoot once before he fell to the ground. Woods then ran for cover as Mulvey took his own weapon from its holster and emptied it at him. The detective then ran to his fallen partner and picked up Lynn's gun. Woods had also emptied his gun and, despite being gravely wounded, attempted to reload it. Mulvey fired two more shots from his partner's weapon and riddled Woods with six bullets. He died only a short time after the shooting at the Bridewell Hospital. Detective-Sergeant Lynn was taken to the Garfield Park Hospital.

Upon arrival, it was discovered that the first bullet Woods fired had fractured Lynn's skull. It was lodged against his brain, leaving no chance for recovery. He died in his hospital bed at 3:25 P.M. The detective was survived by his mother and sister whom he had resided with at 213 N. Austin Boulevard. He was a highly respected officer and his station was flooded with calls inquiring about his welfare as news of the shooting spread. In 1930, Lynn single-handedly stopped a robbery in a Northside restaurant in a shoot out with the robbers that left one of them dead and another wounded. He also killed another robber in a gun battle at a Westside drugstore in 1934. The patrolman was laid to rest at Oak Ridge Cemetery.

After his death, Wood was identified by his fingerprints and found to be an escaped convict from the Missouri State Penitentiary. A map of "EL" stops was found on him, leading police to speculate that he was responsible for a recent string of robberies at various stations.

Patrolman Philip J. Kelly,

STAR #6161, 36th District, 34 years old, was off-duty on May 3, 1939, having drinks in the Eastwood Inn at 4623 N. Western Avenue with group of friends that included another officer, Patrolman Kelly McIntyre and McIntyre's wife, when two gunmen entered and commenced a hold-up. Kelly was talking to a friend, undertaker Alex Ferguson, when the bandits entered a few moments apart and took seats at the bar between the two policemen. After ordering their beers, they stood up and announced the robbery. Patrolman McIntyre immediately moved away from his wife and reached for his gun but it stuck in the holster. Unfortunately, both bandits saw him reach for his gun and opened fire, striking McIntyre, Kelly and Ferguson. McIntyre and Kelly managed to return fire as the battle raged. The bartender, Harry Bonin, managed to slip out a side door for help. When he returned to the tavern after summoning aid he ran into the two bandits, Edward Riley and Orville Watson. Riley was supporting Watson, who had been wounded in the gunfight. When he spotted Bonin, he tried to shoot the terrified man. Luckily, the gun was emptied in the tavern shootout. Realizing the gun was empty the two bandits, ex-convicts from Michigan, made their escape.

When Bonin finally managed to return to the tavern he encountered a tragic scene. Ferguson had been caught in the hail of gunfire and died instantly. McIntyre was wounded by a bullet that entered through the right temple and exited the left. Kelly was shot in the abdomen, right shoulder and right wrist, gravely wounded. Kelly and McIntyre were taken to the Ravenswood Hospital where the prognosis was grim. Officer Larry Dellamaria donated blood for a transfusion Kelly desperately needed, though in the end he could not overcome his wounds. Kelly died seven days after the shooting on May 10, 1939. Kelly's father, John P.; his two brothers, Harold and Edward, and Miss Marion Klauk, a friend of the officer's for five years, were all with him when he drew his last breath. At the time of his death doctors refused to predict Patrolman McIntyre's chances of recovery, but the officer eventually defied all expectations and pulled through.

On the day Kelly died, his killers were apprehended outside of Detroit. Chief of Detectives John L. Sullivan went to Michigan and brought Orville Watson, Edward Riley, and Susanna Smith, back to Chicago. The two men entered pleas of guilty in the death of Alex Ferguson and were sentenced to die in the electric chair on July 7, 1939. Their sentences were suspended until their appeals to the Supreme Court could be heard during its October session. The appeals court upheld the death sentences that were later carried out. Officer Kelly was laid to rest at All Saints Cemetery.

1939

Old Area 6, Damen Avenue
Police Station (1940's). Chicago Police
Department Photo Archive.

Old Area 2, Burnside (1940's).
Chicago Police Department Photo Archive.

Patrolman Harry Francois,

STAR #629, West Park Division, Chicago Park District Police, 37 years old, was on patrol in Humboldt Park with Sergeant Frederick Blank on November 20, 1939 when they stumbled on a suspicious sight. An expensive sedan was stopped on the park's North Drive, an east-west arm of Humboldt Boulevard near North Avenue and Whipple Street. The vehicle was surrounded by three young men. The officers had been surveying the area to expel loiterers during the late night hours when they came upon the vehicle, owned by a union official taking a female companion for a drive. They stopped on the North Drive for only a short time when three armed young men leapt from the surrounding bushes. Two of the men made their way to the passenger side where the female companion sat, while the other stood outside the driver's door. They waved their weapons at the terrified couple and ordered the female to open her door. She lowered her window instead, claiming that the door was locked. Angry at her response, one of the men ordered his companion to shoot her.

Only seconds after that police took the bandits by surprise. Blank and Francois had been able to bring their car within a few feet of the rear of the sedan. They were close enough for Francois to grab one of the gunmen. Francois immediately questioned the men about their business in the park and began to frisk them, but one fired a single shot at close range, which passed through Francois' left arm into his heart.

Sergeant Blank was exiting the car when he heard the fatal shot fired. He ran to the other vehicle only to watch helplessly as the killer and his accomplices fled north. He sent a hail of gunfire after them but did not appear to have wounded any of the criminals. City and Park Police quickly established a working partnership to accelerate the apprehension of Francois' killers. Three suspects were eventually arrested and sentenced to death for their part in Patrolman Francois' murder and a fourth, Jerry Mangano, received 199 years in prison. The patrolman, a 12-year-veteran of the force, left behind his wife, Nellie, and two children, Barbara, 4, and Donald, 2. He was was buried at Acacia Park Cemetery.

Patrolman Charles J. Speaker,

STAR #357, Chicago Park District, 58 years old, died in the line of duty on June 30, 1941. Though Speaker's killer, Bernard "Knifey" Sawicki, was only 19 when he shot the officer, he gained his reputation for violence as far back as fifth grade. He earned his nickname from those who saw him handle a knife. Patrolman Speaker became Sawicki's third murder victim when he pulled him over at 5900 S. Lake Shore Drive in a car that Sawicki had stolen the day before. He used the same .22 caliber pistol as in five other shootings. Sawicki claimed all his shootings were accidents. John J. Miller, a 19-year-old hold-up victim, died when he resisted Sawicki's robbery attempt in Sherman Park. The suspect admitted that the death of his third victim, Momence farmer Henry Allain, was intentional, retribution for Allain having him arrested in the past. Sawicki was also responsible for a violent attack on of Charles Kwasinski, 17, a St. Charles parolee like Sawicki, who had been taken to St. Luke Hospital with a grave gunshot wound. He apparently quarreled with Sawicki over whether to rob a hotel at State and 16th Streets and ended up shot. The trigger-happy psychopath also fired at Clarence Swak, 16, but missed.

Sawicki was transported to the Stockyards Station after shooting Patrolman Speaker. He showed no remorse for his actions while in custody and even claimed he did not fear the electric chair since he had always believed he would not live to the age of 21. Sawicki's own mother called him a black sheep during a newspaper interview, claiming that he had always been going in a bad direction. She stood behind her harsh words, despite the fact that Sawicki was apprehended on her front steps in the process of bringing her candy. Sawicki was found guilty of Officer Speaker's death and died in the electric chair on January 17, 1942 after a lengthy and contentious public trial.

Patrolman Charles H. Williams,

STAR #210, Chicago Park District Police, 45 years old, was off-duty but still in uniform when two men attempted a robbery in a tavern at 4301 N. Western Avenue on December 10, 1941. The bandits noticed Williams only after they announced their intentions. One of the men fired at Williams six times. The other held the door open to facilitate their escape. Patrolman Williams was able to return the bandits fire before falling near the bar. After the shooting, the robbers fled to a vehicle outside where a third bandit was waiting. However, one of them left his hat behind. It was traced to a store where the clerk was able to give the name of the shooter. His address came from the local draft board.

Confronted by the police, the suspect, John Pantano, admitted to being with the man who shot Patrolman Williams. Pantano claimed he could not provide the police with his associates' full names because he knew them simply as Tom and Eddie. Police were able to work with the information Pantano gave them and eventually arrested two additional suspects. Pantano was electrocuted in September of 1942 and his two accomplices, Charles Theos and Joseph Moreale, received prison sentences. Williams, a 19-year-veteran, succumbed to his wounds at Martha Washington Hospital, leaving behind his wife, Nellie. He was interred at St. Lucas Cemetery.

Patrolman Martin C. McCaw,

STAR #6991, 12th District, 34 years old, was accidentally shot on April 27, 1942. McCaw and his partner, Patrolman Louis Onixt, were chasing two drunken bandits when they entered a vacant lot at 653 W. Blue Island Avenue. McCaw had reached the area first and was in the process of taking one of the bandits into custody when Onixt tripped and his service revolver discharged. The bullet lodged in McCaw's head and caused a fatal injury. The offenders fled the scene after the gunshot was fired. McCaw was quickly taken to Mother Cabrini Hospital and pronounced dead upon arrival.

Patrolman McCaw was awarded the *Chicago Tribune's* Fire and Police Hero Award in January of 1942 after rescuing five people that were trapped inside a burning apartment building. The seven-year-veteran left behind his wife, Mary; and five children. The McCaw resided at 5608 S. Emerald Avenue.

Patrolman Walter J. Storm,

STAR #6891, 28th District, Austin Station, 35 years old, was killed in the line of duty when he unintentionally walked in on a stick-up at a local tavern at 5143 W. North Avenue on July 8, 1942. Storm had just left the Austin Station after changing into his civilian clothes and decided to stop to visit the bartender, who was a good friend of his. As Storm entered, a little after 12:15 A.M., four robbers had already moved the bartender and two customers against the wall and were in the process of searching them for valuables. Two gunmen remained in the tavern while the other two moved through to the liquor store at the back of the building in order to hold-up the clerk, Mrs. Rose Martin, for $9.50. One of the men was identified at the scene as Eugene Guzy, an ex-convict on parole from the Illinois State Penitentiary at Joliet, began to beat bartender Fred Goss. He struck him on the head with his gun at least five times, pushing him into the corner and taking $20 from his wallet. Guzy then retrieved $60 from the cash register just as Storm walked in.

Goss peered from the darkened corner and recognized his friend. He shouted, "Look out Walter, it's a stick-up," causing Storm to immediately draw his weapon and empty it at Guzy The robber fell wounded almost immediately. Despite his injuries, the offender was able to return fire as his three associates fled the scene without coming to his defense or firing a single shot of their own. The bandits quickly fled to a vehicle driven by a female companion, Sharlene O'Neill. Guzy died at the scene. Storm was rushed to St. Anne's Hospital with gunshot wounds in his head and shoulder. He died just as the ambulance arrived at St. Anne, leaving his wife a widow. He was buried at Mount Olive Cemetery.

Patrolman Storm had spent the evening before his death searching local taverns for the very gang that killed him. According to Storm's partner, Detective Edward Capparelli, they had used their time on duty that night to comb local drinking establishments in their districts, hoping that the gang of robbers would show up. They received a tip informing them the gang would strike that night but found nothing by the time their shift ended. Caparelli was still at the station at midnight when Storm had left for home.

After Guzy was identified, police found he had a lengthy criminal record dating back to December 28, 1931. He was sent to the Illinois State Penitentiary at Joliet on November 25, 1935 on a weapons charge. He was released from prison on March 29, 1940 and his parole card was found on his body after his death. Guzy's death led to the discoveries of his accomplices. Nick Gianos, Leo Piscopo, Anthony Moskal and Sharlene O'Neill were all later arrested for their part in Patrolman Storm's death. On November 5, 1942, the three male bandits were sentenced to 35 years each in the Illinois State Penitentiary at Joliet. On November 9, 1942, Sharlene O'Neill was sentenced to two years in the Dwight Reformatory for Women in Dwight, Illinois for driving the getaway car.

1942

Patrolman John J. O'Donnell,

STAR #3590, Cragin Station, 30 years old, was tragically killed while on duty on August 9, 1942. Officer O'Donnell was helping load an accident victim into an ambulance on the late summer day when he was struck by a drunk driver at the intersection of Diversey Avenue and Kilbourn Avenue. The intoxicated motorist apparently did not see the accident scene in time and lacked the motor skills to prevent the vehicle from slamming into the back of the ambulance. O'Donnell sustained life threatening injuries when he was crushed between the ambulance and the other vehicle. The inebriated driver, George Peterson, was arrested and charged with manslaughter.

Patrolman James G. Karl,

STAR #690, Lawndale Station, 32 years old, died on August 13, 1943 in Loretto Hospital after heroically saving the life of a truck driver. At 8:30 A.M. on August 12, 1943, William Bradley, a truck driver for Phillips Petroleum Company, crashed into the Belt Line viaduct at 4600 W. 16th Street. As Bradley approached the viaduct he attempted to avoid two cars in front of him that previously had been in an accident. He swerved his truck and lost control, crashing into a pillar. Bradley was pinned helplessly behind the wheel as gasoline poured from the truck's tank, forming a huge pool around the stalled vehicle.

Officer Karl witnessed the incident and immediately attempted to rescue Bradley from his truck. Fortunately, Karl was able to pull Bradley from the truck before the pool of gasoline exploded. The inferno took the life of Patrolman Karl and injured many. All were taken to Loretto Hospital where the officer died the next day.

Anthony Moskal and Leo Picopo,
killers of Patrolman Walter Storm (1942).
Chicago Tribune Photo Archive.

1943

Detective Ellwood S. Egan, Sr.,

STAR #6257, 28th District, Austin Station, 30 years old, was accidentally shot and killed on October 3, 1944 when a patrolman mistook him for an offender. Egan and his partner were out on the street when they saw a patrol unit turn into an alley off of 505 N. Avers Avenue. They decided to assist the patrolmen and headed towards the alley. As they did so, they saw two suspicious characters run out of a nearby parking garage. The detectives fired warning shots in an attempt to make the fleeing men halt. The patrolmen mistakenly believed the criminals were firing at them. They promptly returned fire and one of the bullets caused a fatal wound in Detective Egan's groin. The fallen officer was quickly taken to St. Anne Hospital where he died a short time later. John Przbylski, Michael Cutish and Nichola Golish, who were seen fleeing the scene after Egan was shot, were eventually apprehended and charged with burglary.

Detective Egan's son always believed that his father's star was retired in the superintendant's "star case," among those who died in the line of duty. But in 1975, while at the Chicago Police Headquarters on business, Egan Jr. learned that his father's star was not among those retired. Immediately, he was relentless in his fight to have his father's star added to the star case. In May 2006, Egan's badge was retired by the Chicago Police Department.

Patrolman Ezra Caldwell,

STAR #2969, 5th district, South Wabash Station, 32 years old,

and Patrolman Samuel M. Black,

STAR #1121, 5th district, South Wabash Station, 53 years old, were on patrol in car #151 on December 16, 1944 when a radio call reporting a domestic disturbance at 5147 S. Prairie Avenue was broadcast. The officers, both African-American, were in the vicinity and went to investigate. Black was the first to enter the residence and was met in the hallway by Kermit Bredlove, also African-American. Bredlove asked if the officer was looking for him and Black answered yes. The conversation then ended as Bredlove drew a weapon and shot the officer point-blank in the face. Patrolman Black fell dead almost instantly while Bredlove took the officer's service revolver. The killer then proceeded down the hallway and out onto the front steps where he was confronted by Patrolman Caldwell, who left the car upon hearing gunfire. Bredlove immediately shot at Caldwell. The patrolman returned fire and managed to wound the offender three times. Caldwell then attempted to take cover behind a truck parked on the street near the Bredlove residence. He slipped in the process and could not regain his feet before Bredlove fired a shot that would prove fatal.

Despite his grave injury, Patrolman Caldwell continued shooting at Bredlove until reinforcements arrived in car #162. Seeing his fallen colleague, Patrolman James McKenna leapt from his squad car and immediately started firing at Bredlove. The offender eventually sustained more than six bullet wounds to the chest and abdominal regions. Once Bredlove was finally subdued, he was taken to the Bridewell Hospital. Black and Caldwell were rushed to Provident Hospital. They were pronounced dead upon arrival.

Meanwhile, investigating officers had discovered further fallout from the domestic disturbance initially reported. Prior to the officers' arrival, Bredlove had shot and killed his wife, Goldine, in their first floor apartment. A quarrel between Bredlove and his wife began because he believed his wife had been flirting with another man at a party. Bredlove then shot his wife six times, leading neighbors to call the police. Patrolmen Black and Caldwell arrived just as Bredlove finished his first shooting spree and began to reload his weapon. Bredlove would recover from his injuries and was booked on three charges of murder. On March 9, 1945 he was found guilty of Patrolman Caldwell's murder and sentenced to

199 years in prison. On April 18, 1945 that sentence was ammended by a guilty verdict that sent him to the electric chair for Patrolman Black's brutal slaying. He was sent to the electric chair on September 14, 1945.

Patrolman Caldwell, a five-year-veteran of the force, was survived by his widow, Catherine. Patrolman Black, who had faithfully served the city for 27 years, left behind his wife, Johnnie, and a reputation as a fearless man of honor. Officer Caldwell was interred at Elmwood Cemetery in Sycamore, Illinois and Officer Black was interred at Mount Glenwood South Cemetery.

Patrolman Eugene L. Reid,

STAR #5408, 4th District, Stanton Avenue Station, 45 years old, was in the Harlem Liquor Store, located at 222 E. 35th Street, on May 7, 1945 speaking with the proprietor, Julius Dinkin when a man entered the store and roughly pulled a female patron outside where a second female waited. Patrolman Reid, an African-American officer, followed the couple outside and attempted to mediate an argument between the man and the two women. Barney Johnson, the man who had just exited the liquor store, became indignant at the officer's intervention. He drew a pistol and fired at Patrolman Reid. The officer managed to return fire, despite being hit in the groin. Reid shot Johnson a total of nine times before succumbing to his own injury. Patrolman Reid and the offender were taken to Michael Reese Hospital. Both were pronounced dead when they arrived. Patrolman Reid was interred at Old Lincoln Cemetery.

Further investigation into Patrolman Reid's killer revealed that an official complaint had been filed by Gladys Dawson, Johnson's common-law wife, on May 2. Mattie Richie was the female who joined the two as the argument began. Reid was carrying two pistols at the time of the confrontation and emptied both at the offender after Johnson fired the initial shot.

Detective Morris Friedman,

STAR #2619, Detective Bureau, 46 years old, was riding patrol with Sergeant Frank Pape and Patrolman Rudolph Friedl on June 25, 1945 when they observed and pursued a suspicious vehicle. The officers had been traveling north on Clark Street when they observed a 1940 Ford convertible coupe driving south on Clark Street at Illinois Street. The automobile had a 1945 Michigan license plate and contained two men and three women. Sergeant Pape motioned for the vehicle to stop but the sergeant's command was ignored and the vehicle continued on. Pape then instructed Patrolman Friedl, who was driving the squad car, to make a u-turn and head west on Illinois Street in pursuit. When the squad car reached LaSalle Street the coupe was coming towards them and they forced it to the curb.

The car barely slowed when one of the male passengers, Lyman Heiman, leapt from it and ran south down LaSalle Street before turning east on Hubbard Street. Pape ordered Friedman and Friedl to pursue Heiman, giving one of his weapons to Friedl. Pape used the other to subdue the remaining passengers in the car. As the officers pursued the bandit, Friedman fired two shots into the air and ordered Heiman to halt. Heiman did not heed the warning. Instead, he chose to jump behind a Cadillac sedan parked in front of 110 W. Hubbard Street. He then started shooting at the officers with both the .32 and .38 caliber handguns he carried. Friedman returned fire but sustained a fatal stomach injury that caused him to stumble and fall to the sidewalk. He died only moments later.

Friedl was only a short distance behind Detective Friedman. He immediately engaged Heiman in a brutal gun battle. The offender ducked behind the sedan, exchanging shots as he and Friedl circled the vehicle. Five bullets burst through the cars windows as the killer and the cop caught momentary glimpses of each other. Finally, Friedl caught sight of

Arial view of mounted traffic policeman (1944).
ICH-i39633, Chicago History Museum.

Heiman as he attempted to slip around the auto's rear fender and shot the bandit through the head. Friedl stepped closer to Heiman's fallen form and fired three more shots.

Sergeant Pape placed the other two occupants of the car, Edward "Bob Ross" Ervin and Mrs. Louis Gregerson, under arrest. Both were from Pontiac, Michigan and, with Heiman, had been involved in a number of robberies in Detroit, Dayton and Indianapolis. They were turned over to the Indianapolis Police to face robbery charges in the State of Indiana.

An investigation of Heiman's past revealed that he was an ex-convict from the Detroit area. His army discharge papers indicated that he had served with heroic distinction in the North African and Sicilian campaigns in World War II. Detective Friedman was remembered as a courageous officer who had been a member of the Robbery Detail for 17 years. He earned a file full of commendations. At the time of his death, Detective Friedman lived with his second wife, Rose, at 3825 W. Fulton Street. He had two grown sons, Jack, a 24-year-old Chief Petty Officer in the Navy, and George, 18 years old, from a previous marriage. The detective was buried at Woodlawn Cemetery.

Detective George H. Helstern,
STAR #1124, 41st District, Rogers Park Station, 54 years old, and
Detective Charles A. Brady, STAR
#6795, 41st District, Rogers Park Station, 34 years old, were in civilian clothes en route to their regular beat around 11:10 P.M. on September 2, 1945 when they observed a suspicious young man at the corner of Lunt Avenue and Clark Street outside a currency exchange. Helstern knew the man did not belong in that area. They decided to investigate. The detectives then crossed the street and positioned themselves out of sight. They identified themselves as police officers and without speaking the young hoodlum drew his weapon and began firing at the officers. The detectives fired a half a dozen shots in return as they fell to the ground, both fatally wounded. Detective Hellstern, a 20-year-veteran of the police force, was hit in the chest and died almost instantly. He was survived by his wife and two daughters.

Detective Brady was taken down by a bullet in his back, but did not immediately lose consciousness. The detective was able to recognize a local civilian, Paul McMahon, and directed him to stop the offender. Brady gave McMahon his service revolver, indicating that McMahon should do his best to the criminal. McMahon fired once at the offender as he escaped down a nearby alley.

A short time later a district squad car returning to the station at 7075 N. Clark Street passed the scene and noticed the crowd milling around the southeast corner of the intersection. Patrolmen Arthur Ackman and George Heckenbech got out to investigate and quickly discovered Detective Brady lying face down. His service revolver and several empty cartridges were scattered nearby. The officers quickly loaded the detective into their car, intending to transport him to the hospital. As they were doing so, one of the witnesses at the scene informed Ackerman that there was another wounded officer close by. The patrolman located Detective Helstern about 75 feet south of the corner. He had a bullet wound through his cheek. Both men were rushed by wagon to St. Francis Hospital in Evanston. Detective Helstern was pronounced dead on arrival. Doctors immediately started treating Detective Brady, although the prognosis was grim.

Police squads all over the city were dispatched to find the killer as Detective Brady valiantly fought for his life. Several witnesses at the scene had given differing descriptions of the shooter and investigators turned to Detective Brady for clarity. Despite receiving continuous blood transfusion, Brady did his best to provide a description of the murderous bandit who had taken his partner's life. The detective described a dirty-faced young man wearing a blue shirt, dark pants, a slouch hat and a black rubber glove on his left hand, leading investigators to believe he may have had a prosthetic limb.

Detective Brady, a former Loyola University football player, eventually succumbed to his injuries three and a half hours after the first shot was fired, dying on September 3, 1945 after a Catholic priest had administered the Last Sacraments. He was the father to nine children; and his wife, Bernice, was expecting their tenth at the time of his death. He was buried at All Saints Cemetery in DesPlaines. Detective Helstern was survived by his wife and two daughters. He was laid to rest at St. Joseph Cemetery.

The young shooter, Cecil "Red" Smith, was never prosecuted for the double homicide. He was murdered before standing trial. He met a different justice. Members of his gang, fearful that he might expose them to police, silenced him for good at the end of 1945.

Patrolman Spencer Thornton, Jr.,

STAR #327, Chicago Park District Police, 37 years old, was patrolling the 2nd Ward Democratic picnic at the 31st Street Beach on September 3, 1945 when he was shot and killed in the line of duty. Thornton of 820 E. 42nd Street, an African-American officer, noticed two men, also African-American, quarreling at the event. He attempted to intervene as one of the men produced a gun and began firing. Both Thornton and the other man involved in the quarrel were fatally injured. Patrolman Edward Hall of the Chicago Lawn Station and Park Policeman Joseph Ryan, also assigned to patrol the event, shot the offender in the shoulder, side and the face after hearing sounds of gunfire. The men involved in the original argument were Will Robinson, age 45 of 3129 Indiana S. Avenue, and the killer, James Coppage, age 44 of 4757 S. Prairie Avenue. After the incident Thornton was quickly taken to Michael Reese Hospital. He died soon after his arrival. Robinson also died from his wounds. Coppage was originally brought to Michael Reese Hospital before being moved to Bridewell Hospital, where he recovered from his wounds. A year later, Coppage was found guilty on two murder charges. He was sentenced to two life sentences to be served consecutively. The fallen officer was laid to rest at Lincoln Cemetery.

Patrolman Roy W. Costello,

STAR #471, Motorcycle Division, 44 years old, died when the rear of his motorcycle was struck on October 25, 1945 at Archer and Ashland Avenues. Officer Costello had been following his routine patrol at the time of the accident. The policeman had been a member of the Chicago Police Department for 21 years and was survived by his wife, Pearl, and their four children. Costello had resided at 857 W. 52nd Street.

View down 30th Street looking northeast
(1944, © CHM). *Chicago Daily News*
Collection, Chicago History Museum.

Patrolman Richard E. Pegue,

STAR #371, Chicago Park District Police, 25 years old, had been a temporary patrolman for only five months when he was killed in the line of duty on July 3, 1946. Pegue, an African-American World War II veteran, was on the look out for an alleged rapist attacking in the Washington Park area. Three days prior to the shooting a woman lodged an official complaint claiming that a man had tried to attack her in a boat in the park lagoon. She provided a description of the assailant and Pegue believed he spotted the man near the park's boathouse with a female companion. Pegue investigated and decided to take the couple, who were also African-American, into custody. He was standing with them just outside the boathouse when James Cantrell, the park's concessions operator, pulled up in a Ford truck around 9:40 P.M.

Pegue hailed Cantrell and asked where Nate, the caretaker of the boathouse, could be found. The patrolman wanted to locate the caretaker to ascertain whether he could identify the man in custody as the rapist. Cantrell informed the officer that Nate had left the park so Pegue requested that Cantrell transport him and the couple to the station. Accounts of the next sequence of events differ, but it is agreed that as the couple drove to the Wabash Avenue Station, with Pegue riding on the truck's running board, the female in custody produced a bottle and struck Cantrell in the head in front of 437 E. 60th Street. In the ensuing chaos the male suspect was able to steal the patrolman's service revolver and shoot Pegue through the heart. The two assailants then fled the scene and witnesses could only provide police with vague descriptions of the killer and his companion. There is no record of what happened to Pegue's killer. He was survived by his wife, Laura, and their son. Patrolman Pegue lived at 6218 S. Eberhart Avenue. He was buried at Lincoln Cemetery.

Patrolman Robert E. Oman,

STAR #188, Chicago Park District Police, 42 years old, was on patrol on November 7, 1946 when his motorcycle slipped on a patch of gravel and he sustained life-ending injuries near the 4100 block of Marine Drive. Police records indicate that Frederick West, a psychology teacher at Illinois Institute of Technology who witnessed the accident, reported that Oman had swerved his motorcycle to avoid a collision and the machine left the pavement and overturned. The patrolman suffered a fractured skull and was pronounced dead at American Hospital. Oman, who had been a patrolman since 1933, left behind his widow, Jeanette, and an 11-year-old daughter.

Detective Roderick D. MacLeay

STAR # Unavailable, 36 years old and

Detective Edwin C. Rach, STAR

Unavailable, were killed in an automobile accident at the corner of 29th and State Streets by John Trencan, age 24, on December 29, 1946. Trencan was believed to have been intoxicated after consuming alcohol at six different taverns. He was driving his new automobile on the wrong side of the road when he crashed into the detectives' vehicle. The widows of the victims, Mrs. Edna MacLeay of 8000 S. Maryland Avenue and Mrs. Ella Rach of 6046 S. Whipple Street, filed suit against the six different taverns, which included Club Mars, 8 Ball Tavern, Pink Poodle, Troendero, Club Rondavoo, and Mildred's Tavern. Under the Dram Shop Act, legal action can take place against the seller of alcoholic beverages when an injury or death occurs as a result of intoxication. This law allowed the widows to demand damages of $75,000. In addition, the widows requested $10,000 each from Trencan.

Patrolman Donald Schodrof,

STAR #4382, 32 years old, was involved in a fatal motorcycle crash while chasing a speeding vehicle on Western Avenue on January 19, 1947. The policeman was in pursuit when another vehicle pulled in front of him and caused him to crash into a parked car. The driver that caused the accident was charged with reckless driving. Schodrof, who died the following day, had been on the force for four years and left behind a wife and six children.

Detective Louis A. Abbott,

STAR #762, 5th District, Wabash Avenue Station, 39 years old, was investigating a series of robberies in the 5th and 27th Districts when he was fatally shot at around 11:10 P.M. on February 14, 1947. He had been working on the cases throughout the day with Detectives Louis Cella and Barney Halperin and they had managed to take two of the men involved into custody. In addition, a detail stationed at the apartment of a third suspect, William McKinley, learned information about his whereabouts certain to lead to his arrest. The officers at the residence at 5244 S. Dearborn Street nabbed a teenager named John Forsythe who told them that McKinley had sent him there to pick up clothing. He told investigators he had last seen McKinley at the corner of 43rd St. Lawrence Avenue. The officers relayed the information to the detectives who searched for McKinley but did not find him. Cella and Halperin decided to give up the hunt for that evening around 11:00 P.M. and returned to the station. Abbott decided to continue the search and was alone when he discovered McKinley near 53rd and State streets. As he stopped to question him, the suspect drew his weapon and fired. Despite a critical wound to his liver, Abbott drove himself to Provident Hospital.

About 15 minutes after they entered the station, Detectives Cella and Halperin received a report that Abbott was being treated for a gunshot wound at Provident Hospital. They discovered the identity of Abbott's shooter and a massive manhunt for McKinley spread across the city. He was located and shot to death only a few hours later. Detective Abbott outlived his killer by three weeks, valiantly fighting for his life before dying on March 3, 1947. He was described by the Chief of Uniformed Police, Raymond Crane, as "one of the finest detectives I know," according to the *Chicago Times*. Crane claimed that Abbott had made ten times more burglary arrests than any other man in the department. He was remembered by others as a "lone wolf" who dedicated many of his off hours to hunting criminals. Detective Abbott was interred at Laurel Hill Cemetery in Erie, Pennsylvania.

Ashland Avenue looking south
(1941, © CHM). Chicago History Museum.

Patrolman George T. Freeman,

STAR #2370, 5th District, Wabash Avenue Station, was beaten to death while patrolling his beat at 47th and Champlain Streets on April 26, 1947. Police had no witnesses to the incident and could only assume certain facts once the physicians at Provident Hospital confirmed that Freeman had been assaulted with a heavy weapon. The officer was still alive when he arrived at the hospital, but soon lost consciousness and died moments later. He was not able to provide details about the attack. Police discovered Edward Lee Weaver near the spot where Freeman was found and held him for questioning.

It turned out that earlier Officer Freeman encountered Weaver in front of 556 E. 47th Street around 11:15 P.M. and was walking east with him on 47th when Weaver turned on him. The assailant struck Patrolman Freeman, knocked him to the ground and began kicking him in the head and body as he lay on the sidewalk. A citizen, Johnny Gardnier, standing in the doorway of Cooper's Tavern at 624 E. 47th Street came to Freeman's defense. Weaver and Gardnier exchanged blows and the offender attempted to flee but he could not overpower the civilian hero who held him until the police arrived. Seven other witnesses to the incident all eventually came forward and corroborated Gardnier's account of the events. Weaver was indicted for murder in May of 1947, but found not guilty on December 5, 1947. Patrolman Freeman was laid to rest at Lincoln Cemetery.

Detective Dewey L. Littleton,

STAR #6884, Detective Bureau, 41 years old, was responding to a call reporting a domestic disturbance at 3247 S. Wentworth Avenue on August 13, 1947 when he was shot and killed in the line of duty. Littleton was joined by Detectives John Blyth, Michael Egan and Milburn Wallace at the scene. The report indicated a disturbance was taking place on the 2nd floor of the building so the officers proceeded up the stairway with Detective Littleton in the lead. Littleton spotted the offender, Otis Williams, in the doorway on the 2nd floor landing and motioned the other officers to keep their distance. Williams had been drinking for most of the evening and flew into a rage that peaked when he shot his wife. Despite receiving two bullet wounds, his wife was able to escape to a downstairs apartment where the neighbors called the police. Only seconds after Littleton had warned his colleagues to stay back Williams opened fire and fatally shot the detective in the stomach.

Blythe, Egan and Wallace quickly returned fire but Williams was able to take cover in his living room, leaving the detectives no clear shot. Blyth and Wallace stayed in the apartment doorway attempting to bring Littleton out while Egan ran to the street and fired tear gas into the residence. More police swarmed onto the scene and set up searchlights that soon danced across Williams' apartment as they tried to locate the killer. Over 35 policemen participated in the effort to take Williams into custody as over 3,000 spectators looked on. Machine guns and handguns shattered the building's windows as police and the offender exchanged fire.

Inside, Blyth and Wallace waged their own gun battle with the offender, shouting for his surrender. At the high point of the struggle, Williams left his cover and attempted to cross his living room. Detective Blythe took advantage of his open position. He fired two shotgun blasts directly at Williams, killing him instantly and ending the standoff that had already cost one brave officer his life. Detective Littleton was a 13-year-veteran of the force and a squad leader at the time of his death. He was interred at Lincoln Cemetery.

Two Chicago Police Officers search a manhole where the gun used to kill Patrolman David Keating was found (1949). *Chicago Tribune* Photo Archive.

Murder reenactment for jury members (1949). ICH-i39642, Chicago History Museum.

Patrolman Thomas J. Carroll,

STAR # unavailable, Albany Park Police, 54 years old, died at Cook County Hospital where he had transported a stroke victim on March 20, 1949. Carroll and his partner, Patrolman Henry Kosinski, were carring a paralytic stroke victim up hospital stairs because the elevators were out of order. When the officers reached an upper landing, Carroll began to complain of chest pains. He then went and sat in a nearby chair. Shortly after he sat down, he had a heart attack and died.

Patrolman David F. Keating,

STAR #2259, 18th district, 34 years old, was standing at the corner of Root Street and Wentworth Avenue talking with friends on September 20, 1949 when he saw two suspicious young men across the street. Keating was in uniform working the 12:00 A.M. to 8:00 A.M. shift when he noticed the boys at around 1:25 A.M. He told his companions that one of the young men was holding a package that looked similar to a shot gun, a situation that he needed to investigate. His friends warned him to be cautious and then stepped into a nearby tavern. They had been inside for only a moment when over a half a dozen automatic pistol shots rang out. They rushed outside to find Patrolman Keating near death on the sidewalk and no sign of the suspects he had approached.

Keating, a World War II veteran, died en route to Evangelical Hospital. He left behind his wife, Dorothy; and their four children, David, Jr., Kathy, Maureen and Robert. Keating was buried at Holy Sepulchre Cemetery. He had been a policeman for ten years with the exception of a two and a half year leave, taken when he served in the Navy during World War II. After his shooting police squads swarmed the district in search of the killers. Their first clue came from Ella Evans, a 16-year-old, who was apparently the girlfriend of one of the offenders. The two boys were eventually identified as Sydney Johnson, 17 years old, and Roosevelt Baccus, 15 years old.

Over 100 policemen were combing the area for the offenders when Johnson and Baccus unexpectedly turned themselves in to an off-duty officer, Lester Davidson. They confessed and stated that they had just left Ella Evans' home at 4121 S. Wentworth Avenue at the time of the shooting. The automatic pistol that had been used to kill Patrolman Keating was recovered, as was the shotgun he suspected one of the young men was carrying. Johnson and Baccus were both indicted for murder in September of 1949. The murder charge against Baccus was eventually dropped. He was tried and sentenced to five to 14 years on an armed robbery charge. Johnson was convicted of Patrolman Keating's murder and sentenced to death on May 26, 1950. He was given four stays of execution over the next eleven months. His sentence was eventually commuted to 199 years in the Illinois State Penitentiary at Joliet on April 18, 1951.

Patrolman Thomas J. Costello,

STAR #5331, Kensington Station, 32 years old, was killed in an automobile accident on November 21, 1949 while transporting a heart attack victim to a hospital via a police sqaudrol. The ambulance collided with a truck at the intersections of 71st Street, Cottage Grove Avenue and South Chicago Avenue. Costello was in the ambulance with Officer Frank Krasula and Fireman Walter Rucinski. They were on their way to Chicago Osteopathic Hospital with Mrs. Pauline Swarczewski, 33, and her husband John, 35, at the time of the accident. Russell Phillips was driving the truck, full of produce, at the time of the collision. Fireman Rucinski immediately began to pull everyone from the squadrol. Patrolman Costello was taken to Jackson Park Hospital, but nothing could be done to save him. The other passengers suffered from various injuries, but nothing that proved to be fatal. Patrolman Costello had been on the force since 1945 and was the son of James Costello, a retired policeman. Costello was survived by his wife, Mary. They lived at 1406 W. 88th Street.

Patrolman Thomas Costello.
Chicago Tribune Photo Archive.

Patrolman William B. Murphy,

STAR #867, 4th District, Stanton Avenue Station, 52 years old, was on his way home after working the 4:00 P.M. to 12:00 A.M. shift on April 24, 1950 when he decided to stop in to see a friend who worked at the Normal Park Liquor Store at 455 W. 59th Street. Murphy often stopped there on his way home. On this particular evening his friend, James Speirs, was waiting to warn him of an armed robbery in progress at the store. Four bandits entered the store around the time that Patrolman Murphy left work. After robbing two customers and Speirs, they rifled through the back cash register before noticing an additional register at the front. One of the bandits ordered Speirs out of the refrigerator room where victims were taken and brought him to the front of the store. He was ordered to open the second machine.

Patrolman Murphy, a 25-year-veteran of the force, entered just as the offenders were helping themselves to an additional $150. Speirs saw Murphy and told the men to hurry, as the cops were on their way. Ignoring his warning, they insisted on getting a bottle of scotch before leaving. Murphy sensed something was amiss. He called through the store's screen door to Speirs, inquiring if anything was wrong. Speirs replied all was fine, but he was not very convincing. The patrolman entered the establishment and immediately saw one of the bandits standing beside the door. Murphy reached for his revolver. Before he could secure his weapon the bandit produced one of his own and fired. Patrolman Murphy fired only a single shot before he fell mortally wounded.

He took bullets to the head, chest, abdomen and back. As he laid on the store's floor the gunman brutally kicked him before they fled the scene. Officer Murphy died before reaching Englewood Hospital. In addition to the fatal gunshot wounds, his assailants fractured his arm and nose as well as lacerating his chin. Murphy's wife had died the year before. His sons, Robert, 17, Thomas, 18, and William, Jr., 24, and daughters, Lona, 19, and Rita Gannon, 21, laid their father to rest at Holy Sepulchre Cemetery.

Speirs, who dropped to the floor when the shooting began, was certain he could identify Murhpy's killers. He reported as many as ten shots fired. One bullet hit a home across the street. Few clues were left behind for police. Speirs said one of the killers was called Ted. At 1:20 A.M. police received a break when Provident Hospital reported a patient seeking treatment for a gunshot wound to the back. Police questioned the man, Emile Washington. A positive identification by Speirs confirmed their suspicions. Washington confessed to being one of the robbers, but claimed he was not the shooter. Emmanuel Scott was also arrested and identified by Speirs. Both Washington and Scott were held for murder while the search for the other two men continued. Eventually, Emmanuel Scott and Leroy Lindsey were sentenced to death for the murder of Officer Murphy.

1950

Sidney Johnson is escorted by
Deputy Sheriffs; on the left is Lou Kasper,
Chair of the Cook County Republican
Organization (1950). ICH-32379,
Chicago History Museum Photo Archive.

A Chicago Police Department mug shot.
Chicago Police Department Photo Archive.

Detective Donald E. McCormick,

STAR #7330, Detective Bureau, 39 years old, and

Detective Edward T. Crowley,

STAR #929, Detective Bureau, 43 years old, were attempting to arrest an armed robbery suspect when the offender gained control of a weapon and fatally shot both officers on July 14, 1950. The detectives were working with Patrolman Patrick Driscoll on the investigation of a robbery complaint from Weirton, West Virginia. Dean Davis was identified as a West Virginia robbery suspect through the automobile license number of his vehicle. Police also discovered that he resided in Chicago. The detectives and Patrolman Driscoll, all from the robbery detail, were assigned to ascertain if the suspect, accused of stealing $500, had returned to his residence on the 2nd floor of 2343 W. Maypole Avenue. They were ordered to arrest Davis if he was found there. Once they reached the address, Driscoll stayed in the car while Crowley and McCormick went up to the 2nd floor.

Davis' 18-year-old wife, Dolores, answered the door and informed the officers her husband was not home. Crowley stated they wanted to look around the apartment to make certain Davis wasn't there. They quickly found the suspect hiding in the bedroom closet in his underwear. Davis dressed and then Crowley sat beside him on the couch as he put his shoes on. Unbeknownst to the detectives, Davis stashed a weapon between the cushions of the couch. He produced the weapon after reaching down to tie his shoelaces. Davis brandished the gun and told the detectives that if they did not move they would not get injured, but McCormick quickly fired two shots. The offender returned fire, fatally injuring McCormick. Davis then turned to Crowley who had drawn his own weapon as his partner fell. He fired at Detective Crowley and fatally wounded him, but not before the dying officer engaged the offender in a struggle. Davis found his gun empty and used it to fracture Detective Crowley's skull and lacerate his face. He then fled the scene.

Patrolman Driscoll entered the apartment to find Crowley sprawled over the threshold, while McCormick lay in the hall. He immediately called for help. Rushed to Cook County Hospital, they both died shortly after their arrival. Davis meanwhile commandeered a car at gunpoint from a local resident before abandoning the vehicle at 1043 W. 14th Street.

The police search for the killer revealed bloodspots in a third floor bedroom on 14th Street. They discovered Davis, shot in the right knee, once again hiding in a closet. He still held the .38 caliber pistol used to gun down McCormick and Crowley. Davis was taken into custody, admitting he was the man they were looking for. The suspect confessed to the double homicide as well as a third murder in 1949. Davis was tried on three counts of murder. He was later sentenced to death. Detectives McCormick and Crowley were both buried at All Saints Cemetery, DesPlaines.

No Chicago Policemen were killed in 1951

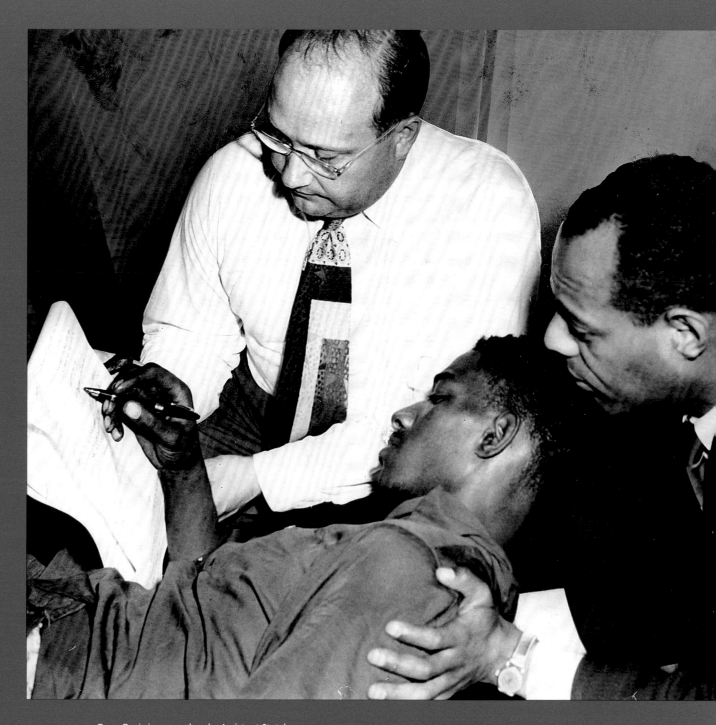

Dean Davis is propped up by Assistant State's
Attorney Joseph J. Atwell as he signs a
confession held by Assistant State's Attorney
William Brumlik, admitting guilt in the double
murder of Detectives Donald E. McCormick
and Daniel T. Crowley (July 16, 1950).
Chicago Tribune Photo Archive.

54th Street and Cottage Grove Avenue (1951). ICH-i23195, Chicago History Museum Photo Archive.

Slums on South Federal Street (1951). ICH-i31720, Chicago History Museum Photo Archive.

63rd Street and Cottage Grove Avenue (1952). ICH-i39629, Chicago History Museum Photo Archive.

A Chicago Police Department squad car (1952). ICH-i21469, Chicago History Museum Photo Archive.

Patrolman George J. Sperakos,

STAR #669, 29th District, Racine Avenue Station, 41 years old, was sitting in the rear room of a tavern at 1807 W. Division Street , around 2:00 A.M., having coffee with the owner, Stanley Kozieniak, and his wife, Cecilia, on April 24, 1952. Sperakos was dressed in his uniform cap, trousers and a civilian sweater as he sat in a back room and visited with his friends. He usually worked the midnight shift but was not on-duty that night. An account later given by his captain, John Ryan of the Racine Avenue Station, stated that Sperakos had just returned from driving his mother-in-law to her home when he decided to stop at the tavern to say hello. He wore a portion of his uniform because he had attended a special drill session earlier that same day and had no time to change completely.

Suddenly, three men entered and ordered refreshments. After a few drinks they drew their guns and announced a robbery. The first bandit shoved the bartender aside, firing a warning shot to discourage any acts of heroism from patrons or employees. He then took $200 from the cash register. Cecilia Kozieniak and her 14-year-old daughter, Dorothy, were lined up against the tavern wall by one of the other bandits. Her husband heard the sounds of the hold-up and immediately stepped to the doorway to assess the situation. He reported the details to Sperakos, who immediately walked to the door and fired three shots. The gunmen turned towards Sperakos and one of them announced to his companions that a "copper" was in the back room. Two of the bandits opened fire on the patrolman. Sperakos dashed back behind the door of the backroom and emerged again. He fired three more shots before a bullet entered the center of his forehead, mortally wounding him. After watching him fall, the suspects fled south on Wood Street in a light-colored vehicle driving east on Division Street.

Patrolman Sperakos was rushed to Presbyterian Hospital where he died at 10:55 A.M. on the morning of April 24, eight hours after the shooting. Fifteen separate squads spread out across the city searching for the gunmen. It was believed one of the shooters may have been wounded by Patrolman Sperakos. It was also thought that the bandits may have been the same men who had robbed Mike's Tavern, 1700 W. Cermak Road, earlier in the evening. Witnesses described the bandits as either Mexican or Italian, between the ages of 25 and 30, of medium height with dark, wavy hair. Sperakos joined the police department in 1943. He was survived by his wife and daughter who buried him at St. Adalbert Cemetery.

Detective Martin J. Moylan, Jr.,

STAR #1112, Austin Avenue Station, 55 years old, was directing traffic after an accident involving two trucks at the intersection of Austin and Wabansia Streets in October of 1950 when he was fatally struck by an automobile driven by a teenage boy. Moylan's leg was broken in five places, his ankle bone was cracked and his skull was fractured as a result of the accident. Two years later, Moylan's back was bothering him so he went to St. Anne Hospital where he developed pneumonia. The doctors sent him home and three weeks later the combination of the pneumonia and the previous injuries he sustained caused his death at his home, at 1425 N. Parkside Avenue, on May 17, 1952.

Moylan's funeral mass was held at St. Angela Church. His burial was at Mount Carmel Cemetery on May 21. He was survived by his wife Margaret nee Conroy; a son, Martin, Jr.; three daughters, Juleann, Marguerite, and the late Mrs. Mary Ellen Long; and six grandchildren. Moylan was a policeman for 30 years, sixteen of which were spent serving the Austin Station with the stolen auto detail. His other fourteen years were spent at the Stockyards, Maxwell and Cragin Stations. Moylan received several citations of honor during his career. He was a member of the Police Post Drum and Bugle corps, American Legion. He served with the famous Princess Pats Regiment of Canada during World War I.

Patrolman William A. Fuller,

STAR #3327, 1st District, Central Station, 49 years old, was shot to death while off-duty on his way home from the station on Wednesday evening, April 2, 1953. Fuller, of 450 W. Surf Street, stopped at Mickey's Liquor Mart at 2316 N. Clark Street. While seated at the bar with a friend, three men arrived and took seats at the bar, just five stools away from Fuller. After ordering drinks two of the men then went to the washroom at the rear of the tavern and emerged with guns drawn. Just then bartender Gordon Swahn, 44, of 2339 W. Geneva Terrace, returned with change for the beers he had served them. A third man, later identified as 25-year-old James Boswell, Jr., rose and stuck a gun in the back of the man seated next to Officer Fuller, Charles Burkart, 50, of 500 W. Belden Avenue. Swahn was taken to the rear of the premises as the thieves emptied the till. Boswell then announced a stick-up and ordered Burkart to move away from the bar. At that point, Officer Fuller was able to reach his service revolver. When Burkart moved out of the line of fire, Fuller proceeded to shoot at Boswell. They exchanged bullets with each other from a distance of no more than four feet. Both men fell to the floor fatally wounded. Fuller had taken a bullet to the heart. Another customer, Nathan Pector, 32, of 2041 W. Pierce Street, was wounded in the shootout, receiving a bullet in the arm. Once gunfire ceased, Boswell's two unknown accomplices fled the scene, running out the door of the tavern onto Clark Street heading south.

Both Officer Fuller, and his killer, James Boswell, Jr., were taken to nearby Augustana Hospital at 2035 N. Lincoln Avenue, where they were pronounced dead on arrival.

Two wallets were discovered in Boswell's pockets by police, his own, giving his address as 822 N. Trumbell Avenue, and the other belonging to his 21-year-old girlfriend, Dorothy Perry, of 615 N. Ada Street. Perry was helpful to police, providing names and addresses to trace Boswell's accomplices. Around 10:00 P.M. that evening, Chicago Police Sergeant Howard Pierson and Detective William Healy of the Homicide Division spotted the men, 19-year-old Robert Stanley of 1619 W. North Avenue and 19-year-old Salvatore LoSchiavo of 709 W. Grand Avenue walking in the vicinity of Grand Avenue and Halsted Street. Though they insisted they had only gone to Mickey's Liquor Store to purchase beer, they were soon identified by three witnesses, Burkart, Swahn and Martin Mulligan, 45, of 2244 N. Cleveland Avenue. The two suspects soon made full confessions to their involvement in the crime. It was learned that James Boswell had been released that year after serving a four-year-sentence at the Illinois State Penitentiary at Pontiac for a series of gas station robberies.

A Solemn High Requiem Mass for Officer Fuller was held at Our Lady of Sorrows Basilica on Jackson Boulevard. Burial followed at Queen of Heaven Cemetery. He was mourned by his wife, Thelma, and his 17-year-old daughter, Mary. Fuller had been with the Chicago Police Department for 27 years and would have observed his anniversary that month. The *Chicago Tribune* reported that he was mourned not only by his fellow policemen at the 1st District Central Station, but also by Chicago newspaper reporters. One reporter was quoted as saying that Fuller "was never too busy to help get the facts for a story." Fuller was well liked and had been an Assistant Desk Sergeant at the Central Station.

1953

The Chicago Police Department marches up State Street in Chicago's Christmas Parade (1952). ICH-i39643, Chicago History Museum Photo Archive.

Detective Charles C. Kraatz,

STAR #5702, 2nd District, Prairie Avenue Station, 54 years old, was working the 3rd Watch from 4:00 P.M. to midnight, on Wednesday, May 7, 1953 when he was killed in the the line of duty. Kraatz and his partner, Patrolman John Sullivan, were in plain clothes and riding in squadrol, #181. Officer Kraatz was filling in for the regular officer assigned to this car. Not long after 9:00 P.M., Kraatz and Sullivan, as well as Squadrol #295 carrying Patrolmen Julian Ford and William Page, arrived simultaneously at 724 E. 36th Street to assist in the investigation of a report of a man firing a gun in the hallway of an apartment building. Officers Kraatz, Ford and Page all exited their cars while Patrolman Sullivan drove squad #181 to an open space at the curb. The attention of the three officers was directed to a crowd of people who had gathered at the corner of 36th Street and Ellis Avenue. When the officers were about ten feet away, people in the crowd gestured that James Knight of 3601 S. Ellis Avenue had the gun. Officer Kraatz ordered Knight to handover his weapon. Knight then fired the gun point-blank at Kraatz. As he fell to the sidewalk mortally wounded, he fired his weapon once at his assailant. Knight then fired two more shots at the wounded officer as he layed in the street. He hit Kraatz's right shoulder, hip and stomach. Immediately, Officers Ford and Page emptied their weapons at Knight, killing him. Officer Kraatz was taken to nearby Michael Reese Hospital. At 8:30 P.M. the next night, May 8, 1953, he died from the three bullet wounds he received. James Knight, it was later learned was on probation for carrying a concealed weapon.

Detective Kraatz lived at 8823 S. Emerald Street and had been on the Chicago Police Force for 24 years since March 22, 1929. He was laid to rest in Evergreen Park Cemetery.

Patrolman Anthony Cannata,

STAR #2216, Racine Avenue Station, 36 years old, was killed during a high speed chase on June 15, 1953. Cannata and his partner, Officer Redd Posner, were approaching Chicago Avenue and Noble Street when they saw a parked car without a license plate, similar to one used the Thursday before in the kidnapping of State Representative Clem Graver. The men in the auto sped away and the two officers began their pursuit. As the chase approached Milwaukee Avenue, near Walton Street, a car swerved into their path, forcing the officers to hit a light post. Cannata was killed upon impact, while Posner was taken to Henrotin Hospital where his injuries were deemed critical but not life-ending. Meanwhile, the offenders made their escape following the crash and were never found. Patrolman Cannata joined the force on July 30, 1951 and left behind his wife, Eleanor; son, two daughters and his mother. He was laid to rest at St. Joseph Cemetery on June 18, 1953. Fifty-three years later, on May 25, 2006, his star was retired and placed in the Superintendant's Star Case at Chicago Police Headquarters.

Detective Oreste E. Gonzales,

STAR #6362, Homicide Detective Division, 27 years old, and Patrolman Robert V. Walsh, were working the 1st Watch, midnight to 8 A.M., in Homicide Investigations on Otober 8, 1953. Around 3:00 A.M. they were riding in car #56 when they heard the report of a taxi-cab stick-up at 56th and Rockwell Streets. Gonzales and Walsh immediately raced to the scene. As they were driving, another report broadcast stated that the taxi-cab had been located at 74th Street and Western Avenue. As they drove south on Western Avenue, the officers passed a man standing in front of White Castle Hamburgers at 71st Street. They noticed him because of the hour and the fact that he was all alone. Upon arriving at the site of the stolen taxi-cab, they were given a detailed description of the thief. They realized it fit the man whom they had just passed. The two then drove back northbound on Western Avenue to 71st Street where the suspect was standing on the northwest corner. They approached him with their guns drawn. Officer Gonzales then searched the suspect from the front, while Officer Walsh searched him from the back. He even inspected the White Castle bag and was satisfied that the offender was unarmed. The suspect identified himself as Charles H. Metzger, 27 years old of 6915 S. Yale Avenue. He was placed in the rear seat of the squad car. Detective Gonzales sat beside him while Officer Walsh drove. The prisoner was being transported so the robbery victim would have an opportunity to identify the suspect. Officer Walsh made a u-turn in the car and then a right hand turn to bring them near to the taxi-cab and squads from the 16th District. Suddenly, the back seat of squad #56 became a battle zone with both Metzger and Gonzales exchanging gunfire. "There was a fusillade of shot," Officer Walsh later recalled. "I released the wheel and attempted to draw my revolver. The left front door flew open and I fell out. The squad car rolled by me and sideswiped another squad car," he later told the *Chicago Tribune*. Officer Walsh quickly jumped to his feet and ran to the squad to find both Officer Gonzales and the suspect lumped in the back seat. Officer Gonzalez appeared to be bleeding from a head wound, but sitting upright against the back seat. Metzger's head was resting on Officer Gonzalez knees. Officer Walsh reached into the back seat and took an automatic pistol from Metzger's hand, shoving him back down on the seat. He then drove the Squad Car to nearby Holy Cross Hospital where both Officer Gonzalez and Metzger were pronounced dead on arrival.

Metzger was identified by the cab driver, Louis Lukadunos, 60 years old of 1542 E. 67th Street, as the one who hailed his cab, held him up for $35 and then stole his taxi-cab. The suspect's fingerprints later revealed he had served five years for manslaughter in Chillicothe, Ohio. Police also discovered he had been paroled from the Illinois State Penitentiary at Joliet on a robbery conviction on April 20, 1953.

Officer Gonzalez, a-five-year-veteran of the Chicago Police Department, was survived by his young wife, Helen, who was expecting their first child at the time of his death. The patrolman was buried at St. Joseph Cemetery.

It is believed that Officer Gonzales is the first Hispanic Chicago Policeman to die in the line of duty.

16th District Station on Gale Street
in Jefferson Park, 1960s style.
Chicago Police Department Archive.

Detective Jeremiah Lucey,
STAR #1831, 32nd District, 60 years old, and
Patrolman Roman C. Steinke, Star
#4706, 32nd District, 42 years old, were involved in a gun battle with a Chinese laundryman, James Lee-Fong, on February 6, 1954. Earlier in the week, Stephen Malenk, Jr., 11 years of age, was looking in the doorway and window of Lee-Fong's shop when Lee-Fong became annoyed and started to chase the boy. Malenk, Jr., was caught by Lee-Fong and slapped in the face. The boy reported this to his father, Stephen Malenk, Sr., who then went to the laundry and confronted Lee-Fong. The laundryman then proceeded to assault Malenk, Sr., with a piece of a pipe. Malenk, Sr., went to the police on February 5th to obtain a warrant charging James Lee-Fong with assault. The next day Officers Lucey and Steinke went with the father and son to identify the landryman.

When they arrived at the laundry, located at 2705 W. Diversey Parkway, Lee-Fong admitted to slapping the boy. He was informed of the warrant and told he had to accompany them to the station. Lee-Fong went to the back of the laundry for his coat, but came back with a .38 caliber rifle instead. He opened fire on the police and the Malenks. He hit Malenk, Sr., first in the chest and upper arm. Lee-Fong continued to fire, hitting Lucey in his chest and Steinke in several places. Steinke, though shot in the wrist, was able to wound Lee-Fong in the head. Lee-Fong then fled to the back of the shop, giving the officers enough time to get out to the sidewalk to be taken to the hospital. While in the back of the shop, Lee-Fong obtained another weapon, a .16 gage shotgun, and began to open fire on the police coming into the shop in response to a radio call. Police forced open the back door as the firing stopped. There they found the shooter lying on the floor.

Lucey died in Alexian Brothers Hospital on the February 7, 1954. He was survived by his wife, Mary, and two children, Gerald and Maureen. He was buried in Queen of Heaven Cemetery. Steinke died on February 13, 1954 in St. Elizabeth Hospital. He was buried at St. Adalbert Cemetery, leaving behind a wife and two children.

James Lee-Fong, the suspect, was taken to Cook County Hospital, where he told investigators he opened fire on the police because he was scared. He claimed that he thought the officers were there to beat him up because they were in plainclothes, not the typical uniform. On April 27, 1954 Lee-Fong succumbed to his wounds.

Sergeant Richard J. Roushorn,
STAR #374, Crime Detection Laboratory Division, 40 years old, was driving south on South Park Avenue, near the intersection of 63rd Street, when a City of Chicago garbage truck hit the car that he was driving on September 11, 1954. Livingston McGraw, the driver of the truck, pulled his vehicle over at 6320 S. South Park Avenue. An argument ensued between the two men when McGraw denied hitting Roushorn's vehicle. Roushorn announced he was going to take McGraw to the station. McGraw told Roushorn that he would not be so confrontational if the officer did not have a gun, so Roushorn took off the gun and placed it on the front seat of his car. While the Sergeant was distracted, McGraw ran to the car and took Roushorn's gun. He said "I'm on this end now." Without notice, he proceeded to fire at Roushorn who was advancing toward him. McGraw emptied the gun and hit the Sergeant three times. Roushorn died later that day at Woodlawn Hospital. The 19-year-veteran, later, was cremated at Mount Hope Cemetery.

Officer Virgil M. Poole observed McGraw run to Roushorn's car and place the gun back on his front seat. Poole approached McGraw and took him into police custody. On June 14, 1955, Livingston McGraw was sentenced to 14 years in the Illinois State Penitentiary at Joliet.

Detective Charles P. Annerino,

STAR #7936, Detective Bureau Robbery Detail, 30 years old, was with his partners, Detectives William Murphy and John Bosquette, in search of the escaped convict Agostino "Gus" Amedeo when he was shot and killed by him on October 22, 1954. On June 28, 1954 Amedeo, who was serving a burglary sentence, escaped from the bull-pen elevator of the Criminal Court Building with fellow inmate Anthony Gambino. Shortly after the escape Gambino was recaptured and returned to jail. Amedeo remained at large. In the following months Annerino, Murphy, and Bosquette spent many hours searching for the offender. On the night of October 22, the detectives went to the Circle Lounge, 1756 W. Lawrence Avenue, in search of Amedeo.

Detectives Annerino and Murphy went inside the bar at approximately 11:55 P.M. while Bosquette stayed inside their squad car. Once inside, the two detectives split up to search for the offender. Murphy approached a man sitting alone and asked him for identification. The man produced a gun instead of his identification. Murphy immediately grabbed a hold of him and yelled to Annerino for help. As Annerino approached the two, the offender fired two fatal shots and took off, leaving behind a wallet which identified him as Agostino Amedeo. Annerino was struck below the heart and succumbed to his wound a short time later. A massive man-hunt followed as hundreds of police officers and detectives covered the Northside in search of Amedeo. On October 29, an informant arranged with the police to have the 26-year-old killer at the corner of Berwyn and Clark Streets. Police set up a dragnet around the intersection and confronted Amedeo, ordering him to halt. He fired upon the police, who fired back and instantly killed him.

Annerino was survived by his wife, Rose, and their two children, Theresa and Charles, Jr. He had been on the force since May 6, 1946. A Funeral Mass for the officer was held at St. Jerome Church. He was buried at St. Mary Cemetery.

63rd Street and Woodlawn Avenue
under the "EL" (1954). ICH-i13748,
Chicago History Museum Photo Archive.

Patrolman Albert H. Brown,

STAR #2806, 32nd District, Shakespeare Avenue Station, 57 years old, was the temporary lockup keeper on-duty July 5, 1955 at the Shakespeare Avenue Station when he was fatally shot by 16-year-old Ronald Dean of 2141 W. Caton Street. Dean, who had been arrested on July 4 for tampering with an automobile at 2140 W. Concord Place, found a beer can opener in his cell and used it to pry open the cell door and make his escape. Before fleeing, the offender found Officer Brown's gun lying on a desk and shot the officer in the abdomen, left arm and right hand. After firing the three fatal shots Dean fled the scene. The wounded officer was taken to Alexian Brothers Hospital where he remained until he succumbed to his wounds on July 19, two weeks later. Officer Brown was survived by his wife, Hattie, and two sons, Albert, Jr., and Walter. The Brown family resided at 3025 W. Belden Avenue and buried their hero at Forest Home Cemetery. Later that same year Brown's son, Albert, was killed in an auto accident. Officer Brown's star was the last of the old "pie plate" style badges to be enshrined in the Superintendent's Honored Star Case.

Dean was apprehended two days after the shooting at the North Avenue Beach. Police had received a tip saying Dean was seen at the beach. Detective Anthony J. Osterkorn and Juvenile Officer William Touhey found the boy there. He admitted who he was and was taken into police custody. Dean was a former inmate at Illinois State Training School for Boys in Kane County. On December 13, Dean plead guilty to murdering Patrolman Brown and was sentenced to life in prison by Judge James R. Bryant.

Patrolman William J. Murphy,

STAR #7438, Detective Bureau, 34 years old, was shot and killed on the Roosevelt Road "EL" platform on August 15, 1955 while arresting Richard Carpenter. The offender initially agreed to be placed under arrest while on the train, but once on the platform he produced a gun and shot Murphy in the chest three times. Carpenter then fled onto the street and forced a 67-year-old driver, Charles Koerper, to take him to Madison and Dearborn Streets, where he jumped out and fled.

Murphy, who died before he could be taken to a hospital, was survived by his wife and two daughters. Both his father and brother were Chicago Policemen. He was laid to rest at All Saints Cemetery.

After a citywide manhunt, Richard Carpenter was discovered in the Biltmore Theater, 2046 W. Division Street, on August 17 by Officer Clarence Kerr, who attempted to arrest him. Carpenter shot Kerr and fled again. The offender then traveled to the home of Leonard Powell at 2040 W. Potomac Avenue, where he forced Powell's family, at gunpoint, to house, feed and aid him. Powell eventually notified police, who surrounded the house until Carpenter surrendered on August 18. Carpenter was found guilty of the death of Murphy and the shooting of Kerr. He was executed on December 18, 1958.

1955

Ronald Dean, Patrolman Albert
Brown's killer, stands with
his mother, Mrs. Bernice Dean
(December 13, 1955).
Chicago Tribune Photo Archive.

Shakespeare Avenue Station,
32nd District. Chicago Police
Department Archive.

A crowd is gathered outside of 2040
W. Potomac Avenue where police
captured Richard Carpenter, Detective
William J. Murphy's killer (August 19,
1955). *Chicago Tribune* Photo Archive.

Richard Carpenter is escorted
by deputy sheriffs after inquest into
Detective Murphy's murder
(August 23, 1955). *Chicago Tribune*
Photo Archive.

left to right

Robert Powell, in whose apartment Carpenter hid out during the 23 hour manhunt, has his testimony interrupted by Coroner Walter McCarron who argues over a statement made by Carpenter's attorney, Kevin Gillogy (August 23, 1955). *Chicago Tribune* Photo Archive.

Officers Max Stone and Ben Kruisicki, who both assisted in the capture of Richard Carpenter, congratulate each other in the West North Avenue Station after the suspect was captured. *Chicago Tribune* Photo Archive.

Richard Carpenter, who attempted to change his appearance to avoid capture by shaving his head, sits bandaged, consulting with his attorney, James O'Malley (August 23, 1955). *Chicago Tribune* Photo Archive.

Witness C.A. Koerper identifies Richard Carpenter as the shooter at Officer Murphy's inquest (August 23, 1955). *Chicago Tribune* Photo Archive.

Officer Ted Sparrow gives evidence at inquest into the murder of Detective William Murphy (August 23, 1955). *Chicago Tribune* Photo Archive.

Patrolman Lyons Kelliher,

STAR #6695, 27th District, 52 years old, was fatally shot during a narcotics investigation on January 25, 1956. He and his partner, Officer William Derrig, were in a tavern at the Boulevard Hotel, 2801 W. Warren Boulevard. They approached two men, James Worthy and Donald Lawrence, who were suspects in an investigation. Derrig was speaking to Lawrence, while Kelliher searched Worthy, when Lawrence drew a gun and shot Derrig in the foot. He then shot Kelliher as he tried to apprehend him. Lawrence escaped from the scene while Worthy was arrested.

Kelliher and Derrig were taken to Illinois Research Hospital, where Kelliher died. Derrig made a full recovery. Officer Kelliher was buried in Mount Carmel Cemetery. His father, Captain Patrick Kelliher, had retired from the police force in 1936 after 36 years of service.

Lawrence was later discovered to be an AWOL U.S. Soldier and located in the stockade at Fort Sheridan. The Army sent him to the 27th Police District, where he was held for Kelliher's murder.

Patrolman John J. Blyth, Jr.,

STAR #1395, 18th District, 42 years old, was killed in a gun battle on June 16, 1956. He and his partner, Officer Daniel Rolewicz, were talking with a fireman in the 4600 block of S. Wentworth Avenue when they heard shots fired near 47th and Wells Streets. They proceeded there and found that the shots had come from an alley just north of 4715 S. Wells Streets. The shooter, James Dukes, had been released from Pontiac Reformatory in 1941 after serving time for armed robbery.

Dukes fired at the officers several times as he ran away from them, hitting Blyth in the chest. Blyth was taken to Evangelical Hospital, where he was met by his wife and four children. The policeman died a short time later. His two oldest children, John Jr., 18, and Mary Ann, 17, had recently graduated from St. Ignatius and St. Xavier High Schools respectively. Blyth was buried at Holy Sepulchre Cemetery.

Although the offender initially escaped, he was later found wounded and trapped underneath a station wagon in a parking lot on Wentworth Avenue. He was charged with Blyth's murder and became the last man to be executed at Cook County Jail on August 24, 1962. Blyth's partner witnessed the execution.

Patrolman Robert R. Golden,

STAR #420, Chicago Park District Police, 35 years old, was killed on November 14, 1956 when he tried to stop a robbery in progress inside the Bel-Mar Tavern at Higgins and Bartlett Roads. The officer drew his service revolver, but was struck by a shotgun blast and died instantly. Golden left behind a wife and two children. He was buried at Queen of Heaven Cemetery.

Three people were named as suspects in Golden's shooting: Edward Pack, 19; his half brother Robert Lord, 18; and Robert Brimhall, 18. Brimhall, the shooter, joined the U.S. Navy and moved to California with his 15-year-old wife the day of the murder. After the Navy detained him, he confessed to the crime and was sent back to Chicago .

Golden was the last member of the Chicago Park District Police to die in the line of duty. The group was disbanded in 1957 and merged into the Chicago Police Department by Mayor Richard J. Daley.

1956

Detective John Blyth's family attends his funeral at St. Adrian Church near Marquette Park. Left to right: William, Norrine, John, Jr., Mrs. Blyth and Mary Ann (June 20, 1956). *Chicago Tribune* Photo Archive.

Patrolman Osbourn Sims,

STAR #4848, 22nd District, 34 years old, and his partner, Officer Donald Burns, received a call on December 6, 1956 reporting a burglary in progress at 702 S. Ada Street. The crime was observed by a neighborhood resident, Nick Riccio, who ran outside and seized the burglar, Hector Garcia, and held him until police arrived on the scene. When Officers Sims and Burns arrived, Garcia broke free. Sims ordered Garcia to stop, but he continued to flee and began to open fire at Sims. The officers chased him to a gangway at 1445 W. Lexington Avenue They then split up to find Garcia; Sims went to the front of the residence and Burns to the rear. Sims found another suspect and was preparing to take him back to the car when he ran into Hector Garcia. The suspect was ordered to stop but continued running. He again turned around and opened fire on Sims. The police-man was shot twice and the unknown man that Sims had in custody fled during the melee.

Garcia entered the W. Lexington Avenue apartment building and threatened the occupants with his gun. He then barricaded himself in the basement of the building. Police fired tear gas into the basement and subsequently shot the assailant who was killed instantly.

Sims was buried in Elmhurst Cemetery in Joliet, Illinois. He was survived by his wife, Bertha; a son, Kenneth; twin daughters, Cynthia and Charlene; and a step-daughter, Katherine. Sims was known for his courage, though he had been a policeman for only 18 months. He served in the navy in World War II and was later drafted into the army during the Korean War.

Patrolman James E. Mitchell,

STAR #9840, 13th District, Morgan Park Station, 24 years old, and his partner, Patrolman Henry Jelderks, were responding to a report of a shooting on April 14, 1957 when tragedy struck. Mitchell and Jelderks went to 1313 W. 109th Street to investigate the report and discovered that two other officers, Patrolmen J. Havlick and J. Wallenda, had already arrived. Mitchell and Jelderks learned from the other two officers that Lee Foster was being sought for the shooting. He had fled the scene in a 1952 green and yellow Mercury sedan. Both teams of officers returned to their vehicles and began to search for the offender.

They headed in the direction of Foster's home address and discovered him sitting in front of his home in the vehicle described. He spotted them as well and quickly sped away. Havlick and Wallenda saw the flashing light of Mitchell and Jelderks' squad car and heard the radio transmission describing the suspect's vehicle. Both cars were in pursuit as the offender sped away. A chase ensued, with speeds of over 70 MPH. Havlick and Wallenda fell behind and lost sight of both the other squad car and Foster's vehicle. When they caught up they discovered both vehicles stopped and abandoned.

Mitchell and Jelderk had forced Foster to halt. The suspect then disappeared behind a resi-dence at 1347 W. 109th Street. The officers headed him off and a struggle began. That was the sight Mitchell and Jelderk found when they reached the scene. A single shot was heard and Patrolman Mitchell staggered towards them repeating "I'm shot" over and over again. Havlick went to aid Jelderk, who was still struggling with the offender, while Wallenda aided Officer Mitchell.

Police learned that Mitchell had been accidently shot when Officer Jelderk's gun dis-charged while scuffling with Foster. The wounded officer was rushed to Roseland Hospital but pronounced dead upon arrival. He had joined the police department only eight months before, on September 1, 1956, and had only recently finished his probationary period.

After Foster was taken into custody his gun was discovered not far from the scene. It was speculated that he may have thrown it from his vehicle when he realized police would apprehend him. Officer Mitchell was buried at St.Mary Cemetery.

Patrolman Arthur J. Eiberg,

STAR # unavailable, Park District Police, 62 years old, was stricken with a fatal heart attack on the night of May 3, 1957 while walking his beat near the intersection of Addison Street and Kilbourn Avenue. His death in 1957 occurred during the period of transition when the various branches of the Park Police were merging into the Chicago Police Department. He lived at 1801 N. Austin Boulevard and was survived by his wife, Eleanor. Officer Eiberg was buried at All Saints Cemetery in DesPlaines.

Patrolman Michael E. Lukaszewski,

STAR #7165, 35th District, 24 years old, had been on the force for a little over a year and a half when he lost his life in the line of duty. Lukaszewski, a former football star at St. Patrick High School, and his partner, Patrolman Anthony Concialdi, were on-duty on the night of June 29, 1957 when they received a call requesting that a police squadrol be sent to transport an offender back to lock-up. The two patrolmen met Detectives M. Smith and T. Bell at 342 W. Chicago Avenue and took custody of the suspect, Lavern Jamison.

When questioned by detectives, Jamison said he was going to break every window in a nearby hotel after a fight with a man in the hotel over a woman. Jamison appeared to be intoxicated.

Lukaszewski and Concialdi brought Jamison back to the lock-up around 12:45 A.M. and began processing his detention. He was joined there by three other offenders, all of whom the officers lined up with their backs against the cell bars across from the lock-up keeper's desk. Lukaszewski was filling out the suspects' arrest slips when Jamison suddenly lunged from his spot against the bars and snatched the patrolman's gun from its holster. They began to struggle and Concialdi turned around just as Jamison fired a single shot. Lukaszeski fell to the ground with a bullet wound to the head as Concialdi rushed toward the offender. Jamison fired again and struck Concialdi in the right forearm before attempting to flee, still armed, down the lock-up's west corridor.

Concialdi returned fire. He wounded Jamison five times. The assailant was then quickly subdued by two lock-up officers who had rushed to the patrolmen's aid at the sound of gunfire. Concialdi rushed back to his partner's side and both officers were taken to St. Luke Hospital. Jamison was also taken there and survived only three hours before succumbing to his wounds at 3:40 A.M. Patrolman Lukaszewski followed an hour and a half later, leaving behind his high school sweetheart, Judy Gallagher, who he had married only six months before. He was buried at St. Joseph Cemetery.

Further investigation revealed that Jamison had been registered at the hotel where he was arrested as Lamar Simmons. His rap sheet contained three arrests for robbery and disorderly conduct.

Patrolman Bernard Poe,

STAR #6509, 23rd District, Marquette Station, 24 years old, had been with the police department for just over a year when he lost his life in the line of duty while attempting to help a fellow officer. Poe, who was assigned a street post on Roosevelt Road from Whipple Street to Kedzie Avenue, was patrolling his beat on November 8, 1957 when he saw Patrolman William McDonagh struggling with an offender. McDonagh had been called to State Jewelers and Clothiers at 3150 W. Roosevelt Road at 4:45 P.M. by the establishment's manager, Hy Rozin. He informed McDonagh that a man was attempting to purchase a watch with a stolen check. According to the employees of State Jewelers, two men had entered the store around 4:30 P.M. and chosen a watch. They then told the clerk assisting them that they wanted to buy the piece on credit and were taken to the store's Credit Department. There one of the men presented a check from the Monarch Box and Paper Company, located at 1212 S. Morgan Street. A phone call to that company to verify the check's authenticity indicated it had been stolen from the company on October 31.

Upon learning a customer was trying to pass a stolen check, Rozin signaled to Patrolman McDonagh, walking the beat by the store. McDonagh entered, was updated on the situation and promptly placed the offender under arrest. The suspect, identified as Elijah White according to the driver's license he had provided while attempting to authenticate the check, objected to his arrest. McDonagh called the station and requested a patrol car to retrieve the offender.

As McDonagh and the suspect waited for the squad car White began hitting McDonagh in the mouth. A struggle caused both men to fall to the sidewalk. As they fell, Officer McDonagh shouted for help and Officer Poe, who was at the corner of Troy Street and Roosevelt Road, rushed to his aid. Poe reached the two men as White was attempting to remove McDonagh's weapon from its holster. Poe was pulling the offender off McDonagh when White managed to grab the officer's weapon and fired at Patrolman Poe. McDonagh caught White by the arm as the offender fired again, leaving both officers wounded. McDonagh, shot in the right elbow, lost his grip on White and the suspect fled east down Roosevelt Road, disappearing at the southwest corner of Troy Street and Roosevelt Road. One of the employees from State Jewelers and Clothiers rushed from the store and grabbed Patrolman Poe's gun, firing after White as he escaped.

Officer Poe sustained a fatal gunshot wound to the chest and was rushed to Illinois Research Hospital. He died there several hours after his arrival. He was was interred at Restvale Cemetery.

Investigators immediately began a search for White. It was discovered that the suspect had an uncle in Muskegon, Michigan with whom he was in close contact. Officers contacted Michigan authorities and requested that they be notified if White was spotted in that state. On November 9, 1957, Baldwin, Michigan authorities contacted the Chicago Police Department and stated they had someone in custody that they believed was White. A squad of Chicago police then went to Michigan, where they used fingerprint technology to confirm White's identity. In addition to White, police also took custody of William Green, the man who was originally in the store with White and helped him escape to Michigan. Once they returned to Chicago, both men gave statements implicating themselves in the events surrounding Patrolman Poe's death. White was found guilty of the murder of Officer Poe and the wounding of Officer McDonagh and sentenced to 99 years in prison. Willie Green was named as an accessory.

Detective Bernard "Barney" L. Halperin,

STAR #7214, 5th District, Wabash Avenue Station, 49 years old, had been with the Chicago Police Department for over 22 years and investigated more than 200 homicides when he was killed in the line of duty on December 20, 1957. Detective Halperin had just finished his shift at 8:00 A.M. that morning and was sitting in the drug store of Jerome Ehrenreich at 4301 S. Michigan Avenue when a neighborhood resident reported a robbery in progress at Alvin's Eat Shop at 116 E. 43rd Street. Though off-duty, Halperin immediately raced to the scene and found his partner, Detective Walter Johnson, who had been only half a block from the scene, and Probationary Patrolman Young Hobson. Also off-duty at the time, they rushed over when they heard of the robbery. Detective Halperin ordered the two officers to cover the rear of the restaurant while he approached the front entrance.

Halperin encountered the robber, Thomas E. Gooden, attempting to flee the scene. According to later reports, Gooden entered the restaurant, ordered a meal, ate a portion of it and then said he needed to step out for a moment. He returned carrying a rifle. He asked employees and 35 customers to place their wallets on the counter. He gathered up the wallets and fired three shots into the cash register when it would not open.

When Gooden realized police surrounded the restaurant, he exited with his gun blazing and immediately wounded Detective Halperin in the head. Despite his grave injury, the detective returned fire and wounded Gooden before dropping unconscious to the sidewalk. Gooden then approached the fallen officer and pumped at least five more bullets into his back before jumping into a 1957 Chevrolet parked in front of the restaurant and trying to flee the scene by way of the alley. He was quickly confronted by the officers covering the rear.

In the alley Johnson and Hobson were joined by Patrolmen Harold Carr and Robert Christian. As Gooden attempted to escape, he refused to obey their commands to stop and surrender. All four officers then opened fire on him. His get away car had barely moved before it crashed into a nearby telephone pole. The four officers then advanced on the vehicle, still firing their weapons. Gooden's body was sprawled across the front seat and riddled with bullets. His identity was later ascertained from papers found on his body after the shooting.

Detective Halperin's wife, Nettie, was brought the news of her husband's death as she recovered from a recent surgery at Jackson Park Hospital. Halperin's mother, Tillie, and two brothers, Joseph G. and Samuel, joined Nettie in mourning Officer Halperin. He was buried in West Lawn Cemetery.

Patrolman John W. Quirk,

STAR #9866, 32nd District, Shakespeare Avenue Station, 23 years old, was off-duty in the early morning hours of January 13, 1958 when circumstances forced him into a police action that led to his death in the line of duty.

Patrolman Quirk had spent the evening of January 12 on a first date with Miss Caroline Smith, an 18-year-old student/model. The young officer had been eager to make a favorable impression and began their date with a visit to the Shakespeare Avenue Station at 2131 N. California Avenue. After touring the station they moved on to a restaurant at 3801 W. Fullerton Avenue where, unbeknownst to Quirk, his partner was also eating dinner. The chance meeting prolonged the young couple's evening and it was almost 2:30 A.M. when Quirk pulled up in front of the Towne Home Girls' Residence at 22 E. Banks Street, where Miss Smith resided.

Quirk and Smith were sitting in his car saying good night when they were suddenly siezed by two armed robbers. The men entered the car from each side and slid into the backseat with their weapons on the young pair. Taking the couple's money and jewelry, they ordered Quirk to drive around. Feeling he had no choice, the officer complied with their instructions. Somewhere around Wisconsin and Cleveland Streets he realized that some action was necessary to protect his companion. He rammed his vehicle into a street lamp, bringing the car to an abrupt stop. Quirk then drew his service revolver and began firing into the backseat of the automobile as he shielded Miss Smith from harm with his own body. The assailants in the back seat quickly returned fire. Patrolman Quirk was mortally wounded within seconds and died at the scene. His heroic actions left Miss Smith uninjured and she used the vehicle's horn to summon help as the bandit's fled the scene.

A citywide manhunt was undertaken after Quirk's death. Only an hour and a half after the shooting the first suspect was discovered at Henrotin Hospital seeking treatment for a gunshot wound to the right hand that he would not explain. After intense questioning the suspect, who identified himself as Nick LaPapa, Jr., admitted to being one of the assailants who attempted to rob Patrolman Quirk and provided the name of his accomplice, George Starcevic. Starcevic became the sole focus of the ensuing police manhunt that swept the city. The gunman eventually turned himself in to two FBI agents at 51st Street and Racine Avenue in the presence of his attorney, Thomas Kilroy. The FBI quickly turned the suspect over to the Chicago Police Department and he was identified by Caroline Smith. Both men gave full confessions. A Grand Jury indicted both men for murder. LaPapa, an apprentice plumber and part-time candy vendor, and Starcevic, a four time escapee of the Illinois State Training School for Boys in Kane County, admitted to having five weapons with them when they robbed the young couple. LaPapa claimed he injured his right hand when he dropped his own weapon during the gun battle. Quirk's weapon was found among the cache of guns to which the suspects directed investigating officers.

LaPapa was sentenced to life at the Illinois State Penitentiary at Joliet, but repeatedly petitioned to have his sentence reduced. In the end he only served eight years of his sentence. Starcevic was sentenced to 199 years at the Illinois State Penitentiary at Joliet. Officer Quirk lived with his parents at 1052 N. Central Avenue. He was a three-year-veteran of the United States Marines Corps and, like LaPapa, had been an apprentice plumber. The patrolman joined the Chicago Police Department only fifteen months before his death on September 1, 1956. He had been promoted to 1st class patrolman in October of 1957. Quirk had received a celebrated mention only four days before his death for his actions during the arrest of a man accused of selling drugs to a 15-year-old boy. Officer Quirk was laid to rest at Queen of Heaven Cemetery.

1959

The electric chair in the basement of
Cook Count Jail where many police killers
met their fate (December 8, 1958).
Chicago Tribune Photo Archive.

Caroline Smith, who was on a date with
Patrolman John Quirk at the time of his death,
testifies at inquest (January 15, 1958).
Chicago Tribune Photo Archive.

George Starcevic (5th from the left, partially hidden) and Nick LaPapa (2nd from the right) are among seven gang members awaiting proceedings in Felony Court for the murder of Officer Quirk. (January 15, 1958). *Chicago Tribune* Photo Archive.

Detective Roy A. Carney,

STAR #7292, Woodlawn Station, 35 years old, was murdered on April 18, 1958 during a gun battle with two robbers at 160 E. Marquette Road.

Two young men sitting at the bar of a tavern that Carney's wife, Carrie, was running drew their guns and announced a robbery. All of the patrons, Detective Carney included, were forced to the back of the tavern. Carney resisted and began wrestling with one of the assailants. The second gunman fired two shots at the detective. One of the bullets hit Carney in the left temple. He was rushed to St. Bernard Hospital where he was pronounced dead. Carney, who was the son of a police officer, had been on the force for 10 years. In 1955 the detective shot a robber at a Southside cleaning shop and earned a departmental honorable mention.

After the attempted robbery and murder, the two gunmen sped away down 66th Street near State Street. The men were soon stopped by Officer James Brooks driving in the wrong direction on a one way street. Brooks, unaware of the recent murder, let the men go.

About a month after the incident John Henry Davis, age 26, was identified as the shooter and arrested in Alexandria, Louisiana. Not long after Davis' arrest Larry Oden, age 26, was also arrested. Davis and Oden were tried and found guilty of Officer Carney's death on November 21, 1958 and sentenced to the electric chair. Over the next few years their execution date was postponed multiple times. In May of 1961 they were tried for a second time after the Illinois Supreme Court ordered a retrial. The duo were again found guilty, but sentenced to 199 years in prison. Officer Carney was buried in Burr Oak Cemetery.

Detective Joseph Borcia,

STAR# unavailable, Rogers Park Police Station, 52 years old, died in an automobile accident on October 13, 1958 at Touhy and Ashland Avenues. Detectives Borcia and George Gannon were on their way to the site of a robbery at 1206 W. Jarvis Avenue, heading east on Touhy Avenue, when Gannon's car collided with the vehicle Detective John L. Curtin and Officer Robert J. Schirmang were driving north on Ashland Avenue. The impact of the collision ejected Detective Borcia from the automobile and inflicted fatal injuries. Borcia was pronounced dead on arrival at St. Francis Hospital, Evanston. The other officers suffered minor injuries.

The fallen officer had just been promoted to detective in July. He had previously been assigned to the Chicago Avenue Station. Borcia, of 5834 N. Mulligan Avenue, left behind a wife and an 18-year-old daughter.

Patrolman Mitchell A. Stone,

STAR #4030, 1st District, 38 years old, was on patrol with his partner, Patrolman Gerald Marzillo, waiting to make a left turn on Roosevelt Road from Wabash Avenue on April 29, 1959 when their vehicle was approached by a female who attempted to enter the squad car. Marzillo locked the vehicles doors and then rolled down a window to inquire what the woman wanted. She said she was looking for a cab. Upon learning they were the police, she pointed to a man in a white jacket and told the officers he was carrying a gun. Acting on the tip, Stone and Marzillo followed the man to an alley at the rear of a parking lot at 1241 S. Michigan Avenue. They lost sight of the suspect as they turned into the alley, leading them to exit the squad car for a more thorough search. Using their flashlights in the darkened alley and parking lot, they combed the area for the armed man.

Stone spotted the suspect and asked Marzillo to follow him in the squad car. Marzillo ran for their vehicle, watching as his partner pursued the suspect across the alley and through the adjoining lot towards Michigan Avenue before they disappeared from view. Marzillo took the car and cut across Michigan Avenue in an attempt to cut off the suspect's escape. He had not gone very far when shots rang out. He quickly sent out a radio call that an officer was in trouble and began to look for Stone. He found his partner bleeding on the asphalt from a severe stomach wound, insisting on giving a full description of his assailant. Backup quickly arrived at the scene and Stone was transported to St. Luke Hospital. Doctors discovered that the bullet had entered two inches below the navel and nothing could be done. Patrolman Stone died at 5:10 A.M. as his fellow officers searched the city for his killer.

A cab driver later informed police a man matching the description of the assailant tried to hail his cab. He watched in his rearview mirror as the man entered a gas station at 11th Street and Wabash Avenue. Police dispatched to the gas station and were informed that the man they were seeking was in the restroom. The suspect, William Witherspoon, was taken into custody and then transported to St. Luke Hospital. Marzillo and Stone both identified him as the man they had been chasing. Investigating officers returned to the gas station and searched the washroom. They found a Radon 9mm automatic pistol in the lavatory flush box. In addition, a spent 9mm casing was found in the parking lot where Officer Stone was shot. The offender promptly confessed to the shooting.

Witherspoon, an ex-convict, came to Chicago from Michigan with partner Frank Dydra, to escape FBI agents seeking them in connection with the armed robbery of a jewelry store in Detroit. Diamonds from that robbery were eventually found in a leather bag under the gravel of the parking lot where Marzillo and Stone had followed Witherspoon. Dydra was arrested on April 29. Both men were indicted, Witherspoon for murder and Dydra as an accessory. Witherspoon's was found guilty of Officer Stone's murder in April of 1960 and sentenced to die in the electric chair. Police later arrested two more men in connection with the original robbery; brothers Daniel and Lewis Wilhite from Detroit. Witherspoon's sentence was voided by the U.S. Supreme Court and he received a 50-year-prison term. He was quietly paroled from prison in 1979 after serving 20 years. Patrolman Stone was survived by his wife, Eppie, and their young son. He was buried at St. Adalbert Cemetery.

1959

Chicago Police Department three-wheel motorcycle officers (1959). ICH-i39634, Chicago History Museum Photo Archive.

A Chicago Police Department traffic stop (1959). ICH-i3883, Chicago History Museum Photo Archive.

Motorcycle policemen at the Fillmore Street
Station, 25th District (1959). ICH-i24408,
Chicago History Museum Photo Archive.

Tavern Row, 4200 S. Ashland Avenue
(1950). ICH-i22794, Chicago History Museum
Photo Archive Photo Archive.

Patrolman Leonard F. Baldy,

STAR #1451, Traffic Division, 33 years old, was a beloved figure who provided Chicagoans with live traffic reports during the morning and evening rush hours. Patrolman Baldy, assigned to the Police Department's Traffic Division: Driver's Educational Unit, was a familiar voice to millions of drivers who depended on his view from the WGN helicopter to help them navigate their rush hour commutes. Preparing to report on the evening drive on May 2, 1960, he tragically lost his life in the line of duty.

Baldy, an eight-year-veteran of the Chicago Police Department, reported for duty that afternoon at the WGN newsroom in the Tribune Tower around 3:45 P.M. He then proceeded to Meigs Field to prepare for takeoff. The helicopter took off after his arrival with Horace G. Ferry in the pilot's seat. The manager at Meigs Field later testified that the chopper's takeoff appeared normal and visibility was unlimited. There was no further communication between the copter and the control tower at the field after takeoff. Patrolman Baldy's voice was then heard at 4:20 P.M. as he checked in with the WGN Master Control Station. Hearing the officer's voice over the radio frequency, the announcer calling the Chicago Cubs game asked Baldy for his location. He told the officer that he could hear the helicopter but couldn't see it. Baldy replied that he was right over center field enjoying the game.

At 4:45 P.M. Baldy was preparing to deliver his traffic report as the copter flew southeast towards the Loop about 200 feet above the Chicago and North Western railway line near the intersection of Hubbard and Union Streets along Milwaukee Avenue. Various witnesses provided an account of the heartbreaking sequence of events that followed. According to those reports, the helicopter's main rotor blade separated from the chopper and fell away. The aircraft then began to spiral downwards. Seconds later an explosion ripped the helicopter apart and it was consumed by flames.

The wreckage hit the north parapet of the railway embankment, just west of the overpass of tracks running over the street. Parts of the machine scattered across this area, with the fuselage landing on the railroad tracks. The remainder crashed onto Union and Hubbard Streets. A tail section of the helicopter separated from the main body of the machine and landed in a back yard at 707 W. Grand Avenue. The wreckage miraculously missed the cars and drivers stuck in rush hour traffic as it went down, but Patrolman Baldy and Ferry, the pilot, both lost their lives. Baldy's wife was listening to the Cubs broadcast at home, 7343 W. Howard Street, when her mother heard the news report of the crash and called with the news. Officer Baldy left three young children, Raymond, Judith Marie and Timothy. His family laid him to rest at All Saints Cemetery.

Patrolman Joseph E. Chapman, Jr.,

Star #6239, Bureau of Operational Services, 56 years old, had gone into the Hi-Spot Liquor Store, 5302 S. Indiana Avenue, on May 8, 1960 to pick-up soft drinks for his grandchildren when he was called to duty and fatally injured. Chapman had originally gone to the store at 3:00 P.M. to enjoy a sandwich with the proprietor, a personal friend of more than 25 years, before returning with refreshments for a Mother's Day celebration at his home that evening. After finishing his sandwich and soda at around 4:40 P.M., the patrolman went to the rear of the store to use the restroom. As he did so, a strange man entered the establishment and went to the rear counter. Hi-Spot's owner, Herman Baum, glanced over at the man just in time to see him jump over the counter, pull a weapon and announce a stick-up. He brandished his gun at Baum and the store's clerk, Starling Bitting, as three terrified customers looked on. Bitting moved towards the back of the store to get Chapman's attention, but he was stopped by the gunman.

A Chicago Police Department helicopter
does surveillance over a southwest portion
of the city as part of Operation Falcon,
a program designed to supplement crime
detection by providing an aerial view.
Chicago Tribune Photo Archive.

Chapman emerged from the rear, quickly assessed the scene and announced he was a cop. He commanded the offender, Larry C. Harvey, to lay his weapon down. The perpetrator responded with gunfire. The patrolman returned fire and both men fell mortally wounded. The gun battle was over as quickly as it began and help was immediately summoned. Both men were rushed to Provident Hospital. Chapman was hit five times and died at 5:00 P.M. on the operating table as the doctors worked feverishly to save his life. Harvey lingered for another eight hours and was moved to the Bridewell Hospital where he died at 1:30 A.M.

As Patrolman Chapman fought for his life, his wife, six daughters and their families awaited his return home at 456 W. 21st Street. Chapman's wife, Frances, was also a police officer with the Department's Youth Bureau. On March 4, 1956, Joseph Chapman shot and wounded a robber at the same liquor store where he lost his life. Patrolman Chapman had spent 31 years with the Chicago Police Department and had been planning to retire in two months on July 2. He was interred at St. Mary Cemetery.

Patrolman Melvin L. Gossmeyer,

STAR #9775, Task Force, 33 years old, was on a three-wheeled motorcycle performing his regular patrol on July 17, 1960 when he was struck and killed by a motorist fleeing the scene of an accident. Larry Benford, 22 years old, hit the rear of a vehicle belonging to William Lynch at 3400 E. 106th Street and caused damage to the fender. Benford fled the scene and Lynch pursued him down 106th Street. Lynch was soon joined in the chase by Policeman Clyde Hughes of the Accident Investigation Unit. Benford's car then spun out of control at 106th and Ewing Streets and struck Patrolman Gossmeyer on his motorcycle. The vehicle then sped across the intersection and hit four pedestrians, fatally injuring one. Albert Eiermann was flung 70 feet and hit another bystander, Miss Elaine Sundin, who suffered multiple lacerations. Officer Gossmeyer was taken to Chicago Hospital and succumbed to his injuries shortly after arrival. Benford and a passenger in his vehicle were transported to the Cook County Hospital and treated for cuts and bruises after the car ended up hitting a telephone pole. Officer Gossmeyer was on the job four years and had received 59 creditable mentions during his short career. He lived at 412 W. 103rd Place and was survived by his wife and three children. Benford was charged with reckless homicide after receiving treatment for his injuries. Patrolman Gossmeyer was buried at Evergreen Park Cemetery.

Patrolman William A. Flowers,

STAR #1872, 27th District, Warren Avenue Station, 32 years old, was on the 3rd Watch in civilian clothes on October 26, 1960 when a man came into lodge a complaint against another citizen. Henry Sanders asked to file a grievance against his neighbor, Johnny Barker. Sanders claimed Barker was having an affair with his wife, Mary Sanders, and had threatened him several times. Flowers was at the station with his partner, Patrolman Henry Pates, and they agreed to investigate the complaint. Sanders informed them that Barker was not currently at his residence and offered to return to their apartment building and call the officers when the suspect returned. At 9:00 P.M., Flowers and Pates received a call from Sanders notifying them that Barker had returned. The officers proceeded to the apartment at 53 N. Washtenaw Avenue.

Sanders met police when they arrived. All three men headed to the building manager's office to gain more details on the suspect. The manager informed them that Barker was definitely at home but warned the patrolmen that they had to be cautious because the offender was notorious for keeping several weapons in his apartment. The officers then went outside with Sanders to identify Barker's apartment from a nearby alley. As Flowers and Pates assessed the situation, Barker entered the alley from the other end with a gun in his hand.

He opened fire on the officers without speaking, fatally wounding Flowers. Officer Pates drew his own weapon and returned fire. Barker ran from Pates who pursued him down the alley. The offender then ran up the building's back staircase into his third floor apartment, exchanging fire with Pates until the door closed behind him.

Pates waited for back-up to arrive before breaking down the apartment door. They found the offender lying wounded on the floor with a .25 caliber automatic pistol still in his grip. Both Flowers and his killer were taken to the Illinois Research Hospital where the policeman was pronounced dead on arrival. Patrolman Flowers, who lived at 3249 W. 16th Street, was a Chicago Policeman for four years. Just days before the shooting, Pates and Flowers had been honored for the arrest of two suspects involved in a fatal shooting on October 15, 1960. Officer Flowers was laid to rest at Lincoln Cemetery. Though Barker sustained six gunshot wounds, none proved fatal. On March 6, 1961, Barker was sentenced to 25 years in the Illinois State Penitentiary at Joliet for Patrolman Flower's murder and received an additional 5 to 14 years on an assault to murder charge to which he pleaded guilty on May 1, 1961.

Detective William R. Johnson,

STAR #6996, Detective Bureau, 37 years old, was rushing to respond to a report on a suspected rapist when he was involved in a fatal car crash with three other vehicles on November 18, 1960. The accident took place at 59th Street and Cottage Grove Avenue when Detective Johnson's vehicle was broadsided by another car. The detective, who was riding with his partner Detective Jerry Howard, was thrown from his automobile and sustained multiple life threatening injuries. Howard, who worked with Johnson in the Sex Bureau, and four civilians were also injured. Johnson was a twelve-year-veteran of the police force and resided at 7408 S. Union Avenue. He left behind a wife and three children. He was buried at Lincoln Cemetery.

Detective Headquarters, 740 E. 56th Place
in Washington Park. Today it is the DuSable
Museum of African-American History.
Chicago Police Department Photo Archive.

Patrolman LaVaughn V. White, Sr.

STAR #7473, 15th district, 38 years old, was off-duty on June 5, 1961 when he was called to service and lost his life at the Poincina Inn, 121 E. 79th Street. Patrolman White had been relaxing at the Inn when four men entered and ordered beers around 1:30 A.M. Officer White retired to his residence above the establishment about 15 minutes after the men arrived. Moments later, the four customers pulled out weapons and announced a hold-up. One of the robbers was in the process of emptying the cash register when Patrolman White passed by while walking his dog. Realizing a crime was underway White burst through the door, with his gun drawn, allowing the Inn's owner to run out and seek help. The robbers took cover as White entered and opened fire on the officer from behind various tables and chairs. The patrolman was able to empty his revolver and hit one of the criminals before falling fatally wounded. Officer White was interred at Holy Sepulchre Cemetery.

Police arrived on the scene after being alerted of the hold-up by the Inn's proprietor and found their fellow officer fatally injured. Unable to help Patrolman White, they were determined to bring his killers to justice. One of the assailants had dropped his wallet when he fled. A photo ID inside the billfold allowed witnesses to tentatively identify him as Joseph Prewett, and the search for him began. He was arrested wearing blood-stained shoes only hours later. He admitted to being at the Inn when White was shot but claimed that he had not fired the fatal shot. He also stated that he was unaware which of his accomplices might have done so. A search of his car revealed two guns; one police believed was Officer White's.

Harold McEwen, the offender White shot, sought treatment for a bullet wound at University of Illinois Hospital shortly after the shooting. He was quickly apprehended. Thomas Jackson and Donald Curry were also arrested and charged with being involved in the shootout at the Poincina Inn. All four men were indicted on June 22, 1961 for murder. They elected to take a bench trial before Judge Alexander Napoli. During trial, all four pled guilty. Judge Napoli sentenced each of them to 99 years in the Illinois State Penitentiary at Joliet for their part in the murder of Patrolman White.

1961

Patrolman James O. Sexton,

STAR # unavailable, 38 years old, was performing training exercises in the canine department at 7900 S. County Line Road on July 25, 1962 when he lost his life. Patrolman Daniel Scanlon was using Sexton's gun which he believed was empty, to train a dog by threatening it. The revolver went off as Officer Scanlon was passing the gun back to Officer Sexton. The patrolman was hit below the heart and died later the same day in the Hinsdale Sanitarium. Sexton lived at 5658 S. Moody Avenue and left behind his wife, Helene, and three daughters, Susan, Kathleen and Colleen. He was interred at St. Joseph's Cemetery.

Patrolman Samuel H. Hall,

STAR #5190, Area #1 Task Force, 33 years old, was driving near 36th Street and Wabash Avenue with his partner, Patrolman Bishop Pamon, around 3:30 A.M. on October 1, 1962 when they heard a shot ring out. It came from the direction of State Street and Hall quickly drove his squad car toward the noise. When they reached the intersection of 36th and State Streets, the officers saw two suspicious individuals standing on the corner. They pulled up next to the curb and one of the men approached the officers' vehicle on the driver's side. As Patrolman Hall exited the squad car the offender drew even closer and opened fire on both officers with an automatic pistol. Hall, struck three times, fell back into the car and slumped over the steering wheel fatally wounded. Pamon jumped from the car and returned fire. Alva Perkins, the other assailant, fell fatally injured.

Police rushed to the scene and discovered that the original gunshot was fired at Perkins by someone he was attempting to rob on the street.

Hall had lived at 7115 S. Union Avenue with his wife, Frances;, sons Samuel, Jr. and Edward and daughter, Maureen. He was also survived by his mother, two brothers and sister. He was laid to rest at Lincoln Cemetery.

No police killed in 1963.

Patrolman John P. Jasper,

STAR # 6894, 8th District, 37 years old, was killed when his squad car crashed and exploded on September 11, 1964. Jasper, a World War II veteran, had been chasing a speeding vehicle southbound on Pulaski Road when he was struck by a westbound vehicle at 83rd Street. Patrolman Jasper's squad car then swerved into a light post. The other vehicle was driven by Thomas Flickinger who was not injured. A ten-year-veteran of the Chicago Police Department, Jasper was pronounced dead at Christ Community Hospital in Oak Lawn. He was survived by his wife, Barbara; and four children, Janet, John, Jr., Cathryn and Laura Lynn.

Two teens were recognized for their efforts to save Officer Jasper. After the crash a stream of gasoline trickled under the car and caught fire. Tom Trahey, age 19, and John Gardner, age 18, saw Jasper's vehicle catch fire and, without hesitation, attempted to pull him from the squad car. The boys did not give up until onlookers forced them away from the vehicle. They were given The Award of Heroism Medal, which was presented by the Chicago Stock Yards' American legion post.

12th Street Store at 1155 S. Halsted Street
in the Maxwell Street District (1964). ICH-i35069,
Chicago History Museum Photo Archive

Mrs. Jean Eichorst, the widow of Sergeant
Charles E. Eichorst, looks on as her son,
Charles Jr., accepts a citation on behalf of his
father from Police Superintendent O.W. Wilson
(August 21, 1965). *Chicago Tribune*
Photo Archive.

Sergeant Charles E. Eichorst,

STAR #1364, 20th District, 43 years old, was on routine patrol at 9:30 A.M. on the morning of August 4, 1965 when a radio call alerted him to a robbery in progress at the Treasure Island Food Mart located at 2540 W. Lawrence Avenue. Two robbers, brothers Holice and Richard Black, had entered the store shortly after it opened and announced a hold-up. According to the store manager, Gerry Komas, Richard acted as a lookout while Holice forced his way to the cashier cage at the back of the store. He emptied $3,000 from the safe into a paper bag, and did not notice the cashier activate the burglar alarm. Sergeant Eichorst, who had been examining a broken parking meter, proceeded to the scene after instructing a bystander to inform a nearby police cruiser of the crime.

When Eichorst reached the store he noticed a man walking away from the front door and ordered him to halt and place his hands against the wall. The man, continued walking, and gave a warning whistle to his accomplice as the sergeant ordered him to stop. When Eichorst pulled his service revolver from its holster the bandit finally complied. While Eichorst was searching Richard Black his brother, Holice, emerged from the store, approached Eichorst, and fired two shots, hitting him in the right temple. He staggered a short distance across the parking lot before collapsing to the ground.

When Lieutenant Joseph Fitzgerald arrived he discovered that Sergeant Eichorst was dead. Police began investigating the scene. They discovered that the Black brothers left a trail of fingerprints during their escape, as well as a shirt containing a parking citation issued to Holice Black. The robbers escaped without any of the $3,000 because of a hole in the paper bag they used. Police located a 1955 Buick with an application for state license plates in Holice Black's name attached to the windshield. A picture of Holice Black was shown to witnesses who confirmed the man in the photo was one who had shot Eichorst. After this a manhunt for the killers began.

The killers were successful in eluding police and convinced a friend to drive them to Gary, Indiana. A nationwide manhunt for the Black brothers began when the F.B.I. issued Unlawful Flight to Avoid Prosecution warrants. On December 15, 1965, the F.B.I. arrested Holice Black in Miami, Florida. His brother turned himself into the Chicago office of the F.B.I two weeks later. Both men were indicted for murder on January 5, 1966 and found guilty of the crime on July 29 of the same year. Holice Black received a sentence of 100 to 200 years on the murder charge and 20 to 40 years for the armed robbery. Richard Black received the same robbery sentence and a prison term of 75 to 100 years on the murder charge. Both were sent to the Illinois State Penitentiary at Joliet.

Sergeant Eichorst was survived by his wife, Jean, daughter, Jill, and son, Charles, Jr. He was an 18-year-veteran of the force who began his career in 1947. He was promoted to sergeant on January 1, 1962. Sergeant Eichorst was interred at Ridgewood Cemetery.

1965

Detective Ralph C. Dunn,

STAR #8499, Criminal Investigation Unit, 41 years old, was driving on the Stevenson Expressway near Pulaski on Thursday, March 24, 1966 when his unmarked squad car skidded on a slippery patch of road and crashed into a guard rail. He suffered fatal injuries and was pronounced dead at St. Anthony Hospital. Detective Dunn, an 11-year-veteran of the Chicago Police Department, was promoted to detective in June 1957 and assigned to the Criminal Intelligence Investigation Unit in February of 1965. He had received five commendations over the course of his career. Dunn was survived by his wife, Helen, and children, Anne, Nancy and Steven. He was laid to rest at Memory Gardens Cemetery.

Desk-Sergeant Claude M. Fischer,

STAR #1570, 21st District, Prairie Avenue Station, 39 years old, was off-duty at 1:30 A.M. on April 19, 1966 when three robbers burst into O'Riley's Tavern, 4622 S. Western Avenue. Two of the men were armed; one with a revolver, the other one with a shotgun. Seeing their weapons, Fischer drew his own gun. Both men fired. Desk-Sergeant Fischer, seated at the bar in plain clothes, slumped to the floor almost instantly. He did manage to fire twice, wounding one of the bandits as he fell. All three fled without completing the robbery. Desk-Sergeant Fischer, an 11-year-veteran of the force, died shortly after the shooting. He was survived by his wife, Gloria, and their five children. He was buried at St. Mary Cemetery.

The gunmen left few clues to their identity at the scene, but were apprehended the next day when one of the men was picked up for his part in another crime. Alfred Armstrong was taken into custody for his role in an attack on a teacher at Marshall High School. During interrogation, police discovered that Armstrong had gunshot wounds in the left hand and forearm. They then noticed Armstrong closely resembled the description of one of Fischer's killers. In a line-up he was identified by two witnesses. Police went to Armstrong's residence at 2744 W. Arthington Street, where his wife gave permission for their home to be searched. A revolver and shotgun, later identified as the murder weapons, were quickly discovered. Armstrong confessed to his part in the crime and named his three accomplices: Jerry Sumlin, Andrew L. Hale and Vern Rhodes, all teenagers. They were quickly arrested and each admitted to being present at the tavern during Fischer's shooting.

Sumlin admitted to firing the revolver during the hold-up. Armstrong admitted to holding the shotgun but claimed he could not remember if he had fired the weapon. It was later determined that revolver bullets had killed Sergeant Fischer. All four men were indicted for murder and two counts of robbery. Sumlin pleaded guilty while the other three offenders stood trial. Hale was found not guilty when it was established that he had waiting outside the tavern as the robbery took place. In October of 1966, Armstrong and Rhodes were both found guilty. Sumlin and Rhodes each received a sentence of 50 to 100 years while Armstrong was given a prison term of 100 to 150 years. All three men were sent to the Illinois State Penitentiary at Joliet.

1966

Detective Daniel J. Quinnan,

STAR #7899, 1st District, Central Station, 38 years old, was killed in the line of duty on September 20, 1966 when he interrupted an armed robbery while on routine patrol. His killer, Paul E. Thedford, had been at the Dinerama Lounge, a restaurant and go-go lounge at 646 S. Wabash Avenue, for about an hour and a half before robbing the place. While there he consumed about seven whiskey sours and conversed with bartender Michael Albanese. According to Albanese's account, Thedford showed him a gun and then hid it under the bar. He ordered Albanese to give him all the money in the cash register. The bartender placed $150 into a brown paper bag and handed it to the offender. Thedford took the money and started to make his way down the bar with his gun in hand. He stopped near the lounge's front entrance and ordered a patron to empty his pockets, adding $65 to paper bag. The robber went to exit just as Detective Quinnan entered.

Quinnan, a vice squad detective in civilian clothes, stepped inside the Dinerama Lounge. Albanese saw the officer enter at 9:45 P.M. Before the officer could heed the bartender's warning, Thedford ran into him. In response, Quinnan grabbed him by the arm and the two men began a struggle. Thedford shot Quinnan before he had an opportunity to draw his own revolver. The robber then fled the scene as Quinnan slumped to the floor.

Police obtained a description of the assailant from the witnesses at the lounge. A task force of more than 100 officers searched the Loop and near-Loop bars and hotels looking for Thedford. His description was broadcast across the city by radio. Less than four hours after the shooting, a cab driver reported that he had seen a man matching Thedford's description at the Harrison Hotel, 609 S. Wabash Avenue. Police turned their attention to the area surrounding the Harrison. They discovered Thedford attempting to check into a room at the YMCA, 628 S. Wabash Avenue. He had only $1 and a bottle of whiskey sour in his possession. He arrived in Chicago from Dallas only the day before after serving a prison term in Texas for burglary. He was indicted for murder and two counts of robbery on October 5, 1966 and pleaded guilty on March 17, 1967. He was sentenced to 30 to 75 years in the Illinois State Penitentiary at Joliet.

Detective Quinnan was rushed to Presbyterian St. Luke Hospital shortly after the shooting, he died soon after arrival. He was a thirteen-year-veteran of the force with a file that included over 30 commendations. He became a detective only the year before his death. Detective Quinnan was survived by his wife, Dorothy, and laid to rest at St. Mary Cemetery.

Patrolman William Y. Bell,

STAR #3565, 2nd District, Wabash Avenue Station, 26 years old, was accidentally killed on February 6, 1967 when he joined fellow officers chasing a robbery suspect. Bell was off-duty in civilian clothes when he observed Grand Crossing police, and store employees from the Jewel Food Store at 1709 E. 71st Street, chasing a robber. William Baird, moments earlier, robbed the South Shore supermarket of $1,200. After a lengthy chase he was hiding in a vestibule at 1647 W. 69th Street just as Officer Bell joined the chase. Police following Baird were unaware of Bell's presence. This error led to the patrolman's death, described to the *Chicago Tribune* by Deputy Chief of Detectives Michael Spiotto as a "ghastly mistake."

A shootout began between the barricaded offender and responding officers. Confusion reigned as the bullets flew. Bell mistook some of the other officers for hold-up men while officers assumed he was an accomplice of Baird's. Bell wounded Patrolmen James Knightly and James Reynolds. Officer Reynolds lost his uniform cap pursuing Baird, and Bell was unable to identify him as an officer. The Grand Crossing police returned fire and both Bell and Baird were hit. Bell had been with the police department for three years and was described as an outstanding policeman by his superiors. Officer Bell, who lived at 6938 S. Jeffrey Boulevard, was survived by his wife, Valerie, and buried at Lincoln Cemetery.

Patrol-Sergeant Gerald E. Doll,

STAR #477, 15th District, 38 years old, was believed to have been pursuing a pair of robbery suspects on March 29, 1967 when he was shot and killed in the line of duty. Doll had observed a station wagon with a male driver and female passenger traveling at a high speed. He attempted to make a traffic stop. The driver refused to stop so Doll set off in pursuit. The chase ended a few minutes later when the suspect's car, later discovered as stolen, crashed turning east onto Shakespeare Avenue from Cicero Avenue. Sergeant Doll stepped from his vehicle and approached the disabled station wagon as the man and women emerged. Without provocation the driver opened fire on the sergeant with a sawed-off shotgun, hitting him squarely in the chest. Doll was able to return fire about half a dozen times before crumpling to the sidewalk.

Patrolman William Redden pulled up to the scene as the offenders fled. He followed them into an alley at the 4700 W. block of Palmer Street and opened fire in an attempt to halt their flight. The male suspect managed to escape, but the female passenger, Miss Delia Ann Jones, was found hiding in a garage at 4733 W. Palmer Street with gunshot wounds to the back, leg and thigh. Transported to Belmont Hospital, she was taken to surgery. A citywide search began for her companion, Gary Horton. Police believed they were a dangerous hold-up team plaguing the area. Horton, a 25-year-old Oak Park man, had been released from Stateville Penitentiary in February of 1967. His dead body was found in the early morning hours of March 30 in a yard at 2218 N. Keating, just blocks from the shooting. He had apparently sustained fatal wounds in his exchanged with the sergeant. Miss Jones was later sentenced to 20 years in prison for her role in the shooting.

Sergeant Doll was survived by his wife, Mary, expecting their fourth child at the time of his death, plus a daughter and two sons. He had joined the force in 1955 and was promoted to Patrol Sergeant in March of 1965. Before becoming a police officer, he had been an accountant and served in Japan from 1950 to 1953 with the United States Army. His exemplary law enforcement career was illustrated by a file that contained a dozen letters of commendation and multiple honorable mentions. Sergeant Doll was interred at St. Joseph Cemetery.

1967

Patrolman Herman Stallworth,

STAR #10965, 3rd District, 37 years old, was fatally shot in the line of duty on May 23, 1967 after a routine traffic stop turned deadly. Stallworth and his partner, Patrolman Eugene Ervin, pulled a vehicle over at Cottage Grove Avenue and Marquette Road and discovered that neither of the two men in the car had valid identification. Ervin returned to the squad car to radio in the vehicles license plate while Stallworth remained to question the men. Suddenly, the driver drew a gun and opened fire. Stallworth, standing next to the vehicle, was struck in the chest and abdomen. Ervin was attempting to exit the squad car to assist his partner when he was also hit. Despite his injuries, he was able to radio for help and 20 units quickly responded to his call.

The scene was soon crawling with police intent on finding Stallworth's killer. Patrolman Edward G. Carey, one of the responding officers, was approached at the scene by Charles Harper, the passenger of the vehicle Stallworth and Ervin had stopped. Harper had remained among the crowd gathered around the wounded officer and identified himself to Carey about an hour after his companion, Joseph R. Hurst, had been taken into custody. Hurst had locked himself in the bathroom of a third floor apartment at 6434 S. Maryland Street after the shooting, firing at the officers who pursued him. Two patrolmen seeing him flee radioed for help. Soon the Maryland Street address was also swarming with policemen. Hurst remained barricaded until he ran out of ammunition. He then threw his .38 caliber automatic pistol into the hallway and surrendered without a struggle. He was taken into custody and transported to Woodlawn Hospital where he was treated for cuts to his head and face. At the time of the shooting the offenders were out on bond on a narcotics charge. Hurst was later convicted of Officer Stallworth's murder on February 16, 1968 and sentenced to death in the electric chair on March 1, 1968. He was later resentenced to 100 to 300 years in prison after the United States Supreme Court ruling of 1972 which invalidated state death penalty statutes.

Patrolman Stallworth had been taken to Billings Hospital for treatment after the shooting and died during surgery there at 1:45 A.M., May 24, 1967. He was an eight-year-veteran of the police force, as well as a Navy veteran, and had received two honorable mentions and three department citations. He was survived by his wife, Geraldine; and four children, ages four months to 13 years old. Officer Stallworth was buried at Lincoln Cemetery.

Patrolman John S. Collins,

STAR #11835, 7th District, Englewood Station, 30 years old, was off-duty Christmas shopping with his wife and 10-year-old son around 8:00 P.M., December 13, 1967 at Sears, Roebuck and Co., located at 79th Street and Kenwood Avenue, and became separated from the boy while choosing gifts. Unable to locate their son in the crowded store, the Collins decided to return to their car with the hope that the boy would have the same idea. When they reached their vehicle they noticed that it had been tampered with and the vent of one window had been forced open. Collins spotted a man attempting to open a car nearby without keys and moved to question him. Although he was in civilian clothes, Collins was carrying his revolver and removed the weapon as he approached the man. The man claimed that he had mistaken their car for his own. Collins did not believe the offender's story and stepped towards him as he identified himself as a police officer.

The suspect ran around to the other side of the vehicle and grabbed his own pistol. He fired at Collins and the officer returned fire, but neither man was hit. The offender then seized Mrs. Collins by the neck in an effort to use her as a human shield. He quickly decided that flight was a better option and threw her to the ground before fleeing the parking lot. Collins caught the offender on a gangway alongside a building at 7808 S. Kenwood Avenue. The two engaged in a struggle that ended with a single shot fatally wounding Patrolman Collins.

Police discovered Collins on the gangway and rushed him to Jackson Park Hospital where he died a short time after arrival. Police originally detained six suspects in the shooting who matched the description of the shooter, but none proved to be the killer. Collins joined the police department on August 19, 1966, 16 months before his death. He continued a family tradition of public service exemplified by his father, Wilbert Collins, who was a Chicago Fire Department Lieutenant. Patrolman Collins was survived by his wife, Barbara, and son, Robert, and laid to rest at St. Mary Cemetery.

Charles Clark, an unemployed laborer, was arrested on January 4, 1968. He was charged with Officer Collin's murder after being identified as the shooter by the officer's wife. A jury found Clark guilty on May 28 and recommended that he be sentenced to death, a recommendation Judge Frank J. Wilson followed two months later when he sentenced Clark to die in the electric chair.

Patrolman Charles W. Pollard,

STAR #5540, 10th District, Marquette District Lock-up Keeper, 44 years old, was found shot to death on December 14, 1967 in the parking lot behind his apartment building at 4038 W. 21st Street. His empty wallet was found at the scene but there was no sign of his service revolver or police identification. Police theorized he may have been killed with his own gun. Police later arrested Eugene Armstrong and Clifton Hill.

Armstrong and Hill eventually provided the investigators with an account of the events leading up to Patrolman Pollard's death, although both continued to claim the other fired the fatal shot. The two offenders had stolen a vehicle, originally intending to hold-up two female victims. However, they soon changed their minds and went after Officer Pollard, approaching him as he locked up his vehicle in the parking lot behind his residence, catching him off guard. The hold-up unraveled when Pollard announced he was a policeman and attempted to place them under arrest. Within seconds Pollard was fatally shot and the offenders fled the scene.

Armstrong and Hill were both charged with murder and robbery and received separate trials. The jury trying Armstrong returned a guilty verdict on the murder charge and sentenced the offender to death. Hill's trial ended with his conviction on the robbery and murder counts. He was sentenced to serve 50 to 100 years on the murder charge and 10 to 20 years for the robbery. Patrolman Pollard, a 15-year-veteran of the force, was survived by his wife, Ruth and two children, Charles, Jr. and Careen. He was buried at Restvale Cemetery.

Detective Young Clifton Hobson,

STAR #11118, Detective Division-Area #4 (Auto Theft), 40 years old, was off-duty at the Halsted Liquor Store, 1330 S. Halsted Street, on May 3, 1968 when he noticed that a customer had a pistol stuck in his belt. Detective Hobson approached the man and inquired whether he was legally carrying the weapon. Another man standing at the bar then pulled out a weapon and shot the detective five times. Both offenders escaped the store and were running north on Halsted Street when Detectives Frank Haidinyak and Robert Gushi spotted them fleeing with their weapons in hand. The detectives set off in pursuit of the two assailants and captured David Walsh at 1315 S. Halsted Street. They confiscated the .38 caliber revolver he carried, believed to be the murder weapon. The second offender escaped west down Maxwell Street.

Hobson was taken to Presbyterian St. Luke Hospital, where he died a short time after arrival. Hobson was a rookie cop in 1957, with only six months on the job, when his role in the pursuit and capture of the gunman who killed Detective Barney Halperin earned him the first of many promotions. Detective Hobson was survived by his wife, Robyn, and laid to rest at Restvale Cemetery. Walsh pleaded guilty to Detective Hobson's murder and was sentenced to 20 to 40 years in prison on July 18, 1969.

Patrolman Henry L. Peeler,

STAR #11174, 7th District, Englewood Station, 28 years old, was shot and killed on June 5, 1968 by a killer who had already taken the life of at least one other law enforcement officer. Peeler and his partner, Patrolman Ronald Lillwitz, were on patrol around 9:00 P.M. when they noticed three men lying on the lawn in front of an apartment building at 57th and Morgan Streets with open bottles of liquor. The officers approached and one of the men, Lyon Herbert, tried to flee. Peeler set off in pursuit of the suspect as Lillwitz detained the other two. Lillwitz was in the midst of questioning one of the suspects, Raymond Sharps, when shots rang out. Fearing for his partner, the patrolman headed towards the sound, dragging Sharps along with him. The officer found Patrolman Peeler lying in the gangway at 5659 S. Morgan Street suffering from multiple gunshot wounds in the head and left hand. Before Lillwitz could help his injured partner, Herbert leapt out of the gangway and fired. Patrolman Lillwitz quickly returned fire, in spite of being hit in the right arm and left hand, and killed the offender.

Sharps was taken into custody by police at the scene. The third offender, Charles Childress, was also apprehended, found hiding behind a boiler in the basement of the apartment building with a .38 caliber revolver police believed he may have used to shoot Peeler. All three men had outstanding warrants in East St. Louis for armed robbery and murder relating to the death of Sergeant Jack Armstrong of the Southern Railroad Police Department in East St. Louis, Illinois. It was also revealed that the men were members of an African-American organization called Black Culture, Inc. The group had provided them with money to flee East St. Louis after the shooting and buy the gun used to kill Patrolman Peeler.

According to Sharps, who gave investigators a detailed statement after the shooting, the men had been hiding out in the Morgan Street apartment for several days. Patrolman Peeler, a two-year-veteran of the force, was survived by his wife, Judy and two daughters, Keely and Sherrie. He was interred at Restvale Cemetery.

A broken window at the Malibu Lounge, 1300 N. Sedgwick Street, near Cabrini Green, following the Martin Luther King riots (1968). ICH-i03618, Chicago History Museum Photo Archive.

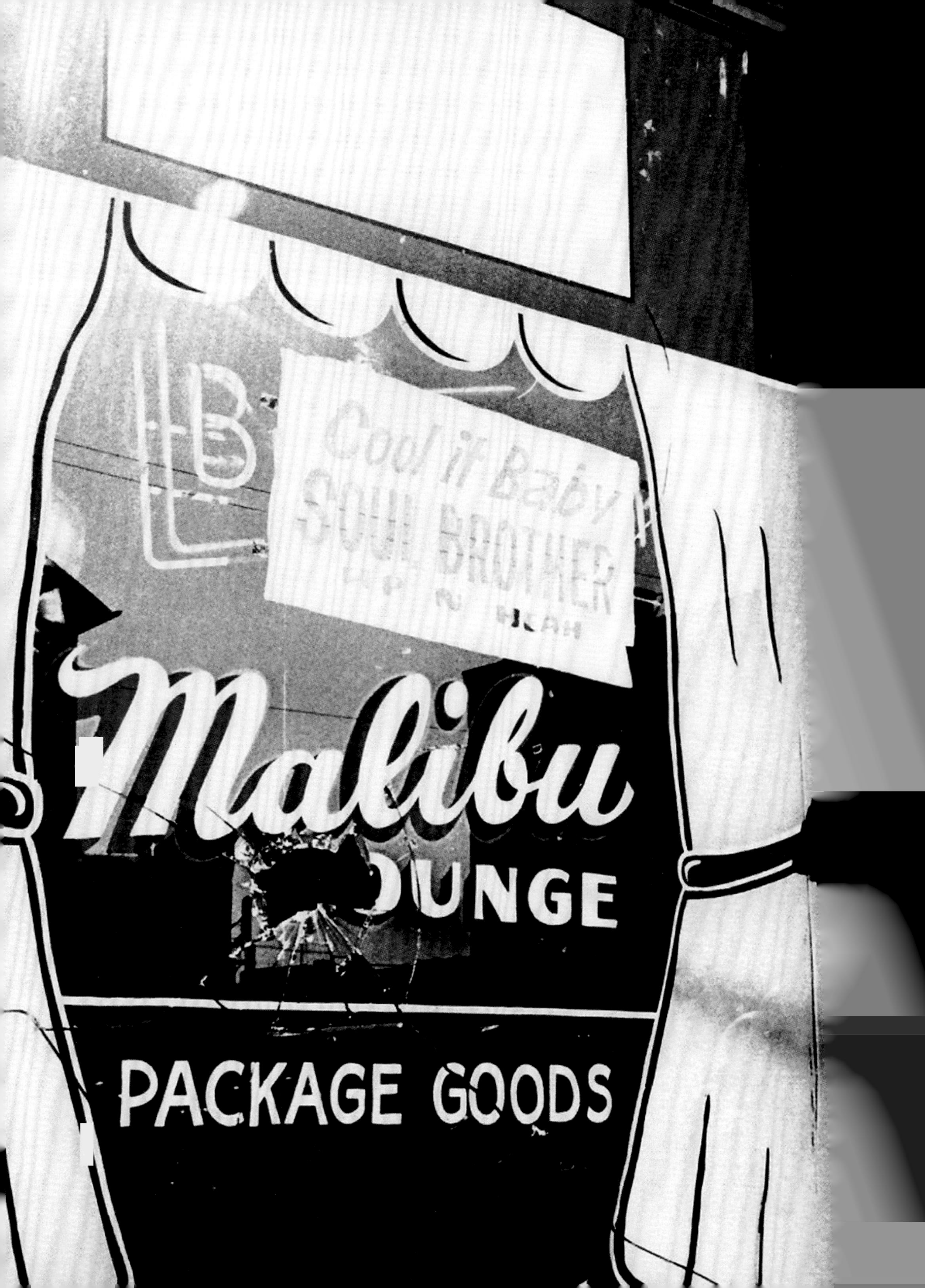
Cool it Baby
SOUL BROTHER
Malibu
OUNGE
PACKAGE GOODS

Chicago Police Department in riot gear on South Michigan Avenue during the Democratic National Convention in August 1968. ICH-i20689, Chicago History Museum Photo Archive.

Englewood Station, 7th District (1960s).
Chicago Police Department Photo Archive.

Patrolman John R. Tucker,

STAR #9168, 4th District, 34 years old, was making a deposit at the Standard Bank and Trust Company, 7919 S. Ashland Avenue, on October 8, 1968, when a bank robbery turned deadly. Tucker, who was off-duty at the time, had just made a deposit into his savings account when Clemmie Johnson appeared at a nearby teller's window carrying a gun. Johnson approached three separate tellers, showed them his weapon and ordered them to stuff a pillowcase he had brought with money. Tucker approached Johnson from behind as he stood at one of the teller's windows and identified himself as a police officer. The offender spun around with his gun and fired, hitting Patrolman Tucker in the chest three times. He fell to the ground fatally injured.

Unbeknownst to Tucker, a bank guard set off an alarm when the robbery began. Police were waiting in the bank lobby to apprehend the suspect, not entering the bank to avoid injury to the 20 bank employees and 12 customers inside at the time. The sound of gunfire, however, quickly brought waiting police into the bank. Upon seeing the armed offender, they opened fire and Johnson was hit three times. He was swiftly arrested.

Patrolman Tucker never regained consciousness and died en route to Little Company of Mary Hospital in Evergreen Park. He had been cited for bravery five times during his career. He lived at 952 W. 52nd Street and was survived by his wife, Jean, and their three children, James, Janice and John, Jr. He was buried in Restvale Cemetery. In 1969, Johnson was sentenced to 100 to 190 years in prison for of Patrolman Tucker's murder.

Detective Clayton Robinson,

STAR #6166, Detective Division-Area #6 (Robbery), Damen Avenue Station, 39 years old, was fatally shot on October 25, 1968 when he stopped a suspect for questioning at the northeast corner of Larrabee and Blackhawk Streets. Detective Robinson detained George Robinson, no relation, and called for a Paddy Wagon after placing him under arrest. Two task force officers in the area, Michael Gedmin and Ronald Uselton, headed to the intersection. As they pulled up they saw the detective speaking with the suspect. They were exiting their vehicle to take the offender into custody when George Robinson pulled out a weapon and shot the detective point blank in the left eye. The responding officers immediately pulled their own guns, ordering him to drop the weapon. When the suspect turned towards them with his own gun raised they opened fire and critically wounded him. He was taken to Henrotin Hospital for treatment, but his injury proved fatal and he died the following day.

Detective Robinson received 15 commendations during his six year career and was promoted to detective on May 12, 1966. His wife, Mamie, was called to her wounded husband's side from her job as an elevator operator at the nearby Drake Hotel. The detective died at Henrotin Hospital at 1:30 A.M. on October 26, 1968. In addition to Mamie, Detective Robinson was survived by his sons Randy, 15, and Michael, 16, and daughters Annette, 17, and Deborah, 11. Detective Robinson was laid to rest at St. Mary Cemetery.

Patrolman Joseph F. Ferguson,

STAR #6892, 2nd District, Wabash Avenue Station, 25 years old, and his partner, Patrolman Daniel Cambric, were on patrol on December 27, 1968 when they spotted a man with a suspicious bulge under his coat walking with two companions. The patrolmen stopped the three men in front of 3834 S. Indiana Avenue and recognized one as a parolee and another as a known drug user. The third man, Al Sanders, claimed that he was not associated with the other two and was simply on his way to work at a barbershop. The officers searched all three men and discovered that the parolee and drug abuser were both carrying guns but that Sanders was not. They let Sanders proceed to his job and placed the other two men under arrest. As Ferguson and Cambric took the offenders into custody, Sanders returned to the scene with a gun retrieved from the barbershop. He disarmed the officers before forcing them to get into the squad car. As the patrolmen entered the vehicle Cambric drew a concealed weapon and opened fire on Sanders.

The offender fired in return and six shots were exchanged. Patrolman Ferguson was hit in the face, neck, left arm and stomach, falling to the ground as the three men fled. Patrolman Cambric, with minor wounds, summoned aid for his partner. Ferguson was rushed to Michael Reese Hospital, where he later died. Sanders was arrested within three hours and was later convicted of Patrolman Ferguson's murder. He received a life sentence and died in jail. Patrolman Ferguson, a graduate of Kelly High School, became a policeman in June of 1965. He was survived by his wife, Tanya; son, Joseph F. Jr.; and daughter, Elizabeth Ann. Officer Ferguson was buried in St. Mary Cemetery.

Sergeant James R. Schaffer,

STAR #824, 4th District, 48 years old, and

Detective Jerome A. Stubig,

STAR #9127, Bomb and Arson Unit, 40 years old, died together in the line of duty on April 14, 1969 at 96th Street and Exchange Avenue. The men had been sent to the apartment of Frank Kulak, a suspect in the South Chicago Goldblatt's bombing, with several officers to question him. Kulak, a trained army sniper, killed both men. Their bodies were later found on the back porch of his apartment. Detective Stubig was conducting the bomb investigation at Kulak's apartment when other police officers attempted to seize the suspect. Stubig attempted to help police by blocking the rear route of Kulak's escape. On the porch he met the gunman, who fatally shot him. Sergeant Schaffer heard the shot that killed Detective Stubig and raced to the back porch. Kulak fired on police. Schaffer, undeterred, returned fire and was mortally wounded in the ensuing gun battle.

Stubig, survived by his wife and six children, was a decorated hero whose reputation for persistence and tenacity left few cases under his watch unsolved. Over the course of his 16-year career he received three letters of commendation, seven "thank you" letters from the public and three honorable mentions. Before joining the Chicago Police Department he served his nation as a signal corps lineman in the U.S. Army. He and his family lived at 6352 N. Odell Avenue. He was buried in St. Joseph Cemetery.

Schaffer was also a military veteran who served with the U.S. Marines in Okinawa at the same time Kulak was also stationed there with the U.S. Army. A 21-year-veteran with the Chicago Police Department, Schaffer also was a colonel in the Army Reserve. Upon hearing the news of Schaffer's death, Speaker of the House John McCormack immediately phoned his condolences to the officer's widow and told the *Chicago Tribune*, "It's a great personal loss for me and my family." Schaffer guarded Speaker McCormack during the 1968

Democratic National Convention and they became close friends. Schaffer, who was survived by his wife and daughter, was held in high regard by his fellow officers, some whom even went so far as to call him "the most fearless policeman we ever knew" according to the *Chicago Tribune*. Schaffer had made his home at 2839 W. 82nd Street. He was interred in St. Mary Cemetery.

In February of 1970, Kulak was declared incompetent to stand trial due to paranoid schizophrenia. Prosecutors asked that he be confined to the state prison for the criminally insane at Chester and pledged to prosecute him for murder if he was ever found competent or released from the facility.

Patrolman Erwin Jackson,

STAR #12433, Area #4 Task Force, 33 years old, was shot and killed in the line of duty on April 24, 1969 when he and his partner, Patrolman Charles Spearman, responded to a report of a man brandishing a gun inside the Heat Wave Lounge at 3320 W. Roosevelt Road. At the tavern they encountered the man who had originally made the report with a female companion. The armed suspect, Bernard E. Barry, followed close behind. The officers ordered the man to drop his weapon. Barry refused. They then tried to disarm him by force. As Jackson and Spearman struggled with the suspect, three shots were fired. Two of the bullets struck Barry, a third struck Jackson in the chest. Officer Jackson was transported to Cook County Hospital and pronounced dead on arrival. Patrolman Jackson, a marine veteran who had joined the force on May 30, 1966, lived at 11538 S. Elizabeth Street with his wife, Caroline, his son, Darell, and two daughters, Stephanie and Kimberly. He was laid to rest at Burr Oak Cemetery.

Three guns were confiscated at the crime scene. One was found behind the bar of the lounge, the second was the weapon belonging to the assailant, and the third was Officer Spearman's service revolver. Analysis of the weapons showed that only Patrolman Spearman's gun had been fired, confirming Barry had attempted to discharge his own weapon but misfired. The offender recovered from his injuries and was charged with attempted murder of a policeman and unlawful use of a weapon. He was sentenced to 5-8 years in the Illinois State Penitentiary.

Patrolman John Stachnik,

STAR # unavailable, Central District, Motorcycle Division, 28 years old, was traveling south on Wabash Avenue on April 28, 1969 when he was thrown from his motorcycle during his routine patrol. Patrolman Stachnik was preparing to make a right turn onto 11th Street when the throttle of his motorcycle suddenly became stuck. He was thrown from his vehicle and struck his head on a street sign. Patrolman Stachnick was rushed to Mercy Hospital immediately after the accident and underwent emergency brain surgery. Despite these efforts, the officer succumbed to his injuries shortly after the operation.

Patrolman Leroy N. Berry, Jr.,

STAR #12789, 5th district, 27 years old, was shot and killed at 9540 S. Harvard Avenue in the parking lot of St. Thaddeus Catholic Church on October 9, 1969. Berry, who usually patrolled in a three man unit, was on duty alone that night. His two partners were reassigned because their station was short-handed after officers were transferred to the Near North Side to quell disorder there. Their absence left many questions surrounding Berry's death unanswered.

Patrolmen Berry was discovered lying next to his squad car by two priests from St. Thaddeus shortly after 10:00 P.M. on the night of October 9. Reverend Thomas Rafferty, the pastor of the church, and Reverend John Cassidy, an assistant pastor, had heard gunfire, approximately seven shots, around 9:50 P.M. Teenagers in the neighborhood had been using the church parking lot for drinking sprees and previously shot out nearby street lights. Father Rafferty and Father Cassidy eventually decided to approach the officer's vehicle because the squad's siren would not stop.

The priests saw two young men running across the nearby Chicago and Indiana railroad tracks as they found Patrolman Berry with multiple gunshot wounds. Investigating officers later theorized Berry took the two offenders into custody and placed them in the back of the squad car. While questioning them, one drew a weapon and fired at the officer from the back seat. Three bullet holes were found in the vehicle, one in the roof and one each in the two front, side windows. The two assailants then set off the car's siren, part of the vehicle's alarm system, when they opened the trunk to steal two shotguns. They took the officer's service revolver and police star before fleeing the scene.

Father Rafferty gave the Last Rites to the dying officer. He later blamed his death on the reduced patrolling in the area. Reports scattered across the floor of Berry's squad were carefully scrutinized to see if they could any clue to the identity of the assailants. Patrolman Berry, who was single, had joined the police force three years before his death. He was buried at Washington Memorial Cemetery in Homewood.

Sedrick Moore and Jonathan Brown were eventually arrested based on descriptions of the assailants provided by Fathers Rafferty and Cassidy and an unidentified witness.

Patrolman John J. Gilhooly,

STAR #3502, 2nd District, 21 years old, and

Patrolman Frank G. Rappaport,

STAR #12256, 3rd District, 32 years old, were responding to a false report of a man with a gun when they were ambushed and fatally shot by members of the Black Panthers on November 13, 1969. Gilhooly and Rappaport, part of a larger group of police sent to investigate the report, were trapped in the courtyard of a vacant building at 5801 S. Calumet Avenue. It was an ambush, "filled with ricocheting shotgun pellets and pieces of brick and cement from the buildings," according to a description given to the *Chicago Tribune* by the one of the policemen present at the scene.

Patrolmen Rappaport and Gilhooly were shot emerging from a gangway near the front porch of the building. Black Panther Spurgeon Winters, Jr., under the porch where the police officers stood, opened fire, hitting Rappaport in the chest and Gilhooly in the face and neck. Winters delivered the fatal shot to Patrolman Rappaport as he lay immobile and injured. Officer Robert Tracey came around the corner as the offender fired the final shot. He opened fire in Winters' direction, joined by Officer Phillip Prerosi. Prerosi, standing behind Rappaport when Winters started shooting, attempted to take the offender out but was momentarily incapacitated by a shotgun blast. He recovered in time to help Tracey. Winters was fatally injured in the gun battle.

When police gained control of the situation, it became clear that the bloodshed was extensive. Besides Rappaport and Gilhooly's fatal wounds, seven police officers were injured and another Black Panther was hurt. Officers Donald Miley and Daniel Coffman were both hospitalized with multiple gunshot wounds, while Black Panther Lawrence S. Bell was taken into custody after he was shot in the leg and right arm when he tried to flee the scene. He would eventually be charged with murder. Patrolman Gilhooly was transported to Billings Hospital with four gunshot wounds, paralyzed. He died shortly after midnight on November 14, 1969. Gilhooly, the 57th officer shot in the line of duty in 1969, was a second generation cop whose father, John Gilhooly, Sr., was a policeman in the Automotive Division of the Englewood District. In addition to his father, Patrolman Gihooly was survived by his brother, Francis, his sister Mrs. Patricia Olson and his fiancée. His mother died just the month before on October 13, 1969. Officer Gilhooly was laid to rest at Holy Sepulchre Cemetery.

Patrolman Rappaport was survived by his wife, Constance, and three young children Susan, Michael and Patricia. He had joined the police force on April 11, 1966. Officer Rappaport was buried in Cedar Park Cemetery.

Patrolman Samuel G. Lynch,

Star # unavailable, Central Station, Motorcycle Division, 46 years old, died on November 11, 1969, the victim of a hit-and-run driver at the intersection of Clark and Polk Streets. Lynch was discovered near his overturned three-wheel motorcycle. He was rushed Presbyterian-St. Luke Hospital, where he later died of his traumatic injuries. Officer Lynch, who joined the police force in 1957, lived with his wife, Astor, at 51 E. 87th Street.

Detective Oliver J. Singleton,

STAR #2131, Crime Intelligence Section, 42 years old, passed away on November 27, 1969, ten months after a gun battle at the Bell and Howell, Co. plant at 7100 N. McCormick Boulevard in Lincolnwood, Illinois left him paralyzed. Police had received a report that a Thillens, Inc. armored car would be held-up when it arrived to cash checks for the Bell and Howell, Co. night crew on January 24, 1969. Detective Singleton and his partner, Detective Frank Edwards, were part of a team of 18 police officers assigned to guard the plant after the information was received. They were stationed outside the factory when Larry Gibson, Tyron L. Oby and James Allen, attempted to pull off the robbery. Police engaged in a gun battle with the three robbers and killed Gibson and Oby. Singleton was fatally injured by a bullet to the back. The third suspect, Allen, was taken into custody and treated for a non-fatal wound to the back. Police sought another suspect, Nathan Wright, believed to be the mastermind behind the crime.

Allen was arrested and charged with attempted murder, attempted armed robbery, aggravated battery and conspiracy. On October 30, 1969, Detective Singleton testified from a hospital stretcher about the events that led to his paralysis, leading to Allen's conviction on all charges. Singleton passed away only days before the offender's sentencing and prosecutors decided to amend the charges against Allen to include murder. Allen and another accomplice, Nathan Wright, were indicted for murder on December 5, 1969. Both men were convicted of Detective Singleton's murder. Allen was sentenced to 100 to 200 years while Wright received 75 to 150 years in prison.

Detective Singleton, a World War II veteran, died at the Veteran's Administration Research Hospital and was buried in his native Springfield, Illinois a week after his death. The sixteen-year-veteran was survived by his wife Patricia, parents Oliver and Rosalia Singleton, two sisters Mrs. Doralyn Young and Mrs. Sally Hynes and his brother Robert Singleton. The detective had met his wife when she was employed as a civilian worker at the Westside detective headquarters in 1961. Visitation was held at the Griffin Funeral Home, 3232 S. King Drive with the funeral mass held at the Episcopal Cathedral of St. James, 33 E. Huron Street. He was buried in Springfield, Illinois.

Lieutenant James E. O'Connor,

STAR #434, 5th District, Kensington Station, 62 years old, was killed while attempting to stop an armed robbery on January 28, 1970. O'Connor was at the Imperial Credit Company, 11048 S. Michigan Avenue, with Officer Raymond Calabrese when the offender, Michael Miller, entered the office with a gun in one hand and the other hand covering his face. Officer O'Connor spotted the gun in Miller's hand and lunged at him. A struggle began and Miller's gun went off. The bullet hit the lieutenant and the offender fled. As Calabrese chased the offender he was joined by Detectives Peter Valesares and John L. Sullivan, who were in a restaurant across the street at the time of the gunfire. They cornered Miller in a parking lot at 111th and State Streets. A short gun battle erupted before Miller was arrested. A .38-caliber revolver with two empty chambers was found in the parking lot.

Police also arrested Ronnie Johnson as Miller's accomplice. He waited in a getaway car near the credit company. Both were charged with murder. On March 20, 1970, Ronnie Johnson was found hanged in his cell at Cook County Jail. After his accomplice's death, Miller pled guilty and was sentenced 50 to 100 years for the murder of Lieutenant O'Connor. Miller was also given 10 to 14 years for attempted armed robbery.

Lieutenant O'Connor was planning to retire in August after 37 years service. He joined the force on March 23, 1933 and was appointed lieutenant on August 1, 1954. Police work was a family occupation for the O'Connor family with three siblings, two brothers and a sister, sworn police officers. The lieutenant was survived by his wife, Theresa, three daughters, Mary Therese, Kathleen, and Patricia and two sons, James Jr. and Timothy. He was interred at Holy Sepulchre Cemetery.

Patrolman Thomas J. Kelly,

STAR #12145, Area 1 Task Force, 26 years old, died from a gunshot wound inflicted during a routine traffic stop on March 3, 1970. Kelly and his partner, Officer Thomas C. Neustrom, observed a traffic violation and stopped a car with two men at 360 E. 44th Street. As they approached the car, Kelly stood outside as Neustrom searched the interior. Suddenly, one of the vehicle's occupants pulled a gun, fatally shooting Patrolman Kelly. Upon hearing the gunshots, Neustrom tried to draw his own gun but was struck twice and incapacitated before he could return fire. When they attempted to shoot Patrolman Neustron a third time, their gun misfired and they escaped on foot.

Charles H. Connolly and Frank Luckett were discovered later that same day at 6543 S. Wood Street. More than 100 police and firemen surrounded the building and fired tear gas through windows. Connolly was later found guilty of the murder of Patrolman Kelly and aggravated battery in connection with the shooting of Patrolman Neustrion. He received the death penalty until the courts ruled against it. The sentence was changed to life in prison.

Patrolman Neustrom made a full recovery. Officer Kelly's injuries proved fatal and he was pronounced dead on his arrival at Provident Hospital. Kelly, a four-year veteran of the force, was survived by his parents, John and Anne; brothers, Jack and Robert; and his fiancée, Joanne Polo. He was buried at St. Mary Cemetery.

Patrolman Casey Tristano,

STAR #1304, Shakespeare Avenue Station, Area Youth Division, 45 years old, suffered a fatal a heart attack while trying to break up a fight at Our Lady Help of Christian Catholic Church on March 13, 1970. Officer Tristano was called to the church, 832 N. Leclair Avenue, when a fight broke out during a dance being held at the adjacent school. Upon his arrival, Tristano found Officer William Healy struggling with Joseph Maltese, age 17. Officer Tristano was struck in the mouth and nose by Maltese as he attempted to help Healy subdue the offender. Tristano's breathing became labored shortly after he was hit and he died before he could be transported to the hospital.

A total of five youths were arrested in connection with the confrontation at the dance. Four were released after posting a $25 bond while Maltese was required to post a $1,000 bond. Maltese was eventually charged with battery, resisting arrest and disorderly conduct. In the end, he was fined only $25 for his part in the altercation. The charges against the other four young men were dropped. Officer Tristano had been on the force for 16 years at the time of his death and was survived by his wife, Marilyn, and two children, Maria and Casey, Jr. He and his family lived at 6800 N. Ionia Street and his funeral Mass was celebrated at St. Mary of the Woods Church. Interment took place at Queen of Heaven Cemetery.

Patrolman Melvin E. Brown,

STAR #12360, 3rd District, 30 years old, was investigating the shooting of an off-duty police officer when he lost his life in the line of duty on June 2, 1970. Officer Brown was at the New Pioneer Lounge, 1200 E. 71st Street, talking with the bartender, Hershell Spencer, when a man entered and asked for a sandwich. When Spencer said the kitchen was closed, the man moved toward the bathroom. Brown and Spencer, were lost in conversation when the stranger suddenly turned around and pulled a gun. Patrolman Brown tried to wrestle the weapon away from the offender rather than risk a gun battle amid bystanders. He managed to subdue the assailant and was placing him under arrest when the offender's two accomplices entered the lounge and fired several shots at the patrolman. The officer fired back twice before his gun jammed. Brown and Spencer, both hit by the gunfire, were taken to Billings Hospital. Spencer survived, but Brown died on June 3, 1970. Patrolman Brown was survived by his wife, Albertyne, and his daughter, Lezah, and buried in Lincoln Cemetery.

Patrolman Kenneth G. Kaner,

STAR #2662, 7th District, Englewood Station, 33 years old, was sitting in his squad car at 74th Street and Union Avenue filing a missing persons report on June 19, 1970 when he was killed in the line of duty. Kaner had just finished questioning five men he believed might have information about a missing individual. When he returned to his squad car a shotgun blast shattered his window. Kaner was hit in the head by the blast and died en route to St. Bernard Hospital. Five armed men were arrested three blocks from the scene after being pulled over for an unrelated traffic violation. Bruce Sharp, 24, whose brother was a Chicago Police Officer, admitted to shooting the officer and was indicted for his murder along with Dwight Cavin, 17, Bradely Green, 23, William Redwine, 23 and Jerome Amos, 23. All of the men but Amos were found guilty and given varying prison sentences. Sharp was given 30 to 125 years.

Officer Kaner, a nine-year-veteran of the force, was survived by his wife, Pauline; his daughter, Kimberly; and his son, Kurt, who is now a member of the Chicago Police Department. Kaner, who had been a Golden Gloves Middleweight Boxing Champion, was honored posthumously for his heroism. He was laid to rest in St. Mary Cemetery.

Mayor Richard J. Daley stands in front of the statue commemorating policemen who lost their lives in the Haymarket riot shortly after its restoration following damage by a bomb (May 5, 1970). *Chicago Tribune* Photo Archive.

Patrolman Anthony N. Rizzato,
STAR #12407, Area 6 Task Force, 37 years old, and
Sergeant James L. Severin,
STAR #1319, Area 6 Task Force, 38 years old, were killed on
July 17, 1970 while patrolling the Cabrini-Green housing
project near Seward Park in the vicinity of West Division and North Larabee Streets.
The two officers were assigned to the "Walk and Talk" program, intended to decrease the
growing anti-police sentiment in the public housing projects. Police came under almost
nightly gunfire in the months since the program was established.

Rizzato and Severin were walking through a baseball field in Seward Park on a
routine patrol when they were cut down by sniper fire from the nearby high-rises. Police
cars quickly arrived on the scene and formed a shield between the fallen officers and the
project buildings so that Rizzato and Severin could be placed in the cars and transported
to Henrotin Hospital. They were both pronounced dead on arrival.

After the siege at Seward Park ended, Deputy Superintendent James M. Rochford set
in motion an apartment-by-apartment search of the complex to find the killers. Four young
men, Johnnie Veal, 18, George Knight, 23, Sidney Bennett, 18, and Vernon Baker, 14, were
arrested during the search. All were eventually charged with murder. Veal and Knight
were each tried and sentenced to 199 years in prison in 1972.

Officer Rizzato was survived by his wife, Rosarino; daughter, Rose, and son,
Anthony. His Funeral Mass was celebrated at Queen of Angeles Catholic Church and he
was buried in St. Joseph Cemetery. Officer Severin was survived by his mother, Catherine;
brother, William and two sisters, Catherine and Joan. His Funeral Mass was celebrated at
Immaculate Conception Catholic Church and he was interred at All Saints Cemetery.

Patrolman James A. Alfano, Jr.,
STAR #4707, Gang Intelligence Section, 30 years old, died on August 16,
1970, two days after being fatally shot in the line of duty. Alfano had been
in an unmarked police car in an alley behind the Southmoor Hotel at 6646
S. Stony Island Avenue when he was hit by two bullets fired by a sniper.
He was ambushed in the alley, leading investigators to believe that the shooting was a
conspiracy aimed at killing a policeman.

Alfano was transported to Billings Hospital after the incident. He survived for
over 70 hours, enduring numerous operations. More than 250 people donated Alfano's rare
AB-positive blood type to the hospital, hoping to save the much decorated officer. He
received 28 "honorable mentions" in his eight years on the police force. Alfano, who was
an ex-Marine and avid skydiver in his free time, was remembered as a "tough but gentle"
man who believed it was his duty to be in hot spots and dangerous locations. He was
survived by his wife, Judy, two children and his parents. Patrolman Alfano was buried him
in St. Mary Cemetery.

Police believed the Black P Stone Nation, a gang that had taken over the Southmoor
Hotel in recent months, was responsible for the officer's death, as well as a large amount
of additional violence across the city. Twenty-three persons were arrested in the aftermath
of the killing. Three men believed to be leaders of the gang were eventually charged with
conspiracy to murder. Tony Carter, 17, one of the suspected leaders of the Black P Stone
Nation, surrendered on a murder warrant in late September. Seven men were eventually
tried for the officer's murder but all were acquitted on January 17, 1971.

Patrolman John J. Matonich,

STAR # 5760, Task Force Detail, 33 years old, was killed in the line of duty on October 16, 1970 near the old Chicago Stadium. The events leading up to Officer Matonich's death began when Ronald Davis hailed a cab from Union Station to 1600 W. Adams Street. As the cab approached the address, the driver, Mark Osberg, was told to go to Madison Street and Winchester Avenue instead. As the cab arrived at the intersection, Davis pulled out a pistol and told Osberg to get out of the vehicle. The offender then fled the scene in Osberg's cab.

Osberg hailed the first policeman that he saw, Officer Warren Lindvig, and the two began to chase after the offender. A short time later, Davis crashed the cab into two parked cars near the Gate 1 entrance of the old Chicago Stadium, where a game between the Chicago Bulls and the Los Angeles Lakers was about to begin. Realizing that the vehicle was unusable, the offender attempted to escape on foot. Officer Matonich and Sergeant Timothy Allman were running to the accident scene to offer aid when Davis opened fire on them, hitting Matonich numerous times. Matonich returned fire three times before he collapsed and died. Officer Lindvig, who had snuck up behind Davis, fired two fatal shots at the offender, hitting him in the head and shoulder. Davis, who had an arrest record but no convictions, was taken to Cook County Hospital and pronounced dead on arrival. Patrolman Matonich had been on the force for nine years at the time of his death. The officer was survived by his wife, Irene, and buried at Holy Cross Cemetery.

Patrolman Paul G. Thomas, Jr.,

STAR #5620, 6th District, Gresham Station, 43 years old, was shot during an armed robbery on November 4, 1970. The officer was with his father in the rear office of a news agency he operated at 556 W. 103rd Street when two men entered through the back door. Thomas' father went to investigate and struggled with one of the armed offenders. When Officer Thomas saw that the man was carrying a gun, he drew his own weapon. He barely had time to aim his gun before the assailant opened fire, hitting him in the chest, right thigh and right hand. Thomas managed to return fire as he fell, but the two men were able to escape. After the shooting, Officer Thomas was rushed to Presbyterian-St. Luke Hospital and received treatment. He was eventually discharged from the hospital, but later developed an infection which caused a high fever and internal bleeding. Taken to Roseland Community Hospital, he died on November 20, 1970. He was survived by his wife, Barbara, three sons, and a daughter and buried in St. Casimir Cemetery. Otis Haywood and Alphonso Newman, who were arrested in 1972 on separate murder charges, were ultimately identified as Officer Thomas' killers.

Foster Avenue Station, 20th District (1960s).
Chicago Police Department Photo Archive.

Patrolman Paul G. Thomas, Jr.'s widow,
Barbara, stands with her two of her children,
Paul Thomas III and Connie, outside St. Helena
of the Cross Catholic Church after the
officer's Funeral Mass (November 11, 1970).
Chicago Tribune Photo Archive.

Patrolman Edgar J. Bronson, Jr.,

STAR #13534, 11th District, Filmore Station, 27 years old, was an eight-year-veteran of the Chicago Police Department when he was killed on January 30, 1971 attempting to settle a gambling dispute at a cab stand at 4021 W. 16th Street. Bronson, a Community Service Officer, had been called to the cab stand by a friend who had lost money to a notorious gambler known as "Big Red." Bronson arrived and confronted "Big Red," also known as Eddie Outley, Jr.

At some point during the argument, Outley pulled out a hand gun, leading the man who had summoned the patrolman to inform the assailant that Bronson was a cop. "Big Red" placed his weapon against the officer's head and took a single shot before calmly walking away. A massive police search for Outley quickly spread across the Southside of the city where he was believed to live. He was arrested and tried for the officer's murder but was acquitted. Bronson, who lived at 1501 S. Karlov Street, was transported to Mount Sinai Hospital and pronounced dead shortly after arrival. Bronson, who was unmarried and lived with his aunt, Mrs. Juanita Mayfield, was interred at Lincoln Cemetery.

Patrolman Melvin A. Galloway, Jr.,

STAR #13794, 15th District, Austin District Tactical Team, 30 years old, was slain on March 21, 1971 during a plain clothes vice investigation at the Sabre Cocktail Lounge at 5611 W. Grand Avenue. Galloway was working on the investigation with several other officers, including Patrolmen James Ahern; Joseph Herman, Patrick Crowley and Sergeant William Alexander. Homicide detectives were later able to determine that the five policemen were sitting at the bar when an argument broke out between them and several patrons. Allegedly, the argument was over the length of Galloway's sideburns.

A brawl ensued, during which Amzi Freeman, a 26-year-old railroad switchman, drew a knife and stabbed Galloway, Ahern, Alexander, and Crowley. It is believed that, amidst the confusion of the fight, Freeman took one of the policemen's service revolvers and used it to shoot Galloway. Patrolman Crowley fired back at Freeman, killing him in the tavern. Patrolman Galloway was taken to St. Anne Hospital where he was pronounced dead on arrival. The other officers at the scene were treated for cuts and bruises and released. Galloway was survived by his son, David, and buried in Memory Gardens Cemetery in Arlington Heights.

1971

Patrolman Irwin F. 'Irv' Hayden,

STAR # 4005, Traffic Division, was killed in a helicopter crash on August 10, 1971. Assigned to temporarily replace Helicopter Officer Leonard Baldy after Baldy crashed in 1960, he stayed on in the position for more than a decade. Hayden was a member of the Education and Safety Unit of the Traffic Patrol Division and gave lectures regarding traffic safety in his free time. Over the years Hayden had logged 11,000 hours of flight time while broadcasting traffic reports to drivers in and around the Chicago area. On August 10, the traffic helicopter struck a utility pole and high-voltage power lines before exploding on the ground at an empty baseball field in Bellwood near the Eisenhower Expressway. The pilot, David Demarest, was also killed in the crash. The helicopter may have been buffeted out of control by high winds moving into the area. Officer Hayden was a police veteran of 23 years and had lived at 1536 W. Thome Avenue. He was survived by his wife, Margaret, and their three grown children, Margarat, Thomas and Patricia. The family interred the officer at St. Joseph Cemetery.

Fillmore Street Station, 11th District (1960s).
Chicago Police Department Photo Archive.

Patrolman William H. Johnson,

STAR # unavailable, 18th District, Cabrini-Green Project Patrol, 38 years old, was shot and killed on September 26, 1971 outside his apartment. Johnson, who had been sent home from work early due to illness, returned to his home at 344 S. Hamlin Avenue and left his 1971 Cadillac EL Dorado double parked with the blinkers on while he went inside his home to change clothes. He returned to his car around 2:00 A.M. and was in the process of placing his uniform, gun and badge inside the trunk when several shots were fired. Neighbors rushed outside and found Johnson lying on the ground next to his car, fatally injured by bullet wounds to his heart. Johnson was rushed to Garfield Park Hospital. He was pronounced dead on arrival.

Two days after Johnson's death, Homicide Commander William Keating reported that Johnson's pocket contained $768 in cash. Additional information later revealed that a .38 caliber snub-nose revolver, which Johnson always carried with him when he was off-duty, was missing from his body when he was discovered.

Several days later, David Sanders, 31, and James Willie Woods, 23, were arrested after bullets fired at a jewelry store robbery on Jackson Boulevard were found to be identical to those that killed Johnson. Sanders and Woods, both heroin addicts with lengthy jail records, were denied bail and soon confessed to killing Johnson after a failed robbery attempt. In their panic, they left the $768 in Johnson's wallet when they fled. The offenders were tried but acquitted of Patrolman Johnson's murder.

Johnson, a 14-year-veteran of the police force, was originally part of the Albany Park Police in the 19th District. Johnson lived alone and was survived by his brother, John, and his two sisters, Lessie and Tillie.

Patrolman Melvin Cohen,

STAR # unavailable, Shakespeare District Traffic Unit, 38 years old, was pursuing a speeding motorist on his police motorcycle on Lake Street on December 7, 1971 when he lost control of the three wheeled vehicle and struck a pillar of the Lake Street "EL" at 4702 W. Lake Street. The speeding motorist escaped and was never located. Cohen, who joined the force in 1955 and had received numerous commendations, was a member of the National Guard, and an avid scuba diver. He was buried at B'nal Jehoshua Cemetery and survived by his wife, Minette; daughter, Jodie; and son, Steven.

Patrolman Robert L. Gallowitch,

STAR #15442, 5th District, Kensington Station, 30 years old, was fatally shot on May 24, 1972 while attempting to stop a robbery at Wittgren Jewelers, 8649 S. Cottage Grove Avenue. Gallowitch responded to a burglar alarm with fellow officers, Kenneth Jacobs and Paul McGrath. He stationed himself in the back alley while the other two policemen went to the front of the store. He encountered three men disguised as telephone repairmen, who opened fire on him and shot him in the abdomen. Gallowitch returned fire and hit Frederick C. Lancaster in the arm and leg.

Lancaster tried to escape in an Illinois Bell Telephone truck that the robbers had stolen, but he was blocked by Gallowitch's parked car. He was arrested by Officers Jacobs and McGrath and turned in his fellow conspirators, Galvin Jackson and Wilbert Droughns. Gallowitch was taken to Jackson Park Hospital where he died several hours later, survived by his parents, brother and stepsister. His funeral was held at Annunciata Church Burial in Evergreen Park Cemetery. Gallowitch had been on the police force for 17 months.

All three offenders were later charged with murder, robbery, unlawful restraint and conspiracy to commit robbery. Lancaster pled guilty to Officer Gallowitch's murder and was sentenced to 20 to 40 years in prison. The offender, who suffered from kidney disease and needed frequent dialysis, was released from prison at one point but ordered to return in 1982 by a higher court.

Patrolman James R. Scannell,

STAR # unavailable, 47 years old, suffered a heart attack on July 7, 1972 while attempting to arrest Christopher Pacelli, 24, in front of the Rush Up Lounge at 909 N. Rush Street. Scannell was with Officers Marion Sykes and George Alvarado when they tried to place Pacelli into the squadrol. After Pacelli was finally put in the car, a man passing by opened the door to the police car and the offender exited the vehicle. A second struggle ensued and Scannell collapsed to the ground. Skyes and Alvarado performed mouth-to-mouth resuscitation to save Scannell but they were unsuccessful. The officers did arrest Pacelli and he was charged with disorderly conduct and resisting arrest. Officer Scannell left behind a wife and nine children.

1972

The Starr Hotel, a Madison Street flop house that once counted the infamous mass murderer Richard Speck among its guests (c.1960s). Chicago History Museum Photo Archive.

Detective Edward M. Madden,

STAR #7711, Crime Intelligence Division, Area 6 Robbery Section, 26 years old, was fatally wounded by accidental gunfire on September 28, 1972 while investigating a suspicious individual at an apartment at 1464 W. Olive Street. Madden and his partner, who both worked out of the Damen Avenue Robbery Unit, were searching the apartment for a robbery suspect at the same time as another officer, Glenn Shurtleff. He was working the case independently and had come to the Olive Street address in search of a man who had disarmed him earlier in the day. When Shurtleff saw Madden appear on the second floor of the building, he opened fire thinking he was the suspect. Patrolman Madden was fatally wounded in the back of the neck and died in Edgewater Hospital on October 2, 1972. He was buried at St. Joseph Cemetery, survived by his parents and five siblings.

Patrolman Edgar DeCuir,

STAR # unavailable, 2nd District, was working in the detention facility on December 22, 1972 when he suffered a fatal heart attack. While processing a prisoner, he was assaulted and a struggle ensued. The prisoner was subdued, but Officer DeCuir experienced a heart attack, dying instantly.

Patrolman Robert F. Wenzel,

STAR #7495, Traffic Division Area 6, 36 years old, was killed in the line of duty on January 19, 1973, while in his squad at 1900 N. Lake Shore Drive in Lincoln Park. The occupants of the car he had pulled over began firing at him. Witnesses from a city engineering crew told police that Wenzel fired six shots before he collapsed near his squad car. He was taken to Augustana Hospital and pronounced dead upon arrival, shot twice in the chin, once in the neck and once in the back.

The shooter, Richard Luckey, hit by multiples bullets, was found near the scene not far from the officer's vehicle. He was charged with murder as police began looking for his alleged accomplice, Jospeh Lee Bolden or Bolten. Luckey, a paraplegic as the result of a bullet lodged near his spine, told police that he and Bolten were looking for a place to rob after leaving a tavern when they ran into Officer Wenzel. Luckey was found guilty of his death and sentenced to 75 to 100 years in the Illinois State Penitentiary at Joliet. Bolten was never found.

Wenzel, an 11-year-veteran, was laid to rest in Acacia Park Cemetery. He left a widow, Rose, three sons, Michael, Daniel, and Robert; and one daughter, Colleen.

Sergeant Michael F. Maguire,

STAR # unavailable, Damen Avenue Station, 45 years old, was a 16-year-veteran of the Chicago Police Department and a sergeant since 1965. He resided at 7123 N. Ottawa Avenue with his wife and three children until he was found shot to death on January 24, 1973.

Sergeant Maguire was found in the parking area of Martha Washington Hospital at 2319 W. Belle Plaine Avenue, shot through the head. His police star was found beneath his body and his .38 caliber service revolver was near his hand. It was reported that Maguire had gone to dinner alone around 8:00 P.M., stopping at a nearby restaurant before he, for unknown reasons, walked to the hospital parking area.

A hospital security guard heard three shots fired at about 9:00 P.M. and found the sergeant's body lying in the parking lot. Maguire was given emergency care and then rushed to Ravenswood Hospital for neurosurgery. The officer died before the surgery was performed.

The police department was left mystified as to why the sergeant was killed. Investigations found no reasons for suicide. Burial was in All Saints Cemetery.

Patrolman Robert Wenzel's widow, Rose, clutches her husband's posthumous award for bravery, which she accepted on his behalf (October 9, 1973). *Chicago Tribune* Photo Archive.

Patrolman Wendell H. Hicks,

STAR #11561, 5th District, Kensington Station, 41 years old, was killed in the line of duty on March 29, 1973. Hicks, who was unarmed, had just finished bowling at 7500 S. Prairie. He was leaving the bowling alley when he witnessed a CTA driver, Clarence Turner, being robbed and attempted to help the victim. Patrolman Hicks called out he was a policeman and ordered the assailants to stop. One of the offenders fled by foot while the second jumped into Turner's car and took off. Hicks followed in his own vehicle and chased the suspect to an alley on 69th Street between Michigan and Indiana Avenues. The assailant's vehicle skidded on wet pavement and crashed into a fence. The offender then got out of the stolen car and shot Officer Hicks before taking both his service revolver and police star. When police arrived on the scene Hicks had a bullet wound to the chest and was pronounced dead. The assailants, Charles Thompson and Herman Reese, were later caught and convicted of murder and armed robbery.

Hicks, who lived at 8054 S. Dante Avenue, was buried in Burr Oak Cemetery and survived by his wife, Celestine, and two daughters, Sharon and Alicia. He had served with the Chicago Police Department for 14 years and had been shot and wounded in 1968 in the line of duty. During his career Hicks received 15 honorable mentions as well as a department commendation. Hicks' was also awarded the blue star and the silver star for his heroic actions on the night of his death.

Patrolman Louis Cullotta,

STAR #11801, 20th District, Foster Avenue Station, 29 years old, was shot to death in The Lunch Pail restaurant at 1038 W. Wilson Avenue on July 26, 1973. Cullotta, of 3651 N. Tripp Avenue, was working part time at the restaurant when he was killed. The assailant was identified as 22-year-old George E. Lyons, a man with two previous counts of attempted murder. Lyons allegedly walked into the restaurant, shot Cullotta who was working behind the counter, and then ran out of the establishment. He was quickly apprehended by two nearby on-duty officers, Sergeants Joseph Mackey and Robert Geib, who had heard the shot and given chase when they were told of the shooting by a bystander. Captain George A. McMahon admitted that police were not certain of the killer's motive, but added that this could have been a grudge slaying since Cullotta was "well-known among persons he arrested." Later investigation showed that Cullotta had interrogated Lyons three years earlier, which could have prompted the 1973 murder.

Cullotta was pronounced dead upon arrival at Weiss Memorial Hospital. He left behind a wife, Elizabeth; and two sons, Michael and James. Patrolman Cullota was buried at St. Joseph Cemetery.

Patrolman Thomas J. Adams, Jr.,

STAR #2210, Police Training Division, Fillmore Station, was found dead on the porch of a home at 3339 W. Douglas Boulevard on Sunday, August 26, 1973. Adams had joined the police force because of his concern over street crime in the city. The officer had recently asked for a transfer because he felt that he was not able to fulfill his obligations as a policeman at his current post. Joe Adams, the brother of the deceased, said his brother was in the Starfire Lounge at Homan Avenue and Grenshaw Street on Saturday night before his death. Patrolman Adams, there with his sister, pointed out two women he had once arrested on prostitution charges. He was later seen leaving the tavern around 2:30 A.M. with the two women, who entered his car with him and drove away.

Marquette District Police later responded to a call of shots fired in the 3300 block of W. Douglas and found Adams' body. A .38 caliber was found at the scene, which authorities believed was used to kill the officer. Adams' gun, wallet and keys were missing. Police traced the weapon they found, registered to Darryl "Doc" Smith. It was believed that Adams had gone to investigate a disturbance at the Douglas Boulevard address and was fatally shot by Smith. The offender surrendered to the Wentworth Robbery Detectives two days after the shooting. Patrolman Adams had been on the force since February and was survived by his wife, Dorothy; and sons, Mark and Daryl. He was buried at Washington Memorial Cemetery in Homewood.

Patrolman Edward L. Barron,

STAR #14571, 4th District, 36 years old, died in the line of duty on September 28, 1973 while pursuing a robbery suspect on the Southside. Barron, who lived at 9475 S. Ewing Avenue, and his partner, Patrolman Daniel P. Abate, followed a 16-year-old suspect, Joseph Bigsby, into an alley on S. Colfax Avenue. Bigsby had reportedly robbed an elderly man.

Barron and Abate were called to the scene along with Sergeants John Mitchell and Anthony Norka. The sergeants had already been in a fire fight with Bigsby before he encountered Barron and Abate. Both shouted at the teen to halt. Then Bigsby fired at them with a 9 mm automatic pistol. Abate hit the gunman in the calf at the same moment Barron fell to the ground with a bullet wound to the head.

After subduing the shooter, Abate tended to Barron, his partner since 1970. The two were very close and often talked about the possibility of dying on the job. Barron was survived by wife, Nancy; son Paul, 14; and daughter Linda, 13. He was interred at St. Mary Cemetery.

Bigsby, the 16-year-old shooter, was arrested and charged with murder, attempted murder and armed robbery. The youth had already accumulated a lengthy juvenile record. He was convicted of the policeman's murder on May 29, 1975 and sentenced to 100 to 200 years in prison.

Patrolman James W. Campbell,

STAR #15250, 9th District, Deering Station, was shot inside a Currency Exchange at 5111 S. Halsted Street on February 1, 1974. Campbell regularly stopped at the exchange, and other area businesses, each day to provide a visible police presence to the neighborhood residents. As the officer was filling out his money order two unknown assailants entered, took Campbell's gun from the holster and shot him four times in the back. The shots severed his spinal cord, partially paralyzing him. Officer Campbell was taken to Billings Hospital, where he died on February 9 after undergoing open-heart surgery necessitated by two heart attacks. He was survived by his fiancée, Yvette Stamps, and two children, Antionette and Darren. The officer was interred at Burr Oak Cemetery. Campbell was a member of the U. S. Air Force from 1963 to 1967 and joined the Chicago Police Department in 1971.

Alderman Anna Langford of the 16th Ward expressed grief over the death of the officer and many people sent their sympathy to the family with the hopes that it would help them cope. The alderman and the Chicago Police Captains Association each offered a $1,000 reward for any information regarding the two robbers. The Community Currency Exchange Association of Illinois offered a $5,000 reward for any leads regarding the incident. Patrolman Campbell's murderer was never apprehended.

Patrolman Bruce N. Garrison,

STAR #14775, Special Operations Group Area 6, 29 years old, and

Patrolman William C. Marsek,

STAR #14086, Special Operations Group Area 6, 28 years old, were both killed in Raven's Pub at 1818 W. Foster Avenue on February 27, 1974 by a wanted fugitive. The two officers were on patrol in their squad car when they noticed a suspicious person enter the tavern, located at the northwest corner of Foster Avenue and Honore Street. Witnesses described the man as conservatively dressed, around 30 years old and said he had been drinking alone for 45 minutes when he left, only to return 20 minutes later.

Garrison and Marsek followed him into the tavern so quickly that they left both doors of the squad car open. A struggle ensued, during which the killer drew a pistol and shot each of the policemen twice. Both died instantly from wounds to the head and chest. Garrison and Marsek had been partners for two and a half years and both had received numerous commendations for good police work. Officer Garrison was buried in Oak Ridge Cemetery. Officer Marsek was laid to rest in Maryhill Cemetery.

The killer, later identified as Jacob Cohen, also known as Paul Robson, had previously served seven years in Stateville Prison for auto theft and burglary. After robbing a Schaumburg jewelry store in 1973, he failed to appear in court, resulting in an FBI warrant against him. After his latest crime, Cohen fled to Wisconsin, where he was killed in a gun battle with the Milwaukee Police.

Patrolman William S. Bodnar, Jr.

STAR #14642, Central District Station, 24 years old and

Patrolman Thomas A. Wodarczyk,

STAR #10530, Central District Station, 34 years old, were killed during a vehicle pursuit on April 8, 1974. The two officers had been chasing a white 1964 Oldsmobile, believed to have been stolen. Frank Scimica, a truck driver traveling north on Morgan Street, collided with the policemen at Van Buren and Morgan Streets. Scimica had an obstructed view and did not see the oncoming squad car. The officers' vehicle crashed into the rear of Simica's produce truck as he proceeded through a green light. Both patrolmen were immediately killed on impact. The stolen Oldsmobile fled. It was found abandoned a short distance from the accident. Officer Bodnar was survived by his wife, Gloria; and two young children, William and Wendy. He had been on the force for four years. Officer Wodarczyk had just celebrated his first year on the force. He left behind a wife, Patricia; and three children, Mark, Anita and David. Both officers were buried at St. Mary Cemetery.

Patrolman Robert J. Strugala,

STAR #10236, 10th District, Marquette Station, 29 years old, was killed in the line of duty on June 16, 1974 in a tavern at 3157 W. 26th Street. Strugala was stopped at a traffic light at 26th Street and Kedzie Avenue with his partner, Patrolman John Wasco, when they heard gunshots coming from the tavern. Multiple gunmen were firing shots at the bartender, Julian Ortiz. The two went to investigate.

Strugala and Wasco entered the tavern from different doors with guns drawn and ordered the assailants to drop their weapons. One of the assailants fired at Wasco with an automatic pistol, knocking Wasco out the door with the force of the gun. It is unknown whether it was the same gunman or one of his accomplices who proceeded to shoot Strugala in the chest, killing him instantly. The firefight lasted less than 30 seconds. A barmaid, Guadalupe Lazzaraga, and another patron, Jesus Posatos, were injured in the attack. One of the offenders, Jose Guillen, was also injured. He was later charged with Strugala's murder.

Strugala, survived by his wife, Christine; and son, Robert, was interred in Resurrection Cemetery. Patrolman Wasco was taken to Mount Sinai Hospital, where he made a full recovery and returned to duty. On June 15, 2004 Wasco retired. Guillen, who had been sentenced to 50 to 100 years in State Prison for Strugala's murder, was released from custody on July 19, 2004, after serving only 30 years of his sentence. Guillen was also charged with attempted murder of Wasco and was sentenced to 10 to 30 years; the two sentences were served concurrently. Antonio Guillen was also wanted for the crime but was never found.

Sergeant Otha M. LeMons,

Star #1048, 5th District, 54 years old, was fatally shot in the line of duty on August 5, 1974 while checking in on his uncle, Arthur Hadley, owner of the Pepsi Lounge at 62 E. 103rd Street. Three weeks prior, the lounge had been the scene of a robbery and LeMons had been stopping by during his free time to keep on eye on the place. Early on the morning of August 5, three armed men came into the lounge and announced a robbery. It was believed that the robbers knew LeMons was a member of the police force despite his plain clothes. They shot LeMons six times before jumping into a tan 1970 Buick Electra without license plates, escaping with a large amount of cash. A suspect's fingerprints were found on the bar and valuable descriptions of the men were provided by six witnesses to the shooting. Willie "Will Kill" Jefferson was identified as the officer's killer two days after the shooting. He was charged with murder and four counts of armed robbery. Larry Collins, 16 years old, was identified in a juvenile petition as Jefferson's accomplice. Three other gang members were also arrested for their part in the shooting and robbery.

LeMons was buried in St. Mary Cemetery. He was survived by his wife, Veradun; his daughter, Babette;, and two grandchildren, Monet and Byron. The policeman had been on the force for 24 years, promoted to sergeant in 1972. LeMons was originally attached to the Kensington Street Station.

Chicago Lawn Station, 8th District (1960s).
Chicago Police Department Photo Archive.

Patrolman Thomas J. Glynn,

STAR # 6933, Chicago Lawn Station, 41 years old, collapsed on September 20, 1974 in front of the district station at 3515 W. 63rd Street after being involved in a fight in Hale Park, located at 6258 W. 62nd Street. Officer Glynn and his partner, Officer William Murphy, were patrolling the park when they spotted a woman previously arrested and ordered to stay away from the area. When Officers Glynn and Murphy asked the woman to leave her male companion, David Bridges, attacked the two policemen, leaving both of them with torn shirts and bruises. Officer Glynn, a 21-year-veteran, suffered a heart attack after the altercation. Efforts were made to save him, but he died at Holy Cross Hospital. Patrolman Glynn left a wife and seven children. Bridges was charged with two counts of aggravated battery and one count of obstructing police. Officer Glynn was buried at St. Mary Cemetery.

Patrolman Harl G. Meister, Jr.

STAR #10054, 10th District, 36 years old, was shopping with his eight-year-old son, Harold, when he was shot and killed at 5601 S. Cicero Avenue on December 23, 1974. Meister and his son had just finished some last minute Christmas shopping when they were approached by four youths announcing a stickup with a .22 caliber revolver. Meister reached his own gun but was unable to stop the shooter from firing, fatally wounding him and severely wounding young Harold in the jaw and shoulder. Harold survived, but his father was pronounced dead on arrival at Holy Cross Hospital.

Anthony Freeman, 16, was identified as the gunman and tried as an adult for Patrolman Meister's murder. He was convicted and sentenced to 20 to 50 years in prison. One accomplice, Anthony Reese, 16, was convicted of felony murder and sentenced to 14 to 20 years in prison. The two other young men, Charles Jakes, 18, and Nathaniel Dudley, 17, were each sentenced to 3 to 9 years for attempted armed robbery.

Officer Meister was buried in St. Mary Cemetery. He was survived by his wife, Judith; son, Harold; and two daughters, Jennifer and Nancy. Throughout his career he was awarded a number of honorable mentions. He also served as treasurer of the Confederation of Police in 1969 and 1970.

Patrolman Daniel E. Howard,

STAR #5983, 21st District, Prairie Avenue District, 26 years old, and **Patrolman Donald E. Andrews,** STAR #1570, 21st District, Prairie Avenue District, 35 years old, were killed in a car accident on January 1, 1975 while responding to a call. Their cruiser crashed into another squad car, injuring Patrolmen John Griffin, 26, and Edward Czoski, 26, both of the Wentworth Avenue District. All four officers were on their way to investigate a report involving a man who had a shotgun on a CTA train. They were heading toward the 47th Street "EL" Station to apprehend the suspect when the collision occurred at the intersection of 43rd Street and Michigan Avenue. Officers Howard and Andrews' car flipped over, traveling a total of 40 feet before crashing. The CTA suspect was arrested at the scene by other police responding to the emergency call. Officer Howard was buried at St. Mary Cemetery and Officer Andrews at Holy Sepulchre Cemetery.

Patrolman Jesse J. Brown,

STAR #10329, 4th District, South Chicago Station, 28 years old, was accidentally shot by another officer on February 11, 1975. Two squads of officers were attempting to restrain a man who had barricaded himself in the basement of a Southside apartment complex, located at 8906 S. Brandon Avenue, when Officer Brown was killed. Darris Ambrose had stationed himself in the basement and taunted police to come get him, threatening to kill any who tried.

Ambrose was in hiding because he had threatened Ms. Shirley Driver and her mother in the apartment complex earlier that day. Driver called police to report the threats, but officers could not find Ambrose when they arrived. After the police left, Ambrose returned and harassed Driver again. She called the police for a second time. Police returned and discovered Ambrose with a revolver, shotgun and 25 shotgun shells.

Completely surrounded by two squads of police, Ambrose was wrestling with Brown when his gun discharged. In response, Patrolman Gene Taylor fired at Ambrose, but his bullet struck Patrolman Brown. Brown was taken to South Chicago Community Hospital, where he died while in surgery. Brown was on the force less than two years and was a former Marine Corps Sergeant who served in Vietnam. Brown lived at 8418 S. Crandon Avenue and was buried in Oakwoods Cemetery.

Murder charges were filed against Ambrose because his actions precipitated the events that led to Brown's death. No charges were filed against Patrolman Taylor. Ambrose was held by the court without bail and charged with five counts of attempted murder, four counts of armed violence, one count of resisting arrest and miscellaneous gun charges.

Patrolman Joseph F. Higgins,

STAR #9956, Gresham Station, 43 years old, suffered a fatal heart attack after wrestling with a fleeing burglar on March 23, 1975. Higgins was one of several officers who trapped a burglar in a vacant house at 1735 W. 99th Street. Police wrestled with George Williams, age 61, fighting him to the ground in order to subdue him. Patrolman Higgins collapsed after the altercation. Rushed to Little Company of Mary Hospital in Evergreen Park, the 18-year-veteran was pronounced dead on arrival. Williams was charged with burglary and resisting arrest. Officer Higgins was survived by his wife, Barbara Ann; three daughters, Margaret, Mary, and Nora Ann, and son, Bill. Officer Higgins was interred at Holy Sepulchre Cemetery.

Patrolman Joseph P. Cali,

STAR #3271, 13th District, 31 years old, was struck by a sniper's bullet on May 19, 1975 while writing a ticket for an illegally parked car at 2103 W. Lake Street near the Henry Horner Housing Project. Cali, working on his day off, discovered a 1966 Chevrolet illegally parked at a bus stop. He was ticketing the vehicle as he was shot. His partner, Patrolman James Kehoe was waiting in the squad car.

The shooter, John J. Brown, Jr., had just robbed a convenience store at 2001 W. Lake Street, and returned to the project boasting to friends that he would kill a police officer with his .22 caliber rifle. After ambushing Cali a massive manhunt ensued. Bystanders threw bricks and bottles at the more than 20 policemen and canine units that had assembled. Brown was later arrested at the Parkside Hotel and sentenced to 20 to 25 years in prison but only served half of his sentence before being paroled in 1986.

Cali, meanwhile, was taken to Cook County Hospital, dying the following day. The patrolman, a Vietnam Veteran and an officer for 2 years, received multiple awards and commendations. Cali was interred at St. Joseph Cemetery in River Grove. He was survived by his wife; Neva and two daughters, Jennifer and Caryin.

Mangled wreckage of the police vehicle in which Patrolmen Daniel Howard and Donald Andrews were riding when they were killed at 43rd Street and Michigan Avenue (January 2, 1975). *Chicago Tribune* Photo Archive.

Wood Street Station, 13th District (1960s). Chicago Police Department Photo Archive.

Police search the scene where Narcotics Investigator Patrick J. Crowley was killed at 6243 S. Aberdeen Street (September 13, 1976). *Chicago Tribune* Photo Archive.

Patrolman Patrick J. Crowley,

STAR #3614, 6th District, 32 years old, was on a narcotics raid on September 13, 1976 when he was fatally shot. He and his partners, Patrolmen James McKeon and James Duignan, received a tip about ongoing drug activity at 6243 S. Aberdeen Street. The three attempted to catch the crime in progress. At the address they observed the situation for a short time before nabbing one of the customers. He tried to trade a stereo for drugs but failed to obtain any narcotics. Urging him to make a second attempt, they planned for Patrolman Duignan to blink a flashlight if he heard a successful sale made. The informant agreed and made the transaction. Duignan shined the flashlight to signal to the other two officers hiding nearby. Crowley ran up the back stairs to make the arrest. The suspect, Willie C. Lewis, spotted him and fired four shots, striking Crowley in the head. McKeon fired two shots but missed. Two suspects, a male and a female, were apprehended in the home and taken in for questioning. Investigators found .22 caliber and .41 magnum handguns in the house, along with several vials of narcotics. Lewis was convicted of murdering Officer Crowley and received a sentence of 500 to 1,000 years in prison, the first four digit prison sentence in the history of Cook County.

Crowley was buried at Holy Sepulchre Cemetery. He was survived by his wife, Joanne, and two children. According to the *Chicago Tribune*, Lieutenant Joseph Curtin, the Brighton Park Homicide Commander, said, "He was the perfect model of the perfect officer."

Patrolman Terrence E. Loftus,

STAR #5701, 14th District, Shakespeare District Tactical Team, 36 years old, was shot in the line of duty while trying to stop a street fight between two rival gangs, the Gaylords and the Lawndale Imperial Gangsters, at Fullerton and Central Park Avenues on October 10, 1976. He was on his way home after finishing his shift when he was fatally injured. His accused shooter, Ronald Carrasquillo, a member of the Lawndale Imperial Gangsters, was arrested hours after the crime and confessed. Carraquillo said he hid the murder weapon in his basement. Police later found two sawed off shotguns, several clips of ammunition, and jars of black powder used to make bombs there. A total of 30 gang members between the ages of 15 and 19 were questioned by police investigators, including nine female suspects. Ronnie L. Carrasquillo was indicted for murder, convicted and sentenced to between 200 and 600 years in prison on January 17, 1978.

The bullet that hit Officer Loftus caused severe brain damage. He was kept on life support at St. Elizabeth Hospital until October 12. Patrolman Loftus, a 15-year-veteran of the force, was survived by his wife, Carol. He was buried in All Saints Cemetery.

1976

Sergeant Michael R. Palese,

STAR #1514, 17th District, was killed by a Milwaukee Road commuter train on March 22, 1977 while looking for a missing 6-year-old girl, Patricia Ann Dunne, a first grader at Scammon Elementary School.

Palese, a 20-year-veteran, found several holes in a wire fence alongside railroad tracks near Kilbourn Park. Neighborhood children often played there and Palese surmised that the child might have wandered onto the tracks. Palese and Patrolman Michael Walsh were creeping along the tracks in a blinding snow storm at 12:45 A.M. when a northbound train appeared out of the darkness. Walsh was able to jump over a concrete wall to safety, but Palese could not escape and was struck by the train while running on the trestle over Roscoe Street. The sergeant, with 48 honorable mentions in his career, was buried in Mount Carmel Cemetery. He was survived by his mother, Josephine; brother, Robert and son, Robert. Dunne, the missing girl, arrived at school the next day after spending the night at a friend's house without telling her parents.

Patrolman James E. O'Connell,

STAR #4142, 19th District, Area 3, 46 years old, died at the Illinois Masonic Hospital on May 20, 1978. O'Connell was injured while dealing with a rowdy prisoner causing a commotion while being moved in a patrol wagon in January of the same year. After subduing the prisoner, O'Connell began to complain of chest pains. He was taken to Illinois Masonic Hospital where doctors decided that his condition was too fragile to operate and made arrangements for the officer to have surgery the following May 20. Officer O'Connell died shortly after surgery began. He lived at 5226 N. Neenah Avenue and was survived by his wife, Katherine; and two children, Kevin and Kathleen. O'Connell was buried in Saint Adalbert Cemetery in Niles, Illinois.

Patrolman James W. Koumoundouros,

STAR #4514, 17th District, 30 years old, was off duty when he was called into service at the First National Bank of Lincolnwood at 6201 N. Lincoln Avenue. On September 7, 1977, Koumoundouros, working as a bank guard, was approached by a gunman, demanding he disarm. After discreetly pushing the alarm button, Koumoundouros continued to calmly talk to the robber as he drew his weapon from its holster. He shot the offender, who returned fire and struck the officer in the head.

The assailant, Erasmo "Roberto" Ramirez, tried to escape the scene by car but crashed his vehicle. The wound that Ramirez received from Koumoundouros, combined with the injuries he received from the crash, made escape impossible. Ramirez, an escapee from Leavenworth Federal Penitentiary in Kansas, was being sought for robbing the same bank of $14,533 the previous month. Thanks to Patrolman Koumoundouros, Ramirez left the bank with nothing.

Both men were taken to Swedish Covenant Hospital. Patrolman Koumoundouros was pronounced dead and Ramirez was treated for his wounds. Officer Koumoundouros was survived by his wife, Karen, and father, Lambros, also a policeman. He was buried in Elmwood Park Cemetery.

Ramirez was convicted and sentenced to death after his recovery. His sentence was commuted by Illinois Governor George Ryan on January 11, 2003 when he and 166 other inmates on death row were given life sentences.

Sergeant Anthony F. Janowski,

STAR #1555, was on his way to Illinois Masonic Hospital to investigate a traffic fatality on September 14, 1978 when his car was struck by a drunk driver speeding through a red light. The impact sent the squad car over a curb and into a light post before crashing into a nearby building. The driver was charged with failure to stop, driving while intoxicated and reckless homicide. Janowski, a veteran of 29 years, left behind a wife, Angela, and daughter, Gloria Anne. He was buried at St Adalbert Cemetery, Niles.

Patrolman James Days,

STAR #6154, Prairie Avenue District, 52 years old, suffered a fatal heart attack on November 10, 1978 after chasing an offender on foot for several blocks.

Policeman Days and his partner, Officer Phyilis Townsend, were on patrol when they witnessed a man driving erratically on the 1300 block of E. 50th Street. The policemen pursued the car until the offender crashed the vehicle. The driver and passenger then exited the car and fled on foot. Officer Days ran after the driver but was later found unconscious on a sidewalk a short distance from the car.

Officer Days was taken to Billings Hospital where he died a short time later. The offender, Prince Willis, was eventually caught by University of Chicago Police responding to the radio call made by Days. Days was a veteran of 17 years.

The Police Honor Guard forms a
ceremonial arch with their batons as the
coffin of Patrolman Roger Van Schaik is
carried from a funeral home (March 7, 1979)
Chicago Tribune Photo Archive

Patrolman William P. Bosak,

STAR #3319, 5th District, 33 years old, and

Patrolman Roger W. Van Schaik,

STAR #14299, 5th District, 31 years old, were both killed in an ambush on March 3, 1979. The two undercover narcotics investigators were heading west on 115th Street when they stopped alongside a brown 1972 Ford LTD. As one officer approached, the men inside immediately began firing upon him. The other officer, still in the car, was able to radio a 10-1 (officer needs assistance) call before he too was fatally shot at point blank range.

Both officers, veterans of the force for more than a decade, were rushed to Roseland Community Hospital where they were pronounced dead. Bosak was the father of two daughters. Van Shaik had a five-month-old child. Both were buried at Holy Sepulchre Cemetery.

Kenneth Allen, 36, was later apprehended and charged with two counts of murder. Evidence pointed to Allen after police gathered statements from witnesses who said he owned the brown 1972 Ford LTD. Allen was sentenced to death, but he was one of the 166 prisoners whose sentences were commuted to life in prison by Governor George Ryan on January 11, 2003.

Captain Nicholas J. McNamara,

STAR #170, Traffic Division, died of a heart attack on May 9, 1979 while in Arizona attending a police training program. Captain McNamara was last seen alive at 10:00 P.M. on May 8 returning from dinner with Lieutenant Gerald Clough of Philadelphia; who had the room next door. At approximately 5:25 A.M. the next morning, Clough knocked on McNamara's door to wake him but received no response. Concerned, the lieutenant notified the hotel engineer, Fred Wisenburg, who entered McNamara's room. The captain's lifeless body was found lying across his bed.

An investigation determined the captain died of natural causes, suffering a fatal heart attack. McNamara was survived by his wife, Delores, and their four children, Nicholas, 16; Patrick, 15; Timothy, 7; and daughter Mary, 19 years old. The McNamara's had two daughters, Patricia and Susan; who both lost their life when they were young children. Captain McNamara's family resided at 5424 W. Grace Street. The family laid their hero to rest at Queen of Heaven Cemetery.

Patrolman Jose M. Torres,

STAR #13988, 10th District, was killed by a speeding car on August 5, 1979 while investigating a traffic accident at 2350 S. Blue Island Avenue. Torres, inspecting the identification number of an automobile, was hit when a vehicle traveling east at 60 MPH ran through a stop sign. Torres was thrown into a parked car. Several hours later, police arrested Jesus Morales based on witnesses' descriptions of the car. He was charged with reckless driving, leaving the scene of an accident, striking a pedestrian in the roadway and failure to buy a city sticker.

Officer Torres was taken to Mount Sinai Hospital where he fought his injuries for 15 days before dying on August 21. He was buried at Mount Calvary Cemetery in Puerto Rico.

No police deaths in 1980.

Chicago Police Officers march in formation during the St. Jude League Parade.

Maxwell Street Station, the face of
"Hill Street Blues." Chicago Police Department
Photo Archive.

Area 3, 19th District at Belmont and
Western Avenues. Chicago Police Department
Photo Archive.

Area 4, 11th District, 3151 W. Harrison Street.
Chicago Police Department Photo Archive.

Patrolman Richard F. Gipson,

STAR #3451, 56 years old, suffered a heart attack on February 4, 1981 on duty at O'Hare International Airport. Officer Gipson, due to retire on the following day, February 5, was directing traffic outside when he was called to the American Airlines office where two suspicious individuals were being held. They first attempted to buy tickets at Trans World Airlines and then later tried to make a purchase at American Airlines. The pair were sent away from Trans World Airlines because their three forms of identification did not match their check. Trans World Airlines then alerted each airline at O'Hare to warn them about the pair. Upon arriving at American Airlines, they were taken to an office to wait for Patrolman Gipson. Once he arrived, Gipson began questioning the duo. As he spoke, one of the offenders stole the check in question and attempted to swallow it. A struggle then ensued between the suspects and Officer Gipson.

Gipson, a beloved member of the police force, suffered a heart attack during the altercation and was pronounced dead at Resurrection Hospital. Over his 24 years on the force many people praised him for his outstanding work. Prior to assignment at O'Hare International Airport, Officer Gipson was a member of the Police Training Detail at the firing range. He and his wife, Irene, had been planning to travel to Florida on Saturday, February 7 to look for a home for their retirement; instead, over 250 people attended a memorial service honoring the officer. The two suspects, Brandie Mason and Denise Herlihy, involved in the dispute, were transferred to Area 5 Violent Crimes charged with aggravated battery and forgery. Patrolman Gipson was buried at All Saints Cemetery.

Patrolman Robert Marousek,

STAR #15453, Monroe Street District, 35 years old, was an 11-year-veteran of the Chicago Police Department when he suffered a fatal heart attack. The incident that led to his heart attack occurred on Saturday, February 28, 1981, when Marousek and his partner, Policeman William Kent, were loading a corpse into their squad car.

The two police officers received a call to pick up the body of an unidentified man left on the sidewalk at 15 S. Aberdeen Street. When the men attempted to load the body into the squadron, Officer Marousek suddenly collapsed to the ground. Officer Kent responded immediately with cardiopulmonary resuscitation. Marousek was taken to University of Illinois Hospital and pronounced dead at 8:52 A.M. Officer Marousek was survived by his wife and son. He was interred in the family plot.

Policeman patrols inside Cabrini Green (1980).
Chicago Tribune Photo Archive.

First Deputy Police Superintendent James J. Riordan,

STAR #103, Bureau of Operational Services, 57 years old, was shot in Johnny Lattner's Restaurant in Marina City, 300 N. State Street, on June 6, 1981.

The First Deputy Superintendent was having dinner around 9:00 P.M. after leaving work. Witnesses said he was seated near the bar with a man and two women. A man identified as Leon Washington, in the bar for several hours, reportedly tried to speak with the two women. Riordan and the other man seated with him attempted to keep him from annoying their companions. They then moved Washington into a hallway that separated the bar from a neighboring coffee shop.

At that point, according to witnesses, the assailant pulled a .380 caliber handgun and fired at Riordan at close range. Riordan collapsed into a fountain there as Washington ran down the hallway towards the exit. Washington did not get far as police in the building quickly detained him. He was later convicted and sentenced to life in prison.

Riordan was rushed to Northwestern Memorial Hospital and immediately underwent surgery. His wife, Loretta; four of his children, his brother, Mayor Jane Byrne and several other top-ranking city officials came to the hospital to await word of his condition. Riordan was conscious and had his eyes open going into surgery but died of multiple gunshot wounds in his chest and neck. Riordan, for whom Chicago's new Police Headquarters at 35th and Michigan is named, was buried at Calvary Cemetery. He remains Chicago's highest ranking police officer to be killed.

Patrolman Edgar A. Clay, Jr.,

STAR #10425, 2nd District, Wentworth Station, Area I Youth Division, died on January 25, 1982, eighteen days after being attacked by a juvenile offender. On January 7, 1982, Clay encountered a student who had reportedly stolen goods from Hyde Park Academy, 6220 S. Stony Island Avenue. He detained the offender and began a search of the student's belongings. Clay recovered a .22 caliber pistol before the young man became hostile and struck him. Clay fell to the ground during the attack and was hospitalized for a knee injury. A blood clot formed in his knee which then caused a heart attack. Bilateral pulmonary embolism was the cause of death. The officer was a 25-year-veteran and was survived by his wife, daughter, two sons and brother. He also left five grandchildren.

Patrolman James E. Doyle,

STAR #9093, 6th District, Gresham Station, Recruit Training Division, 34 years old, was killed in the line of duty on February 5, 1982 on a Chicago Transit Authority bus while trying to detain a robbery suspect. Doyle, a recruit who had joined the department less than nine months prior, boarded the CTA bus at 79th Street and Cicero Avenue with his partner, Officer Robert M. Mantia. The officers had been informed by a distressed citizen that he had recently been robbed and that the attacker, Edgar Hope, had boarded the Route 79 bus. As the officers argued with Hope, attempting to remove him from the bus, the offender pulled a gun and fired at both officers. Hope hit Doyle in the upper right side of his chest but missed his partner. The shooting occurred near the intersection of 79th Street and Lafayette Avenue around 10:00 P.M. The suspect was also injured during the struggle. He was taken to St. Bernard Hospital and later transferred to Cook County Hospital. Doyle was also taken to St. Bernard Hospital and died there a few hours later. Several other bystanders on the bus were also injured and taken to Jackson Park Hospital.

Doyle was survived by his 70-year-old mother and interred at Holy Sepulchre Cemetery. The offender was charged with murder and robbery from the outstanding warrant. Hope was convicted of Patrolman Doyle's murder and sentenced to death.

Doyle's shooting occurred one week after Mayor Jane Byrne announced a crackdown on "hooliganism" on CTA routes after she had ridden a CTA bus and described the experience as "terrible." As a result of the program, 230 additional police officers were added to patrols on CTA vehicles.

Patrolman Richard J. O'Brien,

STAR #5337, Gang Crimes Enforcement Division South, 33 years old, and

Patrolman William P. Fahey, Jr.,

STAR #4194, Gang Crimes Enforcement Division, 34 years old, were making a routine traffic stop at 81st and Morgan Streets on February 9, 1982 when they were killed. The two officers exited their vehicle as did the driver of the car they pulled over. Reportedly, O'Brien asked for the driver's license and the driver refused, so he began to pat him down. Fahey went to question a second man in the front seat of the car. Searching for weapons, he noticed something suspicious and decided to take the man into custody. Fahey and his assailant began to struggle and Fahey's gun was taken and used to shoot him. The gunman then turned on O'Brien, shooting him three times. Both officers were taken to Little Company of Mary Hospital in Evergreen Park. O'Brien died on February 9 and Fahey followed the next day, February 10. The killers, brothers Andrew and Jackie Wilson, were apprehended. They were later found guilty of the double homicide.

Police Supt. Richard Brzeczek using the
telephone at Little Company of Mary Hospital
after Patrolmen Richard O'Brien and
William Fahey were shot and killed (1982).
Chicago Tribune Photo Archive.

O'Brien, a nine-year-veteran, had received six honorable mentions and many letters of appreciation. He was the son of a former Chicago Police Sergeant and was survived by his mother. Patrolman O'Brien was buried in Holy Sepulchre Cemetery.

Patrolman Fahey was a ten-year-veteran of the department and had received 19 honorable mentions and numerous letters of appreciation. He was survived by his wife and three children and also was buried in Holy Sepulchre Cemetery.

Patrolman John F. Lynch,

STAR #11189, 7th District, Englewood Station, 46 years old, died on August 19, 1982 of a heart attack after transporting a body to a hospital. Officer Lynch and his partner were assigned to process a deceased body discovered inside a city residence. They carried the body on a portable stretcher from the house to their police vehicle, transporting it to St. Bernard Hospital. Inside the emergency room, Patrolman Lynch suffered a massive heart attack and died.

Lynch was a 20 year veteran of the Chicago Police Department. He was survived by his wife JoAnn; and three children, Michael, James and Joan. The Funeral Mass for Lynch was said at St. Mary Star of the Sea Catholic Church.

Patrolman Martin E. Darcy, Jr.,

STAR #6444, 22nd District, Morgan Park District, 52 years old, spent 28 years as a police officer and was planning his imminent retirement when he was gunned down on September 27, 1982. Darcy wanted to finish his watch on the streets, not behind the desk where he had spent the last two years working. Early on the morning of September 27, a man entered the Southtown Health Foods Store at 2148 W. 95th Street and announced that he wanted all the big bills from the cash register. The cashier, wife of the store manager Emil Mahler, gave the robber the money as he instructed. Once the offender was gone Mrs. Mahler went and informed her husband of the hold-up. Mahler immediately ran to the street and attempted to apprehend the robber, who turned and shot him in the abdomen. The suspect then jumped into a gold Chevrolet and sped off.

Mahler was able to provide a full description of the gunman and vehicle to Officer Darcy and his partner, Officer Edward Ryan. Darcy and Ryan found the gold colored car and chased it into a parking lot at 95th Street and Western Avenue. The suspect, Aaron Washington, alias Jessie Lee Anderson, exited the vehicle in the parking lot and ran into a nearby home. Washington entered Kathleen Frantz's house and ordered her to hand over her keys. When Frantz did not cooperate Washington shot her in the shoulder. Frantz then ran to the back of her home and escaped out the rear door. Darcy was walking between houses when Washington spotted the officer and fired several shots in his direction. One of the bullets struck Patrolman Darcy and he fell to the ground. Michael Gasea, a part-time Evergreen Park Police Officer and neighborhood resident, rushed toward the scene. Gasea was able to come to Frantz's aid and saved her from further harm.

As Washington fled he encountered Officer Jerry Johnson, one of the many officers combing the area in hopes of apprehending the offender. The offender immediately opened fire on the officer, wounding him in his abdomen and left hand. Washington continued to flee as numerous shots were fired in his direction. He then received four gunshot wounds and was taken into police custody. Washington had a lengthy arrest record.

Officer Darcy was survived by his wife, Patricia; and four daughters, Paula Kedan, a fellow policeman; Diane Higgins, Christina Fairbanks, Patricia; son, Martin; and brother, Police Sergeant Michael Darcy. Patrolman Darcy was buried at Holy Sepulchre Cemetery.

Officer and police dog hunt for clues to Sergeant Hamp McMikel Jr.'s death near South Shore Drive. *Chicago Tribune* Photo Archive.

Sergeant Hamp T. McMikel, Jr.,

STAR #1541, 5th District, 55 years old, was shot and killed during an armed robbery attempt at 4135 S. Lake Shore Drive on November 20, 1982. Sergeant McMikel, off-duty, was using a pay phone when a gang of gunmen ambushed him at around 8:20 P.M. The offenders, believed to be a group of modern-day highwaymen, were preying on motorists. A police stake-out of the crime-ridden area had been called off several days before McMikel's shooting.

The body of one of the gunmen, 20-year-old Michael A. Merrell, was found near Illinois Central Gulf Railroad tracks just west of Lake Shore Drive. Because of the dirt and scratches on his body, investigators believed that he had been dragged there by the other gunmen and left for dead. Ray Greer eventually confessed to McMikel's murder and was sentenced to life in prison.

Sergeant McMikel was taken to Michael Reese Hospital and died in the emergency room at 10:00 P.M. McMikel was the sixth Chicago Police officer killed in 1982, in what was one of the bloodiest 18-month periods in the department's history. He was buried in Holy Sepulchre Cemetery. Sergeant McMikel was a 32-year-veteran of the Chicago Police Department. On May 2, 1982, a mile-long parade was staged through downtown Chicago. An estimated 6,000 police officers, half the force, marched in honor of their comrades who had fallen in the line of duty in the previous 18 months.

Patrolman Larry J. Vincent,

STAR #15161, 2nd District, Wentworth Station, 29 years old, was shot on January 14, 1983 during a gun battle with two robbery suspects. Vincent and his partner, Patrolman George Lipinski, had been called to 5131 S. Calumet Avenue along with another pair of officers, Patrolman Clarence Spraggins and Jackie Stewart. The three-story house was believed to be a flat belonging to suspected narcotics dealers. It had been reported that alleged robbers were trying to steal money from the narcotics dealers, although no money was discovered on the scene. Vincent and Spraggins entered the building while the other two officers remained outside to provide support.

Once Vincent and Spraggins entered the building, they found the suspects attempting to escape through a first-floor window. At that point six shots were reportedly fired, after which Vincent and Spraggins stumbled through the door and collapsed bleeding in the snow. Spraggins was immediately taken to the Provident Hospital in a squad car while Vincent was transported to Billings Hospital in a Fire Department Ambulance. Spraggins' arm wound was treated and he was listed in stable condition. Patrolman Vincent had suffered a wound to the head and was pronounced dead later that day.

Five people, including one woman, were taken into custody following the gun battle and detectives questioned them at police headquarters at Wentworth Avenue and 51st Street. Nicky Cozart, age 28, and Darnell Davis, age 24, were charged with murder, home invasion, aggravated battery, residential burglary, armed robbery, armed violence and unlawful use of weapons. Later, Larry Love, age 28, and Sidney Steve, age 20, were also indicted on charges of murder, armed robbery, armed violence, aggravated battery, burglary, home invasion and unlawful use of a weapon.

Patrolman Vincent was on the force for three years and was survived by his expectant wife, Marilyn, and two sons, Jason and Anthony. Both his father and uncle were Chicago Police Officers. Officer Vincent was buried at Holy Sepulchre Cemetery.

Patrolman Wayne J. Klacza,

STAR #16469, Public Housing Division North, 32 years old, was struck by a car near the Harrison Area Headquarters at 6:00 P.M. on June 28, 1983. As a car swerved in the path of a pedestrian, Jackie Coffey, Officer Klacza jumped to push him out of way. Coffey was unharmed, but Klacza was struck violently by the vehicle, throwing him onto the windshield before he hit the ground. Patrolman Klacza was taken to Mt. Sinai Hospital where he died from the injuries he sustained in the area of 3148 W. Harrison Street. Sandra Little, the 25-year old driver of the vehicle, continued down the street and only stopped when she drove into a utility pole. She was charged with reckless homicide. Little was originally taken to Mt. Sinai Hospital. She was treated for a fractured left arm and multiple bruises and then transported to Cook County Hospital.

Patrolman Klacza was survived by his wife, Barbara; two sons, Wayne and John; daughter, Mary Ann; his parents John and Sophie; and two brothers. The officer was buried at Resurrection Cemetery. Klacza had been a member of the force for seven years.

Little was charged by the Cook County Grand Jury with reckless homicide, possession of a controlled substance and driving under the influence of drugs. Bond was set at $100,000.

Patrolman Anthony L. Creed,

STAR #3245, Mounted Patrol Unit, 35 years old, sustained fatal neck injuries while doing a routine exercise at the department's Mounted Equestrian Unit Headquarters at Old South Shore Country Club, 7059 S. South Shore Drive, on August 30, 1983. Creed's horse, Buster, stumbled while walking down an incline near the lakefront, causing the officer to fall to the ground and sustain head injuries. Creed was taken to Jackson Park Hospital where he was pronounced dead. The patrolman was the first mounted policeman to die since the department was reactivated in 1974.

Creed was a decorated officer who had received the Carter Harrison Award, the city's highest police award for heroism, in 1979, after he was shot in the head by a suspect he was questioning. He was also awarded the Blue Star, given to all officers who are shot or killed in the line of duty. The patrolman joined the force in 1973 and had been a mounted officer since 1980. Creed served in the Marines from 1968 to 1970, and was discharged as a corporal. The fallen officer was survived by his wife, Geri; daughter, Toni; son, Gerald; and parents, Chicago Police Department Lieutenant Gerald Creed and Rosalle. He was buried in Oakwoods Cemetery.

Mounted Chicago Police Officer on
East Washington Street (1982). ICH-i39631,
Chicago History Museum.

Patrolman Fred Eckles, Jr.,

STAR #13561, 41 years old, was assigned to search a home, located at 8051 S. Maryland Avenue, for narcotics on January 17, 1984. He and seven other officers went to the home with a search warrant for cocaine and a man named Neil. With no reply to their knock on the door, they forcefully opened it. Inside three armed men opened fire on the officers. Despite being immediately hit, Eckles managed to fire two shots. He was taken to South Chicago Hospital where he died from multiple gunshot wounds. Patrolman Eckles was buried in Cedar Park Cemetery and survived by his five children.

A suspect killed at the scene was eventually identified as 22-year-old Neil Young. Three other suspects were also found; two men in the front room and a woman hiding in a closet. Neighbors said that the home was owned by an elderly woman who had been in the hospital for over a month after suffering a stroke. Her home was being used for drug deals during her absence. Neither she, nor her daughter who lived with her, were in the home during the raid.

Patrolman Dorelle C. Brandon,

STAR #2684, 3rd District, 35 years old, will forever be remembered as the first Chicago policewoman killed in the line of duty. She was accidentally shot during an undercover drug raid on January 25, 1984. Brandon and her partner, Patrolman Clarence Keith, had received information about ongoing narcotics sales at 10742 S. Calumet Avenue and proceeded to the address with their informant and two other plainclothes officers. The informant had called ahead to the suspect, Anthony Brown, and arranged to buy a quantity of cocaine for himself and his "girlfriend," Brandon.

When the party approached the house, Brandon accompanied the informant while Officer Keith concealed himself in a hallway. She and the informant were told to use the rear entrance to the apartment and Brandon told Keith to follow her in 30 seconds. Once she and the informant entered the apartment, Brown pulled a set of burglar bars across the rear entrance. Once inside, when Brandon witnessed Brown sell one gram of cocaine for $100, she informed Brown she was a police officer and drew a .38 caliber snubnose revolver. She then attempted to place Brown under arrest. The officer and the offender struggled for her gun and Brandon called for her partner to help. Keith, unable to enter because of the locked gates, fired through them at Brown. One of his bullets struck Brandon in the head, fatally injuring her.

Brown, who was seriously wounded in the firefight, was charged with murder under a provision of Illinois law that allows a suspect to be charged with murder if a death occurs in connection with a felony. He was also charged with attempted murder and delivery and possession of narcotics. Brown was convicted on the drug charges during his first trial but a mistrial was declared on the other two counts when the jury could not come to an agreement concerning the murder charges. Dorelle Brandon holds the sad honor of being the first female officer killed in the 171 years of the Chicago Police Department. Women became sworn officers of the Chicago Police Department in 1913. Since then, women have served with distinction and honor. Patrolman Brandon was buried at St. Mary Cemetery.

1984

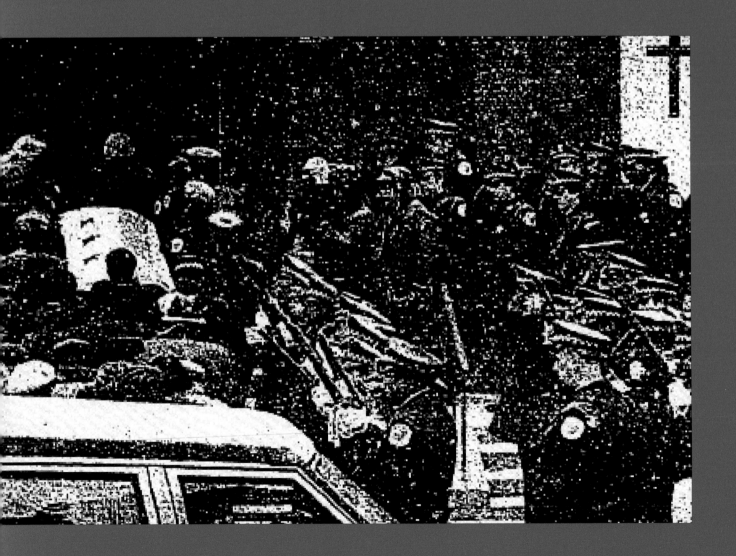

Patrolman Dorelle Brandon's funeral procession, the first woman to die on duty. *Chicago Tribune* Photo Archive.

Sergeant John J. Collins,

STAR #1006, Traffic Division, Highway Enforcement Unit, 52 years old, died on February 7, 1984 when he suffered a fatal heart attack while on patrol. The sergeant was driving along the 2800 block of W. Van Buren Street when his trauma occurred. As a result, his squad car slammed into the rear of a parked truck. Collins was taken to Mount Sinai Hospital, where he was treated for his cardiac condition. He later died. Sergeant Collins had been a 27-year-veteran of the force and was buried at St. Mary Cemetery.

Patrolman Curtis R. Baker,

STAR #12212, 45 years old, was killed at 1:30 A.M. while escorting a woman into a building at 4500 S. State Street on June 2, 1984. Baker, a member of the tactical team, had been assigned to the Mass Transit Unit. He was helping a female into the Robert Taylor Homes when three men who had been trailing them shouted "stickup". Baker attempted to draw his revolver but was fatally shot in the chest by one of the assailants. The 16-year-veteran of the Chicago Police Department was pronounced dead 30 minutes later at Michael Reese Hospital. Baker was survived by his wife, son and daughter.

Three suspects were charged with murder and conspiracy to commit armed robbery. They were identified as Bernard Lash, 22, the alleged shooter; David Govan, 26; and Eugene Jackson, 19. The three were held without bond.

Patrolman Martin P. Clarke,

STAR #13453, Monroe Street Station, 26 years old, was killed on August 26, 1984 when his squad car was broadsided by a speeding vehicle that had ignored a stop sign. Officer Clarke and his partner, Officer Richardo Mancha, were on their routine patrol when the accident occurred at 13th and Paulina Streets. Clarke was thrown from the vehicle while Mancha was seriously injured in the collision. Willie White, a 22-year-old factory worker, was later arrested and charged with reckless homicide. The offender originally fled the scene of the accident by foot.

The officer was pronounced dead upon arrival at Rush-Presbyterian-St.Luke Medical Center. Clarke came from a family of Chicago Police officers; his father was a retired Lieutenant and his sister was a member of the Morgan Park District. Patrolman Clarke had been on the force for 18 months and was survived by his parents, brother, sister and fiancée. Officer Clarke was buried at Queen of Heaven Cemetery, Hillside.

Chicago Police Investigators comb the murder scene of Patrolman John Martin, in an alley at 3200 N. Wilton Avenue. *Chicago Tribune* Photo Archive.

Detective Wayne G. King,

STAR #7413, Office of Municipal Investigations, 53 years old, was shot and killed on July 12, 1985 while investigating a man posing as a police officer and city inspector. The offender, Roosevelt Carr, had spent the afternoon illegally impersonating city officials and retrieving cash payoffs in multiple shakedowns on the Southside. He had apparently convinced an Army recruiter and prospective enlistee to drive him around the area as he pursued these criminal activities. A businessman at one of the shakedown locations recognized Carr as a known grifter and called the Municipal Office of Investigations (OMI) to report him. A warrant was already issued seeking Carr for his phony activities. The offender was well known to King and other OMI detectives who had arrested him several times before. Officers spread out across the Southside to search for Carr. Soon King and his partner, Cherise Morgan, spotted Carr at the corner of 51st Street and Michigan Avenue. King approached Carr, who recognized the detective and attempted to flee. King pursued and caught up with the offender half a block away in front of the Most Worshipful Grand Lodge at 5047 S. Michigan Avenue. Detective King ordered Carr to place his hands against the wall but he refused and attacked the detective instead. As they wrestled, Carr was able to grab King's service revolver from its holster. He used it to shoot the detective in the chest and stomach.

Carr ran from the scene, but was apprehended at 50th Street and Prairie Avenue by tactical unit officers. He offered no resistance when officers took him into custody and confiscated King's revolver. The detective had attempted to follow Carr after the shooting but could not regain his feet due to the severity of his wounds. He died only 30 minutes later. Detective King was survived by his wife Marie; and daughters Lori and Jennifer. The 24-year-veteran was considering retirement at the time of his death. He was laid to rest in St. Mary Cemetery. Carr, who attempted to blame a drug abuse problem for his behavior, was convicted of Detective King's murder and sentenced to life in prison.

Chicago Police Department squad car passing
Auditorium Building on Congress Parkway
(1985). ICH-i39631, Chicago History Museum.

Patrolman Richard Wayne Clark,

STAR #13034, 19th District, 48 years old, was killed in the line of duty on April 3, 1986 when he responded to a complaint of a "man with a gun." At 1429 W. Lill Avenue, he discovered John Pasch, Jr., had taken his landlord, Leslie Shearer, hostage. Pasch was a tool and die maker who neighbors described as a loner. He shot and killed both Officer Clark and Shearer before barricading himself in his 74-year-old neighbor's house and taking her hostage. Police reinforcements arrived at the scene and a stand-off began lasting from the afternoon of April 3 well into the morning of April 4. The offender fired on officers continuously for the first hour of the confrontation and police were forced to evacuate residents from the area in order to ensure their safety.

Pasch, reached by phone during the siege, told police he would not turn himself in until he watched the film *Battle of the Bulge* on WGN-TV, scheduled to be shown from 3:00 A.M. to 5:00 A.M. Despite a televised request by Police Superintendent Fred Rice, Pasch refused to surrender. He later threatened to shoot himself when the movie was over. The offender did not harm his hostage during the long stand-off, though he killed her two dogs and threw them out the window. Officers surrounding the house could see Pasch inside watching television with a shotgun across his lap.

Police eventually removed Pasch from the house without any injuries to him or his elderly hostage. He was later convicted and sentenced to death for the double homicide of Patrolman Clark and Leslie Shearer. He died on death row while awaiting execution. Officer Clark had been a police officer for 23 years at the time of his death. He was survived by his wife, daughter and son who later carried on his father's legacy and became a Chicago Police Officer. Patrolman Clark was buried in Memory Gardens Cemetery in Arlington Heights.

Patrolman George T. Bryja,

STAR #12557, Morgan Park District, 45 years old, died of a heart attack on Sunday, July 27, 1986 after chasing a would-be arsonist in his Southwest Side neighborhood. At about 3:00 A.M., the policeman was awakened by the family car alarm, set off by his wife to summon help. Mrs. Bryja had witnessed two men attempting to set a nearby garage on fire after they had spray-painted it with graffiti. Policeman Bryja and his 18-year-old son chased the vandals through an alley for four blocks before they lost them. The officer returned home sweating profusely and complaining of chest pains before he collapsed. Officer Bryja was taken to Holy Cross Hospital and pronounced dead there at 4:51 A.M. The 20-year-veteran of the force was survived by his wife and two children. Bryja's son followed in his footsteps and became a member of the Chicago Police Department.

Sergeant Richard Davenport, Jr.,

STAR #2280, 9th District, Deering Street Station, 55 years old, was off-duty on August 4, 1986 when his son informed him that five offenders were attempting to steal his car parked near their home. Davenport, a 26-year-veteran of the Chicago Police Department, confronted the suspects.

The sergeant approached the offenders at 10:30 P.M. at the intersection of 93rd Street and Stony Island Avenue and spoke with them for only a short time before one of the car thieves pulled a gun and fired six shots. Davenport was carrying his service revolver but was unable to return fire after being hit in the mouth, chest and left calf. Sergeant Davenport was taken to South Chicago Community Hospital where he died at 11:27 P.M. He was laid to rest at Oakwoods Cemetery. He was survived by his wife, Evelyn, who said, "I lost my best friend."

Police initiated an intense investigation after the shooting and were in the process of questioning multiple suspects and witnesses the morning after the crime. Dwayne Thomas, 16 years old at the time of the shooting, was charged as an adult with the officer's murder. He was acquitted of all charges on June 15, 1987 after claiming he thought Officer Davenport was a gang member who was going to kill his friend.

Patrolman Jay F. Brunkella,

STAR #3429, 24th District, Rogers Park District Tactical Team, 39 years old, and his partner, Officer Fred Hattenberg, were part of a plain clothes narcotics surveillance team assigned to Stephen F. Gale Community Academy, 1631 W. Jonquil Terrace, when Brunkella was fatally shot on September 22, 1986. They had assigned to this detail because of complaints from neighborhood residents about drug deals taking place outside of the school. The officers were stationed at the public elementary school on the Northside at 2:00 P.M. when they spotted a narcotics deal taking place and requested that the dealer be arrested. As the three-officer arrest team arrived, Brunkella and Hattenberg saw an offender, Allison Jenkins, make another transaction and felt that immediate action must to be taken. Jenkins had the drugs he was selling in a potato chip bag. The officers saw him reach into the bag before handing an object to a passenger in an idling car full of young people. As they moved towards the vehicle, the offender threw the chip bag under the car before attempting to flee. Hattenberg, with his weapon in his right hand and his radio in his left hand, caught up to Jenkins and a struggle began. The men fought for several moments before they fell to the ground. Hattenberg's gun hand hit the pavement, causing the weapon to accidentally discharge. Brunkella, attempting to overpower the assailant, was hit in the left rib cage and critically wounded.

Brunkella was rushed to St. Francis Hospital in Evanston and underwent emergency surgery. On October 4, 1986, the officer, an 18-year-veteran, succumbed to his injury. Officer Brunkella left behind a wife, son, mother and brother and was buried in Rosehill Cemetery. Jenkins was arrested and charged with aggravated battery, felony possession of marijuana and resisting arrest. The potato chip bag was later recovered and found to contain an undetermined amount of marijuana. Prosecutors also eventually charged Jenkins with murder, arguing that his actions led to the circumstances that caused Brunkella's death. Jenkins was convicted of murder on October 2, 1987 and sentenced to 20 years in prison.

Patrolman William M. Morrison, Jr.,

STAR #9593, 16th District, 51 years old, was working a special assignment on September 4, 1987 when he was broadsided by a speeding drunk driver. Morrison and four other officers, none of whom were scheduled for regular duty that day, were working a an extra duty assignment. Police received a report of a juvenile with a shotgun in the area near 14th Street and Ashland Avenue. They were going to investigate the claim when the accident occurred. The squad car was traveling west on 15th Street a little after 8:00 P.M. when it collided with a brown Oldsmobile Cutlass traveling north on Ashland that failed to yield the right of way.

Normally, five officers did not travel together in a squad car, but the policemen who worked special assignment often traveled in larger groups because they frequently patrolled and answered calls at Chicago Housing Authority sites. All five officers in the squad car sustained injuries that required hospitalization. Only Morrison's injuries proved fatal. Patrolman Morrison, who worked out of the Jefferson Park District, was rushed to Cook County Hospital after the accident and died there at 9:51 P.M. The 29-year-veteran of the department was survived by his wife, son and two daughters. Officer Morrison was laid to rest at All Saints Cemetery. The civilian driver, Juan Soliz, remained in stable condition at St. Luke Hospital after the crash. He was placed under arrest and charged with driving under the influence.

Patrolman Gregory R. Edwards,

STAR #4562, Grand Crossing District, 27 years old, was killed during a hold-up by an armed assailant on September 29, 1987. Edwards was in a first-floor room at the Roberts Motel, 6625 S. Martin Luther King, Jr. Drive, when Marvin Wright, 24, needing money to complete a drug deal, went to the Roberts Motel to rob its occupants. Wright came to the door of Patrolman Edwards' room and attempted to gain entrance. When the officer identified himself as a policeman a quarrel ensued during which Edwards was fatally shot. The patrolman died at University of Chicago's Bernard Mitchell Hospital from wounds to his head and chest. Wright was arrested at a garage near the scene of the crime and charged with the murder of Officer Edwards. The patrolman had been on the force for 13 months.

Patrolman Arthur O. Jackson,

STAR #8622, Marquette District Tactical Team, 66 years old, suffered a fatal heart attack after chasing a young man on foot for three blocks on September 30, 1987. Robert Richardson, age 18, was an auto-theft suspect whom Jackson chased into the hands of waiting police officers. After the chase, Jackson drove a fellow officer back to his car and then collapsed in his own police vehicle. The patrolman had spent all but one of his 33 years as an officer with the Marquette District. He also spent one year serving as the first African-American officer assigned to the Marine Unit. In 1965, he became one of the first members to join the district's Tactical Unit. A Navy veteran and amateur boxer, Officer Jackson was one of the unit members who helped clean up the reputation of the Marquette District after a police scandal. Jackson was survived by his three children, Gayle, Artis and Brian. A fourth child, Philip, had served in the Vietnam War and was killed in combat there.

1987

Patrolman Lee R. Seward,

STAR #15906, 23rd District, Town Hall Station, 43 years old, and his partner responded to reports of a disturbance at 4126 N. Sheridan Road twice on the night of December 30, 1987. When they reached the scene the first time, they spoke with two neighbors having a dispute over noise levels. The officers left the four story apartment building with the understanding that a peaceable agreement had been reached. They later received a call to return to the Sheridan Road address with a complaint relating to the same parties. The situation was more complicated than they had originally believed. They requested that back-up be sent. When the officers reached the building they climbed to the second floor landing and attempted to arrest a man they found there. However, the offender, John Rogers, was extremely uncooperative and the officers were compelled to use force.

Seward and his partner were attempting to place handcuffs on Rogers when he suddenly reached out and grabbed Patrolman Seward's gun. The assailant then shot the patrolman twice before turning and firing at the backup officers who had just reached the stairs. Rogers managed to empty the gun before he was fatally wounded by return fire. Seward was taken to Weiss Memorial Hospital where he was pronounced dead from a gunshot to the mouth at 10:44 P.M. Patrolman Seward was a 16-year-veteran of the force. He was a patrol specialist in charge of on-the-job training for new officers. He was survived by his wife and son. Officer Seward was buried in Montrose Cemetery.

Patrolman Helen P. Cardwell,

STAR #11815, Senior Citizens Service Division, 50 years old, was killed in an automobile accident on May 19, 1988 while on her way to exchange a temporary patrol car for her regular vehicle. As she was driving south down Sacramento Boulevard her car spun off the road and hit two trees. Patrolman Cardwell was rushed to Mount Sinai Hospital, where she died shortly after her arrival. Cardwell was an 18-year-veteran of the Chicago Police Department. Over the course of her career she had received 127 letters of commendation. Officer Cardwell was survived by her husband, son and brother and buried at St. Mary Cemetery.

Patrolman John W. Mathews,

STAR #9827, 4th District, 26 years old, was off-duty on the night of May 21, 1988 when he heard a police radio call describing a disturbance about a block from his home on South Avenue M in southeast Chicago. Drinking and drag racing had become common in the area on the weekends. Mathews was aware responding officers might need his help. Wearing blue jeans and a t-shirt, he walked over to the location and helped the on-duty officers clear the scene and make one arrest. As the squad cars pulled away, Mathews headed back down the dirt road that led from the site to his home. Five young men emerged from the woods bordering Wolf Lake and approached him. They asked about the cars that had become damaged in the disturbance. Their intimidating demeanor moved Mathews to announce he was a police officer. He asked the men to back up. Instead of dispersing, one of the men, James Kennedy, struck Patrolman Mathews in the back of the head with a baseball bat and the others then joined in hitting the officer. Mathews was able to draw his service weapon and fire a single shot but did not hit any of his assailants. The offenders then knocked the gun from his hand and continued hitting the patrolman until he was motionless. They then remained searching for the gun until they heard the sound of an approaching siren and fled the scene.

1988

A Chicago Policeman examines the wreckage
of Patrolman Helen Cardwell's car crash
along S. Sacramento Avenue. *Chicago Tribune*
Photo Archive.

South Chicago patrol officers discovered Officer Mathews at 12:10 A.M. Police later found his weapon along the dirt road where he was attacked. The baseball bat was located floating in Wolf Lake. Two cars police believed belonged to the suspects were impounded at the scene. A watch, believed to have been Patrolman Mathews', was found in the lake by police divers. Patrolman Mathews, an 18-month-veteran of the force, was survived by his wife, Lorraine; three children, Joseph, John, Jr. and Anne Marie; parents, three sisters and a brother. He was the son and son-in-law of retired Chicago Police Officers. Officer Mathews was buried in Holy Cross Cemetery.

Police arrested two suspects in the fatal beating within 24 hours. Dean Chavez and Edward Manzo, both teenagers, were taken into custody after the registration from one of the cars confiscated at the scene led police to their doors. They were both charged with murder. Police also issued warrants for the arrest of Chavez's brother Tony, Ralph "Tony Garcia" Gabriel and James Kennedy, on charges of murder. All five men were eventually arrested. Manzo plead guilty to his part in the officer's beating and received a two to four year sentence on the charge of concealing a homicide in exchange for testifying against the Chavez brothers. The other four men were all convicted of taking part in the crime. The Chavez brothers both received 27 year prison sentences, while Kennedy and Gabriel received 20 and 10 year terms respectively. All four offenders served their sentences and have been released from prison.

Patrolman Irma C. Ruiz,

STAR #16823, Area #4-Youth Division, Harrison Street Station, 40 years old, and her partner, Patrolman Greg Jaglowski, were at the Moses Montefiore School, 1300 S. Ashland Avenue, on September 22, 1988 when they were confronted by a crazed gunman. Ruiz and Jaglowski operated as a mobile unit that responded to calls from local area schools. On September 22, they were to escort an unruly Montefiore student home. While picking up their charge the officers received a report that an armed offender had entered the school. The man, described as a deranged gunman, had already killed three people and wounded another when Ruiz and Jaglowski engaged him. The assailant opened fire on the officers and Patrolman Ruiz was hit in the chest and sustained a fatal wound. The gunman then fired at Jaglowski, striking him twice in the leg. Despite severe injuries, Officer Jaglowski returned fire and killed the offender. Jaglowski was rushed to Mount Sinai Hospital after the shooting and listed in fair condition the next day.

The officers' presence at the school and quick action prevented more lives from being taken that day. Patrolman Ruiz was remembered by her colleagues, family and friends as a dedicated police officer who loved her job and the chance it gave her to work with children in the area. She graduated from the police academy on October 18, 1976 and became one of the first women assigned to the Grand Crossing District. During her 12 years on the force she earned four complimentary letters, three honorable mentions and a department commendation for her work in a seven week investigation of a hit-and-run accident that led to the driver's arrest. Officer Ruiz was survived by her husband, daughter and three sons. She was laid to rest at St. Mary Cemetery.

Patrolman William J. "Pinky" Luce,

STAR #14287, 45 years old, died of cancer at Michael Reese Hospital on August 14, 1989. Luce had previously been exposed to radiation while on duty, an incident that led to the development of the fatal disease. Luce was testing new weapons when a scope on one of the weapons exploded, causing radiation burns to the officer's face and body. The FBI investigated the accident, but little information was ever disclosed in what remains a secret incident. Luce's radiation burns and exposure were extremely serious and contributed to his death. The patrolman had been on the force for 20 years and had worked in the Special Operations Group as well as the Narcotics Unit. He was also a veteran of the Vietnam War. Officer Luce was survived by his wife, Janet; three sons, Richard, Nick and Brian; and two daughters, Janet Lynn and Lisa. The Luce family laid the fallen officer to rest at St. Mary Cemetery.

Patrolman Bruce Roman Niedorborski,

STAR #17196, Wentworth District, 42 years old, was killed in an accident on Friday, August 18, 1989. It was believed that the officer may have had a heart attack while operating his patrol car, but autopsy reports showed no sign of one. The official cause of death was attributed to the injuries that he sustained during the crash. However, witnesses did report to investigating police that the patrolman had slumped over the wheel of his car before swerving into oncoming traffic in the 4600 block of South Halsted Street. The police vehicle crashed into a truck at about 5:30 P.M. Patrolman Niedoborski was survived by his daughter.

Patrolman Elijah Harris,

STAR #15208, 6th District, Gresham Station, 52 years old, had just finished writing a ticket for an illegally parked vehicle on 79th Street on July 31, 1989 when a local resident informed him a young man riding a white bicycle in the area was carrying a gun. Officer Harris soon spotted the rider on 79th Street and stopped him. He placed the suspect, Andrew Jordan, against a car and began to search him. Jordan then leaned down, took his .22 caliber handgun from the waistband of his pants, turned and shot Patrolman Harris in the abdomen. At 11:05 P.M., Harris sent a distress call over the radio asking for assistance, saying he had been shot. Officers rushed to the scene and transported Harris to Christ Hospital. Harris, a 22-year-veteran, regularly worked as an evidence technician and instructor prior to his death. He had spent the last 14 years working out of the Gresham Station. Over the course of his career he had received 29 honorable mentions and one unit meritorious award. Officer Harris was working the 3:00 P.M. to 11:00 P.M. shift on the night he was shot, his last stint on duty before his vacation was scheduled to begin. He was usually very strict about wearing his bulletproof vest but the heat of the July night led him to go without it.

Officer Harris spent over four months at the hospital. His condition appeared to be improving until about a week and half before his death when he was placed in the Intensive Care Unit. Until then Harris had been keeping his spirits up by taking walks around the hospital and watching Cubs games with friends. He succumbed to his injury on November 16, 1989. Patrolman Harris, a United States Marine Corps veteran, was survived by his four children, mother, sister and brother. Funeral services for Officer Harris were held at Tabor Evangelical Lutheran Church on November 21, 1989. He was interred in Restvale Cemetery. Andrew Jordan, 16 years old, was arrested and held in Cook County Jail on charges of aggravated battery and attempted murder. Prosecutors were considering upgrading the charge to murder at the time of Patrolman Harris' death.

1989

Patrolman Gregory A. Hauser,

STAR #14680, 25th District,
Grand Central District, 43 years old, and

Patrolman Raymond C. Kilroy,

STAR #14686, 25th District, Grand Central District, 47 years
old, were shot to death on the night of May 13, 1990. The patrolmen were responding to
Florence Chavez's call for help in a domestic disturbance involving her 22-year-old grandson
Roman Chavez at 2158 N. Nordica Avenue. The officers had been talking to Florence and Roman
for a few moments when they decided to bring Roman Chavez to the garage to continue questioning him. Suddenly, he grabbed one of the officer's weapons and fired several shots, fatally
wounding both officers. Chavez then fled, still armed with one of the officer's weapons.

After learning that Chavez had escaped his grandmother's home, police quickly
fanned out across the Monteclare neighborhood. More than 100 police officers searched the
area the next morning in a desperate attempt to find the officers' killer. Police went door to
door searching for the offender. Neighbors told the story of a solitary young man, interested
in cars, with a history of causing his grandmother trouble. Police revealed that he had
been released from the Cook County Jail only a short time before the shootings. He had
been arrested the previous February for leading Elmhurst Police on a four mile chase.
Police apprehended Chavez at 2:30 A.M. on May 14, 1990 at 2012 N. Harlem Avenue. He was
arrested, convicted, and sentenced to life in prison for the double homicides.

After the shooting Patrolman Hauser was taken to Lutheran General Hospital, while
Patrolman Kilroy was transported to Illinois Masonic Medical Center. Each was pronounced
dead on arrival. Patrolman Hauser was buried in Elmwood Park Cemetery and Patrolman
Kilroy was laid to rest at Ridgewood Cemetery. Hauser and Kilroy began their careers
together on a March morning 20 years earlier and worked together ever since. They had
both been celebrating Mother's Day with their families earlier in the day. Kilroy was
survived by his wife and three children. Hauser, who was single, left behind his mother.

Patrolman Johnny L. Martin,

STAR #16576, 13th District, Wood Street Station, 31 years old, stepped out of his
home at 3228 N. Wilton Avenue to help a friend on June 28, 1990 and lost his
life in the line of duty. A short time before the officer's death, his neighbor,
Roberto Pizzaro, had noticed a man tampering with his car, parked a short
distance down the street. Pizzaro confronted the offender, Lionel Myles and exchanged words.
Myles left the scene and Martin stepped out into the street to inquire about the raised voices he
had heard. As he and Pizzaro were discussing the incident, Myles returned on a bicycle,
armed with a gun. A confrontation occurred and Myles fired at the officer, fatally injuring him.
Despite a bullet wound to the heart, Patrolman Martin was able to retrieve his weapon from
his ankle holster and fire two shots as Myles escaped. The offender was arrested on his front
porch on the evening of the killing and charged with murder the next morning. Myles was
found guilty of killing Patrolman Martin in January of 1991. Patrolman Martin was buried in
Rosehill Cemetery. He had been a police officer for four years and was survived by his mother,
five sisters, and two brothers.

1990

Patrolman Eddie N. Jones, Jr.,

STAR #11120, 10th District, 28 years old, was fatally shot by a drug informant he and his partner, Patrolman Dennis Dobson, were transporting to a heavily drug-infested area. The officers arrested Alexis Green on drug charges earlier in the day and he offered to lead them to his narcotics source in exchange for the chance of leniency. Once they reached their destination, Green was expected to point out several individuals involved in illegal activities. The officers were unaware that Green, though handcuffed, was in possession of a weapon. The offender managed to get his gun, forcing the officers to pull over in the parking lot of Fairplay Finer Foods, 2200 S. Western Avenue. There he shot the officers from the back of the squad car, injuring Dobson and fatally wounding Jones. Green fled with Dobson's gun. Jones died in the trauma unit of Cook County Hospital on January 7, 1991.

Patrolman Jones left behind a wife and daughter and was laid to rest in Oakwoods Cemetery after being cremated. Arrested 15 times as a juvenile and with three convictions on his adult record, the offender was caught and convicted of officer Jones's death. He was sentenced to life in the State Penitentiary at Joliet.

Patrolman Robert H. Perkins,

STAR #16557, 3rd District, Grand Cross Station, 45 years old, was killed on March 7, 1992 as he questioned a suspect he believed was connected to an earlier crime on the Southside of Chicago near the Dan Ryan Expressway. Perkins was working alone when he was alerted to two men who had allegedly burglarized a man's home near 61st Street and Wabash Avenue. He pulled his vehicle over in front of Betsy Ross Elementary School, 6059 S. Wabash, and began to question the two men. A struggle ensued and one of the men drew a handgun. Four shots were fired and the officer was hit in the left arm and right shoulder. Perkins was unable to fire his own revolver.

The patrolman was taken to Cook County Hospital, where attempts to revive him were unsuccessful. The Vietnam veteran died around 1:00 P.M., several hours after the altercation. Perkins was a father of three and a 16-year-veteran of the force. He was buried at Cedar Park Cemetery.

Chicago Police recovered a handgun and clothing between 60th Street and Michigan Avenue, items believed to have been discarded by Perkin's killer. The items recovered proved useful and Perkins' killer, Stanley Davis, was eventually apprehended and convicted. Davis, paroled in May of 1991 after serving time for another murder, received a life sentence.

Patrolman John J. Lyons,

STAR #3124, Belmont Station, 55 years old, was driving with his partner on October 5, 1992 in the 3400 block of N. Kimball Avenue when he was killed in the line of duty. The officers were responding to a call to assist another unit with a DUI arrest when their squad car spun out of control and hit a tree. The vehicle continued to spin until it struck a lamp post. Officer Lyons was ejected from the vehicle and sustained fatal injuries. His partner, a probationary officer, was taken to the Illinois Masonic Medical Center. He was not able to remember any details of the crash. It was speculated that they might have swerved to avoid hitting another vehicle. Patrolman Lyons, a 25-year-veteran of the department, was survived by his wife and four children.

Patrolman Gerald L. Wright,

STAR #3845, 6th District, 46 years old, was killed at Pat's Food and Liquor at 934 W. 79th Street when he stopped to visit the owner, Jeber Sweis, on August 7, 1993, after his shift ended. About an hour after he arrived at the store, in the Gresham neighborhood, Wright was hit in the aorta by a bullet fired by a gang member. The shooter was aiming at a 17-year-old male, Marlon Brown, with whom Wright was speaking. Patrolman Wright knew Brown from his patrol and was apparently warning him. Brown was targeted in retaliation for a shooting earlier in the week. Four more shots rang out and Wright fell in the doorway. The divorced father of three children was taken to Christ Hospital, where he later died. He was buried at Mount Hope Cemetery. Wright wore the same badge number as his 78-year-old father, a retired Chicago Police veteran.

Police arrested 18-year-old Steven Haas, identified as the shooter by several witnesses at the scene, and charged him with Officer Wright's murder. A second teenager, Rafael Jackson, 16, was also arrested and charged as Haas' accomplice. Jackson testified that he and Haas had planned the shooting in retaliation for the death of a fellow gang member earlier in the week. Jackson plead guilty to murder and was sentenced to 55 years in prison. In January of 1996, almost three years after the shooting, Haas was convicted of Officer Wright's murder and sentenced to 100 years in prison.

No police deaths in 1994

1993

Patrolman Daniel J. Doffyn,

STAR #14030, Recruit Training, Austin District, 40 years old, had been a Chicago police officer for 8 months when he was killed while answering a burglary-in-progress call on March 8, 1995. He and Officer Milan "Mike" Bubalo had just ended their shift and were walking from the 15th District police station to their separate vehicles when they heard a burglary report for a location across the street from the station at 750 N. Lorel Avenue. They joined responding officers and approached the building. The officers heard glass breaking coming from the back of the apartment and ran towards the sound. They discovered two men walking away from the building. Doffyn caught the younger suspect as the other opened fire, striking him in areas not covered by his bulletproof vest. The man then fired three shots at Bubalo, who returned fire and wounded the offender, preventing his escape.

Doffyn was taken to Cook County Hospital and died in surgery five hours later. Three men, Murray Blue, Jimmy Parker and Clyde Cowley, were ultimately arrested. All of the suspects had lengthy criminal records. The men had panicked about having been involved in a shooting a half an hour before they were nabbed by Doffyn and Bubalo. They were all sentenced to life in prison without the possibility of parole for their parts in Officer Doffyn's death. Their sentences were vacated and new trials ordered for all of the men by the Illinois Supreme Court on October 17, 2003.

Patrolman Doffyn, the divorced father of an 8-year-old daughter, was interred at Rosehill Cemetery after a service attended by hundreds of Chicago police officers at Immaculate Heart of Mary Church.

Patrolman James M. O'Connor,

STAR #4573, 23rd District, 27 years old, was off duty on September 16, 1995 when he intervened in a robbery. O'Connor was in his car talking to a woman outside El Jardin, a restaurant located at Clark and Roscoe Streets, around 3:00 A.M. when a car drove by and a young boy stole the woman's purse. The car was being driven by 22-year-old Franklin Matthews of Bolingbrook who was believed to have committed previous robberies with the 14-year-old purse snatcher.

O'Connor gave chase and cut off Matthews' vehicle in the 4100 block of Marine Drive, near Lake Shore Drive and Irving Park Road. As he approached the car fierce gunfire erupted. O'Connor was hit twice and died before he could make it back to his car. Matthews drove off but did not get far. O'Connor had shot him twice and his injuries caused him to crash into a brick wall. He was found dead behind the steering wheel. The boy, whose name was not released due to his age, was arrested and charged with robbery of the woman's purse and, shortly thereafter, murder.

Officer O'Connor had been with the police department for 17 months. He was praised as a dedicated, companionable officer. The patrolman was survived by his parents, Thomas and Louise O'Connor; three brothers, Thomas, Daniel and Tim; and his grandmother, Martha Rossdeutcher. He lived on the northwest side of Chicago with his parents and was buried at All Saints Cemetery.

Patrolman Dell Fountain,

STAR #18247, 15th District, 40 years old, was killed on March 22, 1996 as he entered an apartment located above his own residents on the 3900 block of W. Van Buren Avenue. Fountain's son had been denied entrance to their two-flat by a male who fled to the 2nd floor apartment when the young man called to his father for assistance. Officer Fountain, who was off-duty at the time, pursued Tajuan Murray, and the two men began to struggle. As they fought, Murray was able to gain control of the officer's service weapon and used it to shoot Officer Fountain in the leg. The patrolman was rushed to Cook County Hospital where he died due to massive blood loss. Murray was arrested and convicted of Patrolman Fountain's murder. He was sentenced to life in prison on October 6, 1998. His conviction was overturned in 2001 and a new trial was ordered.

Fountain was a father of two who lived with his 16 year-old son. Officer Fountain had been on the force for almost three years at the time of his death and was buried in Belzoni, Mississippi.

Patrolman David C. Evans,

STAR #9398, 6th District, 39 years old, was driving in his car at 12:35 A.M. on the morning of August 25, 1997 with his partner, Patrolman Estella Johnson, when they received a call reporting paramedics needed assistance at 7933 S. Vernon Avenue. Evans turned the vehicle but had to swerve to avoid pedestrians in the road. The squad car crashed onto a curb before smashing through the barrier of the 79th Street overpass and falling onto the northbound lanes of the Dan Ryan Expressway. Patrolman Evans was an eleven-year-veteran of the force who had enough seniority to work days but chose to work nights to spend more time with his family. He was buried in Oak Woods Cemetery and survived by his wife, Micheline; a son, Brandon King; and two daughters, Burgundy King and Ashlee.

Patrolman Gregory I. Young,

STAR #16148, 15th District, 41 years old, was killed on September 17, 1997 during a robbery attempt in Garfield Park on the 3500 block of W. Lake Street. Young was seated in his car with a companion when two assailants, Chris Davis and Tory Robertson, approached the vehicle and demanded that Officer Young turn over anything of value.

Young reportedly told them he was a police officer and showed his badge. A fusillade of gunfire erupted and Young was shot at close range. He was mortally wounded but still managed to fire several shots and gravely injure Davis. The offender, a three time ex-con once acquitted of a double murder charge, was taken to Cook County Hospital in a coma. He would later make a full recovery and be convicted of Patrolman Young's murder. Sentenced to death, Davis received a commutation from Governor George Ryan on January 11, 2003.

Young was also taken to Cook County Hospital and pronounced dead at 9:47 P.M. Officer Young was survived by his wife, Gladys; his daughter, Rashida; and son, Jason. He was buried at Forest Home Cemetery.

Patrolman Frank Balzano,

STAR #10528, O'Hare Airport, 65 years old, was working at his part-time job as security guard at the Harlem-Irving Plaza when he tried to break up a fight between two teenage girls on November 12, 1997. Policeman Balzano was arresting one of the girls for attacking a security officer when she called out to her boyfriend for help. Her boyfriend, Bob Benjamin, also known as Zbigniew "Ziggy" Kreseckowski, age 16, knocked Balzano to the ground. The officer sustained a fatal injury in the fall and died the following day, November 13, 1997. The girl, Amy Landers, age 17, was charged with first-degree murder; her boyfriend was also charged.

Officer Balzano was to retire in the next few months. He had joined the force in 1958, spending the majority of his career in the canine unit. Balzano had been assigned to O'Hare International Airport working with the canine bomb unit since the early 1990s. His partner was Max, a yellow Labrador. Max was more than just Officer Balzano's partner, he was the family pet, who remained with the Balzano family after the officer's death. Officer Balzano left behind his wife, Jean Balzano; mother, Louise Nelson; two sons, Frank Jr. and Dan; a daughter, Cathy Zak; three grandchildren; two brothers; and a sister.

In 2000, Kreseckowski and Landers pled guilty to involuntary manslaughter. Ziggy was sentenced to four years in prison and Landers was sentenced to three years of probation, including a year of intense anger management counseling.

Patrolman Richard R. Schott,

STAR #12028, 9th District, Deering Street Station, 46 years old, suffered a heart attack, December 3, 1997, after attempting to detain a prisoner in the Deering District's lockup facility. Schott and his partner had just finished taking fingerprints from Sergio DeLeon, arrested for possession of a controlled substance, when a struggle broke out. The officers were able to subdue DeLeon, but Schott fell to the ground unconscious shortly afterwards. Officers at the scene administered CPR and called an ambulance. Schott arrived at Michael Reese Hospital in cardiac arrest and was pronounced dead at 2:00 A.M. The medical examiner's office stated that clogged arteries made the officer extremely susceptible to a heart attack. Patrolman Schott was interred at Holy Sepulchre Cemetery and was survived by his ex-wife and son. He had been an officer since 1973 and had received 48 honorable mentions during his time on the force.

DeLeon was charged with first degree murder along with three counts of aggravated battey. He was convicted on the aggravated battery charges and sentenced to ten years in prison. He also received an additional three year sentence after being convicted in the original drug arrest that led to the struggle with Officer Schott.

Patrolman Michael A. Ceriale,

STAR #17429, 2nd District, 26 years old, died in Cook County Hospital on August 21, 1998 after suffering a bullet wound to the abdomen on August 15. Ceriale and his partner were working an undercover narcotics surveillance around the Robert Taylor Homes when they recognized a drug deal occurring at 4101 S. Federal Street. Parking their car behind the brick high-rise, they observed the men in front of the building. As the officers watched, someone in the group fired a shot from 60-70 yards away. The bullet lodged in Ceriale's lower abdomen, inches from the protection of his bulletproof vest. Seven men were later arrested for their part in the shooting and four were eventually charged with the officer's murder. One of the men, George Alexander, pleaded guilty and was sentenced to 30 years in prison in September of 2001. Prosecutors believe he alerted other gang members to the officers' presence. Willie Hunter and Robert Brandt also pleaded guilty. Hunter was sentenced to 30 years, while Brandt was given 20 years in prison. The final offender, Jonathan Tolliver, was identified as the actual shooter. He was tried twice for Officer Ceriale's murder. The first trial ended in a hung jury when a single juror refused to change his vote for acquittal. The second jury found Tolliver guilty and he was sentenced to 60 years in prison.

After the shooting, Ceriale was rushed to Cook County Hospital. While there, he underwent several surgeries and received more than 200 pints of blood donated by concerned officers and citizens. His funeral at St. Nicholas Ukranian Cathedral was attended by thousands of officers from the Chicago area, Wisconsin, and even Michigan. Patrolman Ceriale, who was unmarried and the only child of two surviving parents, was buried at All Saints Cemetery. The patrolman had been on the force for 15 months.

1998

Patrolman John C. Knight,

STAR #5119, 22nd District Tactical Unit, Morgan Park District, 38 years old, was a plainclothes tactical officer who lost his life in the line of duty on January 9, 1999. Knight and his partner, Patrolman James Butler, spotted a brown 1986 Chevrolet Caprice parked on 99th Street believed to be stolen. When they drove up to the car two men within slid down in their seats to avoid being seen. The officers stopped their unmarked squad and got out. The Caprice then took off west on 99th Street, going the wrong way down a one-way street.

As the officers followed, the Caprice collided with another automobile at 99th Street and Parnell Avenue. The occupants exited the damaged Caprice and began to run. Butler and Knight exited their vehicle as one of the men turned and opened fire with an automatic handgun with a laser sight. Knight was shot three times with other bullets going through the squad car, breaking several windows. Butler was able to return fire, hitting the gunman and bringing him to the ground. The gunman reloaded his weapon, shot Butler in the hip, and then escaped on foot.

A massive police manhunt ensued, with 40 squads and several helicopters searching to find the killers. A trail of blood in the snow led police to James Scott. The offender claimed he did not know the men were police officers. Scott was convicted of Patrolman Knight's murder and sentenced to life in prison without parole.

Fellow officers described John Knight as a happy, good-natured policeman. Knight was survived by a wife, Joan; and three children. He was buried in Holy Sepulchre Cemetery. The policeman had been on the force for 11 years and was the son of a retired Chicago Police Officer.

Patrolman James H. Camp,

STAR #3934, 21st District Tactical Unit, Prairie District, 34 years old, was in plain clothes on March 9, 1999 when he and his partner, Patrolman Kenny King, noticed a suspicious car as they walked out of the Madden Park Homes public housing complex on the 3800 block of South Cottage Grove. They realized that the car had been stolen when they observed that the steering column of the vehicle had been pulled back. Camp approached the driver of the car, Kevin Dean, and ordered him to get out. Dean refused and Camp pulled him out of the car. A struggle ensued and Dean managed to gain control of the patrolman's gun, which he then used to fatally shoot Camp. The woman in the front passenger seat, Yvonne Harris, fled the scene after the shooting. Officer Earl Carter, on patrol nearby, spotted the fleeing offender and fired, halting Dean's escape.

The incident occurred near Albert Einstein Elementary School. Teachers had to instruct the children to duck under their desks below the windows to avoid the gunfire.

Dean was arrested and charged with possession of a stolen car, disarming an officer and Patrolman Camp's murder. He was acquitted of the murder charge and sentenced to a maximum of two consecutive 30 year terms for disarming an officer and possession of a stolen car. He later appealed and his sentence was reduced to a total of 28 years.

Camp, a Marine veteran who had been with the police department for four years, was buried in Oakwoods Cemetery. He was survived by his wife, Opal, who he had married only three months before his death.

Sergeant Alane M. Stoffregen,

STAR #1203, Marine Unit, 50 years old, was a police diver who died during a scuba training exercise on June 2, 2000. She and another officer were diving off the wreck of the USS Iowa in Lake Michigan at approximately 35 feet when Officer Stoffregen became distressed. Her diving partner noticed she appeared disoriented and heroically held her above water until help arrived. Marks were discovered on her forehead that led investigators to believe that she was pushed against the boat by the three foot waves that made the water extremely turbulent that day and may have incapacitated her. Despite all the efforts of the paramedics and her diving partner, Stroffregen was pronounced dead at Northwestern Memorial Hospital a short time after being pulled from the water. She was buried in St. Jude Cemetery and survived by her mother, Agnes; six siblings, Timothy, Kenneth, Gale, Ronald, James, and Marybeth; as well as a number of nieces and nephews. Stoffregen had been a member of the Chicago Police Department for 22 years.

Patrolman Brian T. Strouse,

STAR #15806, 12th District Tactical Unit, 33 years old, responded to a report of gang activity near 18th Place and Loomis Avenue in Pilsen with his two partners on June 30, 2001. Strouse was not supposed to have been on duty that Saturday morning but had volunteered to work because he knew that the area was being terrorized by gang warfare. Strouse and the other officers arrived at an alley behind 1835 S. Loomis Avenue around 2:00 A.M. and began surveillance. They soon heard the sound of gunfire and Strouse stepped out and approached the shooter. He yelled that he was a police officer and to cease shooting. The 16-year-old, Hector Delgado, working as security for his gang's drug trade, continued to shoot. Strouse tried to take shelter behind a car but was struck twice before he could. The first shot was stopped by his bulletproof vest, but the second bullet caused a fatal head wound. The boy was taken into custody moments later and charged with first degree murder.

Delgado was put on trial for the murder of Officer Strouse after making a taped confession with his parents present. On September 17, 2003, he was convicted of first degree murder and sentenced to life in prison on December 8, 2003.

Strouse was a six-year-veteran of the force and had received 61 commendations and the department's Life Saving Award for exceptional courage. He was survived by his parents and three sisters, one of whom is also a Chicago Police Officer. Strouse was buried in Mount Emblem Cemetery.

Patrolman Eric D. Lee,

STAR #16947, 7th District, 37 years old, was fatally shot in the line of duty on the night of August 19, 2001, becoming the fourth tactical officer to be shot in Chicago in two years. Lee and two other officers saw a man being beaten in an alley near 63rd and Aberdeen Streets. They approached, intending to intervene, and informed the assailants that they were police officers. They were immediately fired upon with one shot hitting Officer Lee in the head. Other officers at the scene were able to quickly apprehend the shooter, Aloysius Oliver. The offender had beaten the other man in the alley because he relieved himself on a trashcan behind Oliver's house. Oliver was tried for Patrolman Lee's murder, convicted by a jury in January 2004 and sentenced to life in prison on September 17, 2004.

Lee was taken to Christ Hospital, where he died several hours later. The 9-year-police veteran was highly decorated and respected. He was a former Marine with a magna cum laude university degree. At his funeral, attended by over 1,000 people, he was hailed as a family man, role model and excellent officer. Lee had worked in the crime-ridden neighborhood of Englewood, where he had grown up, for almost 10 years. Officer Lee was buried in Oak Woods Cemetery.

Sergeant Hector A. Silva,

STAR #1760, Special Operations Group, 36 years old, died on October 2, 2001 after participating in a Special Operations training exercise on September 30, 2001. Silva collapsed after sprinting two flights of stairs during a training exercise in which he carried sandbags weighing a total of 55 pounds. The exercise was intended to simulate working in protective gear while dealing with chemical agents.

Silva, who feared he had suffered a heart attack six weeks earlier, died on October 2 during an operation at Mount Sinai Hospital to remove a blood clot from his brain. The officer had been on the force for 11 years and had earned 54 honorable mentions as well as the Superintendent's Award of Valor, the Carter Harrison Medal, in 1997, after jamming his hand in an assailant's pistol in order to disarm and apprehend him. Silva was survived by his wife and two daughters and buried in Mary Hill Cemetery.

Patrolman Donald J. Marquez,

STAR #8620, Corporation Counsel Detail, 47 years old, was serving a warrant around 10:00 P.M. on Monday, March 18, 2002 when he was shot to death by the man he was trying to present with the summons. The warrant, for Housing Court violations was issued to Henry Wolk, 77. The offender had failed to appear in Housing Court for several months in spite of numerous attempts to serve him.

Marquez and his partner arrived at the two-story building at 2451 N. Avers Avenue and enlisted neighbors to help them persuade Wolk to open his door. After 10 minutes of "one-sided" conversation, the suspect, quick-tempered and unstable, had still not opened his door. Marquez resolved to break down the door with a sledgehammer and take the offender into custody. As soon as the door was down Wolk, with a gun in each hand, opened fire and struck Marquez in the head, chest and abdomen. He then engaged responding officers in a ten minute gun battle before he was fatally wounded. He was transported to Mt. Sinai Hospital where he later died. Wolk had previously told neighbors that he would never go to court or leave the home he had lived in since he was two years old.

Marquez died March 19 at 2:25 A.M., succumbing to fatal injuries from a semiautomatic handgun. The officer, a 20-year-veteran of the force, was described as a "policeman's policeman." He was mourned by his wife and four children, one of whom had recently given birth to his first grandchild. Patrolman Marquez was interred in Resurrection Cemetery.

Patrolman Benjamin Perez,

STAR #12225, Marquette District, 32 years old, was killed when he was struck by a train on September 18, 2002 while on a drug stakeout. Perez and his partner, Patrolman Ron Zuniga, received a tip that a drug deal was taking place near the Burlington Northern-Santa Fe railroad tracks on the Westside near Cermak and Spaulding. The officers went to investigate. They climbed an embankment and moved along a set of railroad tracks in order to gain a better sight line. While on the trestle, a Metra commuter train bound for Aurora approached and Patrolman Perez was pulled underneath the train and killed instantly. Perez, who was born in Zacatecas, Mexico, was a distinguished, 4-year-veteran of the Chicago Police Department. He was survived by his wife, Michele; and three children, Katarina, Benjamin and Rebecca; and buried in Resurrection Cemetery.

Sergeant Philip J. O'Reilly,

STAR #2321, Foster District, 41 years old, was killed in a car crash when a tow truck struck his squad car on March 16, 2003 at the intersection of Granville and Western Avenues around 5:00 A.M. The impact of a northbound truck ejected him from his vehicle. O'Reilly was taken to the Illinois Masonic Medical Center and pronounced dead there later that morning. The driver of the tow truck was charged with driving too fast for conditions. O'Reilly, the father of six children, was a 16-year-veteran of the force whose brother was also a police officer. Sergeant O'Reilly was buried at Calvary Cemetery.

Patrolman Roberto Jackson,

STAR # unavailable, Harrison District, 52 years old, a 22-year-veteran, was accidentally shot to death on the morning of June 11, 2003 by her son, James Hargrett. Known to be mentally ill, he had previously attempted suicide. Hargrett ran in front of traffic on the 1600 block of N. Mobile Avenue in an attempt to get hit by a car and end his life. His mother, Officer Jackson, ran after him and gave him a bear hug, hoping to calm him down. However, Hargrett pulled out a TEC-9 semiautomatic pistol and shot himself in the chest. The bullet passed through his body and struck his mother.

Officer Jackson was taken to Mount Sinai Hospital, where she succumbed to her injury. Her son was taken to Stroger Hospital of Cook Country and listed in critical condition. He was later charged with aggravated unlawful use of a weapon. Patrolman Jackson was survived by her son and a daughter.

Patrolman Michael Patrick Gordon,

STAR #18751, Harrison District, 30 years old, was patrolling with Officer John Dalcason on August 8, 2004 when their squad car was hit by a drunk driver. The offender, Luis Calle, was legally intoxicated when his car collided with Officer Gordon's vehicle at the intersection of Jackson Boulevard and Sacramento Avenue. Both officers were ejected from the car on impact. It was later learned that Calle's blood alcohol level was .177, more than twice the legal limit of .08. Gordon was rushed to Stroger Hospital, where he later died. Dalcason was taken to Mount Sinai Hospital and recovered from his injuries. Calle was killed in the crash.

Before joining the Chicago Police Department, Officer Gordon had served as a military officer in Bosnia and South Korea as part of the Army's 82nd Airborne Division. After his military service he became a policeman in Riverside, Illinois and transferred to the Chicago Police Department in 2002. He was survived by his wife, Guin; their daughter, Grace; two sons from a previous marriage, Malik and Cullen; and a stepson, David Lopez; parents, Robert, Jr., and Carol; and two brothers, John and Robert III. Gordon's funeral was held at Blake-Lamb Funeral Home and he was interred at Mount Vernon Memorial Estates. Shortly before Officer Gordon's death his father, Robert Jr., had retired from his position as Assistant Chief of Police in Riverside, Illinois. His brother is a police officer in Broadview, Illinois and an uncle and cousin are both Chicago Police Officers. Police work was described as a family business for the Gordon family.

No police deaths in 2005

Patrolman Eric Solorio,

STAR #13609, Targeted Response Unit, 26 years old, was patrolling with his partner at 10:45 P.M. on January 17, 2006 when they spotted a speeding car in the Englewood neighborhood near 67th and Union Streets and set off in pursuit. The officers were traveling east on 67th Street when the squad car hit a patch of black ice and spun out of control, colliding with a tree and a church at 701 W. Marquette Road before coming to a stop. Officer Solorio was rushed to Christ Medical Center after the accident and underwent surgery for a spinal injury that left him able to move only his shoulders and arms. He eventually regained consciousness and was able to speak with the dozens of visitors who came to his hospital room over the next month. However, his condition never truly improved and he died on February 12, 2006. Solorio's partner suffered minor injuries and was released from the hospital a short time after the crash. Patrolman Solorio was survived by his mother, Amelia; two sisters, Richelle Romo and Rosa Solorio; and a brother, Richard Carillo. Funeral services were held at Holy Cross Church and he was laid to rest at Resurrection Cemetery.

Patrolman Solorio, a graduate of Loyola University, was a three-year-veteran of the force. He enrolled at Loyola as a student at St. Joseph College Seminary before switching his major to premed and finally deciding that police work was his true calling. He had been chosen for the Targeted Response Unit, a division sent to city "hot spots" to deal with areas where gangs, guns, drugs and homicides were rampant. In March 2006, the Granville Police Office, a new satellite police station located under the Granville Red Line "EL" stop in the Edgewater neighborhood, was dedicated in Officer Solorio's honor.

Chicago Police Officer Eric Solorio's funeral at Holy Cross Church. His mother Amelis Solorio follows the casket draped in the Chicago flag and police pallbearers. *Chicago Tribune* Photo Archive.

2006

Number of Arrests and Number of Sworn Officers

Year	Arrests	Officers	Year	Arrests	Officers
1835	Not Available	3	1878	31,713	450
1836	Not Available	1	1879	28,480	453
1837	Not Available	7	1880	27,338	473
1838	Not Available	3	1881	27,208	557
1839	Not Available	3	1882	32,800	637
1840	Not Available	4	1883	37,187	924
1841	Not Available	2	1884	40,998	926
1842	Not Available	2	1885	44,261	1,036
1843	Not Available	6	1886	46,505	1,145
1844	Not Available	9	1887	50,432	1,225
1845	Not Available	16	1888	48,119	1,624
1846	Not Available	6	1889	62,230	1,900
1847	Not Available	22	1890	70,550	2,306
1848	Not Available	18	1891	89,833	2,726
1849	Not Available	12	1892	96,976	3,189
1850	Not Available	19	1893	88,323	3,188
1851	Not Available	37	1894	83,464	3,255
1852	Not Available	37	1895	96,847	3,033
1853	2,449	48	1896	83,680	3,117
1854	Not Available	49	1897	77,441	3,304
1855	5,008	103	1898	71,349	3,267
1856	Not Available	124	1899	70,438	3,314
1857	Not Available	117	1900	69,442	3,250
1858	Not Available	118	1901	70,314	3,168
1859	Not Available	136	1902	77,763	3,205
1860	Not Available	66	1903	66,344	2,316
1861	8,782	72	1904	79,026	2,676
1862	Not Available	71	1905	78,392	4,077
1863	9,601	84	1906	58,002	4,529
1864	14,014	82	1907	63,385	4,733
1865	21,721	179	1908	66,695	4,706
1866	23,315	180	1909	77,218	4,260
1867	22,528	268	1910	80,649	4,926
1868	Not Available	291	1911	83,853	4,955
1869	22,643	368	1912	109,764	4,443
1870	26,488	374	1913	111,461	5,093
1871	21,931	450	1914	114,625	5,331
1872	31,585	450	1915	111,587	5,277
1873	24,899	546	1916	129,270	5,199
1874	19,206	590	1917	105,632	4,706
1875	27,291	591	1918	91,457	5,120
1876	28,035	517	1919	87,197	5,152
1877	27,208	443	1920	117,719	5,140

Year	Arrests	Officers	Year	Arrests	Officers
1921	132,290	6,184	1964	244,739	10,282
1922	181,980	5,965	1965	247,701	11,126
1923	242,602	6,010	1966	251,462	11,428
1924	264,494	5,862	1967	256,094	11,928
1925	211,317	6,080	1968	264,094	12,678
1926	161,239	6,078	1969	265,444	12,678
1927	150,885	6,098	1970	280,222	13,181
1928	194,999	5,776	1971	275,335	13,180
1929	183,434	6,393	1972	265,208	13,751
1930	150,197	6,253	1973	288,505	13,470
1931	176,915	6,020	1974	333,668	13,146
1932	148,664	6,163	1975	288,415	13,040
1933	147,630	5,969	1976	258,771	13,155
1934	198,428	6,302	1977	278,814	13,075
1935	211,872	6,273	1978	295,459	13,026
1936	291,055	6,253	1979	317,774	13,293
1937	226,831	6,408	1980	336,153	12,724
1938	206,497	6,281	1981	412,965	12,374
1939	232,024	6,274	1982	301,863	12,360
1940	284,490	6,427	1983	260,863	12,809
1941	227,026	6,037	1984	246,640	12,530
1942	181,228	6,075	1985	229,309	12,570
1943	235,112	6,020	1986	226,139	12,926
1944	242,634	6,401	1987	255,654	12,931
1945	332,788	7,477	1988	276,912	12,504
1946	333,079	7,319	1989	306,367	12,585
1947	84,558	7,384	1990	316,551	12,137
1948	139,036	7,219	1991	306,369	12,730
1949	133,013	7,070	1992	294,734	12,351
1950	162,495	7,101	1993	294,631	12,809
1951	189,803	7,087	1994	305,255	13,324
1952	186,087	7,261	1995	301,890	13,468
1953	208,470	7,492	1996	292,182	13,439
1954	201,429	8,230	1997	276,986	13,484
1955	207,312	8,862	1998	276,986	13,484
1956	207,041	9,590	1999	268,132	13,755
1957	193,792	9,677	2000	252,802	13,683
1958	209,558	9,997	2001	233,455	13,739
1959	Not Available	10,712	2002	237,706	13,705
1960	Not Available	10,026	2003	238,961	13,619
1961	Not Available	10,716	2004	244,193	13,423
1962	Not Available	10,667	2005	238,636	13,323
1963	253,112	10,258	2006	Not Available	13,540

Causes of Deaths

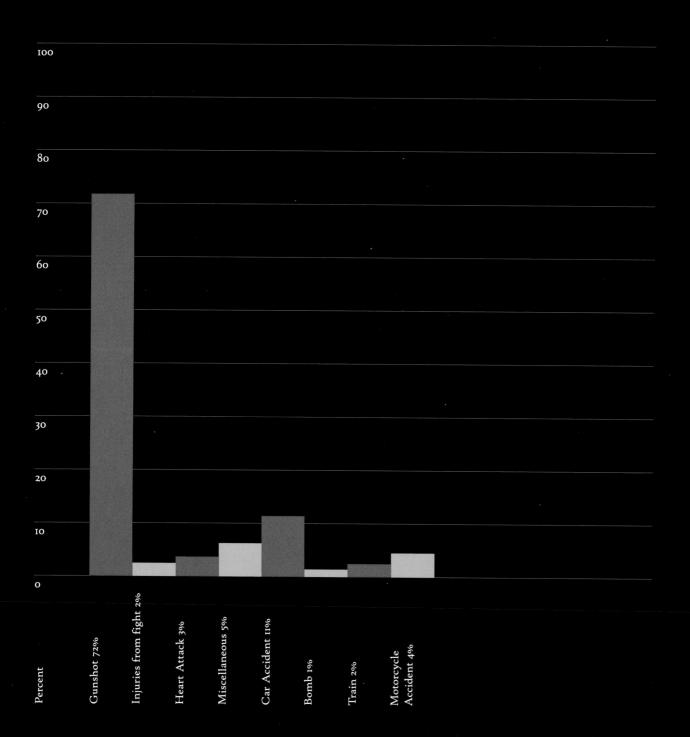

100

90

80

70

60

50

40

30

20

10

0

Percent

Gunshot 72%

Injuries from fight 2%

Heart Attack 3%

Miscellaneous 5%

Car Accident 11%

Bomb 1%

Train 2%

Motorcycle Accident 4%

Number of CPD Deaths by Rank
above Patrolman Grade

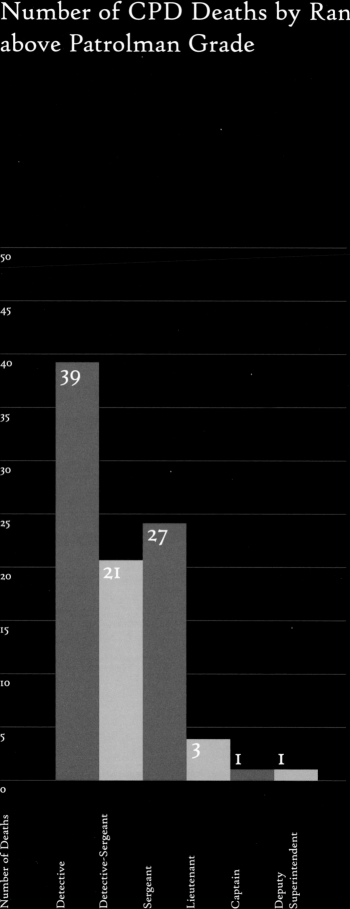

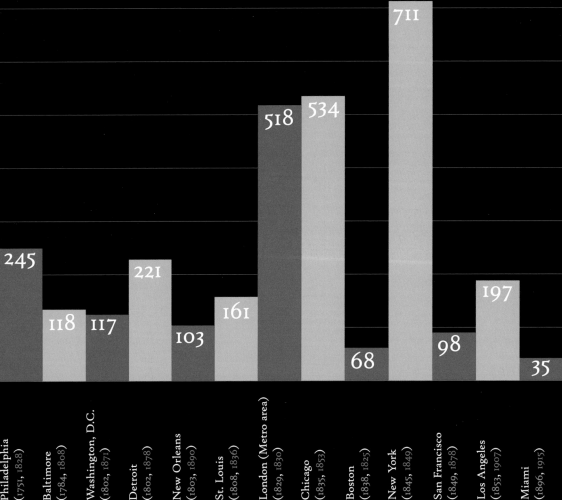

| 245 | 118 | 117 | 221 | 103 | 161 | 518 | 534 | 68 | 711 | 98 | 197 | 35 |

Philadelphia
(1751, 1828)

Baltimore
(1784, 1808)

Washington, D.C.
(1802, 1871)

Detroit
(1802, 1878)

New Orleans
(1803, 1890)

St. Louis
(1808, 1836)

London (Metro area)
(1829, 1830)

Chicago
(1835, 1853)

Boston
(1838, 1825)

New York
(1845, 1849)

San Francisco
(1849, 1878)

Los Angeles
(1853, 1907)

Miami
(1896, 1915)

Years Between Municipal Police Department Founding and First Line of Duty Deaths

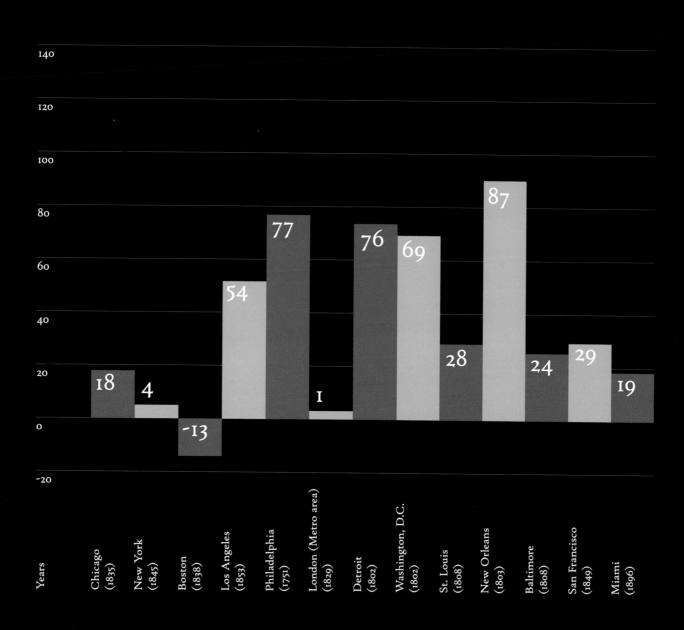

140

120

100

80   77
                              76
60   69   87

54
40

28   29
20 18   24
        4   19
0   I
    -13

-20

Years

Chicago (1835)

New York (1845)

Boston (1838)

Los Angeles (1853)

Philadelphia (1751)

London (Metro area) (1829)

Detroit (1802)

Washington, D.C. (1802)

St. Louis (1808)

New Orleans (1803)

Baltimore (1808)

San Francisco (1849)

Miami (1896)

Officers Killed by Year

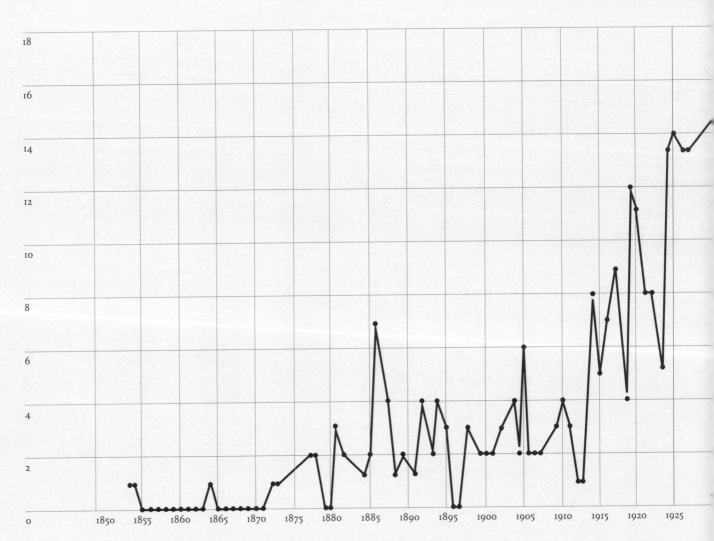

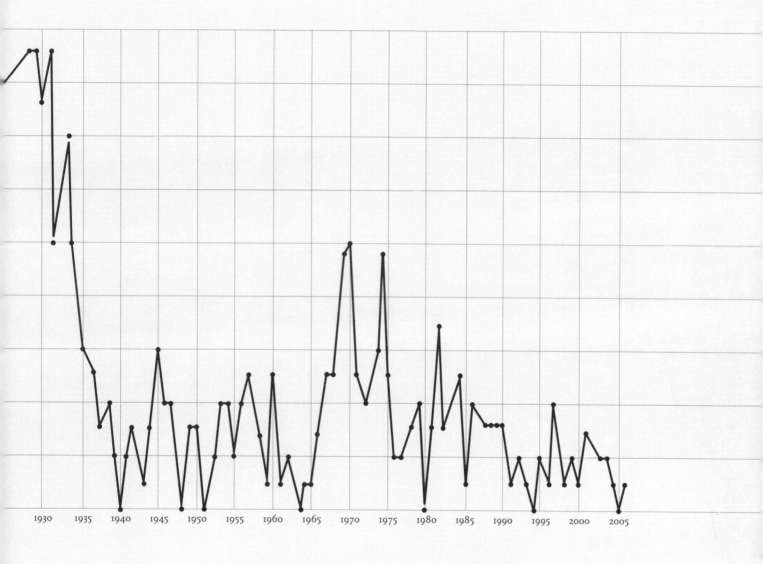

1930   1935   1940   1945   1950   1955   1960   1965   1970   1975   1980   1985   1990   1995   2000   2005

Mounted Chicago Policeman rides his horse
down a ramp onto sidewalk at teh headquarters of
the Mounted Squad at 1121 S. State Street, 1906.
Chicago Daily News photo archive;
Chicago History Museum.

Index

Fogarty, Patrolman Patrick 184
Foley, Patrolman Matthew J. 221
Fountain, Patrolman Dell 543
Francois, Patrolman Harry 399
Freeman, Patrolman George T. 416
Fredericks, Patrolman Bruno H. 212
Freichel, Patrolman John 391
Friedman, Detective Morris 405
Fryer, Patrolman Adam 125
Fuller, Patrolman William A. 426
Furst, Patrolman Louis F. 388

G
Gagler, Patrolman William G. 365
Gallagher, Patrolman Patrick J. 352
Gallagher, Patrolman William 334
Galloway, Patrolman Melvin R. 489
Gallowitch, Patrolman Robert L. 492
Garrison, Patrolman Bruce N. 498
Gartley, Patrolman Andrew 188
Gaster, Patrolman Harry 268
Gibbons, Patrolman Robert 255
Gibbs, Patrolman John 216
Gilhooly, Patrolman John 480
Gillespie, Patrolman Vincent 311
Gilman, Detective Jesse C. 183
Gipson, Patrolman Richard F. 513
Giovanni, Patrolman George F. 336
Glynn, Patrolman Thomas J. 501
Golden, Patrolman Robert R. 437
Gonzales, Detective Oreste 429
Gordon, Patrolman Michael P. 549
Gossmeyer, Patrolman Melvin L. 458
Granger, Patrolman Robert H. 362
Grant, Patrolman Leo 302
Gray, Sergeant Harry J. 281
Guiltanane, Patrolman John J. 347

H
Hagberg, Patrolman Herbert N. 330
Hall, Patrolman Samuel 462
Hallaran, Detective William S. 111
Halloran, Patrolman Edwin 297
Halperin, Detective Barney L. 442
Hansen, Patrolman Nels 110
Harrington, Patrolman James 251
Harris, Patrolman Elijah 536
Hart, Patrolman Peter M. 188
Hartnett, Jr., Patrolman Lawrence C. 261
Hastings, Patrolman Joseph P. 374
Hauser, Patrolman Gregory A. 537
Hauswirth, Patrolman Andrew 132
Hayden, Patrolman Irwin F. 489
Healy, Patrolman Thomas J. 308
Heilman, Patrolman Fred 145
Helstern, Detective George H. 408

Hennessy, Detective-Sergeant
    William E. 243
Henry, Patrolman James A. 289
Hicks, Patrolman Wendell H. 496
Higgins, Patrolman Joseph F. 502
Hoard, Patrolman William E. 375
Hobson, Detective Young C. 472
Holmes, Patrolman William 273
Hosna, Detective-Sergeant
    James L. 222
Howard, Patrolman Daniel E. 502
Howe, Patrolman Luke 319
Huebner, Patrolman John 96
Hults, Patrolman Jesse D. 332
Hulton, Patrolman Eugene 291

I
Isola, Patrolman Joseph 389
Issacs, Patrolman Joseph V. 357

J
Jackson, Patrolman Arthur O. 532
Jackson, Patrolman Erwin 479
Jackson, Patrolman Roberto 549
Jacobs, Patrolman Christian 83
Jagla, Patrolman Leonard T. 319
Janowski, Sergeant Anthony F. 507
Jasper, Patrolman John P. 462
Johnson, Patrolman Bror A. 208
Johnson, Patrolman Thomas J. 356
Johnson, Patrolman William H. 491
Johnson, Detective William R. 459
Johnston, Detective-Sergeant
    Robert L. 294
Johnston, Patrolman Roscoe C. 370
Jones, Patrolman Charles T. 186
Jones, Jr., Patrolman Eddie 540

K
Kakacek, Patrolman James 304
Kaner, Patrolman Kenneth G. 484
Karl, Patrolman James G. 403
Kavanaugh, Patrolman Raymond 351
Kearney, Patrolman John P. 176
Keating, Patrolman David F. 418
Keefe, Patrolman James J. 154
Keegan, Patrolman Eugene J. 312
Keegan, Patrolman John 120
Kehoe, Sergeant Thomas 306
Kelliher, Patrolman Lyons 437
Kelly, Patrolman John 308
Kelly, Patrolman Philip J. 397
Kelly, Patrolman Raymond 362
Kelly, Patrolman Thomas J. 483
Kelma, Patrolman Thomas 387
Kennedy, Patrolman Hugh 351

Kenny, Patrolman John F. 209
Keogh, Patrolman John 324
Keogh, Patrolman Richard J. 364
Keon, Patrolman James 88
Kilroy, Patrolman Raymond C. 537
King, Detective Wayne G. 528
King, Patrolman William J. 240
Klacza, Patrolman Wayne J. 521
Klinke, Patrolman Bernard 393
Klocek, Patrolman Joseph 388
Knight, Patrolman John C. 546
Knudson, Patrolman Martin 360
Koumoundouros, Patrolman
    James W. 506
Kraatz, Detective Charles C.P. 428
Krum, Patrolman George 132
Kuebler, Patrolman Bernard A. 138
Kurtz, Patrolman Joseph 248

L
Langan, Patrolman Michael T. 337
Lange, Patrolman Henry 324
Lauer, Constable Casper 73
Larson, Patrolman Charles C.P. 213
Leach, Patrolman Edward 140
Lee, Patrolman Eric D. 547
LeMons, Sergeant Otha M. 499
Lenehan, Detective-Sergeant
    Bernard J. 235
Leonard, Patrolman Earl K. 331
Lilly, Detective Walter E. 313
Littleton, Detective Dewey L. 416
Locashio, Patrolman Thomas 347
Loftus, Patrolman Terrance 505
Looney, Patrolman James F. 221
Love, Patrolman Robert M. 225
Luce, Patrolman William J. 536
Lucey, Detective Jeremiah E. 431
Lukaszewski, Patrolman Michael A. 440
Lundy, Patrolman William D. 365
Lutke, Patrolman Stanley J. 369
Lynch, Patrolman John F. 518
Lynch, Patrolman Michael 321
Lynch, Patrolman Samuel G. 481
Lynch, Sergeant Thomas 311
Lynn, Detective-Sergeant Edward J. 396
Lyons, Patrolman John J. 540
Lyons, Sergeant Terrence 254

M
MacLeay, Detective Roderick D. 413
Madden, Detective Edward M. 494
Madden, Patrolman Patrick 364
Madigan, Patrolman Michael A. 291
Maguire, Sergeant Michael F. 494
Maher, Patrolman John F. 209

Traffic policeman, Sergeant Edwin Cowing, directs the flow on the street in downtown Chicago, 1917. DN-0068612, *Chicago Daily News* Photo Archive, Chicago History Museum.

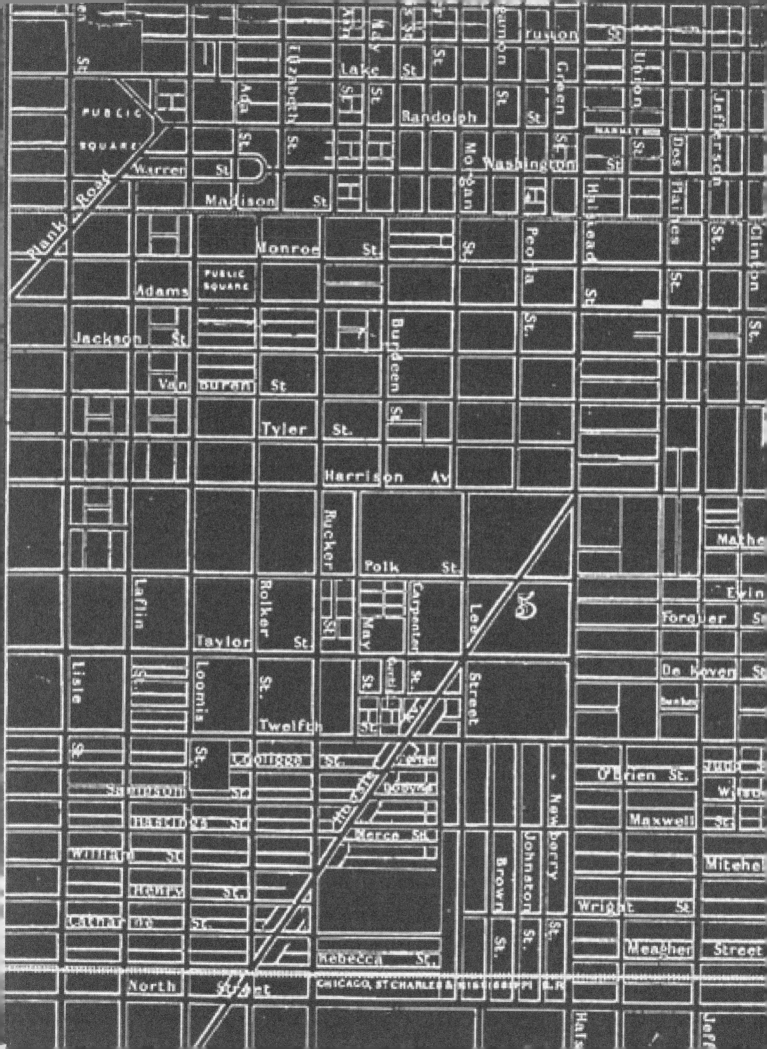